Lecture Notes in Computer Scienc

T0250740

Commenced Publication in 1973
Founding and Former Series Editors:
Gerhard Goos, Juris Hartmanis, and Jan van Leeuwen

Rudolf Freund   Gheorghe Păun
Grzegorz Rozenberg   Arto Salomaa (Eds.)

Membrane Computing

6th International Workshop, WMC 2005
Vienna, Austria, July 18-21, 2005
Revised Selected and Invited Papers

 Springer

Volume Editors

Rudolf Freund
Vienna University of Technology
Faculty of Informatics
Favoritenstr. 9–11, 1040 Vienna, Austria
E-mail: rudi@emcc.at

Gheorghe Păun
Institute of Mathematics of the Romanian Academy
P.O. Box 1-764, 014700 Bucureşti, Romania
and
Sevilla University, Dept. of Computer Science and AI
Research Group on Natural Computing
Avda. Reina Mercedes s/n, 41012 Sevilla, Spain
E-mail: gpaun@us.es

Grzegorz Rozenberg
Leiden University
Leiden Center of Advanced Computer Science (LIACS)
Niels Bohrweg 1, 2333 CA Leiden, The Netherlands
E-mail: rozenber@liacs.nl

Arto Salomaa
Turku Centre for Computer Science (TUCS)
Leminkäisenkatu 14, 20520 Turku, Finland
E-mail: asalomaa@cs.utu.fi

Library of Congress Control Number: 2005937334

CR Subject Classification (1998): F.1, F.4, I.6, J.3

LNCS Sublibrary: SL 1 – Theoretical Computer Science and General Issues

ISSN   0302-9743
ISBN-10   3-540-30948-9 Springer Berlin Heidelberg New York
ISBN-13   978-3-540-30948-2 Springer Berlin Heidelberg New York

Springer is a part of Springer Science+Business Media

springer.com

© Springer-Verlag Berlin Heidelberg 2006
Printed in Germany

Typesetting: Camera-ready by author, data conversion by Scientific Publishing Services, Chennai, India
Printed on acid-free paper   SPIN: 11603047   06/3142   5 4 3 2 1 0

Preface

The present volume is based on papers presented at the 6th Workshop on Membrane Computing, WMC6, which took place in Vienna, Austria, in the period July 18–21, 2005. The first three workshops were organized in Curtea de Argeş, Romania – they took place in August 2000 (with the proceedings published in *Lecture Notes in Computer Science*, volume 2235), in August 2001 (with a selection of papers published as a special issue of *Fundamenta Informaticae*, volume 49, numbers 1–3, 2002), and in August 2002 (with the proceedings published in *Lecture Notes in Computer Science*, volume 2597). The fourth and the fifth workshops were organized in Tarragona, Spain, in July 2003, and in Milan, Italy, in June 2004, with the proceedings published as volumes 2933 and 3365, respectively, of *Lecture Notes in Computer Science*.

The pre-proceedings of WMC6 were published by the Institute for Computer Languages of the Vienna University of Technology, and they were available during the workshop. Conforming with tradition, this workshop, too, was a lively scientific event, with many questions and engaged discussions following presentations of papers.

The current volume is based on a selection of papers from the pre-proceedings. These papers were significantly modified according to the discussions that took place during the workshop, and all the selected papers were additionally refereed. The papers in this volume cover all the main directions of research in membrane computing, ranging from theoretical topics in mathematics and computer science, to application issues, especially in biology. More specifically, these papers present research on topics such as: computational power and complexity classes, new types of P systems, relationships to Petri nets, quantum computing, and brane calculi, determinism vs. nondeterminism, hierarchies, the size of small families, algebraic approaches, and designing polynomial solutions to **NP**-complete problems through the use of membrane systems. Like the previous workshops, the scientific program of WMC6 included invited lectures by leading researchers in membrane computing (all the invited talks are represented in this volume) as well as contributed talks based on refereed papers. Altogether, the volume is a faithful illustration of the current state of research in membrane computing (a comprehensive source of information about this fast emerging area of natural computing is the website `http://psystems.disco.unimib.it`).

The workshop was organized by the Institute for Computer Languages of the Vienna University of Technology, under the auspices of the European Molecular Computing Consortium (EMCC).

The Program Committee consisted of Erzsebeth Csuhaj-Varjú (Budapest, Hungary), Rudolf Freund (Vienna, Austria) – Co-chair, Marian Gheorghe (Sheffield, UK), Hendrik Jan Hoogeboom (Leiden, The Netherlands), Oscar H. Ibarra (Santa Barbara, USA), Natasha Jonoska (Tampa, Florida), Kamala Krithivasan

(Madras, India), Vincenzo Manca (Verona, Italy), Maurice Margenstern (Metz, France), Gheorghe Păun (Bucharest, Romania, and Seville, Spain) – Co-chair, Mario J. Pérez-Jiménez (Seville, Spain), Grzegorz Rozenberg (Leiden, The Netherlands, and Boulder, Colorado, USA), Petr Sosík (Opava, Czech Republic), and Claudio Zandron (Milan, Italy).

The editors are indebted to the participants of WMC6 and in particular to the contributors of this volume. Special thanks go to Springer for the efficient cooperation in the timely production of this volume.

November 2005

Rudolf Freund
Gheorghe Păun
Grzegorz Rozenberg
Arto Salomaa

Table of Contents

Computational Power of Symport/Antiport: History, Advances, and Open Problems

Artiom Alhazov[1,2], Rudolf Freund[3], and Yurii Rogozhin[2]

[1] Research Group on Mathematical Linguistics,
Rovira i Virgili University, Pl. Imperial Tàrraco 1, 43005 Tarragona, Spain
`artiome.alhazov@estudiants.urv.es`
[2] Institute of Mathematics and Computer Science
of the Academy of Sciences of Moldova,
Str. Academiei 5, Chişinău, Moldova
`{artiom, rogozhin}@math.md`
[3] Faculty of Informatics, Vienna University of Technology,
Favoritenstr. 9–11, A–1040 Vienna, Austria
`rudi@emcc.at`

Abstract. We first give a historical overview of the most important results obtained in the area of P systems and tissue P systems with *symport/antiport* rules, especially with respect to the development of computational completeness results improving descriptional complexity parameters. We consider the number of membranes (cells in tissue P systems), the weight of the rules, and the number of objects. Then we establish our newest results: P systems with only one membrane, symport rules of weight three, and with only seven additional objects remaining in the skin membrane at the end of a halting computation are computationally complete; P systems with minimal cooperation, i.e., P systems with symport/antiport rules of size one and P systems with symport rules of weight two, are computationally complete with only two membranes with only three and six, respectively, superfluous objects remaining in the output membrane at the end of a halting computation.

1 Introduction

P systems with *symport/antiport* rules, i.e., P systems with *pure communication rules assigned to membranes*, were introduced in [38]. Symport rules move objects across a membrane together in one direction, whereas antiport rules move objects across a membrane in opposite directions. These operations are very powerful, i.e., P systems with symport/antiport rules have universal computational power with only one membrane, e.g., see [15], [22], [17].

After establishing the necessary definitions, we first give a historical overview of the most important results obtained in the area of P systems and tissue P systems with *symport/antiport* rules and review the development of computational completeness results improving descriptional complexity parameters, especially concerning the number of membranes and cells, respectively, and the weight of

R. Freund et al. (Eds.): WMC 2005, LNCS 3850, pp. 1–30, 2006.

the rules as well as the number of objects. Moreover, we establish our newest results: first we prove that P systems with only one membrane and symport rules of weight three can generate any Turing computable set of numbers with only seven additional symbols remaining in the skin membrane at the end of a halting computation, which improves the result of [21] where thirteen superfluous symbols remained. Then we show that P systems with minimal cooperation, i.e., P systems with symport/antiport rules of weight one and P systems with symport rules of weight two, are computationally complete with only two membranes modulo some initial segment. In P systems with symport/antiport rules of weight one, only three superfluous objects remain in the output membrane at the end of a halting computation, whereas in P systems with symport rules of weight two six additional objects remain. For both variants, in [5] it has been shown that two membranes are enough to obtain computational completeness modulo a terminal alphabet; in this paper, we now show that the use of a terminal alphabet can be avoided for the price of superfluous objects remaining in the output membrane at the end of a halting computation. So far we were not able to completely avoid these additional objects, hence, it remains as an interesting question how to reduce their number.

2   Basic Notions and Definitions

For the basic elements of formal language theory needed in the following, we refer to [45]. We just list a few notions and notations: $\mathbb{N}$ denotes the set of natural numbers (i.e., of non-negative integers). V^* is the free monoid generated by the alphabet V under the operation of concatenation and the empty string, denoted by λ, as unit element; by $\mathbb{N}RE$, $\mathbb{N}REG$, and $\mathbb{N}FIN$ we denote the family of recursively enumerable sets, regular sets, and finite sets of natural numbers, respectively. For $k \geq 1$, by $\mathbb{N}_k RE$ we denote the family of recursively enumerable sets of natural numbers excluding the initial segment 0 to $k - 1$. Equivalently, $\mathbb{N}_k RE = \{k + L \mid L \in \mathbb{N}RE\}$, where $k + L = \{k + n \mid n \in L\}$.

Let $\{a_1, \ldots, a_n\}$ be an arbitrary alphabet; the number of occurrences of a symbol a_i in x is denoted by $|x|_{a_i}$; the *Parikh vector* associated with x with respect to $a_1, \ldots, a_n$ is $\left(|x|_{a_1}, \ldots, |x|_{a_n}\right)$. The *Parikh image* of a language L over $\{a_1, \ldots, a_n\}$ is the set of all Parikh vectors of strings in L. A (finite) multiset $\langle m_1, a_1 \rangle \ldots \langle m_n, a_n \rangle$ with $m_i \in \mathbb{N}$, $1 \leq i \leq n$, can be represented by any string x the Parikh vector of which with respect to $a_1, \ldots, a_n$ is $(m_1, \ldots, m_n)$.

The family of recursively enumerable sets of vectors of natural numbers is denoted by $PsRE$.

2.1   Register Machines and Counter Automata

The proofs of the main results discussed in this paper are based on the simulation of register machines or counter automata, respectively; with respect to register machines, we refer to [37] for original definitions, and to [13] for definitions like those we use in this paper.

A (non-deterministic) *register machine* is a construct

$$M = (d, Q, q_0, q_f, P),$$

where:

- d is the number of registers,
- Q is a finite set of label for the instructions of M,
- q_0 is the initial label,
- q_f is the final label, and
- P is a finite set of instructions injectively labelled with elements from Q.
  The labelled instructions are of the following forms:
  1. $q_1 : (A(r), q_2, q_3)$;
     add 1 to the contents of register r and proceed to one of the instructions (labelled with) q_2 and q_3 ("ADD"-instruction).
  2. $q_1 : (S(r), q_2, q_3)$;
     if register r is not empty, then subtract 1 from its contents and go to instruction q_2, otherwise proceed to instruction q_3 ("SUBTRACT"-instruction).
  3. $q_f : halt$;
     stop the machine; the final label q_f is only assigned to this instruction.

A (non-deterministic) register machine M is said to generate a vector of natural numbers $(s_1, \ldots, s_k)$ if, starting with the instruction with label q_0 and all registers containing the number 0, the machine stops (it reaches the instruction $q_f : halt$) with the first k registers containing the numbers $s_1, \ldots, s_k$ (and all other registers being empty).

The register machines are known to be computationally complete, equal in power to (non-deterministic) Turing machines: they generate exactly the sets of vectors of natural numbers which can be generated by Turing machines, i.e., the family $PsRE$. More precisely, from the main result in [37] that the actions of a Turing machine can be simulated by a register machine with two registers (using a prime number encoding of the configuration of the Turing machine) we know that any recursively enumerable set of k-vectors of natural numbers can be generated by a register machine with $k+2$ registers where only "ADD"-instructions are needed for the first k registers.

A non-deterministic *counter automaton* is a construct

$$M = (d, Q, q_0, q_f, P),$$

where:

- d is the number of counters, and we denote $D = \{1, \ldots, d\}$;
- Q is a finite set of states, and without loss of generality, we use the notation $Q = \{q_i \mid 0 \le i \le f\}$ and $F = \{0, 1, \ldots, f\}$,
- $q_0 \in Q$ is the initial state,
- $q_f \in Q$ is the final state, and
- P is a finite set of instructions of the following forms:

1. $(q_i \rightarrow q_l, k+)$, with $i, l \in F$, $i \neq f$, $k \in D$ ("increment"-instruction).
   This instruction increments counter k by one and changes the state of
   the system from q_i to q_l.
2. $(q_i \rightarrow q_l, k-)$, with $i, l \in F$, $i \neq f$, $k \in D$ ("decrement"-instruction). If
   the value of counter k is greater than zero, then this instruction decrements it by 1 and changes the state of the system from q_i to q_l. Otherwise
   (when the value of register k is zero) the computation is blocked in state
   q_i.
3. $(q_i \rightarrow q_l, k = 0)$, with $i, l \in F$, $i \neq f$, $k \in D$ ("test for zero"-instruction).
   If the value of counter k is zero, then this instruction changes the state
   of the system from q_i to q_l. Otherwise (the value stored in counter k is
   greater than zero) the computation is blocked in state q_i.
4. *halt*. This instruction stops the computation of the counter automaton,
   and it can only be assigned to the final state q_f.

A transition of the counter automaton consists in updating/checking the value
of a counter according to an instruction of one of the types described above and
by changing the current state to another one. The computation starts in state q_0
with all counters being equal to zero. The result of the computation of a counter
automaton is the value of the first k counters when the automaton halts in state
$q_f \in Q$ (without loss of generality we may assume that in this case all other
counters are empty). A counter automaton thus (by means of all computations)
generates a set of k-vectors of natural numbers. As for register machines, we
know that any set of k-vectors of natural numbers from $PsRE$ can be generated
by a counter automaton with $k+2$ counters where only "increment"-instructions
are needed for the first k counters.

A special variant of counter automata uses a set C of pairs $\{i, j\}$ with $i, j \in Q$
and $i \neq j$. As a part of the semantics of the *counter automaton with conflicting
counters* $M = (d, Q, q_0, q_f, P, C)$, the automaton stops without yielding a result
whenever it reaches a configuration where, for any pair of conflicting counters,
both are non-empty.

Given an arbitrary counter automaton, we can easily construct an equivalent
counter automaton with conflicting counters: For every counter i which shall
also be tested for zero, we add a conflicting counter $\bar{i}$; then we replace all "test
for zero"-instructions $(l \rightarrow l', i = 0)$ by the sequence of instructions $(l \rightarrow l'', \bar{i}+)$,
$(l'' \rightarrow l', \bar{i}-)$. Thus, in counter automata with conflicting counters we only use
"increment"-instructions and "decrement"-instructions, whereas the "test for
zero"-instructions are replaced by the special conflicting counters semantics.

Another special variant of a counter automaton is called *partially blind (multi)
counter automaton* (or machine, [23]); we shall use the abbreviation PBCA for
this restricted type of counter automata which consists of a finite number (we call
the number m) of counters that can add one and subtract one, but cannot test
for zero. If there is an attempt to decrement a zero counter, the system aborts
and does not accept. The first k counters (for some $k \leq m$) are input counters.
The system is started with some nonnegative integers $(n_1, \ldots, n_k)$ in the input
counters and the other counters set to zero. The input tuple is accepted if the

system reaches a halting state and all the counters are zero. Hence, the language accepted by a PBCA is the set of k-tuples of nonnegative integers accepted by the system.

Formally a PBCA is defined as $M = (m, B, l_0, l_h, R)$ where m is the number of partially blind counters in the system, B is the set of instruction labels, l_0 is the starting instruction, l_h is the halting instruction, and R is the set of labelled instructions. These labelled instructions in R are of the forms:

- $l_i : (ADD(r), l_j)$,
- $l_i : (SUB(r), l_j)$,
- $l_i : HALT$,

where l_i and l_j are instruction labels and r is the counter that should be added/ subtracted.

For notational convenience, we will denote the family of sets of tuples of natural numbers accepted by some PBCA as $aPBLIND$ and the family of sets of tuples of natural numbers accepted by PBCAs with m counters as m-$aPBLIND$.

A related model called *blind (multi)counter automaton* (or machine, see [23]) is a (multi)counter automaton that can add one and subtract one from a counter, but cannot test a counter for zero. The difference between this model and a partially blind counter automaton is that a blind counter automaton does not abort when a zero counter is decremented. Thus, the counter can store negative numbers. Again, an input is accepted if the computation reaches an accept state and all the counters are zero.

We note that blind counter automata are equivalent in power to reversal bounded counter automata [23] which are equivalent to semilinear sets [30]. Partially blind counter automata are strictly more powerful than blind counter automata [23].

We have defined a PBCA as an acceptor for k-tuples of nonnegative integers. One can also define a partially blind counter automaton that is used as a generator of k-tuples of nonnegative integers [29]. A *partially blind counter generator* (PBCG) M consists of m counters, where the first $k \leq m$ counters are distinguished as the *output counters*. M starts with all counters set to zero. Again, at each step, each counter can be incremented/decremented by 1 (or left unchanged), but if there is an attempt to decrement a zero counter, the system aborts and does not generate anything. If the system halts in a final state with zero in counters $k + 1, \ldots, m$, then the tuple $(n_1, \ldots, n_k)$ in the first k counters is said to be generated by M.

A restricted variant of a counter automaton is called *linear-bounded multi-counter automaton* (or machine).

A *deterministic* multicounter automaton Z is linear-bounded if, when given an input n in one of its counters (called the input counter) and zeros in the other counters, it computes in such a way that the sum of the values of the counters at any time during the computation is at most n. One can easily normalize the computation so that every increment is preceded by a decrement (i.e., if Z

wants to increment a counter C_j, it first decrements some counter C_i and then increments C_j) and every decrement is followed by an increment. Thus we can assume that every instruction of Z, which is not "Halt", is of the form:

p: If $C_i \neq 0$, decrement C_i by 1, increment C_j by 1,
and go to k else go to state l

where p, k, l are labels (states). We do not require that the contents of the counters is zero when the automaton halts.

If in the instruction as defined above there is a "choice" for states k and/or l, then the automaton is called *non-deterministic*.

2.2   P Systems with Symport/Antiport Rules

The reader is supposed to be familiar with basic elements of membrane computing, e.g., from [40]; comprehensive information can be found on the P systems web page http://psystems.disco.unimib.it.

A *P system with symport/antiport rules* is a construct

$$\Pi = (O, \mu, w_1, \ldots, w_k, E, R_1, \ldots, R_k, i_0),$$

where:

1. O is a finite alphabet of symbols called *objects*;
2. μ is a *membrane structure* consisting of k membranes that are labelled in a one-to-one manner by $1, 2, \ldots, k$;
3. $w_i \in O^*$, for each $1 \leq i \leq k$, is a finite multiset of objects associated with the region i (delimited by membrane i);
4. $E \subseteq O$ is the set of objects that appear in the environment in an infinite number of copies;
5. R_i, for each $1 \leq i \leq k$, is a finite set of symport/antiport rules associated with membrane i; these rules are of the forms (x, in) and (y, out) *(symport rules)* and $(y, out; x, in)$ *(antiport rules)*, respectively, where $x, y \in O^+$;
6. i_0 is the label of an elementary membrane of μ that identifies the corresponding output region.

A P system with symport/antiport rules is defined as a computational device consisting of a set of k hierarchically nested membranes that identify k distinct regions (the membrane structure μ), where to each membrane i there are assigned a multiset of objects w_i and a finite set of symport/antiport rules R_i, $1 \leq i \leq k$. A rule $(x, in) \in R_i$ permits the objects specified by x to be moved into region i from the immediately outer region. Notice that for P systems with symport rules the rules in the skin membrane of the form (x, in), where $x \in E^*$, are forbidden. A rule $(x, out) \in R_i$ permits the multiset x to be moved from region i into the outer region. A rule $(y, out; x, in)$ permits the multisets y and x, which are situated in region i and the outer region of i, respectively, to be exchanged. It is clear that a rule can be applied if and only if the multisets involved by this rule are present in the corresponding regions. The weight of a symport rule (x, in) or (x, out) is given by $|x|$, while the weight of an antiport rule $(y, out; x, in)$ is given by $max\{|x|, |y|\}$.

As usual, a computation in a P system with symport/antiport rules is obtained by applying the rules in a non-deterministic maximally parallel manner. Specifically, in this variant, a computation is restricted to moving objects through membranes, since symport/antiport rules do not allow the system to modify the objects placed inside the regions. Initially, each region i contains the corresponding finite multiset w_i, whereas the environment contains only objects from E that appear in infinitely many copies.

A computation is successful if starting from the initial configuration, the P system reaches a configuration where no rule can be applied anymore. The result of a successful computation is a natural number that is obtained by counting all objects (only the terminal objects as it done in [5], if in addition we specify a subset of O as the set of terminal symbols) present in region i_0. Given a P system Π, the set of natural numbers computed in this way by Π is denoted by $N(\Pi)$. If the multiplicity of each (terminal) object is counted separately, then a vector of natural numbers is obtained, denoted by $Ps(\Pi)$, see [40]. For short, we shall also speak of a *P system* only when dealing with a *P system with symport/antiport rules* as defined above.

By

$$\mathbb{N}O_n P_m(sym_s, anti_t)$$

we denote the family of sets of natural numbers (non-negative integers) that are generated by a P system with symport/antiport rules having at most $n > 0$ objects in O, at least $m > 0$ membranes, symport rules of size at most $s \geq 0$, and antiport rules of size at most $t \geq 0$. By

$$\mathbb{N}_k O_n P_m(sym_s, anti_t)$$

we denote the corresponding families of recursively enumerable sets of natural numbers without initial segment $\{0, 1, \ldots, k - 1\}$. If we replace numbers by vectors, then in the notations above $\mathbb{N}$ is replaced by Ps. When any of the parameters m, n, s, t is not bounded, it is replaced by $*$; if the number of objects n is unbounded, we also may just omit n. If $s = 0$, then we may even omit sym_s; if $t = 0$, then we may even omit $anti_t$.

It may happen that P systems with symport/antiport (symport) rules can simulate deterministic register machines (i.e., register machines where in each ADD-instruction $q_1 : (A(r), q_2, q_3)$ the labels q_2 and q_3 are equal) in a deterministic way, i.e., from each configuration of the P system we can derive at most one other configuration. Then, when considering these P systems as accepting devices (the input from a set in $PsRE$ is put as an additional multiset into some specified membrane of the P system), we can get deterministic accepting P systems; the corresponding families of recursively enumerable sets of natural numbers then are denoted in the same way as before, but with the prefix aD; e.g., from the results proved in [18] and [14] we immediately obtain

$$PsRE = aDPsOP_1(anti_2).$$

Sometimes, the results we recall use the intersection with a terminal alphabet, in that way avoiding superfluous symbols to be counted as a result of a halting computation. In that case, we add the suffix $_T$ at the end of the corresponding notation.

2.3   Tissue P Systems with Symport/Antiport Rules

Tissue P systems were introduced in [34], and tissue-like P systems with channel states were investigated in [19]. Here we deal with the following type of systems (omitting the channel states).

A *tissue P system* (of degree $m \geq 1$) with symport/antiport rules is a construct

$$\Pi = \left(m, O, w_1, \ldots, w_m, ch, \left(R_{(i,j)}\right)_{(i,j) \in ch}\right),$$

where:

- m is the number of cells,
- O is the alphabet of *objects*,
- $w_1, \ldots, w_m$ are strings over O representing the *initial* multisets of *objects* present in the cells of the system (it is assumed that the m cells are labelled with $1, 2, \ldots, m$) and, moreover, we assume that all objects from O appear in an unbounded number in the environment,
- $ch \subseteq \{(i,j) \mid i,j \in \{0,1,2,\ldots,m\}, (i,j) \neq (0,0)\}$ is the set of links (*channels*) between cells (these were called *synapses* in [19]; 0 indicates the environment), $R_{(i,j)}$ is a finite set of symport/antiport rules associated with the channel $(i,j) \in ch$.

A *symport/antiport rule* of the form y/λ, λ/x, or y/x, respectively, $x, y \in O^+$, from $R_{(i,j)}$ for the ordered pair (i,j) of cells means moving the objects specified by y from cell i (from the environment, if $i = 0$) to cell j, at the same time moving the objects specified by x in the opposite direction. For short, we shall also speak of a *tissue P system* only when dealing with a *tissue P system with symport/antiport rules* as defined above.

The computation starts with the multisets specified by $w_1, \ldots, w_m$ in the m cells; in each time unit, a rule is used on each channel for which a rule can be used (if no rule is applicable for a channel, then no object passes over it). Therefore, the use of rules is sequential at the level of each channel, but it is parallel at the level of the system: all channels which can use a rule must do it (the system is synchronously evolving). The computation is successful if and only if it halts.

The result of a halting computation is the number described by the multiplicity of objects present in cell 1 (or in the first k cells) in the halting configuration. The set of all (vectors of) natural numbers computed in this way by the system Π is denoted by $N(\Pi)$ (resp., $Ps(\Pi)$). The family of sets $N(\Pi)$ $(Ps(\Pi))$ of (vectors of) natural numbers computed as above by systems with at most $n > 0$ symbols and $m > 0$ cells as well as with symport rules of weight $s \geq 0$ and antiport rules of weight $t \geq 0$ is denoted by

$$\mathbb{N}O_n t' P_m(sym_s, anti_t) \quad (\text{resp.}, \ PsO_n t' P_m(sym_s, anti_t)).$$

When any of the parameters m, n, s, t is not bounded, it is replaced by $*$.

In [19], only channels (i,j) with $i \neq j$ are allowed, and, moreover, for any i,j only one channel out of $\{(i,j),(j,i)\}$ is allowed, i.e., between two cells (or one cell and the environment) only one channel is allowed (this technical detail may influence considerably the computational power). The family of sets $N(\Pi)$ (resp., $Ps(\Pi)$) of (vectors of) natural numbers computed as above by systems with at most $n > 0$ symbols and $m > 0$ cells as well as with symport rules of weight $s \geq 0$ and antiport rules of weight $t \geq 0$ is denoted by

$$\mathbb{N}O_n tP_m(sym_s, anti_t) \quad (\text{resp., } PsO_n tP_m(sym_s, anti_t)).$$

3 Descriptional Complexity – A Historic Overview

In this section we review the development of computational completeness results with respect to descriptional complexity parameters, especially concerning the number of membranes (cells in tissue P systems), the weight of the rules, and the number of objects.

3.1 Rules Involving More Than Two Objects

We first recall results where rules involving more than two objects are used. As it was shown in [38], two membranes are enough for getting computational completeness when rules involving at most four objects, moving up to two objects in each direction, are used, i.e.,

$$\mathbb{N}RE = \mathbb{N}OP_2(sym_2, anti_2).$$

Using antiport. The result stated above was independently improved in [15], [17], and [22] – one membrane is enough:

$$\mathbb{N}RE = \mathbb{N}OP_1(sym_1, anti_2).$$

In fact, only one symport rule is needed; this can be avoided for the price of one additional object in the output region:

$$\mathbb{N}_1 RE = \mathbb{N}_1 OP_1(anti_2).$$

It is worth mentioning that the only antiport rules used are those exchanging one object by two objects.

Using symport. The history of P systems with symport only is longer. In [33] the results

$$\mathbb{N}RE = \mathbb{N}OP_2(sym_5) = \mathbb{N}OP_3(sym_4) = \mathbb{N}OP_5(sym_3)$$

were proved, whereas in [21]

$$\mathbb{N}_{13} RE = \mathbb{N}_{13} OP_1(sym_3)$$

was shown; the additional symbols can be avoided if a second membrane is used:

$$\mathbb{N}RE = \mathbb{N}OP_2(sym_3).$$

In this paper we now will show that we can bound the number of additional symbols by 7:

$$\mathbb{N}_7 RE = \mathbb{N}_7 OP_1(sym_3).$$

Determinism. It is known that deterministic P systems with one membrane using only antiport rules of weight at most 2 (actually, only the rules exchanging one object for two objects are needed, see [18], [11]) or using only symport rules of weight at most 3 (see [18]) can accept all sets of vectors of natural numbers (in fact, this is only proved for sets of numbers, but the extension to sets of vectors is straightforward), i.e.,

$$PsRE = aDPsOP_1(anti_2) = aDPsOP_1(sym_3).$$

3.2   Minimal Cooperation

Already in [38] it was shown that

$$\mathbb{N}RE = \mathbb{N}OP_5(sym_2, anti_1),$$

i.e., five membranes are already enough when only rules involving two objects are used. However, both types of rules involving two objects are used: symport rules moving up to two objects in the same direction, and antiport rules moving two objects in different directions.

Minimal cooperation by antiport. We now consider P systems where symport rules move only one object and antiport rules move only two objects across the a membrane in different directions. The first proof of the computational completeness of such P systems can be found in [9]:

$$\mathbb{N}RE = \mathbb{N}OP_9(sym_1, anti_1),$$

i.e., these P systems have nine membranes. This first result was improved by reducing the number of membranes to six [31], five [10], and four [20, 32], and finally in [46] it was shown that

$$\mathbb{N}_5 RE = \mathbb{N}_5 OP_3(sym_1, anti_1),$$

i.e., three membranes are sufficient to generate all recursively enumerable sets of numbers (with five additional objects in the output membrane).

In [6], a stronger result was shown where the output membrane did not contain superfluous symbols:

$$PsRE = PsOP_3(sym_1, anti_1).$$

In [5] it was shown that even two membranes are enough to obtain computational completeness, yet only modulo a terminal alphabet:

$$PsRE = PsOP_2(sym_1, anti_1)_T.$$

In this paper we now will show that we can bound the number of additional symbols by 3:

$$\mathbb{N}_3 RE = \mathbb{N}_3 OP_2(sym_1, anti_1).$$

Minimal cooperation by symport. We now consider P systems moving only one or two objects by a symport rule; these systems were shown to be computationally complete with four membranes in [22]:

$$NRE = NOP_4(sym_2).$$

In [6], this result was improved down to three membranes even for vectors of natural numbers:

$$PsRE = PsOP_3(sym_2).$$

Moreover, in [6] it was also shown that even two membranes are enough to obtain computational completeness (modulo a terminal alphabet):

$$PsRE = PsOP_2(sym_2)_T.$$

In this paper we will show that the number of additional objects in the output region can be bound by six:

$$N_6RE = N_6OP_2(sym_2).$$

The tissue case. If we do not restrict the graph of communication to be a tree, certain advantages appear. It was shown in [48] that

$$NRE = NOtP_3(sym_1, anti_1),$$

i.e., three cells are enough when using symport/antiport rules of weight one. This result was improved in [8] to two cells, again without additional objects in the output cell, and an equivalent result holds if antiport rules of weight one are replaced by symport rules of weight two:

$$PsRE = PsOtP_2(sym_1, anti_1) = PsOtP_2(sym_2).$$

Moreover, it was shown in the same article that accepting can be done deterministically:

$$PsRE = aDPsOtP_2(sym_1, anti_1) = aDPsOtP_2(sym_2).$$

A nice aspect of the proof is that it not only holds true for P systems with channels operating sequentially (as it is usually defined for tissue P systems), but also for P systems with channels operating in a maximally parallel way (like in standard P systems, generalizing the region communication structure of P systems to the arbitrary graph structure of tissue P systems).

Below computational completeness. In [8], it was also shown that

$$NOP_1(sym_1, anti_1) \cup NOtP_1(sym_1, anti_1) \subseteq NFIN.$$

Together with the counterpart results for symport systems,

$$NOP_1(sym_2) \cup NOtP_1(sym_2) \subseteq NFIN$$

obtained in [21], this is enough to state the optimality of the computational completeness results for the two-membrane/two-cell systems.

The most interesting open questions remaining in the cases considered so far concern the possibility to reduce the number of extra objects in the output region in some of the results stated above.

3.3   Small Number of Objects

In the preceding subsections, a survey of computational completeness results depending on the number of *membranes* or *cells* and the *weights* of the rules has been given. We now follow another direction of descriptional complexity: we try to keep the number of *membranes* or *cells* and especially the number of *objects* small, yet on the other hand allow rules of unbounded weight.

P Systems. A quite surprising result was presented in [42]: using symport/ antiport rules of unbounded weight, P systems with four membranes are computationally complete even when the alphabet contains only three symbols:

$$NRE = NO_3 P_4(sym_*, anti_*).$$

Then it has been shown in [1] that

$$NRE = NO_5 P_1(sym_*, anti_*),$$

i.e., for P systems with one membrane, even five objects are enough for getting computational completeness.

The original result was improved in [3]; in sum, the actual computational completeness results for P systems can be found there:

$$NRE = NO_n P_m(sym_*, anti_*) = aNO_n P_m(sym_*, anti_*)$$
$$\text{for } (n, m) \in \{(5, 1), (4, 2), (3, 3), (2, 4)\}.$$

The results mentioned above are presented as part of a general picture ("complexity carpet"), including results for generating/accepting/computing functions on vectors of specified dimensions.

Below computational completeness. The same article ([3]) presents undecidability results for the families

$$(a)NO_2 P_3(sym_*, anti_*), \quad (a)NO_3 P_2(sym_*, anti_*), \quad (a)NO_4 P_1(sym_*, anti_*);$$

moreover, it was shown that

$$NO_1 P_2(sym_*, anti_*) \cap NO_2 P_1(sym_*, anti_*) \supseteq NREG;$$
$$aNO_3 P_1(sym_*, anti_*) \cap aNO_2 P_2(sym_*, anti_*) \supseteq NREG;$$
$$NO_1 P_1(sym_*, anti_*) = NFIN;$$
$$aNO_2 P_1(sym_*, anti_*) \supseteq NFIN.$$

The last result has been improved in [29]; in the same article, also some results on one-symbol P systems are presented:

$$aNO_2 P_1(sym_*, anti_*) \supsetneq NREG;$$
$$aNO_1 P_{5m+3}(sym_*, anti_*) \supsetneq am\text{-}PBLIND;$$
$$NO_1 P_{5m+3}(sym_*, anti_*) \supseteq m\text{-}PBLIND.$$

The parameter $5m + 3$ in the last two results can even be reduced to $2m + 3$, i.e., $2m + 3$ membranes are enough to simulate partially blind counter automata/generators (these results will appear in the final version of [29].

Several questions are still open; the most interesting one is to determine the computational power of P systems with one symbol (we conjecture that they are not computationally complete, even if we can use an unbounded number of membranes and symport/antiport rules of unbounded weight).

Tissue P Systems. The question concerning systems with only one object has been answered in a positive way in [16] for tissue P systems:

$$NRE = NO_1 t P_7(sym_*, anti_*) = NO_1 t' P_6(sym_*, anti_*).$$

In [2] the "complexity carpet" for tissue P systems was completed:

$$NRE = NO_n t P_m(sym_*, anti_*)$$
$$\text{for } (n, m) \in \{(4, 2), (2, 3), (1, 7)\},$$

but

$$NREG = NO_* t P_1(sym_*, anti_*) = NO_2 t P_1(sym_*, anti_*)$$

and

$$NFIN = NO_1 t P_1(sym_*, anti_*) = NO_1 t' P_1(sym_*, anti_*).$$

Using two channels between a cell and the environment, one cell can sometimes be saved, and one-cell systems become computationally complete:

$$NRE = NO_n t' P_m(sym_*, anti_*)$$
$$\text{for } (n, m) \in \{(5, 1), (3, 2), (2, 3), (1, 6)\}.$$

3.4   Computational Completeness - Summary

We now finish our historical review with repeating (some of) the best known results of computational completeness:

One membrane:
  $aDPsOP_1(anti_2) = aDPsOP_1(sym_3) = PsRE,$
  $N_1 RE = N_1 OP_1(anti_2),$
  $N_7 RE = N_7 OP_1(sym_3).$

P systems - minimal cooperation:
  $PsRE = PsOP_2(sym_1, anti_1)_T = PsOP_2(sym_2)_T,$
  $N_3 RE = N_3 OP_2(sym_1, anti_1),$
  $N_6 RE = N_6 OP_2(sym_2).$

Tissue P systems – minimal cooperation:
  $PsRE = aDPsOtP_2(sym_1, anti_1) = aDPsOtP_2(sym_2),$
  $PsRE = PsOtP_2(sym_1, anti_1) = PsOtP_2(sym_2).$

P systems – small number of objects:
  $NRE = NO_n P_m(sym_*, anti_*)$
  $\qquad \text{for } (n, m) \in \{(5, 1), (4, 2), (3, 3), (2, 4)\}.$

Tissue P systems – small number of objects:
$$NRE = NO_n tP_m(sym_*, anti_*)$$
$$\text{for } (n, m) \in \{(4, 2), (2, 3), (1, 7)\},$$
$$NRE = NO_n t' P_m(sym_*, anti_*)$$
$$\text{for } (n, m) \in \{(5, 1), (3, 2), (2, 3), (1, 6)\}.$$

3.5 Bounded Symport/Antiport Systems

The question whether or not the deterministic version is weaker than the non-deterministic version of a specific variant of (tissue)P systems is an interesting and fundamental research issue in membrane computing, in particular for P systems with symport/antiport rules (see [41], [18], [26]).

Let us consider P systems that are used as acceptors. A symport/antiport P systems is called *bounded* if the only rules allowed are of the form $(u, out; v, in)$ such that u, v are multisets of objects with the restriction that $|u| = |v|$. (Note that all the rules are antiport rules). The power of these systems is exactly equivalent to that of linear-bounded (multi)counter automata or $log\,(n)$ space-bounded Turing machines (see [27]).

The deterministic and non-deterministic versions of such systems are equivalent if and only if deterministic and non-deterministic linear-bounded automata are equivalent, the latter problem being a long-standing open problem in complexity theory (see [27, 28]). This is in contrast to the fact that deterministic and non-deterministic 1-membrane unrestricted symport/antiport systems are equivalent and are universal (see, for example, Subsection 3.1 of this paper).

4 New Results

We first improve the result $\mathbb{N}_{13}OP_1(sym_3) = \mathbb{N}_{13}RE$ from [21]. For the proof, we use the variant of counter automata with conflicting counters and implement the semantics that if two conflicting counters are non-empty at the same time, then the computation is blocked without producing a result.

Theorem 1. $\mathbb{N}_7 OP_1(sym_3) = \mathbb{N}_7 RE$.

Proof. Let L be an arbitrary set from $\mathbb{N}_7 RE$ and consider a counter automaton $M = (d, Q, q_0, q_f, P, C)$ with conflicting counters generating $L - 7$ $(= \{n - 7 \mid n \in L\})$; C is a finite set of pair sets of conflicting counters $\{i, \bar{\imath}\}$. We construct a P system simulating M:

$$\Pi = (O, E, [_1 \ ]_1, w_1, R_1, 1),$$
$$O = \{x_i \mid 1 \leq i \leq 6\} \cup Q \cup \{(p, j) \mid p \in P, 1 \leq j \leq 6\}$$
$$\cup \{a_i, A_i \mid i \in C\} \cup \{\#, b, d\},$$
$$E = \{a_i, A_i \mid i \in C\} \cup \{x_2, x_3, \#\}$$
$$\cup Q \cup \{(p, j) \mid p \in P, j \in \{2, 4, 5, 6\}\},$$
$$w_1 = l_0 dx_1 x_4 x_5 x_6 \prod_{p \in P} (p, 1) (p, 3) b.$$

The following rules allow us to simulate the counter automaton M:

- The rules $(da_i a_{\bar{i}}, out)$ implement the special semantics of conflicting counters $\{i, \bar{i}\}$ with leading to an infinite computation by applying the rules $(d\#, out)$ and $(d\#, in)$.
- The simulation of the instructions of M is initiated by also sending out x_1 in the first step; the rules $(x_1 x_2 x_3, in)$ as well as $(x_2 x_4 x_5, out)$ and $(x_3 x_6, out)$ then allow us to send out the specific signal variables x_4, x_5, and x_6 which are needed to guide the sequence of rules to be applied.
- The instruction $p : (l \rightarrow l', i-)$ is simulated by the sequence of rules

$$
\begin{aligned}
&(l(p,1)x_1, out), \\
&((p,1)x_4(p,2), in), \\
&((p,2)(p,3)a_i, out), \quad ((p,2)(p,3)d, out), \\
&((p,3)x_5(p,4), in), \\
&((p,4)(p,5), out), \\
&((p,5)x_6 l', in).
\end{aligned}
$$

In case that no symbol a_i is present (which corresponds to the fact that counter i is empty), the rule $((p,2)(p,3)d, out)$ leads to an infinite computation by applying the rules $(d\#, out)$ and $(d\#, in)$. Otherwise, decrementing is successfully accomplished by applying the rule $((p,2)(p,3)a_i, out)$.

- The instruction $p : (l \rightarrow l', i+)$ is simulated by the sequence of rules

$$
\begin{aligned}
&(l(p,1)x_1, out), \\
&((p,1)x_4(p,2), in), \\
&((p,2)(p,3)A_i, out), \\
&((p,3)x_5 l', in), \\
&(A_i x_6 a_i, in).
\end{aligned}
$$

The symbol A_i is sent out to take exactly one symbol a_i in.

- A simulation of M by Π terminates with sending out the symbols from $\{(p,1), (p,3) \mid p \in P\} \cup \{A_i \mid i \in C\}$ which were used during the simulation of the instructions of M as soon as the halting label l_h of M appears:

$(l_h bx, out),$
$x \in \{(p,1), (p,3) \mid p \in P\} \cup \{A_i \mid i \in C\},$
$(l_h b, in).$

If the system halts, the objects inside correspond with the contents of the output registers, and the extra symbols are $l_h, d, b, x_1, x_4, x_5, x_6$, i.e., seven in total.   □

We now show that two membranes are enough to obtain computational completeness with symport/antiport rules of minimal size 1 with only three additional objects remaining in halting computations.

Theorem 2. $\mathbb{N}_3 OP_2(sym_1, anti_1) = \mathbb{N}_3 RE$.

Proof. We simulate a counter automaton $M = (d, Q, q_0, q_f, P)$ which starts with empty counters. We also suppose that all instructions from P are labelled in a one-to-one manner with elements of $\{1, \ldots, n\} = I$; I is the disjoint union of $\{n\}$ as well as I_+, I_-, and $I_{=0}$ where by I_+, I_-, and $I_{=0}$ we denote the set of labels for the "increment"-, "decrement"-, and "test for zero"-instructions, respectively. Additionally we suppose, without loss of generality, that on the first counter of the counter automaton M only "increment" instructions – of the form $(q_i \rightarrow q_l, c_1+)$ – are operating.

We construct the P system Π_1 as follows:

$$\Pi_1 = (O, [_1 \, [_2 \,]_2 \,]_1, w_1, w_2, E, R_1, R_2, 2),$$
$$O = E \cup \{I_c, q_0', F_1, F_2, F_3, F_4, F_5, \#_1, \#_2, b_j, b_j' \mid j \in I\},$$
$$E = Q \cup \{a_j, a_j', a_j'' \mid j \in I\} \cup C \cup \{F_2, F_3, F_4, F_5\},$$
$$w_1 = q_0' I_c \#_1 \#_1 \#_2 \#_2,$$
$$w_2 = F_1 F_1 F_1 \prod_{j \in I} b_j \prod_{j \in I} b_j',$$
$$R_i = R_{i,s} \cup R_{i,r} \cup R_{i,f}, \quad i = 1, 2.$$

The functioning of this system may be split into two stages:

1. simulating the instructions of the counter automaton;
2. terminating the computation.

We code the counter automaton as follows:

Region 1 will hold the current state of the automaton, represented by a symbol $q_i \in Q$; region 2 will hold the value of all counters, represented by the number of occurrences of symbols $c_k \in C$, $k \in D$, where $D = \{1, \ldots, d\}$. We also use the following idea realized by the phase "START" below: from the environment, we bring symbols c_k into region 1 all the time during the computation. This process may only be stopped if all stages finish correctly; otherwise, the computation will never stop.

We split our proof into several parts that depend on the logical separation of the behavior of the system. We will present the rules and the initial symbols for each part, but we remark that the system we present is the union of all these parts. The rules R_i are given by three phases:

1. START (stage 1);
2. RUN (stage 1);
3. END (stage 2).

The parts of the computations illustrated in the following describe different stages of the evolution of the P system given in the corresponding theorem. For simplicity, we focus on explaining a particular stage and omit the objects that do not participate in the evolution at that time. Each rectangle represents a membrane, each variable represents a copy of an object in a corresponding membrane (symbols outside of the outermost rectangle are found in the environment). In each step, the symbols that will evolve (will be moved) are written in boldface. The labels of the applied rules are written above the symbol $\Rightarrow$.

1. START.

$$R_{1,s} = \{\mathbf{1s1} : (I_c, in), \quad \mathbf{1s2} : (I_c, out; c_k, in), \quad \mathbf{1s3} : (c_k, out) \mid c_k \in C\}$$
$$\cup \{\mathbf{1s4} : (q'_0, out; q_0, in)\},$$
$$R_{2,s} = \emptyset$$

Symbol I_c brings one symbol c_k from the environment into region 1 (rules $\mathbf{1s1}$, $\mathbf{1s2}$), where it may be used immediately during the simulation of the "increment" instruction and then moved to region 2. Otherwise symbol c_k returns to the environment (rule $\mathbf{1s3}$). Rule $\mathbf{1s4}$ is used for synchronizing the appearance of the symbols c_k and q_i in region 1.

We illustrate the beginning of the computation as follows:

2. RUN.

$$R_{1,r} = \{\mathbf{1r1} : (q_i, out; a_j, in) \mid (j : q_i \rightarrow q_l, c_k\gamma) \in P, \gamma \in \{+, -, = 0\}\}$$
$$\cup \{\mathbf{1r2} : (b_j, out; a'_j, in), \quad \mathbf{1r3} : (a_j, out; b_j, in),$$
$$\mathbf{1r4} : (\#_1, out; b_j, in) \mid j \in I\}$$
$$\cup \{\mathbf{1r5} : (a'_j, out; a''_j, in) \mid j \in I_+ \cup I_-\} \cup \{\mathbf{1r6} : (\#_1, out; \#_1, in)\}$$
$$\cup \{\mathbf{1r7} : (b'_j, out; a''_j, in), \quad \mathbf{1r8} : (a'_j, out; b'_j, in),$$
$$\mathbf{1r9} : (\#_1, out; b'_j, in) \mid j \in I_{=0}\}$$
$$\cup \{\mathbf{1r10} : (a''_j, out, q_l, in) \mid (j : q_i \rightarrow q_l, c_k\gamma) \in P, \gamma \in \{+, -, = 0\}\}$$
$$\cup \{\mathbf{1r11} : (b_j, out), \quad \mathbf{1r12} : (b'_j, out) \mid j \in I\},$$
$$R_{2,r} = \{\mathbf{2r1} : (b_j, out; a_j, in) \mid j \in I\}$$
$$\cup \{\mathbf{2r2} : (a_j, out; c_k, in) \mid (j : q_i \rightarrow q_l, c_k+) \in P\}$$
$$\cup \{\mathbf{2r3} : (a'_j, in) \mid j \in I_+\}$$
$$\cup \{\mathbf{2r4} : (a'_j, out; b_j, in) \mid j \in I_+ \cup I_-\}$$
$$\cup \{\mathbf{2r5} : (a_j, out) \mid j \in I_- \cup I_{=0}\}$$
$$\cup \{\mathbf{2r6} : (c_k, out; a'_j, in) \mid (j : q_i \rightarrow q_l, c_k\gamma) \in P, \gamma \in \{-, = 0\}\}$$
$$\cup \{\mathbf{2r7} : (b'_j, out; b_j, in), \quad \mathbf{2r8} : (b'_j, in) \mid j \in I_{=0}\}$$
$$\cup \{\mathbf{2r9} : (a_j, out; \#_2, in) \mid j \in I_+\} \cup \{\mathbf{2r10} : (\#_2, out; \#_2, in)\}.$$

"Increment"-instruction:

$$\mathbf{a_j} a'_j a''_j q_l \boxed{\mathbf{q_i} c_k \# _1 \# _1 \boxed{b_j}} \Rightarrow^{1r1} a'_j a''_j q_i q_l \boxed{\mathbf{a_j} c_k \# _1 \# _1 \boxed{b_j}} \Rightarrow^{2r1}$$

$$\mathbf{a'_j} a''_j q_i q_l \boxed{\mathbf{b_j} c_k \# _1 \# _1 \boxed{a_j}} \Rightarrow^{1r2,2r2} \mathbf{b_j} a''_j q_i q_l \boxed{\mathbf{a_j} a'_j \# _1 \# _1 \boxed{c_k}}$$

Now there are two possibilities: we may either apply
   a) rule **1r5** or
   b) rule **2r3**.

It is easy to see that **case a)** leads to an infinite computation:

$$\mathbf{b_j} a''_j q_i q_l \boxed{\mathbf{a_j} a'_j \# _1 \# _1 \boxed{c_k}} \Rightarrow^{1r5,1r3}$$

$$a_j a'_j q_i \mathbf{q_l} \boxed{\mathbf{b_j} a''_j \# _1 \# _1 \boxed{c_k}} \Rightarrow^{1r2,1r10} a_j \mathbf{b_j} q_i a''_j \boxed{\mathbf{a'_j} \mathbf{q_l} \# _1 \# _1 \boxed{c_k}}$$

After that rule **1r4** will eventually be applied, object $\# _1$ will be moved to the environment and then applying rule **1r6** leads to an infinite computation.

Now let us consider **case b)**:

$$\mathbf{b_j} a''_j q_i q_l \boxed{\mathbf{a_j} a'_j \# _1 \# _1 \boxed{c_k}} \Rightarrow^{1r3,2r3} a_j a''_j q_i q_l \boxed{\mathbf{b_j} \# _1 \# _1 \boxed{a'_j c_k}}$$

We cannot apply rule **1r2** as this leads to an infinite computation (see above). Hence, rule **2r4** has to be applied:

$$a_j a''_j q_i q_l \boxed{\mathbf{b_j} \# _1 \# _1 \boxed{a'_j c_k}} \Rightarrow^{2r4} a_j a''_j q_i q_l \boxed{\mathbf{a'_j} \# _1 \# _1 \boxed{b_j c_k}} \Rightarrow^{1r5}$$

$$a_j a'_j q_i \mathbf{q_l} \boxed{\mathbf{a''_j} \# _1 \# _1 \boxed{b_j c_k}} \Rightarrow^{1r10} a_j a'_j a''_j q_i \boxed{\mathbf{q_l} \# _1 \# _1 \boxed{b_j c_k}}$$

In that way, q_i is replaced by q_l and c_k is moved from region 1 into region 2.

"Decrement"-instruction:

$$\mathbf{a_j} a'_j a''_j q_l \boxed{\mathbf{q_i} \# _1 \# _1 \boxed{b_j c_k}} \Rightarrow^{1r1} a'_j a''_j q_i q_l \boxed{\mathbf{a_j} \# _1 \# _1 \boxed{b_j c_k}} \Rightarrow^{2r1}$$

$$\mathbf{a'_j} a''_j q_i q_l \boxed{\mathbf{b_j} \# _1 \# _1 \boxed{a_j c_k}} \Rightarrow^{1r2,2r5} \mathbf{b_j} a''_j q_i q_l \boxed{\mathbf{a_j} a'_j \# _1 \# _1 \boxed{c_k}} \Rightarrow^{1r3,2r6}$$

$$a_j a''_j q_i q_l \boxed{\mathbf{b_j} c_k \# _1 \# _1 \boxed{a'_j}} \Rightarrow^{2r4} a_j \mathbf{a'_j} q_i q_l \boxed{\mathbf{a'_j} c_k \# _1 \# _1 \boxed{b_j}} \Rightarrow^{1r5}$$

$$a_j a'_j q_i \mathbf{q_l} \boxed{\mathbf{a''_j} c_k \# _1 \# _1 \boxed{b_j}} \Rightarrow^{1r10} a_j a'_j a''_j q_i \boxed{\mathbf{q_l} c_k \# _1 \# _1 \boxed{b_j}}$$

In the way described above, q_i is replaced by q_l and c_k is removed from region 2 to region 1.

"Test for zero"-instruction:

q_i is replaced by q_l if there is no c_k in region 2, otherwise a'_j in region 1 exchanges with c_k in region 2 and the computation will never stop.

(i) *There is no c_k in region 2:*

$$\mathbf{a_j}a'_j a''_j q_l \; \boxed{\mathbf{q_i}\#_1\#_1 \boxed{b_j b'_j}} \;\Rightarrow^{1r1}\; a'_j a''_j q_i q_l \; \boxed{\mathbf{a_j}\#_1\#_1 \boxed{b_j b'_j}} \;\Rightarrow^{2r1}$$

$$a'_j a''_j q_i q_l \; \boxed{\mathbf{b_j}\#_1\#_1 \boxed{\mathbf{a_j} b'_j}}$$

Now there are two possibilities: we apply either
   a) rule **2r7** or
   b) rule **1r2**.

It is easy to see that **case a)** leads to an infinite computation:

$$a'_j a''_j q_i q_l \; \boxed{\mathbf{b_j}\#_1\#_1 \boxed{\mathbf{a_j} b'_j}} \;\Rightarrow^{2r7,2r5}\; a'_j a''_j q_i q_l \; \boxed{\mathbf{a_j b'_j}\#_1\#_1 \boxed{\mathbf{b_j}}} \;\Rightarrow^{2r1,2r8}$$

$$a'_j a''_j q_i q_l \; \boxed{\mathbf{b_j}\#_1\#_1 \boxed{\mathbf{a_j} b'_j}} \;\Rightarrow^{2r7,2r5}\; \cdots \;\Rightarrow^{2r1,2r8}\; a_j a'_j a''_j q_i q_l \; \boxed{\mathbf{b_j}\#_1\#_1 \boxed{\mathbf{a_j} b'_j}}$$

$$\Rightarrow^{1r2,2r5}\; \mathbf{b_j} a''_j q_i q_l \; \boxed{\mathbf{a_j} a'_j \#_1\#_1 \boxed{b'_j}} \;\Rightarrow^{1r3}\; a_j a''_j q_i q_l \; \boxed{\mathbf{b_j} a'_j \#_1\#_1 \boxed{b'_j}}$$

Again there are two possibilities: we can apply either
   c) rule **1r2** or
   d) rule **2r7**.

Case c) leads to an infinite computation (rules **1r4** and **1r6**).

Now let us consider **case d)**:

$$a_j a''_j q_i q_l \; \boxed{\mathbf{b_j} a'_j \#_1\#_1 \boxed{b'_j}} \;\Rightarrow^{2r7}\; a_j a''_j q_i q_l \; \boxed{\mathbf{b'_j} a'_j \#_1\#_1 \boxed{b_j}} \;\Rightarrow^{1r7}$$

$$a_j \mathbf{b'_j} q_i q_l \; \boxed{\mathbf{a''_j} a'_j \#_1\#_1 \boxed{b_j}} \;\Rightarrow^{1r8,1r10}\; a_j a'_j a''_j q_i \; \boxed{\mathbf{q_l} b'_j \#_1\#_1 \boxed{b_j}}$$

There are two possibilities: we can apply either
   e) rule **1r7** or
   f) rule **2r8**.

Case e) leads to infinite computation (rules **1r9** and **1r6**).

In **case f)**, the object b'_j comes back to region 2.

(b) *There is some c_k in region 2:*
   Consider again **case d)**:

$$a_j a''_j q_i q_l \; \boxed{\mathbf{b_j} a'_j \#_1\#_1 \boxed{\mathbf{b'_j} c_k}} \;\Rightarrow^{2r7,2r6}\; a_j a''_j q_i q_l \; \boxed{\mathbf{b'_j} c_k \#_1\#_1 \boxed{a'_j b_j}} \;\Rightarrow^{1r7}$$

$$a_j \mathbf{b'_j} q_i q_l \; \boxed{\mathbf{a''_j} c_k \#_1\#_1 \boxed{a'_j b_j}} \;\Rightarrow^{1r9,1r10}\; a_j a''_j \#_1 q_i \; \boxed{\mathbf{q_l} b'_j c_k \#_1 \boxed{a'_j b_j}}$$

Now the application of rule **1r6** leads to an infinite computation.

Finally, let us notice that applying the rules **1r11** and **1r12** during the phase RUN leads to infinite computation. Hence, we model correctly the "test for zero" instruction.

3. END.

$$R_{1,f} = \{\mathbf{1f1} : (F_1, out; F_2, in), \quad \mathbf{1f2} : (F_2, out; F_3, in),$$
$$\mathbf{1f3} : (F_3, out; F_4, in), \quad \mathbf{1f4} : (F_4, out; F_5, in)\},$$
$$R_{2,f} = \{\mathbf{2f1} : (F_1, out; q_f, in), \quad \mathbf{2f2} : (q_f, out; I_c, in),$$
$$\mathbf{2f3} : (q_f, out; \#_1, in), \quad \mathbf{2f4} : (q_f, out; \#_2, in), \quad \mathbf{2f5} : (F_5, out),$$
$$\mathbf{2f6} : (b_j, out; F_5, in), \quad \mathbf{2f7} : (b'_j, out; F_5, in)\}.$$

We illustrate the end of computations as follows:

$$F_2 F_3 F_4 F_5 I_c c_{k_1} c_{k_2} \boxed{q_f \#_1 \#_1 \#_2 \#_2 \boxed{F_1 F_1 F_1 b_{j_1} b'_{j_2}}} \Rightarrow^{\mathbf{2f1,1s1}}$$

$$F_2 F_3 F_4 F_5 c_{k_1} c_{k_2} \boxed{I_c \#_1 \#_1 \#_2 \#_2 F_1 \boxed{q_f F_1 F_1 b_{j_1} b'_{j_2}}} \Rightarrow^{\mathbf{2f3,1s2,1f1}}$$

$$F_2 F_3 F_4 F_5 I_c c_{k_2} F_1 \boxed{F_2 c_{k_1} \#_1 \#_2 \#_2 q_f \boxed{\#_1 F_1 F_1 b_{j_1} b'_{j_2}}} \Rightarrow^{\mathbf{1s1,1s4,1f2,2f1}}$$

$$F_2 F_3 F_4 F_5 c_{k_1} c_{k_2} F_1 \boxed{F_3 I_c \#_1 \#_2 \#_2 F_1 \boxed{q_f \#_1 F_1 b_{j_1} b'_{j_2}}} \Rightarrow^{\mathbf{1s2,1f1,1f3,2f3}}$$

$$F_2 F_3 F_4 F_5 c_{k_1} I_c F_1 F_1 \boxed{F_2 F_4 c_{k_2} \#_2 \#_2 q_f \boxed{\#_1 \#_1 F_1 b_{j_1} b'_{j_2}}} \Rightarrow^{\mathbf{1s1,1s4,1f2,1f4,2f1}}$$

$$F_2 F_3 F_4 F_5 c_{k_1} c_{k_2} F_1 F_1 \boxed{F_3 F_5 I_c \#_2 \#_2 F_1 \boxed{q_f \#_1 \#_1 b_{j_1} b'_{j_2}}}$$

Notice that now rule **2f2** will eventually be applied, as otherwise the application of rule **2f4** will lead to an infinite computation (rule **2r10**). Hence, we continue as follows:

$$F_2 F_3 F_4 F_5 c_{k_1} c_{k_2} F_1 F_1 \boxed{F_3 F_5 I_c \#_2 \#_2 F_1 \boxed{q_f \#_1 \#_1 b_{j_1} b'_{j_2}}} \Rightarrow^{\mathbf{1f1,1f3,2f2,2f6}}$$

$$F_2 F_3 F_4 F_5 c_{k_1} c_{k_2} F_1 F_1 F_1 \boxed{F_2 F_4 \#_2 \#_2 b_{j_1} q_f \boxed{I_c \#_1 \#_1 F_5 b'_{j_2}}} \Rightarrow^{\mathbf{1f2,1f4,1r11,2f5}}$$

$$F_2 F_3 F_4 F_5 c_{k_1} c_{k_2} F_1 F_1 F_1 b_{j_1} \boxed{F_3 F_5 F_5 \#_2 \#_2 q_f \boxed{I_c \#_1 \#_1 b'_{j_2}}}$$

We continue in this manner until all objects b_j, b'_j, $j \in I$ from the elementary membrane 2 have been moved to the environment. Notice that the result in the elementary membrane 2 (multiset c_1^t) cannot be changed during phase END, as object I_c now is situated in the elementary membrane and cannot bring symbols c_1 from the environment. Recall that the counter automaton can only increment the first counter c_1, so all other computations of P system Π_1 cannot change the number of symbols c_1 in the elementary membrane. Thus, at the end of a terminating computation, in the elementary membrane there are the result (multiset c_1^t) and only the three additional objects $I_c, \#_1, \#_1$. □

A "dual" class of systems with minimal cooperation is the class where two objects are moved across the membrane in the same direction rather than in the opposite ones. We now prove a similar result for this class using six additional symbols.

Theorem 3. $N_6OP_2(sym_2) = N_6RE$.

Proof. As in the proof of Theorem 1 we simulate a counter automaton $M = (d, Q, q_0, q_f, P)$ that starts with empty counters. Again we suppose that all instructions from P are labelled in a one-to-one manner with elements of $\{1, \ldots, n\} = I$ and that I is the disjoint union of $\{n\}$ as well as I_+, I_-, and $I_{=0}$ where by I_+, I_-, and $I_{=0}$ we denote the set of labels for the "increment"-, "decrement"-, and "test for zero"-instructions, respectively. Moreover, we define $I' = \{1, 2, \ldots, n + 4\}$, $Q_k = \{q_{i,k}\}$, $1 \le k \le 5$, $i \in K$, $K = \{0, 1, \ldots, f\}$, and $C = \{c_i \mid 1 \le i \le d\}$.

We construct the P system Π_2 as follows:

$$\Pi_2 = (O, [_1 [_2]_2]_1, w_1, w_2, E, R_1, R_2, 2),$$

$$O = \{\#_0, \#_1, \#_2, \$_1, \$_2, \$_3, \hat{a}, \hat{b}, I_c\} \cup \{a_k \mid 1 \le k \le 5\} \cup Q \bigcup_{1 \le k \le 5} Q_k$$

$$\cup\, C \cup \{a_j, a_j', \breve{a}_j, \hat{a}_j, b_j, d_j, d_j', d_j'' \mid j \in I\} \cup \{e_t, h_t \mid t \in I'\},$$

$$E = \{a_1, a_3, a_5, \#_0\} \cup \{a_j, a_j' \mid j \in I\} \cup \{h_t \mid t \in I'\} \cup Q \cup Q_2 \cup Q_4 \cup C,$$

$$w_1 = \#_1 \hat{a} \hat{b} a_2 a_4 \$_3 \prod_{j \in I} \breve{a}_j \prod_{j \in I} d_j' \prod_{j \in I} d_j'' \prod_{t \in I'} e_t \prod_{i \in K} \hat{q}_i \prod_{i \in K} q_{i,1} \prod_{i \in K} q_{i,3} \prod_{i \in K} q_{i,5},$$

$$w_2 = \#_2 \$_1^{n+1} \$_2 \prod_{j \in I} \hat{a}_j \prod_{j \in I} b_j \prod_{j \in I} d_j,$$

$$R_i = R_{i,s} \cup R_{i,r} \cup R_{i,f}, i \in \{1, 2\}.$$

The functioning of this system again may be split into two stages:

1. simulating the instructions of the counter automaton;
2. terminating the computation.

We code the counter automaton as in Theorem 1 above: region 1 will hold the current state of the automaton, represented by a symbol $q_i \in Q$; region 2 will hold the value of all counters, represented by the number of occurrences of symbols $c_k \in C$, $k \in D$, where $D = \{1, \ldots, d\}$. We also use the following idea (called "*circle*") realized by phase "START" below: from the environment, we bring symbols c_k into region 1 all the time during the computation. This process may only be stopped if all stages finish correctly; otherwise, the computation will never stop.

We split our proof into several parts that depend on the logical separation of the behavior of the system. We will present the rules and the initial symbols for each part, but we remark that the system that we present is the union of all these parts.

The rules R_i again are given by three phases:

1. START (stage 1);
2. RUN (stage 1);
3. END (stage 2).

1. START.

$$R_{1,s} = \{1s1 : (I_c, out), \quad 1s2 : (I_c c_k, in), \quad 1s3 : (c_k, out) \mid k \in D\},$$
$$R_{2,s} = \emptyset.$$

Symbol I_c brings one symbol $c \in C$ from the environment into region 1 (rules 1s1, 1s2) where it may be used immediately during the simulation of an "increment"-instruction and moved to region 2. Otherwise symbol c returns to the environment (rule 1s3).

2. RUN.

$R_{1,r} = \{1r1 : (q_i \hat{q}_i, out) \mid i \in K\}$

$\cup \{1r2 : (a_j \hat{q}_i, in) \mid (j : q_i \rightarrow q_l, k\gamma) \in P, \gamma \in \{+, -, = 0\}, k \in D\}$

$\cup \{1r3 : (a_j \hat{a}, out) \mid j \in I_+ \cup I_-\} \cup \{1r4 : (a_j \hat{b}, out) \mid j \in I_{=0}\}$

$\cup \{1r5 : (\#_2, out), \quad 1r6 : (\#_2, in)\} \cup \{1r7 : (b_j \breve{a}_j, out) \mid j \in I\}$

$\cup \{1r8 : (b_j \#_1, out) \mid j \in I\} \cup \{1r9 : (\hat{a}_j \#_1, out) \mid j \in I\}$

$\cup \{1r10 : (\#_0 \#_1, in), \quad 1r11 : (\#_0 \hat{b}, in)\} \cup \{1r12 : (a'_j b_j, in) \mid j \in I\}$

$\cup \{1r13 : (\hat{a} a_1, in), \quad 1r14 : (a_1 a_2, out), \quad 1r15 : (a_2 a_3, in)\}$

$\cup \{1r16 : (a_3 a_4, out), \quad 1r17 : (a_4 a_5, in), \quad 1r18 : (a_5, out)\}$

$\cup \{1r19 : (a'_j q_{l,1}, out) \mid (j : q_i \rightarrow q_l, k\gamma) \in P, \gamma \in \{+, -, = 0\}, k \in D\}$

$\cup \{1r20 : (q_{i,1} q_{i,2}, in), \quad 1r21 : (q_{i,2} q_{i,3}, out), \quad 1r22 : (q_{i,3} q_{i,4}, in) \mid i \in K\}$

$\cup \{1r23 : (q_{i,4} q_{i,5}, out), \quad 1r24 : (q_{i,5} q_i, in) \mid i \in K\}$

$\cup \{1r25 : (d_j \hat{a}, out), \quad 1r26 : (d_j \#_0, in) \mid j \in I_+ \cup I_-\}$

$\cup \{1r27 : (d_j \breve{a}_j, in) \mid j \in I\} \cup \{1r28 : (d_j \#_1, out) \mid j \in I_+ \cup I_-\}$

$\cup \{1r29 : (d_j d'_j, out) \mid j \in I_{=0}\} \cup \{1r30 : (d'_j \hat{b}, in) \mid j \in I_{=0}\},$

$R_{2,r} = \{2r1 : (a_j \breve{a}_j, in) \mid j \in I\} \cup \{2r2 : (b_j \breve{a}_j, out) \mid j \in I\}$

$\cup \{2r3 : (a_j c_k, out) \mid (j : q_i \rightarrow q_l, k\gamma) \in P, \gamma \in \{-, = 0\}, k \in D\}$

$\cup \{2r4 : (a_j \#_2, out) \mid j \in I_-\} \cup \{2r5 : (a_j \hat{a}_j, out) \mid j \in I_+\}$

$\cup \{2r6 : (\#_0, in), 2r7 : (\#_0, out)\}$

$\cup \{2r8 : (c_k \hat{a}_j, in) \mid (j : q_i \rightarrow q_l, k+) \in P, k \in D\}$

$\cup \{2r9 : (a'_j b_j, in) \mid j \in I\} \cup \{2r10 : (a'_j d_j, out) \mid j \in I\}$

$\cup \{2r11 : (d_j a_5, in) \mid j \in I_+ \cup I_-\} \cup \{2r12 : (a_5, out)\}$

$\cup \{2r13 : (d_j d''_j, in) \mid j \in I_{=0}\} \cup \{2r14 : (a_j d''_j, out) \mid j \in I_{=0}\}.$

"Increment"-instruction:

$$a_j c \boxed{\mathbf{I_c q_i \hat{q}_i} \breve{a}_j \hat{a}\, \boxed{b_j \hat{a}_j}} \Rightarrow^{1r1,1s1} q_i \hat{q}_i \mathbf{a}_j \mathbf{I_c c} \boxed{\breve{a}_j \hat{a}\, \boxed{b_j \hat{a}_j}} \Rightarrow^{1r2,1s2}$$

$$q_i \boxed{I_c c \hat{q}_i a_j \breve{a}_j \hat{a}\, \boxed{b_j \hat{a}_j}} \text{ where } c \in C$$

Now there are two variants of computations (depending on the application of rule 2r1 or rule 1r3). It is easy to see that the application of rule 1r3 leads to an infinite computation (by *"circle"*). Consider applying rule 2r1:

$$q_i c_k \boxed{\mathbf{I_c c} \hat{q}_i \mathbf{a}_j \breve{a}_j \hat{a}\, \boxed{b_j \hat{a}_j}} \Rightarrow^{2r1,1s1,1s3}$$

$$q_i \mathbf{I_c c_k} c \boxed{\hat{q}_i \hat{a}\, \boxed{\mathbf{b_j} \breve{a}_j \mathbf{a}_j \hat{a}_j}} \Rightarrow^{2r2,2r5,1s2}$$

$$q_i c \boxed{I_c c_k \hat{q}_i \hat{a} b_j \breve{a}_j a_j \hat{a}_j \boxed{}}$$

Notice that object $\hat{a}_j$ cannot be idle, as the application of the rules 1r9, 1r10, 2r6, 2r7 leads to an infinite computation. Hence, rule 2r8 will be applied and object c_k will be moved to region 2 (thus, we increase the number of objects c_k in region 2 by one and model the increment-instruction of the counter automaton). In an analogous way, object b_j cannot be idle, as applying rules 1r8, 1r10, 2r6, 2r7 leads to an infinite computation. Thus, rule 2r1 cannot be applied and rule 1r7 will eventually be applied.

$$c a'_j a_1 a_3 a_5 \boxed{\mathbf{I_c c_k} \hat{q}_i \hat{a} b_j \breve{a}_j \mathbf{a}_j \hat{a}_j a_2 a_4 q_{l,1} \boxed{}}$$

$$\mathbf{I_c c a'_j b_j} \breve{a}_j a_j \hat{\mathbf{a}} \mathbf{a}_1 a_3 a_5 \boxed{\hat{q}_i a_2 a_4 q_{l,1} \boxed{\hat{a}_j c_k}} \Rightarrow^{1r12,1r13,1s2}$$

$$\breve{a}_j a_j a_3 a_5 \boxed{I_c c \hat{q}_i \hat{a} a_1 a_2 a_4 q_{l,1} a'_j b_j \boxed{\hat{a}_j c_k}}$$

Notice that applying rule 1r19 leads to an infinite computation, as object b_j cannot be idle. Thus, rule 2r9 will eventually be applied.

$$\breve{a}_j a_j a_3 a_5 q_{l,2} q_{l,4} \boxed{\mathbf{I_c c} \hat{q}_i \hat{a} \mathbf{a}_1 a_2 a_4 q_{l,1} \mathbf{a}'_j \mathbf{b}_j q_{l,3} q_{l,5} \boxed{d_j \hat{a}_j c_k}}$$

$$\Rightarrow^{2r9,1r14,1s1,1s3}$$

$$\mathbf{I_c c} \breve{a}_j a_j a_1 \mathbf{a}_2 \mathbf{a}_3 a_5 q_{l,2} q_{l,4} \boxed{\hat{q}_i \hat{a} a_4 q_{l,1} q_{l,3} q_{l,5} \boxed{\mathbf{d}_j \mathbf{a}'_j b_j \hat{a}_j c_k}}$$

$$\Rightarrow^{2r10,1r15,1s2}$$

$$\breve{a}_j a_j a_1 a_5 q_{l,2} q_{l,4} \boxed{\mathbf{I_c c} \hat{q}_i a_2 \mathbf{a}_3 \mathbf{a}_4 \hat{\mathbf{a}} \mathbf{d} \mathbf{j} \mathbf{a}'_j \mathbf{q}_{l,1} q_{l,3} q_{l,5} \boxed{b_j \hat{a}_j c_k}}$$

$$\Rightarrow^{1r19,1r25,1r16,1s1,1s3}$$

$$\mathbf{I_c c} a_j \breve{\mathbf{a}}_j \mathbf{d}_j \hat{\mathbf{a}} \mathbf{a}_1 a_3 \mathbf{a}_4 \mathbf{a}_5 a'_j \mathbf{q}_{l,1} \mathbf{q}_{l,2} q_{l,4} \boxed{\hat{q}_i a_2 q_{l,3} q_{l,5} \boxed{b_j \hat{a}_j c_k}}$$

$$\Rightarrow^{1r27,1r13,1r17,1r20,1s2}$$

$$a_j a_3 a'_j q_{l,4} \boxed{I_c c \hat{q}_i \hat{a} a_1 a_2 a_4 \breve{a}_j d_j a_5 q_{l,1} q_{l,2} q_{l,3} q_{l,5} \boxed{b_j \hat{a}_j c_k}}$$

Now we can apply the rules $1r25$, $1r18$ or $2r11$. It is easy to see that applying rule $1r25$ leads to an infinite computation (rules $1r26, 2r6, 2r7$), which is true for rule $1r18$, too (rules $1r28, 1r10, 2r6, 2r7$). Hence, now consider applying rule $2r11$.

$$a_j a_3 a'_j q_{l,4} q_l \boxed{\mathbf{I_c c}\hat{q}_l \hat{q}_i \hat{a} \mathbf{a_1 a_2} a_4 \breve{a}_j \mathbf{d_j a_5} q_{l,1} \mathbf{q}_{l,2} \mathbf{q}_{l,3} q_{l,5} \boxed{b_j \hat{a}_j c_k}}$$

$$\Rightarrow^{2r11,1r21,1r14,1s1,1s3}$$

$$\mathbf{I_c c} a_j a_1 \mathbf{a_2 a_3} a'_j q_{l,2} \mathbf{q}_{l,3} \mathbf{q}_{l,4} q_l \boxed{\hat{q}_l \hat{q}_i \hat{a} a_4 \breve{a}_j q_{l,1} q_{l,5} \boxed{d_j \mathbf{a_5} b_j \hat{a}_j c_k}}$$

$$\Rightarrow^{2r12,1r15,1r22,1s2}$$

$$a_j a_1 a'_j q_{l,2} q_l \boxed{\mathbf{I_c c}\hat{q}_l \hat{q}_i \hat{a} a_2 \mathbf{a_3 a_4 a_5} \breve{a}_j q_{l,1} q_{l,3} \mathbf{q}_{l,4} \mathbf{q}_{l,5} \boxed{d_j b_j \hat{a}_j c_k}}$$

$$\Rightarrow^{1r16,1r18,1r23,1s1,1s3}$$

$$\mathbf{I_c c} a_j a_1 a_3 \mathbf{a_4 a_5} a'_j q_{l,2} q_{l,4} \mathbf{q}_{l,5} \mathbf{q}_l \boxed{\hat{q}_l \hat{q}_i \hat{a} a_2 \breve{a}_j q_{l,1} q_{l,3} \boxed{d_j b_j \hat{a}_j c_k}}$$

$$\Rightarrow^{1r17,1r24,1s2}$$

$$a_j a_1 a_3 a'_j q_{l,2} q_{l,4} \boxed{\mathbf{I_c c q}_l \hat{\mathbf{q}}_l \hat{q}_i \hat{a} a_2 a_4 \mathbf{a_5} \breve{a}_j q_{l,1} q_{l,3} q_{l,5} \boxed{d_j b_j \hat{a}_j c_k}}$$

$$\Rightarrow^{1r1,1r18,1s1,1s3}$$

$$I_c c a_j a_1 a_3 a_5 a'_j q_{l,2} q_{l,4} q_l \hat{q}_l \boxed{\hat{q}_i \hat{a} a_2 a_4 \breve{a}_j q_{l,1} q_{l,3} q_{l,5} \boxed{d_j b_j \hat{a}_j c_k}}$$

Thus, we begin a new circle of modelling.

"Decrement"-instruction.

If there is an object c_k in region 2, we obtain the following computation:

$$a_j \boxed{\mathbf{q_i}\hat{\mathbf{q}}_\mathbf{i} \breve{a}_j \hat{a} \boxed{b_j c_k \#_2}} \Rightarrow^{1r1} q_i \hat{\mathbf{q}}_\mathbf{i} \mathbf{a_j} \boxed{\breve{a}_j \hat{a} \boxed{b_j c_k \#_2}} \Rightarrow^{1r2}$$

$$q_i \boxed{\hat{q}_i a_j \breve{a}_j \hat{a} \boxed{b_j c_k \#_2}}$$

Now there are two variants of computations (depending on the application of rule $2r1$ or rule $1r3$). It is easy to see that the application of rule $1r3$ leads to an infinite computation (by *"circle"*). Now consider applying rule $2r1$:

$$q_i \boxed{\hat{q}_i \mathbf{a_j} \breve{a}_j \hat{a} \boxed{b_j c_k \#_2}} \Rightarrow^{2r1} q_i \boxed{\hat{q}_i \hat{a} \boxed{\mathbf{b_j} \breve{a}_j \mathbf{a_j} \mathbf{c_k} \#_2}} \Rightarrow^{2r2,2r3}$$

$$q_i \boxed{\hat{q}_i b_j \breve{a}_j \hat{a} a_j c_k \boxed{\#_2}}$$

Thus, object c_k is moved from region 2 to region 1 (i.e., we decrease the number of objects c_k in region 2 by one and in that way model the "decrement"-instruction of the counter automaton).

The case when there is no object c_k in region 2 leads to an infinite computation (rules $2r4, 1r5, 1r6$), hence, again we correctly model the "decrement"-instruction. The further behavior of the system is the same as in the case of modelling the "increment"-instruction.

"Test for zero"-instruction:

q_i is replaced by q_l if there is no c_k in region 2 (case a)), otherwise the computation will never stop (case b)).

Case a):

$$a_j \boxed{\mathbf{q_i\hat{q}_i}\check{a}_j\hat{b}d'_j d''_j \boxed{b_j d_j \#_2}} \Rightarrow^{\mathbf{1r1}} q_i\mathbf{\hat{q}_i a_j} \boxed{\check{a}_j\hat{b}d'_j d''_j \boxed{b_j d_j \#_2}} \Rightarrow^{\mathbf{1r2}}$$

$$q_i \boxed{\hat{q}_i a_j \check{a}_j \hat{b}d'_j d''_j \boxed{b_j d_j \#_2}}$$

Now there are two variants of computations (depending on the application of rule 2r1 or rule 1r4). It is easy to see that the application of rule 1r4 leads to an infinite computation (by *"circle"*). Consider the application of rule 2r1:

$$q_i q_{l,2} q_{l,4} q_l a'_j \boxed{\hat{q}_i \mathbf{a_j \check{a}_j} q_{l,1} q_{l,3} q_{l,5} \hat{b}d'_j d''_j \boxed{b_j d_j \#_2}} \Rightarrow^{\mathbf{2r1}}$$

$$q_i q_{l,2} q_{l,4} q_l a'_j \boxed{\hat{q}_i q_{l,1} q_{l,3} q_{l,5} \hat{b}d'_j d''_j \boxed{a_j \mathbf{\check{a}_j b_j} d_j \#_2}} \Rightarrow^{\mathbf{2r2}}$$

$$q_i q_{l,2} q_{l,4} q_l a'_j \boxed{\hat{q}_i \mathbf{\check{a}_j b_j} q_{l,1} q_{l,3} q_{l,5} \hat{b}d'_j d''_j \boxed{a_j d_j \#_2}} \Rightarrow^{\mathbf{1r7}}$$

$$q_i q_{l,2} q_{l,4} q_l \check{a}_j \mathbf{b_j a'_j} \boxed{\hat{q}_i q_{l,1} q_{l,3} q_{l,5} \hat{b}d'_j d''_j \boxed{a_j d_j \#_2}} \Rightarrow^{\mathbf{1r12}}$$

$$q_i q_{l,2} q_{l,4} q_l \check{a}_j \boxed{\hat{q}_i b_j a'_j q_{l,1} q_{l,3} q_{l,5} \hat{b}d'_j d''_j \boxed{a_j d_j \#_2}}$$

Again there are two variants of computations, depending on the application of rule 1r19 or rule 2r9. Notice that applying rule 1r19 leads to an infinite computation, as object b_j cannot be idle (rules 1r8, 1r10, 2r6, 2r7). Hence, we only consider the case of applying rule 2r9:

$$q_i q_{l,2} q_{l,4} q_l \check{a}_j \boxed{\hat{q}_i \mathbf{b_j a'_j} q_{l,1} q_{l,3} q_{l,5} \hat{b}d'_j d''_j \boxed{a_j d_j \#_2}} \Rightarrow^{\mathbf{2r9}}$$

$$q_i q_{l,2} q_{l,4} q_l \check{a}_j \boxed{\hat{q}_i q_{l,1} q_{l,3} q_{l,5} \hat{b}d'_j d''_j \boxed{a_j b_j \mathbf{a'_j d_j} \#_2}} \Rightarrow^{\mathbf{2r10}}$$

$$q_i q_{l,2} q_{l,4} q_l \check{a}_j \boxed{\hat{q}_i a'_j q_{l,1} q_{l,3} q_{l,5} \hat{b}d_j d'_j d''_j \boxed{a_j b_j \#_2}}$$

Now there are two variants of computations, depending on the application of rule 2r13 and 1r29. It is easy to see that applying rule 2r14 leads to an infinite computation (rules 2r14, 1r4, 1r11, 2r6, 2r7). Hence, consider applying rule 1r29:

$$q_i q_{l,2} q_{l,4} q_l \check{a}_j \boxed{\hat{q}_i \mathbf{a'_j q_{l,1}} q_{l,3} q_{l,5} \hat{b} \mathbf{d_j d'_j} d''_j \boxed{a_j b_j \#_2}} \Rightarrow^{1r29,1r19}$$

$$q_i a'_j \mathbf{q_{l,1} q_{l,2}} q_{l,4} q_l \check{\mathbf{a}}_j \mathbf{d_j} d'_j \boxed{\hat{q}_i q_{l,3} q_{l,5} \hat{b} d''_j \boxed{a_j b_j \#_2}} \Rightarrow^{1r20,1r27}$$

$$q_i a'_j q_{l,4} q_l d'_j \boxed{\hat{q}_i q_{l,1} \mathbf{q_{l,2} q_{l,3}} q_{l,5} \hat{b} \check{a}_j \mathbf{d_j} d''_j \boxed{a_j b_j \#_2}} \Rightarrow^{1r21,2r13}$$

$$q_i a'_j q_{l,2} \mathbf{q_{l,3} q_{l,4}} q_l d'_j \boxed{\hat{q}_i q_{l,1} q_{l,5} \hat{b} \check{a}_j \boxed{d_j \mathbf{d''_j} a_j b_j \#_2}} \Rightarrow^{1r22,2r14}$$

$$q_i a'_j q_{l,2} q_l d'_j \boxed{\hat{q}_i q_{l,1} q_{l,3} \mathbf{q_{l,4} q_{l,5}} d''_j \mathbf{a_j} \hat{b} \check{a}_j \boxed{d_j b_j \#_2}} \Rightarrow^{1r4,1r23}$$

$$q_i a'_j q_{l,2} q_{l,4} \mathbf{q_{l,5} q_l} a_j \hat{\mathbf{b}} d'_j \boxed{\hat{q}_i q_{l,1} q_{l,3} d''_j \check{a}_j \boxed{d_j b_j \#_2}} \Rightarrow^{1r24,1r30}$$

$$q_i a'_j q_{l,2} q_{l,4} a_j \boxed{\hat{q}_i q_{l,1} q_{l,3} q_{l,5} q_l \hat{b} d'_j d''_j \check{a}_j \boxed{d_j b_j \#_2}}$$

Thus, q_i is replaced by q_l in region 1.

Case b):

$$a_j \boxed{\mathbf{q_i \hat{q}_i} \check{a}_j \hat{b} \boxed{c_k b_j d_j \#_2}} \Rightarrow^{1r1} q_i \hat{\mathbf{q}}_i \mathbf{a_j} \boxed{\check{a}_j \hat{b} \boxed{c_k b_j d_j \#_2}} \Rightarrow^{1r2}$$

$$q_i \boxed{\hat{q}_i a_j \check{a}_j \hat{b} \boxed{c_k b_j d_j \#_2}}$$

Again there are two variants of computations (depending on the application of rule 2r1 or rule 1r4). It is easy to see that the application of rule 1r4 leads to infinite computation (by *"circle"*). Consider the applying of rule 2r1:

$$q_i \boxed{\hat{q}_i \mathbf{a_j} \check{\mathbf{a}}_j \hat{b} \boxed{c_k b_j d_j \#_2}} \Rightarrow^{2r1} q_i \boxed{\hat{q}_i \hat{b} \boxed{\mathbf{c_k a_j} \check{\mathbf{a}}_j \mathbf{b_j} d_j \#_2}} \Rightarrow^{2r2,2r3}$$

$$q_i \boxed{\hat{q}_i \check{a}_j b_j c_k a_j \hat{b} \boxed{d_j \#_2}}$$

There are two variants of computations, depending on the application of rule 2r1 or rule 1r4. Notice that they both lead to infinite computations. Indeed, if rule 2r1 will be applied, then rules 1r8, 1r10, 2r6, 2r7 will be applied (applying rules 2r6, 2r7 leads to an infinite computation). If rule 1r4 will be applied, it again leads to an infinite computation (rules 1r11, 2r6, 2r7). Thus, we correctly model a "test for zero"-instruction.

3. END.

$$\begin{aligned}
R_{1,f} = &\left\{ \mathbf{1f1} : (\$_1 \check{a}_j, out) \mid j \in I \right\} \\
&\cup \left\{ \mathbf{1f2} : (\$_2 e_1, out), \mathbf{1f3} : (\$_1 \$_3, out) \right\} \\
&\cup \left\{ \mathbf{1f4} : (e_t h_t, in) \mid t \in I' \right\} \\
&\cup \left\{ \mathbf{1f5} : (h_t e_{t+1}, out) \mid 1 \le t \le n+3 \right\},
\end{aligned}$$

$$R_{2,f} = \{2\mathtt{f}1 : (q_f, in), 2\mathtt{f}2 : (q_f\$_1, out), 2\mathtt{f}3 : (q_f\$_2, out)\}$$
$$\cup \{2\mathtt{f}4 : (\$_1\hat{a}, in), 2\mathtt{f}5 : (\$_1\#_1, in), 2\mathtt{f}6 : (\$_1 I_c, in)\}$$
$$\cup \{2\mathtt{f}7 : (h_{n+4}, in)\}$$
$$\cup \{2\mathtt{f}8 : (h_{n+4}\hat{a}_j, out) \mid j \in I\}$$
$$\cup \{2\mathtt{f}9 : (h_{n+4}b_j, out) \mid j \in I\}$$
$$\cup \{2\mathtt{f}10 : (h_{n+4}d_j, out) \mid j \in I\}.$$

At first, all objects $\breve{a}_j$ will be moved to the environment and the objects $\hat{a}, \#_1, I_c$ to region 2 (thus, we stop without continuing the loop) and after that all objects $\hat{a}_j, b_j, d_j$ will be moved from region 2 to region 1. Hence, in region 2 now there are only the objects c_1 (representing the result of the computation) and the six additional objects $\#_1, \#_2, \hat{a}, I_c, q_f, h_{n+4}$. □

Both constructions from Theorem 2 and Theorem 3 can easily be modified to show that

$$PsOP_2(sym_1, anti_1)_T = PsRE \text{ and}$$
$$PsOP_2(sym_2)_T = PsRE,$$

i.e., the results proved in Theorem 2 and Theorem 3 can be extended from sets of natural numbers to sets of vectors of natural numbers.

5 Final Remarks

In this paper we have proved the new results that P systems with minimal cooperation, i.e., P systems with symport/antiport rules of size one, are computationally complete with only two membranes: they generate all recursively enumerable sets of vectors of nonnegative integers excluding (at most) the initial segment $\{0, 1, 2\}$. In an analogous manner, P systems with symport rules of size two are computationally complete with only two membranes: they generate all recursively enumerable sets of vectors of nonnegative integers excluding (at most) the initial segment $\{0, 1, 2, 3, 4, 5\}$. On the other hand it is known that systems with such rules in only one membrane cannot be universal, see [21, 47, 7]. Hence, the results we have proved in this paper are optimal with respect to the number of membranes. Notice that for *tissue* P systems with minimal cooperation this problem has already been solved successfully ([8]), i.e., it was proved that two cells are enough to generate all recursively enumerable sets of natural numbers.

Moreover, for P systems with symport rules of weight three we already obtain computational completeness with only one membrane modulo the initial segment $\{0, 1, 2, 3, 4, 5, 6\}$, which improves the result of [21], where thirteen objects remained in the skin membrane at the end of a halting computation.

As so far we have not been able to completely avoid additional symbols that remain after a computation has halted, the interesting open question remains to find the minimal numbers of these additional objects that permit to obtain computationally completeness in the cases described above.

Acknowledgements

The first author is supported by the project TIC2002-04220-C03-02 of the Research Group on Mathematical Linguistics, Tarragona. The first author and the third author acknowledge the U.S. Civilian Research and Development Foundation (CRDF) and the Moldavian Research and Development Association (MRDA), Award No. MM2-3034 for providing a challenging and fruitful framework for cooperation. This article was written during the first author's stay at the Vienna University of Technology.

References

1. A. Alhazov, R. Freund: P systems with one membrane and symport/antiport rules of five symbols are computationally complete. In [25], 19–28.
2. A. Alhazov, R. Freund, M. Oswald: Tissue P systems with antiport rules and a small number of symbols and cells. In *Developments in Language Theory, 9th International Conference, DLT 2005* (C. De Felice, A. Restivo, eds.), Palermo, Italy, July 4 – 8, 2005, LNCS 3572, Springer, Berlin, 2005, 100–111.
3. A. Alhazov, R. Freund, M. Oswald: Symbol/membrane complexity of P systems with symport/antiport rules. In [12], 123–146.
4. A. Alhazov, R. Freund, Yu. Rogozhin: Computational power of symport/antiport: history, advances and open problems. In [12], 44–78.
5. A. Alhazov, R. Freund, Yu. Rogozhin: Some optimal results on communicative P systems with minimal cooperation. In [24], 23–36.
6. A. Alhazov, M. Margenstern, V. Rogozhin, Yu. Rogozhin, S. Verlan: Communicative P systems with minimal cooperation. In [36], 161–177.
7. A. Alhazov, Yu. Rogozhin: Minimal cooperation in symport/antiport P systems with one membrane. In [25], 29–34.
8. A. Alhazov, Yu. Rogozhin, S. Verlan: Symport/antiport tissue P systems with minimal cooperation. In [24], 37 – 52.
9. F. Bernardini, M. Gheorghe: On the power of minimal symport/antiport. In *Pre-proceedings of Workshop on Membrane Computing, WMC-2003* (A. Alhazov, C. Martín-Vide, Gh. Păun, eds.), Tarragona, July 17–22, 2003, Technical Report RGML 28/03, Universitat Rovira i Virgili, Tarragona, 2003, 72–83.
10. F. Bernardini, A. Păun: Universality of minimal symport/antiport: five membranes suffice. In *Membrane Computing, International Workshop, WMC 2003, Tarragona, July 2003, Selected Papers* (C. Martin-Vide, G. Mauri, Gh. Păun, G. Rozenberg, A. Salomaa, eds.), LNCS 2933, Springer, Berlin, 2004, 43–45.
11. C.S. Calude, Gh. Păun: Bio-steps beyond Turing. *BioSystems*, 77 (2004), 175–194.
12. R. Freund, G. Lojka, M. Oswald, Gh. Păun, eds.: *Pre-proceedings of Sixth International Workshop on Membrane Computing, WMC6*, Vienna, July 18–21, 2005.
13. R. Freund, M. Oswald: GP systems with forbidding context. *Fundamenta Informaticae*, 49 (2002), 81–102.
14. R. Freund, M. Oswald: A short note on analysing P systems with antiport rules. *Bulletin of the European Association for Theoretical Computer Science*, 78 (2002) 231–236.
15. R. Freund, M. Oswald: P systems with activated/prohibited membrane channels. In [44], 261–268.

16. R. Freund, M. Oswald: Tissue P systems with symport/antiport rules of one symbol are computationally universal. In [24], 187–200.
17. R. Freund, A. Păun: Membrane systems with symport/antiport: universality results. In [44], 270–287.
18. R. Freund, Gh. Păun: On deterministic P Systems. Manuscript, 2003 (available at http://psystems.disco.unimib.it).
19. R. Freund, Gh. Păun, M.J. Pérez-Jiménez: Tissue-like P systems with channel states. In [43], 206–223, and *Theoretical Computer Science*, 330 (2005), 101–116.
20. P. Frisco: About P systems with symport/antiport. In [43], 224–236.
21. P. Frisco, H.J. Hoogeboom: P systems with symport/antiport simulating counter automata. *Acta Informatica*, 41 (2004), 145–170.
22. P. Frisco, H.J. Hoogeboom: Simulating counter automata by P systems with symport/antiport. In [44], 288–301.
23. S. Greibach: Remarks on blind and partially blind one-way multicounter machines. *Theoretical Computer Science*, 7 (1978), 311–324.
24. M.A. Gutiérrez-Naranjo, Gh. Păun, M.J. Pérez-Jiménez, eds.: *Cellular Computing. Complexity Aspects*. Fenix Editora, Sevilla, 2005.
25. M.A. Gutierrez-Naranjo, A. Riscos-Núñez, F.J. Romero-Campero, D. Sburlan, eds.: *Proceedings of the Third Brainstorming Week on Membrane Computing*, Sevilla (Spain), January 31 – February 4, 2005.
26. O.H. Ibarra: On determinism versus nondeterminism in P systems. *Theoretical Computer Science*, to appear.
27. O.H. Ibarra, S.Woodworth: On bounded symport/antiport P systems. *Proc. DNA11*, UWO, London, Ontario, 2005, 37–48, and LNCS, to appear.
28. O.H. Ibarra: Some recent results concerning deterministic P systems. In [12], 24–25.
29. O. Ibarra, S. Woodworth: On symport/antiport P systems with one or two symbols. In *Pre-Proceedings of the Workshop on Theory and Applications of P Systems*, Timişoara, September 26-27, 2005, 75–82.
30. O.H. Ibarra, S. Woodworth, H. Yen, Z. Dang: On symport/antiport systems and semilinear sets. In [12], 312–335.
31. L. Kari, C. Martín-Vide, A. Păun: On the universality of P systems with minimal symport/antiport rules. In *Aspects of Molecular Computing. Essays Dedicated to Tom Head on the Occasion of His 70th Birthday* (N. Jonoska, Gh. Păun, G. Rozenberg, eds.), LNCS 2950, Springer, Berlin, 2004 254–265.
32. M. Margenstern, V. Rogozhin, Yu. Rogozhin, S. Verlan: About P systems with minimal symport/antiport rules and four membranes. In [35], 283–294.
33. C. Martín-Vide, A. Păun, Gh. Păun: On the power of P systems with symport rules, *Journal of Universal Computer Science*, 8 (2002), 317–331.
34. C. Martín-Vide, J. Pazos, Gh. Păun, A. Rodríguez-Patón: Tissue P systems. *Theoretical Computer Science*, 296 (2003), 295–326.
35. G. Mauri, Gh. Păun, C. Zandron, eds.: *Pre-Proceedings of Fifth Workshop on Membrane Computing (WMC5)*, Universitá di Milano-Bicocca, Italy, June 14–16, 2004.
36. G. Mauri, Gh. Păun, M.J. Pérez-Jiménez, G. Rozenberg, A. Salomaa, eds.: *Membrane Computing. 5th Inter. Workshop, WMC5, Milan, Italy, June 2004, Revised Selected and Invited Papers*. LNCS 3365, Springer, Berlin, 2005.
37. M.L. Minsky: *Finite and infinite machines*. Prentice Hall, Englewood Cliffs, New Jersey, 1967.
38. A. Păun, Gh. Păun: The power of communication: P systems with symport/antiport. *New Generation Computing*, 20 (2002), 295–305.

39. Gh. Păun: Computing with membranes. *Journal of Computer and Systems Science*, 61 (2000), 108–143.
40. Gh. Păun: *Membrane computing. An Introduction*. Springer-Verlag, 2002.
41. Gh. Păun: Further twenty six open problems in membrane computing. In [25], 249–262.
42. Gh. Păun, J. Pazos, M.J. Perez-Jimenez, A. Rodriguez-Paton: Symport/antiport P systems with three objects are universal. *Fundamenta Informaticae*, 64 (2005), 1–4.
43. Gh. Păun, A. Riscos-Núñez, A. Romero-Jiménez, F. Sancho-Caparrini, eds.: *Second Brainstorming Week on Membrane Computing*. Technical report of Research Group on Natural Computing, University of Seville, TR 01, 2004.
44. Gh. Păun, G. Rozenberg, A. Salomaa, C. Zandron, eds.: *Membrane Computing. International Workshop, WMC-CdeA 02, Curtea de Arges, Romania, August 19–23, 2002. Revised Papers*. LNCS 2597, Springer, Berlin, 2003.
45. G. Rozenberg, A. Salomaa, eds.: Handbook of formal languages (3 volumes). Springer, Berlin, 1997.
46. Gy. Vaszil: On the size of P systems with minimal symport/antiport. In [35], 422–431.
47. S. Verlan: Optimal results on tissue P systems with minimal symport/antiport. Presented at *EMCC meeting*, Lorentz Center, Leiden, The Netherlands, 22–26 November, 2004.
48. S. Verlan: Tissue P systems with minimal symport/antiport. In *Developments in Language Theory, DLT 2004* (C.S. Calude, E. Calude, M.J. Dinneen, eds.), LNCS 3340, Springer, Berlin, 2004, 418–430.

Structural Operational Semantics of P Systems

Oana Andrei[1], Gabriel Ciobanu[2], and Dorel Lucanu[1]

[1] "A.I.Cuza" University of Iaşi, Faculty of Computer Science,
Str. General Berthelot 16, Iaşi, Romania
[2] Romanian Academy, Institute of Computer Science,
Blvd. Carol I nr.8, 700505 Iaşi, Romania
{oandrei, gabriel, dlucanu}@info.uaic.ro

Abstract. The paper formally describes an operational semantics of P systems. We present an abstract syntax of P systems, then the notion of configurations, and we define the sets of inference rules corresponding to the three stages of an evolution step: maximal parallel rewriting, parallel communication, and parallel dissolving. Several results assuring the correctness of each set of inference rules are also presented. Finally, we define simulation and bisimulation relations between P systems.

1 Introduction

Structural operational semantics (SOS) provides a framework of defining a formal description of a computing system. It is intuitive and flexible, and it became more attractive during the years by the developments presented by Plotkin [14], Kahn [7], and Milner [9]. Configurations are states of transition systems, and computations consist of sequences of transitions between configurations, and terminating (if they terminate) in a final configuration. In the usual style of structural operational semantics, computations proceed by small steps through intermediate configurations.

In this paper we present a structural operational semantics of P systems. The operational semantics of P systems is given in a rather big-step style, each step representing the collection of parallel steps due to the maximal parallelism principle. In P systems a computation is regarded as a sequence of parallel application of rules in various membranes, followed by a communication step and a dissolving step. An SOS of P systems emphasizes the deductive nature of the membrane computing by describing the transition steps by using a set of inference rules. Considering a set $\mathcal{R}$ of inference rules of form $\frac{premises}{conclusion}$, we can describe the computation of a P system as a deduction tree. As a consequence, given two configurations C, C' of a P system, SOS provides a formal method to show that C' is obtained in a transition step from C, i.e., $\mathcal{R} \vdash C \Rightarrow C'$.

First we give an abstract syntax of P systems, and then we define an appropriate notion of configuration. We introduce three sets of inference rules corresponding to distinct phases in the evolution of a P system. We prove the soundness of our inference rules. The (bi)simulation relations between P systems are also defined; they allow to compare the evolution behaviour of two P systems. The

R. Freund et al. (Eds.): WMC 2005, LNCS 3850, pp. 31–48, 2006.

structure of the paper is as follows. Section 2 presents briefly the P systems. Section 3 represents the principal part of the paper; it presents the structural operational semantics of the P systems. Conclusion and references end the paper.

2   Definition of P Systems

P systems represent a new abstract model of parallel and distributed computing inspired by cell compartments and molecular membranes [12]. A cell is divided in various compartments, each compartment with a different task, and all of them working simultaneously to accomplish a more general task of the whole system. P systems provide a nice abstraction for parallel systems, and a suitable framework for distributed and parallel algorithms [3].

A detailed description of P systems can be found in [12]. A P system consists of a hierarchy of membranes that do not intersect, with a distinguishable membrane, called the *skin membrane*, surrounding them all. A membrane without any other membranes inside is *elementary*, while a non-elementary membrane is a *composite* membrane. The membranes produce a demarcation between *regions*. For each membrane there is a unique associated region. The space outside the skin membrane is called the *outer region*. Because of this one-to-one correspondence we sometimes use membrane instead of region. Regions contain multisets of *objects*, *evolution rules* and possibly other membranes. Only rules in a region delimited by a membrane act on the objects in that region. The multisets of objects from a region correspond to the "chemicals swimming in the solution in the cell compartment", while the rules correspond to the "chemical reactions possible in the same compartment". The rules must contain target indications, specifying the membrane where the new objects obtained after applying the rule are sent. The new objects either remain in the same region when they have a *here* target, or they pass through membranes, in two directions: they can be sent *out* of the membrane which delimits a region from outside, or can be sent *in* one of the membranes which delimit a region from inside, precisely identified by its label. In a step, the objects can pass only through one membrane. We consider that all the objects are enclosed in messages together with the target indication. Therefore we have *here* messages of typical form $(w, here)$ with w a possibly empty multiset of objects, *out* messages of typical form (w, out), and *in* messages of typical form (w, in_L), both with w a non-empty multiset of objects. For the sake of simplicity, we consider that the messages with the same target indication merge into one message, such that

$(w_1, here) \ldots (w_n, here) = (w, here)$,
$(w_1, in_L) \ldots (w_n, in_L) = (w, in_L)$, and
$(w_1, out) \ldots (w_n, out) = (w, out)$,

where $w = w_1 \ldots w_n$.

A membrane is *dissolved* by the symbol δ resulted after a rule application; this action is important when discussing about adaptive executions. When such an action takes place, the membrane disappears, its contents (objects and membranes) remain free in the membrane placed immediately outside, and the evolution rules of the dissolved membranes are lost. The skin membrane is never dissolved. The application of evolution rules is done in parallel, and it is eventually regulated by *priority* relationships between rules.

A P system has a certain structure represented by a tree (with the skin membrane as its root and elementary membranes as leaves), or by a string of correctly matching parentheses, placed in a unique pair of matching parentheses; each pair of matching parentheses corresponds to a membrane. Graphically, a membrane structure is represented by a Venn diagram in which two sets can be either disjoint, or one is a subset of the other. This representation makes clear that the order of sibling membranes is irrelevant (as they float around), while, on the contrary, the inclusion relationship (or parent-child relationship in the tree-like representation) between membranes is essential. The membranes (and the corresponding regions) are labelled in a one-to-one manner with labels from a given set, usually ranging from 1 to the total number of membranes.

Formally, a *P system* is a structure $\Pi = (O, \mu, w_1, \ldots, w_m, (R_1, \rho_1), \ldots, (R_m, \rho_m), i_o)$, where:

- O is an alphabet of objects;
- μ is a membrane structure;
- for each membrane $i = 1, \ldots, m$, w_i is the initial multiset over O;
- R_i is a finite set of evolution rules over O associated with the membrane i; the typical form of a rule is $u \to v$, with u a multiset over O, and v consisting of messages and/or the dissolving symbol δ;
- ρ_i is a partial order relation over R_i, specifying a *priority* relation among the rules: $(r_1, r_2) \in \rho_i$ iff $r_1 > r_2$ (i.e., r_1 has a higher priority than r_2);
- i_0 is either a number between 1 and m specifying the *output* membrane of Π, or it is equal to 0 indicating that the output is the outer region.

Since the skin is not allowed to be dissolved, we consider that the rules of the skin do not involve δ. These are the *general P systems*, or *transition P systems*; many other variants and classes were introduced [12].

The membranes preserve the initial labelling, evolution rules, and priority relation among them in all subsequent configurations. Therefore in order to describe a membrane we consider its label and the current multiset of objects together with its structure. We use the mappings *rules* and *priority* to associate to a membrane label the set of evolution rules and the priority relation: $rules(L_i) = R_i$, $priority(L_i) = \rho_i$, and the projections L and w which return from a membrane its label and its current multiset, respectively.

Notation. If X is a set, then X_c^* denotes the set of the finite multisets defined over X, and X_c^+ denotes X_c^* without the empty multiset. These notations are inspired by the one-to-one correspondence from the set of the finite multisets defined over X onto the free commutative monoid generated by X.

Formally, the set of *membranes for a P system Π*, denoted by $\mathcal{M}(\Pi)$, and *the membrane structure* are inductively defined as follows:

– if L is a label, and w is a multiset over $O \cup (O_c^* \times \{here\}) \cup (O_c^+ \times \{out\}) \cup \{\delta\}$, then $\langle\, L \mid w \,\rangle \in \mathcal{M}(\Pi)$; $\langle\, L \mid w \,\rangle$ is called *simple (or elementary) membrane*, and it has the structure $\langle\rangle$;

– if $M_1, \ldots, M_n \in \mathcal{M}(\Pi)$ with $n \geq 1$, the structure of M_i is μ_i for all $i \in [n]$, L is a label, w is a multiset over $O \cup (O_c^* \times \{here\}) \cup (O_c^+ \times \{out\}) \cup (O_c^+ \times \{in_{L(M_j)} | j \in [n]\}) \cup \{\delta\}$, then $\langle\, L \mid w \,;\, M_1, \ldots, M_n \,\rangle \in \mathcal{M}(\Pi)$; $\langle\, L \mid w; M_1, \ldots, M_n \,\rangle$ is called *a composite membrane*, and it has the structure $\langle \mu_1, \ldots, \mu_n \rangle$.

A finite multiset of membranes is usually written as $M_1, \ldots, M_n$. We denote by $\mathcal{M}^+(\Pi)$ the set of non-empty finite multisets of membranes. The union of two multisets of membranes $M_+ = M_1, \ldots, M_m$ and $N_+ = N_1, \ldots, N_n$ is written as $M_+, N_+ = M_1, \ldots, M_m, N_1, \ldots, N_n$. An element from $\mathcal{M}^+(\Pi)$ is either a membrane, or a set of sibling membranes.

A *committed configuration* for a P system Π is a skin membrane which has no messages and no dissolving symbol δ, i.e., the multisets of all regions are elements in O_c^*. We denote by $\mathcal{C}(\Pi)$ the set of committed configurations for Π, and it is a proper subset of $\mathcal{M}^+(\Pi)$. We have $C \in \mathcal{C}(\Pi)$ iff C is a skin membrane of Π and $w(M)$ is a multiset over O for each membrane M in $\mathcal{C}$.

An *intermediate configuration* is a skin membrane in which we have messages or the dissolving symbol δ. The set of intermediate configurations is denoted by $\mathcal{C}^{\#}(\Pi)$. We have $C \in \mathcal{C}^{\#}(\Pi)$ iff C is a skin membrane of Π such that there is a membrane M in C with $w(M) = w'w''$, $w' \in (Msg(O) \cup \{\delta\})_c^+$, and $w'' \in O_c^*$. By $Msg(O)$ we denote the set $(O^* \times \{here\}) \cup (O^+ \times \{out\}) \cup (O^+ \times \{in_L(M)\})$.

A *configuration* is either a committed configuration or an intermediate configuration. Each P system has an initial committed configuration which is characterized by the initial multiset of objects for each membrane and the initial membrane structure of the system.

Example 1. We give an example of a deterministic P system computing n^2 for a given n. The initial configuration of such a system is:

and it is written as $\langle\, 1 \mid empty \,;\, \langle\, 2 \mid empty \,;\, \langle\, 3 \mid a^n cf \,\rangle, \langle\, 4 \mid empty \,\rangle \,\rangle \,\rangle$.

3   Structural Operational Semantics of P Systems

Structural operational semantics descriptions of systems start from abstract syntax. Specifications of abstract syntax introduce symbols for syntactic sets, metavariables ranging over those sets, and notation for constructor functions. Some of the syntactic sets are usually regarded as basic, and left open or described only informally. The abstract syntax for P systems is given as follows:

Objects:	$o \in O$
Multisets of objects:	$w \in O_c^*$
Labels:	$L \in \{Skin\} \cup \mathcal{L}$
Messages:	$(w, here), (w, in_L), (w, out) \in Msg(O)$
Dissolving symbol:	δ

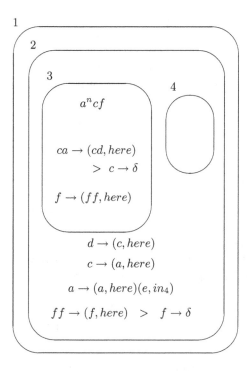

Fig. 1. An example of a P system

Membrane contents:	$w \in (O \cup Msg(O) \cup \{\delta\})_c^*$
Membranes:	$M \in \mathcal{M}(\Pi)$
	$M ::= \langle L \mid w \rangle \mid \langle L \mid w; M_+ \rangle$
Sibling membranes:	$M_+ \in \mathcal{M}^+(\Pi) = \mathcal{M}(\Pi)_c^+$
Committed configurations:	$C \in \mathcal{C}(\Pi)$
Intermediate configurations:	$C \in \mathcal{C}^{\#}(\Pi)$

In structural operational semantics, the evolution of systems is modelled by a transition system inductively specified by rules. The transition system for a P system Π is intuitively defined as follows. For two committed configurations C_1 and C_2 of Π, we say that there is a *transition* from C_1 to C_2, and write $C_1 \Rightarrow C_2$, if the following *steps* are executed in the following given order:

1. *the maximal parallel rewriting step*, written $C_1 \overset{mpr}{\Longrightarrow} C_2'$, is consisting in non-deterministically assigning objects to evolution rules in every membrane, and executing them in a maximal parallel manner;

2. *the parallel communication of objects through membranes*, written $C_2' \overset{tar}{\Longrightarrow} C_2''$, is consisting in sending the existing messages;

3. *the parallel membrane dissolving*, written $C_2'' \overset{\delta}{\Longrightarrow} C_2$, consisting in dissolving the membranes which contain the δ symbol.

The last two steps are executed only if there are messages or δ symbols resulted from the first step, respectively. If the first step is not possible, consequently neither the other two steps, then we say that the system has reached a *halting configuration*. A halting configuration is always a committed one.

Next we present in the terms of SOS each of the three steps.

3.1   Maximal Parallel Rewriting Step

We can pass from a configuration to another one by using the evolution rules. This is done in parallel: all objects from all membranes evolve simultaneously according to the evolution rules and their priority relation. The rules of a membrane are using its current objects as much as this is possible in a parallel and non-deterministic way. However, an object introduced by a rule cannot evolve at the same step by means of another rule. The use of a rule $u \to v$ in a region with a multiset w means to subtract the multiset identified by u from w, and then adding the objects of v according to the form of the rule.

We denote the maximal parallel rewriting on membranes by $\overset{mpr}{\Longrightarrow}$ and by $\overset{mpr}{\Longrightarrow}_L$ the maximal parallel rewriting over the multisets of objects of the membrane labelled by L (we omit the label whenever it is clear from the context). The SOS definition of $\overset{mpr}{\Longrightarrow}$ uses two predicates regarding mpr-irreducibility and (L, w)-consistency.

Definition 1. *The irreducibility property w.r.t. the maximal parallel rewriting relation for multisets of objects, messages, and δ, for membranes, and for sets of sibling membranes is defined as follows:*

- *a multiset w consisting only of objects is L-**irreducible** iff there are no rules in $rules(L)$ applicable to w w.r.t. the priority relation $priority(L)$;*
- *a multiset containing at least a message or the dissolving symbol δ is L-**irreducible**;*
- *a simple membrane $\langle\, L \mid w \,\rangle$ is **mpr-irreducible** iff w is L-irreducible;*
- *a non-empty set of sibling membranes $M_1, \ldots, M_n$ is **mpr-irreducible** iff M_i is mpr-irreducible, for every $i \in [n]$;*
- *a composite membrane $\langle L | w; M_1, \ldots, M_n \rangle$, with $n \geq 1$, is **mpr-irreducible** iff w is L-irreducible, and the set of sibling membranes $M_1, \ldots, M_n$ is mpr-irreducible.*

Definition 2. *Let M be a membrane labelled by L, and w a multiset of objects. A non-empty multiset $R = (u_1 \to v_1, \ldots, u_n \to v_n)$ of evolution rules is (L, w)-**consistent** iff:*

- *$R \subseteq rules(L)$,*
- *$w = u_1 \ldots u_n z$, so that all the rules in R are applicable in parallel over w,*
- *$(\forall r \in R, \forall r' \in rules(L))$ r' applicable on w implies $(r', r) \notin priority(L)$,*
- *$(\forall r', r'' \in R)$ $(r', r'') \notin priority(L)$,*
- *the dissolving symbol δ has at most one occurrence in the multiset $v_1 \ldots v_n$.*

The **maximal parallel rewriting relation** $\overset{mpr}{\Longrightarrow}$ is defined by the following inference rules:

- For each $w = u_1 \ldots u_n z \in O_c^+$ such that z is L-irreducible, and (L, w)-consistent rules $(u_1 \to v_1, \ldots, u_n \to v_n)$,

$$(\mathbf{R_1}) \; \frac{}{u_1 \ldots u_n z \overset{mpr}{\Longrightarrow}_L v_1 \ldots v_n z}$$

- For each $w \in O_c^+$, $w' \in (O \cup Msg(O) \cup \{\delta\})_c^+$, and label L,

$$(\mathbf{R_2}) \; \frac{w \overset{mpr}{\Longrightarrow}_L w'}{\langle L \mid w \rangle \overset{mpr}{\Longrightarrow} \langle L \mid w' \rangle}$$

- For each $w \in O_c^+$, $w' \in (O \cup Msg(O) \cup \{\delta\})_c^+$, $M_+, M_+' \in \mathcal{M}^+(\Pi)$, and label L,

$$(\mathbf{R_3}) \; \frac{w \overset{mpr}{\Longrightarrow}_L w', M_+ \overset{mpr}{\Longrightarrow} M_+'}{\langle L \mid w \; ; \; M_+ \rangle \overset{mpr}{\Longrightarrow} \langle L \mid w' \; ; \; M_+' \rangle}$$

- For each $w \in O_c^+$, $w' \in (O \cup Msg(O) \cup \{\delta\})_c^+$, mpr-irreducible $M_+ \in \mathcal{M}^+(\Pi)$, and label L,

$$(\mathbf{R_4}) \; \frac{w \overset{mpr}{\Longrightarrow}_L w'}{\langle L \mid w \; ; \; M_+ \rangle \overset{mpr}{\Longrightarrow} \langle L \mid w' \; ; \; M_+ \rangle}$$

- For each L-irreducible $w \in O_c^*$, and $M_+, M_+' \in \mathcal{M}^+(\Pi)$, and label L,

$$(\mathbf{R_5}) \; \frac{M_+ \overset{mpr}{\Longrightarrow} M_+'}{\langle L \mid w \; ; \; M_+ \rangle \overset{mpr}{\Longrightarrow} \langle L \mid w \; ; \; M_+' \rangle}$$

- For each $M, M' \in \mathcal{M}(\Pi)$, and $M_+, M_+' \in \mathcal{M}^+(\Pi)$,

$$(\mathbf{R_6}) \; \frac{M \overset{mpr}{\Longrightarrow} M', M_+ \overset{mpr}{\Longrightarrow} M_+'}{M, M_+ \overset{mpr}{\Longrightarrow} M', M_+'}$$

- For each $M, M' \in \mathcal{M}(\Pi)$, and mpr-irreducible $M_+ \in \mathcal{M}^+(\Pi)$,

$$(\mathbf{R_7}) \; \frac{M \overset{mpr}{\Longrightarrow} M'}{M, M_+ \overset{mpr}{\Longrightarrow} M', M_+}$$

Example 2. Considering the P system of Example 1, the inference tree for

$$\langle 1 \mid empty; \langle 2 \mid aaf; \langle 4 \mid ee \rangle \rangle \rangle \overset{mpr}{\Longrightarrow} \langle 1 \mid empty; \langle 2 \mid (aa, here)(ee, in_4)\delta; \langle 4 \mid ee \rangle \rangle \rangle$$

is:

$$\frac{(R_5) \; \dfrac{(R_4) \; \dfrac{(R_1) \; \dfrac{}{aaf \overset{mpr}{\Longrightarrow}_2 (aa, here)(ee, 4)\delta}}{\langle 2 \mid aaf \; ; \; \langle 4 \mid ee \rangle \rangle \overset{mpr}{\Longrightarrow} \langle 2 \mid (aa, here)(ee, in_4)\delta \; ; \; \langle 4 \mid ee \rangle \rangle}}{\langle 1 \mid empty \; ; \; \langle 2 \mid aaf \; ; \; \langle 4 \mid ee \rangle \rangle \rangle \overset{mpr}{\Longrightarrow}}{\langle 1 \mid empty \; ; \; \langle 2 \mid (aa, here)(ee, in_4)\delta \; ; \; \langle 4 \mid ee \rangle \rangle \rangle}$$

Lemma 1. *If $w \overset{mpr}{\Longrightarrow}_L w'$, then w' is L-irreducible.*

Proof. We get $w \overset{mpr}{\Longrightarrow}_L w'$ only applying (R_1) using a (L, w)-consistent multiset of rules. Then we have $w' = w''z$ such that $w'' \in (Msg(O) \cup \{\delta\})_c^+$, and $z \in O_c^*$ is L-irreducible. Then w' is L-irreducible by definition because it contains messages or δ. $\square$

Lemma 2. *If $M_+ \overset{mpr}{\Longrightarrow} M'_+$ then M'_+ is mpr-irreducible.*

Proof. Let M_+, M'_+ be two non-empty sets of membranes such that $M_+ \overset{mpr}{\Longrightarrow} M'_+$. We prove that M'_+ is mpr-irreducible by induction on the depth of the associated inference tree. We consider all possible cases for the final step of the inference:

(i) $M_+ \overset{mpr}{\Longrightarrow} M'_+$ is inferred by (R_2). Then $M_+ = \langle L|w \rangle$ and $M'_+ = \langle L|w' \rangle$ with $w \overset{mpr}{\Longrightarrow} w'$. By Lemma 1 w' is L-irreducible, therefore M'_+ is mpr-irreducible by definition.

(ii) $M_+ \overset{mpr}{\Longrightarrow} M'_+$ is inferred by (R_3). Then $M_+ = \langle L \mid w ; N_+ \rangle$ and $M'_+ = \langle L \mid w' ; N'_+ \rangle$ with $w \overset{mpr}{\Longrightarrow}_L w'$ inferred by (R_1), and $N_+ \overset{mpr}{\Longrightarrow} N'_+$ inferred by a shorter inference tree. By Lemma 1 w' is L-irreducible, and by inductive hypothesis, N'_+ is mpr-irreducible. Therefore M'_+ is mpr-irreducible by definition.

(iii) $M_+ \overset{mpr}{\Longrightarrow} M'_+$ is inferred by (R_4). Then $M_+ = \langle L \mid w ; N_+ \rangle$ and $M'_+ = \langle L \mid w' ; N_+ \rangle$ with $w \overset{mpr}{\Longrightarrow} w'$ (therefore w' is L-irreducible by Lemma 1) and N_+ mpr-irreducible. By definition we obtain that M'_+ is mpr-irreducible.

(iv) $M_+ \overset{mpr}{\Longrightarrow} M'_+$ is inferred by (R_5). Then $M_+ = \langle L \mid w ; N_+ \rangle$ and $M'_+ = \langle L|w ; N'_+ \rangle$ with w L-irreducible and $N_+ \overset{mpr}{\Longrightarrow} N'_+$ inferred by a shorter inference tree. By inductive hypothesis N'_+ is mpr-irreducible, therefore M'_+ is mpr-irreducible.

(v) $M_+ \overset{mpr}{\Longrightarrow} M'_+$ is inferred by (R_6). Then $M_+ = M, N_+$ and $M'_+ = M', N'_+$ where $M \overset{mpr}{\Longrightarrow} M'$ and $N_+ \overset{mpr}{\Longrightarrow} N'_+$ are inferred by shorter inference trees. By inductive hypothesis M' and N'_+ are mpr-irreducible, therefore M', N'_+ is mpr-irreducible.

(vi) $M_+ \overset{mpr}{\Longrightarrow} M'_+$ is inferred by (R_7). Then $M_+ = M, N_+$ and $M'_+ = M', N_+$ where $M \overset{mpr}{\Longrightarrow} M'$ is inferred by a shorter inference tree, and N_+ is mpr-irreducible. By inductive hypothesis M' is mpr-irreducible, therefore M', N_+ is mpr-irreducible by definition.

This completes the proof. $\square$

Theorem 1. *Let Π be a P system. If $C \in \mathcal{C}(\Pi)$ and $C' \in \mathcal{C}^\#(\Pi)$ such that $C \overset{mpr}{\Longrightarrow} C'$, then C' is mpr-irreducible.*

The proof follows straightforward from Lemma 1 and Lemma 2.

3.2 Parallel Communication of Objects

Communication through two membranes M_1 and M_2 can take place only if one is inside the other.

We say that a multiset w is *here-free/in_L-free/out-free* if it does not contain any *here/in_L/out* messages, respectively. For w a multiset of objects and messages, we introduce the operations *obj*, *here*, *out*, and *in_L* as follows:

$obj(w)$ is obtained from w by removing all messages,

$$here(w) = \begin{cases} empty & \text{if } w \text{ is } here\text{-free,} \\ w'' & \text{if } w = w'(w'', here) \wedge w' \text{ is } here\text{-free,} \end{cases}$$

$$out(w) = \begin{cases} empty & \text{if } w \text{ is } out\text{-free,} \\ w'' & \text{if } w = w'(w'', out) \wedge w' \text{ is } out\text{-free,} \end{cases}$$

$$in_L(w) = \begin{cases} empty & \text{if } w \text{ is } in_L\text{-free,} \\ w'' & \text{if } w = w'(w'', in_L) \wedge w' \text{ is } in_L\text{-free.} \end{cases}$$

We recall that all the messages with the same target merge in one message.

Definition 3. *The* **tar-irreducibility** *property for membranes and for sets of sibling membranes is defined as follows:*

1. *a membrane* $\langle\, L \mid w \,\rangle$ *is* **tar-irreducible** *iff* $L \neq Skin \vee (L = Skin \wedge w$ *is out-free);*
2. *a non-empty set of sibling membranes* $M_1, \ldots, M_n$ *is* **tar-irreducible** *iff* M_i *is tar-irreducible, for every* $i \in [n]$;
3. *a composite membrane* $\langle\, L \mid w \,;\, M_1, \ldots, M_n \,\rangle$, $n \geq 1$, *is* **tar-irreducible** *iff:*
   (a) $L \neq Skin \vee (L = Skin \wedge w$ *is out-free),*
   (b) w *is* $in_{L(M_i)}$*-free, for every* $i \in [n]$,
   (c) *for all* $i \in [n]$, $w(M_i)$ *is out-free,*
   (d) *the set of sibling membranes* $M_1, \ldots, M_n$ *is tar-irreducible.*

Notation. We treat the messages of form $(w', here)$ as a particular communication inside their membranes consisting in substitution of $(w', here)$ by w'. We denote by $\overline{w}$ the multiset obtained by replacing $(here(w), here)$ by $here(w)$ in w. For instance, if $w = a\,(bc, here)\,(d, out)$ then $\overline{w} = abc\,(d, out)$, where $here(w) = bc$. We note that $in_L(\overline{w}) = in_L(w)$, and $out(\overline{w}) = out(w)$.

The **parallel communication relation** $\x!\stackrel{tar}{\Longrightarrow}$ is defined by the following inference rules:

For each tar-irreducible $M_1, \ldots, M_n \in \mathcal{M}^+(\Pi)$, label L, and multiset w such that
$$here(w) \neq empty, \text{ or } L = Skin \wedge out(w) \neq empty, \text{ or it exists } i \in [n] \text{ with}$$
$$in_{L(M_i)}(w)out(w(M_i)) \neq empty \text{ or } here(w(M_i)) \neq empty,$$

$$(\mathbf{C_1}) \frac{}{\langle\, L \mid w \,;\, M_1, \ldots, M_n \,\rangle \xrightarrow{tar} \langle\, L \mid w' \,;\, M_1', \ldots, M_n' \,\rangle}$$

where
$$w' = \begin{cases} obj(\overline{w})\, out(w(M_1))\ldots out(w(M_n)) & , \text{if } L = Skin \\ obj(\overline{w})\,(out(w), out)\, out(w(M_1))\ldots out(w(M_n)) & , \text{otherwise} \end{cases}$$
and
$$w(M_i') = obj(\overline{w(M_i')})\, in_{L(M_i)}(w), \text{ for all } i \in [n]$$

For each $M_1, \ldots, M_n, M_1', \ldots, M_n' \in \mathcal{M}^+(\Pi)$, multiset w, and label L,

$$(\mathbf{C_2})\,\frac{M_1, \ldots, M_n \overset{tar}{\Longrightarrow} M_1', \ldots, M_n'}{\langle\, L \mid w\,;\, M_1, \ldots, M_n\,\rangle \overset{tar}{\Longrightarrow} \langle\, L \mid w''\,;\, M_1'', \ldots, M_n''\,\rangle}$$

where
$$w'' = \begin{cases} obj(\overline{w})\, out(w(M_1'))\ldots out(w(M_n')) & \text{if } L = Skin, \\ obj(\overline{w})\,(out(w), out)\, out(w(M_1'))\ldots out(w(M_n')) & \text{otherwise,} \end{cases}$$
and each M_i'' is obtained from M_i' by replacing its resources by
$$w(M_i'') = obj(\overline{w(M_i')})\, in_{L(M_i')}(w), \text{ for all } i \in [n]$$

For each multiset w such that $here(w)\, out(w) \neq empty$,

$$(\mathbf{C_3})\,\frac{}{\langle\, Skin \mid w\,\rangle \overset{tar}{\Longrightarrow} \langle\, Skin \mid obj(\overline{w})\,\rangle}$$

For each $M, M' \in \mathcal{M}(\Pi)$, and tar-irreducible $M_+ \in \mathcal{M}^+(\Pi)$,

$$(\mathbf{C_4})\,\frac{M \overset{tar}{\Longrightarrow} M'}{M, M_+ \overset{tar}{\Longrightarrow} M', M_+}$$

For each $M \in \mathcal{M}(\Pi)$, $M_+ \in \mathcal{M}^+(\Pi)$,

$$(\mathbf{C_5})\,\frac{M \overset{tar}{\Longrightarrow} M', M_+ \overset{tar}{\Longrightarrow} M_+'}{M, M_+ \overset{tar}{\Longrightarrow} M', M_+'}$$

Example 3. Considering the P system of Example 1, the inference tree for

$$\langle 1 \mid empty\,;\, \langle 2 \mid (aa, here)(ee, in_4)\delta\,;\, \langle 4 \mid ee\,\rangle\,\rangle\,\rangle \overset{tar}{\Longrightarrow} \langle 1 \mid empty\,;\, \langle 2 \mid aa\delta\,;\, \langle 4 \mid eeee\,\rangle\,\rangle\,\rangle$$

is:

$$(C_1)\,\frac{}{(C_2)\,\frac{\langle\, 2 \mid (aa, here)(ee, in_4)\delta\,;\, \langle\, 4 \mid ee\,\rangle\,\rangle \overset{tar}{\Longrightarrow} \langle\, 2 \mid aa\delta\,;\, \langle\, 4 \mid eeee\,\rangle\,\rangle}{\langle 1 \mid empty\,;\, \langle\, 2 \mid (aa, here)(ee, in_4)\delta\,;\, \langle\, 4 \mid ee\,\rangle\,\rangle\,\rangle \overset{tar}{\Longrightarrow}}}$$
$$\langle 1 \mid empty\,;\, \langle\, 2 \mid aa\delta\,;\, \langle\, 4 \mid eeee\,\rangle\,\rangle\,\rangle$$

Lemma 3. *If* $M_+ \overset{tar}{\Longrightarrow} M_+'$, *then* M_+' *is tar-irreducible.*

Proof. Let M_+, M'_+ be two non-empty sets of membranes such that $M_+ \overset{tar}{\Longrightarrow} M'_+$. We prove that M'_+ is tar-irreducible by induction on the depth of the associated inference tree. We consider all possible cases for the final step of the inference tree, i.e., each of the five rules for communication:

(i) $M_+ \overset{tar}{\Longrightarrow} M'_+$ is inferred by (C_1). Then $M_+ = \langle\, L \mid w \;;\; M_1, \ldots, M_n \,\rangle$, $M'_+ = \langle\, L \mid w' \;;\; M'_1, \ldots, M'_n \,\rangle$ where $M_1, \ldots, M_n$ is a tar-irreducible set of membranes, and $(here(w) \neq empty$, or $L = Skin \wedge out(w) \neq empty$, or it exists $i \in [n]$ with $in_{L(M_i)}(w)out(w(M_i)) \neq empty$ or $here(w(M_i)) \neq empty)$. Then M'_+ is tar-irreducible by Definition 3.3.

(ii) $M_+ \overset{tar}{\Longrightarrow} M'_+$ is inferred by (C_2). Then $M_+ = \langle\, L \mid w \;;\; M_1, \ldots, M_n \,\rangle$, $M'_+ = \langle\, L \mid w'' \;;\; M''_1, \ldots, M''_n \,\rangle$ and the hypothesis $M_1, \ldots, M_n \overset{tar}{\Longrightarrow} M'_1, \ldots, M'_n$ is inferred by a shorter inference tree. $M'_1, \ldots, M'_n$ is tar-irreducible by inductive hypothesis. For the membrane M'_+, w'' is *out*-free if $L = Skin$, w'' is $in_{L(M_i)}$-free and $w(M''_i)$ is *out*-free, for all $i \in [n]$. Moreover, the sibling membranes $M''_1, \ldots, M''_n$ are tar-irreducible. Then M'_+ is tar-irreducible by Definition 3.3.

(iii) $M_+ \overset{tar}{\Longrightarrow} M'_+$ is inferred by (C_3). Then $M_+ = \langle Skin|w\rangle$, $M'_+ = \langle Skin|obj(\overline{w})\rangle$, where $out(w) \neq empty$, and $w(M'_+)$ is *out*-free. Then M'_+ is tar-irreducible by Definition 3.1.

(iv) $M_+ \overset{tar}{\Longrightarrow} M'_+$ is inferred by (C_4). Then $M_+ = M, N_+$, $M'_+ = M', N_+$ where N_+ is tar-irreducible, and $M \overset{tar}{\Longrightarrow} M'$ is inferred by a shorter inference tree. It follows that M' is tar-irreducible by inductive hypothesis. Therefore M'_+ is tar-irreducible by Definition 3.2.

(v) $M_+ \overset{tar}{\Longrightarrow} M'_+$ is inferred by (C_5). Then $M_+ = M, N_+$, $M'_+ = M', N'_+$ where $M \overset{tar}{\Longrightarrow} M'$ and $N_+ \overset{tar}{\Longrightarrow} N'_+$ are inferred by shorter inference trees. M' and N'_+ are tar-irreducible by inductive hypothesis. It follows that M', N'_+ is a tar-irreducible by Definition 3.2.

The proof is complete. $\square$

Theorem 2. *Let Π be a P system. If $C \in \mathcal{C}^{\#}(\Pi)$ with messages and $C \overset{tar}{\Longrightarrow} C'$, then C' is tar-irreducible.*

The proof follows straightforward from Lemma 3.

3.3 Parallel Membrane Dissolving

If the special symbol δ occurs in the multiset of objects of a membrane labelled by L, the membrane is dissolved producing the following changes in the system:

- its evolution rules and the associated priority relation are lost, and
- its contents (objects and membranes) are added to the contents of the region which was immediately external to the dissolved membrane.

We consider the extension of the operator w (previously defined over membranes) to non-empty sets of sibling membranes by setting $w(M_1, \ldots, M_n) = w(M_1) \ldots w(M_n)$. We say that a multiset w is δ-*free* if it does not contain the special symbol δ.

Definition 4. *The* δ-**irreducibility** *property for membranes and for sets of sibling membranes is defined as follows:*

1. *a simple membrane is* δ-**irreducible**;
2. *a non-empty set of sibling membranes* $M_1, \ldots, M_n$ *is* δ-**irreducible** *iff every membrane* M_i *is* δ-**irreducible**, *for* $1 \le i \le n$;
3. *a composite membrane* $\langle L \,|\, w ; M_+ \rangle$ *is* δ-**irreducible** *iff* M_+ *is* δ-*irreducible*, *and* $w(M_+)$ *is* δ-*free*.

The **parallel dissolving relation** $\overset{\delta}{\Longrightarrow}$ is defined by the following inference rules:

For each multisets of objects w_1, w_2, and labels L_1, L_2,

$$(\mathbf{D_1}) \frac{}{\langle L_1 \,|\, w_1 ; \langle L_2 \,|\, w_2\delta \rangle \rangle \overset{\delta}{\Longrightarrow} \langle L_1 \,|\, w_1 w_2 \rangle}$$

For each $M_+ \in \mathcal{M}^+(\Pi)$, multiset w_2, and labels L_1, L_2 such that $\langle L_2 | w_2\delta ; M_+ \rangle$ is δ-irreducible,

$$(\mathbf{D_2}) \frac{}{\langle L_1 \,|\, w_1 ; \langle L_2 \,|\, w_2\delta ; M_+ \rangle \rangle \overset{\delta}{\Longrightarrow} \langle L_1 \,|\, w_1 w_2 ; M_+ \rangle}$$

For each $M_+ \in \mathcal{M}^+(\Pi)$, δ-free multiset w_2, and labels L_1, L_2,

$$(\mathbf{D_3}) \frac{\langle L_2 \,|\, w_2 ; M_+ \rangle \overset{\delta}{\Longrightarrow} \langle L_2 \,|\, w_2' \rangle}{\langle L_1 \,|\, w_1 ; \langle L_2 \,|\, w_2 ; M_+ \rangle \rangle \overset{\delta}{\Longrightarrow} \langle L_1 \,|\, w_1 ; \langle L_2 \,|\, w_2' \rangle \rangle}$$

For each $M_+, M_+' \in \mathcal{M}^+(\Pi)$, δ-free multiset w_2, multisets w_1, w_2', and labels L_1, L_2

$$(\mathbf{D_4}) \frac{\langle L_2 \,|\, w_2 ; M_+ \rangle \overset{\delta}{\Longrightarrow} \langle L_2 \,|\, w_2' ; M_+' \rangle}{\langle L_1 \,|\, w_1 ; \langle L_2 \,|\, w_2 ; M_+ \rangle \rangle \overset{\delta}{\Longrightarrow} \langle L_1 \,|\, w_1 ; \langle L_2 \,|\, w_2' ; M_+' \rangle \rangle}$$

For each $M_+ \in \mathcal{M}^+(\Pi)$, multisets w_1, w_2, w_2', and labels L_1, L_2

$$(\mathbf{D_5}) \frac{\langle L_2 \,|\, w_2\delta ; M_+ \rangle \overset{\delta}{\Longrightarrow} \langle L_2 \,|\, w_2'\delta \rangle}{\langle L_1 \,|\, w_1 ; \langle L_2 \,|\, w_2\delta ; M_+ \rangle \rangle \overset{\delta}{\Longrightarrow} \langle L_1 \,|\, w_1 w_2' \rangle}$$

For each $M_+ \in \mathcal{M}^+(\Pi)$, multisets w_1, w_2, w_2', and labels L_1, L_2

$$(\mathbf{D_6}) \frac{\langle L_2 \,|\, w_2\delta ; M_+ \rangle \overset{\delta}{\Longrightarrow} \langle L_2 \,|\, w_2'\delta ; M_+' \rangle}{\langle L_1 \,|\, w_1 ; \langle L_2 \,|\, w_2\delta ; M_+ \rangle \rangle \overset{\delta}{\Longrightarrow} \langle L_1 \,|\, w_1 w_2' ; M_+' \rangle}$$

For each $M_+, N_+ \in \mathcal{M}^+(\Pi)$, multiset w', and label L such that $\langle L \mid w ; N_+ \rangle$ is δ-irreducible,

$$(\mathbf{D_7}) \frac{\langle L \mid w ; M_+ \rangle \overset{\delta}{\Longrightarrow} \langle L \mid w' \rangle}{\langle L \mid w ; M_+, N_+ \rangle \overset{\delta}{\Longrightarrow} \langle L \mid w' ; N_+ \rangle}$$

For each $M_+, M'_+, N'_+ \in \mathcal{M}^+(\Pi)$, multisets w', w'', and label L such that $\langle L \mid w ; N_+ \rangle$ is δ-irreducible,

$$(\mathbf{D_8}) \frac{\langle L \mid w ; M_+ \rangle \overset{\delta}{\Longrightarrow} \langle L \mid w' ; M'_+ \rangle}{\langle L \mid w ; M_+, N_+ \rangle \overset{\delta}{\Longrightarrow} \langle L \mid w' ; M'_+, N_+ \rangle}$$

$$(\mathbf{D_9}) \frac{\langle L \mid w ; M_+ \rangle \overset{\delta}{\Longrightarrow} \langle L \mid ww' \rangle \quad \langle L \mid w ; N_+ \rangle \overset{\delta}{\Longrightarrow} \langle L \mid ww'' \rangle}{\langle L \mid w ; M_+, N_+ \rangle \overset{\delta}{\Longrightarrow} \langle L \mid ww'w'' \rangle}$$

$$(\mathbf{D_{10}}) \frac{\langle L \mid w ; M_+ \rangle \overset{\delta}{\Longrightarrow} \langle L \mid ww' \rangle \quad \langle L \mid w ; N_+ \rangle \overset{\delta}{\Longrightarrow} \langle L \mid ww'' ; N'_+ \rangle}{\langle L \mid w ; M_+, N_+ \rangle \overset{\delta}{\Longrightarrow} \langle L \mid ww'w'' ; N'_+ \rangle}$$

$$(\mathbf{D_{11}}) \frac{\langle L \mid w ; M_+ \rangle \overset{\delta}{\Longrightarrow} \langle L \mid ww' ; M'_+ \rangle \langle L \mid w ; N_+ \rangle \overset{\delta}{\Longrightarrow} \langle L \mid ww'' ; N'_+ \rangle}{\langle L \mid w ; M_+, N_+ \rangle \overset{\delta}{\Longrightarrow} \langle L \mid ww'w'' ; M'_+, N'_+ \rangle}$$

Example 4. Considering the P system of Example 1, the inference tree for

$$\langle 1 | empty; \langle 2 | empty; \langle 3 | dffff\delta \rangle, \langle 4 | empty \rangle \rangle \rangle \overset{\delta}{\Longrightarrow} \langle 1 | empty; \langle 2 | dffff; \langle 4 | empty \rangle \rangle \rangle$$

is:

$$(D_4) \frac{(D_7) \frac{(D_1) \frac{}{\langle 2 | empty ; \langle 3 | dffff\delta \rangle \rangle \overset{\delta}{\Longrightarrow} \langle 2 | dffff \rangle}}{\langle 2 | empty ; \langle 3 | dffff\delta \rangle, \langle 4 | empty \rangle \rangle \overset{\delta}{\Longrightarrow} \langle 2 | dffff ; \langle 4 | empty \rangle \rangle}}{\substack{\langle 1 | empty ; \langle 2 | empty ; \langle 3 | dffff\delta \rangle, \langle 4 | empty \rangle \rangle \rangle \overset{\delta}{\Longrightarrow} \\ \langle 1 | empty ; \langle 2 | dffff ; \langle 4 | empty \rangle \rangle \rangle}}$$

Lemma 4. *If* $M_+ \overset{\delta}{\Longrightarrow} M'_+$, *then* M'_+ *is δ-irreducible.*

Proof. Let M_+, M'_+ be two non-empty sets of membranes such that $M_+ \overset{\delta}{\Longrightarrow} M'_+$. We prove that M'_+ is δ-irreducible by induction on the depth of the associated inference tree. We consider all possible cases for the final step of the inference:

(i) $M_+ \overset{\delta}{\Longrightarrow} M'_+$ is inferred by (D_1). Since M'_+ is a simple membrane, M'_+ is δ-irreducible by Definition 4.1.

(ii) $M_+ \overset{\delta}{\Longrightarrow} M'_+$ is inferred by (D_2). Then $M_+ = \langle\, L_1 \mid w_1\,;\, \langle\, L_2 \mid w_2\delta\,;\, N_+ \,\rangle\,\rangle$ and $M'_+ = \langle\, L_1 \mid w_1 w_2\,;\, N_+ \,\rangle$, where $\langle\, L_2 \mid w_2\delta\,;\, N_+ \,\rangle$ is δ-irreducible. It follows that $w(N_+)$ is δ-free, and M'_+ is δ-irreducible by Definition 4.3.

(iii) $M_+ \overset{\delta}{\Longrightarrow} M'_+$ is inferred by (D_3). Then $M_+ = \langle L_1 \mid w_1\,;\, \langle L_2 \mid w_2\,;\, N_+ \rangle\rangle$ and $M'_+ = \langle\, L_1 \mid w_1\,;\, \langle\, L_2 \mid w'_2 \,\rangle\,\rangle$, where $\langle\, L_2 \mid w_2\,;\, N_+ \,\rangle \overset{\delta}{\Longrightarrow} \langle\, L_2 \mid w'_2 \,\rangle$ is inferred by a shorter inference tree, and w_2 is δ-free. $\langle\, L_2 \mid w'_2 \,\rangle$ is δ-irreducible by inductive hypothesis. Since w_2 is δ-free and no dissolving rule preserves δ, it follows that w'_2 is δ-free. Then M'_+ is δ-irreducible by Definition 4.3.

(iv) $M_+ \overset{\delta}{\Longrightarrow} M'_+$ is inferred by (D_4). We proceed in a similar way as for (D_3).

(v) $M_+ \overset{\delta}{\Longrightarrow} M'_+$ is inferred by (D_5). M'_+ is δ-irreducible by Definition 4.1.

(vi) $M_+ \overset{\delta}{\Longrightarrow} M'_+$ is inferred by (D_6). Then $M_+ = \langle\, L_1 \mid w_1\,;\, \langle\, L_2 \mid w_2\delta\,;\, N_+ \,\rangle\,\rangle$ and $M'_+ = \langle\, L_1 \mid w_1 w'_2\,;\, N'_+ \,\rangle$, where $\langle\, L_2 \mid w_2\delta\,;\, N_+ \,\rangle \overset{\delta}{\Longrightarrow} \langle\, L_2 \mid w'_2\delta\,;\, N'_+ \,\rangle$ is inferred by a shorter inference tree. $\langle\, L_2 \mid w'_2\delta\,;\, N'_+ \,\rangle$ is δ-irreducible by inductive hypothesis, and hence N'_+ is δ-irreducible, and $w(N'_+)$ is δ-free. M'_+ is also δ-irreducible by Definition 4.3.

(vii) $M_+ \overset{\delta}{\Longrightarrow} M'_+$ is inferred by (D_7). Then $M_+ = \langle\, L \mid w\,;\, N'_+, N''_+ \,\rangle$ and $M'_+ = \langle\, L \mid w'\,;\, N''_+ \,\rangle$, where $\langle\, L \mid w\,;\, N'_+ \,\rangle \overset{\delta}{\Longrightarrow} \langle\, L \mid w' \,\rangle$ is inferred by a shorter inference tree, and $\langle\, L \mid w\,;\, N''_+ \,\rangle$ is δ-irreducible. It follows that $w(N''_+)$ is δ-free, and M'_+ is δ-irreducible by Definition 4.3.

(viii) $M_+ \overset{\delta}{\Longrightarrow} M'_+$ is inferred by (D_8). Then $M_+ = \langle\, L \mid w\,;\, N^1_+, N^2_+ \,\rangle$ and $M'_+ = \langle L \mid w'\,;\, N^3_+, N^2_+ \rangle$, where $\langle L \mid w\,;\, N^1_+ \rangle \overset{\delta}{\Longrightarrow} \langle L \mid w'\,;\, N^3_+ \rangle$ is inferred by a shorter inference tree, and $\langle L \mid w\,;\, N^2_+ \rangle$ is δ-irreducible. N^3_+ is δ-irreducible and $w(N^3_+)$ is δ-free by inductive hypothesis and Definition 4.3. It follows that N^3_+, N^2_+ is δ-irreducible by Definition 4.2. Since $w(N^3_+, N^2_+)$ is δ-free, we get that M'_+ is δ-irreducible by Definition 4.3.

(ix) $M_+ \overset{\delta}{\Longrightarrow} M'_+$ is inferred by (D_9). M'_+ is δ-irreducible by Definition 4.1.

(x) $M_+ \overset{\delta}{\Longrightarrow} M'_+$ is inferred by (D_{10}). Then $M_+ = \langle\, L \mid w\,;\, N^1_+, N^2_+ \,\rangle$ and $M'_+ = \langle\, L \mid ww'w'' \,;$
$N^3_+ \,\rangle$, where $\langle L \mid w;\, N^1_+ \rangle \overset{\delta}{\Longrightarrow} \langle L \mid ww' \rangle$ and $\langle L \mid w;\, N^2_+ \rangle \overset{\delta}{\Longrightarrow} \langle L \mid ww''\,;\, N^3_+ \rangle$ are inferred by shorter inference trees. $\langle\, L \mid ww''\,;\, N^3_+ \,\rangle$ is δ-irreducible by inductive hypothesis, and hence N^3_+ is δ-irreducible, and $w(N^3_+)$ is δ-free. Then M'_+ is δ-irreducible by Definition 4.3.

(xi) $M_+ \overset{\delta}{\Longrightarrow} M'_+$ is inferred by (D_{11}). Then $M_+ = \langle\, L \mid w\,;\, N^1_+, N^2_+ \,\rangle$ and $M'_+ = \langle\, L \mid ww'w'' \,;$
$N^3_+, N^4_+ \,\rangle$, where $\langle\, L \mid w\,;\, N^1_+ \,\rangle \overset{\delta}{\Longrightarrow} \langle\, L \mid ww'\,;\, N^3_+ \,\rangle$ and $\langle\, L \mid w\,;\, N^2_+ \,\rangle \overset{\delta}{\Longrightarrow} \langle\, L \mid ww'' \,;\, N^4_+ \,\rangle$ are inferred by shorter inference trees. Both N^3_+ and N^4_+ are δ-irreducible, and both $w(N^3_+)$ and $w(N^4_+)$ are δ-free by inductive hypothesis and Definition 4.3. Therefore N^3_+, N^4_+ is also δ-irreducible, and $w(N^3_+, N^4_+)$ is δ-free. It follows that M'_+ is δ-irreducible by Definition 4.3.

This completes the proof. $\square$

Theorem 3. *Let Π be a P system. If $C \in \mathcal{C}^{\#}(\Pi)$ is mpr- and tar-irreducible and $C \overset{\delta}{\Longrightarrow} C'$, then $C' \in \mathcal{C}(\Pi)$, i.e., C' is a committed configuration.*

The proof follows straightforward from Lemma 4.

Proposition 1. *Let Π be a P system. If $C \overset{mpr}{\Longrightarrow} C'$ and $C' \overset{tar}{\Longrightarrow} C''$ such that $C \in \mathcal{C}(\Pi)$, $C' \in \mathcal{C}^{\#}(\Pi)$, and C'' is δ-irreducible, then $C'' \in \mathcal{C}(\Pi)$.*

Proof. C' is mpr-irreducible by Theorem 1, and C'' is tar-irreducible by Theorem 2. Therefore C'' does not contain both messages and δ, and hence it is a committed configuration, i.e., $C'' \in \mathcal{C}(\Pi)$. □

Proposition 2. *Let Π be a P system. If $C \overset{mpr}{\Longrightarrow} C'$ and $C' \overset{\delta}{\Longrightarrow} C''$ such that $C \in \mathcal{C}(\Pi)$, $C' \in \mathcal{C}^{\#}(\Pi)$, and C' is tar-irreducible, then $C'' \in \mathcal{C}(\Pi)$.*

Proof. C' is mpr-irreducible by Theorem 1, and C'' is δ-irreducible by Theorem 3. Therefore C'' does not contain both messages and δ, and hence it is a committed configuration, i.e., $C'' \in \mathcal{C}(\Pi)$. □

Proposition 3. *Let Π be a P system. If $C \overset{mpr}{\Longrightarrow} C'$, $C' \overset{tar}{\Longrightarrow} C''$, and $C'' \overset{\delta}{\Longrightarrow} C'''$ such that $C \in \mathcal{C}(\Pi)$, and $C', C'' \in \mathcal{C}^{\#}(\Pi)$, then $C''' \in \mathcal{C}(\Pi)$.*

Proof. C' is mpr-irreducible by Theorem 1, C'' is tar-irreducible by Theorem 2, and hence C'' does not contain messages. C''' is δ-irreducible by Theorem 3, and hence it does not contain both messages and δ. Therefore C''' is a committed configuration, i.e., $C''' \in \mathcal{C}(\Pi)$. □

Definition 5. *Let Π be a P system. A transition step in Π is defined by the following inference rules:*

For each $C, C'' \in \mathcal{C}(\Pi)$, and δ-irreducible $C' \in \mathcal{C}^{\#}(\Pi)$,

$$\frac{C \overset{mpr}{\Longrightarrow} C', C' \overset{tar}{\Longrightarrow} C''}{C \Rightarrow C''}$$

For each $C, C'' \in \mathcal{C}(\Pi)$, and tar-irreducible $C' \in \mathcal{C}^{\#}(\Pi)$,

$$\frac{C \overset{mpr}{\Longrightarrow} C', C' \overset{\delta}{\Longrightarrow} C''}{C \Rightarrow C''}$$

For each $C, C''' \in \mathcal{C}(\Pi)$, and $C', C'' \in \mathcal{C}^{\#}(\Pi)$,

$$\frac{C \overset{mpr}{\Longrightarrow} C', C' \overset{tar}{\Longrightarrow} C'', C'' \overset{\delta}{\Longrightarrow} C'''}{C \Rightarrow C'''}$$

The consistency of this definition follows from the previous three propositions.

A sequence of transition steps represents a *computation*. A computation is successful if this sequence is finite, namely there is no rule applicable to the objects present in the last committed configuration. In a halting committed configuration, the result of a successful computation is the total number of objects present either in the membrane considered as the output membrane, or in the outer region.

3.4   Bisimulation

Operational semantics provides us with a formal and mechanizable way to find out which transitions are possible for the current configurations of a P system. It provides an abstract interpreter for P systems, as well as the basis for the definition of certain equivalences and congruences between P systems. Moreover, given an operational semantics, we can reason about the rules defining the semantics.

Operational semantics allows a formal analysis of membrane computing, permitting the study of relations between systems. Important relations include simulation preorders and bisimulation. These are especially useful in the context of P systems, allowing to compare two P systems.

A simulation preorder is a relation between transition systems associated to P systems expressing that the second one can match the transitions of the first one. We present a simulation as a relation over the states in a single transition system rather than between the configurations of two systems. Often a transition system consists intuitively of two or more distinct systems, but we also need our notion of simulation over the same transition system. Therefore our definitions relate configurations within one transition system, and this is easily adapted to relate two separate transition systems by building a single transition system consisting of their disjoint union.

Definition 6. *Let Π be a P system.*

1. *A* simulation *relation is a binary relation R over $\mathcal{C}(\Pi)$ such that for every pair of configurations $C_1, C_2 \in \mathcal{C}(\Pi)$, if $(C_1, C_2) \in R$, then for all $C_1' \in \mathcal{C}(\Pi)$, $C_1 \Rightarrow C_1'$ implies that there is a $C_2' \in \mathcal{C}(\Pi)$ such that $C_2 \Rightarrow C_2'$ and $(C_1', C_2') \in R$.*
2. *Given two configurations $C, C' \in \mathcal{C}(\Pi)$, C simulates C', written $C' \leq C$, iff there is a simulation R such that $(C', C) \in R$. In this case, C and C' are said to be similar, and $\leq$ is called the* similarity *relation.*

The similarity relation is a preorder. Furthermore, it is the largest simulation relation over a given transition system. A bisimulation is an equivalence relation between transition systems associated to systems which behave in the same way, in the sense that one system simulates the other and vice-versa. Intuitively two systems are bisimilar if they match each other's transitions, and their evolutions cannot be distinguished.

Definition 7. *Let Π be a P system.*

1. *A* bisimulation *relation is a binary relation R over $\mathcal{C}(\Pi)$ such that both R and R^{-1} are simulation preorders.*
2. *Given two configurations $C, C' \in \mathcal{C}(\Pi)$, C is bisimilar to C', written $C \sim C'$, iff there is a bisimulation R such that $(C, C') \in R$. In this case, C and C' are said to be bisimilar, and $\sim$ is called the* bisimilarity *relation.*

The bisimilarity relation $\sim$ is an equivalence relation. Furthermore, it is the largest bisimulation relation over a given transition system.

4 Conclusion and Related Work

Structural operational semantics is an approach originally introduced by Plotkin [14] in which the operational semantics of a programming language or a computational model is specified in a logical way, independent of a machine architecture or implementation details, by means of rules that provide an inductive definition based on the elementary structures of the language or model.

We have two main approaches in SOS. *Big-step semantics* is also called *natural semantics* by Kahn [7], Gunter [5], and Nielson and Nielson [11], and *evaluation semantics* by Hennessy [6]. In this approach, the main inductive predicate describes the overall result or value of executing a computation, ignoring the intermediate steps. On the other hand, in *small-step semantics* the main inductive predicate describes in more detail the execution of individual steps in a computation, with the overall computation roughly corresponding to the transitive closure of such small steps. Small-step semantics is also called *structural operational semantics* by Plotkin [14] and Nielson and Nielson [11], *computational semantics* by Hennessy [6], and *transition semantics* by Gunter [5]. In general, the small-step style tends to require a greater number of rules that the big-step style, but this is outweighed by the fact that the small-step rules also tend to be simpler. The small-step style facilitates the description of interleaving [10].

In this paper we present an abstract syntax of the membrane systems, and we define a structural operational semantics of P systems by means of three sets of inference rules corresponding to maximal parallel rewriting, parallel communication, and parallel dissolving. The inference rules come together with correctness results. The simulation and bisimulation relations between P systems are also defined. The inference rules provide a big-step operational semantics due to the parallel nature of the model. As a continuation of this work, we translated this big-step operational semantics of P systems into rewriting logic [8], and so we get a small-step operational description. Moreover, by using an efficient implementation of rewriting logic as Maude [4], we obtain an interpreter for membrane systems, and we can verify various properties of these systems by means of a `search` command (a semi-decision procedure for finding failures of safety properties), and a LTL model checker. These achievements are presented in [2].

Acknowledgements

This work has been supported by the research grant CNCSIS 1426/2005.

References

1. O. Andrei, G. Ciobanu, D. Lucanu: Executable specifications of the P systems. In *Membrane Computing, International Workshop, WMC5, Milano, Italy, 2004, Selected Papers* (G. Mauri, Gh. Păun, M.J. Pérez-Jiménez, G. Rozenberg, A. Salomaa, eds.), LNCS 3365, Springer, Berlin, 2005, 127–146.
2. O. Andrei, G. Ciobanu, D. Lucanu: Operational semantics and rewriting logic in membrane computing. *Proceedings SOS Workshop*, 2005, to appear in *ENTCS*.

3. G. Ciobanu: Distributed algorithms over communicating membrane systems. *Biosystems*, 70 (2003), 123–133.
4. M. Clavel, F. Durán, S. Eker, P. Lincoln, N. Martí-Oliet, J. Meseguer, J.F. Quesada: Maude: Specification and programming in rewriting logic. *Theoretical Computer Science*, 285 (2002), 187–243.
5. C. Gunter: Forms of semantic specification. *Bulletin of the EATCS*, 45 (1991), 98–113.
6. M. Hennessy: *The Semantics of Programming Languages: An Elementary Introduction Using Structural Operational Semantics*. Wiley, 1990.
7. G. Kahn: *Natural semantics*. Technical Report 601, INRIA Sophia Antipolis, 1987.
8. N. Marti-Oliet, J. Meseguer: Rewriting logic as a logical and semantical framework. In *Handbook of Philosophical Logic*, 2nd. edn., Kluwer Academic, 2002, 1–87.
9. R. Milner: Operational and algebraic semantics of concurrent processes. In *Handbook of Theoretical Computer Science* (J. van Leeuwen, ed.), vol. B, Elsevier, 1990, 1201–1242.
10. P. Mosses: Modular structural operational semantics. *BRICS RS* 05-7, 2005.
11. H.R. Nielson, F. Nielson: *Semantics with Applications: A Formal Introduction*. Wiley, 1992.
12. Gh. Păun: *Membrane Computing. An Introduction*. Springer, Berlin, 2002.
13. A. Pitts: *Semantics of Programming Languages*. Lecture Notes, University of Cambridge, 1989.
14. G. Plotkin: Structural operational semantics. *Journal of Logic and Algebraic Programming*, 60 (2004), 17–139.

Some Recent Results Concerning Deterministic P Systems

Oscar H. Ibarra

Department of Computer Science,
University of California,
Santa Barbara, CA 93106, USA
ibarra@cs.ucsb.edu

Abstract. We consider P systems that are used as acceptors (recognizers). In the standard semantics of P systems, each evolution step is a result of applying all the rules in a maximally parallel manner: at each step, a maximal multiset of rules are nondeterministically selected and applied in parallel to the current configuration to derive the next configuration (thus, the next configuration is not unique, in general). The system is deterministic if at each step, there is a UNIQUE maximally parallel multiset of rules applicable. The question of whether or not the deterministic version is weaker than the nondeterministic version for various models of P systems is an interesting and fundamental research issue in membrane computing.

Here, we look at three popular models of P systems – catalytic systems, symport/antiport systems, and communicating P systems. We report on recent results that answer some open problems in the field. The results are of the following forms:

1. The deterministic version is weaker than the nondeterministic version.
2. The deterministic version is as powerful as the nondeterministic version.
3. The question of whether the deterministic version is weaker than the nondeterministic version is equivalent to the long-standing open problem of whether deterministic linear-bounded automata are weaker than nondeterministic linear-bounded automata.

1 Catalytic Systems

An interesting subclass of symport/antiport system [8, 9, 10] was studied in [3] – each system is *deterministic* in the sense that the computation path of the system is unique, i.e., at each step of the computation, the maximal multiset of rules that is applicable is unique. It was shown in [3] that any recursively enumerable unary language $L \subseteq o^*$ can be accepted by a deterministic 1-membrane symport/antiport system. Thus, for symport/antiport systems, the deterministic and nondeterministic versions are equivalent and both are universal. It also follows from the construction in [13] that for another model of P systems, called communicating P systems, the deterministic and nondeterministic versions are

R. Freund et al. (Eds.): WMC 2005, LNCS 3850, pp. 49–54, 2006.
© Springer-Verlag Berlin Heidelberg 2006

equivalent as both can accept any unary recursively enumerable language. However, the deterministic-versus-nondeterministic question was left open in [3] for the class of catalytic systems (these systems have rules of the form $Ca \rightarrow Cv$ or $a \rightarrow v$), where the proofs of universality involve a high degree of parallelism [13, 2]. For a discussion of this open question and its importance, see [1, 11]. We resolved this question in the negative in [7]. Since nondeterministic catalytic systems are universal, this result also gives the first example of a P system for which the nondeterministic version is universal, but the deterministic version is not.

For a catalytic system serving as a *language acceptor*, the system starts with an initial configuration wz, where w is a fixed string of catalysts and noncatalysts not containing any symbol in z, and $z = a_1^{n_1} \ldots a_k^{n_k}$ for some nonnegative integers $n_1, \ldots, n_k$, with $\{a_1, \ldots, a_k\}$ a distinguished subset of noncatalyst symbols (the input alphabet). At each step, a maximal multiset of rules is nondeterministically selected and the rules are applied in parallel to the current configuration to derive the next configuration (note that the next configuration is not unique, in general). The string z is accepted if the system eventually halts.

Unlike nondeterministic 1-membrane catalytic system acceptors (with 2 catalysts) which are universal, we showed in [7] using a graph-theoretic approach that the Parikh map of any language which is included in $a_1^* \ldots a_k^*$ is accepted by any deterministic catalytic system is a simple semilinear set which can be effectively constructed. This result gives the first example of a P system for which the nondeterministic version is universal, but the deterministic version is not. We also proved that for deterministic 1-membrane catalytic systems using only rules of type $Ca \rightarrow Cv$ (i.e., purely catalytic rules), the set of reachable configurations from a given initial configuration is effectively semilinear. In contrast, the reachability set is no longer semilinear in general if rules of type $a \rightarrow v$ are also used. Our results generalized to multi-membrane catalytic systems.

We also considered in [7] deterministic catalytic systems which allow rules to be prioritized. We investigated three types of such systems, namely, *totally prioritized*, *strongly prioritized*, and *weakly prioritized* catalytic systems. For totally prioritized systems, the rules are divided into different priority groups, and if a rule in a higher priority group is applicable, then no rules from a lower priority group can be used. For both strongly prioritized and weakly prioritized systems, the underlying priority relation is a *strict partial order* (i.e., irreflexive, asymmetric, and transitive). Under the semantics of strong priority, if a rule with higher priority is used, then no rule of a lower priority can be used even if the two rules do not compete for objects. For weakly prioritized systems, a rule is applicable if it cannot be replaced by a higher priority one.

For these three prioritized systems, we obtained contrasting results by showing that deterministic strongly and weakly prioritized catalytic systems are universal, whereas totally prioritized systems only accept semilinear sets.

2 Restricted Symport/Antiport Systems

2.1 Bounded S/A Systems

As we already noted, it is known that for 1-membrane symport/antiport systems, the deterministic and nondeterministic versions are equivalent and they are universal [3]. It also follows from the results in [13] that for another model of P systems, called communicating P systems, the deterministic and nondeterministic versions are equivalent as both can accept any unary recursively enumerable language.

In [6], we looked at some restricted versions of these systems. One model, called *bounded S/A system*, have rules are of the form: $(u, out; v, in)$, where u, v are strings representing multisets of objects (i.e., symbols) with the restriction that $|u| \geq |v| \geq 1$. Actually, the result in [6] was for when $|u| = |v| \geq 1$, but it also holds for our case. (Note that we are only interested in the multiplicities of the objects.) An input $z = a_1^{n_1} \ldots a_k^{n_k}$ (each n_i is a nonnegative integer) is accepted if the system when started with wz, where w is a fixed string independent of z and not containing a_i $(1 \leq i \leq k)$ eventually halts. We showed the following:

1. A language $L \subseteq a_1^* \ldots a_k^*$ is accepted by a bounded S/A system if and only if it is accepted by a *log n* space-bounded Turing machine, and if and only if it is accepted by a two-way multihead finite automaton. This result holds for both deterministic and nondeterministic versions.
2. Deterministic and nondeterministic bounded S/A systems over a unary input alphabet are equivalent if and only if deterministic and nondeterministic linear-bounded automata (over an arbitrary input alphabet) are equivalent. The latter problem is a long-standing open question in complexity theory [12].

2.2 Multi-membrane Bounded S/A Systems

We also studied multi-membrane S/A systems, called special S/A systems, which are restricted in that only rules of the form $(u, out; v, in)$, where $|u| \geq |v| \geq 1$, can appear in the skin membrane. Thus, the number of objects in the system during the computation does not increase. Let E be the alphabet of symbols in the environment (note that there may be other symbols in the system that are not transported into the environment and, therefore, not included in E). We showed that for every nonnegative integer t, special S/A systems with environment alphabet E of t symbols has an infinite hierarchy in terms of the number of membranes. Again, this holds for both deterministic and nondeterministic versions.

2.3 Bounded S/A Systems Accepting String Languages

We also investigated in [6] another model – a (one-membrane) bounded S/A system whose alphabet of symbols V contains a distinguished input alphabet Σ. We assume that Σ contains a special symbol $\$$, called the (right) end marker. The rules are restricted to be of the forms:

(1) $(u, out; v, in)$
(2) $(u, out; vc, in)$

where u is in V^+ and v is in $(V - \Sigma)^+$ with $|u| \geq |v| \geq 1$, and c is in Σ. The second type of rule is called a *read-rule*. There is an abundance of symbols from $V - \Sigma$ in the environment. The only symbols from Σ available in the environment are in the input string $z = a_1 \ldots a_n$ (where a_i is in $\Sigma - \{\$\}$ for $1 \leq i < n$, and $a_n = \$$), which is provided online externally.

There is a fixed string w in $(V - \Sigma)^*$, which is the initial configuration of the system. Maximal parallelism in the application of the rules is assumed as usual. Hence, in general, the size of the multiset of rules applicable at each step is unbounded. In particular, the number of instances of read-rules (i.e., rules of the form $(u, out; vc, in)$) applicable in a step is unbounded. However, clearly, the number of read-rules in an applicable multiset cannot exceed the number of symbols remaining to be read, and the symbols in these read-rules, say there are s of them, must be consistent with the next s symbols of the input string z that have not yet been processed. Note that rules of types 1 do not consume any input symbol from z.

The input string $z = a_1 \ldots a_n$ (with $a_n = \$$) is accepted if, after reading all the input symbols, the system eventually halts.

As described above, the system is nondeterministic. In the deterministic case, the maximally parallel multiset of rules applicable at each step of the computation is unique. In [6] we showed that the deterministic version is strictly weaker than the nondeterministic version: There are languages accepted by the nondeterministic version that cannot be accepted by the deterministic version. An example is the language $L = \{x\#^p \mid x \text{ is a binary number with leading bit 1 and } p \neq 2val(x)\}$, where $val(x)$ is the value of x. It was shown in [6] (using a similar result in [5]) that L can be accepted by the nondeterministic version but not by the deterministic version.

Let NBSA (DBSA) be the class of languages accepted by the nondeterministic (deterministic) acceptors defined above. The following was also shown in [6] (again, using similar results in [5]):

1. NBSA is closed under union and intersection, but not under complementation.
2. DBSA is closed under union, intersection, and complementation.

3   Restricted Communicating P Systems

The model we investigated in [5] is a restricted version of the communicating P system (CPS). A CPS, first introduced and studied in [13], has multiple membranes labeled $1, 2, \ldots$, where 1 is the skin membrane. The rules are of the form:

1. $a \rightarrow a_x$,
2. $ab \rightarrow a_x b_y$,
3. $ab \rightarrow a_x b_y c_{come}$,

where a, b, c are objects, x, y (which indicate the directions of movements of a and b) can be *here*, *out*, or in_j. The designation *here* means that the object remains in the membrane containing it, *out* means that the object is transported to the membrane directly enclosing the membrane that contains the object (or to the environment if the object is in the skin membrane). The designation in_j means that the object is moved into the membrane, labeled j, that is directly enclosed by the membrane that contains the object. A rule of the form (3) can only appear in the skin membrane. When such a rule is applied, c is imported through the skin membrane from the environment and will become an element in the skin membrane. In one step, all rules are applied in a maximally parallel manner.

An RCPS [4, 5] is a restricted CPS where the environment does not contain any object initially. The system can expel objects into the environment but only expelled objects can be retrieved from the environment. Hence, at any time during the computation, the objects in the system (including in the environment) are always the same.

Let o be a distinguished object (called the *input symbol*) in V. Assume that an RCPS has m membranes, with a distinguished *input membrane*. We say that the system accepts o^n if, when started with o^n in the input membrane initially (with no o's in the other membranes), the system eventually halts. Note that objects in $V - \{o\}$ have fixed numbers and their distributions in the different membranes are fixed initially. Also, at any time during the computation, the number of each object $a \in V - \{o\}$ in the whole system (including the environment) remains the same, although the distribution of the a's among the membranes may change at each step. The RCPS model can be generalized to have k input membranes (see [5]). Such a system then accepts a language which is a subset of $a_1^* \ldots a_k^*$.

A nondeterministic (deterministic) RCPS is one in which there may be more than one (at most one) maximally parallel multiset of rules that is applicable at each step. It turns out that nondeterministic (deterministic) RCPSs are equivalent to nondeterministic (deterministic) bounded S/A systems (of Section 2.1) (see [6, 5]. Hence, we have:

1. The following are equivalent for a language $L \subseteq a_1^* \ldots a_k^*$:
   (a) L is accepted by an RCPS.
   (b) L is accepted by a bounded S/A system.
   (c) L is accepted by a *log n* space-bounded Turing machine
   (d) L it is accepted by a two-way multihead finite automaton.
   The above holds for both deterministic and nondeterministic versions.
2. Deterministic and nondeterministic bounded RCPSs over a unary input alphabet are equivalent if and only if deterministic and nondeterministic linear-bounded automata (over an arbitrary input alphabet) are equivalent.

Finally, we mention that a restricted multi-membrane CPS that is an acceptor of string language, called SCPA, was introduced in [5], and this model is equivalent to the the bounded S/A system accepting string languages of Section 2.3. Hence, the results cited in that section hold for SCPAs as well.

Acknowledgements

This work was supported in part by NSF Grants CCF-0430945, IIS-0451097, and CCF-0524136. Some of the results reported here were obtained jointly with Sara Woodworth and Hsu-Chun Yen.

References

1. C.S. Calude, Gh. Păun: *Computing with Cells and Atoms: After Five Years.* New text added to Russian edition of the book with the same title first published by Taylor and Francis Publishers, London, 2001. To be published by Pushchino Publishing House, 2004.
2. R. Freund, L. Kari, M. Oswald, P. Sosik: Computationally universal P systems without priorities: two catalysts are sufficient. *Theoretical Computer Science*, 330, 2 (2005), 251–266.
3. R. Freund, Gh. Păun: On deterministic P systems. Manuscript, 2003 (available at `http://psystems.disco.unimib.it`).
4. O.H. Ibarra: The number of membranes matters. In *Membrane Computing. Intern. Workshop, WMC2003, Tarragona*, LNCS 2933, Springer, Berlin, 2004, 218–231.
5. O.H. Ibarra: On determinism versus nondeterminism in P systems. *Theoretical Computer Science*, to appear.
6. O.H. Ibarra, S. Wood: On bounded symport/antiport systems. *Pre-proceedings of 11th International Meeting on DNA Computing*, UWO, London, Ontario, 2005, 37–48.
7. O.H. Ibarra, H. Yen: On deterministic catalytic systems. *Pre-proceedings of 10th International Conference on Implementation and Application of Automata*, 2005, to appear.
8. A. Păun, Gh. Păun: The power of communication: P systems with symport/antiport. *New Generation Computers*, 20, 3 (2002), 295–306.
9. Gh. Păun: Computing with membranes. *Journal of Computer and System Sciences*, 61, 1 (2000), 108-143.
10. Gh. Păun: *Membrane Computing: An Introduction.* Springer, Berlin, 2002.
11. Gh. Păun: Further twenty six open problems in membrane computing. *Proc. Third Brainstorming Week on Membrane Computing*, Sevilla, 2005, RGNC Report 01/2005, 249–262. Available at *http://psystems.disco.unimib.it*.
12. W. Savitch: Relationships between nondeterministic and deterministic tape complexities. *J. Comput. Syst. Sci.*, 4, 2 (1970), 177–192.
13. P. Sosik: P systems versus register machines: two universality proofs. In *Pre-Proceedings of Workshop on Membrane Computing (WMC-CdeA2002), Curtea de Arges, Romania*, 2002, 371–382.

Membrane Algorithms

Taishin Y. Nishida

Faculty of Engineering,
Toyama Prefectural University,
Imizu, 939-0398 Toyama, Japan
nishida@pu-toyama.ac.jp

Abstract. A new type of approximate algorithms for optimization problems, called membrane algorithms, is proposed, which can be seen as an application of membrane computing to evolutionary computing. A membrane algorithm consists of several membrane separated regions, where subalgorithms and tentative solutions to the optimization problem to be solved are placed, as well as a solution transporting mechanism between adjacent regions. The subalgorithms improve tentative solutions simultaneously. After that, the best and worst solutions in a region are sent to adjacent inner and outer regions, respectively. By repeating this process, a good solution will appear in the innermost region. The algorithm terminates if a terminate condition is satisfied. A simple condition of this type is the number of iterations, while a little more sophisticated condition becomes true if the good solution is not changed during a predetermined period. Computer experiments show that such algorithms are rather efficient in solving the travelling salesman problem.

1 Introduction

An NP-complete (or, even more difficult, NP-hard) problem has a large number of possible solutions (at least $O(2^n)$ for an instance of size n) and no (up to now) effective deterministic procedure to decide the optimum solution. As a consequence, it is of interest, and there are many investigations in this respect, to find approximate algorithms for them. Such approximate algorithms are tractable in time complexity and provide close to optimal solutions. This is the case with genetic algorithms, simulated annealing, tabu search, neural networks, ant colony algorithm, and so on [1]. An approximate algorithm is better than another one if the former obtains solutions closer to the optimum solution than the latter.

It is obvious that the simple random search algorithm which randomly selects a solution from $O(2^n)$ candidates is the worst approximate algorithm. On the other hand, any local search algorithm which transforms a tentative solution into a new solution by modifying a part of the tentative solution often falls into local optima and cannot find better solutions even if such solutions exist. That is why many approximate algorithms consist of a pool of tentative solutions, a stochastic mechanism of changing them, and a rule which selects the next pool of solutions from the changed solutions.

R. Freund et al. (Eds.): WMC 2005, LNCS 3850, pp. 55–66, 2006.
© Springer-Verlag Berlin Heidelberg 2006

The present paper contributes to this area of research by making use of some attractive features of membrane computing [11]. The starting point is the observation that P systems provide a natural framework for approximate algorithms: a multiset of objects represents a pool of tentative solutions and transition rules correspond to change and select mechanisms. Moreover, the P systems paradigm can bring to the approximate algorithms area "space" and "time" varying strategies: membrane structures and dynamic behaviors of rules and membranes. In the evolutionary computing literature, there are many researches on algorithms with spatial and/or temporal structures (e.g., simulated annealing, ant colony algorithm, spatially structured evolutionary algorithms [14], etc.). They all have limitations, because they only use their specific features; for example, a simulated annealing algorithm never uses the recombination mechanism of genetic algorithms. On the other hand, a P systems inspired algorithm, called below a *membrane algorithm*, can both use any existing approximate algorithm, and can bring new ideas into the stage, inspired from the cell biology, such as, hierarchical compartmentalization, dynamical membrane structure, communication across membranes, etc.

In the next section, the basic ideas of membrane algorithms are explained. Then two types of membrane algorithms, which solve the travelling salesman problems approximately, are defined and computer experiments with these algorithms are shown in Section 3.

2   The Framework of Membrane Algorithms

Here we explain the new type of algorithms, called *membrane algorithms*, as introduced and discussed already in [7, 8, 9].

A membrane algorithm consists of three different kinds of components:

1. A number of regions which are separated by nested membranes (Figure 1).
2. For every region, a subalgorithm and a few tentative solutions of the optimization problem to be solved.
3. Solution transporting mechanisms between adjacent regions.

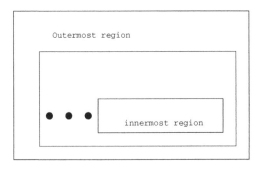

Fig. 1. A membrane structure of a membrane algorithm

After initial settings, a membrane algorithm works as follows:

1. For every region, the tentative solutions are updated by the subalgorithm associated with that region, simultaneously in all regions.
2. In every region, the best and worst solutions, with respect to the optimization criteria, are sent to the adjacent inner and outer regions, respectively.
3. In every region, the next population of tentative solutions is selected from the solutions left in the region and received from the adjacent regions. The selection is done by the subalgorithm associated with that region.
4. One repeats updating and transporting until a terminate condition is satisfied.
5. During the execution, a membrane algorithm can change the membrane structure or even produce a new membrane structure, and then repeat procedures 1 − 3.
6. After all terminate conditions are satisfied, the best solution in the innermost regions of all membrane structures will be the output of the algorithm.

A membrane algorithm can have a number of subalgorithms which are any approximate algorithm for the optimization problem, for example, genetic algorithms, tabu search, simulated annealing, local search, and so on. A membrane algorithm is expected to be able to escape from local optimal solutions by using in upper regions a subalgorithm which is similar to random search. On the other hand, it can preserve (and may sometimes improve) good solutions in the inner regions by a subalgorithm which resembles local search. So, assigning appropriate subalgorithms for the given problem, the performance of a membrane algorithm can be improved.

3   Computer Experiments in Solving the Travelling Salesman Problem

In this section we fix the components of membrane algorithms to solve the travelling salesman problem (TSP for short). Then the algorithm is implemented and experimented on a computer.

3.1   Travelling Salesman Problem

An instance of TSP with n nodes contains n pairs of real numbers (x_i, y_i) $(i = 0, 1, \ldots, n-1)$ which correspond to points in the two dimensional space. The distance between two nodes $v_i = (x_i, y_i)$ and $v_j = (x_j, y_j)$ is the geometrical distance $d(v_i, v_j) = \sqrt{(x_i - x_j)^2 + (y_i - y_j)^2}$. A solution (or a tour) is a list of nodes $(v_0, v_1, \ldots, v_{n-1})$ in which no nodes appear twice, i.e., $\forall i, j \; i \neq j$ implies $v_i \neq v_j$. The *value* of a solution $v = (v_0, v_1, \ldots, v_{n-1})$, denoted by $W(v)$, is given by

$$W(v) = \sum_{i=0}^{n-2} d(v_i, v_{i+1}) + d(v_{n-1}, v_0).$$

For two solutions u and v, v is better than u if $W(v) < W(u)$. The solution which has the minimum value from all possible solutions is said to be the *strict solution* of the instance. A solution which has a value close to the strict solution is called an *approximate solution*.

3.2   Simple Membrane Algorithms

First we examine a simple realization of a membrane algorithm.

Let m be the number of membranes and let region 0 be the innermost and region $m - 1$ be the outermost regions, respectively.

A simple membrane algorithm has one tentative solution in region 0 and two solutions in regions 1 to $m - 1$.

We use a tabu search as the subalgorithm in region 0. Tabu search searches a neighbor of the tentative solution by exchanging two nodes in the solution. In order for the same solution not to appear twice, tabu search has a tabulist which consists of solutions already appeared. Solutions in the tabulist do not appear again. Tabu search resets the tentative solution and the tabulist if one of the next three conditions occurs:

1. The value of the neighboring solution is less than that of the tentative solution. The neighboring solution becomes the tentative solution.
2. The value of the best solution in region 1 is less than that of the tentative solution. The best solution in region 1 becomes the new tentative solution.
3. Neighbor search exceeds a predetermined number of turns (in this case $\frac{n}{5}$). The tentative solution remains. Only the tabulist is reset.

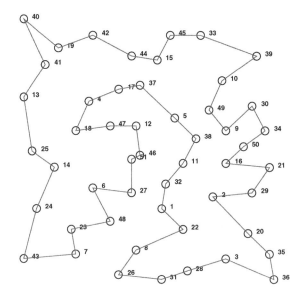

Fig. 2. An example tour (solution) obtained by a simple membrane algorithm. The instance is eil51.

In case 3, no improvement occurs. However, tabu search tries to search other neighbors, since there are many unsearched neighbors.

The tentative solutions in regions 1 to $m - 1$ (there are two solutions in each region) are improved by the subalgorithm summarized below:

1. If the two solutions have the same value, then a part of one solution (which is selected probabilistically) is reversed.
2. The two solutions are recombined and two new solutions are produced.
3. The two new solutions are modified by point mutations. In the i-th region, a mutation occurs with probability $\frac{i}{m}$.
4. From the four solutions (the two old solutions and the two newly produced solutions), the best solution is sent to the adjacent inner region and the worst solution is sent to the adjacent outer region.
5. The best two solutions are selected from the four solutions (two remaining solutions and two received solutions).

Obviously, the subalgorithm described above resembles the genetic algorithm. However, the subalgorithm always recombines the two solutions in a region while the genetic algorithm randomly selects solutions to be recombined. If the two solutions in a region are identical, then recombination makes no new solutions. In this case, step 1 introduces a new solution using the reverse operation, which is a kind of mutation.

The overall algorithm looks as follows:

1. An instance of TSP is given.
2. One tentative solution is made for region 0 and two tentative solutions are made for every region 1 to $m - 1$, randomly.
3. 3.1 to 3.3 are repeated d times (d is given as a parameter).
   3.1 Tentative solutions are modified simultaneously in every region using the subalgorithms from the regions.
   3.2 For every region i ($1 \leq i \leq m - 2$), the best among the solutions in the region (old solutions and modified solutions) is sent to region $i - 1$ and the worst solution to region $i + 1$. (In region 0, the worst solution is sent to region 1 and in region $m - 1$, the best solution is sent to region $m - 2$.)
   3.3 For every region 1 to $m - 1$ all solutions but the best two are erased.
4. The tentative solution in region 0 becomes the output of the algorithm.

3.3 Computer Experiments

We have implemented the algorithm above using Java programming language. By using Java, modifications of the algorithm have been easily tested on a computer. For example, we have implemented several recombination methods and have found that the edge exchange recombination (see [4] and the Appendix) is superior to other methods.

Tables 1 and 2 show results of the program for TSP benchmark problems eil51 and kroA100 from TSPLIB [12]. Results of genetic algorithm [5], simulated annealing [17], temperature parallel simulated annealing [3], ant colony algorithm [6], and neural network [15] are also shown in the tables.

Table 1. Results of membrane algorithm (MA), genetic algorithm (GA), simulated annealing (SA), temperature parallel simulated annealing (TPSA), and ant colony algorithm (AC) for the benchmark problem eil51 whose optimum value is 426. The membrane algorithm repeats step 3 100,000 times. The number of membranes is 50 and the number of trials is 100. NA stands for no data available for the worst case of the ant colony algorithm.

Algorithm	MA	GA	SA	TPSA	AC
Best	426	426	430	426	426
Average	430	428	438	427	427
Worst	438	432	445	427	NA

Table 2. Results for benchmark problem kroA100 whose optimum value is 21282. NN stands for neural network. The conditions for the membrane algorithm are the same as for eil51. There are no data for GA and AC for the problem.

Algorithm	MA	SA	TPSA	NN
Best	21319	21369	21384	22246
Average	21937	21763	21418	22765
Worst	23389	22564	21482	23167

It should be noted that all simulations of Tables 1 and 2 and the optimum values are computed with integer distances between nodes, that is, for nodes $v_i = (x_i, y_i)$ and $v_j = (x_j, y_j)$, the distance $d(v_i, v_j)$ is the rounded integer of $\sqrt{(x_i - x_j)^2 + (y_i - y_j)^2}$. In the previous papers [7, 8, 9] computations have been done with real distances (without rounding).

3.4   Shrink Membrane Algorithm

Now we incorporate in our algorithms a central feature of membrane comput- ing, that of dynamically changing membrane structures, thus leading to *shrink membrane algorithms*.

A shrink membrane algorithm consists of two phases. The first phase starts with m membranes and subalgorithms of GA type in all regions, where m is a parameter. If the best solution in region 0 does not change during $100n$ iterations (where n is the size of the instance, i.e., number of nodes), then the number of membranes becomes 2, with tabu search in region 0 and a GA type subalgorithm in region 1. The two regions have the same initial solutions, which are the best solution obtained so far. Then the algorithm improves solutions until the solution in region 0 does not change during $300n$ iterations.

The first phase has a number, say t, of membrane structures. All structures do the same computation independently. They get different solutions because the subalgorithms use a probabilistic choice[1].

---
[1] Of course, the results of the first phase may be unique if the strict solution is ob- tained.

The second phase of the shrink membrane algorithm has one membrane structure with $\frac{t}{2}$ regions. The t solutions obtained in the first phase are sorted and put into the $\frac{t}{2}$ regions. The best solution is put into the innermost region. The subsequent solutions are put into regions 1 to $\frac{t}{2}$, two in each region, and better solutions are put in inner regions. In other words, the results of the first phase become the initial solutions of the second phase. The subalgorithms of the second phase are identical to those of simple membrane algorithms, but the shrink membrane algorithm terminates if the best solution does not change during $100n$ iterations.

Figure 3 and Table 3 illustrate the evolution and the parameters of the shrink membrane algorithm. The parameters shown in Table 3 are selected by several preliminary experiments of solving eil51 and kroA100 with various combinations of parameters.

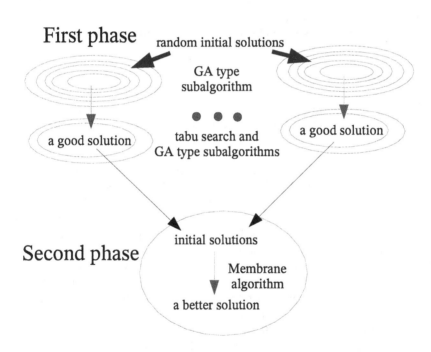

Fig. 3. Shrink membrane algorithm

Table 3. Parameters of shrink membrane algorithm used in the computer experiment

Phase	number of		subalgorithms	terminate conditions
	structures	membranes		unchange during
1–1	$t = 100$	$m = 5$	GA type only	$100n$
1–2	$t = 100$	2	GA type and tabu search	$300n$
2	1	$\frac{t}{2} = 50$	GA type and tabu search	$100n$

Table 4. Results of 10 trials of simple and shrink MAs for various benchmark problems

Problem	best		average		worst	
	shrink	simple	shrink	simple	shrink	simple
eil51	429	429	431	434	436	444
eil76	547	556	556	564	561	575
eil101	655	669	667	684	677	693
kroA100	21299	21651	21504	22590	21750	24531
ch150	6751	7073	6889	7320	6961	7633
tsp225	4031	4073	4112	4154	4172	4239

Table 4 shows results of simple and shrink membrane algorithms for benchmark problems in TSPLIB. We can see that the shrink algorithm yields a good approximate solution in every trial. The results shown in Table 4 are obtained with real distances between nodes (see the note of Subsection 3.3), hence the results cannot be compared to the results in Tables 1 and 2 nor the optimum values.

4   Conclusion

In this paper, the idea of membrane algorithms and several computer experiments in solving the traveller salesman problem are presented. Such algorithms incorporate several basic features of P systems, such as compartmentalization, communication among compartments, dynamic membrane structure.

We have considered two types of membrane algorithms, simple and shrink algorithms, and we examined their behaviors in solving the traveller salesman problem on a computer. We have observed that simple membrane algorithms provide as good approximate solutions as other approximate algorithms. On the other hand, shrink membrane algorithms always finds quite good approximate solutions. The programs used in the computer experiments are available from the web-site [10].

Membrane algorithms inherit the parallelism of P system. Therefore, membrane algorithms are naturally implemented on a parallel hardware, while the other approximate algorithms must be modified before being implemented on a parallel computer (cf [13]). A preliminary experiment shows that the shrink membrane algorithms become $30 \sim 40$ % faster if they are implemented on a loosely coupled multiprocessing computer with two CPU's (SUN Blade 1000).

Finally, it is worth mentioning that membrane algorithms have a possibility of avoiding the "No Free Lunch Theorem" [2, 16], because membrane algorithms can use various algorithms as subalgorithms.

References

1. C.A. Floudas, P.M. Pardalos, eds.: *Encyclopedia of Optimization*. Kluwer, Dordrecht, 2001.
2. C. Igel, M. Toussaint: On classes of functions for which No Free Lunch results hold. *Information Processing Letters*, 86 (2003), 317–321.

3. K. Konishi et al.: An application of temperature parallel simulated annealing to the travelling salesman problem and its experimental analysis. *Trans. IEICS D-I*, J80-DI (1997), 127–136 (in Japanese).

4. K. Maekawa et al.: A solution of travelling salesman problem by genetic algorithm. *SICE*, 31 (1995), 598–605 (in Japanese).

5. K. Maekawa et al.: A genetic solution for the travelling salesman problem by means of a thermodynamical selection rule. *SICE*, 33 (1997), 939–946 (in Japanese).

6. Y. Nakamichi et al.: The effects of diversity control based on random selection in ant colony optimization. *Journal of IPSJ*, 43 (2002), 2939–2947 (in Japanese).

7. T.Y. Nishida: An application of P-system: A new algorithm for NP-complete optimization problems. In *Proceedings of The 8th World Multi-Conference on Systems, Cybernetics and Informatics* (N. Callaos et al., eds.), 2004, vol V, 109–112.

8. T.Y. Nishida: An approximate algorithm for NP-complete optimization problems exploiting P-systems. In *Proceedings of Brainstorming Workshop on Uncertainty in Membrane Computing*, Palma de Majorca, 2004, 185–192.

9. T.Y. Nishida: Membrane algorithms. Approximate algorithms for NP-complete optimization problems. In *Application of Membrane Computing* (G. Ciobanu, Gh. Păun, M.J. Pérez-Jiménez, eds.), Springer, Berlin, 2005, 301–312.

10. T.Y. Nishida: URL http://www.comp.pu-toyama.ac.jp/nishida/.

11. Gh. Păun: Computing with membranes. *Journal of Computer and System Sciences*, 61 (2000), 108–143.

12. G. Reinelt: TSPLIB, URL http://www.iwr.uni-heidelberg.de/groups/comopt/software/TSPLIB95/.

13. M. Tomassini: Parallelism and evolutionary algorithms. *IEEE Trans. Evolutionary Computation*, 6 (2002), 443–462.

14. M. Tomassini: *Spatially Structured Evolutionary Algorithms*. Springer, Berlin, 2005.

15. T. Tanaka et al.: Performance comparisons of two Hopfield neural networks for large-scale travelling salesman problem. *Journal IPSJ*, 38 (1997), 2157–2164.

16. D.H. Wolpert, W.G. Macready: No Free Lunch Theorem for optimization. *IEEE Transactions on Evolutionary Computation*, 1 (1997), 67–82.

17. M. Yoneda: URL http://www.mikilab.doshisha.ac.jp/dia/research/person/yoneda/research/2002_7_10/SA/07-sareslut.html

Appendix: Edge Exchange Crossover

We describe here the edge exchange crossover algorithm.

For a positive integer n, let $[n]$ denote the set $\{0, 1, \ldots, n-1\}$. An instance of TSP with n nodes is a weighted complete graph of n nodes[2]. A (pseudo) tour of a TSP instance of n nodes is a function $X : [n] \to [n]$. If X is a bijection, then X is a tour of the instance; otherwise, X is a pseudo tour. For every $i \in [n]$, $X(i)$ stands for the i-th node of the (pseudo) tour X.

For a (pseudo) tour X and an integer $i \in [n]$, $E(X, i)$ stands for the i-th edge of the (pseudo) tour, i.e., $E(X, i) = (X(i), X((i + 1) \bmod n))$. For an edge e of a (pseudo) tour X, $s(e)$, and $t(e)$ denote the beginning and the ending nodes of e, respectively. The following equations are obvious:

---

[2] The definition here corresponds to all types of weights, not only to the geometrical distance in the two dimensional space.

$$s(E(X, i)) = X(i),$$
$$t(E(X, i)) = X((i + 1) \bmod n).$$

In the sequel, all additions and subtractions are those of the modulo-n residue ring.

The edge exchange crossover (EXX for short) is the algorithm described below.

Algorithm EXX:
Input: A TSP instance and two tours A, B
Output: Recombined tours A', B'
  1. Select $i \in [n]$ randomly.
  2. Let j be an integer such that $s(E(B, j)) = s(E(A, i))$.
  3. Make new (pseudo) tours A', B' by

$$A'(k) = \begin{cases} A(k) & 0 \le k \le i, \ i + 2 \le k \le n - 1 \\ t(E(B, j)) & k = i + 1 \end{cases}$$

$$B'(k) = \begin{cases} B(k) & 0 \le k \le j, \ j + 2 \le k \le n - 1 \\ t(E(A, i)) & k = j + 1 \end{cases}$$

  4. While $t(E(A, i)) \ne t(E(B, j))$ do
     /* If $t(E(A, i)) = t(E(B, j))$, then A' and B' are tours and the algorithm terminates. See Lemma 1. */
  5.   Let i' and j' be integers such that $s(E(A, i')) = t(E(B, j))$ and $s(E(B, j')) = t(E(A, i))$.
  6.   Make (pseudo) tours A'' and B'' by
        case $i < i'$

$$A''(k) = \begin{cases} A'(k) & 0 \le k \le i + 1 \text{ or } i' \le k \le n - 1 \\ A(i + i' + 1 - k) & i + 2 \le k \le i' - 1 \end{cases}$$

        case $i' < i$

$$A''(k) = \begin{cases} A'(k) & i' \le k \le i + 1 \\ A(i + i' + 1 - k) & 0 \le k \le i' - 1 \text{ or } i + 2 \le k \le n - 1 \end{cases}$$

        case $j < j'$

$$B''(k) = \begin{cases} B'(k) & 0 \le k \le j + 1 \text{ or } j' \le k \le n - 1 \\ B(j + j' + 1 - k) & j + 2 \le k \le j' - 1 \end{cases}$$

        case $j' < j$

$$B''(k) = \begin{cases} B'(k) & j' \le k \le j+1 \\ B(j+j'+1-k) & 0 \le k \le j'-1 \text{ or } j+2 \le k \le n-1 \end{cases}$$

7. Let $i \leftarrow i'$, $j \leftarrow j'$, $A \leftarrow A''$, $B \leftarrow B''$
8. Make new (pseudo) tours A', B' by

$$A'(k) = \begin{cases} A(k) & 0 \le k \le i-1 \text{ or } i+2 \le k \le n-1 \\ B(j) & k = i \\ t(E(B,j)) & k = i+1 \end{cases}$$

$$B'(k) = \begin{cases} B(k) & 0 \le k \le j-1 \text{ or } j+2 \le k \le n-1 \\ A(i) & k = j \\ t(E(A,i)) & k = j+1 \end{cases}$$

/* the end of "while" loop */

Example 1. If tours A and B are given by the following table

x	0	1	2	3	4	5	6	7
$A(x)$	0	1	2	3	4	5	6	7
$B(x)$	1	4	3	0	5	6	2	7

and i is selected to 1, then the algorithm EXX calculates $j = 0$, $i' = 4$, and $j' = 6$. The pseudo tours A'' and B'' are given by

x	0	1	2	3	4	5	6	7
$A''(x)$	0	1	4	3	4	5	6	7
$B''(x)$	1	2	6	5	0	3	2	7

Now, $i = 4$, $j = 6$, $i' = 7$, and $j' = 3$. The next A'' and B'' become

x	0	1	2	3	4	5	6	7
$A''(x)$	0	1	4	3	2	7	6	7
$B''(x)$	6	2	1	5	0	3	4	5

Then $i = 7$ and $j = 3$ and the terminate condition of the algorithm becomes true obtaining the tours

x	0	1	2	3	4	5	6	7
$A'(x)$	0	1	4	3	2	7	6	5
$B'(x)$	6	2	1	7	0	3	4	5

Lemma 1. *Let A, B, A', B', A'', B'', i, j, i', and j' be the symbols defined in the algorithm EXX. The following conditions are equivalent.*

1. A' and B' are not tours.
2. $t(E(A, i)) \neq t(E(B, j))$, $A''(i') = A''(i + 1)$, $B''(j') = B''(j + 1)$, $\forall x, y \in [n] - \{i', i+1\}$ $x \neq y$ implies $A''(x) \neq A''(y)$, and $\forall x, y \in [n] - \{j', j+1\}$ $x \neq y$ implies $B''(x) \neq B''(y)$.

Proof. The proof of $2 \to 1$ is obvious.

We prove the $1 \to 2$ by induction on the "while" loop.

At the first execution of the loop, A' has $t(E(B, j))(= B(j + 1))$ at $A'(i + 1)$ and B' has $t(E(A, i))(= A(i + 1))$ at $B'(j + 1)$. If $A(i + 1) \neq B(j + 1)$, then there exist $i', j' \in [n]$ such that $i \neq i'$, $j \neq j'$, $A(i') = A'(i') = A'(i + 1)$, and $B(j') = B'(j') = B'(j + 1)$ because A and B are tours. Then all assertions of 2 hold.

Next let 1 and 2 be equivalent until the previous execution of the loop. In this case we have $A'(i) = B(j)$, $A'(i + 1) = t(E(B, j))$, $B'(j) = A(i)$, and $B'(j + 1) = t(E(A, i))$. If $A(i + 1) \neq B(j + 1)$, then there exist $i', j' \in [n]$ such that $i \neq i'$, $j \neq j'$, $A(i') = A'(i') = A'(i + 1)$, and $B(j') = B'(j') = B'(j + 1)$ because of the hypothesis of induction. Then assertions of 2 hold. $\square$

Lemma 2. *The algorithm EXX always terminates.*

Proof. It is easily seen that the algorithm EXX is reversible, that is, given A'', B'', i, j, i', and j', A, and B are uniquely determined. The observation implies that the algorithm EXX is an injection on the direct product of the sets of pseudo tours. Then the lemma follows from Lemma 1 and the fact that the domain of the algorithm is finite. $\square$

Lemmas 1 and 2 prove the next theorem.

Theorem 1. *The algorithm EXX always terminates and outputs recombined tours.*

On Evolutionary Lineages of Membrane Systems

Petr Sosík[1,2] and Ondřej Valík[2]

[1] Facultad de Informática, Universidad Politécnica de Madrid,
Campus de Montegancedo s/n, Boadilla del Monte 28660, Madrid, Spain
[2] Institute of Computer Science, Silesian University,
74601 Opava, Czech Republic
{petr.sosik, ondrej.valik}@fpf.slu.cz

Abstract. We introduce a simple model of P system motivated by certain restrictions found in biological systems. Its computational power is rather limited and corresponds to that of a finite transducer. An important characteristics of the model is its interactive behavior. Then we study the computational power of evolutionary lineages of such P systems. Referring to known results from the structural complexity theory (Karp and Lipton, Wiedermann and van Leeuwen), we show that a super-Turing computational potential can emerge in non-uniform lineages of these restricted P systems.

Furthermore, key features of our model are related to lineages of biological systems. In this way, our results provide another argument supporting the thesis from [14] and others that a super-Turing potential is *naturally and inherently present* in evolution of living organisms.

1 Introduction

Membrane systems (currently called P systems) are biologically inspired (particularly, cell inspired) formal computational models introduced in [8]. For an overview of membrane computing theory we refer the reader to [9]. Computational operations in P systems are motivated by some properties of living cells which are mathematically abstracted and generalized. Many of the recently studied variants of P systems achieve universal (in Turing sense) computational power, provided that their membranes can contain an unlimited number of objects.

In this paper, however, we attempt to relate (although freely) our theoretical results to limits of computational potential of biological cells and their lineages. Therefore, we adopt the assumption that *each living cell or a multicellular organism is a finite body and its behavior can in principle be modelled by a finite-size model, however complicated.* A similar approach can be found also in the recently developed model of *P colonies* [7]. One can argue that organisms can use their (potentially infinite) environment as an external memory, but even then there is a barrier of their limited length of life during which only a limited portion of "memory" can be used.

An important part of our model are certain properties of living organisms which, due to [12, 14], give them power beyond the level of classical formal automata:

R. Freund et al. (Eds.): WMC 2005, LNCS 3850, pp. 67–78, 2006.
© Springer-Verlag Berlin Heidelberg 2006

(i) *interactivity*, i.e., a continuous flow of information, contrasting with a beforehand-given input of conventional automata;

(ii) *unpredictability* of interactions and information exchange (notice the difference from a nondeterministic Turing machine where all possible configurations can be found and simulated by its deterministic variant);

(iii) *continuous lineage of individuals*, transferring information from one generation to another, and capable of continuous changes due to intensive interactions with their environment.

Also nowadays computers connected into a worldwide network possess exactly the same properties (i)–(iii). Indeed, they intensively interact in an unpredictable manner (often too unpredictable to our taste). When solving difficult problems, they can consult other network machines. They get continuous upgrade through the network, often without our knowledge. Last, but not least, there exists a continuity between their generations. Therefore, the original paradigm of a computer as a Turing machine does not correspond to the recent situation and maybe the time has come for its change [13].

Based on this argumentation, we incorporate the properties (i)–(iii) into our P system model and study its power. Rather surprisingly, we show that the resulting lineage of simple P systems reaches a *super-Turing computational potential.*

The history of super-Turing computation originates, paradoxically, in the Turing's dissertation thesis [11], where the modified variant of the Turing machine augmented with the *oracle device* has been introduced and its power studied. The machine has a special *oracle tape* and a corresponding query state. The machine can write a question on the oracle tape and enter the query state. Then in one step, an (in principle uncomputable) answer appears on the oracle tape. There have been also considered limitations on the size of the oracle's answer. In 1980 there was defined the weaker *advice Turing machines* [6]. The advice differs from the oracle in the following: while the oracle assigns an individual answer to each query, the advice provides an answer due to the *length* of the query and ignores its content. Therefore, all queries with the same length are given the same answer. Usually, length of the advice is polynomially restricted with respect to the length of the query. We denote an advice Turing machine by TM/A. We refer the reader, e.g., to [1] for more information on non-uniform complexity classes.

In 1980's and 1990's many super-Turing models were studied, such as Interaction Machines, Site and Internet Machines, π-kalkul, \$-kalkul, etc. The reader is referred to [3] or [4] for an overview. We mention two super-Turing computational models with biological inspiration. In [2], authors show a super-Turing power of deterministic P systems which can speed up their operations gradually (a reversed Achilles and Tortoise principle). Another paper [15] introduces the model called *bacterioid* which combines computational and non-computational mechanisms. The bacterioid conforms with the requirements for a minimal artificial life and exhibits also rudimentary cognitive properties.

In this context we argue together with [12, 14] and others that a super-Turing potential can naturally emerge in evolutionary lineages of finite (biological or other) systems. Indeed, the requirements (i)–(iii) form elementary components of biological evolutionary processes. Together with the finiteness of living organisms we obtain a reasonable scenario suggesting that a super-Turing potential is not only possible, but probably rather necessary phenomenon during biological evolution.

2 Interactive Finite Machines

In this section we focus on the first natural property of the living entities – *interactivity*. We fix some basic notation first. An *alphabet* Σ is a finite and nonempty set of symbols. The set of all words over Σ is denoted by Σ^*. This set includes the *empty word* ϵ. The set of all nonempty words $\Sigma^* \setminus \{\epsilon\}$ is denoted by Σ^+. The length of a word w is denoted by $|w|$. For a nonnegative integer n and a word w, we use w^n to denote the word that consists of n concatenated copies of w. For more information on formal language theory we refer the reader to [10].

Now we present a canonical model of an interactive finite machine – the *interactive finite transducer (IFT)*, introduced in [12], which is an analog of Mealy automaton. Recall that a Mealy automaton is a finite-state machine which at each computational step inputs and outputs symbols from a given alphabet. Of course, when considering suitable computational models for embodiment of the lineages of evolving organisms, we may think about finite-state neural networks or other models with evolutionary capabilities. However, as they are in general finite-state machines, IFT's appear to be a proper choice for the study of their computational limits due to their simplicity.

Definition 1. *A* Mealy automaton *is a six-tuple* $\mathcal{M} = (I, O, Q, \delta, \rho, q_0)$, *where*

- *I is an input alphabet,*
- *O is an output alphabet,*
- *Q is a finite nonempty set of states,*
- *$\delta : Q \times I \longrightarrow Q$ is a transition function,*
- *$\rho : Q \times I \longrightarrow O$ is an output function,*
- *$q_0 \in Q$ is an initial state.*

The input of a Mealy automaton is an input tape containing a finite word over the input alphabet. At each step, the Mealy automaton reads a symbol from the input tape, changes eventually its state due to δ, and outputs a symbol from the output alphabet selected by ρ.

IFT's differ from Mealy automata mainly in their computational scenario. Unlike a Mealy automaton, an IFT inputs a (potentially infinite) input stream over an input/output alphabet Σ via its input channel and outputs a (potentially infinite) output stream. Therefore we do not assume that the whole input is fixed and written on a tape beforehand. Let Σ^ω denote the *set of all infinite streams* over the alphabet Σ. Hence an IFT realizes a *translation* $\phi : \Sigma^\omega \longrightarrow \Sigma^\omega$. In the sequel, however, we use Mealy automata as a formal representation of IFT's.

2.1   Interactive Finite P Systems

Membrane computing offers a computational framework in which the assumptions (i)–(iii) from Section 1 can be naturally implemented. We build on a "classical" variant of P system computing with multisets of objects. However, we impose some restrictions motivated by reflections in Section 1. Also, communication with the outer environment is performed via an *input* and an *output* channel similarly as in P automata with communication rules [5]. At each step our model can receive at most one symbol via its input channel and send at most one symbol via its output channel. Of course, living organisms receive at each moment an n-tuple of "inputs" via their "input channels", but let us assume that n is limited from above and hence the the set of all such n-tuples can be mapped one-to-one into a finite alphabet. The resulting model is called *Interactive Finite P System (IFPS)*. We note that an alterative variant of an interactive finite P systems might be also considered using the formalism of ω-P automata [5].

Definition 2. *An* interactive finite P system *of degree* n, $n \geq 1$, *is a construct*

$$\Pi = (\Sigma, \Gamma, \sqcup, \mu, w_1, \ldots, w_n, R_1, \ldots, R_n),$$

where:

- Σ *is an alphabet; its elements are called objects;*
- $\Gamma \subset \Sigma$ *is an input/output alphabet;*
- $\sqcup \in \Gamma$ *is a special symbol denoting an undefined input/output;*
- μ *is a hierarchical structure of* n *membranes, with membranes denoted by integers* $1, \ldots, n$; *the outermost membrane is called also the* skin *membrane;*
- w_i, $1 \leq i \leq n$, *is an initial content of region* i *of the membrane structure* μ; *formally,* w_i *is a word in* Σ^* *representing by its Parikh vector a multiset* $m(w_i)$ *over* Σ;
- R_i, $1 \leq i \leq n$, *is a finite set of evolutional rules* $u \to v$ *over* Σ *belonging to region* i *of the structure* μ; *forms of the rules can be:*
  - *(a)* $a \to b_\tau$, $a, b \in \Sigma$, $\tau \in (\{here\} \cup \{in_j \mid 1 \leq j \leq n\})$; *if* $[_i\ ]_i$ *is not the skin membrane, then it is also allowed that* $\tau = out$;
  - *(b)* $ab \to a_{\tau_1} c_{\tau_2}$, $a, b, c \in \Sigma$, $\tau_1, \tau_2 \in (\{here\} \cup \{in_j \mid 1 \leq j \leq n\})$; *if* $[_i\ ]_i$ *is not the skin membrane, then it is also allowed that* $\tau_1 = out$ *or* $\tau_2 = out$ *or both;*
  - *(c)* $ab \to a_\tau b_{out} c_{come}$, $a \in \Sigma$, $b, c \in \Gamma$, $\tau \in (\{here\} \cup \{in_j \mid 1 \leq j \leq n\})$; *these rules can exist only within the skin membrane.*

The components $w_1, \ldots, w_n$ form an initial state of Π. Generally, each n-tuple $w'_1, \ldots, w'_n$ is called a *configuration* of Π. For two configurations $C_1 = (w'_1, \ldots, w'_n)$ and $C_2 = (w''_1, \ldots, w''_n)$ we write $C_1 \Longrightarrow C_2$, and we say that we have a *transition* from C_1 to C_2, if we can pass from C_1 to C_2 by using the evolution rules appearing in $R_1, \ldots, R_n$ in the following manner:

- If an object appears in v in a form a_{here}, then it will remain in the same region i (instead of a_{here} we often write simply a).

- If an object appears in v in a form a_{out}, then a will exit the membrane i and will become an element of the region immediately outside it; or, in case of (c)-type rules, it is sent out of the system via its output channel.
- If an object appears in a form a_{in_q}, then a will be added to the multiset $m(w'_q)$, provided that a is adjacent to the membrane q.
- If an object appears in a form a_{come}, then a is imported into the skin membrane via the input channel. *At each step, only one rule of type (c) can be applied.*

All these operations are done in parallel, for all possible applicable rules $u \rightarrow v$, for all occurrences of multisets u in the region associated with the rules, for all regions at the same time. The system continues these parallel steps until there remain any applicable rules in any compartment of Π. Both an input and an output of the system are infinite streams of symbols in Γ^ω.

In this paper we restrict ourselves to *deterministic* IFPS's, which at each configuration C_1 and for each symbol in the input channel can pass to at most one possible configuration C_2 and send at most one possible symbol to its output channel.

Definition 3. *A translation mapping* $\phi : \Sigma^\omega \longrightarrow \Sigma^\omega$ *is called an* interactive translation *realized by a deterministic IFPS Π if the following holds:* $\phi(x) = y$ *iif Π with the input x never halts and outputs y, for $x, y \in \Sigma^\omega$.*

It follows by the above definition that those IFPS's which halt after a finite number of steps, as well as those which input/output only a finite number of symbols, do not realize an interactive translation.

Example 1. The following IFPS Π_{ab} searches the input stream for strings ab, see Fig. 1. Its response to such a string is the output $\#$. In other cases the system just copies an input string to the output.

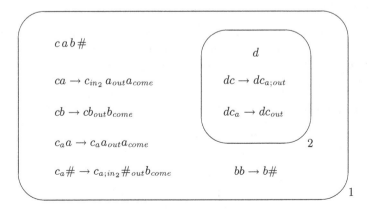

Fig. 1. Interactive finite P system Π_{ab}

Let $\Pi_{ab} = (\Sigma, \Gamma, \sqcup, \mu, w_1, w_2, R_1, R_2)$ be an IFPS of degree 2, where

$$
\begin{aligned}
\Sigma &= \{a, b, c, c_a, d, \sqcup, \#\}, \\
\Gamma &= \{\sqcup, a, b, \#\}, \\
\mu &= [_1[_2\ ]_2]_1, \\
w_1 &= cab\#, \\
w_2 &= d, \\
R_1 &= \{r_1 : ca \rightarrow c_{in_2} a_{out} a_{come}, \\
&\qquad r_2 : cb \rightarrow cb_{out} b_{come}, \\
&\qquad r_3 : c_a a \rightarrow c_a a_{out} a_{come}, \\
&\qquad r_4 : c_a\# \rightarrow c_{a;in_2} \#_{out} b_{come}, \\
&\qquad r_5 : bb \rightarrow b\#\}, \\
R_2 &= \{r_6 : dc_a \rightarrow dc_{out},\ r_7 : dc \rightarrow dc_{a;out}.\}
\end{aligned}
$$

The system Π_{ab} works as follows:

1. In the initial configuration only the rules r_1 or r_2 are applicable. If the input is
   - a, then r_1 is applied, the object a is copied to the output and c is sent to region 2; we continue by step 2;
   - b, then r_2 is applied, b is sent to the output and we continue in the same configuration.
2. In region 2 the rule r_7 is now applicable, rewriting c to c_a and sending it to region 1.
3. Now in region 1 the rules r_3 or r_4 are applicable. If the input is
   - a, then r_3 is applied, copying a to the output without a change of the recent configuration;
   - b, then r_4 is applied, sending $\#$ to the output as an indicator of the input ab, sending simultaneously c_a into region 2, and we continue by step 4.
4. Rules r_5 and r_6 are simultaneously applied, turning the system back into the initial configuration, and we continue by step 1.

2.2   Equivalence of IFT and IFPS

We show that interactive P systems compute exactly the same translation functions as IFT's. Our result extends Theorem 1 in [14] which states the equivalence of IFT with several other computational models, such as discrete neural nets or combinatorial circuits.

Theorem 1. *For a translation $\phi : \Sigma^\omega \rightarrow \Sigma^\omega$ the following is equivalent:*

(i) ϕ is realized by an interactive finite transducer;
(ii) ϕ is realized by a deterministic interactive finite P system.

Proof. $(i){\Rightarrow}(ii)$ Let $\mathcal{M} = (I, O, Q, \delta, \sqcup, q_0)$ be a Mealy automaton, where $I = \{x_1, \ldots, x_k\}$, $O = \{y_1, \ldots, y_l\}$, and $Q = \{q_0, \ldots, q_n\}$.

We construct a deterministic interactive P system $\Pi_\mathcal{M} = (\Sigma, \Gamma, \sqcup, \mu, w_1, \ldots, w_m, R_1, \ldots, R_m)$ of degree $m = n + 2$ realizing the same translation.

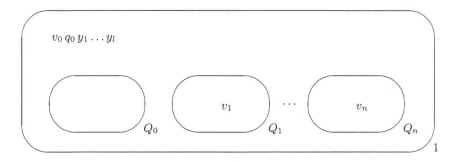

Fig. 2. An interactive P system simulating an IFT

- $\Gamma = \{\sqcup, x_1, \ldots, x_k, y_1, \ldots, y_l\}$,
- $\Sigma = \{q_0, \ldots, q_n, p_0, \ldots, p_n\} \cup \Gamma$,
- $\mu = [_1 [_{Q_0}]_{Q_0} \cdots [_{Q_n}]_{Q_n}]_1$,
- $w_1 = q_0 p_0 y_1 \ldots y_l$, $w_{Q_0} = \epsilon$ and $w_{Q_i} = p_i$, $1 \leq i \leq n$,
- R_1 is constructed as follows: for each pair of rules $\delta(q_i, x) = q_j$, $\rho(q_i, x) = y$, $q_i, q_j \in Q$, $x \in I$, $y \in O$, we add to R_1 the rules:

$$p_i y \rightarrow p_{i;in_{Q_i}} y_{out} x_{come}, \tag{1}$$

$$q_i x \rightarrow q_{i;in_{Q_j}} y, \tag{2}$$

- $R_{Q_i} = \{p_i p \rightarrow p_{i;out} q_{i;out} \mid \delta(p, x) = q_i, \text{ for some } p \in Q, x \in I\}$, $0 \leq i \leq n$.

Each step of the automaton $\mathcal{M}$ is simulated by the P system $\Pi_{\mathcal{M}}$ as follows.

1. *Input and output of a symbol:* the presence of an object p_i, $0 \leq i \leq n$, in the skin membrane represents the state q_i of $\mathcal{M}$. An application of a rule $\rho(q_i, x) = y$ of $\mathcal{M}$ is simulated by a rule of type (1). Notice that a complete set of output objects $y_1, \ldots, y_l$ is present within the skin membrane.
2. *State transition – phase I:* A rule of type (2) completes the set of output objects within the skin membrane. Simultaneously it sends the object q_i into the membrane Q_j which is equivalent to the rule $\delta(q_i, x) = q_j$ of $\mathcal{M}$.
3. *State transition – phase II:* Now the membrane Q_j contains objects p_j and q_i. The object q_i is rewritten to q_j and sent to the skin membrane together with p_j to represent the new state q_j of $\mathcal{M}$.

It follows by the above description that the deterministic IFPS $\Pi_{\mathcal{M}}$ realizes the same translation as the IFT $\mathcal{M}$.

$(i) \Leftarrow (ii)$ Let $\Pi = (\Sigma, \Gamma, \sqcup, \mu, w_1, \ldots, w_n, R_1, \ldots, R_n)$ be a deterministic IFPS which realizes a translation ϕ. Let us denote by $\mathcal{C}_{\Pi}$ the set of all configurations of Π. The number of all possible configurations is determined by the membrane structure μ, the size of the alphabet $l = |\Sigma|$, and the initial number of objects within the system, $m = |w_1| + |w_2| + \ldots + |w_n|$. Observe that the number of objects does not change during the work of the system. The reader can verify that the system has $|\mathcal{C}_\Pi| = (m + ln - 1)!/(m!(ln - 1)!)$ possible configurations.

Then the IFPS Π can be simulated by a Mealy automaton $\mathcal{M}_\Pi = (\Gamma, \Gamma, Q, \delta, \rho, C_0)$, where:

- $Q = \{C_0\} \cup \{C \in \mathcal{C} \mid C_0 \Rightarrow^* C' \Rightarrow_r C, r = ab \rightarrow a_\tau b_{out} c_{come}\}$,
- $\delta(C, c) = C'$ and $\rho(C, c) = b, b, c \in \Gamma$, if and only if $C \Rightarrow_\Pi^+ C'$, and this sequence of transitions involves exactly one application of a rule $ab \rightarrow a_\tau b_{out} c_{come}$ in its last step, for some $a \in \Sigma, \tau \in (\{here\} \cup \{in_j \mid 1 \leq j \leq n\})$.

Due to the determinism of Π, it is guaranteed that the sequence of transitions $C \Rightarrow_\Pi^+ C'$ is unique for a given $c \in \Gamma$. The above description shows that the translation ϕ realized by Π is identical with the translation realized by $\mathcal{M}_\Pi$.

3   From Machines to Lineages

In this section we consider the other two mentioned properties of communities of living organisms: continuous lineages of unpredictably evolving individuals. Similarly as in the previous section, we present first a canonical model of lineage [12] based on the theory of finite automata. We denote by $\mathcal{U}$ the universe of possible states of all automata in the lineage.

Definition 4. Let $\mathcal{A} = \{A_1, A_2, \ldots\}$ be a sequence of IFT's over an input/output alphabet Σ and let $Q_i \subseteq \mathcal{U}$ be a set of states of A_i. Let $G = \{G_1, G_2, \ldots\}$ be a sequence of states from $\mathcal{U}$ such that $G_i \subset Q_i$ and $G_i \subseteq G_{i+1}$, $i \geq 1$. Then $\mathcal{A}$ together with G is called a sequence of IFT's with global states.

The sequence $\mathcal{A}$ is *non-uniform*, i.e., there is no algorithmic way how to describe its members. The only way how to define the sequence is to list all its members. The set $\bigcup_i G_i \subseteq \mathcal{U}$ is called the *set of global states* of $\mathcal{A}$. The sequence $\mathcal{A}$ processes an infinite input stream from Σ^ω as follows. At the beginning, the automaton A_1 processes the input stream using its local states $Q_1 - G_1$. At a certain moment A_1 enters a global state $g \in G_1$, finishes its computation and passes the control to A_2. The input stream is redirected to the input of A_2 which starts its computation in the same state $g \in G_2$ and processes another symbol. After a certain number of steps in its local states, A_2 enters a global state g', passes control to A_3, and so on. Although it is not explicitly mentioned in the definition, it is assumed that the number of states of automata $\{A_1, A_2, \ldots\}$ increases, although possibly non-monotonically (unlike the monotonic sequence $G_1 \subseteq G_2 \subseteq G_3 \subseteq \ldots$).

Therefore, the input stream is processed by automata with an increasing index i. The next active automaton represents a new generation with potentially richer configuration space. This mechanism allows for a transfer and improvement of structural information from the previous generation. These improvements are understood as a result of unpredictable interactions of an individual (transducer) with its environment and other individuals.

3.1   Computational Potential of Lineages of IFT's

We use an *interactive advice Turing machine* to characterize the computational power of non-uniform lineages of IFT's. The interactive Turing machine (ITM) is – similarly as an IFT – a computational device working over infinite input and output streams. Unlike an IFT, however, an ITM has an internal architecture of a Turing machine with an infinite tape and therefore its configuration space is infinite. Besides tape operations in spirit of Turing machines, at each step an ITM reads a symbol from its input channel and sends a symbol to its output channel. Moreover, after receiving a *nonempty* symbol from its input channel, the ITM is required to send a *nonempty* symbol to its output channel within a finite number of steps. In this way the ITM realizes an interactive translation $\phi : \Sigma^\omega \longrightarrow \Sigma^\omega$. We refer the reader to [12] for more details.

The computational power of ITM's is in principle equivalent to that of a standard Turing machine. Indeed, an input/output of a standard TM can be a part of input/output streams of an ITM, on one hand. On the other hand, each translation of an ITM, $\mathrm{Pref}(x) \longrightarrow \mathrm{Pref}(y)$ for finite prefixes of x and y of the same length, is Turing-computable. The ingredient we add to ITM's to increase their power is the *advice function* introduced in Section 1.

Definition 5. *An* advice *is a function* $f : \mathbb{N}^+ \longrightarrow \{0,1\}^*$. *We say that an* advice f *is* $S(m)$-bounded *if* $|f(m)| \leq S(m)$ *for each* $m \in \mathbb{N}$.

The resulting device is called an *interactive advice Turing machine* (ITM/A). See [13] for motivation and more results about ITM/A. An ITM/A can in a step t ask only a query of length $t_1 \leq t$. To get an advice, the ITM/A is equipped with a special *advice tape* and an *advice state*. When ITM/A writes an argument t_1 on the advice tape and enters the advice state, the value of $f(t_1)$ rewrites in one step the original content of the advice tape. Due to the possible non-computability of the advice, an ITM/A is a super-Turing computational device [12]. The following result can be found in [14].

Theorem 2. *A translation* $\phi : \Sigma^\omega \rightarrow \Sigma^\omega$ *can be realized by a sequence of IFT's with global states iff it can be realized by an ITM/A.*

3.2   Lineages of IFPS's

Theorem 2 can be naturally extended to sequences of interactive finite P systems. Consider an IFPS

$$\Pi = (\Sigma, \Gamma, \sqcup, \mu, w_1, \ldots, w_m, R_1, \ldots, R_m)$$

with a configuration $C = (w_1, \ldots, w_m)$. A *state* of Π is a pair (μ', C'), where C' is obtained from C by omitting all empty strings ϵ corresponding to membranes containing no objects, and μ' is obtained from μ by omitting these membranes. The *universe of states* $\mathcal{U}$ is the set of all possible states (including all possible membrane structures).

Consider further a sequence of IFPS's $\mathcal{P} = \{\Pi_1, \Pi_2, \ldots\}$ such that each Π_i has assigned a finite set of states $Q_i \subseteq \mathcal{U}$ determined by its structure and possible contents of its membranes. Some selected states form a set $G_i \subset Q_i$ of global states. The sequence $\mathcal{P}$ must satisfy the conditions of Definition 4: $G_i \subseteq G_{i+1}$, $i \geq 1$. Then $\mathcal{P}$ is called an *evolutionary sequence of interactive P systems*.

Example 2. Let $\mathcal{P} = \{\Pi_1, \Pi_2, \ldots\}$ be a sequence of IFPS's. Denote by Q_i the set of states of Π_i, $i \geq 1$. Let $\Delta_i \subseteq \Gamma_i$ be a nonempty alphabet of *global symbols*, where Γ_i is the alphabet of Π_i. Let further $\Delta_i \subseteq \Delta_{i+1}$, $i \geq 1$. Let *global states* of Π_i be those of its states which contain a symbol from Δ_i.

A transition from Π_i to Π_{i+1} is realized by its mutation, during which:

- a rule can be added/deleted/replaced,
- a symbol can be added to the system's alphabet,
- an empty membrane together with rules can be added.

When Π_i enters a global state, it is changed to Π_{i+1} which starts from the same state. Then Π_{i+1} operates over input/output streams until it enters again a global state. This can happen even in its first step if all global symbols are not removed during this step.

Thus, the sequence of IFPS's $\mathcal{P} = \{\Pi_1, \Pi_2, \ldots\}$ satisfies the conditions of Definition 4 and we have the following result:

Theorem 3. *A translation $\phi : \Sigma^\omega \to \Sigma^\omega$ can be realized by a sequence of IFT's with global states iff it can be realized by an evolutionary sequence of IFPS's.*

Corollary 1. *A translation $\phi : \Sigma^\omega \to \Sigma^\omega$ can be realized by an evolutionary sequence of IFPS's iff it can be realized by an ITM/A.*

Note that all members of the sequence $\mathcal{P}$ operate with the same number of objects. The evolution changes only their alphabet, membrane structure, and rules.

4   Conclusion

We have studied a simple variant of P system called the *interactive finite P system* – IFPS. An IFPS can at each step contain only a fixed, pre-defined number of objects and a fixed number of membranes, therefore its configuration space is finite. It communicates with the outer environment via an input and an output channel. The key ingredient increasing its power is the capability of evolutionary lineages of IFPS's to evolve from one generation to another in an unpredictable, non-computable manner.

We have shown that evolutionary lineages of IFPS's reach the super-Turing computational potential. This result extends the work of [12, 14, 15] and others where one studies the power of lineages of finite-state machines. Our biologically inspired model of IFPS, however, is restricted to use elementary cell-like computational operations. We have therefore settled the open question in [15] how to implement such lineages within the framework of P systems.

One might ask whether now we are able to solve some concrete, a priori given undecidable problems with lineages of IFPS's? On the one hand, it has been shown in [12] that ITM/A's (and in turn also lineages of IFPS's) are *strictly more powerful* than ITM's (and hence than standard Turing machines). In other words, some undecidable problems (e.g., the halting problem) can in principle be solved by lineages of IFPS's in a finite number of steps. On the other hand, computational evolutionary processes are by definition of an interactive and unpredictable nature and cannot be simulated by an equivalent deterministic device in a finite number of steps. (Unlike a nondeterministic TM which can be simulated by a deterministic TM with an exponential slowdown.) Therefore, one cannot solve non-computable problems "on command" with IFPS's. Which problems will be solved and when depends on the evolutionary process. What one can do is to increase the chances for finding answers by providing a "rich and inspirative" evolutionary environment.

There remain many other open questions. For instance, we imposed a few restrictions on the form of evolution of IFPS's. However, in [12] authors show that polynomially bounded lineages of IFT's are computationally equivalent to logarithmic space-bounded ITM's with a polynomially bounded advice. Hence the complexity problems of lineages of IFPS's are subject of further research.

Similar open problems exist for *uniform* lineages of IFPS's with various evolutionary restrictions. We conjecture that NP-complete or PSPACE-complete problems are solvable in polynomial time by certain uniform lineages of IFPS's. An interesting question is whether similar results can be obtained by even simpler membrane computing models, such as the recently introduced *P colonies* [7]. Communities of IFPS's or P colonies can not only reach the computational power exceeding the power of each of its members [7], but they might also be useful for modelling complex social behavior of living cells, e.g., of bacteria.

Acknowledgements

This research was supported by the Silesian University Science Foundation, grant No. 26/2005, and by the Czech Science Foundation, grant No. 201/04/0528. Authors are obliged to A. Alhazov and J. Wiedermann for comments improving the paper.

References

1. J.L. Balcazar, J. Diaz, J. Gabarro: *Structural Complexity I, Second Edition*. Springer, Berlin, 1995.
2. C.S. Calude, Gh. Păun: Bio-steps beyond Turing. *Biosystems*, 77 (2004), 175–194.
3. B.J. Copeland, ed.: *Minds and Machines*. 12, 4 (2002), and 13, 1 (2003).
4. E. Eberbach, P. Wegner: Beyond Turing machines. *Bulletin of the EATCS*, 81 (2003), 279–304.

5. R. Freund, M. Oswald, L. Staiger: ω-P automata with communication rules. In *Membrane Computing, International Workshop, WMC 2003, Tarragona, July 2003, Selected Papers* (C. Martin-Vide, G. Mauri, G. Rozenberg, A. Salomaa, eds.), LNCS 2933, Springer, Berlin, 2004, 203–217.

6. R.M. Karp, R.J. Lipton: Some connections between nonuniform and uniform complexity classes. In *Proc. 12th Annual ACM Symposium on the Theory of Computing* (STOC '80), 1980, 302–309.

7. J. Kelemen, A. Kelemenova, Gh. Păun, P colonies: In *Workshop on Artificial Chemistry*, ALIFE9, Boston, USA (M. Bedan et al., eds.), 2004, 82–86.

8. Gh. Păun: Computing with membranes. *Journal of Computer and System Sciences*, 61, (2000), 108–143.

9. Gh. Păun: *Membrane Computing: An Introduction*. Springer, Berlin, 2002.

10. G. Rozenberg, A. Salomaa, eds.: *Handbook of Formal Languages*. Springer, Berlin, 1997.

11. A.M. Turing: Systems of logic based on the ordinals. *Proceedings of the London Mathematical Society*, 45 (1939), 161–228.

12. J. van Leeuwen, J. Wiedermann: Beyond the Turing limit: evolving interactive systems. In *SOFSEM'01: Theory and Practice of Informatics* (L. Pacholski, P. Rùzièka, eds.), LNCS 2234, Springer, Berlin, 2001, 90–109.

13. J. van Leeuwen, J. Wiedermann: The Turing machine paradigm in contemporary computing. In *Mathematics Unlimited – 2001 and Beyond* (B. Enquist, W. Schmidt, eds.), Springer-Verlag, Berlin, 2001, 1139–1155.

14. J. Wiedermann, J. van Leeuwen: The emergent computational potential of evolving artificial living systems. *AI Communications*, 15 (2002), 205–216.

15. J. Wiedermann: Coupling computational and non-computational processes: minimal artificial life. *Pre-proceedings of the Fifth Workshop on Membrane Computing (WMC5)* (G. Mauri, Gh. Păun, C. Zandron, eds.), University of Milan – Bicocca, 2004, 432–445.

Number of Protons/Bi-stable Catalysts and Membranes in P Systems. Time-Freeness

Artiom Alhazov

Research Group on Mathematical Linguistics,
Rovira i Virgili University,
Pl. Imperial Tàrraco 1, 43005 Tarragona, Spain
artiome.alhazov@estudiants.urv.es
Institute of Mathematics and Computer Science,
Academy of Sciences of Moldova,
Str. Academiei 5, Chişinău, MD 2028 Moldova
artiom@math.md

Abstract. Proton pumping P systems are a variant of membrane systems with both rewriting rules and symport/antiport rules, where a set of objects called protons is distinguished, every cooperative symport or antiport rule involves a proton, but no rewriting rule does. Time-freeness property means the result of all computations does not depend on the time it takes to execute the rules.

The goal of this article is to improve (showing that two membranes are sufficient) the known universality results on proton pumping P systems, establishing at the same time an upper bound on the number of protons, namely one, or four for time-free systems.

All results mentioned hold for proton pumping P systems with non-cooperative rewriting and either symport/antiport rules of weight one (classical variant) or symport rules of weight at most two. As a corollary, we obtain the universality of P systems with one membrane and one bi-stable catalyst, or the universality of time-free P systems with one membrane and four bi-stable catalysts. All universality results are stated as generating RE (except the time-free systems without targets generate $PsRE$).

1 Introduction

Membrane computing is a rapidly developing field, launched in 1998 by Gheorghe Păun; see [14] for a systematic survey and [16] for a comprehensive bibliography. It studies, among others, the computational power of devices with multisets distributed over a tree-like membrane structure and rules rewriting and/or moving objects (elements of these multisets).

In evolution-communication P systems as introduced in [6], there are two types of rules: simple rewriting rules associated to regions and symport/antiport rules associated to membranes. Rules of the first type change the objects in the region where they are, while the latter ones move the objects across the membrane, thus, separating evolution and communication.

R. Freund et al. (Eds.): WMC 2005, LNCS 3850, pp. 79–95, 2006.
© Springer-Verlag Berlin Heidelberg 2006

Proton pumping P systems as introduced in [5] are a restricted variant of evolution-communication P systems: the set of protons is a subset of objects, no evolution rule involves a proton, while every cooperative communication rule has to involve exactly one proton. Thus, a proton is a "catalyst of communication". However, since the proton is also moved to another region, this hints its "multi-stability" (bi-stability if it moves between two regions), allowing the one-proton results of this paper.

It is worth mentioning that these models, although being formal and abstract, are motivated by cell biology (e.g., in many bacteria, the only antiports available are those that can exchange a proton with some chemical objects), see [1] and [15].

Time-freeness is a property introduced in [9],[7]. Consider a fixed P system Π and an arbitrary mapping e from the set of all rules to the set of positive integers. If the result of all halting computations of Π, where the rules are executed in the number of steps specified by e, is independent on e, then Π is called time-free.

It has been established that EC P systems with 2 membranes are universal with non-cooperative evolution and either symport/antiport rules of weight 1 ([2]) or symport rules of weight at most 2 ([11]); moreover, the constructions can be made time-free ([4]). For the proton pumping P systems with non-cooperative evolution and symport/antiport rules of weight 1, three membranes are enough for universality, while considering only one kind of protons and strong or weak priority of proton pumping rules, at least Parikh images of ET0L languages can be generated with two membranes.

In this article we improve the universality result of proton pumping P systems with symport/antiport rules of weight 1 from three membranes and an unbounded number of protons to only two membranes and only 4 protons; moreover, the underlying system is even time-free. We also strengthen the universality result of time-free evolution-communication P systems with two membranes and symport rules of weight at most 2 by proving the same result for proton pumping P systems with 4 protons.

Surprisingly, one can decrease the number of kinds of protons to one by giving up the time-freeness for the proton pumping P systems with non-cooperative evolution, symport of weight 1 and either form of minimal cooperation (antiport of weight 1 or symport of weight 2).

Finally, protons in two-membrane P systems behave like bi-stable catalysts in one region, so the corresponding corollaries hold for one-membrane P systems with bi-stable catalysts, improving results from [12] and [7].

2   Definitions and Preliminaries

2.1   Proton Pumping

We will now recall from [5] the definition of proton pumping P systems. The notation has been changed a little, and the definition has been slightly reformulated (restricted). First, the multiset describing the initial contents of the environment is no longer considered, as the environment is initially empty. Second, all communicative rules are listed together (for a shorter description, symport and antiport rules associated to region i are not divided any more into two sets). Third, we now also require that cooperative symport rules also involve a proton (in [5], cooperative symport rules were not studied). Fourth, the rules involving a proton are now restricted to involve exactly one (like in the catalyst case).

Definition 1. *A* proton pumping P system *of degree* $m \geq 1$, *is defined as*

$$\Pi = (O, P, \mu, w_1, w_2, \cdots, w_m, R_1, \cdots, R_m, R'_1, \cdots, R'_m, i_0), \ where:$$

- O *is the alphabet of objects,* $P \subseteq O$ *is a set of protons;*
- μ *is a membrane structure with* m *membranes injectively labeled by* $1, 2, \cdots, m$;
- w_i *are strings which represent multisets over* O *associated with regions* $1, 2, \cdots, m$ *of* μ;
- R_i, $1 \leq i \leq m$, *are finite sets of simple evolution rules over* O; R_i *is associated with the region* i *of* μ;
- R'_i, $1 \leq i \leq m$, *are finite sets of symport/antiport rules over* O *of a restricted form;* R'_i *is associated with the membrane* i *of* μ;
- $i_0 \in \{0, 1, 2, \cdots, m\}$ *is the output region; if* $i_0 = 0$, *then it is the environment, otherwise* i_0 *is a label of some membrane of* μ.

A simple evolution rule is of the form $u \to v$, *where* u *and* v *are strings over* $O - P$ *(the variant can be extended by allowing to assign the target indications here, out, in_j, to the symbols in v; for evolution–communication P systems this was first used in [11]). The only symport/antiport rules allowed are of the following forms: (a) uniport rules: (a, in), (a, out), $a \in O$ (notice that in this article we never use uniport of protons); (b) antiport rules with a proton on one side: $(x, out; p, in)$, $(p, out; x, in)$, $p \in P$, $x \in (O - P)^+$; (c) symport rules with a proton: (px, out), (px, in), $p \in P$, $x \in (O - P)^+$.*

The m-tuple of multisets of objects present at any moment in the regions of Π represents the configuration of the system at that moment (the m-tuple $(w_1, \cdots, w_m)$ is the initial configuration). A transition between configurations is governed by the mixed application of the evolution rules and of the symport/antiport rules. All rules are applied in a maximally parallel way (no rules are applicable to the objects that remain idle), chosen non-deterministically.

The system continues parallel steps until there remain no applicable rules (evolution rules or symport/antiport rules) in any region of Π. Then the system halts, and we consider the number of objects in the output region i_0 at the moment when the system halts as the result of the computation of Π. The set of all natural numbers computed in this way is denoted by $N(\Pi)$. If instead of the total number, the multiplicities of objects are considered, then the result is denoted by $Ps(\Pi)$. In case of external output, one can also consider the sequence in which the objects are sent into the environment, denoting the result by $L(\Pi)$.

A *bi-stable catalyst* is a pair of symbols $c, c' \in O$ such that all rules where these symbols appear are of the following forms: $ca \to cv$, $ca \to c'v$, $c'a \to cv$, $c'a \to c'v$.

When speaking of a P system with bi-stable catalysts, we will additionally specify the set C_b of bi-stable catalysts in the description of the P system. We use the following notations

$$XProP_m^k(\alpha, tar, sym_i, anti_j)$$

to denote the family of languages $(X = L)$, vector sets $(X = Ps)$ or number sets $(X = N)$ generated by proton pumping P systems with at most m membranes, k different types of protons (i.e., k is the cardinality of the set P), using symport rules of weight at most i, antiport rules of weight at most j, and non-cooperative $(\alpha = ncoo)$ or bi-stable catalytic $(\alpha = 2cat_l)$ with l bi-stable catalysts evolution rules with targets. If targets are not allowed, then tar is removed from the notation (like any other unused feature). If one of the numbers m, k, i, j, l is unbounded, we write $*$ instead). For P systems without protons, we will replace $ProP^k$ by OP in the notation and exclude the specification of the set P, as well as the sets of symport/antiport rules if they are not used, from the description of the P system.

2.2   Time-Freeness

We now recall from [9] the definition of time-free P systems for the case of proton pumping P systems (for P systems without protons it is done in the same way).

Given a time-mapping $e : R_1 \cup \cdots \cup R_m \cup R'_1 \cup \cdots \cup R'_m \longrightarrow \mathbb{N}_1$ and a proton pumping P system Π as defined above, it is possible to construct a *timed proton pumping P system* $\Pi(e)$ working in the following way.

We suppose the existence of an external and global clock that ticks at uniform intervals of time. At each time in the regions of the system we have both rules (both evolution and transport) in execution and rules not in execution. At each time all the evolution and transport rules that can be applied (started) in each region, have to be applied. If a rule $r \in R_i, R'_i, 1 \leq i \leq m$, is applied, then all objects that can be processed by the rule have to evolve by this rule (a rule is applied in a maximally parallel manner as standard in the P system area).

As usual, the rules from R_i are applied to objects in region i and the rules from R'_i govern the communication of objects through membrane i. There is no difference between evolution rules and communication rules: they are chosen and applied in the non-deterministic maximally parallel manner. When an evolution rule or a transport rule r is started at time j, its execution terminates at time $j + e(r)$. If two rules are started in the same time unit, then possible conflicts for using the occurrences of symbol-objects are solved assigning the objects in a non-deterministic way (again, in the way usually defined in the P system area). Notice that when the execution of a rule r is started, the occurrences of objects used by this rule are not anymore available for other rules during the entire execution of r.

A proton pumping P system Π is *time-free* if and only if every system in the set $\{\Pi(e) \mid e : R \longrightarrow \mathbb{N}_1\}$ (where $R = R_1 \cup \cdots \cup R_m \cup R'_1 \cup \cdots \cup R'_m$) produces the same result.

As all $\Pi(e)$ generate the same result, in this case the set of natural numbers (vectors, words) generated by a time-free proton pumping P system Π is denoted by $N(\Pi)$ $(Ps(\Pi),\ L(\Pi))$. For the notation of what is generated by a family of *time-free* P systems, we add f to the notation introduced before: $f\mathbf{X}ProP_{\mathbf{m}}^{\mathbf{k}}(\alpha, tar, sym_i, anti_j)$, $f\mathbf{X}OP_{\mathbf{m}}^{\mathbf{k}}(\alpha, tar, sym_i, anti_j)$.

2.3 Register Machines

In what follows, we will use register machines as an important tool for showing the computational completeness results. Let us recall their definitions from [13].

An n-register machine is a construct $M = (n, l_0, l_h, I)$ where:

- n is the number of registers;
- I is a set of labeled instructions of the form $(l : op(i), l', l'')$ where $op(i)$ is an operation on register i of M; symbols l, l', l'' belong to the set of labels associated in a one-to-one manner with instructions of I;
- l_0 is the initial label;
- l_h is the final label.

The instructions allowed by an n-register machine are:

- $l : (A(i), l', l'')$ – add one to the contents of register i and proceed to instruction l' or to instruction l'';
- $l : (S(i), l', l'')$ – jump to instruction l'' if register i is empty; otherwise subtract one from register i and jump to the instruction labeled by l' (these two cases are often called *zero-test* and *decrement*);
- $l_h : halt$ – finish the computation. This is the unique instruction with label h;
- $l : (write(a), l', l'')$ – write symbol $a \in T$ to the output tape and proceed to instruction l' or to instruction l'' (these instructions are only used in register machines with an output tape, denoted by (n, T, l_0, l_h, I)).

If a register machine $M = (n, l_0, l_h, I)$, starting from the instruction labeled by l_0 with all registers being empty, halts with values n_j in register j, $1 \le j \le m$, and the contents of registers $m + 1, \cdots, n$ being empty, then it generates the vector $(n_1, \cdots, n_k) \in \mathbb{N}^m$. The result of a halting computation of a register machine with an output tape is a sequence of symbols written on that tape.

It is known that register machines with $m + 2$ registers can generate all recursively enumerable sets of m-dimensional vectors (we can also require that the only instructions associated to the output registers are increment instructions). Moreover, register machines with 2 registers and an output tape can generate all recursively enumerable languages.

3 Time-Free Results

Theorem 1. $fPsProP_2^4(ncoo, sym_1, anti_1) = PsRE$.

Proof. We only prove the inclusion $\supseteq$. Consider an arbitrary recursively enumerable set S of m-dimensional vectors. Then there is a register machine $M = (m + 2, l_0, l_h, I)$ generating S. Let $I_- = \{l \mid l : (S(i), l', l'') \in I\}$.

We will construct a P system Π simulating M in such a way that the value of register $i \in W = \{m+1, m+2\}$ is represented by the multiplicity of the object a_i in the skin region. The proton D_i will be used to decrement the value of register i, while E_i will be used to check if the register i is empty.

$$\Pi = (O, P, [_1 [_2]_2]_1, w_1, w_2, R_1, R_2, R'_1, R'_2), \text{ where}$$
$$O = \{a_i \mid 1 \leq i \leq m+2\} \cup \{l_j \mid l \in I_-, 1 \leq j \leq 4\} \cup \{\#_1, \#_2\} \cup I \cup P,$$
$$P = \{D_i, E_i \mid i \in W\},$$
$$w_1 = l_0 D_{m+1} D_{m+2} Z_{m+1} Z_{m+2} \#_1, \ w_2 = \lambda,$$

and the sets of rules are the following:
For each instruction $l : (A(i), l', l'') \in I$,

$$l \rightarrow a_i l', \ l \rightarrow a_i l'' \in R_1.$$

Moreover, for $1 \leq i \leq m$ we have the rules

$$(a_i, out) \in R'_1.$$

For each instruction $l : (S(i), l', l'') \in I$,

$$(l, in) \in R'_2,$$
$$(\text{decrement}) \ l \rightarrow l_4 \in R_2,$$
$$(l_4, out; D_i, in), (D_i, out; a_i, in), (D_i, out; \#_1, in) \in R'_2,$$
$$l_4 \rightarrow l' \in R_1,$$
$$(\text{zero test}) \ l \rightarrow l_1, \ l_2 \rightarrow l_3 \in R_2,$$
$$(E_i, in; l_1, out), \ (E_i, out; a_i, in), \ (E_i, out; l_2, in) \in R'_2,$$
$$(l_3, out) \in R'_2,$$
$$l_1 \rightarrow l_2, \ l_2 \rightarrow \#_2, \ l_3 \rightarrow l'' \in R_1.$$

Finally, we also have the rules

$$\#_1 \rightarrow \#_1 \in R_2,$$
$$\#_2 \rightarrow \#_2 \in R_1.$$

The system constructed in that way simulates the corresponding register machine. The increment instructions are simulated in one step: the instruction symbol changes to a symbol corresponding to the next instruction and a symbol corresponding to the register being incremented.

Decrement: l comes to region 2, changes to l_4 and returns to region 1, bringing D_i to region 2, and then changes to l'. The "duty" of D_i is to decrement register i by returning to region 1 and removing one copy of a_i from region 1. If register i is empty, then D_i exchanges with $\#_1$ and the computation never halts (if decrement is possible, D_i can still exchange with $\#_1$, but this case is not productive).

Zero-test: after l has come to region 2, it changes to l_1 and returns to region 1, bringing E_i to region 2, and then changes to l_2. The "duty" of E_i is to check

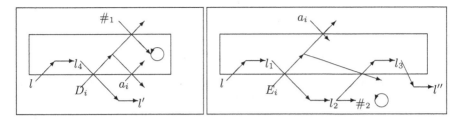

Fig. 1. Using $(ncoo, sym_1, anti_1)$ decrement: left, zero-test: right

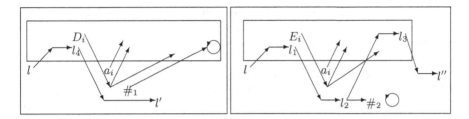

Fig. 2. Using $(ncoo, sym_2)$ decrement: left, zero-test: right

that register i is empty by waiting for l_2. If register i is not empty, then E_i will immediately exchange with a_i and then l_2 will change to $\#_2$, so the computation will never halt (if E_i waits for l_2, l_2 can still change to $\#_2$, but this case is not productive).

The decrement and zero-test are illustrated in Figure 1. From these figures it is clear that the system is time-free: most of the correct simulation is sequential, and we only remark one point – the time it takes to exchange D_i and a_i is not relevant because after the start of the rule a_i is already unavailable in region 1, and, moreover, if D_i still has not returned to region 1 for the next decrement instruction, the system will simply wait for it.   □

Theorem 2. $fPsProP_2^4(ncoo, sym_2) = PsRE$.

Proof. This is a "dual" theorem: the simulation of a register machine is done in exactly the same way, except that the protons that were in region 1 are now in region 2, and vice-versa. The system we consider is:

$$\Pi = (O, P, [_1 [_2]_2]_1, w_1, w_2, R_1, R_2, R'_1, R'_2), \text{ where}$$
$$O = \{a_i \mid 1 \le i \le m+2\} \cup \{l_j \mid l \in I_-, 1 \le j \le 4\} \cup \{\#_1, \#_2\} \cup I \cup P,$$
$$P = \{D_i, E_i \mid i \in W\},$$
$$w_1 = l_0\#_1, \; w_2 = D_{m+1}D_{m+2}Z_{m+1}Z_{m+2},$$
$$R_1 = \{l \to a_il', l \to a_il'' \mid l : (A(i), l', l'') \in I\} \cup \{\#_2 \to \#_2\}$$
$$\quad \cup \{l_4 \to l', l_1 \to l_2, l_2 \to \#_2, l_3 \to l'' \mid l : (S(i), l', l'') \in I\},$$
$$R_2 = \{l \to l_4, l \to l_1, l_2 \to l_3 \mid l : (S(i), l', l'') \in I\} \cup \{\#_1 \to \#_1\},$$

$$R'_1 = \{(a_i, out) \mid 1 \le i \le m\},$$
$$R'_2 = \{(l, in), (l_4 D_i, out), (a_i D_i, in), (\#_1 D_i, in),$$
$$(l_1 E_i, out), (a_i E_i, in), (l_2 E_i, in), (l_3, out) \mid l : (S(i), l', l'') \in I\}.$$

The system constructed above simulates the corresponding register machine. The increment instructions are simulated in one step: the instruction symbol changes to a symbol corresponding to the next instruction and a symbol corresponding to the register being incremented.

Decrement: l comes to region 2, changes to l_4 and returns to region 1 with D_i, and then changes to l'. The "duty" of D_i is to decrement register i by returning to region 2 and removing one copy of a_i from region 1. If register i is empty, then D_i exchanges with $\#_1$ and the computation never halts (if decrement is possible, D_i can still exchange with $\#_1$, but this case is not productive).

Zero-test: after l has come to region 2, it changes to l_1 and returns to region 1 with E_i, and then changes to l_2. The "duty" of E_i is to check that register i is empty by waiting for l_2. If register i is not empty, then E_i will immediately exchange with a_i and then l_2 will change to $\#_2$, so the computation will never halt (if E_i waits for l_2, l_2 can still change to $\#_2$, but this case is not productive).

As in the previous proof, the time-freeness of the system immediately becomes clear from the illustrations in Figure 2.   □

One can consider simulating a register machine with an output tape generating an arbitrary recursively enumerable language L: simulating an instruction $(l : write(a), l', l'')$ is done exactly as simulating $(l : A(i), l', l'')$ by replacing a_i with a. Then the output symbols are generated in the right order; however, generating languages by these constructions is not time-free because the different execution times of the rules sending output symbols to the environment might lead to changing the order of symbols in the output word.

Nevertheless, if target indications are allowed, then, replacing rules $l \to al' \in R_1$, $l \to al'' \in R_1$, $(a, out) \in R'_1$ for $a \in T$ by $l \to a_{out}l' \in R_1$, $l \to a_{out}l'' \in R_1$, one obtains time-free P systems generating RE.

Corollary 1. $fLProP_2^4(ncoo, tar, sym_1, anti_1) = RE$,
$\qquad fLProP_2^4(ncoo, tar, sym_2) = RE$.

4   One Proton

We will now show that even one proton is enough for computational completeness, again with only two membranes.

Theorem 3. $LProP_2^1(ncoo, sym_1, anti_1) = RE$.

Proof. We only prove the inclusion $\supseteq$. Consider an arbitrary recursively enumerable language $L \subseteq T^*$. Then there is a register machine $M = (2, T, l_0, l_h, I)$ generating L.

We will construct a P system Π simulating M in such a way that the value of register $i \in W = \{1,2\}$ is represented by the multiplicity of the object a_i in region i. The proton p will be used to decrement/zero test the value of the working registers.

$$\Pi = (O, P, [_1 \; [_2 \;]_2 \;]_1, w_1, w_2, R_1, R_2, R_1', R_2'), \text{ where}$$
$$O = T \cup \{a_i, a_i' \mid 1 \le i \le 2\} \cup \{l_j \mid l \in I, 1 \le j \le 9\} \cup I \cup P$$
$$\cup \; \{\#, I_{2,4}, I_{1,3}, I_{0,2}\} \cup \{I_j \mid 0 \le j \le 2\} \cup \{O_j \mid 0 \le j \le 5\},$$
$$P = \{p\}, \quad w_1 = pI_1, \quad w_2 = O_0 l_0,$$

and the sets of rules are the following:

Rules related to special objects which "wait" for a certain time and then must exchange with the proton (or else the trap symbol will be introduced):

$$I_{2,4} \to I_{1,3}, \; I_{1,3} \to I_{0,2} \in R_2,$$
$$(I_{0,2}, out) \in R_2',$$
$$I_{0,2} \to I_0 I_2 \in R_1,$$
$$I_{j+1} \to I_j \in R_1, \; 0 \le j \le 1,$$
$$(p, out; I_0, in) \in R_2',$$
$$O_0 \to \lambda, \; I_0 \to \#, \; \# \to \# \in R_1,$$
$$O_{j+1} \to O_j \in R_2, \; 0 \le j \le 4,$$
$$(O_0, out; p, in) \in R_2',$$
$$I_0 \to \lambda, \; O_0 \to \#, \; \# \to \# \in R_2.$$

Rules of interaction of the proton and register symbols:

$$(p, out; a_1, in), \; (a_2, out; p, in) \in R_2'.$$

For each instruction $l : (A(i), l', l'') \in I$,

$$l \to a_i' l_1 O_3 O_1 I_{0,2} \in R_2,$$
$$l_j \to l_{j+1} \in R_2, \; 1 \le j \le 2,$$
$$l_3 \to l', \; l_3 \to l'' \in R_2.$$

The output instructions $l : (write(a), l', l'') \in I$ are simulated exactly as the addition instructions above, replacing a_i' by a.

The register symbols a_i in region i and the output symbols a in the environment are produced by the rules

$$a_2' \to a_2 \in R_2,$$
$$(a_1', out), \; (a, out) \in R_2', \; a \in T,$$
$$a_1' \to a_1 \in R_1,$$
$$(a, out) \in R_1', \; a \in T.$$

For each instruction $l : (S(1), l', l'') \in I$,

$$\text{(decrement)} \quad l \to l_1 O_1 O_3 O_5 I_{2,4} \in R_2,$$
$$l_j \to l_{j+1} \in R_2, \ 1 \le j \le 4,$$
$$l_5 \to l' \in R_2,$$
$$\text{(zero test)} \quad l \to l_6 O_1 O_4 I_{1,3} \in R_2,$$
$$l_j \to l_{j+1} \in R_2, \ 6 \le j \le 8,$$
$$l_9 \to l'' \in R_2.$$

For each instruction $l : (S(2), l', l'') \in I$,

$$\text{(decrement)} \quad l \to l_1 O_3 I_{0,2} \in R_2,$$
$$l_j \to l_{j+1} \in R_2, \ 1 \le j \le 2,$$
$$l_3 \to l' \in R_2,$$
$$\text{(zero test)} \quad l \to l_6 O_2 O_4 I_{1,3} \in R_2,$$
$$l_j \to l_{j+1} \in R_2, \ 6 \le j \le 8,$$
$$l_9 \to l'' \in R_2.$$

For terminating the computation we have

$$l_h \to \lambda \in R_2.$$

The simulation is illustrated by the tables below. Notice that every time an antiport rule is possible it must be executed, otherwise one of the objects O_0, I_0 will change to $\#$, leading to an infinite computation.

The intuitive idea behind this construction is to create a "predefined scenario" for the proton; if the system tries to decrement an empty register or the system zero-tests a non-empty register, then the proton ends up in a "wrong" region and cannot follow the "scenario" anymore. We now list the scenarios for the proton, for different instructions:

- Decrement a_1: p exchanges with O_0, then with I_0, then with O_0, then with a_1, then with O_0, and finally with I_0.
- Zero-test a_1: p exchanges with O_0, then with I_0, then with O_0, then waits one step because there is no a_1, and finally with I_0.
- Decrement a_2: p exchanges with O_0, then with I_0, then with a_2, and finally I_0.
- Zero-test a_2: p exchanges with O_0, then with I_0, then waits one step because there is no a_2, then with O_0, and finally I_0.
- Increment any register or output a symbol: p exchanges with O_0, then with I_0, then with O_0, and finally I_0.

Notice that the first two steps of the simulation are always the same. This is needed to "keep the proton busy" while the object associated to the instruction creates the rest of the scenario. The scenario is created by producing objects O_0 in region 2 and objects I_0 in region 1, with corresponding delays.

When the output register is incremented, the corresponding symbol is sent to the environment, contributing to the result. At the end of the correct simulation, object l_h is erased, registers 1 and 2 are empty, so no objects are present in region 2, while region 1 only contains p.

Instruction	Decrement a_1		Zero-test a_1	
Step	Region 1	Region 2	Region 1	Region 2
1	$a_1 I_1 p$	lO_0	$I_1 p$	lO_0
2	$a_1 I_0 O_0$	$l_1 I_{2,4} O_5 O_3 O_1 p$	$I_0 O_0$	$l_6 I_{1,3} O_4 O_1 p$
3	$a_1 p$	$l_2 I_{1,3} O_4 O_2 O_0 I_0$	p	$l_7 I_{0,2} O_3 O_0 I_0$
4	$a_1 O_0$	$l_3 I_{0,2} O_3 O_1 p$	$I_{0,2} O_0$	$l_8 O_2 p$
5	$I_{0,2} p$	$a_1 l_4 O_2 O_0$	$I_2 I_0$	$l_9 O_1 p$
6	$I_2 I_0 O_0$	$a_1 l_5 O_1 p$	$I_1 p$	$l'' O_0 I_0$
7	$I_1 p$	$a_1 l' O_0 I_0$	Next instr.	Next instr.

Instruction	Decrement a_2		Zero-test a_2	
Step	Region 1	Region 2	Region 1	Region 2
1	$I_1 p$	$a_2 l O_0$	$I_1 p$	lO_0
2	$I_0 O_0$	$a_2 l_1 I_{0,2} O_3 p$	$I_0 O_0$	$l_6 I_{1,3} O_4 O_2 p$
3	$I_{0,2} p$	$a_2 l_2 O_2 I_0$	p	$l_7 I_{0,2} O_3 O_1 I_0$
4	$a_2 I_2 I_0$	$l_3 O_1 p$	$I_{0,2} p$	$l_8 O_2 O_0$
5	$a_2 I_1 p$	$l' O_0 I_0$	$I_2 I_0 O_0$	$l_9 O_1 p$
6	Next instr.	Next instr.	$I_1 p$	$l'' O_0 I_0$

Instruction	Increment a_i/write a		a	$i=1$		$i=2$	Terminate	
Region	1	2	0 1	1	2	1	2	
1	$I_1 p$	lO_0					pI_1	$l_h O_0$
2	$I_0 O_0$	$l_1(a_i'$ or $a)I_{0,2} O_3 O_1 p$					$O_0 I_0$	p
3	$I_{0,2} p$	$l_2 O_2 O_0 I_0$	a	a_{m+1}'	a_{m+2}	p	I_0	
4	$I_2 I_0 O_0$	$l_3 O_1 p$	a	a_{m+1}	a_{m+2}	p		
5	$I_1 p$	$(l'$ or $l'')O_0 I_0$		a_{m+1}	a_{m+2}	Halt	Halt	

Theorem 4. $LProP_2^1(ncoo, sym_2) = RE$.

Proof. This is a "dual" theorem: the simulation of a register machine is done in exactly the same way, except that the proton that was in region 1 is now in region 2, and vice-versa, and except that the halting is slightly modified such that the proton stays in region 1.

Let $I_+ = \{l \mid l : (A(i), l', l'') \in I\}$ and $I_{out} = \{l \mid l : (write(a), l', l'') \in I\}$. We consider the system:

$$\Pi = (O, P, [_1 \ [_2 \ ]_2 \ ]_1, w_1, w_2, R_1, R_2, R_1', R_2'), \text{ where}$$

$$O = T \cup \{a_i, a_i' \mid 1 \le i \le 2\} \cup \{l_j \mid l \in I, 1 \le j \le 9\} \cup I \cup P$$

$$\cup \ \{\#, I_{2,4}, I_{1,3}, I_{0,2}\} \cup \{I_j \mid 0 \le j \le 2\} \cup \{O_j \mid 0 \le j \le 5\},$$

$$P = \{p\}, \ w_1 = I_1, \ w_2 = pO_0 l_0,$$

and the sets of rules are the following:

$$R_1 = \{I_{0,2} \to I_0I_2, O_0 \to \lambda, I_0 \to \#, \# \to \#\}$$
$$\cup \{I_{j+1} \to I_j \in R_1 \mid 0 \le j \le 1\}$$
$$\cup \{a_1' \to a_1\},$$
$$R_2 = \{l \to a_i'l_1O_3O_1I_{0,2}, l_3 \to l', l_3 \to l'' \mid l : (A(i), l', l'') \in I\}$$
$$\cup \{l \to al_1O_3O_1I_{0,2}, l_3 \to l', l_3 \to l'' \mid l : (write(a), l', l'') \in I\}$$
$$\cup \{l_j \to l_{j+1} \mid 1 \le j \le 2, \ l \in I_+ \cup I_{out}\}$$
$$\cup \{l \to l_1O_1O_3O_5I_{2,4}, l_5 \to l', l \to l_6O_1O_4I_{1,3}, l_9 \to l''$$
$$\mid l : (S(1), l', l'') \in I\}$$
$$\cup \{l \to l_1O_3I_{0,2}, l_3 \to l', l \to l_6O_2O_4I_{1,3}, l_9 \to l''$$
$$\mid l : (S(2), l', l'') \in I\}$$
$$\cup \{l_j \to l_{j+1} \mid 1 \le j \le 4, \ l : (S(1), l', l'') \in I\}$$
$$\cup \{l_j \to l_{j+1} \mid 1 \le j \le 2, \ l : (S(2), l', l'') \in I\}$$
$$\cup \{l_j \to l_{j+1} \mid 6 \le j \le 8, \ l : (S(i), l', l'') \in I\}$$
$$\cup \{I_{2,4} \to I_{1,3}, I_{1,3} \to I_{0,2}, I_0 \to \lambda, O_0 \to \#, \# \to \#\}$$
$$\cup \{a_2' \to a_2, l_h \to O_1\} \cup \{O_{j+1} \to O_j \mid 0 \le j \le 4\},$$
$$R_1' = \{(a, out) \mid a \in T\},$$
$$R_2' = \{(I_{0,2}, out), (pI_0, in), (pO_0, out), (pa_{m+1}, in), (pa_{m+2}, out)\}$$
$$\cup \{(a_1', out)\} \cup \{(a, out) \mid a \in T\}.$$

The simulation is illustrated by the tables below. Notice that every time an antiport rule is possible it must be executed, otherwise one of the objects O_0, I_0 will change to $\#$, leading to an infinite computation.

Like in the previous proof, to arrive at a halting configuration, the proton must follow the "predefined scenario" created by instruction objects. If the system tries to decrement an empty register or the system zero-tests a non-empty register, then the proton ends up in a "wrong" region and cannot follow the "scenario". We now list the proton's scenarios.

- Decrement a_{m+1}: p accompanies O_0, then I_0, then O_0, then a_{m+1}, then O_0, and finally I_0.
- Zero-test a_{m+1}: p accompanies O_0, then I_0, then O_0, then waits one step because there is no a_{m+1}, and finally goes with I_0.
- Decrement a_{m+2}: p moves O_0, then I_0, then a_{m+2}, and finally I_0.
- Zero-test a_{m+2}: p accompanies O_0, then I_0, then waits one step because there is no a_{m+2}, then goes with O_0, and finally with I_0.
- Increment or output: p accompanies O_0, then I_0, then O_0, and finally I_0.
- Halt: p accompanies O_0, then I_0, and finally O_0.

Again, the first two steps are the same, to "keep the proton busy" while the object associated to the instruction creates the rest of the scenario. The scenario is created by producing objects O_0 in region 2 and objects I_0 in region 1, with corresponding delays.

When the output register is incremented, the corresponding symbol is sent to the environment, contributing to the result. At the end of the correct simulation, object l_h changes to O_0 in 3 steps, moving p to region 1. Since registers $m+1$ and $m+2$ are empty, no objects are present in region 2, while region 1 only contains p.

Instruction	Decrement a_1		Zero-test a_1	
Step	Region 1	Region 2	Region 1	Region 2
1	a_1I_1	lO_0p	I_1	lO_0p
2	$a_1I_0O_0p$	$l_1I_{2,4}O_5O_3O_1$	I_0O_0p	$l_6I_{1,3}O_4O_1$
3	a_1	$l_2I_{1,3}O_4O_2O_0I_0p$		$l_7I_{0,2}O_3O_0I_0p$
4	a_1O_0p	$l_3I_{0,2}O_3O_1$	$I_{0,2}O_0p$	l_8O_2
5	$I_{0,2}$	$a_1l_4O_2O_0p$	I_2I_0p	l_9O_1
6	$I_2I_0O_0p$	$a_1l_5O_1$	I_1	$l''O_0I_0p$
7	I_1	$a_1l'O_0I_0p$	Next instr.	Next instr.

Instruction	Decrement a_2		Zero-test a_2	
Step	Region 1	Region 2	Region 1	Region 2
1	I_1	a_2lO_0p	I_1	lO_0p
2	I_0O_0p	$a_2l_1I_{0,2}O_3$	I_0O_0p	$l_6I_{1,3}O_4O_2$
3	$I_{0,2}$	$a_2l_2O_2I_0p$		$l_7I_{0,2}O_3O_1I_0p$
4	$a_2I_2I_0p$	l_3O_1	$I_{0,2}$	$l_8O_2O_0p$
5	a_2I_1	$l'O_0I_0p$	$I_2I_0O_0p$	l_9O_1
6	Next instr.	Next instr.	I_1	$l''O_0I_0p$

Instruction	Increment a_i/write a		a	$i=1$	$i=2$	Terminate	
Region	1	2	0 1	1	2	1	2
1	I_1	lO_0p				I_1	l_hO_0p
2	I_0O_0p	$l_1(a'_i \text{ or } a)I_{0,2}O_3O_1$				O_0I_0p	O_1
3	$I_{0,2}$	$l_2O_2O_0I_0p$	a	a'_1	a_2		I_0O_0p
4	$I_2I_0O_0p$	l_3O_1	a	a_1	a_2	O_0p	
5	I_1	$l'/l'' O_0I_0p$		a_1	a_2	p	

Consider either of the theorems above. Remove from the construction all rules (a, out), $a \in T$. The output of the system is now internal: when it halts, one can consider objects $a \in T$ in the elementary membrane as a result (no other objects will be there). Let the superscript int stand for systems with internal output and let subscript ne mean that no rule uses the environment and the skin membrane.

Corollary 2. $PsProP_{2,ne}^{1,int}(ncoo, sym_1, anti_1) = PsRE$,
$$PsProP_{2,ne}^{1,int}(ncoo, sym_2) = PsRE.$$

5   Bi-stable Catalysts

An interesting observation is that, interpreting the same object in different regions of the system as different objects in the same region (encoding regions in objects), one can easily see that the proton becomes a bi-stable catalyst. Let us explain this more formally.

Given a proton pumping P system with two membranes $\Pi = (O, P, [_1 [_2]_2]_1, w_1, w_2, R_1, R_2, R'_1, R'_2)$ such that the communication rules are minimally cooperative (either symport rules of weight at most two and antiport rules of weight 1) and the only rules associated to the skin membrane are the rules that output the terminal symbols, one can construct a P system with bi-stable catalysts in the following way:

$\Pi' = (O', C_b, [_1 \ ]_1, w'_1, R')$ where
$O' = \{a, h(a) \mid a \in O\} \cup \{b_p \mid \{p, h(p)\} \in C_b\}$,
$C_b = \{\{p, h(p)\} \mid p \in P\}$,
$w'_1 = h_b(w_1 h(w_2))$,
$R' = R_1 \cup \{h(u) \rightarrow h(v) \mid (u \rightarrow v) \in R_2\} \cup R''$,
$R'' = \{u \rightarrow u_{out} \mid (u, out) \in R'_1\} \cup \{h(u) \rightarrow u \mid (u, out) \in R'_2\}$
$\quad \cup \{u \rightarrow h(u) \mid (u, in) \in R'_2\} \cup \{h(u)v \rightarrow h(v)u \mid (u, out; v, in) \in R'_2\}$
$\quad \cup \{h(p)b_p \rightarrow pb_p \mid (p, out) \mid R'_2, \ p \in P\}$
$\quad \cup \{pb_p \rightarrow h(p)b_p \mid (p, in) \mid R'_2, \ p \in P\}$,

where $h : O \rightarrow \{a' \mid a \in O\}$ and $h_b : O \rightarrow O^*$ are morphisms defined by $h(a) = a'$ for every $a \in O$, $h(a) = a$ for $a \in O - \{p, p' \mid p \in P\}$, $h(p) = pb_p$ for $p \in P$, and $h(p') = p'b_p$; h is the priming morphism for objects of region 2, and h_b is the morphism adding objects b_p to objects p or p'.

It is easy too see that the behavior of Π' is exactly the same as that of Π: the objects in region 1 of Π are also in Π', while the objects in region 2 of Π are renamed (i.e., primed) and also placed in region 1 of Π, and the rules are changed accordingly. The role of extra objects b_p (one copy for every copy of bi-catalytic symbols in w_1 and w_2) is to transform all non-cooperative proton rules in cooperative bi-stable catalytic rules (because rules $p \rightarrow p'$ or $p' \rightarrow p$, $\{p, p'\} \in C_b$, are forbidden by the definition of P system with bi-stable catalysts).

Clearly, non-cooperative rules (except the uniport of protons) remain non-cooperative, while other rules are changed as follows:

In Π	(pa, out)	(pa, in)	$(p, out; a, in)$	$(a, out; p, in)$
In Π'	$p'a' \rightarrow pa$	$pa \rightarrow p'a'$	$p'a \rightarrow pa'$	$pa' \rightarrow p'a$

In Π	(p, out)	(p, in)
In Π'	$p'b_p \rightarrow pb_p$	$pb_p \rightarrow p'b_p$

We can now claim that during this transformation the proton pumping computational completeness constructions become the computational completeness constructions of P systems with (the same number as protons in the original construction) bi-stable catalysts.

Example 1. Transformed time-free P system from Corollary 1 to Theorem 2 (extra objects are not needed: the construction does not have uniport rules of protons).

$\Pi = (O, C_b, [_1 \ ]_1, w_1, R_1),$ where

$O = T \cup \{a_i, a'_i \mid 1 \le i \le 2\} \cup \{l_j, l'_j \mid l \in I_-, 1 \le j \le 4\}$

$\quad \cup \{\#_1, \#_2, \#'_1, \#'_2\} \cup \{l, l' \mid l \in I\} \cup P,$

$C_b = \{\{D_i, D'_i\}, \{E_i, E'_i\} \mid 1 \le i \le 2\},$

$w_1 = l_0 \#_1 D'_{m+1} D'_{m+2} Z'_{m+1} Z'_{m+2},$

$R_1 = \{l \to a_{out} l^{(1)}, l \to a_{out} l^{(2)} \mid l : (write(a), l^{(1)}, l^{(2)}) \in I\}$

$\quad \cup \{l \to a_i l^{(1)}, l \to a_i l^{(2)} \mid l : (A(i), l^{(1)}, l^{(2)}) \in I\} \cup \{\#_2 \to \#_2\}$

$\quad \cup \{l_4 \to l^{(1)}, l_1 \to l_2, l_2 \to \#_2, l_3 \to l^{(2)} \mid l : (S(i), l^{(1)}, l^{(2)}) \in I\},$

$\quad \cup \{l' \to l'_4, l' \to l'_1, l'_2 \to l'_3 \mid l : (S(i), l^{(1)}, l^{(2)}) \in I\} \cup \{\#'_1 \to \#'_1\},$

$\quad \cup \{l \to l', l'_4 D'_i \to l_4 D_i, a_i D_i \to a'_i D'_i, \#'_1 D'_i \to \#_1 D_i, l'_1 E'_i \to l_1 E_i,$

$\quad a_i E_i \to a'_i E'_i, l_2 E_i \to l'_2 E'_i, l'_3 \to l_3 \mid l : (S(i), l^{(1)}, l^{(2)}) \in I\}.$

Thus we obtain a (clearly, optimal) computational completeness result for systems with one bi-stable catalyst: $LOP_1(2cat_1, tar) = RE$, improving NOP_5 $(cat_2, 2cat_1, tar) = NRE$ from [12]. Another new result (see the example above) is that time-free systems with four bi-stable catalysts are computationally complete: $fLOP_1(2cat_4, tar) = RE$ (improving $fPsOP_1(2cat_*, tar) = PsRE$ from [7]).

6   Concluding Remarks

We have studied proton pumping P systems, a variant of P systems which is both biologically motivated and mathematically elegant. The obtained results are then transferred to P systems with bi-stable catalysts. Since every object only carries a finite amount of information, the cooperation of objects (i.e., the exchange of information) is crucial to obtain any non-trivial computational device. Here, the cooperation is reduced to the minimum: objects can only cooperate directly with protons, by moving together to another region, or with bi-stable catalysts, by changing their state.

Nevertheless, this is enough to reach computational completeness, even with low parameters like rewriting objects in *two regions* and communicating them across *one membrane* using just *one proton*, or rewriting objects in *one region* using just *one bi-stable catalyst*. The latter result nicely correlates with the computational completeness of P systems with two catalysts, [10]. The same systems are computationally complete in a *time-free* way with *four protons/bi-stable catalysts* instead of one.

Yet another point worth mentioning is that the constructions in the proofs have a low number of *cooperative rules: four* for both one-proton constructions and $|I_+| + 2|I_-| + 6$ (where I_+ is the number of ADD instructions and I_- is the number of SUB instructions in the simulated register machine) for both time-free constructions (exactly the same results can be claimed for P system with bi-stable catalysts).

The one-proton results obtained here are optimal for P systems with external output in terms of number of membranes and protons, assuming that the skin membrane is only used to output the result: with only one membrane (i.e., output membrane) or zero protons the behavior of the system is non-cooperative. However, some challenging open problems remain:

- Is rewriting in both regions necessary for completeness (most of the constructions in evolution–communication and proton pumping P systems heavily rely on rewriting in all regions)?
- What is the generative power of proton pumping P systems with one membrane and internal output?
- What about restricted proton pumping P systems, where the only uniport rules allowed are uniport rules of protons (i.e., protons appear in no evolution rules but in all communication rules)?
- Are four protons (or bi-stable catalysts) necessary for time-free computational completeness?

Acknowledgements

The author is thankful to Francesco Bernardini for suggesting to use the register machines to show that four protons are enough, and to Rudolf Freund for the useful discussions of the results on catalytic P systems. The paper was written during the author's visit of the Vienna University of Technology. This article is a final version of [3].

The author is supported by the project TIC2002-04220-C03-02 of the Research Group on Mathematical Linguistics, Tarragona, and acknowledges the Moldovan Research and Development Association (MRDA) and the U.S. Civilian Research and Development Foundation (CRDF), Award No. MM2-3034 for providing a challenging and fruitful framework for cooperation.

References

1. B. Alberts et al.: *Essential Cell Biology, An Introduction to the Molecular Biology of the Cell.* Garland Publ, New York, London, 1998.
2. A. Alhazov: Minimizing evolution-communication P systems and automata. In: [8], 23–31, and *New Generation Computing,* 22 (2004), 299–310.
3. A. Alhazov: Number of protons/bi-stable catalysts and membranes in P systems. Time-freeness. In *Preproceedings of the Workshop on Membrane Computing* (R. Freund, G. Lojka, M. Oswald, Gh. Păun, eds.), Vienna Institute of Technology, 2005, 102–122.
4. A. Alhazov, M. Cavaliere: Evolution-communication P systems: Time-freeness. In *Proceedings of the Third Brainstorming Week on Membrane Computing* (M.A. Gutiérrez-Naranjo, A. Riscos-Núñez, F.J. Romero-Campero, D. Sburlan, eds.), Technical Report 01/2005, Sevilla University, 2005, 11–18.
5. A. Alhazov, M. Cavaliere: Proton pumping P systems. In *Preproceedings of the Workshop on Membrane Computing* (A. Alhazov, C. Martín-Vide, Gh. Păun, Eds.), Technical Report **28/03**, Rovira i Virgili University, Tarragona, 2003, 1–16, and in *Membrane Computing, International Workshop, WMC 2003, Tarragona, 2003, Revised Papers* (C. Martín-Vide, G. Mauri, Gh. Păun, G. Rozenberg, A. Salomaa, Eds.), LNCS 2933, Springer, Berlin, 2004, 1–18.

6. M. Cavaliere: Evolution-communication P systems. In *Membrane Computing. International Workshop, WMC-CdeA 2002, Curtea de Argeş* (Gh. Păun, G. Rozenberg, A. Salomaa, C. Zandron, eds.), LNCS 2597, Springer, Berlin, 2003, 134–145.

7. M. Cavaliere, V. Deufemia: Further results on time-free P systems. In *Proceedings of the ESF PESC Exploratory Workshop on Cellular Computing (Complexity Aspects)* (M.A. Gutiérrez-Naranjo, Gh. Păun, M.J. Pérez-Jiménez, eds.), Fénix Editora, Sevilla, 2005, 95–116.

8. M. Cavaliere, C. Martín-Vide, Gh. Păun, eds.: *Brainstorming Week on Membrane Computing.* Technical Report 26/03, Rovira i Virgili University, Tarragona, 2003.

9. M. Cavaliere, D. Sburlan: Time-independent P systems. In *Membrane Computing, International Workshop WMC5, Milano, Italy, 2004, Selected Papers* (G. Mauri, Gh. Paun, M.J. Pérez-Jiménez, G. Rozenberg, A. Salomaa, eds.), LNCS 3365, Springer, Berlin, 2005.

10. R. Freund, L. Kari, M. Oswald, P. Sosík: Computationally universal P systems without priorities: two catalysts are sufficient. *Theoretical Computer Science*, 330 (2005), 251–266.

11. S.N. Krishna, A. Păun: Some universality results on evolution-communication P systems. In [8], 207–215, and *New Generation Computing*, 22 (2004), 377–394.

12. S.N. Krishna, A. Păun: Three universality results on P systems. In [8], 198–206.

13. M.L. Minsky: *Finite and Infinite Machines.* Prentice Hall, Englewood Cliffs, New Jersey, 1967.

14. Gh. Păun: *Computing with Membranes: An Introduction.* Springer, Berlin, 2002.

15. M.H. Saier, jr.: A functional-phylogenetic classification system for transmembrane solute transporters. *Microbiology and Molecular Biology Reviews*, 2000, 354–411.

16. The P systems Web Page: `http://psystems.disco.unimib.it`

Symbol/Membrane Complexity of P Systems with Symport/Antiport Rules

Artiom Alhazov[1,2], Rudolf Freund[3], and Marion Oswald[3]

[1] Research Group on Mathematical Linguistics,
Rovira i Virgili University,
Pl. Imperial Tàrraco 1, 43005 Tarragona, Spain
`artiome.alhazov@estudiants.urv.es`
[2] Institute of Mathematics and Computer Science,
Academy of Sciences of Moldova,
Str. Academiei 5, Chişinău, MD 2028, Moldova
`artiom@math.md`
[3] Faculty of Informatics, Vienna University of Technology,
Favoritenstr. 9–11, A–1040 Vienna, Austria
{`rudi, marion`}`@emcc.at`

Abstract. We consider P systems with symport/antiport rules and small numbers of symbols and membranes and present several results for P systems with symport/antiport rules simulating register machines with the number of registers depending on the number s of symbols and the number m of membranes. For instance, any recursively enumerable set of natural numbers can be generated (accepted) by systems with $s \geq 2$ symbols and $m \geq 1$ membranes such that $m+s \geq 6$. In particular, the result of the original paper [17] proving universality for three symbols and four membranes is improved (e.g., three symbols and three membranes are sufficient). The general results that P systems with symport/antiport rules with s symbols and m membranes are able to simulate register machines with $\max \{m(s-2), (m-1)(s-1)\}$ registers also allows us to give upper bounds for the numbers s and m needed to generate/accept any recursively enumerable set of k-dimensional vectors of non-negative integers or to compute any partial recursive function $f : \mathbb{N}^\alpha \rightarrow \mathbb{N}^\beta$. Finally, we also study the computational power of P systems with symport/antiport rules and only one symbol: with one membrane, we can exactly generate the family of finite sets of non-negative integers; with one symbol and two membranes, we can generate at least all semilinear sets. The most interesting open question is whether P systems with symport/antiport rules and only one symbol can gain computational completeness (even with an arbitrary number of membranes) as it was shown for tissue P systems in [1].

1 Introduction

In the area of membrane computing there are two main classes of systems: P systems with a hierarchical (tree-like) structure as already introduced in the original

R. Freund et al. (Eds.): WMC 2005, LNCS 3850, pp. 96–113, 2006.

paper of Gheorghe Păun (see [15]) and tissue P systems with cells arranged in an arbitrary graph structure (see [12], [9]). We here consider "classical" P systems using symport/antiport rules for the communication through membranes (these communication rules first were investigated in [14]).

It is well known that equipped with the maximally parallel derivation mode P systems /tissue P systems with only one membrane /one cell already reach universal computational power, even with antiport rules of weight two (e.g., see [4] and [7]); yet on the other hand, in these P systems the number of symbols remains unbounded.

Considering the generation of recursively enumerable sets of natural numbers we may also ask the question how many symbols we need for obtaining computational completeness in a small number of membranes. In [17] the quite surprising result was proved that three symbols are enough in the case of P systems with symport/antiport rules. The specific type of maximally parallel application of at most one rule in each connection (link) between two cells or one cell and the environment, respectively, in tissue P systems allowed for an even more surprising result proved in [10]: The minimal number of one symbol is already sufficient to obtain computational completeness, e.g., it was shown that any recursively enumerable set of natural numbers can be generated by a tissue P system with at most seven cells using symport/antiport rules of only one symbol. The question remained open whether such a result for the minimal number of symbols can also be obtained for "classical" P systems with symport/antiport rules.

The study of the computational power of tissue P systems depending on the number of cells and symbols was continued in [1]; many classes of these tissue P systems characterize the class of recursively enumerable sets of natural numbers, and some of them were shown to characterize or at least to include the families of finite and regular sets of natural numbers, respectively.

In this paper we continue the direction of [2] and consider "classical" P systems with symport/antiport rules simulating register machines with the number of registers depending on the number s of symbols and the number m of membranes. After some definitions in Sections 2 and 3, in Subsection 3.1, we show that P systems with one symbol and one membrane can exactly generate the family of finite sets of non-negative integers. In Subsections 3.2 and 3.3, some general results for the simulation of register machines by P systems with symport/antiport rules with s symbols and m membranes that allow us to give upper bounds for the numbers s and m needed to generate/accept any recursively enumerable set of vectors of non-negative integers or to compute any partial recursive function are elaborated: We show that any recursively enumerable set of natural numbers can be generated (accepted) by systems with $s \geq 2$ symbols and $m \geq 1$ membranes such that $m + s \geq 6$. In particular, the result of the original paper [17] proving universality for three symbols and four membranes is improved (i.e., three symbols and three membranes or two symbols and four membranes are shown to be sufficient). Finally, in Subsection 3.4 we show that P systems with symport/antiport rules with one symbol and two membranes can generate at least all semilinear (i.e., regular) sets of natural numbers. A summary of the obtained results and some open questions conclude the paper.

2   Preliminaries

For the basic elements of formal language theory needed in the following, we refer to any monograph in this area, in particular, to [3] and [19]. We just list a few notions and notations: $\mathbb{N}$ denotes the set of non-negative integers (natural numbers). V^* is the free monoid generated by the alphabet V under the operation of concatenation and the empty string, denoted by λ, as unit element; by RE ($RE(k)$) we denote the family of recursively enumerable languages (over a k-letter alphabet). By $\Psi_T(L)$ we denote the Parikh image of the language $L \subseteq T^*$, and by $PsFL$ we denote the set of Parikh images of languages from a given family FL. $PsRE(k)$ corresponds with the family of recursively enumerable sets of k-dimensional vectors of non-negative integers; for $PsRE(1)$ we also write NRE. $N_l REG$ denotes the family of regular sets of numbers not containing any number smaller than l; if $l = 0$ we simply write $NREG$. $NFIN$ denotes the family of finite sets of natural numbers.

2.1   Register Machines

The proofs of the main results established in this paper are based on the simulation of register machines; we refer to [13] for original definitions, and to [4] for definitions like those we use in this paper:

An *n-register machine* is a construct $M = (n, R, l_0, l_h)$, where n is the number of registers, R is a finite set of instructions injectively labelled with elements from a given set $lab(M)$, l_0 is the initial/start label, and l_h is the final label.

The instructions are of the following forms:

- $l_1 : (A(r), l_2, l_3)$,
  Add 1 to the contents of register r and proceed to one of the instructions (labelled with) l_2 and l_3. (We say that we have an ADD instruction.)
- $l_1 : (S(r), l_2, l_3)$,
  If register r is not empty, then subtract 1 from its contents and go to instruction l_2, otherwise proceed to instruction l_3. (We say that we have a SUB instruction.)
- $l_h : halt$,
  Stop the machine. The final label l_h is only assigned to this instruction.

(Deterministic) Register machines can be used to compute any partial recursive function $f : \mathbb{N}^\alpha \to \mathbb{N}^\beta$; starting with $(n_1, \ldots, n_\alpha) \in \mathbb{N}^\alpha$ in registers 1 to α, M has computed $f(n_1, \ldots, n_\alpha) = (r_1, \ldots, r_\beta)$ if it halts in the final label h with registers 1 to β containing r_1 to r_β. If the final label cannot be reached, $f(n_1, \ldots, n_\alpha)$ remains undefined.

A deterministic register machine can also analyze an input $(n_1, \ldots, n_\alpha) \in \mathbb{N}^\alpha$ in registers 1 to α, which is recognized if the register machine finally stops by the halt instruction with all its registers being empty. If the machine does not halt, the analysis was not successful.

A (non-deterministic) register machine M is said to generate a vector $(s_1, \ldots, s_k)$ of natural numbers if, starting with the instruction with label l_0 and all registers containing the number 0, the machine stops (it reaches the instruction $l_h : halt$) with the first k registers containing the numbers $s_1, \ldots, s_k$ (and all other registers being empty).

Without loss of generality, in the succeeding proofs we will assume that in each ADD instruction $l_1 : (A(r), l_2, l_3)$ and in each SUB instruction $l_1 : (S(r), l_2, l_3)$ the labels l_1, l_2, l_3 are mutually distinct (for a short proof see [9]).

The register machines are known to be computationally complete, equal in power to (non-deterministic) Turing machines: they generate exactly the sets of vectors of natural numbers which can be generated by Turing machines, i.e., the family $PsRE$.

The results proved in [5] (based on the results established in [13]) as well as in [6] and [8] immediately lead to the following results:

Proposition 1. *For any partial recursive function $f : \mathbb{N}^\alpha \to \mathbb{N}^\beta$ there exists a deterministic $(\max\{\alpha, \beta\} + 2)$-register machine M computing f in such a way that, when starting with $(n_1, \ldots, n_\alpha) \in \mathbb{N}^\alpha$ in registers 1 to α, M has computed $f(n_1, \ldots, n_\alpha) = (r_1, \ldots, r_\beta)$ if it halts in the final label h with registers 1 to β containing r_1 to r_β, and all other registers being empty; if the final label cannot be reached, $f(n_1, \ldots, n_\alpha)$ remains undefined.*

In particular we know that $k + 2$-register machines generate/accept any recursively enumerable set of k-dimensional vectors of non-negative integers (see [4], [13]):

Proposition 2. *For any recursively enumerable set $L \subseteq \mathbb{N}^\beta$ of vectors of non-negative integers there exists a non-deterministic $(\beta + 2)$-register machine M generating L in such a way that, when starting with all registers 1 to $\beta + 2$ being empty, M non-deterministically computes and halts with n_i in registers i, $1 \leq i \leq \beta$, and registers $\beta + 1$ and $\beta + 2$ being empty if and only if $(n_1, \ldots, n_\beta) \in L$.*

Proposition 3. *For any recursively enumerable set $L \subseteq \mathbb{N}^\alpha$ of vectors of non-negative integers there exists a deterministic $(\alpha + 2)$-register machine M accepting L in such a way that M halts with all registers being empty if and only if M starts with some $(n_1, \ldots, n_\alpha) \in L$ in registers 1 to α and the registers $\alpha + 1$ to $\alpha + 2$ being empty.*

From the main result in [13] that the actions of a Turing machine can be simulated by a 2-register machine (using a prime number encoding of the configuration of the Turing machine) we also know that the halting problem is undecidable for 2-register machines.

Moreover, it is well-known that 1-register machines can generate/accept $NREG$.

2.2   P Systems with Symport/Antiport Rules

The reader is supposed to be familiar with basic elements of membrane computing, e.g., from [16]; comprehensive information can be found on the P systems web page http://psystems.disco.unimib.it.

A *P system* (of degree $m \geq 1$) *with symport/antiport rules* (in the following we shall only speak of a *P system*) is a construct

$$\Pi = (O, \mu, w_1, \cdots, w_m, R_1, \cdots, R_m),$$

where:

- O is the alphabet of *objects*,
- μ is the *membrane structure* (it is assumed that we have m membranes, labelled with $1, 2, \ldots, m$, the skin membrane usually being labelled with 1),
- w_i, $1 \leq i \leq m$, are strings over O representing the *initial* multiset of *objects* present in the membranes of the system,
- R_i, $1 \leq i \leq m$, are finite sets of *symport/antiport rules* of the form x/y, for some $x, y \in O^*$, associated with membrane i (if $|x|$ or $|y|$ equals 0 then we speak of a symport rule, otherwise we call it an antiport rule).

An antiport rule of the form $x/y \in R_i$ means moving the objects specified by x from membrane i to the surrounding membrane j (to the environment, if $i = 1$), at the same time moving the objects specified by y in the opposite direction. (The rules with one of x, y being empty are, in fact, symport rules, but in the following we do not explicitly consider this distinction here, as it is not relevant for what follows.) We assume the environment to contain all objects in an unbounded number.

The computation starts with the multisets specified by $w_1, \ldots, w_m$ in the m membranes; in each time unit, the rules assigned to each membrane are used in a maximally parallel way, i.e., we choose a multiset of rules at each membrane in such a way that, after identifying objects inside and outside the corresponding membranes to be affected by the selected multiset of rules, no objects remain to be subject to any additional rule at any membrane. The computation is successful if and only if it halts; depending on the function of the system, the input and the output may be encoded by different symbols in different membranes, the input then being added in the initial configuration as the corresponding number of respective symbols in the designated membranes.

The set of all k-dimensional vectors generated/accepted in this way by the system Π is denoted by $g(k) N(\Pi)$ and $a(k) N(\Pi)$, respectively. The family of sets $g(k) N(\Pi)/a(k) N(\Pi)$ of vectors computed as above by systems with at most m membranes and at most s symbols is denoted by $g(k) NO_s P_m$ and $a(k) NO_s P_m$, respectively. The family of functions from k-dimensional vectors to l-dimensional vectors computed as above by P systems with at most m membranes and at most s symbols is denoted by $f(k, l) NO_s P_m$. When any of the parameters k, l, m, s is not bounded, it is replaced by $*$.

3   Results

We now establish our results for P systems with symport/antiport rules and small numbers of membranes and symbols. The main constructions show that a

P system with symport/antiport rules and $m \geq 1$ membranes as well as $s \geq 2$ symbols can simulate a register machine with $\max \{m (s - 2), (m - 1)(s - 1)\}$ registers. For example, in that way we improve the result $NRE = g(1) NO_3 P_4$ as established in [17] to $NRE = g(1) NO_3 P_3 = g(1) NO_2 P_4$.

3.1   One Membrane

The following characterization of $NFIN$ by P systems with only one membrane and only one symbol corresponds with the similar characterization by tissue P systems with only one cell and only one symbol as established in [1].

Example 1. $g(1) NO_1 P_1 = NFIN$.

Consider an arbitrary non-empty set $M \in NFIN$. Then we construct a P system $\Pi = (\{a\}, [_1 \ ]_1, w_1, R_1)$ where $w_1 = a^m$ with $m = \max(M) + 1$ and $R_1 = \{a^m/a^j \mid j \in M\}$.

Clearly, $j < m$ for any $j \in M$, so the computation finishes in one step generating the elements of M as the corresponding number of symbols a in the skin membrane.

The special case of generating the empty set can be done by the following trivial P system: $\Pi = (\{a\}, [_1 \ ]_1, a, \{a/a\})$. A computation in this system will never halt.

The inclusion $NFIN \supseteq g(1) NO_1 P_1$ can easily be argued (like in [1]) as follows:

Consider a P system $\Pi = (\{a\}, [_1 \ ]_1, w_1, R_1)$.

Let $m = \min \{j \mid j/i \in R_1 \text{ for some } i\}$. Then a rule from R_1 can be applied as long as region 1 contains at least m objects. Therefore, $g(1) N(\Pi) \subseteq \{j \mid j < m\}$; hence, $g(1) N(\Pi) \in NFIN$.

Let us recall another relatively simple construction for tissue P systems from [1] that also shows a corresponding result for the membrane case.

Example 2. $g(1) NO_2 P_1 \supseteq NREG$.

We will use the fact that for any regular set M of nonnegative integers there exist finite sets of numbers M_0, M_1 and a number k such that $M = M_0 \cup \{i + jk \mid i \in M_1, j \in \mathbb{N}\}$ (this follows, e.g., from the shape of the minimal finite automaton accepting the unary language with length set M).

We now construct a P system $\Pi = (\{a, p\}, [_1 \ ]_1, w_1, R_1)$ where $w_1 = pp$ and $R_1 = \{pp/a^i \mid i \in M_0\} \cup \{pp/pa, pa/pa^{k+1}\} \cup \{pa/a^i \mid i \in M_1\}$, which generates M as the number of symbols a in the skin membrane in halting computations.

Initially, there are no objects a in region 1, so the system "chooses" between generating an element of M_0 in one step or exchanging pp by pa. In the latter case, there is only one copy of p in the system. After an arbitrary number j of applications of the rule pa/pa^{k+1} a rule exchanging pa by a^i for some $i \in M_1$ is eventually applied, generating $jk + i$ symbols a. Hence, $g(1) N(\Pi) = M_0 \cup \{i + jk \mid i \in M_1, j \in \mathbb{N}\} = M$.

We will now show two simple constructions to illustrate the accepting power of P systems with one membrane.

Example 3. $\{ki \mid i \in \mathbb{N}\} \in a\,(1)\,NO_1P_1$ for any $k \in \mathbb{N}$.

The set of numbers divisible by a fixed number k (represented by the multiplicity of the object a in the initial configuration) can be accepted by the P system $\Pi = (\{a\}, [_1 \ ]_1, w_1, \{a^k/\lambda, a/a\})$; w_1 is the input of the P system in the initial configuration. The rule a^k/λ sends objects out in groups of k, while the rule a/a "keeps busy" all objects not used by the other one. Hence, the system halts if and only if a multiple of k symbols a has been sent out in several steps finally not using the antiport rule a/a anymore.

Example 4. $NFIN \subseteq a\,(1)\,NO_2P_1$.

Any finite set M of natural numbers (represented by the multiplicity of the object a in the initial configuration) can be accepted by the P system $\Pi = (\{a, p\}, [_1 \ ]_1, pw_1, \{a/a, p/p\} \cup \{pa^n/\lambda \mid n \in M\})$; w_1 is the input of the P system in the initial configuration as the number of symbols a in the skin membrane representing the corresponding element from M. The rule pa^n/λ can send out p together with a "correct" number of objects a, while the rules a/a and p/p (in the case of $w_1 = \lambda$) "keep busy" all other objects.

Example 3 illustrates that even P systems with one membrane and one object can accept some infinite sets (as opposed to the generating case, where we exactly get all finite sets). Example 4 shows that when using two objects it is already possible to accept all finite sets.

3.2   At Least Three Symbols

It was already shown in [2] that any d-register machine can be simulated by a P system in one membrane using $d + 2$ symbols. In this subsection we generalize this result: P systems with m membranes and $s \geq 3$ symbols can simulate $m(s - 2)$-register machines:

Theorem 1. *Any mn-register machine can be simulated by a P system with* $2 + n$ *symbols and m membranes.*

Proof. Let us consider a register machine $M = (d, R, l_1, l_{halt})$ with $d = mn$ registers. No matter what the goal of M is (generating/accepting vectors of natural numbers, computing functions), we can construct the P system (of degree m)

$$
\begin{aligned}
\Pi &= (O, \mu, w_1, \cdots, w_m, R_1, \cdots, R_m), \\
O &= \{p, q\} \cup \{a_j \mid 1 \leq j \leq n\}, \\
\mu &= [_1 \ [_2 \ ]_2 \cdots [_m \ ]_m \ ]_1, \\
w_1 &= w_0 \prod_{j=1}^{n} a_j^{r_j}, \\
w_i &= \prod_{j=1}^{n} a_j^{r_j+(i-1)n}, \quad 2 \leq i \leq m,
\end{aligned}
$$

that simulates the actions of M as follows. The symbols p and q are needed for encoding the instructions of M; q also has the function of a trap symbol, i.e., in case of the wrong choice for a rule to be applied we take in so many symbols q that we can never again rid of them and therefore get "trapped" in an infinite loop. Throughout the computation, the value of register $j+(i-1)n$ is represented by the multiplicity of symbol a_j in region i. In the generating case, $w_1 = w_0$ and $w_i = \lambda$ for $2 \leq i \leq m$; in the accepting case and in the case of computing functions, the numbers of symbols a_j as defined above specify the input.

An important part of the proof is to define a suitable encoding $c : \mathbb{N} \to \mathbb{N}$ (a strictly monotone linear function) for the instructions of the register machine: As we will use at most 6 different subsequent labels for each instruction, without loss of generality we assume the labels of M to be positive integers such that the labels assigned to ADD and SUB instructions have the values $6i - 5$ for $1 \leq i < t$, as well as $l_0 = 1$ and $l_{halt} = 6(t - 1) + 1$, for some $t \geq 1$.

For the operations assigned to a label l and working on register r, we will use specific encodings by the symbols p and q which allow us to distinguish between the operations ADD, SUBTRACT, and ZERO TEST. As we have d registers, this yields $3d$ multisets for specifying operations. The number of symbols p and q in these operation multisets is taken in such a way that the number of symbols p always exceeds the number of symbols q. Finally, the number of symbols q can never be split into two parts that could be interpreted as belonging to two operation multisets.

Hence, the range for the number of symbols q is taken as the interval $[3d + 1, 6d]$ and the range for the number of symbols p is taken as the interval $[6d + 1, 9d + 1]$. Thus, with $h = 12d + 1$ we define the following operation multisets:

$$\begin{aligned} ADD: && \alpha_+(r) &= q^{3d+r}p^{h-(3d+r)}, \ 1 \leq r \leq d, \\ SUBTRACT: && \alpha_-(r) &= q^{4d+r}p^{h-(4d+r)}, \ 1 \leq r \leq d, \\ ZEROTEST: && \alpha_0(r) &= q^{5d+r}p^{h-(5d+r)}, \ 1 \leq r \leq d. \end{aligned}$$

The encoding $c : \mathbb{N} \to \mathbb{N}$ which shall encode the instruction l of M to be simulated as $p^{c(l)}$ also has to obey to the following conditions:

- For any i, j with $1 \leq i, j \leq 6t - 5$, $c(i) + c(j) > c(6t - 4)$, i.e., the sum of the codes of two instruction labels has to be larger than the largest code we will ever use for the given M, hence, if we do not use the maximal number of symbols p as interpretation of a code for an instruction (label), then the remaining rest of symbols p cannot be misinterpreted as the code for another instruction label.
- The distance g between any two codes $c(i)$ and $c(i+1)$ has to be larger than any of the multiplicities of the symbol p which appear besides codes in the rules defined above.

As we shall see in the construction of the rules below, we may take

$$g = 2h = 24d + 2.$$

In sum, for a function c fulfilling all the conditions stated above we can take

$$c(x) = g(x + 6t - 4) \text{ for } x \geq 0.$$

For example, with this function, for arbitrary $i, j \geq 1$ we get

$$c\,(i) + c\,(j) = g(i + 6t - 4) + g(j + 6t - 4) > g(6t - 4 + 6t - 4) = c\,(6t - 4)\,.$$

Moreover, for $l_1 = 1$ we therefore obtain

$$c\,(l_1) = g\,(6t - 3) = (24d + 2)\,(6t - 3)$$

as well as

$$w_0 = p^{c(l_1)} = p^{(24d+2)(6t-3)}.$$

Finally, we have to find a number f which is so large that after getting f symbols we inevitably enter an infinite loop with the rule

$$q^f / q^{3f};$$

as we shall justify below, we can take

$$f = c\,(l_{halt} + 1) = 2g(6t - 4).$$

Equipped with this coding function and the constants defined above we are now able to define the following set of symport/antiport rules assigned to the membranes for simulating the actions of the given register machine M:

$$
\begin{aligned}
R_1 = \ & \{p^{c(l_1)}/p^{c(l_2)}a_s, p^{c(l_1)}/p^{c(l_3)}a_s \mid \\
& \quad l_1 : (A(s), l_2, l_3) \in R, 1 \leq s \leq n\} \\
& \cup \{p^{c(l_1)}/p^{c(l_1+1)}\alpha_+(s + (s' - 1)n)a_s, p^{c(l_1+1)}/p^{c(l_1+2)}, \\
& \quad p^{c(l_1+2)}/p^{c(l_1+3)}, p^{c(l_1+3)}\alpha_+(s + (s' - 1)n)/p^{c(l_2)} \\
& \quad p^{c(l_1+3)}\alpha_+(s + (s' - 1)n)/p^{c(l_3)} \mid \\
& \quad l_1 : (A(s + (s' - 1)n), l_2, l_3), 1 \leq s \leq n, 2 \leq s' \leq m\} \\
& \cup \{p^{c(l_1)}a_s/p^{c(l_2)}, p^{c(l_1)}/p^{c(l_1+1)}\alpha_0(s), \\
& \quad p^{c(l_1+1)}/p^{c(l_1+2)}, \alpha_0(s)a_s/q^{3f}, \\
& \quad p^{c(l_1+2)}\alpha_0(s)/p^{c(l_3)} \mid l_1 : (S(s), l_2, l_3) \in R, 1 \leq s \leq n\} \\
& \cup \{p^{c(l_1)}/p^{c(l_1+1)}\alpha_-(s + (s' - 1)n), p^{c(l_1+1)}/p^{c(l_1+2)}, \\
& \quad p^{c(l_1+2)}/p^{c(l_1+3)}, p^{c(l_1+3)}\alpha_-(s + (s' - 1)n)a_s/p^{c(l_2)}, \\
& \quad p^{c(l_1)}/p^{c(l_1+4)}\alpha_0(s + (s' - 1)n), p^{c(l_1+4)}/p^{c(l_1+5)}, \\
& \quad p^{c(l_1+5)}\alpha_0(s + (s' - 1)n)/p^{c(l_3)}, \\
& \quad \alpha_-(s + (s' - 1)n)/q^{3f} \mid \\
& \quad l_1 : (S(s + (s' - 1)n), l_2, l_3), 1 \leq s \leq n, 2 \leq s' \leq m\} \\
& \cup \{p^{c(l_{halt})}/\lambda, p^h/q^{3f}, q^f/q^{3f}\}
\end{aligned}
$$

as well as for $2 \leq s' \leq m$

$$
\begin{aligned}
R_{s'} = \ & \{\lambda/\alpha_+(s + (s' - 1)n)a_s, \alpha_+(s + (s' - 1)n)/\lambda \mid \\
& \quad l_1 : (A(s + (s' - 1)n), l_2, l_3), 1 \leq s \leq n, 2 \leq s' \leq m\} \\
& \cup \{a_s/\alpha_-(s + (s' - 1)n), \alpha_-(s + (s' - 1)n)/\lambda, \\
& \quad a_s/\alpha_0(s + (s' - 1)n) \mid \\
& \quad l_1 : (S(s + (s' - 1)n), l_2, l_3), 1 \leq s \leq n, 2 \leq s' \leq m\}.
\end{aligned}
$$

The correct work of the rules can be described as follows:

1. Throughout the whole computation in Π, it is directed by the code $p^{c(l)}$ for some $l \leq 6t - 5$; in order to guarantee the correct sequence of encoded rules the trap is activated in case of a wrong choice, which in any case guarantees an infinite loop with the symbols q by the "trap rule"

$$q^f/q^{3f}.$$

   The minimal number of superfluous symbols p to start the trap is h and causes the application of the rule p^h/q^{3f}.

2. For each ADD instruction $l_1 : (A(s), l_2, l_3)$ of M, i.e., for incrementing register s for $1 \leq s \leq n$, we use the following rules in R_1:

$$p^{c(l_1)}/p^{c(l_2)}a_s, \text{ and}$$
$$p^{c(l_1)}/p^{c(l_3)}a_s.$$

   In that way, the ADD instruction $l_1 : (A(s), l_2, l_3)$ of M for one of the first n registers is simulated in only one step: the number of symbols p representing the instruction of M labelled by l_1 is replaced by the number of symbols p representing the instruction of M labelled by l_2 or l_3, respectively, in the same moment also incrementing the number of symbols a_s. Whenever a wrong number of symbols p is taken, the remaining symbols cannot be used by another rule than the "trap rule" p^h/q^{3f}, which in the succeeding computation steps inevitably leads to the repeated application of the rule q^f/q^{3f} thus flooding the skin membrane with more and more symbols q.

   On the other hand, incrementing register $s + (s' - 1)n$, for $1 \leq s \leq n$, $2 \leq s' \leq m$, i.e., registers $n + 1$ to nm is accomplished by the rules

$$p^{c(l_1)}/p^{c(l_1+1)}\alpha_+(s + (s' - 1)n)a_s,$$
$$p^{c(l_1+1)}/p^{c(l_1+2)}$$
$$p^{c(l_1+2)}/p^{c(l_1+3)},$$
$$p^{c(l_1+3)}\alpha_+(s + (s' - 1)n)/p^{c(l_2)}$$
$$p^{c(l_1+3)}\alpha_+(s + (s' - 1)n)/p^{c(l_3)}$$

in R_1 as well as by the rules

$$\lambda/\alpha_+(s + (s' - 1)n)a_s,$$
$$\alpha_+(s + (s' - 1)n)/\lambda \text{ in } R_{s'}.$$

Hence, adding one to the contents of registers $n + 1$ to nm now needs four steps: the number of symbols p representing the instruction of M labelled by l_1 is replaced by $p^{c(l_1+1)}$ together with $3d + s + (s' - 1)n$ additional symbols q, $h - (3d + s + (s' - 1)n)$ symbols p and the symbol a_s. In the second step, $p^{c(l_1+1)}$ is exchanged with $p^{c(l_1+2)}$, while at the same time the additional $3d + s + (s' - 1)n$ symbols q and $h - (3d + s + (s' - 1)n)$ symbols p are introduced together with a_s in membrane s'. In the third step, the $c(l_1 + 2)$ symbols p in the skin membrane are exchanged with $c(l_1+2)$ symbols p from the environment, whereas the additional $3d + s + (s' - 1)n$ symbols q and $h - (3d + s + (s' - 1)n)$ symbols p pass out from membrane r. Finally, in the fourth step, these latter symbols together with $p^{c(l_1+3)}$ in the skin membrane are replaced by the number of symbols p representing the next instruction of M labelled by l_2 or l_3, respectively.

3. For simulating the decrementing step of a SUB instruction $l_1 : (S(s), l_2, l_3)$ from R we introduce the following rules:

$$p^{c(l_1)}a_s/p^{c(l_2)}$$

for decrementing the contents of register s, for $1 \leq s \leq n$, represented by the symbols a_s in the skin membrane.

In that way, the decrementing step of the SUB instruction $l_1 : (S(s), l_2, l_3)$ of M now is also simulated in one step: together with $p^{c(l_1)}$ we send out one symbol a_s and take in $p^{c(l_2)}$, which encodes the label of the instruction that has to be executed after the successful decrementing of register s, for $1 \leq s \leq n$.

For decrementing the registers $s + (s' - 1)n$, for $1 \leq s \leq n$, $2 \leq s' \leq m$, we need the following rules:

$$p^{c(l_1)}/p^{c(l_1+1)}\alpha_-(s + (s' - 1)n),$$
$$p^{c(l_1+1)}/p^{c(l_1+2)}$$
$$p^{c(l_1+2)}/p^{c(l_1+3)},$$
$$p^{c(l_1+3)}\alpha_-(s + (s' - 1)n)a_s/p^{c(l_2)} \text{ in } R_1$$

as well as

$$a_s/\alpha_-(s + (s' - 1)n),$$
$$\alpha_-(s + (s' - 1)n)/\lambda \text{ in } R_r.$$

In this case, the SUB instruction is simulated in four steps: $p^{c(l_1)}$ is replaced by $p^{c(l_1+1)}$ together with the "operation multiset" $\alpha_-(s + (s' - 1)n)$, i.e., $q^{4d+r}p^{h-(4d+r)}$, $r = s + (s' - 1)n$, for $1 \leq s \leq n$, $2 \leq s' \leq m$. While in the next two steps, two intermediate exchanges of symbols p with the environment take place, the symbol a_s is exchanged with $\alpha_-(s + (s' - 1)n)$ in membrane r, that, in the third step, goes out again to the skin membrane, where it can now together with $p^{c(l_1+3)}$ be exchanged with $p^{c(l_2)}$, i.e., the representation of the next instruction of M.

Again we notice that if we do not choose the correct rule, then the trap is activated by the rule p^h/q^{3f}, especially if no symbol a_s is present in membrane r, then we have to apply the "trap rule" $\alpha_-(s + (s' - 1)n)/q^{3f}$.

4. For simulating the zero test, i.e., the case where we check the contents of register r to be zero, of a SUB instruction $l_1 : (S(s), l_2, l_3)$ from R for registers 1 to n we take the following rules:

$$p^{c(l_1)}/p^{c(l_1+1)}\alpha_0(s),$$
$$p^{c(l_1+1)}/p^{c(l_1+2)}, \text{ and}$$
$$p^{c(l_1+2)}\alpha_0(s)/p^{c(l_3)} \text{ in } R_1.$$

If the rule $\alpha_0(s)a_s/q^{3f}$ from R_1 can be applied, then in the next step we cannot apply $p^{c(l_1+2)}\alpha_0(s)/p^{c(l_3)}$ from R_1, hence, only a rule using less than $c(l_1+2)$ symbols p can be used together with the "trap rule" p^h/q^{3f}.

For simulating the zero test, i.e., the case where we check the contents of register r to be zero, of a SUB instruction $l_1 : (S(s), l_2, l_3)$ from R for registers $n+1$ to nm we now take the following rules:

$$p^{c(l_1)}/p^{c(l_1+4)}\alpha_0(s+(s'-1)n),$$
$$p^{c(l_1+4)}/p^{c(l_1+5)}, \text{ and}$$
$$p^{c(l_1+5)}\alpha_0(s+(s'-1)n)/p^{c(l_3)} \text{ in } R_1.$$

If the rule $a_s/\alpha_0(s+(s'-1)n)$ from R_r can be applied, then in the next step we cannot apply $p^{c(l_1+5)}\alpha_0(s+(s'-1)n)/p^{c(l_3)}$ from R_1, hence, only a rule using less than $c(l_1+5)$ symbols p can be used together with the "trap rule" p^h/q^{3f}.

5. The number of symbols p never exceeds $c(l_{halt}) = 2g(6t-4)$ as long as the simulation of instructions from R works correctly. By definition, $f = c(l_{halt}+1) = 2g(6t-4)$, hence, there will be at least three times more symbols q in region 1 than symbols p in the system after having applied a "trap rule", thus introducing $3f$ symbols q. As by any rule in R_1, the number of symbols p coming in is less than double the number sent out, the total number of symbols p in the system, in one computation step, can at most be doubled in total, too. As every rule that removes some symbols q from region 1 involves at least as many symbols p as symbols q, the "trap rule" q^f/q^{3f} guarantees that in the succeeding steps this relation will still hold true, no matter how the present symbols p and q are interpreted for rules in Π. Therefore, if as soon as a "trap rule" has been applied, then the number of objects q will grow and the system will never halt.

6. Finally, for the halt label $l_{halt} = 6t - 5$ we only take the rule

$$p^{c(l_{halt})}/\lambda,$$

hence, the work of Π will stop exactly when the work of M stops (provided the trap has not been activated due to a wrong non-deterministic choice during the computation).

From the explanations given above we conclude that Π halts if and only if M halts, and moreover, the final configuration of Π represents the final contents of the registers in M. These observations conclude the proof.   □

As already proved in [2], when using P systems with only one membrane, at most five objects are needed to obtain computational completeness:

Corollary 1. $g(1) NO_5P_1 = a(1) NO_5P_1 = NRE$.

Moreover, from Theorem 1 we can also conclude that P systems with two membranes are computationally complete with only four objects:

Corollary 2. $g(1) NO_4P_2 = a(1) NO_4P_2 = NRE$.

3.3   At Least Two Symbols and at Least Two Membranes

On the other hand, for $s, m \geq 2$, we can show that P systems with s symbols and m membranes can simulate $(s-1)(m-1)$-register machines:

Theorem 2. *Any mn-register machine can be simulated by a P system with $n+1$ symbols and $m+1$ membranes, with $n, m \geq 1$.*

Proof. Consider a register machine $M = (d, R, l_0, l_{halt})$ with $d = mn$ registers. We construct the P system

$$
\begin{aligned}
\Pi &= (O, \mu, w_1, \cdots, w_{m+1}, R_1, \cdots, R_{m+1}), \\
O &= \{p\} \cup \{a_j \mid 1 \leq j \leq n\}, \\
\mu &= [_1 \, [_2 \,]_2 \cdots [_{m+1} \,]_{m+1} \,]_1, \\
w_1 &= w_0, \\
w_{i+1} &= \textstyle\prod_{j=1}^{n} a_j^{r_{j+(i-1)n}}, \quad 1 \leq i \leq m,
\end{aligned}
$$

that simulates the actions of M as follows. The contents of register $j+(i-1)n$ is represented by the multiplicity of symbols a_j in region $i+1$, whereas the symbol p is needed for encoding the instructions of M; this time, too, many copies of a_1 in the skin membrane have the function of trap symbols.

Again, an important part of the proof is to define a suitable encoding $c : \mathbb{N} \to \mathbb{N}$ for the instructions of the register machine, and at most 6 different subsequent labels will be used for each instruction, hence, without loss of generality we assume the labels of M to be positive integers such that the labels assigned to ADD and SUB instructions have the values $6i - 5$ for $1 \leq i < t$, as well as $l_0 = 1$ and $l_{halt} = 6(t-1) + 1$, for some $t \geq 1$.

Since one copy of a_s will be used for addition/subtraction, now the operation multisets will be encoded by even numbers of object a_1, i.e., we take $h = 2(12d+1) = 24d + 2$ and define the following operation multisets:

$$
\begin{aligned}
ADD: &\quad \alpha_+(r) = a_1^{6d+2r} p^{h-(6d+2r)}, \; 1 \leq r \leq d, \\
SUBTRACT: &\quad \alpha_-(r) = a_1^{8d+2r} p^{h-(8d+2r)}, \; 1 \leq r \leq d, \\
ZEROTEST: &\quad \alpha_0(r) = a_1^{10d+2r} p^{h-(10d+2r)}, \; 1 \leq r \leq d.
\end{aligned}
$$

In a similar way as before, we now take

$$
g = 2h = 48d + 4
$$

and define the function c by

$$
c(x) = g(x + 6t - 4) \text{ for } x \geq 0.
$$

For $l_1 = 1$ we therefore obtain

$$
c(l_1) = g(6t - 3) = (48d + 4)(6t - 3)
$$

as well as

$$
w_0 = p^{c(l_1)} = p^{(48d+4)(6t-3)}.
$$

Finally, for f we again take

$$f = c\,(l_{halt} + 1) = 2g(6t - 4)$$

which is so large that after getting f symbols we inevitably enter an infinite loop with the rule

$$a_1{}^f / a_1{}^{3f}.$$

Equipped with this coding function and the constants defined above we are now able to define the following set of symport/antiport rules assigned to the membranes for simulating the actions of the given register machine M:

$$
\begin{aligned}
R_1 = \{ & p^{c(l_1)}/p^{c(l_1+1)}\alpha_+(s + (s' - 1)n)a_s, p^{c(l_1+1)}/p^{c(l_1+2)}, \\
& p^{c(l_1+2)}/p^{c(l_1+3)}, p^{c(l_1+3)}\alpha_+(s + (s' - 1)n)/p^{c(l_2)}, \\
& p^{c(l_1+3)}\alpha_+(s + (s' - 1)n)/p^{c(l_3)} \mid \\
& l_1 : (A(s + (s' - 1)n), l_2, l_3), 1 \le s \le n, 1 \le s' \le m \} \\
\cup \{ & p^{c(l_1)}/p^{c(l_1+1)}\alpha_-(s + (s' - 1)n), p^{c(l_1+1)}/p^{c(l_1+2)}, \\
& p^{c(l_1+2)}/p^{c(l_1+3)}, p^{c(l_1+3)}\alpha_-(s + (s' - 1)n)a_s/p^{c(l_2)}, \\
& \alpha_-(s + (s' - 1)n)/a_1{}^{3f}, \\
& p^{c(l_1)}/p^{c(l_1+4)}\alpha_0(s + (s' - 1)n), p^{c(l_1+4)}/p^{c(l_1+5)}, \\
& p^{c(l_1+5)}\alpha_0(s + (s' - 1)n)/p^{c(l_3)} \mid \\
& l_1 : (S(s + (s' - 1)n), l_2, l_3), 1 \le s \le n, 1 \le s' \le m \} \\
\cup \{ & p^{c(l_{halt})}/\lambda, p^h/a_1{}^{3f}, a_1{}^f/a_1{}^{3f} \}
\end{aligned}
$$

and for $1 \le r \le m$,

$$
\begin{aligned}
R_{r+1} = \{ & \lambda/\alpha_+(s + (s' - 1)n)a_r, \alpha_+(s + (s' - 1)n)/\lambda \mid \\
& l_1 : (A(s + (s' - 1)n), l_2, l_3), 1 \le s \le n, 1 \le s' \le m \} \\
\cup \{ & a_s/\alpha_-(s + (s' - 1)n), \alpha_-(s + (s' - 1)n)/\lambda, \\
& a_s/\alpha_0(s + (s' - 1)n) \mid \\
& l_1 : (S(s + (s' - 1)n), l_2, l_3), 1 \le s \le n, 1 \le s' \le m \}.
\end{aligned}
$$

The operations ADD, SUBTRACT, and ZERO TEST now are carried out for all registers r as in the preceding proof for the registers $r > n$. Hence, we do not repeat all the arguments of the preceding proof, but stress the following important differences:

We now take advantage that the operation multisets additionally satisfy the property that now the number of symbols p can never be split into two parts that could be interpreted as belonging to two operation multisets; this guarantees that during a correct simulation, inside an elementary membrane at most one operation can be executed - and if it is the wrong one (i.e., we do not use all symbols p, but instead use more symbols a_1 from the amount representing the contents of a register), then we return a number of symbols p which is too small to allow the correct rule to be applied from R_1, instead the "trap rule" $p^h/a_1{}^{3f}$ will be applied.   □

From the result proved above we can immediately conclude the following, thus also improving the result from [17] where $g\,(1)\,NO_3P_4 = NRE$ was proved: we can reduce the number of membranes from four to three when using only three objects or the number of symbols from three to two when using four membranes.

Corollary 3. $NRE = g(1)NO_3P_3 = a(1)NO_3P_3 = g(1)NO_2P_4 = a(1)NO_2P_4.$

3.4   One Symbol

If only one symbol is available, then so far we do not know whether computational completeness can be obtained even when not bounding the number of membranes (in contrast to tissue P systems which have been shown to be computationally complete with at most seven cells, see [1]). Yet at least we can generate any regular set of natural numbers in only two membranes (remember that with only one membrane we have got a characterization of $NFIN$, see Example 1).

Example 5. $g\,(1)\,NO_1P_2 \supseteq NREG.$

Any finite set can be generated without using the second membrane (see Example 1), so we proceed with infinite sets. Let $M \in NREG - NFIN$, then there exist finite sets M_0, M_1 with $M_1 \neq \emptyset$ and a number $k > 0$ such that $M = M_0 \cup \{i + jk \mid i \in M_1, j \in \mathbb{N}\}$.

Let m be the smallest element of M such that $m > \max\,(M_0 \cup M_1 \cup \{2k\})$; moreover, let $m' = m + 2k$ (thus, $m' \in M$). Then we consider the P system constructed as follows:

$$\Pi = (\{a\}, [_1\,[_2\,]_2\,]_1, a^{m'}, \lambda, R_1, R_2) \text{ where}$$
$$R_1 = \{a^{m'}/a^i \mid i \in M_0\} \cup \{a^{m'}/a^m, a^m/a^{m+k}\} \cup \{a^m/a^i \mid i \in M_1\},$$
$$R_2 = \lambda/a.$$

We assume the result of a halting computation to be collected in the second membrane, and we claim $g\,(1)\,N(\Pi) = M$:

$$g\,(1)\,N(\Pi) \supseteq M:$$

The elements of M_0 are generated in one step, while the rest of M can be generated by

$$[_1\,a^{m'}[_2\,]_2\,]_1 \Rightarrow [_1\,a^m[_2\,]_2\,]_1 => [_1\,a^{m+k}[_2\,]_2\,]_1 \Rightarrow^{j-1}$$
$$[_1\,a^{m+k}[_2\,a^{(j-1)k}\,]_2\,]_1 \Rightarrow [_1\,a^i[_2\,a^{jk}\,]_2\,]_1 \Rightarrow [_1\,[_2\,a^{i+jk}\,]_2\,]_1$$

or by

$$[_1\,a^{m'}[_2\,]_2\,]_1 \Rightarrow [_1\,a^m[_2\,]_2\,]_1 \Rightarrow [_1\,a^i[_2\,]_2\,]_1 \Rightarrow [_1\,[_2\,a^i\,]_2\,]_1.$$
$$g\,(1)\,N(\Pi) \subseteq M:$$

What other derivations can we get different from those described above?

– If all m' symbols enter membrane 2, $m' \in M$.
– If all m symbols enter membrane 2 (possibly after some additions of k), $m+jk \in M$ (by the definition of m, $m \in M$ and, moreover, it can be prolongued by multiples of k).
– If during the first step m copies of the symbol a are used instead of m' (and $2k$ fall inside), then the system generates some number $2k + (i + jk)$ or $2k + (m + jk)$; all these numbers belong to M, too.

Nothing else can happen, because $m + k < m'$ and $\max(M_0 \cup M_1) < m$ and because all symbols not used by R_1 fall into region 2.

4   Summary and Open Questions

From the main theorems (Theorem 1 and Theorem 2) established in the preceding section showing that P systems with symport/antiport rules and $m \geq 1$ membranes as well as $s \geq 2$ symbols can simulate a register machine with $\max\{m(s-2), (m-1)(s-1)\}$ registers in combination with Propositions 2 and 3 we infer the following general results:

Theorem 3. $g(1)NO_sP_m = a(1)NO_sP_m = NRE$, for $m \geq 1$, $s \geq 2$, $m + s \geq 6$.

We conjecture that these results establishing the computational completeness bounds are optimal.

As the halting problem for d-register machines is undecidable for $d \geq 2$, from Theorems 1 and 2 we also obtain the following result:

Theorem 4. *The halting problem for P systems with symport/antiport rules and $s \geq 2$ symbols as well as $m \geq 1$ membranes such that $m + s \geq 5$ is undecidable.*

As 1-register machines can generate/accept all regular number sets, we obtain the following:

Theorem 5. $NREG \subseteq g(1)NO_3P_1 \cap g(1)NO_2P_2 \cap a(1)NO_3P_1 \cap a(1)NO_2P_2$.

The main results established in this paper now can be summarized in the following table:

$|O|$	1	2	3	4	5	m
1	A	B	B	B	B	B
2	B	1	2 (U)	③	4	$m-1$
3	1	2 (U)	④	6	8	$2m-2$
4	2 (U)	④	**6**	9	12	$3m-3$
5	③	6	9	**12**	16	$4m-4$
6	4	8	12	16	**20**	$5m-5$
s	$s-2$	$2s-4$	$3s-6$	$4s-8$	$5s-10$	$\max\{m(s-2), (m-1)(s-1)\}$

(Membranes)

In the table depicted above, the class of P systems indicated by

A generates exactly $NFIN$;

B generates at least $NREG$;

d can simulate any d-register machine. A box around a number indicates a known computational completeness bound, (U) indicates a known unpredictability bound, and a number in boldface shows the diagonal where Theorem 2 and Theorem 1 provide the same result (because in that case $m(s-2)$ equals $(m-1)(s-1)$); the numbers above this diagonal are taken from Theorem 2, while the numbers below the diagonal are taken from Theorem 1.

Based on these simulation results, we now could discuss in more detail how many symbols s and membranes m at most are needed to accept or generate recursively enumerable sets of vectors of natural numbers or compute functions $\mathbb{N}^k \to \mathbb{N}^l$ (e.g., recursively enumerable sets of d-dimensional vectors, $d \geq 1$, can be generated / accepted by P systems with symport/antiport rules using at most $d + 4$ symbols in one membrane, see also [2]). Yet as all these results are direct consequences of the corresponding computational power of the simulated register machines (see Propositions 3, 2, 1), we do not follow this line any further.

Just recently, the computational power of P systems with symport/antiport rules and small numbers of symbols and membranes has also been investigated in [11]. There the authors show that P systems with symport/antiport rules with one symbol and three membranes or with two symbols and one membrane can accept the non-semilinear set $L = \{2^n \mid n \geq 0\}$. Moreover, they prove that for any $k \geq 1$, the class of sets of k-tuples of non-negative integers accepted by partially blind (multi-)counter machines is a proper subclass of the class of sets of k-tuples accepted by P systems with symport/antiport rules with one object and multiple membranes. Similarly, the class of sets of k-tuples of non-negative integers generated by partially blind counter machines is shown to be a subclass (but is not known to be proper) of the class of sets of k-tuples generated by P systems with one object and multiple membranes.

Yet the interesting question whether or not P systems with one symbol are universal still remains open. (The corresponding result holds for tissue P systems, see [1].)

Acknowledgements

Artiom Alhazov is supported by the project TIC2002-04220-C03-02 of the Research Group on Mathematical Linguistics, Tarragona; he also acknowledges the Moldovan Research and Development Association (MRDA) and the U.S. Civilian Research and Development Foundation (CRDF), Award No. MM2-3034. This paper was written during his stay at the Vienna University of Technology.

The work of Marion Oswald is supported by FWF-project T225-N04.

References

1. A. Alhazov, R. Freund, M. Oswald: Tissue P systems with antiport rules and a small number of symbols and cells. In *Developments in Language Theory, 9th International Conference, DLT 2005* (C. De Felice, A. Restivo, eds.), Palermo, Italy, 2005, LNCS 3572, Springer, Berlin, 2005, 100–111.
2. A. Alhazov, R. Freund: P systems with one membrane and symport/antiport rules of five symbols are computationally complete. In *Proceedings of the Third Brainstorming Week on Membrane Computing* (M.A. Gutiérrez-Naranjo, A. Riscos-Núñez, F.J. Romero-Campero, D. Sburlan, eds.), Sevilla, Spain, 2005, 19–28.
3. J. Dassow, Gh. Păun: *Regulated Rewriting in Formal Language Theory*. Springer, Berlin, 1989.

4. R. Freund, M. Oswald: P Systems with activated/prohibited membrane channels. In [18], 261–268.
5. R. Freund, M. Oswald: GP systems with forbidding context. *Fundamenta Informaticae*, 49 (2002), 81–102.
6. R. Freund, Gh. Păun: On the number of non-terminals in graph-controlled, programmed, and matrix grammars. In *Machines, Computations, and Universality, Third International Conference, MCU 2001* (M. Margenstern, Yu. Rogozhin, eds), Chisinau, Moldavia, May 23-27, 2001, LNCS 2055, Springer, Berlin, 2001, 214–225
7. R. Freund, A. Păun: Membrane systems with symport/antiport rules: universality results. In [18], 270–287.
8. R. Freund, Gh. Păun: From regulated rewriting to computing with membranes: Collapsing hierarchies. *Theoretical Computer Science*, 312 (2004), 143–188.
9. R. Freund, Gh. Păun, M.J. Pérez-Jiménez: Tissue-like P systems with channel states. In *Proceedings of the Brainstorming Week on Membrane Computing* (Gh. Păun, A. Riscos-Núñez, A. Romero-Jiménez, F. Sancho-Caparrini, eds.), Sevilla, February 2004, TR 01/04 of Research Group on Natural Computing, Sevilla University, 206–223, and *Theoretical Computer Science*, 330 (2004), 101–116.
10. R. Freund, M. Oswald: Tissue P systems with symport/antiport rules of one symbol are computationally complete. In *Cellular Computing. Complexity Aspects* (M.A. Gutiérrez-Naranjo, Gh. Păun, M.J. Pérez-Jiménez, eds.) Fénix Editora, Sevilla, 2005, 185–197.
11. O.H. Ibarra, S. Woodworth: On symport/antiport P systems with one or two symbols. In *Proceedings of the first International Workshop on Theory and Applications of P Systems, TAPS '05* (Gh. Păun, G. Ciobanu, eds.), Timişoara, Romania, September 26-27, 2005, IeAT Technical Report 05-11, 2005, 75–82
12. C. Martín-Vide, Gh. Păun, J. Pazos, A. Rodríguez-Patón: Tissue P systems. *Theoretical Computer Science*, 296 (2003), 295–326.
13. M.L. Minsky: *Computation: Finite and Infinite Machines*. Prentice Hall, Englewood Cliffs, New Jersey, 1967.
14. A. Păun, Gh. Păun: The power of communication: P systems with symport/antiport. *New Generation Computing*, 20 (2002), 295–306.
15. Gh. Păun: Computing with membranes. *Journal of Computer and System Sciences*, 61 (2000), 108–143, and TUCS Research Report 208 (1998) (http://www.tucs.fi).
16. Gh. Păun: *Computing with Membranes: An Introduction*. Springer, Berlin, 2002.
17. Gh. Păun, J. Pazos, M.J. Pérez-Jiménez, A. Rodríguez-Patón: Symport/antiport P systems with three objects are universal. *Fundamenta Informaticae*, 64 (2005), 353-367
18. Gh. Păun, G. Rozenberg, A. Salomaa, C. Zandron, eds.: *Membrane Computing. International Workshop WMC 2002, Curtea de Argeş, Romania*. LNCS 2597, Springer, Berlin, 2003.
19. G. Rozenberg, A. Salomaa, eds.: *Handbook of Formal Languages* (3 volumes). Springer, Berlin, 1997.
20. The P Systems Web Page, http://psystems.disco.unimib.it

On P Systems as a Modelling Tool
for Biological Systems

Francesco Bernardini[1], Marian Gheorghe[1], Natalio Krasnogor[2],
Ravie C. Muniyandi[1], Mario J. Pérez-Jímenez[3],
and Francisco José Romero-Campero[3]

[1] Department of Computer Science, The University of Sheffield,
Regent Court, Portobello Street, Sheffield, S1 4DP, UK
{F.Bernardini, M.Gheorghe, R.Muniyandi}@dcs.shef.ac.uk
[2] Automated Scheduling, Optimisation and Planning Research Group,
School of Computer Science and Information Technology,
University of Nottingham, Jubilee Campus, Nottingham NG8 1BB, UK
Natalio.Krasnogor@nottingham.ac.uk
[3] Research Group on Natural Computing,
Department of Computer Science and Artificial Intelligence,
University of Seville, Avda. Reina Mercedes 41012, Sevilla, Spain
{marper, fran}@us.es

Abstract. We introduce a variant of P systems where rules have associated a real number providing a measure for the "intrinsic reactivity" of
the rule and roughly corresponding to the kinetic coefficient which, in
bio-chemistry, is usually associated to each molecular reaction. The behaviour of these P systems is then defined according to a strategy which,
in each step, randomly selects the next rule to be applied depending upon
a certain distribution of probabilities. As an application, we present a P
system model of the quorum sensing regulatory networks of the bacterium *Vibrio Fischeri*. In this respect, a formalisation of the network
in terms of P systems is provided and some simulation results concerning the behaviour of a colony of such bacteria are reported. We also
briefly describe the implementation techniques adopted by pointing out
the generality of our approach which appears to be fairly independent
from the particular choice of P system variant and the language used to
implement it.

1 Introduction

Membrane computing represents a new and rapidly growing research area which
is part of the natural computing paradigm and which was initiated by Gheorghe Păun in 1998 with a seminal paper initially circulated on the web and
later published in [13]. Already a monograph has been dedicated to this subject [14] and some fairly recent results can be found in [15],[9],[10]. Membrane
computing aims at defining computational models which abstract from the functioning and structure of the cell. Specifically, membrane computing starts from
the observation that membranes play a fundamental role in the functioning of

R. Freund et al. (Eds.): WMC 2005, LNCS 3850, pp. 114–133, 2006.
© Springer-Verlag Berlin Heidelberg 2006

a living cell. Membranes are essentially involved in many reactions taking place inside various compartments of a cell, and they act as selective channels of communication between different compartments as well as between the cell and its environment [1].

Membrane computing formalises these essential features of living cells by introducing the notion of *membrane systems*, which are usually called *P systems*. P systems are characterised by four fundamental features: a *membrane structure* where *objects* evolve according to some *evolution rules*, which also determine the *communication* of objects between membranes. Specifically, the *membrane structure* consists in a number of membranes arranged in a hierarchical structure, all of them but one included in an unique main membrane called *skin membrane*. This most external membrane defines the boundary between the inside of the system and its outside, which is called *environment*. A membrane without any membrane inside is called *elementary*. Each membrane identifies a corresponding *region* inside the system: the space between the membrane and the membranes (if any) directly contained in it. A graphical representation of such a membrane structure is reported in Figure 1.

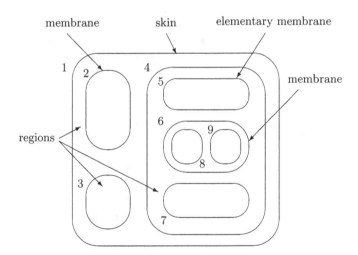

Fig. 1. A membrane structure containing 9 membranes and 9 corresponding regions; labels are used to uniquely identify each distinct membrane in the system.

Some *objects* are then assigned to the regions, each object appearing with a specific multiplicity. That is, each region, in general, contains a *multiset of objects* rather than a set. As well as this, finite sets of *evolution rules* are assigned to the region, one per each region, which are used to modify the objects associated with the regions and to move them across the membrane from one region to the other. Rules have a *local scope*: the rules assigned to a specific region inside the system can be applied only to the objects associated with that same region. P systems were originally introduced to investigate the computational nature of various features of biological membranes [13], with an approach typical to formal language theory and theory of computing, rather than to provide a comprehensive model of the living cell. Nevertheless, some recent researche trends [4], [5], [16] have been actually dedicated to the study of P systems as a modelling tool where P systems are used as a formalism for describing, and possibly simulating, the behaviour of biological systems. Therefore, there is a growing interest in developing implementations for the membrane computing paradigm in order to be able to execute P system models and run simulations of biological phenomena of various interest. In this respect, a number of tools have already been produced (some of them are available from `http://psystems.disco.unimib.it/`, the P systems web pages) but yet correct implementation techniques need to be identified, especially when the quantitative aspects featuring the "reality" of a biological phenomenon are considered in the model.

In this paper, we present a variant of P systems (Section 2) where rules are generalised boundary rules which allow us to express transformations affecting simultaneously the objects placed on both sides of a membrane, that is, both the objects placed inside that compartment and the objects placed into the surrounding region. As well as this, each rule has associated a real number providing a measure for the "intrinsic reactivity" of the rule and roughly corresponding to the kinetic coefficient which, in bio-chemistry, is usually associated to each molecular reaction [16]. Moreover, in this variant, rules are applied according to a strategy which, in each step, randomly selects the next rule to be applied depending upon a certain distribution of probabilities. The main difference with respect to the usual approach adopted in membrane computing is that, in our approach, there is no parallelism in the application of the rules as the system evolves only by means of a rule at a time. Next, in Section 3, we present, as a case-study, a P system model for the quorum sensing system of the marine bacterium *Vibrio fischeri* together with some simulation results obtained by implementing the model in Scilab (a free software package available at `http://scilabsoft.inria.fr/`). The novelty of our approach consists in the fact that we do not only provide a description for the reactions involved in the quorum sensing regulatory network but we are also able to provide a model for an arbitrarily large colony of bacteria. In this respect, we can say our simulations provides a snapshot of the behaviour of the colony as a whole complex system. Finally, the last section describes implementation techniques for our P system model by presenting the data structures and the code that are necessary to support its execution. Moreover, by following [12], we advocate the use of the mark-up language SBML as a "machine-interpretable" language for defining executable specifications of P systems and the corresponding code that can be automatically generated from. In this respect, we want to stress the generality of our approach which appears to be fairly independent of the particular choice of a P system variant, the language used to implement it, and flexible enough with respect to the strategy of applying the rules of the system.

2 Definitions

We start by recalling from [14] some basic notions of formal language theory which are commonly used in the area of membrane computing. An *alphabet* is a finite non-empty set of abstract symbols. Given an alphabet O, we denote by O^* the *set of all possible strings over* O, including the empty string λ. The *length of a string* $x \in O^*$ is denoted by $|x|$ and, for each $a \in O$, $|x|_a$ denotes the number of occurrences of the symbol a in x. A *multiset* over O is a mapping $M : O \longrightarrow N$ such that, $M(a)$ defines the multiplicity of a in the multiset M (N denotes the set of natural numbers). Such a multiset can be represented by a string $a_1^{M(a_1)} a_2^{M(a_2)} \ldots a_n^{M(a_n)} \in O^*$ and by all its permutations with $a_j \in O$, $M(a_j) \neq 0$, $1 \leq j \leq n$. In other words, we can say that each string $x \in O^*$ identifies a finite multiset over O defined by $M_x = \{ (a, |x|_a) \mid a \in O \}$. Moreover, given two strings $x, y \in O^*$, we denote by xy their catenation, which corresponds to the union of the multiset represented by string x and the multiset represented by string y.

Membrane structures are represented as usual by means of strings of matching pairs of square-brackets, with each pair of square-brackets representing a membrane and each one of them being labelled with a different value in $\{1, 2, \ldots, n\}$, for n the number of membranes in the structure. For example, the membrane structure of 1 can be represented by using the following string of matching square brackets:

$$[_1 [_2]_2 [_3]_3 [_4 [_5]_5 [_6 [_8]_8 [_9]_9]_6 [_7]_7]_4]_1$$

where:

- membrane 1 is the *skin membrane*,
- membrane 2, membrane 3, membrane 5, membrane 7, membrane 8 and membrane 9 are *elementary membranes*, Moreover,
- membrane 1 *directly contains* membrane 2, membrane 3 and membrane 4,
- membrane 4 *directly contains* membrane 5, membrane 6 and membrane 7,
- membrane 6 *directly contains* membrane 8 and membrane 9.

We refer to [14] for further details about this representation.

A P system is then defined in the following way.

Definition 1. *A P system is a construct*

$$\Pi = (O, L, \mu, C_1, C_2, \ldots, C_n, R)$$

where:

- *O is a finite alphabet of symbols representing objects;*
- *L is a finite alphabet of symbols representing labels for the compartments;*
- *μ is a membrane structure consisting of $n \geq 1$ membranes;*
- *$C_i = (l_i, w_i)$, for each $1 \leq i \leq n$, is the initial configuration of the compartment i with $l_i \in L$ and $w_i \in O^*$ a finite multiset of objects;*

- R is a finite set containing $m \geq 1$ rules that are labelled in one-to-one manner with values in $\{1, 2, \ldots, m\}$ and that are of the form

$$j : u\,[\,v\,]_l \xrightarrow{k_j} u'[\,v'\,]_l$$

with $1 \leq j \leq m$, $u, v, u', v' \in V^*$ some finite multisets of objects, $l \in L$ a label for the compartment, and k_i a real number.

Thus, a P system is characterised by a finite alphabet O for the objects placed into the compartments, a finite alphabet L for labelling the compartments, a membrane structure μ, an initial configuration for each compartment in the system, and a finite set R containing rules describing transformations that can be applied to the objects placed inside the compartments. Specifically, the initial configuration of a compartment consists of a label from the alphabet L and a finite multiset of objects from O represented as a string in O^*; these objects are those which are initially placed inside that compartment. Compartments can interact each other by means of the rules in R which are of the form $u\,[\,v\,]_l \xrightarrow{k_j} u'[\,v'\,]_l$. Such a rule specifies that a multiset u, which is supposed to be contained in the outside part of a compartment labelled by l, and a multiset v, which is supposed to be contained inside a compartment labelled by l, can be simultaneously replaced by the multisets u', v' in the respective places. Moreover, each rule in R has associated a real constant which is meant to provide a measure of the "reactivity" of the rule in a similar way to what was done in [5], [16]. In other words, in our P systems, multisets of objects are used to model bags or soups of chemicals whereas rules are used to model generic biochemical processes which affect the number and distribution of these objects within the system. All these rules are supposed to consume certain chemicals in order to produce some new ones.

Then, in order to make the system transit from one configuration to the other, a strategy for the application of the rules is adopted that makes the system evolve only by means of a rule at a time. Moreover, in each step, only one rule to be applied inside a specific cell is randomly selected according to a given distribution of probabilities. To this aim, we developed an adaption of Gillespie's algorithm in order to associate a stochastic behaviour to population P systems. Gillespie's algorithm [8] (see also [7] for some recent improvements) provides an exact method for the stochastic simulation of systems of bio-chemical reactions; the validity of the method is rigorously proved and it has been already successfully used to simulate various biochemical processes [11]. As well as this, Gillespie's algorithm is used in the implementation of stochastic π-calculus [17] and in its application to the modelling of biological systems [18] (an implementation of the stochastic pi-machine is avaliable at http://www.doc.ic.ac.uk/~anp/spim/). Here, with respect to the original algorithm, we have to take into account the fact that in P systems we have different cells, each one with its own set of rules, and the fact that the application of a rule inside a cell can affect the content of environment too.

Specifically, let $\Pi = (O, L, \mu, (w_1, l_1), \ldots, (w_n, l_n), R)$ be a P system as specified in Definition 1. At any moment, a configuration of the system Π can be represented as a tuple

$$\Gamma = ((x_1, l_1), \ldots, (x_n, l_n), \mu)$$

where, for each $1 \leq i \leq n$, x_i is the multiset of objects currently contained in compartment i. Thus, given such a configuration, for each $1 \leq i \leq n$, we define the set $R(i)$ of pairs (j, p_j) such that:

- j is the index of a rule in R of the form $u\,[\,v\,]_{l_i} \xrightarrow{k_j} u'[\,v'\,]_{l_i}$, with $x_f = y\,u$ and $x_i = z\,v$, for f the index of the compartment that directly contains i and some $y, z \in O^*$ (i.e., the rule j is applicable inside compartment i because it is labelled by l_i, the surrounding region contains the multiset u, and compartment i contains the multiset v);
- p_j is the probability of the rule j to be applied in the next step of evolution; this probability is computed by multiplying the constant k_j by the number of possible combinations of the objects present on the left-side of the rules with respect to the multisets x_i and x_f (for example, if we have a rule $[\,ab\,]_{l_i} \rightarrow [\,w\,]_{l_i}$, with $a, b \in O$, $w \in O^*$, the probability p_j is given by $k_j * |x_i|_a * |x_i|_b$ (i.e., there are $|x_i|_a * |x_i|_b$ different possible ways of assigning objects to the rule $[\,ab\,]_{l_i} \rightarrow [\,w\,]_{l_i}$);

Then, given these probabilities, the strategy for the application of the rules is defined according to the following procedure.

First, for each compartment i, we compute the index of the next rule to be used inside cell i and its waiting time by using the classical Gillespie's algorithm:

1. construct the sets $R(i)$ containing pairs (j, p_j) where p_j is the probability associated to rule j currently applicable inside compartment i; let us denote by M_i, $M_i \geq 1$, the number of elements of $R(i)$; the pairs in $R(i)$ are supposed to be associated in an one-to-one manner with values in $\{1, \ldots, M_i\}$, i.e. $k : (j_k, p_{j_k})$, for $1 \leq k \leq M_i$;
2. calculate $a_0 = \sum p_j$, for all $(j, p_j) \in R(i)$;
3. generate two random numbers r_1 and r_2 uniformly distributed over the unit interval $(0, 1)$;
4. calculate the waiting time for the next reaction as $\tau_i = \dfrac{1}{a_0} ln(\dfrac{1}{r_1})$
5. take the index h, $1 \leq h \leq M_i$, such that $\sum_{k=1}^{h-1} p_k < r_2 a_0 \leq \sum_{k=1}^{h} p_k$, with $k : (j_k, p_{j_k}) \in R(i)$, and $p_k = p_{j_k}$, for all $1 \leq k \leq h$;
6. return the triple (τ_i, j_h, i), if $h : (j_h, p_{j_h}) \in R(i)$.

Notice that the larger the stochastic constant of a rule and the number of occurrences of the objects placed on the left-side of the rule inside a membrane are, the greater is the chance that a given rule will be applied in the next step of the simulation. There is no constant time-step in the simulation. The time-step is determined in every iteration and it takes different values depending on the configuration of the system.

Next, a step of application of the rules is simulated by using the following procedure:

- **Initialisation**
  - set time of the simulation $t = 0$;
  - for each compartment i in μ compute a triple (τ_i, j, i) by using the procedure described above;
  - sort the list according to each waiting time;
- **Iteration**
  1. extract the first triple, (τ_m, j, m) from the list;
  2. set time of the simulation $t = t + \tau_m$;
  3. update the waiting time for the rest of the triples in the list by subtracting τ_m;
  4. apply the rule j only once changing the number of objects in the compartment and in the surrounding region
  5. if the surrounding region has been affected by the application of the rule then remove the corresponding triple from the list;
  6. re-run the Gillespie algorithm for the compartment m and for the compartment associated with the surrounding region in order to obtain the new corresponding triples; add these new triples to the list;
  7. sort this list according to each waiting time and iterate the process.
- **Termination**
  1. Terminate simulation when time of the simulation t reaches or exceeds a preset maximal time of simulation.

Specifically, in each step, the compartment selected is the cell with the minimal waiting time.

3   Modelling Quorum Sensing in *Vibrio Fischeri*

Bacteria are generally considered to be independent organisms. However it has been observed that certain bacteria, like the marine bacterium *Vibrio Fischeri*, exhibit coordinated behaviour which allows an entire population of bacteria to regulate the expression of certain or specific genes in a coordinated way depending on the size of the population. This cell density dependent gene regulation system is referred to as *quorum sensing* [6], [19], QS for short. In this respect, a comprehensive literature about QS can be found at http://www.nottingham.ac.uk/quorum/ – a web page maintained by the Nottingham Quorum Sensing Group.

This phenomenon was first investigated in the marine bacterium *Vibrio Fischeri*. This bacterium exists naturally either in a free-living planktonic state or as a symbiont of certain luminescent squid. The bacteria colonise specialised light organs in the squid, which cause it to luminesce. Luminescence in the squid is thought to be involved in the attraction of prey, camouflage and communication between different individuals. The source of the luminescence is the bacteria themselves. The bacteria only luminesce when colonising the light organs and do not emit light in the free-living state. The QS process in *Vibrio Fischeri* relies on the synthesis, accumulation and subsequent sensing of a signal molecule, 3-oxo-C6-HSL, an N-acyl homoserine lactone or AHL, we will call it OHHL. When only a small number of bacteria are present these proteins are produced at a low level. OHHL diffuses out of the bacterial cells and into the surrounding environment. At high cell density the signal accumulates in the area surrounding the bacteria and can also diffuse to the inside of the bacterial cells. The signal is able to interact with the LuxR protein to form the complex LuxR-OHHL. This complex binds to a region of DNA called the Lux Box causing the transcription of the luminescence genes, a small cluster of 5 genes, luxCDABE. As well as the transcription of LuxR and OHHL, which are therefore called autoinducers as they activate their own synthesis. In this way, bacteria can effectively communicate each other by responding to changes in the concentration of signal molecules inside and in the surrounding environment.

Next, a model for quorum sensing in *Vibrio fischeri* is obtained by considering a P system consisting of a number of distinct compartments placed inside an unique main membrane, which represents the environment, and where each one of these compartments represents a bacterium and contains rules describing the reactions involved in the regulation of the luminescence genes. Compartments representing bacteria interact each other by sending objects into the environment and receiving some others from it. Specifically, given a population of $m \geq 1$ bacteria, we define the P system $\Pi(m)$ such that

$$\Pi(m) = (O, \{e, b\}, \mu, C_1, C_2, \ldots, C_m, C_{m+1}, R)$$

and where:

- $O = \{OHHL, LuxR, LuxR\text{-}OHHL, LuxBox\} \cup$
  $\cup \{LuxBox\text{-}LuxR\text{-}OHHL\}$,
- $\mu = [\,[\,]_1\,[\,]_2 \cdots [\,]_m\,]_{m+1}$,
- $C_i = (b, LuxBox)$, for each $1 \leq i \leq m$,
- $C_{m+1} = (e, \lambda)$,
- $R = R_b \cup R_e$ with R_b the set of rules to be used inside compartments labelled by b and R_e the set of rules to be used inside the compartment labelled by e. Each compartment labelled by b represents a bacterium whereas the unique compartment labelled by e represents the environment.

Notice that the P system $\Pi(m)$ is a parametric one as its definition depends on the value m, the number of bacteria in the colony.

The set R_b contains the following rules:

An unstressed bacterium produces the signal OHHL and the protein LuxR at basal rates - very low rates:

$$1 : [\, LuxBox \,]_b \xrightarrow{k_1} [\, LuxBox, OHHL \,]_b,$$
$$2 : [\, LuxBox \,]_b \xrightarrow{k_2} [\, LuxBox, LuxR \,]_b.$$

The protein LuxR acts as a receptor and OHHL as its ligand. Both together form the complex LuxR-OHHL which in turn can dissociate into OHHL and LuxR again:

$$3 : [\, LuxR,\ OHHL\,]_b \xrightarrow{k_3} [\, LuxR\text{-}OHHL\,]_b,$$
$$4 : [\, LuxR\text{-}OHHL\,]_b \xrightarrow{k_4} [\, LuxR,\ OHHL\,]_b.$$

The complex LuxR-OHHL acts as a transcription factor or as a promoter binding to a region of the bacterium DNA called LuxBox and starting the transcription of different proteins involved in the production of light. The complex LuxR-OHHL can also dissociate from the LuxBox:

$$5 : [\, LuxBox,\ LuxR\text{-}OHHL\,]_b \xrightarrow{k_5} [\, LuxBox\text{-}LuxR\text{-}OHHL\,]_b,$$
$$6 : [\, LuxBox\text{-}LuxR\text{-}OHHL\,]_b \xrightarrow{k_6} [\, LuxBox,\ LuxR\text{-}OHHL\,]_b.$$

The binding of the complex LuxR-OHHL to the LuxBox produces a massive increase of the production of the signal OHHL and of the protein LuxR. In this sense OHHL and LuxR are autoinducers:

$$7 : [\, LuxBox\text{-}LuxR\text{-}OHHL\,]_b \xrightarrow{k_7} [\, LuxBox\text{-}LuxR\text{-}OHHL,\ OHHL\,]_b,$$
$$8 : [\, LuxBox\text{-}LuxR\text{-}OHHL\,]_b \xrightarrow{k_8} [\, LuxBox\text{-}LuxR\text{-}OHHL,\ LuxR\,]_b.$$

OHHL is a small molecule that diffuses outside the bacterium and so it can accumulate in the environment:

$$9 : [\, OHHL\,]_b \xrightarrow{k_9} OHHL\, [\,]_b.$$

Due to the presence of proteases and other chemical substances OHHL, LuxR and the complex LuxR-OHHL undergo a process of degradation in the bacterium:

$$10 : [\, OHHL\,]_b \xrightarrow{k_{10}} [\,]_b,$$
$$11 : [\, LuxR\,]_b \xrightarrow{k_{11}} [\,]_b,$$
$$12 : [\, LuxR\text{-}OHHL\,]_b \xrightarrow{k_{12}} [\,]_b.$$

The set R_e contains the following rules:

When the signal OHHL accumulates in the environment it can diffuse inside the bacteria. OHHL also undergoes a process of degradation in the environment

$$13 : OHHL\, [\ ]_b \xrightarrow{k_{13}} [\, OHHL\,]_b,$$
$$14 : [\, OHHL\,]_e \xrightarrow{k_{14}} [\ ]_e.$$

4 Simulation Results and Discussion

In order to implement our model in the aforementioned simulator, we have chosen the following set of kinetic constants [5], $k_1 = 2, k_2 = 2, k_3 = 9, k_4 = 1, k_5 = 10, k_6 = 2, k_7 = 250, k_8 = 200, k_9 = 1, k_{10} = 50, k_{11} = 30, k_{12} = 15,$

$k_{13} = 20, k_{14} = 20$. These values have been set such that the degradation rates $(k_{11}, k_{12}, k_{13}, k_{14})$ compensate the basal production of the signal and the protein (k_1, k_2) and such that the production rates when the regulatory region is occupied (k_7, k_8) produce a massive increase in the transcription of the signal and the protein.

We have studied the behaviour of the system for populations of different sizes to examine how bacteria can sense the number of bacteria in the population and produce light only when the number of individuals is big enough. First we have considered a population of 300 bacteria. Next we show in Figure 2 the evolution over time of the number of quorated bacteria and the number of signal (OHHL) in the environment. We say a bacterium is quorated if and only if, the LuxBox is occupied by the complex LuxR-OHHL.

It may be observed that the signal, OHHL, accumulates in the environment until saturation and then, when this threshold is reached, bacteria are able to detect that the size of the population is big enough. At the beginning, a few bacteria get quorated and then they accelerate a process of recruitment that makes the whole population behave in a coordinated way. There exists a correlation between the number of signals in the environment and the number of quorated bacteria such that, when the number of signals in the environment drops, so does the number of quorated bacteria and when the signal goes up it produces a recruitment of more bacteria.

Now we show in Figure 3 the evolution over time of the average bacterium across the population of the number of signal (OHHL), protein (LuxR) and the complex (LuxR-OHHL).

Note that on average there is a correlation among the signal OHHL, the protein LuxR and the complex LuxR-OHHL. Moreover, the patterns in the evolution of the average number of complexes across the population and the number of quorated bacteria are similar.

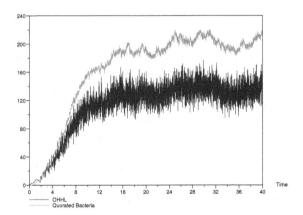

Fig. 2. The evolution of the quorated bacteria and the number of OHHL in the environment

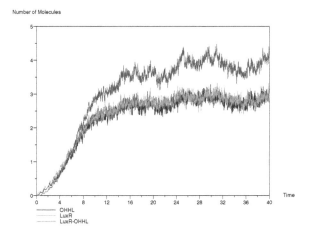

Fig. 3. The evolution of the number of signal molecule (OHHL), protein (LuxR) and the complex (LuxR-OHHL) for the average bacterium

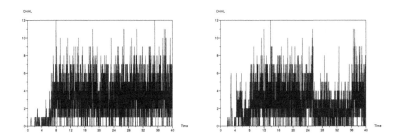

Fig. 4. The correlation between the amount of signal inside each bacterium (left) and the occupation of the LuxBox by the complex (right)

In our approach the behaviour of each individual in the colony can be tracked. We have taken a sample of two bacteria and have studied (see Figure 4) the correlation between the amount of signal inside each bacterium (left) and the occupation of the LuxBox by the complex (right) which represents that the bacterium has been quorated.

In Figure 5 it is shown that the number of signal molecules inside the bacterium has to exceed a threshold in order to recruit the bacterium. It may be observed that when the number of molecules is greater than the threshold the bacterium gets quorated or up-regulated (left), but when there are less signal molecules the bacterium switches off (right) the system and goes down-regulated.

We can also study how rules are applied across the evolution of the system. For instance, we can show the evolution of the number of applications of the rule representing the basal production of the signal OHHL (Figure 6) and the number of applications of the rules representing the production of the signal OHHL after the binding of the complex to the LuxBox (Figure 7).

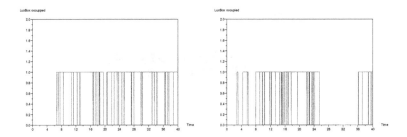

Fig. 5. The number of signal molecules inside bacterium when the level is greater than the threshold (left) and under the threshold (right)

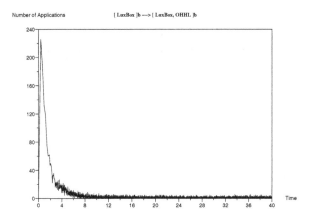

Fig. 6. The evolution of the number of applications of the rule representing the basal production of the signal OHHL

This can be compared with the number of applications of the rules representing the production of the signal OHHL after the binding of the complex to the LuxBox. In this way, we can show how at the beginning the basal production rule is the most applied rule while the other one is seldomly applied. Then, as a result of the recruitment process the bacteria sense the size of the population and they behave in a coordinate way by applying massively the third rule. Thus, the system moves from a down-regulated state to an up-regulated one where the bacteria collectively emit light. Specifically, this can be clearly seen if you compare the last graph above with the next one. Two similar graphs can be obtained for the rules producing the protein LuxR.

Finally, in order to study how bacteria can sense the number of individuals in the colony and get quorated only when the size of the colony is big enough, we have examined the behaviour of a population of only 10 bacteria. In this case, as shown in Figure 8, we observed that the recruitment process does not take place. Only one of the bacteria guessed wrong the size of the popu-

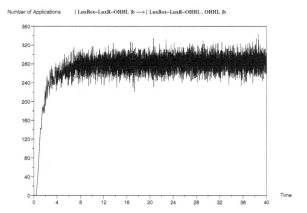

Fig. 7. The evolution of the number of applications of the rule representing the production of the signal OHHL after binding the complex to the LuxBox

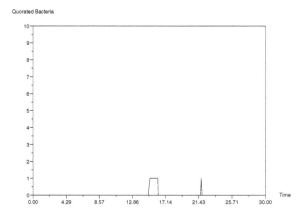

Fig. 8. No recruitment

lation and got up-regulated but then it switches off after sensing that the signal does not accumulate in the environment. The average number of molecules (see Figure 9) shows no pattern which means that the colony is not coordinating its behaviour.

Furthermore, we tracked the behaviour of two bacteria in the colony (see Figure 10) by obtaining that one never got quorated whereas the other one got quorated. Observe that this bacterium got quorated because the amount of signal inside exceeded the threshold.

Summing up, our simulations show that *Vibrio fischeri* has a quorum sensing system where a single bacterium can guess that the size of the population is big enough and starts to produce light. Then this bacterium starts to massively

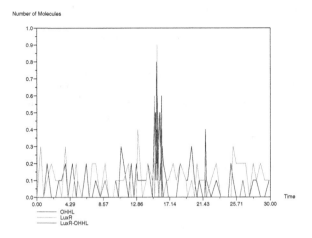

Fig. 9. No pattern of coordinating behaviour

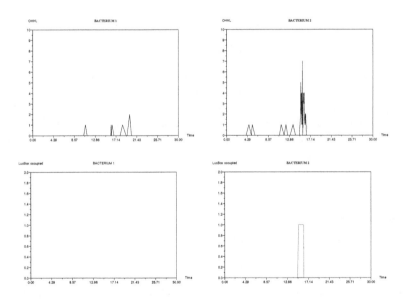

Fig. 10. The behaviour of two bacteria

produce signals, if the signal does not accumulate in the environment meaning that the guess was wrong it switches off. On the other hand if the signal does accumulate in the environment, meaning that the number of bacteria in the colony is big, then a recruitment process takes place that makes the whole population of bacteria to luminesce. These results agree well with in vitro experiments and with results obtained by using differential equations [6].

5 Implementation of the P System Model

We implemented the P system model of Definition 1 by following the approach proposed in [12] that is based on an initial specification in SBML of the model and a subsequent automatic generation of the executable code. In this section, we briefly describe the data structures necessary to support the execution of our variant of P systems. The language chosen is Scilab but similar considerations may apply to other commonly-used programming languages, such as C, Java, MatLab. Moreover, our approach appears to be fairly independent from the particular choice of P system variant. An SBML specification of the P system modelling quorum sensing in *Vibrio fischeri* is reported as an appendix.

The data structures used to represent the different components of P systems are the follows:

- **Rules:**

Recall that we are using rules of the form:

$$j : u \, [\, v \,]_l \xrightarrow{k_j} u' [\, v' \,]_l$$

Which will be represented as:

$$Comp \; father(l) \; l \; k_j \; multisets$$

with $multisets = length(u) \; u \; length(v) \; v \; length(u') \; u' \; length(v') \; v'$ and where $Comp$ represents the compartment where the rule j can be applied, $father(l)$ represents the father of the membrane with label l in the membrane structure, l is the label of the compartment involved in the rule and k_j is the kinetic constant. $length(u)$, $length(v)$, $length(u')$ and $length(v')$ tell us the size of u, v, u' and v', respectively. And u and v are the strings of objects representing the left-hand side (reactants) and u' and v' represent the right-hand side (products) of the rule j.

- **Compartments:**

Each compartment is represented by:

$$label \; n\text{-}copies \; multiplicity\text{-}of\text{-}o_1 \cdots multiplicity\text{-}of\text{-}o_n$$

The first component represents the label associated with the compartment, the second component is the number of instances of the compartment in the initial configuration; the other components describe for each object $o_i \in O$ its corresponding multiplicity inside that compartment.

- **Configurations of the system:**

A configuration of the system is made up of compartments; each compartment is represented:

$$identifier \; label \; multiplicity\text{-}of\text{-}o_1 \cdots multiplicity\text{-}of\text{-}o_n$$

identifier is an index associated in a one-to-one manner with each compartment, *label* is the label of the compartment and the last n components are the multiplicities of the objects in the compartment in the current configuration of the system.

Thus, the operation of a multiset u with a multiset v can be implemented by just subtracting and adding the corresponding vectors to the vectors representing the content of a certain compartment.

6 Conclusions

There is a growing interest in membrane computing in using P systems for modelling biological systems. This often requires the introduction into the model of quantitative aspects featuring the "reality" of the biological phenomenon to be modelled which are not usually considered in the abstract model of P systems. In this paper, these quantitative aspects have been considered for P systems by associating to each rule a real number (i.e., a kinetic constant), and by defining a Gillespie-like strategy for the application of the rules. This approach has been used to model the quorum sensing process in a colony of *Vibrio fischeri* bacteria by obtaining some simulation results which show the transition from a population of down-regulated cells to a population of up-regulated cells.

Our interest for the future is in developing a flexible software platform for running *in silico* experiments that integrates tools for the specification, execution and verification/validation of P system models. The details of the implementation provided in this paper can be viewed as a first step in this direction. A model checking approach is now being investigated that is based on Maude term rewriting tool [2]. In this framework, a central issue is the integration of the specification at individual level (e.g., a bacterium) with the specification at population level (e.g., the colony) such us to allow us to model more complex and larger biological systems. In this respect, a number of case studies need to be identified together with appropriate simulation/validation/ verification techniques.

Acknowledgements

The research of F.B. and M.G. has been supported by the Engineering and Physical Sciences Research Council of United Kingdom (EPSRC), grant GR/R84221/01. N.K. acknowledges the support of the Biotechnological and Biological Sciences Research Council (BBSRC) for supporting his grant BB/C511764/1 and also to the EPSRC for the grant GR/T07534/01. The research of M.P. and F.R. has been supported by the Ministero de Ciencia y Tecnología of Spain, by the Plan Nacional de I+D+I (2002-2003) (TIC-2002-04220-C03-01), co-financed by FEDER funds, and by a FPI fellowship from the Universidad de Seville, Spain.

References

1. Alberts, B., Johnson, A., Lewis, J., Raff, M., Roberts, K., Walter, P., (2002). *The Molecular Biology of The Cell. Fourth Edition.* Garland Publ. Inc., London.
2. Andrei, O., Ciobanu, G., Lucanu, D., (2005). Executable Specifications of P Systems. In [10], 126–145
3. Bernardini, F., Gheorghe, M., (2004). Population P systems. *Journal of Universal Computer Science*, **10**, 509–539.
4. Besozzi, D., (2004). *Computational and Modelling Power of P systems.* PhD Thesis, Università degli Studi di Milano, Milan, Italy.
5. Bianco, L., Fontana, F., Franco, G., Manca, V. (2005). P Systems for Biological Dynamics. In: *Applications of Membrane Computing* (Ciobanu, G., Păun, Gh., Pérez-Jiménez, M.J., eds.), Springer-Verlag, Berlin, Heidelberg, New York, 81–126.
6. Fargerströn, T., James, G., James, S., Kjelleberg, S., Nilsson, P., (2000). Luminescence Control in the Marine Bacterium *Vibrio Fischeri*: An Analysis of the Dynamics of lux Regulation. *Journal of Molecular Biology*, **296**, 1127–1137.
7. Gibson, M.A., Bruck, J., (2000). Efficient Exact Stochastic Simulation of Chemical Systems with Many Species and Many Channels. *Journal of Physical Chemistry*, **104**, 25, 1876–1889.
8. Gillespie, D.T., (1977). Exact Stochastic Simulation of Coupled Chemical Reactions. *The Journal of Physical Chemistry*, **81**, 25, 2340–2361.
9. Martin-Vide, C., Mauri, G., Păun, Gh., Rozenberg, G., Salomaa, A., eds., (2004). Membrane Computing. International Workshop, WMC 2003, Tarragona, Spain, July 2003. Revised Papers. *Lecture Notes in Computer Science*, **2933**, Springer-Verlag, Berlin, Heidelberg, New York.
10. Mauri, G., Păun, Gh., Pérez-Jiménez, M., J., Rozenberg, G., Salomaa, A., eds., (2005). Membrane Computing. International Workshop, WMC 2004, Milan, Italy, June 2004. Revised and Invited Papers. *Lecture Notes in Computer Science*, **3365**, Springer-Verlag, Berlin, Heidelberg, New York.
11. Meng, T.C., Somani S., Dhar, P., (2004). Modelling and Simulation of Biological Systems with Stochasticity. *In Silico Biology*, **4**, 0024.
12. Nepomuceno, I, Nepomuceno, J.,A, Romero-Campero, F., (2005) . A Tool for Using the SBML Format to Represent P System which Model Biological Reaction Networks. In: *Proceeding of the Third Brainstorming Week in Membrane Computing, Seville, Spain, January 31st-February 4th, 2005*, University of Seville, Seville, Spain.
13. Păun, Gh., (2000). Computing with Membranes. *Journal of Computer and System Sciences*, **61**, 1, 108–143.
14. Păun, Gh. (2002). *Membrane Computing. An Introduction.* Springer-Verlag, Berlin, Heidelberg, New York.
15. Păun, Gh., Rozenberg, G., Salomaa, A., Zandron, C., eds., (2003). Membrane Computing. International Workshop, WMC-CdeA 02, Curtea de Arges, Romania, August 19-23, 2002. Revised Papers. *Lecture Notes in Computer Science*, **2597**, Springer-Verlag, Berlin, Heidelberg, New York.
16. Pérez-Jiménez, M.J.; Romero-Campero, F.J.,(2005). Modelling EGFR Signalling Cascade Using Continuous Membrane Systems. In: *Proceedings of the Third International Workshop on Computational Methods in Systems Biology 2005 (CMSB 2005)* (Plotkin, G., ed.), University of Edinburgh, Edinburgh, United Kingdom.
17. Philips, A., Cardelli. L., (2004). A Correct Abstract Machine for the Stochastic Pi-calculus. *Electronical Notes in Theoretical Computer Science*, to appear.

18. Priami, C., Regev, A., Shapiro, E., Silverman, W., (2001). Application of a Stochastic Name-Passing Calculus to Representation and Simulation of Molecular Processes. *Information Processing Letters*, **80**, 25–31.

19. Taga, M., E., Bassler, B., L., (2003). Chemical Communication among Bacteria. *Proceedings of the National Academy of Sciences of the United States of America* (*PNAS*), **100**, 2, 14549–14554.

A   An SBML Specification

Consider the P system $\Pi(m)$, with $m = 100$, defined in Section 3. We start by specifying the structure of the system by listing the compartments present in the system and the relationships of inclusion between them.

```
<listOfCompartments>
  <compartment id="e" />
  <compartment id="b" outside="b"/>
</listOfCompartments>
```

There are two different "types" of compartments: compartments labelled by e and compartment labelled by b; all the compartments labelled by b, the bacteria, are included in a compartment with label e, the environment. Specifically, this is just a shorthand for a membrane structure consisting of a number of membranes, each one associated with a compartment labelled by b, contained inside an unique main membrane associated with a compartment labelled by e. The actual number of bacteria in the system is specified as a parameter of the system together with the constants k_i, $1 \le i \le 14$.

```
<listOfParameters>
    <parameter id="k1" value="2''constant="true"/>
    <parameter id="k2" value="2" constant="ture"/>
    <parameter id="k3" value="9" constant="true"/>
    <parameter id="k4" value="1" constant="true"/>
    <parameter id="k5" value="10" constant="true"/>
    <parameter id="k6" value="2" constant="true"/>
    <parameter id="k7" value="250" constant="true"/>
    <parameter id="k8" value="200" constant="true"/>
    <parameter id="k9" value="1"  constant="true"/>
    <parameter id="k10" value="50" constant="true"/>
    <parameter id="k11" value="30" constant="true"/>
    <parameter id="k12" value="15" constant="true"/>
    <parameter id="k13" value="20" constant="true"/>
    <parameter id="k14" value="20" constant="true"/>
     <parameter id="m" value="100" constant="true"/>
</listOfParameters>
```

Next, we specify the initial distribution of objects inside the system by listing out the species and their initial concentration inside each compartment.

```
<listOfSpecies>
  <specie id="OHHL_e"
  initialConcentration="0" compartment="e" />
  <specie id="OHHL_b"
  initialConcentration="0" compartment="b" />
  <specie id="LuxR_b"
  initialConcentration="0" compartment="b" />
  <specie id="LuxR_OHHL_b"
  initialConcentration="0" compartment="b" />
  <specie id="Lux_Box_b"
  initialConcentration="1" compartment="b" />
  <specie id="Lux_Box_LuxR_OHHL_b"
  initialConcentration="0" compartment="b" />
</listOfSpecies>
```

The objects that can be contained inside the environment are labelled by e whereas the objects that can appear inside a bacterium are labelled by b.

Finally we specify the rules as a list of SBML reactions. We just report here two of them as an example.

```
<reaction name="Reaction1" reversible="false">
  <listOfReactants>
   <specieReference specie="Lux_Box_b" />
  </listOfReactants>
  <listOfProducts>
   <specieReference specie="Lux_Box_b" />
   <specieReference specie="OHHL_b" />
  </listOfProducts>
  <kineticLaw>
    <math xmlns="http://www.w3.org/1998/Math/MathML">
      <apply>
        <times/>
        <ci>k1</ci>
        <ci>Lux_Box_b</ci>
      </apply>
    </math>
  </kineticLaw>
</reaction>

<reaction name="Reaction9" reversible="false">
  <listOfReactants>
   <specieReference specie="OHHL_b" />
  </listOfReactants>
  <listOfProducts>
   <specieReference specie="OHHL_e" />
  </listOfProducts>
  <kineticLaw>
```

```
      <math xmlns="http://www.w3.org/1998/Math/MathML">
        <apply>
          <times/>
          <ci>k9</ci>
          <ci>OHHL_b</ci>
        </apply>
      </math>
    </kineticLaw>
  </reaction>
```

The movement of objects is specified by changing the labels of the products according to the labels of the reactants.

Encoding-Decoding Transitional Systems for Classes of P Systems

Luca Bianco and Vincenzo Manca

University of Verona,
Department of Computer Science,
15 strada Le Grazie – 37134 Verona, Italy
bianco@sci.univr.it, vincenzo.manca@univr.it

Abstract. A useful tool in the research on computation systems, and in particular on P systems, is the translation of a system under investigation into another one which is, in some sense, better known. Such kinds of translations were the bases of many computational universality and equivalence results in formal languages theory and in membrane computing. Here we outline a general framework for comparing systems at various descriptive levels and very different in nature.

1 Introduction

A fundamental aspect in the investigation of computation systems, and especially of P systems, is the use of many translation methods in order to pass from a certain kind of systems to another one. In this way it is possible to perform all computations in the translated system, rather than in the original one. For example, many computational universality and equivalence results on P systems [6, 5, 9] are based on such a technique.

The aim of this work is to define a notion of *computational encoding*, which allows us to extend to complex membrane structures the *metabolic algorithm* [2, 3, 4] that was developed for basic membrane systems and has proved to be very useful in the simulation of many biological phenomena. In this preliminary work, we give fundamental definitions and the main framework of this approach, then we discuss two applications of these concepts.

Our notion of *computational encoding* resembles, in some aspects, the notion of bisimulation developed in concurrency theory [7]. However, computational encoding does not intend to cope with the operational semantics of systems or processes "at the same level", but rather it deals with the reduction of a computation from a "machine" to another one at a different (simpler or more complex) descriptive level. In fact, this notion of encoding is related to the interpretation of a computational system into another one. This aspect is apparent in Figure 1, if we compare the upper computation with the lower one, where in general one step at the upper level corresponds to many steps at the lower level. The ratio between the computation lengths is a parameter related to the different descriptive levels of the two corresponding transitional systems.

R. Freund et al. (Eds.): WMC 2005, LNCS 3850, pp. 134–143, 2006.
© Springer-Verlag Berlin Heidelberg 2006

2   Transitional Systems

Let us start by introducing formally the notion of *transitional system*.

Definition 1. *A* transitional system *is a 7-tuple* $\Pi = (A, C, R, \sigma, \Rightarrow, G, F)$, *where:*

- *– A is the alphabet;*
- *– C is a set of strings defined over A, representing configurations of the system;*
- *– R is a set of rewriting rules, defined over C;*
- *– σ is the* transitional *or* program *function, where* $\forall \mu \in C$, $\sigma(\mu)$ *is a set of sets of rules, that is, every element* $Q \in \sigma(\mu)$ *contains the rules that are simultaneously applicable to the configuration* $\mu \in C$;
- *– $\Rightarrow$ is the* transition, *a ternary relation* $C \times \wp(R) \times C$. *Given two configurations* $\mu, \mu' \in C$ *and a subset of rules* $Q \in \sigma(\mu)$, *we denote by* $\mu \Rightarrow_Q \mu'$ *the transition from* μ *to* μ' *by means of the application of the set of rules Q;*
- *– G is a set of sequences of transitions and its elements are called* computa-tions. *Given an initial configuration* μ_1, *a computation* $\Gamma \in G$ *is denoted by:*

$$\Gamma = (\mu_1 \Rightarrow_{Q_1} \mu_2 \Rightarrow_{Q_2} \cdots \Rightarrow_{Q_{n-1}} \mu_n),$$

  where for each i:
  (a) $\mu_i \in C$,
  (b) $\sigma(\mu_i) = Q_i$,
  (c) $\mu_i \Rightarrow_{Q_i} \mu_{i+1}$,
  (d) $\mu_n \in F$;
- *– $F \subseteq C$ is the set of final configurations.*

Note that if the set of initial configurations is fully specified, then G is completely defined by the other elements of the transitional system. As it is apparent from the notation, the computation $\Gamma = (\mu_1 \Rightarrow_{Q_1} \mu_2 \Rightarrow_{Q_2} \cdots \Rightarrow_{Q_{n-1}} \mu_n)$ is basically a sequence of transitions between configurations, originated from the initial con-figuration μ_1 by means of the application of the rules of the system.

It is useful to denote with $\Gamma(i)$ the ith configuration of the computation Γ and with $l_\Gamma = |\Gamma|$ the length of the computation Γ.

In the following, $\mu \Rightarrow_{*Q} \mu'$ is a compact representation meaning the existence of a computation $\mu \Rightarrow_{Q_1} \mu_2 \Rightarrow_{Q_2} \cdots \Rightarrow_{Q_{n-1}} \mu_n$ for some $n \in \mathbb{N}$ where, for every $1 \le i \le n$, $Q_i \subseteq Q$.

3   Computational Encodings

We introduce two distinct notions of *computational encodings* between different transitional systems.

Definition 2. *A* computational encoding *E from a transitional system* $\Pi = (A, C, R, \sigma, \Rightarrow, G, F)$ *to another transitional system* $\Pi' = (A', C', R', \sigma', \Rightarrow', G', F')$ *is a triple of functions* $E = (\gamma_{conf}, \gamma_{rule}, \gamma_{comp})$ *with:*

- $\gamma_{conf} : C \to C'$ *is an injective function used to encode configurations of* Π *into configurations of* Π',
- $\gamma_{rule} : R \to \wp(R')$ *is an injective function encoding rules of* Π *into a set of rules of* Π', *where* $\wp(R')$ *is the power set of* R',
- $\gamma_{comp} : G \to G'$ *is an injective function used to encode computations of* Π *into computations of* Π',

in which, for every $\Gamma \in G$, *the following conditions are satisfied:*

(i) $\gamma_{conf}(\Gamma(1)) = \gamma_{comp}(\Gamma)(1)$,
(ii) $\gamma_{conf}(\Gamma(l_\Gamma)) = \gamma_{comp}(\Gamma)(l_\Gamma)$.

Given a computational encoding E that encodes a transitional system Π into another one Π', we write $\Pi' = E(\Pi)$.

It is interesting to point out that, due to the injectivity of γ_{conf}, a *mirror principle* holds. In fact, starting from an initial configuration μ of Π, we can encode it in $\mu' = \gamma_{conf}(\mu)$ of $E(\Pi)$ and in this encoded transitional system we can execute the computation Γ' until we reach its last configuration $\Gamma'(l_{\Gamma'})$. After this, we can obtain the final configuration $\Gamma(l_\Gamma) = \gamma_{conf}^{-1}(\Gamma'(l_{\Gamma'}))$ of the computation Γ in the transitional system Π. The mirror principle becomes interesting when we can encode a transitional system into another one, that is more efficient, according to some computational perspective.

Let us introduce a more strict notion of encoding, in which we require a step-by-step correspondence between configurations of a transitional system Π and their corresponding configurations in $E(\Pi)$:

Definition 3. *A computational encoding* $E = (\gamma_{comp}, \gamma_{conf}, \gamma_{rule})$ *from a transitional system* $\Pi = (A, C, R, \sigma, \Rightarrow, G, F)$ *to another one* $\Pi' = (A', C', R', \sigma', \Rightarrow', G', F')$ *is strict (or 1-1 step) if the step commutativity holds for every* $\Gamma \in G$:

(i) $\gamma_{comp}(\Gamma)(i) = \gamma_{conf}(\Gamma(i))$, $\forall\, i, 1 \leq i \leq l_\Gamma$,
(ii) $\Gamma(i) \Rightarrow_Q \Gamma(i+1) \Leftrightarrow \gamma_{conf}(\Gamma(i)) \Rightarrow'_{\gamma_{rule}(Q)} \gamma_{conf}(\Gamma(i+1))$.

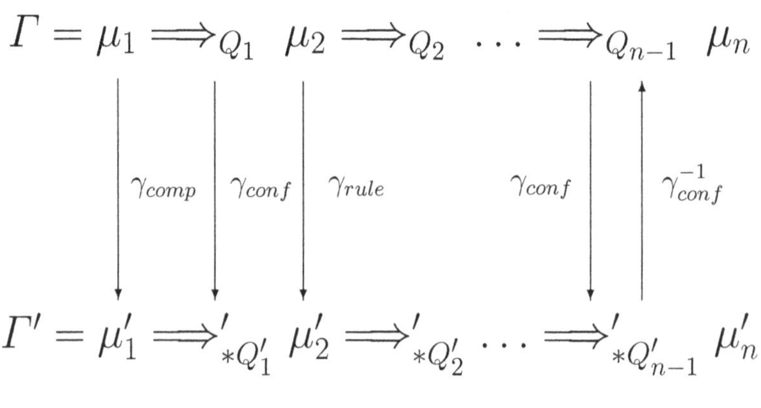

$$\Gamma = \mu_1 \Longrightarrow_{Q_1} \mu_2 \Longrightarrow_{Q_2} \cdots \Longrightarrow_{Q_{n-1}} \mu_n$$

$$\Big|_{\gamma_{comp}} \quad \Big|_{\gamma_{conf}} \quad \Big|_{\gamma_{rule}} \qquad \Big|_{\gamma_{conf}} \qquad \Big|_{\gamma_{conf}^{-1}}$$

$$\Gamma' = \mu'_1 \Longrightarrow'_{*Q'_1} \mu'_2 \Longrightarrow'_{*Q'_2} \cdots \Longrightarrow'_{*Q'_{n-1}} \mu'_n$$

Fig. 1. Schematic representation of a computational encoding

Note that, when a computational encoding E is *strict*, γ_{comp} is *completely determined* by the couple $(\gamma_{conf}, \gamma_{rule})$.

Figure 1 depicts a schematic representation of a computational encoding. The three encoding functions $(\gamma_{conf}, \gamma_{rule}, \gamma_{comp})$ are represented as arrows which connect elements of the computation Γ to the corresponding ones in computation Γ'. In the case of strict encoding the relationship between elements of Γ and the corresponding ones in Γ' can be extended to all elements of computations. This means that in the previous picture we have to remove the symbols * from rules and add arrows going from all up configurations and rules to the corresponding elements on the lower path.

4 Encoding Examples

The definitions of transitional systems and of computational encoding, expressed in previous sections, allow us to use the general schema of Figure 2 to compare the computational dynamics of different systems. In fact, starting from two distinct systems S_1 and S_2 of different nature, we can represent them in terms of transitional systems (respectively Π_1 and Π_2) and then compare their dynamics in the common and homogeneous environment of the transitional systems.

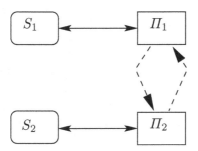

Fig. 2. General framework for systems encodings

4.1 Encoding n-PBR Systems into 0-PBR Systems

We apply a similar schema to that expressed previously (refer to Figure 3) in order to determinate the dynamics of an n-PBR system by means of a 0-PBR system. We have defined the metabolic algorithm [2, 3, 4], only in the case of 0-PBR systems, as a method to compute the dynamics of many interesting biological phenomena. Now we can extend its applicability to the case of n-PBR systems (i.e., PBR systems with $n > 0$ membranes) by using a strict computational encoding.

PBR systems [3, 4] are an extension and generalization of PB systems [1]. They introduce reaction maps needed to describe their time-varying dynamics and generalize PB Systems rules in such a way to obtain forms allowing us to perform an easy translation from multi-membrane (n-PBR) to zero-membrane (0-PBR) systems.

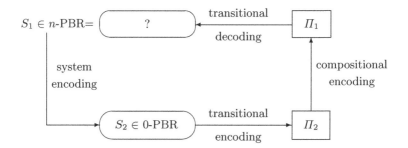

Fig. 3. Simulation of a n-PBR system by means of a 0-PBR system

A n-PBR system (i.e., a PBR system with n membranes) is a construct

$$\Pi = (\mathcal{A}, \mu_0, R, F, E), \tag{1}$$

where:

- $\mathcal{A}$ is the alphabet of *symbols*;
- μ_0, is the initial *configuration*, a string in which alphabet symbols contained in n nested parentheses, labelled $0, \ldots, n-1$, denote the objects contained in corresponding membranes. For instance, the configuration $[_1a[_2bc]_2[_3d]_3]_1$, where $a, b, c, d \in \mathcal{A}$, says a belongs to membrane 1, bc to membrane 2, and d to membrane 3, moreover that membrane 1 contains membranes 2 and 3.
- R is a finite set of *rules* of the following three possible forms, with $\alpha, \beta, \delta, \gamma \in \mathcal{A}^*$:
  - (a) $[_h[_j\alpha[_i\beta \to [_h[_j\delta[_i\gamma$, with $1 \le j, i \le n-1$ and $0 \le h \le n-1$, telling that α is transformed into δ in membrane j and β is transformed into γ in membrane i, moreover that membrane i is contained into membrane j and they are both placed inside membrane h;
  - (b) $[_0\alpha[_i\beta \to [_0\delta[_i\gamma$, with $1 \le i \le n-1$, telling that α is transformed into δ in membrane 0 (e.g., the skin membrane) and β is transformed into γ in membrane i, moreover that membrane i is contained in the skin membrane;
  - (c) $[_0\beta \to [_0\alpha\beta$, telling that α is created inside the skin membrane in presence of β.

  Note that $[_i\alpha[_j\beta$ means that α is a substring of the string representing a multiset of objects contained in membrane i, which in turn contains membrane j comprising β.
- F is a finite set of functions called *reaction maps*, each associated to a rule in a one-to-one manner;
- E is the *environment*, a set of rules of the type (c).

Note that when $n = 0$ there are no membranes in the system. In this case a configuration is simply a string over the alphabet $\mathcal{A}$, rules of type (a) and (b) have the form $\alpha \to \beta$, while rules of type (c) have the form $\beta \to \alpha\beta$, with $\alpha, \beta, \gamma \in \mathcal{A}^*$.

We refer the reader to [3, 4] for more details on reaction maps, their relationship with rules and for an accurate description on how these elements are used by the metabolic algorithm.

The encoding strategy from n-PBR into 0-PBR systems is made of two parts, the former managing configurations, the latter dealing with rules.

The following set of rewriting rules defines an encoding γ_{conf} of n-PBR configurations into 0-PBR configurations:

$$
\begin{aligned}
[_i]_i &\rightarrow \lambda, \\
[_iX &\rightarrow X_i[_i, \\
[_jX_i &\rightarrow X_{j,i}[_j, \\
[_hX_{j,i} &\rightarrow X_{j,i}[_h, \\
X_0 &\rightarrow X_{0,0},
\end{aligned}
\tag{2}
$$

in which $X \in \mathcal{A}$, $0 \leq i, j, h \leq n-1$, with $i \neq j \neq h$. When these rules are applied to configurations of the n-PBR system they provide configurations of the 0-PBR system. The idea behind this encoding is to get rid of membranes, by indexing objects with the identifiers of membranes containing them. To keep track of the whole membrane structure it is sufficient to mark every object with the label j of the membrane containing it in combination with the label i of the immediately outer membrane. We encode an object X within the skin membrane (that is conventionally labelled with 0) as $X_{0,0}$.

Before proceeding any further, let us see an encoding example for the following configuration of a 3 membrane system:

$$
[_0 A [_1 BC]_1 [_2 A]_2 B]_0,
$$

that, according to rules (2), applied in a maximal parallel way, originate the following sequence of strings:

$$
\begin{aligned}
&[_0 A [_1 BC]_1[_2 A]_2 B]_0 \rightarrow A_0 [_0 B_1 [_1 C]_1 A_2 [_2]_2 B]_0 \\
&\rightarrow A_{0,0} [_0 B_1C_1 [_1]_1 A_2B]_0 \rightarrow A_{0,0} B_{0,1} [_0 C_1A_2B]_0 \\
&\rightarrow A_{0,0}B_{0,1}C_{0,1}[_0 A_2B]_0 \rightarrow A_{0,0}B_{0,1}C_{0,1}A_{0,2} [_0 B]_0 \\
&\rightarrow A_{0,0}B_{0,1}C_{0,1}A_{0,2}B_0 [_0]_0 \rightarrow A_{0,0}B_{0,1}C_{0,1}A_{0,2}B_{0,0},
\end{aligned}
\tag{3}
$$

where only the first and the last strings represent admissible configurations, respectively for a 3-PBR system and for a 0-PBR system.

The second part of the encoding deals with meta-rules which establish how to transform n-PBR rules into 0-PBR rules. As defined in (1), an n-PBR system has three types of rules. So, in the 0-PBR system:

- rules of type (a) must be substituted by rules in the form $\alpha_{h,j}\beta_{j,i} \rightarrow \delta_{h,j}\gamma_{j,i}$;
- rules of type (b) must be substituted by rules in the form $\alpha_{0,0}\beta_{0,i} \rightarrow \delta_{0,0}\gamma_{0,i}$;
- rules of type (c) must be substituted with rules in the form $\beta_{0,0} \rightarrow \alpha_{0,0}\beta_{0,0}$.

To summarize, the encoding of an n-PBR into a 0-PBR system changes the configuration and the rules by removing all parentheses (that represent membranes). Localization is now encoded into symbols, this making the alphabet different: every symbol in the 0-PBR system is indexed with the two innermost membranes containing it (in the n-PBR system). Obviously, the alphabet $\mathcal{A}_1$ of a 0-PBR system that has been derived by an n-PBR system can have larger cardinality than $\mathcal{A}$.

It is important to notice that in this case the computational encoding $E = (\gamma_{conf}, \gamma_{rule}, \gamma_{comp})$ is strict, for this reason γ_{comp} is fully specified once we give γ_{conf} and γ_{rule}. Therefore, from the mirror principle we can calculate the dynamics of an n-PBR system by means of a 0-PBR system, and this construction can be used to extend the applicability of the metabolic algorithm to the case of n-PBR systems. The following picture illustrates the underlying schema of the method.

4.2   Encoding a Register Machine into a Cell-Like P System

Inspired from the construction proposed in [5], we represent here another example of transitional encoding, dealing with the case of a register machine [8] and a cell-like P system [9].

A register machine is a theoretical computing device composed by a set of registers containing positive integer values and by a program. The program is made by a sequence of instructions each one of them uniquely associated to a label. Every instruction specifies how to change the value of a register and the instruction that will follow its execution. Following the Minsky formulation, a register machine is a quintuple $M = (m, B, l_0, l_h, P)$, where:

- m is the number of registers;
- $B \subseteq \mathbb{N}$ is the set of instruction labels;
- l_0 is the label of the first instruction;
- l_h is the label of an halting instruction (i.e., an instruction halting the computation of the machine);
- P is a set of instructions that are of three different types:
  - ADD$(r), l_i$: adds 1 to register r and forces the machine to execute instruction l_i;
  - SUB$(r), l_i, l_j$: if register r is not empty the machine subtracts 1 to it and then executes instruction l_i otherwise no subtraction is performed and the machine executes instruction labelled l_j;
  - HALT: stops the computation of the machine.
  Each rule is uniquely identified by its label, for this reason in the following we will denote each rule $\phi \in P$ as $l_\phi : \phi$ where l_ϕ is the label of rule ϕ.

A cell-like P system of degree m (i.e., with m membranes) has the form $\Pi = (O, H, \eta, w_1, \ldots, w_m, \mathcal{R}_1, \ldots, \mathcal{R}_m)$, where:

- O is the alphabet;
- H is a set of unique membrane labels;
- η is the membrane structure composed by m membranes, labelled $1, \ldots, m$ that can be represented, as usual in P systems, by means of a string of matching indexed parentheses [9];

- $w_i \in O^*$, $1 \le i \le m$, is the multiset of objects contained in membrane i;
- $\mathcal{R}_i$ is the set of rules associated to membrane i; rules can be of two distinct types:
  - *multiset processing rules*: $u \to v$ or $u \to v\delta$, with $u \in O^+$, $v \in (O \times TAR)^*$, for $TAR = \{here, out, in\}$, and δ is the special symbol representing membrane dissolution;
  - *membrane creation rules*: $a \to [v]_h$, where $a \in O$, $v \in O^*$, and $h \in H$, saying that an object a creates a membrane labelled h containing the multiset v.

The policy of rules application is a maximally parallel one and objects to evolve are chosen in a nondeterministic way.

In [5] a reduction of a (deterministic) register machine to a cell-like P systems is shown; here we see that such kind of reduction is a transitional encoding.

Let us describe $\Pi_1 = (A_1, C_1, R_1, \sigma_1, \Rightarrow_1, F_1, G_1)$, the transitional system associated with a (deterministic) register machine $M = (m, B, l_0, l_h, P)$:

- $A_1 = \mathbb{N}$;
- $C_1 = \{r_1, r_2, \ldots, r_m, l \mid l, r_i \in \mathbb{N}, 1 \le i \le m\}$, where each r_i is the content of the ith register of M and l represents the label of the current instruction;
- $R_1 = P$;
- given a configuration $\mu = r_1, r_2, \ldots, r_m, l \in C_1$, $\sigma_1(\mu) = p_l$, where $p_l \in P$ is the instruction of M labelled l; note that M is deterministic, and for this reason given a configuration of M we can apply a single instruction to it (i.e., $|\sigma_1(\mu)| = 1$ for every $\mu \in C_1$);
- given two configurations $\mu, \mu' \in C_1$, $\mu \Rightarrow_{1p} \mu'$ if and only if μ' is obtained by μ when applying to it the instruction $p \in P$;
- G_1 is the set of configurations obtained by programs of M when applied to the initial configuration $0, 0, \ldots, 0, l_0$ with $l_0 \in \mathbb{N}$ being the label of the first instruction;
- $F_1 = \{r_1, r_2, \ldots, r_m, l_h \mid l_h, r_i \in \mathbb{N}, 1 \le i \le m\}$ with l_h being the label of the halting instruction.

Let us now describe the transitional system $\Pi_2 = (A_2, C_2, R_2, \sigma_2, \Rightarrow_2, F_2, G_2)$ associated with the P system $\Pi = (O, H, \eta, w_1, \ldots, w_m, \mathcal{R}_1, \ldots, \mathcal{R}_m)$:

- $A_2 = O$;
- C_2 is a string of correctly nested parenthesis, reflecting the membrane structure η, augmented with the multiset of objects contained inside each membrane;
- $R_2 = \mathcal{R}_1 \cup \ldots \cup \mathcal{R}_m$;
- σ_2 is the function used by Π to choose the set of rules appliable to a configuration, fulfilling the nondeterminism and maximal parallelism;
- given two configurations $\mu, \mu' \in C_2$, $\mu \Rightarrow_{2Q} \mu'$ if and only if μ' is obtained by μ when applying to it the set of rules $Q \in R_2$ in a nondeterministic and maximally parallel way;

- G_2 is the set of configuration sequences obtained by applying in a nondeterministic and maximally parallel way the rules of R_2 to the initial configuration $\mu_0 \in C_2$, in which all membranes of η contain the initial multiset of objects w_i and whose last configuration has no appliable rules;
- $F_2 = \{\mu \in C_2 \mid \text{in } \mu \text{ no rules are appliable}\}$.

We are now ready to discuss the encoding of a register machine into a cell-like P system by means of the computational encoding $E = (\gamma_{conf}, \gamma_{rule}, \gamma_{comp})$ defined over the transitional systems Π_1 and Π_2 introduced previously. Note that this construction follows the one proposed in [5], but it is slightly different. The P system we use has a very simple membrane structure, composed by a single membrane. Moreover, a symbol a_i is introduced in the cell-like P system for each register i used by the register machine M. The multiplicity of a_i encodes the value of the ith register and another set of objects is used to encode the current instruction of the register machine. Here are the details of the encoding E:

- $\gamma_{conf} : C_1 \to C_2$.
  Given $\mu = r_1, r_2, \ldots, r_m, l \in C_1$, $\gamma_{conf}(\mu) = a_1^{r_1} a_2^{r_2} \ldots a_m^{r_m} l \in C_2$, where in the configuration $\gamma_{conf}(\mu)$ we have not specified the membrane structure that contains only one membrane holding all elements, each one of them present respectively with the multiplicities obtained by the value of the corresponding register r_i, $1 \le i \le m$.
- $\gamma_{rule} : R_1 \to \wp(R_2)$.
  Rules in R_1 are of three types:
  - *Add rule*: given $\phi = l : \mathrm{ADD}(r), l_i \in R_1$

$$\gamma_{rule}(\phi) = \{l \to a_r l_i\}.$$

  - *Subtract rule*: given $\phi = l : \mathrm{SUB}(r), l_i, l_j \in R_1$,

$$\gamma_{rule}(\phi) = \{l \to l' \, l'', \; l' \, a_r \to \ddot{\imath}, \; l'' \to \hat{\imath}, \; \ddot{\imath} \, \hat{\imath} \to l_i, \; l' \, \hat{\imath} \to l_j\},$$

    where l', l'', $\ddot{\imath}$, $\hat{\imath}$ are newly created objects relative to the instruction labelled l.
  - *Halt rule*: given $\phi = l : \mathrm{HALT} \in R_1$,

$$\gamma_{rule}(\phi) = \{l \to l_{halt}\},$$

    where l_{halt} is a newly created object; note that there is no rule dealing with this symbol and due to the fact that each rule needs a rule label in order to be fired, l_{halt} forces the computation to stop.
- $\gamma_{comp} : G_1 \to G_2$.
  The register machine we encode is deterministic, and for this reason once we specify the initial configuration and the set of rules, then the computation is determined. In this way, given $\Gamma \in G_1$, we can obtain $\gamma_{comp}(\Gamma)$ by encoding $\Gamma(1)$ into the corresponding configuration $\gamma_{conf}(\Gamma_1)$ and then letting the transitional system work until its execution stops, and this gives $\gamma_{comp}(\Gamma)$.

The correctness of this construction follows directly from the proof proposed in [5], but we would like to emphasize that this example of computational encoding is not strict, because the subtraction rule of the register machine is encoded in several steps of the corresponding P system.

5 Conclusions

We have proposed the definition of a general framework in which it is possible to describe translations between different kinds of computational systems, focusing particularly on P systems. The two examples we proposed highlight the implicit presence of our general notions into specific cases of P systems. We plan to refine the notions here outlined in the context of descriptional complexity and of dynamical systems. In fact, a systematic evaluation of the way computational encodings alter some parameters could be very useful in the comparison and simulation of computational systems.

References

1. F. Bernardini, V. Manca: Dynamical aspects of P systems. *BioSystems*, 70 (2002), 85–93.
2. L. Bianco, F. Fontana, G. Franco, V. Manca: P systems for biological dynamics. In [6], 81–126.
3. L. Bianco, F. Fontana, V. Manca: Reaction-driven membrane systems. In *Proc. First International Conference on Advances in Natural Computation* (L. Wang, K. Chen, Y.S. Ong, eds.), LNCS 3611, Springer, Berlin, 2005, 1155–1158.
4. L. Bianco, F. Fontana, V. Manca: P systems with reaction maps. *International J. of Fundations of Computer Science*, to appear.
5. C.S. Calude, Gh. Păun: Bio-steps beyond Turing. *BioSystems*, 77 (2004), 175–194.
6. G. Ciobanu, Gh. Păun, M.J. Pérez-Jiménez, eds.: *Applications of Membrane Computing*. Springer, Berlin, 2006.
7. R. Milner: *Communicating and Mobile Systems: The π-calculus*. Prentice-Hall, Englewood Cliffs, New York, 1999.
8. M. Minsky: *Computation: Finite and Infinite Machines*. Prentice-Hall, Englewood Cliffs, New York, 1967.
9. Gh. Păun: *Membrane Computing. An Introduction*. Springer, Berlin, 2002.

On the Computational Power of the Mate/Bud/Drip Brane Calculus: Interleaving vs. Maximal Parallelism

Nadia Busi

Dipartimento di Scienze dell'Informazione,
Università di Bologna,
Mura A. Zamboni 7, 40127 Bologna, Italy
busi@cs.unibo.it

Abstract. Brane calculi are a family of biologically inspired process calculi proposed in [3] for modeling the interactions of dynamically nested membranes. In [3] two basic calculi are proposed. Mate/Bud/Drip (MBD) is one of such basic calculi, and its primitives are inspired by membrane fusion and fission.

In this paper we investigate the expressiveness of MBD w.r.t. its ability to act as a computational device. In particular, we compare the expressiveness of two different semantics for MBD: the standard interleaving semantics – where a single interaction is executed at each computational step – and the maximal parallelism semantics – according to which a computational step is composed of a maximal set of independent interactions.

For the interleaving semantics, we show a nondeterministic encoding of Register Machines in MBD, that preserves the existence of a terminating computation, but that could introduce additional divergent (i.e., infinite) computations.

For the maximal parallelism semantics, we provide a deterministic encoding of Register Machines, which preserves both the existence of a terminating computation and the existence of a divergent computation.

The impossibilty of providing a deterministic encoding under the interleaving semantics is a consequence of the decidability of the existence of a divergent computation proved in [1].

1 Introduction

Brane calculi [3] are a family of process calculi proposed for modeling the behaviour of biological membranes. In a process algebraic setting, brane calculi represent an evolution of BioAmbients [10], a variant of Mobile Ambients [4] based on a set of biologically inspired primitives of interaction. The main novelty of brane calculi consists in the fact that the active entities reside on membranes, and not inside membranes.

However, the formal investigation of biological membranes has been initiated by G. Păun with membrane computing [8], in the field of automata and formal

R. Freund et al. (Eds.): WMC 2005, LNCS 3850, pp. 144–158, 2006.
© Springer-Verlag Berlin Heidelberg 2006

language theory. Quoting from [5], the objectives of brane calculi and membrane computing [9] are different: "While membrane computing is a branch of natural computing, which tries to abstract computing models, in the Turing sense, from the structure and the functioning of the cell, making use especially of automata, languages, and complexity theoretic tools, brane calculi pay more attention to the fidelity to the biological reality, have as primary target systems biology, and use especially the framework of process algebra." Another difference is concerned with the semantics of the two formalism: whereas brane calculi are usually equipped with an interleaving, sequential semantics (each computational step consists of the execution of a single instruction), the usual semantics in membrane computing[1] is based on maximal parallelism (a computational step is composed of a maximal set of independent interactions).

Despite such differences, some recent papers try to establish some contact points between the two areas. A very preliminary step in this direction is represented by [1], where the computational power of two variants of basic brane calculi is investigated. A more relevant step is [5], where a variant of P systems (the formalism of membrane computing) is defined, inspired by the interaction primitives of the brane calculi, and its computational power is investigated. The present paper goes in the same direction, as it continues the investigation of the computational power of brane calculi started in [1], and investigates an alternative semantics for brane calculi, inspired by the maximal parallelism semantics usually adopted for P systems.

The focus in this paper is on the Mate/Bud/Drip calculus (MBD), a variant of basic brane calculus whose primitives are inspired by membrane fusion (mate) and fission (mito). Because membrane fission can split a membrane at an arbitrary place, it turns out to be a rather uncontrollable process. Hence, it is replaced by two simpler operations: *budding*, that is splitting off one internal membrane, and *dripping*, that consists in splitting off zero internal membranes. This paper originates from an open problem raised in [1], where the expressiveness of two basic brane calculi of [3], namely, MBD and PEP (a basic Brane Calculus with interaction primitives inspired by endocytosis and exocytosis) was investigated.

In [1] an encoding of Register Machines (RAMs) in PEP is defined. Such an encoding provides a very faithful representation of the behaviour of RAMs. In fact, the encoding of RAMs in PEP is deterministic. As RAMs are a deterministic computing device, we have that the RAM can either terminate or diverge, but cannot have both a divergent and a terminated computation. As the encoding has the same property, and the encoding respects the terminating behaviour of the RAM (i.e., the encoding terminates iff the RAM terminates), we obtain the undecidability of both the existential termination (there exists a terminating computation) and the universal termination (all computations terminate) for PEP. In [1] we also prove the decidability of universal termination for MBD, and the decidability of existential termination for MBD was left as an open problem. In this paper we answer to the above question by providing a nondeterministic

---

[1] With the notable exception of, e.g., [6].

encoding of RAMs in MBD, which preservers the existence of a terminating computation. The encoding is nondeterministic because it introduces additional computations which do not follow the expected behaviour of the modeled RAM. However, all these computations are infinite. This ensures that, given a RAM, its modeling has a terminating computation if and only if the RAM terminates. A direct consequence of this result is the undecidability of existential termination for MBD.

The decidability of universal termination for MBD in [1] ensures that we cannot do better, namely, it is impossible to provide a deterministic encoding of RAMs in MBD. It is also impossible to provide a (nondeterministic) encoding of RAMs in MBD that preserves the existence of a divergent computation, or satisfying the following property: the RAM terminates iff all the computations of the encoding terminate.

The computational power of MBD is increased if we move to the maximal parallelism semantics typical of Membrane Computing [9]. According to the maximal parallelism semantics, at each computational step a maximal set of independent reductions is simultaneously executed. Hence, all the membranes that can evolve have to do it. By exploiting such maximal progress hypothesis, we provide a deterministic encoding of RAMs in MBD with maximal parallelism that preserves the existence of a terminated computation (hence also the existence of a divergent computation). Thus we obtain the undecidability of both existential and universal termination for MBD with maximal parallelism. This result confirms the intuition emerging from [6], where the interleaving (sequential) and the maximal parallelism semantics of many variants of P systems are compared: in most cases, the computational power increases when moving from interleaving to maximal parallelism.

The paper is organized as follows: in Section 2 we present the syntax of MBD, and equip MBD with both a standard, interleaving semantics and a maximal parallelism semantics. Section 3 contains the nondeterministic encoding of RAMs in MBD with interleaving semantics, and the deterministic encoding of RAMs in MBD with maximal parallelism semantics. Section 4 reports some conclusive remarks.

2   MBD Calculus: Syntax and Semantics

In this section we recall the syntax and the standard, interleaving semantics of Brane Calculi, and specialize it to MBD [3]. Then, we define an alternative semantics that enforces the execution, at each computational step, of a maximal set of independent operations.

2.1   Syntax and Structural Congruence of Brane Calculi

A system consists of nested membranes, and a process is associated to each membrane.

Definition 1. *The set of systems is defined by the following grammar:*

$$P, Q \quad ::= \quad \diamond \mid P \circ Q \mid !P \mid \sigma (\!| P |\!)$$

The set of membrane processes is defined by the following grammar:

$$\sigma, \tau \quad ::= \quad 0 \mid \sigma | \tau \mid !\sigma \mid a.\sigma$$

Variables a, b range over actions, that will be detailed later.

The term $\diamond$ represents the empty system; the parallel composition operator on systems is $\circ$. The replication operator $!$ denotes the parallel composition of an unbounded number of instances of a system. The term $\sigma (\!| P |\!)$ denotes the membrane that performs process σ and contains system P.

The term 0 denotes the empty process, whereas $|$ is the parallel composition of processes; with $!\sigma$ we denote the parallel composition of an unbounded number of instances of process σ. Term $a.\sigma$ is a guarded process: after performing the action a, the process behaves as σ.

We adopt the following abbreviations: with a we denote $a.0$, with $(\!| P |\!)$ we denote $0 (\!| P |\!)$, and with $\sigma (\!| |\!)$ we denote $\sigma (\!| \diamond |\!)$.

The structural congruence relations on systems and processes is defined as follows:[2]

Definition 2. *The structural congruence $\equiv$ is the least congruence relation satisfying the following axioms:*

$$P \circ Q \equiv Q \circ P \qquad\qquad \sigma \mid \tau \equiv \tau \mid \sigma$$
$$P \circ (Q \circ R) \equiv (P \circ Q) \circ R \qquad\qquad \sigma \mid (\tau \mid \rho) \equiv (\sigma \mid \tau) \mid \rho$$
$$P \circ \diamond \equiv P \qquad\qquad \sigma \mid 0 \equiv \sigma$$

$$!\diamond \equiv \diamond \qquad\qquad !0 \equiv 0$$
$$!(P \circ Q) \equiv !P \circ !Q \qquad\qquad !(\sigma \mid \tau) \equiv !\sigma \mid !\tau$$
$$!!P \equiv !P \qquad\qquad !!\sigma \equiv !\sigma$$
$$P \circ !P \equiv !P \qquad\qquad \sigma \mid !\sigma \equiv !\sigma$$

$$0 (\!| \diamond |\!) \equiv \diamond$$

2.2 Interleaving Semantics of Brane Calculi

We recall the standard, interleaving semantics. At each computational step, a single reaction is chosen and executed. The next definition provides the set of generic reaction rules that are valid for all brane calculi, while the reaction axioms are specific for each brane calculus; the reaction axioms for MBD will be provided in Definition 5.

---

[2] With abuse of notation we use $\equiv$ to denote both structural congruence on systems and structural congruence on processes.

Definition 3. *The basic reaction rules are the following:*

$$\text{(par)} \quad \frac{P \rightarrow Q}{P \circ R \rightarrow Q \circ R} \qquad\qquad \text{(brane)} \quad \frac{P \rightarrow Q}{\sigma(\!|\, P \,|\!) \rightarrow \sigma(\!|\, Q \,|\!)}$$

$$\text{(strucong)} \quad \frac{P' \equiv P \quad P \rightarrow Q \quad Q \equiv Q'}{P' \rightarrow Q'}$$

Rules **(par)** and **(brane)** are the contextual rules that respectively permit to a system to execute also if it is in parallel with another process or if it is inside a membrane, respectively. Rule **(strucong)** ensures that two structurally congruent systems have the same reactions.

With $\rightarrow^*$ we denote the reflexive and transitive closure of a relation $\rightarrow$. Given a reduction relation $\rightarrow$, we say that the system P' is a *derivative* of the system P if $P \rightarrow^* P'$; the set of *derivatives* of a system P is denoted by $Deriv(P)$.

We say that a system P *has a divergent computation* (or infinite computation) if there exist an infinite sequence of systems $P_0, P_1, \ldots, P_i, \ldots$ such that $P = P_0$ and $\forall i \geq 0 : P_i \rightarrow P_{i+1}$. We say that a system P *has a terminating computation* if there exists $Q \in Deriv(P)$ such that $Q \nrightarrow$. We say that *all computations of a system P terminate* if P has no divergent computations.

We use $\prod$ (resp. $\bigcirc$) to denote the parallel composition of a set of processes (resp. systems), i.e., $\prod_{i \in \{1,\ldots,n\}} \sigma_i = \sigma_1 \mid \ldots \mid \sigma_n$ and $\bigcirc_{i \in \{1,\ldots,n\}} P_i = P_1 \circ \ldots \circ P_n$. Moreover, $\prod_{i \in \emptyset} \sigma_i = 0$ and $\bigcirc_{i \in \emptyset} P_i = \diamond$. Finally, $\prod_n \sigma$ (resp. $\bigcirc_n P$) denotes the parallel composition of n copies of process σ (resp. system P).

2.3   Syntax and Interleaving Semantics of MBD

The actions of the MBD calculus, proposed in [3], are inspired by membrane fusion and splitting. To make membrane splitting more controllable, in [3] two more basic operations are used: *budding*, consisting in splitting off one internal membrane, and *dripping*, consisting in splitting off zero internal membranes. Membrane fusion, or merging, is called *mating*.

Definition 4. *Let Name be a denumerable set of names, ranged over by $n, m, \ldots$. The set of actions of MBD is defined by the following grammar:*

$$a \quad ::= \quad mate_n \mid mate_n^\perp \mid bud_n \mid bud_n^\perp(\sigma) \mid drip(\sigma)$$

Actions $mate_n$ and $mate_n^\perp$ will synchonize to obtain membrane fusion. Action bud_n permits to split one internal membrane, and synchronizes with the co-action $bud_n^\perp$. Action $drip$ permits to split off zero internal membranes. Actions $bud^\perp$ and $drip$ are equipped with a process σ, that will be associated to the new membrane created by the membrane performing the action.

Definition 5. *The reaction relation for MBD is the least relation containing the following axioms, and satisfying the rules in Definition 3:*

(mate) $mate_n.\sigma|\sigma_0(\!|\, P \,|\!) \ \circ \ mate_n^\perp.\tau|\tau_0(\!|\, Q \,|\!) \to \sigma|\sigma_0|\tau|\tau_0(\!|\, P \circ Q \,|\!)$

(bud) $bud_n^\perp(\rho).\tau|\tau_0(\!|\, bud_n.\sigma|\sigma_0(\!|\, P \,|\!) \circ Q \,|\!) \to \rho(\!|\, \sigma|\sigma_0(\!|\, P \,|\!) \,|\!) \ \circ \ \tau|\tau_0(\!|\, Q \,|\!)$

(drip) $drip(\rho).\sigma|\sigma_0(\!|\, P \,|\!) \to \rho(\!|\ \,|\!) \ \circ \ \sigma|\sigma_0(\!|\, P \,|\!)$

2.4 Maximal Parallelism Semantics of MBD

In this section we introduce a semantics based on maximal progress, and inspired by the standard semantics of Membrane Computing [9]. The idea is that at each computational step, a maximal set of independent reductions is simultaneously executed. Hence, all the membranes that can evolve have to do it. For example, the system

$$mate_a(\!|P|\!) \ \circ \ drip(0)(\!|Q|\!) \ \circ \ mate_a^\perp(\!|R|\!)$$

performs the maximal progress move

$$mate_a(\!|P|\!) \ \circ \ drip(0)(\!|Q|\!) \ \circ \ mate_a^\perp(\!|R|\!) \Rightarrow 0(\!|P|\!) \ \circ \ 0(\!|Q|\!) \ \circ \ 0(\!|\ |\!) \ \circ \ 0(\!|R|\!)$$

On the other hand, the following move does not involve all the membranes that can evolve, hence it is not allowed:

$$mate_a(\!|P|\!) \ \circ \ drip(0)(\!|Q|\!) \ \circ \ mate_a^\perp(\!|R|\!) \not\Rightarrow 0(\!|P|\!) \ \circ \ drip(0)(\!|Q|\!) \ \circ \ 0(\!|R|\!)$$

At each computational step, a membrane can be involved in at most one reduction rule. Hence, also the following move, where three membranes are simultaneously fused, is not allowed:

$$mate_a|mate_b(\!|P|\!) \ \circ \ mate_a^\perp(\!|Q|\!) \ \circ \ mate_b^\perp(\!|R|\!) \not\Rightarrow 0(\!|P \circ Q \circ R|\!)$$

In such case, one of the following computational steps can be performed:

$$mate_a|mate_b(\!|P|\!) \ \circ \ mate_a^\perp(\!|Q|\!) \ \circ \ mate_b^\perp(\!|R|\!) \Rightarrow$$
$$mate_b(\!|P \circ Q|\!) \ \circ \ mate_b^\perp(\!|R|\!)$$

$$mate_a|mate_b(\!|P|\!) \ \circ \ mate_a^\perp(\!|Q|\!) \ \circ \ mate_b^\perp(\!|R|\!) \Rightarrow$$
$$mate_a(\!|P \circ R|\!) \ \circ \ mate_a^\perp(\!|Q|\!)$$

A maximal parallelism computational step is obtained as a maximal sequence of independent reductions. To formalize this notion, we take a modified reduction semantics, obtained by "freezing" all the processes associated to a membrane, after that such a membrane has been involved in a reduction. After the execution of a maximal parallelism computational step, the frozen processes are "heated" and can be involved in the next computational step.

To this aim, we extend the grammar of systems with a new term, denoting a membrane whose process is frozen:

$$P, Q \quad ::= \quad \dots \ | \ \langle \sigma \rangle (\!| \, P \,|\!)$$

The reaction relation is modified as follows:

Definition 6. *The reaction relation* $\mapsto$ *for MBD is the least relation containing the following axioms, and satisying the rules in Definition 3 (obtained by replacing* $\rightarrow$ *with* $\mapsto$ *):*

(mate) $mate_n.\sigma|\sigma_0(\!| \, P \,|\!) \ \circ \ mate_n^{\perp}.\tau|\tau_0(\!| \, Q \,|\!) \mapsto \langle \sigma|\sigma_0|\tau|\tau_0 \rangle (\!| \, P \circ Q \,|\!)$

(bud) $bud_n^{\perp}(\rho).\tau|\tau_0(\!| \, bud_n.\sigma|\sigma_0(\!| \, P \,|\!) \circ Q \,|\!) \mapsto$
$\qquad \langle \rho \rangle (\!| \, \langle \sigma|\sigma_0 \rangle (\!| \, P \,|\!) \,|\!) \ \circ \ \langle \tau|\tau_0 \rangle (\!| \, Q \,|\!)$

(drip) $drip(\rho).\sigma|\sigma_0(\!| \, P \,|\!) \mapsto \langle \rho \rangle (\!| \ |\!) \ \circ \ \langle \sigma|\sigma_0 \rangle (\!| \, P \,|\!)$

The heating function *heated( )* transforms the frozen processes of a system in active processes.

Definition 7. *The heating function, called heated(P), is defined inductively on the structure of (the extended set of) systems:*

$$
\begin{aligned}
heated(\diamond) &= \diamond \\
heated(P \circ Q) &= heated(P) \circ heated(Q) \\
heated(!P) &= !heated(P) \\
heated(\sigma(\!|P|\!)) &= \sigma(\!|P|\!) \\
heated(\langle \sigma \rangle (\!|P|\!)) &= \sigma(\!|P|\!)
\end{aligned}
$$

Now we are ready to define the maximal parallelism computational step $\Rightarrow$, consisting in a maximal (not extendable) sequence of reductions $\mapsto$.

Definition 8. *Let* P, Q *be MBD systems (not containing frozen processes).* $P \Rightarrow Q$ *iff there exists a system* Q' *such that* $P \mapsto^{+} Q'$ *,* $Q' \not\mapsto$ *and* $Q = heated(Q')$.

3   Computing with MBD

In this section we investigate the computational power of MBD. We show how to model Register Machines (RAMs) [12], a well known Turing powerful formalism. We start by recalling what RAMs are.

Then, we provide a nondeterministic encoding of RAMs in MBD (with interleaving semantics), which preservers the existence of a terminating computation. The encoding is nondeterministic because it introduces additional computations which do not follow the expected behaviour of the modeled RAM. However, all these computations are infinite. This ensures that, given a RAM, its modeling has a terminating computation if and only if the RAM terminates. A direct consequence of this result is the undecidability of existential termination for MBD.

Finally, we provide a deterministic encoding of RAMs in MBD with maximal parallelism that preserves the existence of a terminated computation (hence also the existence of a divergent computation). Thus we obtain the undecidability of both existential and universal termination for MBD with maximal parallelism.

3.1   Register Machines

RAMs are a computational model based on finite programs acting on a finite set of registers. More precisely, a RAM R is composed of the registers $r_1, \ldots, r_n$, that can hold arbitrary large natural numbers, and by a sequence of indexed instructions $(1 : I_1), \ldots, (m : I_m)$. In [7] it is shown that the following two instructions are sufficient to model every recursive function:

- $(i : Succ(r_j))$: adds 1 to the contents of register r_j and goes to the next instruction;
- $(i : DecJump(r_j, s))$: if the contents of the register r_j is not zero, then decreases it by 1 and goes to the next instruction, otherwise jumps to the instruction s.

The computation starts from the first instruction and it continues by executing the other instructions in sequence, unless a jump instruction is encountered. The execution stops when an instruction number higher than the length of the program is reached.

A state of a RAM is modelled by $(i, c_1, \ldots, c_n)$, where i is the program counter indicating the next instruction to be executed, and $c_1, \ldots, c_n$ are the current contents of the registers $r_1, \ldots, r_n$, respectively.

A state $(i, c_1, \ldots, c_n)$ is *terminated* if the program counter i is strictly greater than the number of instructions m. We say that a RAM R *terminates* if its computation reaches a terminated state.

3.2   A Nondeterministic Encoding of RAMs in MBD with Interleaving Semantics

In this section we show how to obtain a nondeterministic encoding of RAMs. The encoding satisfies the following property. If the RAM terminates, then the encoding has at least one terminating computation; otherwise, no computation of the encoding terminates. Hence, even if the RAM terminates, it may happen that a run of the encoding diverges. This is due to the fact that it is not possible to perform a test for zero on the (representation of the) contents of registers. When a *DecJump* instruction is performed, one of the two branches (decrement or jump) is chosen nondeterministically. If the right branch is taken, then the encoding behaves correctly. On the other hand, if the wrong branch is taken, then a system is reached such that any computation starting from such a system will diverge.

The modelling of RAMs is based on an encoding function, which transforms instructions and registers independently.

The basic idea for modelling the natural numbers contained in the registers is the following: the natural number n contained in register r_j is represented by n copies of a system R_j collected inside a register membrane. The increment is performed by fusing the register membrane with a membrane containing one copy of R_j, thus obtaining $n + 1$ copies of R_j inside the register membrane. The decrement is performed by mating the register membrane with a membrane whose process permits to perform a budding of one of the systems R_j contained inside the register membrane, thus leaving $n - 1$ copies of R_j inside the register membrane.

Consider a RAM R with instructions $(1 : I_1), \ldots, (m : I_m)$ and registers $r_1, \ldots, r_n$; the encoding of an initial state $(1, c_1, \ldots, c_n)$ is defined as follows:

$$[\![(1, c_1, \ldots, c_n)]\!] = [\![PC = 1]\!] \circ ! \; [\![(1 : I_1)]\!] \; \circ \; \ldots \; \circ \; ! \; [\![(m : I_m)]\!] \; \circ$$
$$[\![r_1 = c_1]\!] \; \circ \; \ldots \; \circ \; [\![r_n = c_n]\!] \; \circ \; LOOP(\!|\;)$$

where $LOOP =! \, mate_{loop}^{\perp} . drip(mate_{loop})$ is the process on the loop membrane, ensuring that the system will diverge if the wrong branch of the encoding of a $DecJump$ instruction is taken. If a membrane $mate_{loop}(\!|\ldots|\!)$ is produced, then such a membrane may fuse with the loop membrane, and another similar membrane is dripped, that may fuse with the loop membrane, and so on, thus preventing the system to terminate.

The encoding of an initial state of the RAM is composed by the following parts: the program counter, (an unbouded number of occurrences of) the encodings of each instruction, the encodings of the initial contents of registers, and the loop membrane.

The encoding of the contents of the program counter is defined as follows:

$$[\![PC = i]\!] = mate_{p_i}(\!|\;)$$

The presence of such a program counter membrane denotes the fact that the next instruction to be executed is I_i. The encoding of the program counter membrane $[\![PC = i]\!]$ will fuse with the encoding of the i-th instruction to activate the execution of such instruction.

The encoding of the contents of register r_j is

$$[\![r_j = c_j]\!] = mate_{opr_j}^{\perp}(\!| \; \bigcirc_{c_i} \, R_j |\!)$$

where $R_j = (bud_{decr_j} \mid bud_{loopr_j})(\!|\;)$.

If an increment operation on r_j is executed, then a membrane, containing one copy of R_j, is fused with $[\![r_j = c_j]\!]$, thus obtaining a representation of $[\![r_j = c_j + 1]\!]$.

If a decrement operation on r_j is executed, then a membrane – decorated with a budding instruction on name $decr_j$ – is fused with $[\![r_j = c_j]\!]$. At this point, the only operation that can be performed by the register membrane is such a budding. If $c_j > 0$, then at least one copy of R_j is present in the register membrane; by performing action bud_{decr_j}, one copy of R_j is "expelled" from the register membrane. Such an expelled copy is surrounded by a membrane with an empty program, hence becoming an innocuous garbage that can neither perform reductions nor interact with the other membranes. If $c_j = 0$, then the register membrane contains no membranes and no further operation can be performed by the register membrane.

If the zero branch is selected, then a membrane – decorated with a budding instruction – is fused with $[\![r_j = c_j]\!]$, and a new system $[\![r_j = 0]\!]$ is produced. If $c_j = 0$, then the old register membrane contains no membranes inside; as the only instruction that the old register membrane can perform is a budding, it becomes innocuous garbage. If $c_j > 0$, then the old register membrane contains at least one copy of R_j; such R_j can be expelled, and surrounded by a membrane that can activate the loop membrane, thus starting a divergent computation.

The encoding for the instruction $(i : I_i)$ is as follows:

$$[\![(i : Succ(r_j))]\!] \qquad = mate_{p_i}^{\perp}.mate_{opr_j}.drip(mate_{p_{i+1}}).mate_{opr_j}^{\perp}(\!|R_j|\!)$$

$$[\![(i : DecJump(r_j, s))]\!] = DECR_{i,j,s}(\!|\ |\!) \mid ZERO_{i,j,s}(\!|\ |\!)$$

where

$$DECR_{i,j,s} = mate_{p_i}^{\perp}.mate_{opr_j}.drip(mate_{loop}).bud_{decr_j}^{\perp}(0).$$
$$mate_{loop}^{\perp}.drip(mate_{p_{i+1}}).mate_{opr_j}^{\perp}$$
$$ZERO_{i,j,s} = mate_{p_i}^{\perp}.mate_{opr_j}.drip(mate_{opr_j}^{\perp}).drip(mate_{p_s}).$$
$$bud_{loopr_j}^{\perp}(mate_{loop})$$

The encoding of each instruction consists in a membrane, and the encoding of a RAM contains an unbounded number of copies of the encoding of each instruction.

When a program counter system $mate_{p_i}$ appears at top-level, an (occurrence of) instruction $(i : I_i)$ is activated by fusing it with the program counter.

If the i-th instruction is an increment of register r_j, and the actual contents of r_j is k, then the instruction membrane is fused with the register membrane by performing $mate_{opr_j}$. As the instruction membrane for increment, $[\![(i : Succ(r_j))]\!]$, contains one copy of system R_j, now the register+instruction membrane (the result of the fusion of register membrane and instruction membrane) contains $k + 1$ copies of R_j. At this point, the program counter membrane corresponding to instruction $i+1$ is dripped, and the register+instruction membrane becomes the register membrane corresponding to $[\![r_j = k + 1]\!]$, and is ready to accept the execution of new operations on the register.

Suppose that the i-th instruction is a decrement of register r_j, or jump to instruction s if the contents of r_j is zero. Independently of the actual contents of register r_j, the program counter membrane is fused with either the decrement part or the zero part of the instruction, thus selecting nondeterministically one of the two branches of the $DecJump$ instruction.

Suppose that the decrement part is selected. The instruction membrane is fused with the register membrane by performing $mate_{opr_j}$, and a loop activator membrane $mate_{loop}(\!|\ |\!)$ is dripped. Now the register+instruction membrane is ready to perform a budding of a copy of R_j. Two cases can happen:

- If the contents of r_j is not zero, e.g., $r_j = k + 1$, the right branch has been chosen. Moreover, the register+instruction membrane contains at least one copy of R_j. Hence, the budding operation is performed, and the expelled copy of R_j is surrounded by a membrane with an empty program, thus producing innocuous garbage. Now the register+instruction membrane contains k copies of R_j. The loop activator membrane is removed (by fusing it with the register+instruction membrane by operation $mate_{loop}^{\perp}$) and the program counter membrane corresponding to instruction $i+1$ is dripped. At this point, the register+instruction membrane becomes the register membrane $[\![r_j = k]\!]$, and is ready to accept the execution of new operations on the register.
- If $r_j = 0$, then the wrong branch has been chosen. Moreover, the register+instruction membrane contains no membranes. As the only instruction that can be performed by the register+instruction membrane is a budding, no other reduction or interaction can be performed by such a membrane. No other computation is possible, but the fusion of the loop activator membrane with the loop membrane. At this point, the computation can only diverge.

Suppose that the zero part is selected. The instruction membrane is fused with the register membrane by performing $mate_{opr_j}$. A new register membrane $[\![r_j = 0]\!]$ and a program counter $mate_{p_s}$ are produced, thus the computation continues from instruction s. Now the old register+instruction membrane can only perform a budding $bud_{loopr_j}(mate_{loop})$:

- If $r_j = 0$, then the right branch has been chosen. Moreover, the old register+instruction membrane contains no membranes. As the only operation the old register+instruction membrane can perform is a budding, it has become innocuous garbage.
- If the contents of r_j is not zero, e.g., $r_j = k + 1$, the wrong branch has been chosen. Moreover, the old register+instruction membrane contains at least one copy of R_j. Hence, the budding operation is performed, and the expelled copy of R_j is surrounded by a membrane with program $mate_{loop}$, that can fuse with the loop membrane, thus preventing the computation to terminate.

We can now conclude with the Theorem which states that our modelling of RAMs preserves existential termination.

Theorem 1. *Let R be a RAM with program $(1 : I_1), \ldots, (m : I_m)$ and initial state $(1, c_1, \ldots, c_n)$. Then we have that the RAM R terminates if and only if the system $[\![(1, c_1, \ldots, c_n)]\!]$ has a terminating computation.*

3.3   A Deterministic Encoding of RAMs in MBD with Maximal Parallelism Semantics

In this section we show how to obtain an encoding that behaves deterministically under the maximal parallelism hypothesis.

The modeling of the RAM is quite similar to the one of the previous section. The key idea is to use the maximal progress hypothesis to ensure that the right branch of a *DecJump* instruction is taken. Both the decrement and the zero branches of the instruction are activated in parallel, but the execution of the relevant part of the zero branch is delayed by innocuous $drip(0)$ operations, so that the zero branch will be executed only if the decrement branch fails.

The modelling of the contents of registers and of the increment instruction is the same as for the previous encoding, but in the present encoding all the components are surrounded by an external membrane. Such an external membrane permits to bud the garbage membranes that are not innocuous but could interfere with the correct components.

For completeness, here we report the whole encoding, and we highlight the differences.

Consider a RAM R with instructions $(1 : I_1), \ldots, (m : I_m)$ and registers $r_1, \ldots, r_n$; the encoding of an initial state $(1, c_1, \ldots, c_n)$ is defined as follows:

$$[\![(1, c_1, \ldots, c_n)]\!] = EXT(\!|\ [\![PC = 1]\!] \circ$$
$$!\ [\![(1 : I_1)]\!]\ \circ\ \ldots\ \circ\ !\ [\![(m : I_m)]\!]\ \circ$$
$$[\![r_1 = c_1]\!]\ \circ\ \ldots\ \circ\ [\![r_n = c_n]\!]\ |\!)$$

where $EXT =!\ bud_{ext}^{\perp}(0)$ is the process surrounding the external membrane, permitting to expell the garbage membranes.

The encoding of the program counter is the same as in the previous section, whereas the encoding of the contents of registers is slightly simpler (as it is no longer necessary to start a loop in the case the wrong branch is taken):

$$[\![PC = i]\!] = mate_{p_i}(\!|\ |\!)$$
$$[\![r_j = c_j]\!] = mate_{opr_j}^{\perp}(\!|\ \bigcirc_{c_i} R_j |\!)$$

where

$$R_j = bud_{decr_j}(\!|\ |\!)$$

The main difference w.r.t. the previous section is represented by the encoding of the *DecJump* instruction, whereas the encoding of the *Succ* instruction is unchanged:

$$[\![(i : Succ(r_j))]\!] = \qquad mate_{p_i}^{\perp}.mate_{opr_j}.drip(mate_{p_{i+1}}).mate_{opr_j}^{\perp}(\!|R_j|\!)$$

$$[\![(i : DecJump(r_j, s))]\!] = mate_{p_i}^{\perp}.mate_{opr_j}.drip(ZERO_{i,j,s}).$$
$$drip(mate_{dorj}).$$
$$bud_{decr_j}^{\perp}(drip(0).mate_{zero}.bud_{ext}).$$
$$mate_{dorj}^{\perp}.drip(0).drip(0).drip(mate_{p_{i+1}}).$$
$$mate_{opr_j}^{\perp}(\!|\ |\!)$$

where

$$ZERO_{i,j,s} = drip(0).drip(0).drip(0).mate_{dorj}^{\perp}.drip(mate_{opr_j}^{\perp}).$$
$$drip(drip(0).mate_{p_s}).bud_{ext}\ |$$
$$mate_{zero}^{\perp}$$

As in the previous section, instruction $(i : I_i)$ is activated by fusing it with the program counter membrane $mate_{p_i}$.

Suppose that the i-th instruction is a decrement of register r_j, or jump to instruction s if the contents of r_j is zero.

The instruction membrane is fused with the register membrane by performing $mate_{opr_j}$, and a zero branch membrane with process $ZERO_{i,j,s}$ is dripped.

Also a mutual exclusion membrane $mate_{dorj}(\!|\ |\!)$ is dripped, and the zero branch membrane perform the first innocuous $drip(0)$.

Now the register+instruction membrane is ready to perform a budding of a copy of R_j. Two cases can happen:

- If the contents of r_j is not zero, e.g., if $r_j = k+1$, then the register+instruction membrane contains at least one copy of R_j. Hence, the budding operation is performed, and the expelled copy of R_j is surrounded by a the membrane with process $drip(0).mate_{zero}.mate_{garb}$. The zero branch membrane performs the second $drip(0)$.

  Now the register+instruction membrane contains k copies of R_j.

  The register+instruction membrane removes the membrane for mutual exclusion by performing $mate_{dorj}^{\perp}$, the zero branch membrane performs the third $drip(0)$ and the membrane surrounding the expelled R_j performs the $drip(0)$.

  At the next step, the register+instruction membrane performs the first $drip(0)$, and the zero branch membrane fuses with the membrane surrounding the expelled R_j by performing $mate_{zero}^{\perp}$. Note that the zero branch membrane can no longer perform $mate_{dorj}^{\perp}$, because the mutual exclusion membrane has been already been removed.

  At the next step, the register+instruction membrane performs the second $drip(0)$, and the membrane, obtained by fusing the zero branch membrane with the membrane surrounding the expelled R_j, is expelled from the external membrane, and surrounded by a membrane with empty process.

  At the next step, the only active membrane is the register+instruction membrane, that produces the program counter membrane $mate_{p_{i+1}}(\!|\ |\!)$; now the register+instruction membrane has become the register membrane $[\![r_j = k]\!]$, and is ready to accept the execution of new operations on the register.

- If $r_j = 0$, then no membrane is contained in the register+instruction membrane. Hence, the register+instruction membrane is blocked on the budding instruction. As no membrane can be fused with it, the register+instruction membrane has become innocuous garbage. The only active membrane is the zero branch membrane, which performs the two $drip(0)$, then it consumes the mutual exclusion membrane by performing $mate_{dorj}^{\perp}$. A new register membrane $[\![r_j = 0]\!]$ is produced by performing $drip(mate_{opr_j}^{\perp})$. A quasi program counter membrane $drip(0).mate_{p_s}(\!|\ |\!)$ is produced.

  At the next step, the quasi program counter membrane performs the $drip(0)$ and becomes the program counter $mate_{p_s}(\!|\ |\!)$, and the zero branch membrane performs the budding. Hence, the zero branch membrane has been expelled outside the surrounding external membrane, and surrounded by a membrane with empty program, thus becoming innocuous garbage.

We can now conclude with the Theorem which states that our modelling of RAMs faithfully represents the behaviour of the RAM.

Theorem 2. *Let R be a RAM with program $(1 : I_1), \ldots, (m : I_m)$ and initial state $(1, c_1, \ldots, c_n)$. Then we have that the RAM R terminates if and only if all the computations of the system $[\![(i, c_1, \ldots, c_n)]\!]$ terminate.*

4   Conclusion

We investigated the expressiveness of two different semantics (interleaving and maximal parallelism) for the MBD brane calculus w.r.t. the ability to encode computable functions.

Even if the underlying formalisms are different, the present work is intimately connected with the result in [5], namely, the Turing equivalence of P systems with mate and drip operations. A deep comparison of the two formalisms deserves a further investigation; however, at a first sight, it seems that the interaction primitives in the P systems defined in [5] are more powerful that the primitives of the MBD calculus. Moreover, in [5] only the halting computations are considered as successful, but it is not clear if a deterministic encoding of RAMs can be provided in P systems with mate and drip.

As observed in [5], it is not clear if moving to an interleaving semantics leads to a decrease of the computational power.

In [5], only a finite number of membranes is needed to obtain Turing equivalence, whereas in the present paper an unbounded number of membranes is required. The (im)possibility to encode RAMs in MBD with a fixed number of membranes deserves further investigation. Probably the technique adopted in [2] to reduce the process calculus Mobile Ambients on Petri nets [11] could provide some inspiration for an impossibility result.

Finally, an interesting topic is the expressivity of fragments of MBD obtained by dropping some primitive.

For example, [5] shows that in P systems the mate and drip primitives are enough to obtain Turing equivalence. We plan to investigate what is the impact of the removal of budding on the computational expressiveness of the MBD brane calculus.

Regarding the removal of drip, we claim that the results presented in this paper continue to hold in the brane calculus with mate and bud primitives. The basic idea is to encode a drip performed by a membrane with a co-bud operation, and by adding a submembrane ready to perform a bud. For example, the system $drip(\sigma)(\!|P|\!)$ is encoded with the system $bud^\perp_{dop}(\sigma)(\!|\ P\ \circ\ bud_{dop}(\!|\ |\!)\ |\!)$ (we assume that σ does not contain drip operations and that dop is a fresh name not used in P or σ). We plan to investigate the possibility to provide an encoding of the MBD brane calculus in the fragment with mate and bud primitives, that preserves some reasonable behavioural equivalence.

Acknowledgements

I would like to thank the organizers and the participants of WMC6 for the stimulating discussions.

References

1. N. Busi, R. Gorrieri: On the computational power of brane calculi. In *Proc. Third Workshop on Computational Methods in Systems Biology* (CMSB'05), Edinburgh, Scotland, 2005.
2. N. Busi, G. Zavattaro: Deciding reachability in mobile ambients. In *Proc. ESOP'05*, LNCS 3444, Springer, Berlin, 2005, 248–262.
3. L. Cardelli: Brane calculi – Interactions of biological membranes. In *Proc. Computational Methods in System Biology* (CMSB 2004), Paris, France, May 2004. LNCS 3082, Springer, Berlin, 2004, 257–280.
4. L. Cardelli, A.D. Gordon: Mobile ambients. *Theoretical Computer Science*, 240, 1 (2000), 177–213.
5. L. Cardelli, Gh. Păun: An universality result for a (mem)brane calculus based on mate/drip operations. *International Journal of Foundations of Computer Science*, to appear.
6. R. Freund: Asynchronous P Systems and P Systems Working in the Sequential Mode. In *Proc. 5th International Workshop on Membrane Computing, WMC2004, Milan, Italy, 2004. Revised Selected and Invited Papers*, LNCS 3365, Springer, Berlin, 2005, 36–62.
7. M.L. Minsky: *Computation: Finite and Infinite Machines*. Prentice-Hall, 1967.
8. Gh. Păun: Computing with membranes. *Journal of Computer and System Sciences*, 61, 1 (2000), 108–143.
9. Gh. Păun: *Membrane Computing. An Introduction*. Springer, Berlin, 2002.
10. A. Regev, E.M. Panina, W. Silverman, L. Cardelli, E. Shapiro: BioAmbients: An abstraction for biological compartments. *Theoretical Computer Science*, 325, 1 (2004), 141–167.
11. W. Reisig: *Petri Nets: An Introduction*. Springer, Berlin, 1985.
12. J.C. Shepherdson, J.E. Sturgis: Computability of recursive functions. *Journal of the ACM*, 10 (1963), 217–255.

A Membrane Computing System Mapped on an Asynchronous, Distributed Computational Environment

Guido Casiraghi, Claudio Ferretti, Alberto Gallini, and Giancarlo Mauri

DISCo – Dipartimento di Informatica Sistemistica e Comunicazione,
Università degli Studi di Milano–Bicocca,
Via Bicocca degli Arcimboldi 8 – 20126 Milano – Italy
ferretti@disco.unimib.it

Abstract. We show how to simulate a membrane system on a (simulated) distributed and bio-inspired computational architecture (BME). The advantages of this approach are the ease of representing each membrane with a processing element and the perspective of exploiting the expected nano-technological implementation of such an architecture.

By combining these two non-conventional computing architectures, we touch interesting subproblems, such as the trade-off between being synchronous (P systems) and asynchronous (BME), or between structural adjacency and position-independent communications.

1 Introduction

Processing elements (PE) arrays have gained attention as suitable architectures for computational machines based on molecular scale device. Thanks to their regular structure this kind of systems make design simpler, and could allow manufacturing techniques based on molecular self-organization. Lack of a clock avoids signal propagation troubles, but imposes an asynchronous interaction system based on messages exchange. Having such constraints on computational architecture and communication subsystem, the issue about which computational model to employ on them arises.

In this paper, we want to investigate how to map the membrane synchronous computations on such an environment; in particular, we will describe a technique to implement P systems on an asynchronous PE grid by employing a simulation environment for asynchronous parallel computational system, named Bio-Molecular Engine(BME).

BME in short. BME ([2]) is a graphical simulation environment for distributed computational systems architecture. Every simulated system has, as elementary unit, a processing element (PE, or "cell"), characterized by a certain computational capability defined by the virtual machine the user associates to it. Every cell is provided with one or more net-interface to manage messages incoming/outgoing to the computing environment, and all cells are linked together in a toroidal mesh.

R. Freund et al. (Eds.): WMC 2005, LNCS 3850, pp. 159–164, 2006.

Cells dynamically acquire a code to execute from the environment, and they themselves can ask to the environment the availability of a cell to be dedicated to the execution of a certain piece of code. Cells internally execute operations specified by the user who, in the BME simulator, can choose the formalism used to write the code (e.g., a simple specialized programming language, or plain Java). However, a small group of primitives has to be used for environment dependent operations (e.g., assignment of code to cells, communication, and so on). In particular, for our purposes three primitives have been employed:

- Run: used by a cell to dynamically associate a code to another cell in the environment. The new specialized cell executes the code without inheriting constraints from the cell which has instantiated it.
- Send: a cell sends a BME-data-message containing a small amount of information.
- Wait: a cell waits for an incoming BME-data-message.

Motivations. Both BME computing architecture and membrane systems have biological inspiration. In particular, BME considers features like: staminal (redundant) cells, specialization, tissue-like topology, massive parallelism. But there are also significant differences, for instance: P systems have nested structures, while BME has PEs in a lattice structure, the former usually have a clocked synchronous evolution of computation, while the latter has PEs cooperating without a clock.

Given this kind of comparison, we thought that the two models could be interestingly combined, with BME simulating the P systems; we look forward to advantages like the exploitation of current highly flexible and distributed BME simulating environment, but also future (nanoscale) hardware implementation of BME architecture, and thus also of P systems.

2   The Simulated Membrane System Model

We define membrane systems (P systems) omitting some definitions, which can be found, for instance, in [4].

A *P system* is defined by a tuple:

$$\Pi = (O, \mu, w_1, \ldots, w_m, R_1, \ldots, R_m, i_0),$$

where:

1. O is an alphabet, whose elements are called *objects*;
2. μ is a nested membrane structure;
3. w_i, $1 \le i \le m$, are multisets on O, describing objects initially contained in regions $1, 2, \ldots, m$ of μ;
4. R_i, $1 \le i \le m$, are finite sets of evolution rules on strings of objects from O; R_i is the set of rules active in region i of μ; an evolution rule has form $u \to v$, where u is a string on O and v is a string on $O_{tar} = (O^* \times TAR) \cup (O^* \times TAR \times \{\delta\})$, with $TAR = \{here, out, in\} \cup \{in_j \mid 1 \le j \le m\}$;

5. if a rule ends with the symbol δ, then after its application the membrane to which the rule belongs *dissolves*, and the objects contained in that membrane move to its parent membrane;

6. $i_0 \in \{1, 2, \ldots, m\}$ is the label of one of the membranes (*output membrane*).

Evolution rules are applied in each membrane in a *maximally parallel* way, and each membrane applies its rules and then communicates the results in *synchronous parallelism* with other membranes. In case that more than one alternative rule matchings appear, then a *non-deterministic choice* is made. Finally, each evolution rule states, with symbols from TAR, where each of its results have to be sent. If destination is *in*, without subscript, then the result is sent to one of inner membranes, non-deterministically chosen, if available.

A computation in the membrane system ends when no membrane can apply any rule.

3 Simulation of P Systems on the BME Environment

Both P systems and BME simulated architectures are distributed systems, but while BME cells interact asynchronously P systems are synchronous i.e., there is a sort of master clock that forces the transitions of data among membranes to occur together at any tick, defining a function from natural numbers (time axis) and the global states of a P system.

The basic idea of our simulation is to associate a membrane to a single cell, internally keeping a data structure tracing relationships with other membranes (inner membranes and parent membrane). The topology of the membrane system is thus not represented by relative positions of simulating PEs, chosen on the lattice by core algorithms of BME computational model. We use BME-primitives for message exchange to simulate the synchronous behaviour of P systems. A P system has a tree structure and when it is mapped on a BME virtual architecture, it is dynamically built starting from a single cell (the root of the tree), named *skin* membrane, that executes the BME primitive "Run" for each of its inner membranes; the same policy is employed by inner membranes and so on until the leaves of the tree are activated (i.e., membranes with no inner membranes).

The P systems simulator we developed consists of a Java package, which exploits two kinds of messages: *data messages* to pass data between two membranes and *event messages* (both implemented by BME-data-messages) to communicate events about the evolution of system's structure (i.e., when a inner membrane dissolves it communicates the results of this event to its parents and to its inner membranes).

Given the asynchronous nature of the BME sub-system, every cell, i.e., every simulated membrane, evolves autonomously. The evolution of a membrane is a sequence of computational steps, where each step can be described by a loop of four subsequent stages:

1. internal evolution rules application (to objects acquired in the previous iteration);
2. the sending of data to other PEs-membranes, by exploiting BME communication sub-system, and the waiting for incoming data messages;
3. the sending of event messages to signal structural (i.e., inner/parent membranes) changes, and the waiting for incoming event messages;
4. update of local messages buffer, containing messages arrived out of sequence.

In fact, since the evolution of internal state of the membranes is untied with the rest of the environment, it is not possible, at receiver side, to state to which simulated P system's step an incoming message is related.

An approach to this problem is to introduce packets numbering policies in order to associate them to a computational step of the emitting membrane. When a membrane M, at computational step n, receives a message (data or event) emitted by another membrane S at step $n + k$ (k is the communication "window"), M stores it into a buffer. When M will be at step $n + k$, it will be able to consume the received message. The problem is to verify if an upper bound exists for k, so to easily manage incoming traffic.

Another important issue is to maintain the structural consistency of the system: in an asynchronous system, the membranes can expire (dissolve) independently by the state of other membranes.

To solve both "window upper-bound" and "structural consistency" problems we have defined a *message processing protocol* (MPP) at the level of the single membrane that covers the second and the third point of the previously described algorithm for simulated membrane evolution. MPP is essentially organized in such a way that, for instance, a PE-membrane, which has a parent membrane and at least a inner membrane, will strictly alternate the exchange of data messages and event messages.

In this way, it can be proved that, for instance, even if we cannot be sure about delays and reordering of messages traveling along the lattice toward the PE associated to the parent membrane, nonetheless we will receive messages associated to simulated evolutions far at most one step from what we are now simulating in our PE-membrane.

This allowed us to simulate a synchronous P system by means of a set of asynchronous PEs in BME, just by numbering messages and allowing PEs to have a buffer memory for the small amount of messages which can arrive one step apart from what we are simulating.

4   Examples

The P system we want to simulate on BME is described by a set of simple Java modules, one for each membrane, and each of them will be transported to a single PE which will execute it. Inside each module the starting multiset and the set of rules of the associated membrane are defined by simple strings.

A multiset $x_1^{n_1} x_2^{n_2} \ldots x_k^{n_k}$, where $x_1, x_2, \ldots, x_k$ are objects and $n_1, n_2, \ldots \ldots$, $n_k \in N$, is represented by:

```
[(x1:n1),(x2:n2),...,(xk:nk)]
```

For instance, the multiset a^2b^3c is represented by:

```
[(a:2),(b:3),(c:1)]
```

Evolution rules have a LHS, which is a multiset, and a RHS which lists resulting multisets and their destination, e.g., $b_{here}(a^2c)_{out}d_{in}$. This example becomes:

```
[(b:1)].here[(a:2),(c:1)].out[(d:1)].in
```

If the destination is a specific membrane, it can be specified. For instance, $d_{in_{two}}$ becomes:

```
[(d:1)].in_two
```

LHS and RHS are separated by "=>". Operator δ, possibly appearing as suffix of evolution rules is represented by "!". Therefore, a complete evolution rule is:

```
[(a:2),(b:3)] => [(b:1)].here[(a:2),(c:1)].out[(d:1)].in!
```

Each membrane has a name, which also is the name of the corresponding Java module. The skin membrane has always the name `Main()`.

Each module will:

- build a `RuleList` (using also `parse()`);
- build the starting multiset of the membrane (with `parse()` of a corresponding Java class);
- create and instantiate on BME the (possible) inner membranes ("Run" primitive of BME);
- finally, start itself.

An instance membrane follows: it has name "one", it is inside *skin* membrane, and it has an inner membrane named "two". It has the evolution rule $d \rightarrow e^2_{out}f_{in}\delta$ and a starting multiset d^2:

```
one() {

    bmeModuleSig("null");

    rl = new RuleList();
    rl.add(Rule.parse("[(d:1)] => [(e:2)].out[(f:1)].in!"));
    c = MembraneContent.parse("[(d:2)]");
    m = new Membrane(new MembraneName("one"),
                     Membrane.SKIN_MEMBRANE_NAME, c, rl);

    m.addInnerMembraneName(new MembraneName("two"));
    bmeRun("two");

    bmeMembrane = new BmeMembrane(own, m);
    while (!bmeMembrane.stop()) bmeMembrane.evolve();

}
```

5   Discussion

Our approach is not focused on providing a powerful simulator of P systems, but it aims instead at discovering synergies and/or contrasts between the two different non-conventional computing models considered. Results and further references about software simulation of P systems can be found, for instance, in [3].

By using our already well developed BME simulator, rich in graphical visualization tools and in features like tools for doing heavy simulations on distributed high-performance clusters, we easily obtained a good user interface for displaying simulated P systems. Moreover, since BME is being defined together with researchers from the nano-technology field, with the aim of making that computational model implementable on (future) nano-scale devices, we like to think that in this way also P systems could be brought to specialized hardware.

An important detail about the system we presented here, is that our BME-based simulator substitutes non-deterministic choices with random choices, thus making it more suited to simulation of *confluent* P systems (that is, systems where, for a given input, all the computations produce the same output).

Two interesting issues are worth of further development. One is that of how well time-independent P systems ([1]) could be simulated on the asynchronous BME architecture. Another one is that of looking for higher performance by using bigger message buffers in PEs, while exploiting pipelined flow control algorithms to build correct message streams at destination, instead of the current message protocol, essentially corresponding to a pipeline of size 1.

References

1. M. Cavaliere, D. Sburlan: Time-independent P systems. In *Membrane Computing International Workshop WMC 2004, Milan, Italy, 2004, Revised Selected and Invited Papers* (G. Mauri, Gh. Păun, M.J. Pérez-Jiménez, G. Rozenberg, A. Salomaa, eds.), LNCS 3365, Springer, Berlin, 2005, 239–258.
2. A. Gallini, C. Ferretti, G. Mauri: Bio molecular engine: A bio-inspired environment for models of growing and evolvable computation. *Genetic and Evolutionary Computation Conference* (GECCO)'05, 2005.
3. M.A. Gutiérrez-Naranjo, M.J. Pérez-Jiménez, A. Riscos-Nùnez: A simulator for confluent P systems. *Second Brainstorming Week on Membrane Computing*, Sevilla, 2004, 169–184.
4. Gh. Păun: *Membrane Computing. An Introduction.* Springer, Berlin, 2002.

P Systems with Memory

Paolo Cazzaniga, Alberto Leporati, Giancarlo Mauri, and Claudio Zandron

Università degli Studi di Milano–Bicocca,
Dipartimento di Informatica, Sistemistica e Comunicazione,
via Bicocca degli Arcimboldi 8, 20126 Milano, Italy
{cazzaniga, leporati, mauri, zandron}@disco.unimib.it

Abstract. We propose P systems in which the solutions of previously
executed computations can be stored in sub-systems composed by a number of membranes which act as memory elements. When a new input
is inserted into the system, the computation on that input is started
in parallel with the search for the corresponding solution in all memory membranes. If the solution is found in memory, then a copy of it
is expelled from that memory membrane; the search in all other memory membranes is stopped, and the same is done with the computing
sub-system. If no solution for that input is found, then the computation
produces the solution, which is subsequently stored in a memory cell.

1 Introduction

P systems were introduced by Gh. Păun in [3] as a class of distributed parallel
computing devices, inspired by the functioning of living cells. The basic model
consists of a membrane structure composed by several cell-membranes, hierarchically embedded in a main membrane called the skin. The membranes delimit
regions and can contain objects. The objects evolve according to given evolution rules associated with the regions. A rule can modify the objects and send
them outside the membrane or to an inner membrane. Moreover, membranes
can be dissolved. When a membrane is dissolved, all the objects of the dissolved
membrane are released into the membrane placed immediately outside, while
the evolution rules of the dissolved membrane are lost. The skin membrane is
never dissolved.

The evolution rules are applied in a maximally parallel manner: at each step,
all the objects which can evolve should evolve. A computation device is obtained:
we start from an initial configuration and we let the system evolve. A computation halts when no rule can be applied. In such a case, the objects in a specified
output membrane are the result of the computation.

Further information concerning P systems can be found in [7], and at the
Internet web address: http://psystems.disco.unimib.it.

In this paper we propose P systems in which solutions of previously executed
computations can be stored in some static memory cells, to speed-up computations. In fact, one possible way to speed-up computations would be to create new
membranes by means of division (see, e.g., [6]). However, with this approach the

R. Freund et al. (Eds.): WMC 2005, LNCS 3850, pp. 165–180, 2006.

number of membranes can grow exponentially. Here, the defined systems have two main sub–components: the first sub-component is a standard computing P system; the second sub-component is constituted by a fixed number of membranes which act as memory elements. Each time a solution is produced by the computing sub-system, we store that solution in a memory membrane.

When a new input is inserted in the system to start a new computation, we start in parallel the search for the solution in all memory membranes and, at the same time, the computation on that input in the computing sub-system. If the solution is found in one memory cell before the computation ends, then a copy of the solution is expelled from that memory membrane; the search in all other memory membranes is stopped, and the same is done with the computing sub-system. On the other hand, if the solution is not found in any memory membrane, then the computing sub-system produces the new solution, which is then stored in a free memory membrane. In order to keep at least one memory membrane available all the time, oldest solutions are deleted from memory when necessary.

We will show that the search for a solution stored in memory can be done in linear time with respect to the input length. As a consequence, the system could be effectively used in all cases when the computation time order is greater than linear and the output for the same input is requested many times with a high probability within a short time. This occurs, for example, in image and vocal processing applications.

We will implement our systems by means of usual rewriting P systems which make use of the following features:

- **Membranes of variable thickness:** membranes can be made thicker or thinner (also dissolved, as told above), in order to change its permeability with respect to the passage of objects through them.
- **Membrane polarization:** electrical charges are associated to membranes: they can be marked with a "positive" $(+)$, "negative" $(-)$ or "neutral" (0) charge. The rules are applied to strings by taking into account the electrical charges of the membranes.
- **Replicated rewriting rules:** the rules allow to create k copies of the string starting from a single copy. A symbol in the original copy is deleted from the string to create k different strings; in each of these copies the deleted symbol is replaced by a specific sub-string, and each obtained string is then sent to a specific target membrane (as usual, it can remain in the same membrane, it can be sent to the region immediately outside or it can be sent to an immediately inner membrane).

For further details about P systems and the properties of the features described above, we refer the reader to $[1, 2, 4, 8, 9, 11, 12]$.

The remaining of the paper is organized as follows. In section 2, we give some formal definitions concerning rewriting P systems with active membranes. In section 3, we give the description of P systems with memory. In section 4, we describe the functioning of such systems. Finally, section 5 contains the conclusions and some perspectives for future work.

2   Rewriting P Systems with Active Membranes

We will not recall here the basic definitions of P systems. For details, we refer to [7]. For elements of Formal Language Theory, we refer to [10].

In the following, we will make use of *Replicated Rewriting P Systems with polarized membranes of variable thickness*. In such systems, objects can be described by finite strings over a given finite alphabet. The evolution of an object will correspond to a transformation of a string, by means of context free rewriting rules. The evolution of objects will depend also on the electrical charges associated with the membranes. The thickness of membranes can be modified, to dissolve them or to obtain thicker membranes that are impermeable to the passage of objects. Finally, a string can be replicated to obtain more copies starting from a single one.

Formally, such a system of degree $n, n \geq 1$, is defined as follows:

$$\Pi = (V, T, H, \mu, M_1, \ldots, M_n, R_1, \ldots, R_n, i_0),$$

where:

- V is an alphabet (the total alphabet of the system);
- $T \subseteq V$ is the terminal alphabet;
- H is a finite set of labels for membranes;
- μ is a membrane structure, consisting of n membranes, labeled (not necessarily in a one-to-one manner) with elements of H; all membranes in μ are supposed to be initially neutral;
- $M_i, 1 \leq i \leq n$, are finite languages over V;
- i_0 is the label of the output membrane. If i_0 is omitted, then the output is collected in the region outside the skin membrane;
- $R_i, 1 \leq i \leq n$, are finite sets of evolution rules.
  The rules are context free evolution rules of the following form:
  (a) $[_h a \rightarrow v]_h^\alpha$ or $[_h a \rightarrow v\gamma]_h^\alpha$, for $h \in H$, $a \in V$, $v \in V^*$, $\alpha \in \{+, -, 0\}$, $\gamma \in \{\delta, \tau\}$ (string evolution rules),
  (b) $a[_h]_h^{\alpha_1} \rightarrow [_h v]_h^{\alpha_2}$ or $a[_h]_h^{\alpha_1} \rightarrow [_h v\gamma]_h^{\alpha_2}$, where $a \in V$, $v \in V^*$, $h \in H$, $\alpha_1, \alpha_2 \in \{+, -, 0\}$, $\gamma \in \{\delta, \tau\}$ (the symbol a in the string is rewritten as v and the obtained string is introduced in membrane h),
  (c) $[_h a]_h^{\alpha_1} \rightarrow [_h]_h^{\alpha_2} v$ or $[_h a]_h^{\alpha_1} \rightarrow [_h]_h^{\alpha_2} v\gamma$, where $h \in H$, $\alpha_1, \alpha_2 \in \{+, -, 0\}$, $a \in V$, $v \in V^*$, $\gamma \in \{\delta, \tau\}$ (the symbol a in the string is rewritten as v and the obtained string is moved from membrane h to the region immediately outside),
  (d) $[_h a]_h^{\alpha_1} \rightarrow [_h v_1\gamma_1(tar_1)||v_2\gamma_2(tar_2)||\ldots||v_k\gamma_n(tar_k)]_h^{\alpha_2}$, where $h \in H$, $\alpha_1, \alpha_2 \in \{+, -, 0\}$, $a \in V$, $v_i \in V^*$, γ_i is empty or $\gamma_i \in \{\delta, \tau\}$, $1 \leq i \leq k$, $tar_i \in \{here, out, j \mid j$ is the label of a membrane immediately inside membrane $h\}$, $1 \leq i \leq k$ (the string containing the symbol a is replicated in k copies and then a symbol a in each of them is replaced by the corresponding substring v_i; each string is then communicated to a target membrane specified by the target label).

These rules are applied according to the following principles:

1. If a rule contains the special symbol δ and the membrane where this rule is applied has thickness 1, then that membrane is dissolved and it is no longer recreated; the objects in the membrane become objects of the membrane placed immediately outside, while the rules of the dissolved membrane are removed from the system. If the membrane has thickness 2, then this symbol reduces the thickness to 1. The skin membrane is never dissolved.

2. If a rule contains the special symbol τ, then the thickness of the membrane where this rule is applied is increased; the thickness of a membrane of thickness 2 is not further increased. If a membrane has thickness 2, then no object can pass through it. All rules involving a passage through a membrane of thickness 2 cannot be applied until the thickness is reduced to 1 by means of another rule which introduces the symbol δ in that membrane (note that this also applies to the case for replicated rewriting rules: if a replicated string cannot reach its target, then the whole rule cannot be applied).

3. If the symbols δ and τ are simultaneously introduced in the same region (by applying two or more different rules on two or more different objects), then the corresponding membrane preserves its thickness.

4. The communication of objects has priority over the actions of δ and τ; if at the same step an object has to pass through a membrane and a rule changes the thickness of that membrane, then we first transmit the object and after that we change the thickness.

5. All objects evolve in parallel: at each step of computation, an object can be modified by only one rule, non-deterministically chosen among all applicable rules. On the other hand, any object which can evolve by a rule of any form, is forced to evolve.

6. All objects and membranes not specified in a rule and which do not evolve are passed unchanged to the next computation step.

The membrane structure at a given time, together with all the strings associated with the regions defined by the membrane structure, is the *configuration* of the system at that time. The *initial configuration* is $(\mu, M_1, \ldots, M_n)$. A *transition* between two configurations is performed by applying the rules in R according to the principles described above. A *computation* is a sequence of transitions between configurations. A computation *halts* when there is no rule which can be applied to objects and membranes in the current configuration. In such a case, the *output* of the computation consists of all strings in membrane i_0 when the computation halts. A non-halting computation does not produce an output.

3   The Structure of the Storage Device

As told above, the main idea is to define a system which allows to store information of previously executed computations, in order to save computation time. Hence, the final system (we will call it the Storage Device) is obtained by adding to an original computation system (i.e., a P System designed to solve a

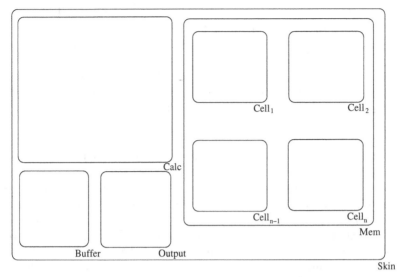

Fig. 1. The general structure of the storage membrane system

given computational problem), a memory sub-system, an output membrane, and a buffer membrane (which is used to store the information needed during the computation). All these components are then surrounded by a skin membrane.

In this section we illustrate the main components of the storage device, and then we formally define it. The detailed functioning of the system will be described in the next section.

The general structure of the storage device is depicted in Fig. 1. As one can see, there are four main sub-systems.

The **computational sub-system** consists of a P system that performs computations on the input strings that are injected from outside. This system does not have an output membrane, but it expels the output strings to its environment, which is the skin membrane of the storage device.

The **memory sub-system** consists of a certain number n of complex cells, where a cell is a region with a complex structure. Each cell is used to store previously computed solutions (together with their corresponding inputs), and to produce them when the same input is injected again in the system at a later time.

The **buffer membrane** is used to store information concerning the solution that the system is currently computing. In particular, the buffer is used when the input string is not stored in the memory sub-system and, as a consequence, the solution has to be calculated by the computational sub-system. As told above, at the end of the computation the storage device has to store the new computed solution, together with the corresponding input string, into the same memory cell. Inside the buffer there are two sub-membranes, used to start up the operations needed to retrieve the string previously stored and to empty the buffer, respectively.

The **output membrane** collects the result of the computation, be it retrieved from the memory sub-system or calculated by the computational sub-system.

The computation in the system proceeds as follows. The input string (injected through the skin membrane) is replicated to obtain three copies: a copy is sent to the computation sub-system, where it will start a computation in order to calculate a new solution, while a second copy is sent into the buffer membrane. At the same time, the third copy is sent to the memory sub-system, where it is replicated and forwarded to all the memory cells, to check (in parallel in all memory cells) if the solution is already stored into the system.

If the solution is found in the memory sub-system, then it is sent to the output membrane and the system proceeds to empty the buffer and to stop the execution in the computational sub-system. Otherwise, the computational sub-system produces the new solution, and sends it both to the output membrane and to the memory sub-system. The solution has to be stored in a memory membrane together with its corresponding input, which is found in the buffer membrane where it was stored at the beginning of the computation. Thus, the system non-deterministically chooses an empty cell in the memory sub-system and sends into this membrane the two strings. The system is now ready to execute a new computation.

Formally, the system is defined as follows:

$$DdM = (\mu, V, W_{Calc}, W_{Buf}, W_{Mem}, R, Output),$$

where:

- $\mu = \begin{bmatrix} _{Skin} \begin{bmatrix} _{Output} \end{bmatrix}_{Output} \begin{bmatrix} _{Calc} \end{bmatrix}_{Calc} \begin{bmatrix} _{Buf} \end{bmatrix}_{Buf} \end{bmatrix}$
  $\begin{bmatrix} _{Mem} \begin{bmatrix} _{Cell_1} \end{bmatrix}_{Cell_1} \cdots \begin{bmatrix} _{Cell_n} \end{bmatrix}_{Cell_n} \end{bmatrix}_{Mem} \end{bmatrix}_{Skin}$
  The internal structure of every cell belonging to Mem is:
  $\begin{bmatrix} _{Cell_i} \begin{bmatrix} _{Count} \end{bmatrix}_{Count} \begin{bmatrix} _{Count\beta} \end{bmatrix}_{Count\beta} \begin{bmatrix} _{Sol} \begin{bmatrix} _{Empty} \end{bmatrix}_{Empty} \begin{bmatrix} _{Double} \end{bmatrix}_{Double}$
  $\end{bmatrix}_{Sol} \begin{bmatrix} _{Input} \begin{bmatrix} _{Compare} \end{bmatrix}_{Compare} \begin{bmatrix} _{Syncro} \begin{bmatrix} _{Empty} \end{bmatrix}_{Empty} \begin{bmatrix} _{Double} \end{bmatrix}_{Double}$
  $\end{bmatrix}_{Syncro} \end{bmatrix}_{Input} \end{bmatrix}_{Cell_i}$, for $1 \leq i \leq n$;
- $V = \{a_1, \ldots, a_k, \alpha, \ldots, \omega, A, \$, \$', \$'', \$_P \Pi, X, X'\} \cup$
  $\{Y, D, \langle, \langle', \langle'', \rangle, th, pol, per, Stop, F, \lambda, =, \neq, \neq'\}$
  is the total alphabet of the system; we assume the alphabet is sorted in increasing order from a_1 to a_k, $k = |V|$;
- W_{Calc} is the family of strings belonging to the $Calc$ region;
- W_{Buf} is the family of strings belonging to the $Buffer$ region. In the initial configuration W_{Buf} is empty.
- W_{Mem} is the family of strings belonging to the Mem region. In the initial configuration, the only set belonging to W_{Mem} is $w_{Compare} = \{\neq\}$.
- $R = \{R_{Skin}, R_{Mem}, R_{Cell_i}, R_{Sol}, R_{Doub.}, R_{Empty}, R_{Input}, R_{Sync.}, R_{Comp}\}$, $i \in \{1, 2, \ldots, n\}$ is the family of rules of the system.

$R_{Skin} = \{$
$r_1 : \begin{bmatrix} _{Skin} X \end{bmatrix}_{Skin} \to \begin{bmatrix} _{Skin} (X, in_{Mem}) \end{bmatrix} \| (X, in_{Buf}) \| (\Pi', in_{Calc}) \end{bmatrix}_{Skin}$
$r_2 : \begin{bmatrix} _{Skin} \$' \end{bmatrix}_{Skin} \to \begin{bmatrix} _{Skin} (\lambda, in_{Out}) \| (\$', in_{Buf}) \| (Stop, here) \end{bmatrix}_{Skin}$

$r_3 : [_{Sk}.\$_P]_{Skin} \rightarrow [_{Sk}.(\$, in_{Buf})||(\lambda, in_{Out})||(\$, in_{Mem})||(Stop, here)]_{Skin}$

$r_4 : \langle [_{Mem}]_{Mem} \rightarrow [_{Mem} \langle]_{Mem}\}$

r_1 replicates and forwards the input string to the *Mem*, *Buffer* and *Calc* membranes at the beginning of each computation.

r_2, r_3 are used to forward the solution string to the *Output*, *Buffer* and *Mem* membranes at the end of each computation.

r_4 sends the input string to the *Mem* membrane, to store it in the system.

$R_{Mem} = \{r_1 : [_{Mem} \$]_{Mem} \rightarrow [_{Mem} \$^-]_{Mem}$

$r_2 : [_{Mem} X]_{Mem} \rightarrow [_{Mem}(X, in_{Cell_1})||(X, in_{Cell_2})|| \ldots ||(X, in_{Cell_n})]_{Mem}$

$r_3 : [_{Mem} \$']_{Mem} \rightarrow [_{Mem}]_{Mem} \$'$

$r_4 : [_{Mem} \langle]_{Mem} \rightarrow [_{Mem} \langle^+]_{Mem}\}$

r_1, r_4 are used to non–deterministically send the input string and the corresponding solution into an empty cell, to store them in the system.

r_2 is used to forward the input string that comes from the environment to all the memory cells in order to start the comparison procedure.

r_3 when a solution is found in memory, this rule is used to send it to the skin membrane, where it will then be sent to the output membrane.

$R_{Cell_i} = \{r_1 : [_{Cell_i} \langle]_{\overline{Cell_i}} \rightarrow [_{Cell_i} [_{Input}\langle'']_{Input}]_{Cell_i}^0$

$r_2 : [_{Cell_i} pol]_{Cell_i} \rightarrow [_{Cell_i}]_{Cell_i}^+ th$

$r_3 : X \rightarrow [_{Input} X]_{Input}$

$r_4 : [_{Cell_i} \$']_{Cell_i} \rightarrow [_{Cell_i}]_{Cell_i} \$'$

$r_5 : [_{Cell_i} F]_{Cell_i} \rightarrow [_{Cell_i} (F, in_{Sol}) || (F, in_{Input})]_{Cell_i}$

$r_6 : [_{Cell_i} \$]_{Cell_i}^+ \rightarrow [_{Cell_i} \$'']_{Cell_i}^-$

$r_7 : [_{Cell_i} \$'']_{Cell_i} \rightarrow [_{Cell_i} (\$, in_{Sol}) || (=, in_{count})]_{Cell_i}\}$

r_1, r_6, r_7 are used to store information concerning the inputs and their corresponding solutions into the sub–membranes of the cell.

r_2, r_5 are used to empty the cell from solutions which become too old.

r_3 sends the input string to be compared into the *Input* sub-membrane.

r_4 is used to expel the solution.

$R_{Sol} = \{r_1 : [_{Sol} \$]_{Sol} \rightarrow [_{Sol} \$^-]_{Sol}$

$r_2 : = [_{Double}]_{Double}^0 \rightarrow [_{Double} th]_{Double}^+$

$r_3 : [_{Sol} th]_{Sol} \rightarrow [_{Sol}]_{Sol} th$

$r_4 : F[_{Empty}]_{Empty}^0 \rightarrow [_{Empty} th]_{Empty}^+$

$r_5 : [_{Sol} \$']_{Sol} \rightarrow [_{Sol}]_{Sol} \$'$

$r_6 : [_{Sol} pol]_{Sol} \rightarrow [_{Sol}]_{Sol} pol\}$

r_1, r_2, r_3, r_5 are used to duplicate the solution and to send out one copy.

r_4, r_6 are used to empty the cell.

$R_{Double} = \{r_1 : [_{Double} th]_{Double} \rightarrow [_{Double}]_{Double} th$

$r_2 : [_{Double} \$]_{Double} \rightarrow [_{Double} (\$', here) || (\$'', here)]_{Double}$

$r_3 : [_{Double} \$']_{Double} \rightarrow [_{Double}]_{Double} \$'$

$r_4 : [_{Double} \$'']_{Double}^+ \rightarrow [_{Double}]_{Double}^0 \$'$

$r_5 : [_{Double} X']_{Double} \rightarrow [_{Double} X]_{Double}$

$r_6 : \ [_{Double} X \ ]^+_{Double} \rightarrow [_{Double} \ ]^0_{Double} \ X$

$r_7 : \ [_{Double} \ \langle \ ]_{Double} \rightarrow [_{Double} \ (\langle, out) \ || \ (\langle', out) \ ]_{Double} \}$

r_1, r_2, r_3, r_4 are used to duplicate the solution string.

r_5, r_6, r_7 are used to duplicate the input string stored within a cell.

$R_{Empty} = \{ r_1 : \ [_{Empty} \$ \ ]^+_{Empty} \rightarrow [_{Empty}]^0_{Empty} \ pol$

$r_2 : \ [_{Empty} \langle \ ]^+_{Empty} \rightarrow [_{Empty}]^0_{Empty} \ th \}$

r_1, r_2 are used to delete solution and input strings, respectively.

$R_{Input} = \{$

$r_1 : \ [_{Input} \ X' \ [_{Comp.}]^+_{Comp.} \ ]_{Input} \rightarrow [_{Input} \ [_{Comp.} \ X' - \ ]^+_{Comp.} \ ]_{Input}$

$r_2 : \ [_{Input} \ X' \ [_{Comp.} \ ]^0_{Comp.} \ ]_{Input} \rightarrow [_{Input} \ [_{Comp.} \ th \ ]^0_{Comp.} \ ]_{Input}$

$r_3 : \ X\alpha \ [_{Compare} \ ]_{Compare} \rightarrow [_{Compare} X\alpha \ ]_{Compare}, \ \forall \ \alpha \in V$

$r_4 : \ \langle \alpha \ [_{Compare} \ ]_{Compare} \rightarrow [_{Compare} \langle \alpha \ ]_{Compare}, \ \forall \ \alpha \in V$

$r_5 : \ XY \ [_{Compare} \ ]_{Compare} \rightarrow [_{Compare} XY \ ]_{Compare}$

$r_6 : \ \langle \rangle \ [_{Compare} \ ]_{Compare} \rightarrow [_{Compare} \langle \rangle \ ]_{Compare}$

$r_7 : \ [_{Input} \ \neq \ ]_{Input} \rightarrow [_{Input} \ ]_{Input} \ th \ \tau$

$r_8 : \ [_{Input} \ X \ ]_{Input} \rightarrow [_{Input} \ ]_{Input} \ th$

$r_9 : \ \neq' \ [_{Compare} \ ]_{Compare} \rightarrow [_{Compare} \ th \ ]_{Compare}$

$r_{10} : \ [_{Input} \ D \ ]_{Input} \rightarrow [_{Input} \ ]_{Input} \ th \ \delta$

$r_{11} : \ [_{Input} \ th \ ]_{Input} \rightarrow [_{Input} \ ]_{Input} \ th$

$r_{12} : \ F \ [_{Syncro}]^+_{Syncro} \rightarrow [_{Syncro} \ F \ ]^0_{Syncro}$

$r_{13} : \ [_{Input} \ pol \ ]_{Input} \rightarrow [_{Input} \ ]_{Input} \ pol$

$r_{14} : \ \langle'' \ [_{Syncro}]^0_{Syncro} \rightarrow [_{Syncro} \ \langle \ ]^+_{Syncro} \}$

r_1 is used to send the input string into the *Syncro* membrane only if the cell actually stores data.

r_2 is used to delete the input string if the cell is empty.

$r_3 - r_{11}$ are used to compare the input string that comes from the environment with the string stored into the cell.

r_{12}, r_{13} are used to empty the cell.

r_{14} is used to store the input string into the cell.

$R_{Syncro} = \{ r_1 : \ [_{Syncro} \ \langle \ ]_{Syncro} \rightarrow [_{Syncro} \ \langle^- \ ]_{Syncro}$

$r_2 : \ X' \ [_{Double}]_{Double} \rightarrow [_{Double} X' \ ]^+_{Double}$

$r_3 : \ [_{Syncro} \ th \ ]_{Syncro} \rightarrow [_{Syncro} \ ]_{Syncro} \ th$

$r_4 : \ [_{Syncro} \ X \ ]_{Syncro} \rightarrow [_{Syncro} \ ]_{Syncro} \ X$

$r_5 : \ [_{Syncro} \ \langle' \ ]_{Syncro} \rightarrow [_{Syncro} \ ]_{Syncro} \ \langle$

$r_6 : \ F \ [_{Empty}]^0_{Empty} \rightarrow [_{Empty} \ th \ ]^+_{Empty} \}$

r_1, r_2 are used to activate the duplication procedure on the input string.

r_3, r_4, r_5 are used to begin the comparison procedure.

r_6 is used to empty the cell.

$R_{Comp} = \{ r_1 : \ [_{Compare} \ X \ Y \ ]_{Compare} \rightarrow [_{Compare} \ X \ z \ ]_{Compare}$

$r_2 : \ [_{Compare} \ X \ \alpha_n]_{Compare} \rightarrow [_{Compare} \ X \ \alpha_{n-1}]_{Compare}$

$r_3 : \ [_{Compare} \ \langle \ \rangle \ ]_{Compare} \rightarrow [_{Compare} \ \langle \ z \ ]_{Compare}$

$r_4 : \ [_{Comp.} \ \langle \ \alpha_n]_{Comp.} \rightarrow [_{Comp.} \ \langle \ \alpha_{n-1}]_{Comp.}, \ \forall \ \alpha \in V \ and \ n \geq 2$

$r_5 :\ [_{Compare}\ X\ a\ ]_{Compare} \rightarrow [_{Compare}\ ]_{Compare} X \lambda\ \tau$

$r_6 :\ [_{Compare}\ \langle\ a\ ]_{Compare} \rightarrow [_{Compare}\ ]_{Compare} \langle \lambda\ \delta$

$r_7 :\ [_{Compare}\ \langle\ ]_{Compare} \rightarrow [_{Compare}\ per\ ]_{Compare}$

$r_8 :\ [_{Compare}\ per\ ]_{Compare} \rightarrow [_{Compare}\ ]_{Compare} th\ \delta\ \}$

The comparison of the string is performed in a left to right manner: the leftmost symbols of the two strings are compared. If they are different, then a negative answer is returned. Otherwise, both symbols are deleted from their corresponding strings and the comparison proceeds with the (new) leftmost symbols. If all symbols are deleted from both strings, then a positive answer is returned.

$r_1 - r_4$ are used to check if the leftmost symbols of the two strings are different.

r_5, r_6 are used to delete the leftmost symbol of the input strings.

r_7, r_8 are used to end the comparison algorithm.

– *Output* is the output membrane.

4 Functioning of the Storage Device

The computation of the system starts when an input string is injected from the environment into the skin region. As told above, the input string is replicated in three copies: the first copy is sent to the computation sub-system, to start a computation which calculates a new solution; the second copy is sent to the buffer membrane, to be eventually used later to store the string and its corresponding solution in a memory cell. The third copy is sent to the memory sub-system, where it is replicated in n copies to be forwarded to all memory cells, to check (in parallel in all memory cells) if the corresponding solution is already stored into the system.

When the solution string is already stored in memory, it is retrieved from the memory cell and then sent to the output membrane. Then, the system proceeds to empty the buffer membrane and to stop the execution of the computational sub-system. On the contrary, if the solution is not stored in the system, then the computational sub-system produces the new solution, which is then sent both to the output membrane and to the memory sub-system. The solution has to be stored in a memory membrane together with its corresponding input string; this last string is thus retrieved from the buffer membrane, where it was stored at the beginning of the computation. The system chooses, in a non–deterministic-way, an empty cell in the memory sub–system, and sends to this membrane both the input and the corresponding solution strings.

In the following, we describe the internal structure of memory cells and (by means of pseudo-code) the tasks executed by them. The structure of a cell included inside the memory of the system is depicted in Fig. 2.

All the cells have different labels; however, they have the same internal structure and the same initial configuration. Every cell is made up of three parts: two of these are used to store the input string and the solution string, while the third part manages the counter of the cell. In the initial configuration of the system

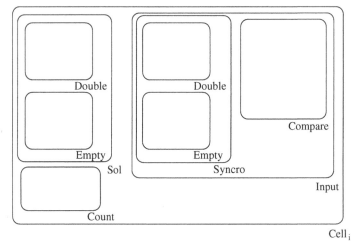

Fig. 2. The structure of a memory cell

all the cells have a positive electrical charge but the sub–membranes, which have null electrical charge. The polarization is used to distinguish empty cells from cells that contain some information. This distinction is useful when the system has to store a new solution: using the polarization of the cell, the system is able to select an empty cell.

When the system stores some information inside a cell, it changes its electrical charge from positive to null, and modifies the polarization of the sub–membrane (from null to positive) where the input string is delivered. This value will be used by the system to detect the cells that contain information when it is needed to compare the input string that comes from the environment with the string stored in the cell.

Inside the membrane where the input string is stored, there is a membrane used to compare the strings. The comparison is carried out by synchronizing the entrance and the going out from this membrane of the strings to be compared. The strings enter into the membrane simultaneously; then, the rules that reduce the symbol value until deleting it are applied. It is clear that if two symbols are equal they will be deleted at the same time, whereas if they are different the deleting rules will be applied at different times. During the delete operations, the strings are also sent out of the comparison membrane and, while going out, the applied rules perform a δ and a τ operation, respectively. In this way, if the strings leave the membrane simultaneously, the operations are executed at the same computation step and they have no effect. On the other hand, by applying one rule before the other one, it is impossible to carry on the algorithm. This is due to the change of thickness, because the membrane is dissolved or its permeability is increased, and the strings are not able to pass through the membrane.

Besides the structure that realizes the algorithm, there are two membranes which are able to duplicate and to erase data, respectively. These membranes are used only when the system explicitly needs to execute these operations. The second region of the cell is used to store the solution strings. Also inside this membrane there are two sub–membranes: one is used to duplicate solution strings when the comparison algorithm successfully ends, and the second to delete it when the system needs to empty the cell.

The last part of the cell is made of two membranes, which are used to manage the counter of the cell. The counter is used to establish when information are obsolete. We assume that the oldest solutions have a low probability of being requested at a later time. The counter starts to count the life time of a solution when this is stored inside a cell; at every computation step, the counter value is decreased. The starting value of the counter can be chosen over an established threshold, so that the solution inside a cell is not deleted too early; the aim is to store information as long as possible before deleting it. When the counter reaches the value zero it produces a special symbol F, which is used to delete the contents of the cell, and to restore its original positive polarization.

Let us show now the three procedures which are used to insert, delete and retrieve the information inside a cell. Moreover, we describe the algorithm used to compare two strings.

Procedure **insert** *(input,solution)*
begin
    If *the memory is full (no cell with positive polarization exists)* **then**
        delete ();
    Choose non–deterministically a cell among those with a positive charge;
    Send into this cell the solution string, and change its charge
        to negative polarization;
    Send the input string in the (unique) membrane
        with negative polarization, changing its charge to neutral;
    Send the solution string in sub-membrane Sol;
    Send the input string in sub-membrane Input and then
        in sub-membrane Syncro;
    Change the charge of membrane Syncro from 0 to +;
end.

The *insert* procedure is executed when the storage device needs to store a new solution. If no free cells are available (i.e., no cells with positive polarization are present), then the system proceeds to free some cells by means of the *delete* procedure (described below). When one or more free cells are available, the solution string and its corresponding input string are non–deterministically sent inside one of them; first, the solution string is sent through the chosen membrane, changing its charge from positive to negative. Then, the input string (which is still inside the memory region) is sent in the same membrane, that can be identified as it is the only one with negative charge. During this passage, the polarization of the membrane is changed to neutral, to label this cell as non-empty. Then, the solution string is sent to the internal sub-membrane *Sol*, while the input string is sent to the internal sub-membrane *Input* and, from here, in the inner region delimited by membrane *Syncro*. During the last passage, the electrical charge of the membrane *Syncro* is changed from neutral to positive; this fact will be exploited when the solution will be searched in a following computation.

After the end of the procedure, the cell starts to count the solution life time.

Procedure **delete** *()*
begin
    Send a special symbol F in sub-membranes Sol and Input;
    Send F in sub-membrane Empty;
    Change the charge of membrane Empty from 0 to +;
    Send solution in Empty;
    Send input in Empty;
    Delete solution;
    Delete input;
end.

The *delete* procedure is executed when the memory is full or when a solution stored into a cell is too old to be held, that is, the age counter of the stored solution reaches the value 0.

In the first case, when all the cells are full and the system needs to store a new solution produced by the current computation, it has to choose a cell and activate from the outside the *delete* procedure. The cell that the system has to empty is non–deterministically chosen, sending inside of it a message marked with the special symbol F. In the second case, when the counter of a cell reaches the value 0, the symbol F is created within the cell.

The *delete* procedure starts when the message marked with F is sent or is created inside a memory cell. The first operation uses a replicated rewriting rule to forward the message inside the membranes *Sol* and *Input*. Now within these membranes, concurrently, the string message is sent to the membrane labelled with *Empty*, that is a sub–membrane belonging to both membranes (*Sol* and *Input*). When the string passes through the membrane, it changes its polarization from null to positive. Now, inside the membranes *Sol* and *Input* it is possible to apply rules to send both strings into the two membranes *Empty*. Inside the two membranes *Empty*, it is now possible to apply the appropriate rules which delete the input and solution strings. When the procedure has ended, the storage device sends out to the environment all the strings that are no longer useful to the system.

Procedure **retrieve** *(inputE)*
begin
    if *cell contains data* **then**
      Send inputE in Syncro
    Duplicate input;
    Send out input and inputE;
    if **Comparison***(input,inputE)* = *TRUE* **then**
    begin
      Duplicate solution;
      Send out solution;
    end
end.

The *retrieve* procedure is used to search inside the memory cell the solution of the current computation. At the beginning of every computation, the input string that comes from the environment (in the above pseudo–code, this string is called *inputE*) is sent to every cell of the system memory. When this string reaches every cell, the *retrieve* procedure starts. This procedure is executed in parallel in every cell.

The first operation is to check if the cell contains data. If it does, then the input string coming from the environment is sent inside the sub–membrane labelled with *Syncro*; otherwise the procedure ends. If the memory cell contains information, then the procedure goes on duplicating the stored input string. Then, in the same computational step, the input string currently stored into the cell and the one that comes from the environment are sent out from the membrane *Syncro*; hence, the *comparison* procedure is started. The two strings are compared symbol by symbol, in a left to right order. We recall from the definition of the storage device that the alphabet of the system is sorted in increasing order from a_1 to a_k, $k = |V|$. The decrement of a symbol of the alphabet $a_i, 1 < i \leq k$, corresponds to replace it with the symbol a_{i-1}. If the comparison procedure successfully ends, then the solution string is duplicated and sent out, otherwise the *retrieve* procedure ends.

The pseudo–code of the comparison algorithm is the following:

Procedure **comparison** *(inputM,inputE)*
begin
    while *(length(InputM) > 0 AND length(InputE) > 0)*
    begin
      Send *inputM,inputE in Compare;*
      while *first char (InputM) $\neq a_1$ AND first char (InputE) $\neq a_1$*
        Decrease first char value;
      if *first char value(InputM) $= a_1$ AND first char value(InputE) $= a_1$*
        Delete first char;
        Send input,inputE out;
      else *return FALSE;*
    end
    if *(length(InputM) = 0 AND length(InputE) = 0)* **then**
      return TRUE
    else *return FALSE*
end.

The comparison algorithm is the main task executed by the storage device: it is used to compare the input string that comes from the environment (*InputE*) with the string contained within a cell (*InputM*). Just like the *retrieve* procedure, the comparison algorithm is executed in parallel in all memory cells.

The algorithm compares every symbol of the two strings in a left to right order and, in case all these symbols are equal, returns a TRUE value, otherwise it returns FALSE. The procedure to check whether the two strings are equal is realized with the synchronized entrance and going out of the strings through a special membrane. The procedure begins by sending the strings inside the comparison membrane at the same computation step, only if their length is positive. Now, within the comparison membrane, some rules are activated that operate on the leftmost symbol of the strings. These rules decrease the symbol value until it becomes a_1 (that is, the first symbol belonging to V).

It is now possible to use the rule that deletes the symbol a_1 and sends the strings to the outside region; then the procedure proceeds to analyze the second symbol of the strings. The procedure works simultaneously on the two strings, as it needs a method to determine if the current leftmost symbols of the two strings are equal. This is done by exploiting the rules that send out the strings from the comparison membrane: when the system executes the rules in order to delete the first character of the strings, δ and τ operations are executed by the rule that sends out the string *InputM* and the rule that sends out the string *InputE*, respectively.

It is clear that if the two rules are concurrently applied, then the effect of the δ and τ operations is null and nothing happens to the membrane. On the contrary, if the two symbols that the system is comparing are different, then the two rules used to send out the strings are applied at different computation steps (due to the different number of rules executed to decrease the value of the leftmost symbol of the two strings). Applying one of these rules before the other means to use a δ or τ operation before the other one. It is clear that the net effect is to dissolve or to increase the thickness of the *compare* membrane. In both cases, it is impossible to carry on the comparison algorithm, and the system determines that the two strings are different.

For instance, if the system is comparing the strings $s_1 = a_3 a_2 a_2 a_1$ and $s_2 = a_3 a_2 a_2 a_1$, first it sends concurrently s_1 and s_2 into the *compare* membrane, and it applies rules like $a_3 \rightarrow (a_2, here)$ on both strings. Now $s_1 = a_2 a_2 a_2 a_1$ and $s_2 = a_2 a_2 a_2 a_1$, and the procedure goes on by applying rules as: $a_2 \rightarrow (a_1, here)$ so that $s_1 = a_1 a_2 a_2 a_1$ and $s_2 = a_1 a_2 a_2 a_1$. The analysis of the leftmost symbol ends with the concurrent execution of the rule $a_1 \rightarrow (\lambda, out)\delta$ on the first string and $a_1 \rightarrow (\lambda, out)\tau$ on the other string. The effect of the δ and τ operations is then null and the system understands that the two characters are equal and can go on to compare the remaining symbols of the strings. Now $s_1 = a_2 a_2 a_1$ and $s_2 = a_2 a_2 a_1$, and the algorithm continues analyzing the current leftmost symbol. When all symbols have been deleted, the algorithm returns the value TRUE.

Let us denote by $T_m(n)$ the computation time of the P system with memory, by $T_P(n)$ the computation time of the original computational system (which is equal to the computational sub-system) and by $T_c(n)$ the time required to compare an input in a memory cell. From the previous description, it is easy to see that the system with memory works with the following computation time:

- If the solution is not stored in memory, then the time required by the system is the time required by the original computational system plus a (constant) time to store the new solution. Thus, $T_m(n) = O(T_p(n))$.
- If the solution is already stored in memory, then the time required by the system with memory is the minimum time between the time to calculate

the new solution and the time to retrieve such solution from memory; thus, $T_m(n) = min\{T_P(n), T_c(n)\}$. It is easy to see that $T_c(n) = O(n)$, as the time required to compare the input and the string stored in memory is linear. Hence we can conclude that, when a solution is stored in memory, $T_m(n) = O(n)$.

Thus, the proposed system requires a constant time to store new solutions, when the input is not (anymore) known, while it allows to cut down the computation time to a linear one, when the input is stored in memory. Therefore, such systems could be effectively used when many computations are requested where the same input is submitted many times with a high probability.

5   Conclusions

We presented P systems in which solutions of previously executed computations can be stored in memory cells, which are added to a standard computing system. Each time a solution is produced by the computing sub-system, the solution is stored in a memory membrane. When a new input is inserted in the system to start a new computation, we start in parallel the search for the solution in all memory membranes and, at the same time, the computation on that input in the computing sub-system.

   If the solution is found in one memory cell before the computation ends, then a copy of the solution is expelled from that memory membrane; the search in all other memory membranes is stopped, and the same is done with the computing sub-system. In case the solution is not found in any memory membrane, then the computing sub-system produces the new solution, which is stored in a free memory membrane. In order to keep at least one memory membrane available all the time, oldest solutions are deleted from memory when necessary. Such system can be used to speed-up computations, when the output for the same input is requested many times with a high probability within a short time. This happens, for example, in image and vocal processing applications.

   We point out that this is a preliminary approach, which could be developed following different lines; as an example, we could consider the possibility to store not only solutions of previously executed computations, but also to store programs.

   An issue related to the system presented above concerns the size of the memory, i.e., the number of memory cells to use. In the solution we proposed here, the memory cells are static. The number of cells has a direct influence on the efficiency of the computations. A small number of cells reduce the probability to find a solution in memory, and requires further computation steps to free one memory cell and to store the new solution. One possible enhancement of the system could be to consider dynamic memory cells, which can be added and removed during the computation. This could be accomplished by means of membrane division (see [5]) and membrane dissolution (already considered in our systems).

Acknowledgements

This work has been supported by the Italian Ministry of University (MURST), under project FIRB-01 "Biomolecular algorithms to solve NP-Complete problems".

The authors wish to thank the anonymous referees for their helpful suggestions, that allowed us to improve a previous version of this paper.

References

1. V. Manca, C. Martin-Vide, Gh. Păun: On the power of P systems with replicated rewriting. *J. Automata, Languages, and Combinatorics*, 6, 3 (2001), 359-374.
2. C. Martin-Vide, Gh. Păun: String objects in P systems. *Proc. of Algebraic Systems, Formal Languages and Computations Workshop*, Kyoto, 2000, RIMS Kokyuroku, Kyoto Univ., 2000, 161-169.
3. Gh. Păun: Computing with membranes. *J. of Computer and System Sciences*, 61, 1 (2000), 108–143.
4. Gh. Păun: Computing with membranes – A variant: P systems with polarized membranes. *Intern. J. of Foundations of Computer Science*, 11, 1 (2000), 167–182.
5. Gh. Păun: Computing with membranes: Attacking NP–complete problems. In *Unconventional Models of Computation* (I. Antoniou, C.S. Calude, M.J. Dinneen, eds.), Springer, London, 2000, 94-115.
6. Gh. Păun: P systems with active membranes: Attacking NP–complete problems. *Journal of Automata, Languages and Combinatorics*, 6, 1 (2001), 75-90.
7. Gh. Păun: *Membrane Computing. An Introduction*. Springer, Berlin, 2002.
8. Gh. Păun, G. Rozenberg, A. Salomaa: Membrane computing with external output. *Fundamenta Informaticae*, 41, 3 (2000), 259–266. (www.tucs.fi).
9. I. Petre: A normal form for P systems. *Bulletin of EATCS*, 67 (Febr. 1999), 165–172.
10. G. Rozenberg, A. Salomaa, eds.: *Handbook of Formal Languages*. Springer, Berlin, 1997.
11. C. Zandron, C. Ferretti, G. Mauri: Two normal forms for rewriting P systems. *Proc. Third. Intern. Conf. on Universal Machines and Computations*, Chisinau, Moldova, 2001, LNCS 2055 (M. Margenstern, Y. Rogozhin, eds.), Springer, Berlin, 2001, 153-164.
12. C. Zandron, C. Ferretti, G. Mauri: Using membrane features in P systems. *Rom. Journ. of Information Science and Technology*, 4, 1-2 (2001), 241–257.

Algebraic and Coalgebraic Aspects
of Membrane Computing

Gabriel Ciobanu[1] and Viorel Mihai Gontineac[2]

[1] Romanian Academy, Institute of Computer Science,
Blvd. Carol I nr.8, 700505 Iaşi, Romania
`gabriel@iit.tuiasi.ro`
[2] "A.I. Cuza" University, Faculty of Mathematics,
Blvd. Carol I nr.11, 700506 Iaşi, Romania
`gonti@uaic.ro`

Abstract. We introduce and study a new class of automata able to consume and produce multisets; we call them Mealy multiset automata. We are interested in their algebraic and coalgebraic properties. After some useful properties of multisets, we present the notions of bisimulation, observability, and behavior for Mealy multiset automata. We give a characterization of the bisimulation between two Mealy multiset automata, and a result relating their general behavior to their sequential behavior. We describe an endofunctor of the category of *Set* such that a Mealy multiset automaton is a coalgebra of this functor. This functor preserves coproducts, coequalizers, and weak pullbacks. Moreover, the new defined bisimulation is an instance of a more general coalgebraic definition.

1 Introduction

Membrane systems described in [11] represent bio-inspired abstract models. We try to connect membrane computing with the classical theory of Mealy automata. The approach is mainly algebraic, identifying the main operations able to describe membrane systems, and some algebraic rules governing their functioning.

Membrane systems are also called P systems, and they represent a new abstract model of parallel and distributed computing inspired by cell [11]. A cell is divided in various compartments, each compartment with a specific duty, and all of them working simultaneously to accomplish the task of the whole system. The membranes of a P system determine regions where objects and evolution rules can be placed. The objects evolve according to the rules associated with each region, and the regions cooperate in order to maintain the proper behavior of the whole system. It is desirable to find more connections with various fields of computer science, including the classical automata theory.

In this paper we present some algebraic properties of multisets, we present Mealy multiset automata [3], and then we define direct and cascade products of Mealy multiset automata corresponding to their parallel and serial connections. We give a characterization of the bisimulation between two Mealy multiset

R. Freund et al. (Eds.): WMC 2005, LNCS 3850, pp. 181–198, 2006.

automata, and a result relating their general behavior to their sequential behavior. Mealy multiset automata satisfy the criteria of general state based systems, namely their behavior depends on internal states which can be invisible for the user, the system interacts with its environment and it is not necessarily terminating, and it has a set of operations through which this interaction takes place. For these systems, the notions of behavior, observability, bisimulation become interesting and important. We describe two distinct concepts of behavior: the sequential behavior dealing with a specific order of consuming multisets, and a more general behavior dealing with the outcome of a Mealy multiset automaton. The concept of observer could be useful, particularly when we deal with complex structures. The behavior of a system can be defined as the set of all possible sequences of configurations during a computation. Rather than being concerned with the computations resulting in new states, coalgebraic approaches of the dynamical systems focus on the observable behavior; the notion of bisimulation is used to formalize observational indistinguishability.

The remarks regarding a coalgebraic approach, as well as other advantages that we emphasize in this paper provide reasons for using category theory as an appropriate formalism. We define the category of Mealy multiset automata, and we prove that we can view every Mealy multiset automaton as a coalgebra of a suitable endofunctor of the category of sets.

2   On Algebra of Multisets

The evolution rules performed by membranes are multiset operators; the multiset operators are associative and commutative, and have also an identity. In this section we look at multisets, providing some of their algebraic properties.

A *multiset* over an alphabet $A = \{a_1, a_2, ..., a_n\}$ is a mapping $\alpha : A \to \mathbb{N}$. It can be represented by $\{(a_1, \alpha(a_1)), (a_2, \alpha(a_2)), ..., (a_n, \alpha(a_n))\}$. As it is mentioned in [11], a multiset can be also represented as a string $a_1^{\alpha(a_1)} a_2^{\alpha(a_2)} ... a_n^{\alpha(a_n)}$ together with all its permutations. A certain extra computation power of P systems comes from the fact that applying a multiset rule $u \to v$ means that we actually apply at most $|u|!|v|!$ classical rules on strings. The use of multiplicative notation for both multisets and strings may produce confusion when we interplay multiset and strings rules. It is therefore useful to have distinct notations for multiset operations and string operations.

There are various approaches to deal with multiplicities of the elements of a set. Multisets could be viewed as a particular case of the so-called *formal power polynomials* [10] (i.e., a formal power polynomial over a finite alphabet). However almost all the studies in formal power series do not take care of multisets, and we think that a lot of specific properties are lost. Inspired from formal power polynomials, we denote by $\mathbb{N}\langle A \rangle = \{\alpha : A \to \mathbb{N} \mid \alpha \text{ is a mapping}\}$ the set of all multisets on A. The structure of $\mathbb{N}\langle A \rangle$ is mainly an additive one, since we add multiplicities of appearance (in fact, it is induced by the addition in $\mathbb{N}$). This argument is sustained also by the chemical reactions that are the base of the biological modeling. They provide a notation for defining the way a biological system evolves.

If $\alpha, \beta \in \mathbb{N}\langle A \rangle$, then their *sum* is the multiset $(\alpha + \beta) : A \rightarrow \mathbb{N}$ defined by $(\alpha + \beta)(a_i) = \alpha(a_i) + \beta(a_i)$, $i = \overline{1, n}$. Moreover, if we consider the letters from A as multisets, i.e., a_i is given by μ_{a_i}, where $\mu_{a_i} : A \rightarrow \mathbb{N}$, $\mu_{a_i}(a_i) = 1$ and $\mu_{a_i}(a_j) = 0$ for all $j \neq i$, then we can express every multiset $\alpha \in \mathbb{N}\langle A \rangle$ as a linear combination of a_i, i.e., $\alpha = \sum_{i=1}^{n} \alpha(a_i) \cdot a_i$ (see also [3]). We can define an external operation $m\alpha = \sum_{i=1}^{n} (m\alpha(a_i)) \cdot a_i$, for all $m \in \mathbb{N}$ and $\alpha \in \mathbb{N}\langle A \rangle$.

Proposition 1. $\mathbb{N}\langle A \rangle$ *has a structure of $\mathbb{N}$-semimodule (semimodule over the semiring of positive integers).*

If we want to deal with strings, and apply both kinds of rules, we can work with multisets over A^*, or formal power polynomials, $\mathbb{N}\langle A^* \rangle = \{\alpha : A^* \rightarrow \mathbb{N} \mid Supp(\alpha) < \infty \}$, where $Supp(\alpha) = \{w \in A^* \mid \alpha(w) \neq 0\}$ is a support set of the multiset α.

The addition of two multisets over strings is defined like in the usual multiset case, and with respect to "+" we have a structure of commutative monoid. In this manner every multiset over A^* may be viewed as a finite linear combination with natural coefficients, i.e., $\alpha = \sum_{w \in A^*}^{*} \alpha(w) \cdot w$.

The Cauchy product induced by the concatenation of strings is defined by $\alpha \bullet \beta = \sum_{w \in A^*}^{*} \sum_{uv=w} \alpha(u)\beta(v) \cdot w$. Note that the star from $\sum_{w \in A^*}^{*}$ means that this sum is finite. Since concatenation is not commutative, the product is also a non-commutative one. Moreover, $(\mathbb{N}\langle A^* \rangle, \bullet)$ is a non-commutative monoid.

Proposition 2. $(\mathbb{N}\langle A^* \rangle, +, \bullet)$ *is a semiring.*

For other properties of formal power series and related subjects we refer to [10]. We use also the *difference* between two multisets over A or A^*, defined by

$$(\alpha - \beta)(w) = \alpha(w) - \beta(w),$$

for all α, β such that $\alpha \supseteq \beta$ (i.e., $\alpha(w) \geq \beta(w)$ for all w).

It is possible to work also with strings of multisets, i.e., with elements from the free monoid $(\mathbb{N}\langle A \rangle)^*$. It is worth to mention that this non-commutative monoid has a different structure than $\mathbb{N}\langle A^* \rangle$. Therefore it is useful to clarify what are the relationships between $\mathbb{N}\langle A \rangle$, $(\mathbb{N}\langle A \rangle)^*$ and $\mathbb{N}\langle A^* \rangle$.

We consider the canonical inclusion $i : \mathbb{N}\langle A \rangle \rightarrow (\mathbb{N}\langle A \rangle)^*$ and the identity map $id : \mathbb{N}(A) \rightarrow \mathbb{N}(A)$. By the universal property of the free monoid $(\mathbb{N}\langle A \rangle)^*$, we know that there exists a unique homomorphism of monoids $\mathbf{I}_A : (\mathbb{N}\langle A \rangle)^* \rightarrow \mathbb{N}\langle A \rangle$ such that $\mathbf{I}_A \circ i = id$. We also know that $\mathbf{I}_A$ is defined by $\mathbf{I}_A(a_1...a_n) = a_1 + ... + a_n$, where a_i are all from $\mathbf{I}_A$. Since id is onto, it follows that $\mathbf{I}_A$ is onto, and so, applying the isomorphism theorem for monoids, we obtain that $(\mathbb{N}\langle A \rangle)^*/ker\mathbf{I}_A \simeq \mathbb{N}\langle A \rangle$. Moreover, we have the following diagrams revealing the connections between $\mathbb{N}\langle A \rangle$, $(\mathbb{N}\langle A \rangle)^*$ and $\mathbb{N}\langle A^* \rangle$.

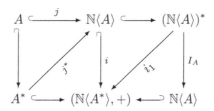

and

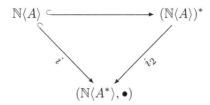

In these diagrams, "$\hookrightarrow$" represents the canonical inclusion, and $j^* : A^* \to \mathbb{N}\langle A \rangle$ represents the unique homomorphism induced by $j : A \to \mathbb{N}\langle A \rangle$.

We mention here the well-known property of universality of the free monoid over a set, in order to explain better the other homomorphisms of our diagram:

Theorem 1. *If Σ is an arbitrary set, Σ^* is the free monoid on Σ and $i : \Sigma \to \Sigma^*$ is the canonical inclusion, then any mapping $f : \Sigma \to M$, where $(M, \star)$ is a monoid, can be uniquely extended to a monoid homomorphism $f^* : \Sigma^* \to (M, \star)$. Moreover, f^* is defined by $f^*(\alpha_1\alpha_2...\alpha_n) = f(\alpha_1) \star f(\alpha_2) \star ... \star f(\alpha_n)$.*

We look back to our diagrams, and we consider $\Sigma = \mathbb{N}\langle A \rangle$ and $f = i : \mathbb{N}\langle A \rangle \hookrightarrow \mathbb{N}\langle A^* \rangle$. We have two cases:

- $(M, \star) = (\mathbb{N}\langle A^* \rangle, +)$. According to the previous theorem, there exists a unique homomorphism $i_1 : (\mathbb{N}\langle A \rangle)^* \to \mathbb{N}\langle A^* \rangle$ extending i. Moreover $i_1(\alpha_1\alpha_2...\alpha_n) = \alpha_1 + \alpha_2 + ... + \alpha_n$, where α_i are from $\mathbb{N}\langle A^* \rangle$. Since i is one-to-one, and its image is $\mathbb{N}\langle A \rangle$, we can conclude that $ker\ i_1 = ker\ \mathbf{I}_A$ and $Im\ i_1 = \mathbb{N}\langle A \rangle$. This means that we do not have any hierarchical relationship between $(\mathbb{N}\langle A^* \rangle, +)$ and $(\mathbb{N}\langle A \rangle)^*$.

- $(M, \star) = (\mathbb{N}\langle A^* \rangle, \bullet)$, where "$\bullet$" is the Cauchy product of formal power polynomials. According to the previous theorem, there exists a unique homomorphism $i_2 : (\mathbb{N}\langle A \rangle)^* \to \mathbb{N}\langle A^* \rangle$ extending i. Moreover $i_2(\alpha_1\alpha_2...\alpha_n) = \alpha_1 \bullet \alpha_2 \bullet ... \bullet \alpha_n$, where α_i are from $\mathbb{N}\langle A^* \rangle$.

We pay a little more attention to the second case because there are a lot of possibilities to confuse the reader. $ker\ i_2 \neq \emptyset$ because $(a + b)(2a + 2b) \neq (2a +$

$2b)(a + b)$ in $(\mathbb{N}\langle A\rangle)^*$, but $(a + b) \bullet (2a + 2b) = (2a + 2b) \bullet (a + b)$ in $\mathbb{N}\langle A^*\rangle$. Once again, we cannot claim any hierarchical relationship between $\mathbb{N}\langle A^*\rangle$ and $(\mathbb{N}\langle A\rangle)^*$. By a hierarchical relationship we understand here any connection of epimorphic or monomorphic type allowing us to express that one structure can be viewed as a substructure of the other.

According to all these considerations, we can say that, when dealing with the *sequential behavior* of P systems, $(\mathbb{N}\langle A\rangle)^*$ is more suitable than $\mathbb{N}\langle A^*\rangle$. The main reason is given by the fact that the Cauchy product of $\mathbb{N}\langle A^*\rangle$ is not able to keep the objects multiplicities; for instance, $2a \bullet 5b \bullet 3(a+b) = 30a \bullet b \bullet (a+b)$ in $\mathbb{N}\langle A^*\rangle$ and, whenever we have $30a \bullet b \bullet (a + b)$, we cannot recover the initial sequences.

3   Mealy Multiset Automata

3.1   Algebraic Description

We introduce and study the notion of *Mealy multiset automata* (MmA). Roughly speaking, an MmA consists of a *storage location* (a *box* for short) in which we place a multiset over an input alphabet, and a device to translate that multiset into a multiset over an output alphabet. MmA works in the following way: we have a detection head able to detect whether a given sub-multiset appears in the multiset available in the box. If the sub-multiset is detected, then it is removed from the box, and MmA inserts a multiset over an output alphabet. MmA stops when no further move is possible. We say that the sub-multiset read by the head was translated to a multiset over the output alphabet.

Definition 1. *A* Mealy multiset automaton *is a construct*

$$\mathcal{A} = (Q, V, O, f, g, q_0),$$

where
  Q is a finite set, the set of states;
  $q_0 \in Q$ is a special state, both initial and final;
  V is a finite set of objects, the input alphabet;
  O is a finite set of objects, the output alphabet, *such that $O \cap V = \emptyset$;*
  $f : Q \times \mathbb{N}\langle V\rangle \to \mathcal{P}(Q)$ is the state-transition *(partial) mapping;*
  $g : Q \times \mathbb{N}\langle V\rangle \to \mathcal{P}(\mathbb{N}\langle O\rangle)$ is the output *(partial) mapping.*

If $|f(q, a)| \leq 1$ we say that $\mathcal{A}$ is *Q-deterministic*, and if $|g(q, a)| \leq 1$ we say that $\mathcal{A}$ is *O-deterministic*. MmA is endowed with a box where it receives a multiset. It begins to process this multiset over V, passing through different *configurations*. It starts with a multiset from $\mathbb{N}\langle V\rangle$, and ends with a multiset from $\mathbb{N}\langle V \cup O\rangle$.

Definition 2. *A* configuration *of $\mathcal{A}$ is a triple $(q, \alpha, \bar{\beta})$ where $q \in Q$, $\alpha \in \mathbb{N}\langle V\rangle$, and $\bar{\beta} \in \mathbb{N}\langle O\rangle$. We say that a configuration $(q, \alpha, \bar{\beta})$ passes to $(s, \alpha - a, \bar{\beta} + \bar{b})$ (or, that we have a transition between these configurations) if there is a $a \subseteq \alpha$ such that $s \in f(q, a)$, and $\bar{b} \in g(q, a)$. We denote this by $(q, \alpha, \bar{\beta}) \vdash (s, \alpha - a, \bar{\beta} + \bar{b})$. We also denote by $\vdash^*$ the reflexive and transitive closure of $\vdash$.*

Remark 1. We could alternatively define a configuration to be a pair (q, α) where $\alpha \in \mathbb{N} \langle V \cup O \rangle$, and the transition relation is $(q, \alpha) \vdash (s, \alpha - a + \bar{b})$, with the same conditions as above.

Definition 3. *A multiset $\alpha \in \mathbb{N} \langle V \rangle$ is said to be a* totally consumed multiset *(tc-multiset) for $\mathcal{A}$ if, starting from the configuration $(q_0, \alpha, \varepsilon)$, MmA can pass through various configurations till it arrives in a configuration $(q_0, \varepsilon, \bar{\beta})$ (i.e., $(q_0, \alpha, \varepsilon) \vdash^* (q_0, \varepsilon, \bar{\beta})$).*

A multiset $\alpha \in \mathbb{N} \langle V \rangle$ is said to be a consumed multiset *(c-multiset) for $\mathcal{A}$ if, starting from a configuration (q, α, ε), MmA can pass through various configurations till it arrives in a configuration $(s, \varepsilon, \bar{\beta})$ (i.e., $(q, \alpha, \varepsilon) \vdash^* (s, \varepsilon, \bar{\beta})$).*

In both cases, we say that α is entirely translated to $\bar{\beta}$. *In all the other situations we say that $\alpha \in \mathbb{N} \langle V \rangle$ is* partially consumed *(pc-multiset), or it is partially translated.*

We denote by $TC(\mathcal{A})$ the set of all tc-multisets of $\mathcal{A}$, by $C(\mathcal{A})$ the set of all c-multisets of $\mathcal{A}$, and by $PC(\mathcal{A})$ the set of all pc-multisets of $\mathcal{A}$. It is clear that $TC(A) \subseteq C(A)$.

Theorem 2. *$TC(\mathcal{A})$ is a $\mathbb{N}$-sub-semimodule of $\mathbb{N} \langle V \rangle$. Moreover, if we define $\mathcal{A}(\alpha) = \bar{\beta}$ for all $\alpha \in TC(\mathcal{A})$ with $(q_0, \alpha, \varepsilon) \vdash^* (q_0, \varepsilon, \bar{\beta})$, we may view $\mathcal{A}$ as an $\mathbb{N}$-homomorphism from $TC(\mathcal{A})$ to $\mathbb{N} \langle O \rangle$.*

Remark 2. In general, $C(\mathcal{A})$ it is not an $\mathbb{N}$-sub-semimodule of $\mathbb{N} \langle V \rangle$. Let us consider $\alpha, \alpha' \in C(\mathcal{A})$. We have $(q, \alpha, \varepsilon) \vdash^* (q', \varepsilon, \bar{\beta})$ and $(s, \alpha', \varepsilon) \vdash^* (s', \varepsilon, \bar{\beta}')$; therefore $(q, \alpha + \alpha', \varepsilon) \vdash^* (q', \alpha', \bar{\beta})$, and it is possible the automaton cannot go further (for instance, we may have $f(q', a') = \emptyset$ for all $a' \subseteq \alpha'$).

It is possible for two multisets $\alpha, \alpha' \in \mathbb{N} \langle V \rangle$ to have their sum in $TC(\mathcal{A})$, even they are not in $TC(\mathcal{A})$. Let us give an example:

Example 1. Consider $\mathcal{A} = (\{s_0, s_1, s_2\}, \{a, b, c\}, \{d, e, l\}, f, g, s_0)$ with

– $f(s_0, 2a) = \{s_1, s_2\}$, $f(s_1, b) = s_0$, $f(s_2, c) = s_0$ for the transition function,
– $g(s_0, 2a) = e$ if $f(s_0, 2a) = s_1$, $g(s_0, 2a) = d$ if $f(s_0, 2a) = s_2$, $g(s_1, b) = e$, $g(s_2, c) = l$ for the output mapping.

It is easy to see that $TC(\mathcal{A}) = \{m(2a + b) + n(2a + c) \mid m, n \in \mathbb{N}\}$. The set of tc-translations is $\mathcal{A}(TC(\mathcal{A})) = \{2me + n(d + l) \mid m, n \in \mathbb{N}\}$. We have also that $a + b$ and a are neither in $TC(\mathcal{A})$, nor in $C(\mathcal{A})$, but their sum belongs to $TC(\mathcal{A})$. Similarly, $6a + b, 2a + 3c \notin TC(\mathcal{A})$, $6a + b, 2a + 3c \in PC(\mathcal{A})$, and their sum is in $TC(\mathcal{A})$.

Remark 3. We do not provide a representation for MmA as a graph like in [5], simply because graphs are strongly related with sequencing and do not permit to express facts like "if we can consume two multisets a and b, and their sum is available in the box, it does not matter the order of consuming them". This is an important difference between MmA and weighted automata [10] (or K-Σ automata [7]).

From now on, we restrict ourselves to the *deterministic* case, i.e., our MmA's are both Q-deterministic and O-deterministic. Moreover, we do not include an initial state in our definition, simply because there is no reason to focus attention to one particular state. In the classical theory of automata, initial states play a certain role, for instance in the definition of the sequential composition of two automata, where all the terminating states of the first automaton are connected to the initial state of the second automaton. Without specifying the initial set of an MmA, all the considerations are valid, except the tc-multiset notion; we consider now only c-multisets and pc-multisets associated with an arbitrary state q.

Definition 4. *Given two MmA's* $\mathcal{A} = (Q, V, O, f, g)$ *and* $\mathcal{A}' = (Q', V, O, f', g')$, *a function* $h : Q \to Q'$ *is called a* morphism *from* $\mathcal{A}$ *to* $\mathcal{A}'$ *if the following conditions*

$$h(f(q, a)) = f'(h(q), a) \text{ and } g(q, a) = g'(h(q), a)$$

are satisfied for all $q \in Q$, *and for all* $a \in \mathbb{N} \langle V \rangle$.

If $h : Q \to Q'$ is a morphism between $\mathcal{A}$ and $\mathcal{A}'$, we denote this by $h : \mathcal{A} \to \mathcal{A}'$. Let $h : \mathcal{A} \to \mathcal{A}'$ be a morphism, and $(q, \alpha, \bar{\beta})$ a configuration of $\mathcal{A}$. Let us suppose that we have the transition $(q, \alpha, \bar{\beta}) \vdash (s, \alpha - a, \bar{\beta} + \bar{b})$. This means that $s = f(q, a), \bar{b} = g(q, a)$. We get that $h(s) = h(f(q, a)) = f'(h(q), a)$, and $\bar{b} = g(q, a) = g'(h(q), a)$, and so we have $(h(q), \alpha, \bar{\beta}) \vdash (h(s), \alpha - a, \bar{\beta} + \bar{b})$. Therefore we have the following result:

Theorem 3. *Let* $h : \mathcal{A} \to \mathcal{A}'$ *be a morphism of MmA's. If the multiset* $\alpha \in \mathbb{N} \langle V \rangle$ *is a c/pc-multiset for* $\mathcal{A}$, *then* α *has the same nature for* $\mathcal{A}'$.

This result underlines that if h is a morphism between two MmA's, then it is not possible to have α both as a pc-multiset for $\mathcal{A}$, and as a c-multiset for $\mathcal{A}'$, i.e., we get a kind of invariance property under morphisms for $C(\mathcal{A})$ and $PC(\mathcal{A})$.

3.2 Series and Parallel Connections

The cascade product. This is a way to make a series connection in the case of Mealy automata, and provides also some results in decompositions of such machines in irreducible ones. Even we are not prepared yet to provide such a decomposition result (this involves a lot of algebra for multisets), we define the cascade product of two MmA's.

Let $\mathcal{A} = (Q, V, O, f, g)$ and $\mathcal{A}' = (Q', V', O', f', g')$ two MmA's. In order to link them by a series connection, we need a multiset mapping to link the output of one of them to the input of the other. This can be done using an $\mathbb{N}$-homomorphism from $\mathbb{N} \langle O' \rangle$ to $\mathbb{N} \langle V \rangle$; this homomorphism can be obtained as usual by using a mapping from O' to V. We denote this homomorphism by $\Lambda : \mathbb{N} \langle O' \rangle \to \mathbb{N} \langle V \rangle$, and we get a mapping $\Omega : Q' \times \mathbb{N} \langle V' \rangle \to \mathbb{N} \langle V \rangle$, defined by $\Omega(q', a') = \Lambda(g'(q', a'))$. This mapping gives us *the cascade product induced by* Ω:

$$\mathcal{A} \Omega \mathcal{A}' = (Q \times Q', V', O, f^{\Omega}, g^{\Omega}),$$

where $f^{\Omega} : (Q \times Q') \times \mathbb{N} \langle V' \rangle \to Q \times Q'$, $g^{\Omega} : (Q \times Q') \times \mathbb{N} \langle V' \rangle \to O$ are given by $f^{\Omega}((q, q'), a') = (f(q, \Omega(q', a')), f'(q', a'))$, and $g^{\Omega}((q, q'), a') = g(q, \Omega(q', a'))$ for all $a' \in \mathbb{N} \langle V' \rangle$, $(q, q') \in Q \times Q'$.

The transition relation becomes $((q, q'), \alpha', \bar{\beta}) \vdash ((s, s'), \alpha' - a', \bar{\beta} + \bar{b})$ if there is $a' \subseteq \alpha'$ such that $(s, s') \in f^{\Omega}((q, q'), a')$, $\bar{b} \in g^{\Omega}((q, q'), a')$, where $a', \alpha' \in \mathbb{N} \langle V' \rangle$, $(q, q') \in Q \times Q'$, and $\bar{\beta} \in \mathbb{N} \langle O \rangle$.

We can alternatively define the transition relation by

$$((q, q'), \alpha' + \bar{\beta}) \vdash ((s, s'), \alpha' - a' + \bar{\beta} + \bar{b})$$

if there is $a' \subseteq \alpha'$ such that $s \in f(q, \Lambda(g'(q', a')))$, $s' \in f'(q', a')$, and $\bar{b} \in g(q, \Lambda(g'(q', a')))$, where $a', \alpha' \in \mathbb{N} \langle V' \rangle$, $(q, q') \in Q \times Q'$, and $\bar{\beta} \in \mathbb{N} \langle O \rangle$.

As we already mention in [3], in order to simulate an elementary membrane, we also need a kind of direct product of MmA's. We consider only a restricted variant because the input alphabets (and also the output alphabets) are the same for all MmA's involved.

Restricted direct product. Let $\mathcal{A}_i = (Q_i, V, O, f_i, g_i)$ be a finite family of Mealy multiset automata, and B_i their corresponding boxes, $i = \overline{1, n}$. We can connect them in *parallel* in order to obtain the *restricted direct product* of $\mathcal{A}_i$ defined by $\mathcal{A} = \bigwedge_{i=1}^{n} \mathcal{A}_i = (\times_{i=1}^{n} Q_i, V, O, f, g)$, where:

- $f((q_1, q_2, ..., q_n), a) = (f_1(q_1, a), f_2(q_2, a), ..., f_n(q_n, a))$;
- $g((q_1, q_2, ..., q_n), a) = (g_1(q_1, a), g_2(q_2, a), ..., g_n(q_n, a))$;
- the box B of $\mathcal{A}$ is the disjoint union $\bigsqcup_{i=1}^{n} B_i$;
- a *configuration* of $\mathcal{A}$ is a triple $(q, \alpha, \bar{\beta})$, where $q = (q_1, q_2, ..., q_n)$, $\alpha = (\alpha_1, \alpha_2, ..., \alpha_n)$, and $\bar{\beta} = (\bar{\beta}_1, \bar{\beta}_2, ..., \bar{\beta}_n)$;
- the *(asynchronous) transition relation* of $\mathcal{A}$: $(q, \alpha, \bar{\beta}) \vdash (s, \alpha - a, \bar{\beta} + \bar{b})$ if and only if there is at least an $i \in \overline{1, n}$ such that $s_i \in f_i(q_i, a_i)$, and $\bar{b}_i \in g_i(q_i, a_i)$, where $a = (a_1, a_2, ..., a_n)$, and $\bar{b} = (\bar{b}_1, \bar{b}_2, ..., \bar{b}_n)$.

3.3   Bisimulation and Observability

The **bisimulation** relation between states of a transition system was originally introduced by Park and Milner, in order to formalize the behavioral equivalence of concurrent processes.

Definition 5. *A bisimulation between two MmA's $\mathcal{A} = (Q, V, O, f, g, q_0)$ and $\mathcal{A}' = (Q', V, O, f', g', q'_0)$ is a relation $R \subseteq Q \times Q'$ such that for all $a \in \mathbb{N} \langle V \rangle$, if qRq', then $g(q, a) = g'(q', a)$ and $f(q, a)Rf'(q', a)$.*

It can be verified without difficulty that union and (relational) composition of bisimulations are bisimulations again. We write $q \sim q'$ whenever there exists a bisimulation R with qRq'. This relation is the union of all bisimulations and, therewith, the largest bisimulation. The largest bisimulation on the same automaton, again denoted by $\sim$, is called the *bisimilarity* relation, and it is an equivalence relation.

Two states related by a bisimulation relation are *observationally indistinguishable* in the sense that

1. they provide the same output, and
2. performing the same experiment on both states, we get states that are indistinguishable again.

We can relate the notion of MmA morphism to that of bisimulation [4].

Theorem 4. *A function $h : Q \to Q'$ is a morphism from $\mathcal{A}$ to $\mathcal{A}'$ if and only if its graph relation $G(h) = \{(q, h(q)) \mid q \in Q\}$ is a bisimulation.*

Regarding the **observability**, we can remark that one of the main features of our Mealy multiset automata is that we have an intrinsic *observer* given by the *output mapping*. As we can see in our previous example, there are transitions that cannot be observed from outside, i.e., transitions for which the output mapping is the empty multiset ε.

A state q is *observable* from an other state s if there exist a multiset α such that $(s, \alpha, \varepsilon) \vdash (q_1, \alpha - a_1, b_1) \vdash (q_2, \alpha - a_1 - a_2, b_1 + b_2) \vdash ... \vdash (q_n, \alpha - a_1 - ... - a_n, b_1 + ... + b_n)$, $q_n = q$ and $b_n \neq \varepsilon$.

One of the main differences between MmA and the classical automata is given by the possibility of the detection head of MmA to choose, in a given state, various sub-multisets from the input multiset. This means that for the same input multiset, we can have various possibilities to go further from a given state. This remark emphasize the important role played by the output mapping as an observer.

3.4   Behavior

Behavior is often appropriately viewed as consisting of both dynamics and observations, namely state-transition and output mappings. The main advantage of an MmA is given by its output function playing an important role in observability (we do not construct other machinery to describe the behavior of our MmA).

Definition 6. *Let $\mathcal{A} = (Q, V, O, f, g)$ be a Mealy multiset automaton. The general behavior of a state $q \in Q$ is a function $\mathbf{beh}(q)$ that assigns to every input multiset $\alpha \in \mathbb{N} \langle V \rangle$ the output multiset obtained after consuming α.*

When talking about behavior of a state, we have to consider a specific order of consuming multisets in terms of strings of multisets. A certain feature for MmA is that its behavior is always finite because we cannot go further after consuming the given multiset. On the other hand, since the outputs go back into the box and it can become larger, it is possible that we cannot track the sequence of intermediate states. If we are interested only on the outcome of our machine, we should not take care of the intermediate states, but if the input multiset is partially consumed (i.e., is a pc-multiset), it should be of interest to know the state where the MmA arrives, in order to (possibly) provide the box with a supplementary multiset, or in order to make the initial multiset a consumed multiset. These considerations lead us to the following notion.

Definition 7. Let $\mathcal{A} = (Q, V, O, f, g)$ be a Mealy multiset automaton. The sequential behavior of a state $q \in Q$ is a function $\mathbf{seqbeh}(q)$ that assigns to every multiset $\alpha \in \mathbb{N}\langle V \rangle$ all the sequences of the output multisets obtained during consuming α.

Example 2. Suppose that we have the following sequence of transitions $(q, \alpha, \varepsilon) \vdash (q_1, \alpha - a_1, b_1) \vdash (q_2, \alpha - a_1 - a_2, b_1 + b_2) \vdash \ldots \vdash (q_n, \alpha - a_1 - \ldots - a_n, b_1 + \ldots + b_n)$ and suppose that this MmA stops. Then $\mathbf{beh}(q)(\alpha) = b_1 + \ldots + b_n$, and $\mathbf{seqbeh}(q)(\alpha)$ contains $b_1 \ldots b_n$. Moreover, $b_1 + \ldots + b_n$ belongs to $\mathbb{N}\langle O \rangle$, while $b_1 \ldots b_n$ belongs to $(\mathbb{N}\langle O \rangle)^*$, the free monoid on $\mathbb{N}\langle O \rangle$.

We consider the canonical inclusion $i : \mathbb{N}\langle O \rangle \rightarrow (\mathbb{N}\langle O \rangle)^*$, and the identity $id : \mathbb{N}\langle O \rangle \rightarrow \mathbb{N}\langle O \rangle$. As we have already mentioned, there exists a unique homomorphism of monoids $\mathbf{I}_O : (\mathbb{N}\langle O \rangle)^* \rightarrow \mathbb{N}\langle O \rangle$ such that $\mathbf{I}_O \circ i = id$. This homomorphism $\mathbf{I}_O$ is defined by $\mathbf{I}_O(b_1 \ldots b_n) = b_1 + \ldots + b_n$. Since id is onto, it follows that $\mathbf{I}_O$ is onto, and by applying the isomorphism theorem for monoids, we have that $(\mathbb{N}\langle O \rangle)^*/ker\mathbf{I}_O \simeq \mathbb{N}\langle O \rangle$. Moreover, $\mathbf{I}_O \circ (\mathbf{seqbeh})(q) = \mathbf{beh}(q)$.

Example 3. Consider $\mathcal{A} = (\{s_0, s_1, s_2, s_3\}, \{a, b\}, \{c, d\}, f, g)$ with the transition function f given by $f(s_0, 2a) = s_1$, $f(s_0, a) = s_2$, $f(s_1, 2b) = s_2$, $f(s_0, 2b) = s_3$, $f(s_0, 3b) = s_2$, $f(s_1, 2a + b) = s_3$, $f(s_1, a) = s_3$, $f(s_2, a) = s_3$, $f(s_2, b) = s_1$, and the output function g given by $g(s_0, 2a) = 2c$, $g(s_0, a) = c$, $g(s_1, 2b) = d$, $g(s_0, 2b) = 2c + d$, $g(s_0, 3b) = \varepsilon$, $g(s_1, 2a + b) = c$, $g(s_1, a) = \varepsilon$, $g(s_2, a) = \varepsilon$, $g(s_2, b) = c$, where ε corresponds to the transitions that cannot be "viewed" by an external observer. Then $\mathbf{seqbeh}(s_0)(3a + 2b)$ contains $(2c)d\varepsilon$ for the sequence of transitions $(s_0, 3a + 2b, \varepsilon) \vdash (s_1, a + 2b, 2c) \vdash (s_2, a, 2c + d) \vdash (s_3, \varepsilon, 2c + d)$. The same input multiset can also be consumed in the following ways: $(s_0, 3a + 2b, \varepsilon) \vdash (s_1, a + 2b, 2c) \vdash (s_0, 2b, 2c) \vdash (s_3, \varepsilon, 2c + d)$, or
$(s_0, 3a + 2b, \varepsilon) \vdash (s_2, 2a + 2b, d) \vdash (s_1, 2a + b, c + d) \vdash (s_3, \varepsilon, 2c + d)$.

Hence $\mathbf{seqbeh}(s_0)(3a + 2b) = \{(2c)d, dcc\}$. Therefore, independent of the consuming sequences, the general behavior of s_0 is $\mathbf{beh}(s_0)(3a + 2b) = 2c + d$.

It is interesting to remark that our bisimulation preserves $\mathbf{seqbeh}$. If q, q' are two bisimilar states, i.e., $q \sim q'$, then they have the same sequential behavior $\mathbf{seqbeh}(q) = \mathbf{seqbeh}(q')$. This implies that they also have the same behavior $\mathbf{beh}(q) = \mathbf{beh}(q')$. Since the reciprocal statement is not true, we can define a weaker equivalence relation, namely

$$q \approx q' \Leftrightarrow \mathbf{beh}(q) = \mathbf{beh}(q')$$

We have the following result:

Proposition 3. $q \approx q'$ if and only if $(\mathbf{seqbeh}(q), \mathbf{seqbeh}(q')) \in ker\mathbf{I}_O$ for all $\alpha \in \mathbb{N}\langle V \rangle$.

Since this weaker equivalence relation over states is given by the general behavior $\mathbf{beh}$, we can say that this relation is independent of the order of consuming resources from the box, and we call it an *output conservative equivalence*. The importance of this equivalence is given mainly by the idea of consuming and producing *resources* by over passing the sequential framework represented by **seqbeh**. This problem appears to be of interest when we consider the concurrent processes competing for resources.

4   Category Theory and Mealy Multiset Automata

The aim of this section is to explore some of the current ideas from category theory that enable various mathematical descriptions of hierarchical structures, and membrane systems in particular. The abstraction level of category theory allows us to work with objects and morphisms without considering their internal structure. This seems to be an appropriate setting for membrane computing. The categorical approach is based on the definition of a category whose objects model system components, and whose morphisms represent how systems are composed, simulated, refined, etc. Complex systems can be modeled as diagrams in category theory. This approach is best suited for modeling systems based on shared resources (see also eMMA of [3, 4]), sharing being expressed through morphisms.

4.1   Categories and Functors

Definition 8. *A category* $\mathcal{C}$ *consists of: – a class of* objects;

– *a class of* morphisms *(arrows)*;
– *for each morphism* f, *one object as* domain, *and another as* codomain *of* f;
– *for each object* A, *an* identity morphism id_A;
– *for each pair of morphisms* $f : A \rightarrow B$ *and* $g : B \rightarrow C$ *(cod(f)=dom(g))*, *a composite morphism* $g \circ f : A \rightarrow C$. *This composition have to satisfy the following rules:*
– Associativity: *For each set of morphisms* $f : A \rightarrow B, g : B \rightarrow C, h : C \rightarrow D$,
$$h \circ (g \circ f) = (h \circ g) \circ f.$$
– Identity: *For each morphism* $f : A \rightarrow B$, $f \circ id_A = f$, $id_B \circ f = f$.

The *functorial character* of a categorial construction is important for at least two reasons:
– working within categories, we make explicit the morphisms which correspond to appropriate notions of simulation or refinement between systems;
– functors act on objects and behave consistently on their simulations, preserving them (moreover, when functors are adjoint, they preserve limits or colimits, yielding good compositional properties, since complex systems can be expressed as (co)limits of their simpler components).

Definition 9. *Given two categories* $\mathcal{C}$ *and* $\mathcal{D}$, *a functor* between them $F : \mathcal{C} \rightarrow \mathcal{D}$ *is a pair* $F = (F_{ob}, F_{mor})$, *where:*
$F_{ob} : Ob(\mathcal{C}) \rightarrow Ob(\mathcal{D})$ *the object mapping;*

$F_{mor} : Mor\mathcal{C}(A, B) \rightarrow Mor\mathcal{D}(F_{ob}(A), F_{ob}(B))$ *the* morphism mapping, *such that if* $f : A \rightarrow B$ *then* $F_{mor}(f) : F_{ob}(A) \rightarrow F_{ob}(B)$, *satisfying the following axioms:*

Compositionality: $F_{mor}(gf) = F_{mor}(g)F_{mor}(f)$,
Identity: $F_{mor}(id_A) = id_{F_{mor}(A)}$.

Interesting examples of categories in computer science include the category $\mathcal{MAUT}$ of Mealy automata, and the category $\mathcal{BEH}$ of behaviors. We emphasize the functorial connection between the category of Mealy automata and the category of their behaviors.

Example 4. Let $\mathcal{A} = (Q, V, O, f, g, s_0)$ be a Mealy automaton with a distinguished state s_0, where Q, V, O are the sets of states, input symbols and output symbols, respectively; f is the transition function, and g is the output function. We denote, as usual, with the same letters f and g the extension of f from $Q \times V$ to $Q \times V^*$, and the extension of g from $Q \times O$ to $Q \times O^*$. For every state we can define $beh_A : V^* \rightarrow O^*$ by $beh_A(w) = g(s_0, w)$. We consider now the following categories:

$\mathcal{MAUT}$: the category of Mealy automata. It has Mealy automata as objects, and a morphism $\alpha : \mathcal{A} \rightarrow \mathcal{A}'$ is a triple $(\alpha_1, \alpha_2, \alpha_3)$, $\alpha_1 : Q \rightarrow Q'$, $\alpha_1(s_0) = s_0'$, $\alpha_2 : V \rightarrow V'$ and $\alpha_3 : O \rightarrow O'$ such that $\alpha_1(f(s, a)) = f'(\alpha_1(s), \alpha_2(a))$ and $\alpha_3(g(s, a)) = g'(\alpha_1(s), \alpha_2(a))$.

$\mathcal{BEH}$: the category of behaviors. It has triples $(V, O, beh : V \rightarrow O)$ as objects, and a morphism $\beta : (V, O, beh) \rightarrow (V', O', beh')$ is a pair (β_1, β_2), $\beta_1 : V \rightarrow V'$, $\beta_2 : O \rightarrow O'$ such that $\beta_2 \circ beh = beh' \circ \beta_1$.

We can define a functor $Beh : \mathcal{MAUT} \rightarrow \mathcal{BEH}$:
  – on objects: $Beh(\mathcal{A}) = (V, O, beh_A)$,
  – on morphisms: if $\alpha : \mathcal{A} \rightarrow \mathcal{A}'$ is a morphism in $\mathcal{MAUT}$, then $Beh(\alpha) = (\alpha_2, \alpha_3)$.

We can also organize Mealy multiset automata as a category.

Proposition 4. *For fixed alphabets V and O, the collection of Mealy multiset automata together with their morphisms form a category denoted by $\mathcal{MA}_{VO}$.*

More notions and results of the category theory are available in [2]. As we have already explained, the lack of a comprehensive approach for the algebra of multisets, together with the necessity of some mechanisms to connect and compose several MmA's, lead us to initiate a study of the category $\mathcal{MA}_{VO}$. We have two possible approaches to prove the existence of some usual constructions (e.g., limits and colimits like (co)products, pushout, pullback, (co)equalizers) in the category of Mealy multiset automata. We can either use the classical way, i.e., we can construct step by step everything we need, consuming a lot of effort and without visible benefits, or, more elegant, we can use the categorial coalgebraic point of view for transition-like systems. Moreover, this latter approach permits us to work easier with concepts like bisimulation, bisimilarity, and behavior.

4.2   Short Introduction to Coalgebra

We introduce briefly some of the basic notions of coalgebra, homomorphism, and bisimulation relation; see [12] for more details.

Let $\mathcal{C}$ be a category, and $F : \mathcal{C} \to \mathcal{C}$ be a functor. An F-*coalgebra* or F-*system* is a pair (S, α_S) consisting of an object S and a morphism $\alpha_S : S \to F(S)$. The object S is called the *carrier* of the system, also to be called the *set of states*; the morphism α_S is called the F-*transition structure* of the system. When no explicit reference to the functor is needed, we simply speak of system and transition structure. Moreover, when no explicit reference to the transition structure is needed, we often use S instead of (S, α_S).

Definition 10. *Let* (S, α_S) *and* (T, α_T) *be two* F-*systems, where* F *is again an arbitrary functor. A morphism* $f : S \to T$ *is a* homomorphism *of* F-*systems, or* F-*homomorphism, if* $F(f) \circ \alpha_S = \alpha_T \circ f$, *i.e., the following diagram is commutative:*

$$
\begin{array}{ccc}
S & \xrightarrow{\ \alpha_S\ } & F(S) \\
{\scriptstyle f}\downarrow & & \downarrow{\scriptstyle F(f)} \\
T & \xrightarrow{\ \alpha_T\ } & F(T)
\end{array}
$$

Intuitively, homomorphisms are functions that preserve and reflect F-transition structures. We sometimes write $f : (S, \alpha_S) \to (T, \alpha_T)$ to express that f is an F-homomorphism. The identity function of an F-system (S, α_S) is a homomorphism, and the composition of two homomorphisms is again a homomorphism. Thus the collection of all F-systems together with F-system homomorphisms is a category, denoted by $\mathcal{C}_F$.

Definition 11. *Let* F *be an arbitrary functor* $F : \mathcal{C} \to \mathcal{C}$ *and let* $(S, \alpha_S), (T, \alpha_T)$ *be* F-*coalgebras. An object* (R, α_R) *from* $\mathcal{C}_F$, *together with two morphisms* $p : R \to S, q : R \to T$ *(called* projections*), is called a* bisimulation *between* (S, α_S) *and* (T, α_T) *if* p *and* q *are also homomorphisms of* F-*coalgebras, i.e.,* $F(p) \circ \alpha_R = \alpha_S \circ p$ *and* $F(q) \circ \alpha_R = \alpha_T \circ q$. *See also the following diagram:*

$$
\begin{array}{ccccc}
S & \xleftarrow{\ p\ } & R & \xrightarrow{\ q\ } & T \\
{\scriptstyle \alpha_S}\downarrow & & \downarrow{\scriptstyle \alpha_R} & & \downarrow{\scriptstyle \alpha_T} \\
F(S) & \xleftarrow[F(p)]{} & F(R) & \xrightarrow[F(q))]{} & F(T)
\end{array}
$$

A special case is obtained when $\mathcal{C}$ is *Set*, the category of sets. For a comprehensive approach we refer to [12]. We mention here only some facts. A subset $R \subseteq S \times T$ of the Cartesian product of S and T is called an F-*bisimulation* between S and T if there exists an F-transition structure $\alpha_R : R \to F(R)$ such that the projections from R to S and T are F-homomorphisms. We say that (R, α_R) is a bisimulation between (S, α_S) and (T, α_T). If $(S, \alpha_S) = (T, \alpha_T)$, then (R, α_R) is called a *bisimulation* on (S, α_S). A *bisimulation equivalence* is a bisimulation that is also an equivalence relation. Two states s and t are called *bisimilar* if there exists a bisimulation R with $(s, t) \in R$. According to [12], a fundamental relationship between homomorphisms and bisimulations is given by

Theorem 5. *Let (S, α_S) and (T, α_T) be two systems. $f : S \to T$ is a homomorphism if and only if its graph $G(f)$ is a bisimulation between (S, α_S) and (T, α_T).*

5   Mealy Multiset Automata as Coalgebras

Coalgebra can be understood as a theory that deals with behavioral aspects of dynamic systems in a rather wide sense. Behavior is often appropriately viewed as consisting of both dynamics and observations, which have to do with change of states and partial access to states, respectively. Bisimulation was introduced into the world of coalgebra by Aczel and Mendler [1], who gave a categorical definition of bisimulation that applies to arbitrary coalgebras. Let us consider two alphabets V and O and the functor $F : Set \to Set$ defined by

- $F(Q) = (Q \times \mathbb{N}\langle O \rangle)^{\mathbb{N}\langle V \rangle}$
- if $h : Q \to Q'$ is a mapping (i.e., morphism in *Set*), then $F(h) : (Q \times \mathbb{N}\langle O \rangle)^{\mathbb{N}\langle V \rangle} \to (Q' \times \mathbb{N}\langle O \rangle)^{\mathbb{N}\langle V \rangle}$ is defined by $F(h)(k) = \langle h, id_{\mathbb{N}\langle O \rangle} \rangle \circ k$

Definition 12. *A coalgebra for F is a set Q together with a morphism $\alpha_Q : Q \to F(Q) = (Q \times \mathbb{N}\langle O \rangle)^{\mathbb{N}\langle V \rangle}$.*

It is obvious that, starting from a coalgebra (Q, α_Q), we can obtain an MmA $\mathcal{A} = (Q, V, O, f, g)$ where $f(q, a)$ is the first component of $\alpha_Q(q)(a)$, and $g(q, a)$ is the second component of $\alpha_Q(q)(a)$. Of course, if $\mathcal{A} = (Q, V, O, f, g)$ is an MmA, we can obtain a coalgebra for F with $\alpha_Q : Q \to F(Q) = (Q \times \mathbb{N}\langle O \rangle)^{\mathbb{N}\langle V \rangle}$ defined by $\alpha_Q(q)(a) = (f(q, a), g(q, a))$.

Let $h : (Q, \alpha_Q) \to (Q', \alpha_{Q'})$ be an F-morphism, i.e., $F(h) \circ \alpha_Q = \alpha_{Q'} \circ h$, and $\mathcal{A} = (Q, V, O, f, g)$, $\mathcal{A}' = (Q', V, O, f', g')$ their attached MmA's. This implies that for all $q \in Q$ and for all $a \in \mathbb{N}\langle V \rangle$ we have $(F(h) \circ \alpha_Q)(q)(a) = (\alpha_{Q'} \circ h)(q)(a) \Leftrightarrow F(h)(\alpha_Q(q))(a) = \alpha_{Q'}(h(q))(a) \Leftrightarrow \langle h, id_{\mathbb{N}\langle O \rangle} \rangle (\alpha_Q(q)(a)) = (f'(h(s), a), g'(h(s), a)) \Leftrightarrow \langle h, id_{\mathbb{N}\langle O \rangle} \rangle (f(q, a), g(q, a)) = (f'(h(q), a), g'(h(q), a)) \Leftrightarrow (h(f(q, a)), g(q, a)) = (f'(h(s), a), g'(h(s), a))$.

Proposition 5. *$h : (Q, \alpha_Q) \to (Q', \alpha_{Q'})$ is an F-morphism if and only if $h : Q \to Q'$ is a morphism between their associated automata.*

It can be proved that the classical MmA bisimulation is an instance of the general coalgebraic definition.

Theorem 6. *If $R \subseteq Q \times Q'$ is an F-bisimulation between coalgebras (Q, α_Q) and $(Q', \alpha_{Q'})$, then R is a bisimulation between their corresponding MmA's $\mathcal{A} = (Q, V, O, f, g,)$ and $\mathcal{A}' = (Q', V, O, f', g',)$.*

If we want to prove statements like: "the union of a collection of bisimulations is again a bisimulation"; "the quotient of a system with respect to a bisimulation equivalence is again a system"; and: "the kernel of a homomorphism is a bisimulation equivalence" we need three basic constructions in the category of F-systems: coproducts (sums), coequalizers, and (weak) pullbacks. The first two constructions exist according to Theorem 4.2 from [12]:

Theorem 7. *Let* $F : Set \rightarrow Set$ *be any functor. In the category* Set_F *of* F-*coalgebras, all coproducts and coequalizers exist, and are constructed as in* Set.

As a corollary, we obtain directly that all coproducts and coequalizers exist in the category of Mealy multiset automata.

Therefore we have to construct only the pullbacks. Following some results from [12], we get the following theorem:

Theorem 8. *Let* $F : Set \rightarrow Set$ *be any functor,* Set_F *the category of* F-*coalgebras, and* $U : Set_F \rightarrow Set$ *the forgetful functor.*

1. *If* F *preserves pullbacks, then pullbacks exist in* Set_F.
2. *If* F *preserves weak pullbacks, and let* $f : (S, \alpha_S) \rightarrow (T, \alpha_T)$ *and* $g : (Q, \alpha_Q) \rightarrow (T, \alpha_T)$ *be homomorphisms of* F-*coalgebras. Then the pullback* (P, π_1, π_2) *of* f *and* g *in* Set *is a bisimulation between* S *and* T.
3. *The functor* $U : Set_F \rightarrow Set$ *creates colimits. This means that any type of colimit in* Set_F *exists, and it is obtained by first constructing the colimit in* Set *and next supplying it (in a unique way) with an* F-*transition structure.*

In order to obtain our desired construction, the only thing that we have to do is to prove that our functor F introduced in the beginning of this section preserves weak pullbacks.

Let $f : S \rightarrow T$ and $g : Q \rightarrow T$ be morphisms in Set, (P, π_1, π_2) a weak pullback of f and g in Set $(P = \{(s, q) \in S \times Q \mid f(s) = g(q)\})$, and our functor $F : Set \rightarrow Set$ which is defined by $F(-) = (- \times \mathbb{N} \langle O \rangle)^{\mathbb{N} \langle V \rangle}$. We have to prove that $(F(P), F(\pi_1), F(\pi_2))$ is a weak pullback of $F(f)$ and $F(g)$.

Let us consider the following diagram

$$
\begin{array}{ccc}
F(P) & \xrightarrow{F(\pi_1)} & F(S) \\
{\scriptstyle F(\pi_2)}\downarrow & & \downarrow{\scriptstyle F(f)} \\
F(Q) & \xrightarrow{F(g)} & F(T)
\end{array}
$$

Since $f \circ \pi_1 = g \circ \pi_2$, and F is a functor, we have $F(f) \circ F(\pi_1) = F(g) \circ F(\pi_2)$, and so the above diagram is commutative.

It remains to prove the property of universality, i.e., for all (P', p_1, p_2) such that $F(f) \circ p_1 = F(g) \circ p_2$, there is a morphism $h : P' \rightarrow F(P)$ such that $F(\pi_1) \circ h = p_1$, $F(\pi_2) \circ h = p_2$. This means that the following diagram is commutative:

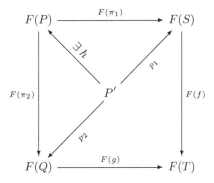

Consider $r \in P'$. It follows that $p_1(r) \in F(S)$, $p_2(r) \in F(Q)$. Denote by $p_j^i(r)(a)$ the i-th component of $p_j(r)(a)$. From $F(f) \circ p_1 = F(g) \circ p_2$ we obtain $F(f)(p_1(r)) = F(g)(p_2(r))$, and so $\langle f, id_{\mathbb{N}\langle O \rangle} \rangle \circ p_1(r) = \langle g, id_{\mathbb{N}\langle O \rangle} \rangle \circ p_2(r)$. This means that for all $a \in \mathbb{N}\langle V \rangle$ we have $(\langle f, id_{\mathbb{N}\langle O \rangle} \rangle \circ p_1(r))(a) = (\langle g, id_{\mathbb{N}\langle O \rangle} \rangle \circ p_2(r))(a)$, and so $(f(p_1^1(r)(a)), p_1^2(r)(a)) = (g(p_2^1(r)(a)), p_2^2(r)(a))$. The latter equality leads us to $f(p_1^1(r)(a)) = g(p_2^1(r)(a))$ and $p_1^2(r)(a) = p_2^2(r)(a)$. Since P contains all the pairs that have the same image under f and g, we have $(p_1^1(r)(a), p_2^1(r)(a)) \in P$. This enables us to say that $(p_1(r), p_2(r)) \in F(P)$.

The so-called "mediating morphism" that we need for the universality property is $h : P' \to F(P)$ defined by $h(r) = (p_1(r), p_2(r))$. We check now that it satisfies the commutativity of the diagram. $(F(\pi_1) \circ h)(r) = F(\pi_1)(h(r)) = \langle \pi_1, id_{\mathbb{N}\langle O \rangle} \rangle \circ h(r) = \langle \pi_1, id_{\mathbb{N}\langle O \rangle} \rangle \circ (p_1(r), p_2(r)) = p_1(r)$ for all r from P'.

Similarly, it can be proved that $F(\pi_2) \circ h = p_2$.

Theorem 9. *The functor* $(- \times \mathbb{N}\langle O \rangle)^{\mathbb{N}\langle V \rangle} : Set \to Set$ *preserves weak pullbacks.*

Combining this last theorem with the results of Section 5 in [12], we get the following result:

Theorem 10. *Let* $(S, \alpha_S), (T, \alpha_T), (Q, \alpha_Q)$ *be three coalgebras associated to the functor* $(- \times \mathbb{N}\langle O \rangle)^{\mathbb{N}\langle V \rangle} : Set \to Set$. *The following assertions are true:*

1. *The diagonal* Δ_S *of a system* S *is a bisimulation.*
2. *Let* (R, α_R) *be a bisimulation between* S *and* T. *The inverse* R^{-1} *of* R *is a bisimulation between* T *and* S.
3. *The composition* $R \circ R'$ *of two bisimulations* $R \subseteq S \times T$ *and* $R' \subseteq T \times Q$ *is a bisimulation between* S *and* Q.
4. *The union* $\bigcup_k R_k$ *of a family* $\{R_k\}$ *of bisimulations between systems* S *and* T *is again a bisimulation. In particular, the largest bisimulation between* S *and* T *exists, and it is the union of all bisimulations.*
5. *The kernel* $K(f)$ *of a homomorphism* $f : S \to T$ *is a bisimulation equivalence.*
6. *Let* $f : S \to T$ *be a homomorphism. If* $R \subseteq S \times S$ *is a bisimulation on* S, *then* $f(R)$ *is a bisimulation on* T. *If* $R' \subseteq T \times T$ *is a bisimulation on* T, *then* $f^{-1}(R')$ *is a bisimulation on* S.

6   Conclusion and Related Work

The purpose of this paper is to present a class of automata able to work with resources represented by multisets. Roughly speaking, a Mealy multiset automaton is a machine able to consume and produce multisets. Mealy multiset automata could be related to the multiset automata presented in [5] as a particular accepting MmA having a "two letters" output alphabet. While [5] deals with multiset grammars and Chomsky hierarchy, we are mainly interested in algebraic, categorial and coalgebraic properties, emphasizing on their bisimulations, observation, and behavior. The results presented in this paper guarantee useful properties of our multiset automata, including that the (relational) product of bisimulations is a bisimulation, the largest bisimulation is an equivalence relation, and kernels of homomorphisms are always bisimulations. The link between MmA and P systems is initiated in [3], where the description of elementary Mealy membrane automata is based on Mealy multiset automata [4].

We give here only the first results regarding an algebraic and categorical approach to Mealy multiset automata, and we begin to develop the formal instruments for a further approach to membrane computing based on these notions. The algebraic constructions are useful for defining and operating with notions like bisimulation, observability, and behavior.

We have used elementary categorical language to model Mealy multiset automata and their behavior. The idea of this approach is that a categorical formal language is rich enough to describe and analyze various aspects of complex systems, and it could be applicable to membrane systems. The first paper in category theory was written by Eilenberg and MacLane in 1945 [8]. It aimed to describe both interactions and comparisons within a given context (topological spaces, groups, other algebraic structures, etc.), and interactions between different contexts. For instance, within the area of pure mathematics known as algebraic topology, problems in the theory of spaces are attacked by assigning various types of algebraic requirements to spaces, thus translating the topological problem to a more tractable algebraic one. Some links of category theory with the modeling of biological systems are briefly explored in [9]. Some categorical aspects of the theory of hierarchical systems are presented in [6].

Acknowledgements

This work has been supported by the research grant CNCSIS 875/2005.

References

1. P. Aczel, N. Mendler: A final coalgebra theorem. LNCS 389, Springer, Berlin, 1989, 357–365.
2. M. Barr, C. Wells: *Category Theory Lecture Notes for ESSLLI*. Available on-line at http://www.let.uu.nl/esslli/Courses/barr/barrwells.ps.

3. G. Ciobanu, M. Gontineac: Mealy membrane automata and P systems complexity. In *Cellular Computing; Complexity Aspects* (M.A. Gutiérrez-Naranjo, Gh. Păun, M.J. Pérez-Jiménez, eds.), ESF Workshop, Fenix Editora, Sevilla, 2005, 149–164.

4. G. Ciobanu, M. Gontineac: Mealy multiset automata. *International Journal of Foundations of Computer Science*, to appear in 2006.

5. E. Csuhaj-Varju, C. Martin-Vide, V. Mitrana: Multiset automata. *Multiset Processing. Mathematical, Computer Science, and Molecular Computing Points of View* (C. Calude, Gh. Păun, G. Rozenberg, A. Salomaa, eds.), LNCS 2235, Springer-Verlag, Berlin, 2001, 69–83.

6. A.C. Ehresmann, J.-P. Vanbremersch: Hierarchical evolutive systems: A mathematical model for complex systems. *Bull. of Math. Biol.*, 49 (1987), 13–50.

7. S. Eilenberg: *Automata. Languages and Machines*, vol. A. Academic Press, 1976.

8. S. Eilenberg, S. MacLane: The general theory of natural equivalences. *Trans. Amer. Math. Soc.*, 58 (1945), 231–294.

9. M.J. Fisher, G. Malcolm, R.C. Paton: Spatio-logical processes in intracellular signalling. *Biosystems*, 55 (2000), 83–92.

10. W. Kuich, A. Salomaa: *Semirings, Automata, Languages*. Springer, Berlin, 1986.

11. Gh. Păun: *Membrane Computing. An Introduction*, Springer, Berlin, 2002.

12. J. Rutten: Universal coalgebra: a theory of systems. *Theoretical Computer Science*, 249 (2000), 3–80.

P Systems and the Modeling
of Biochemical Oscillations

Federico Fontana, Luca Bianco, and Vincenzo Manca

University of Verona,
Department of Computer Science,
15 strada Le Grazie – 37134 Verona, Italy
{federico.fontana, vincenzo.manca}@univr.it,
bianco@sci.univr.it

Abstract. In this paper we discuss the role that P systems have in the description of oscillatory biochemical processes once the membrane system evolution depends on the process parameters. This discussion focuses on a specific application example, meanwhile it includes a general definition of oscillation based on which we want to explore the meaning of oscillatory behaviors more deeply. The symbolic-based approach to biochemical processes such as that provided by P systems has recently resulted in insightful model descriptions. For this reason we expect it to turn useful in computational systems biology, whose models must deal with the twofold nature of the cell that is a *continuous* biochemical reactor ruled by *discrete* information contained in the DNA.

1   Introduction

Originally conceived to assess the expressive power of grammars and to classify formal languages [21], rewriting systems more recently have been applied to the analysis of biological structures—for instance, they have demonstrated capability to represent the development of living species such as the growing of some simple organisms [13, 20]. Inspired by these investigations, P systems [17, 18, 16] have been concerned particularly with the dynamic aspect of rewriting and its application to biology and biochemistry [23, 1, 3]. Dynamic rewriting systems have led to alternative representations of several biological phenomena [22] and to exploratory models of known pathological processes [14, 19].

   Along this direction of research, we have recently presented a symbolic rewriting algorithm [2] in which production rules are given along with *reaction maps*, each one specifying the "strength" of a rule in modifying a population of symbols (denoting concentrations of chemical reactants, individuals, molecules, and so on) in the system. This algorithm has successfully simulated some well-known biochemical models, such as the Lotka-Volterra population dynamics [25], and the Brusselator model of the BZ chemical reaction [9]. These early results, along with the inherent advantages that rewriting systems offer in terms of modeling flexibility, ask for doing further tests on more elaborate biochemical models such as those presented in this paper.

R. Freund et al. (Eds.): WMC 2005, LNCS 3850, pp. 199–208, 2006.
© Springer-Verlag Berlin Heidelberg 2006

After a brief description of the algorithm, we show results obtained simulating an extensive model of circadian rhythms in *Drosophila melanogaster* [12], whose clarity and richness of quantitative data allows to make effective comparisons between the numerical solutions of the differential equations found in that model and the solutions coming out from our rewriting system. Although still partial in front of the huge amount of simulations of circadian rhythms that have been carried out through differential equation system models, these results, along with those achieved in the simulation of the aforementioned dynamics, confirm the effectiveness of our approach in modeling elaborate biochemical behaviors such as those emerging in circadian rhythms.

Inspired by the flexibility and power of this model we have started thinking about how to investigate on the meaning of oscillation taken as a phenomenon *per se*. We have in fact discovered that no clear definition of this phenomenon exists. This lack of a definition reflects an inherent difficulty to characterize oscillation in formal (and consequently quantitative) terms, as opposite to periodicity for which a huge amount of theoretical results have been found, the Fourier analysis being on top of them [10].

Unlike ideal oscillatory systems, biochemical processes never show exact periodic behavior [6]. In the meantime it is crucial to find if, and how, they oscillate. Gaining insight on the ultimate meaning of oscillation may be useful to define formal tools that help giving an answer to these two questions.

2   Algorithm Quick Overview

A detailed description of the algorithm we use to control the evolution of a system has been previously given [2]; furthermore, a comprehensive formalization of this algorithm in specific P system-based constructs is ongoing. Here, we briefly recall the concepts that are necessary to set up a representation of the circadian model.

Let a single-membrane system be made of a set $R = \{r_1, \ldots, r_k\}$ of rewriting rules working over strings on an alphabet $\mathcal{A} = \{X, Y, \ldots\}$ containing k symbols:

$$r_1 : \alpha_{r_1} \to \beta_{r_1}, \quad r_2 : \alpha_{r_2} \to \beta_{r_2}, \quad \ldots \quad r_k : \alpha_{r_k} \to \beta_{r_k}, \tag{1}$$

in which α_ρ and β_ρ are strings denoting consumed and produced objects for each rule $\rho \in R$, respectively.

Let the *state* of our system be a k-uple $\langle q(X), q(Y), \ldots \rangle$ containing the number of objects $X, Y, \ldots$ in the system at every temporal step (here we will make every step correspond to a system transition, however in general this is not necessarily true). To every rule we associate a corresponding *reaction map* $F_{r_1}, F_{r_2}, \ldots, F_{r_k}$, i.e., a real function of the state of the system affecting the rule in the way we explain below.

By denoting with $\alpha(i)$ the ith symbol in a string α, with $|\alpha|$ the length of the same string, and with $|\alpha|_X$ the number of occurrences of the symbol X in

α, then we define the *reaction weight* $W_r(\alpha_r(i))$ for $r : \alpha_r \to \beta_r$ with respect to the symbol $\alpha_r(i)$:

$$W_r(\alpha_r(i)) = \frac{F_r}{\sum\limits_{\rho \in R \,|\, \alpha_r(i) \in \alpha_\rho} F_\rho}, \quad i = 1, \ldots, |\alpha_r|. \tag{2}$$

Note that at the denominator we sum only over the rules containing the symbol $\alpha_r(i)$ in their left part.

If at this point we consider that every rule r cannot consume more than the amount of the symbol (called also *reactant*) whose availability in the system is lowest, then for every rule we have to minimize among all reactants—each one taken with its own multiplicity in α_r—participating to the reaction. In this way for every symbol we find the population a rule applies to during a transition of the system:

$$\Lambda_r = \min_{i=1,\ldots,|\alpha_r|} \left\{ W_r(\alpha_r(i)) \frac{q(\alpha_r(i))}{|\alpha_r|_{\alpha_r(i)}} \right\}. \tag{3}$$

In the end, for every symbol $X \in \mathcal{A}$ the change in the number of objects due to r is equal to $|\beta_r|_X - |\alpha_r|_X$ times Λ_r:

$$\Delta_r(X) = \Lambda_r \left(|\beta_r|_X - |\alpha_r|_X \right). \tag{4}$$

A detailed explanation of the algorithm structure, in particular the way it works with discrete populations rather than concentrations, and its extension to multiple reaction environments made using membrane systems, is given in [2].

3   Application to Circadian Rhythms

We have applied the algorithm discussed in Section 2 to the simulation of a known model of circadian cycles (or *rhythms*) in *Drosophila melanogaster*, involving the oscillation of the Period (PER) and Timeless (TIM) proteins [5]. Existing in every living organism, circadian rhythms are biochemical cycles evoked by variations in the expression level of specific genes. Such variations give rise to a surprisingly robust biological clock, synchronized with daylight and performing a complete cycle about every 24 hours.

According to this model the genes involved in the process code for PER and TIM proteins, meanwhile their expression is inhibited by the presence of a PER-TIM protein complex, in its own made of PER and TIM. Under certain conditions, this complex forms in the cytosol, then migrates inside the nucleus where it behaves as a PER and TIM suppressor. Taken together, gene expression and suppression result in a negative feedback network of signal transduction that has been formalized by a non-trivial system made of several nonlinear differential equations [6, 12].

A graphical scheme of the model is depicted in Figure 1.

Details of its functioning can be found in [12]. At least it is interesting to note that the formation of the PER-TIM complex is regulated by the degradation induced on mature TIM (denoted as T_2) by light. However, in our study we do not include the effects of light.

In spite of its complexity, the PER and TIM model results in emergent oscillatory concentrations of the biochemical elements considered. The temporal evolution of such concentrations exhibits clear mutual relationships between concentration onsets and decays. These relationships disclose the causality existing between gene expression and the consequent change in concentration of the transcribed mRNA and, hence, of the coded proteins.

Symbolic rewriting allows to describe this model by means of a set of rules, avoiding the classical approach based on differential equations. By looking at Figure 1 it is not difficult to figure out the following rewriting rules:

$$
\begin{aligned}
r1 &: \lambda & \to & \ M_P, & \qquad r2 &: \lambda & \to & \ M_T, \\
r3 &: M_P & \to & \ \lambda, & \qquad r4 &: M_T & \to & \ \lambda, \\
r5 &: M_P & \to & \ M_P P_0, & \qquad r6 &: M_P & \to & \ M_T T_0, \\
r7 &: P_0 & \to & \ P_1, & \qquad r8 &: T_0 & \to & \ T_1, \\
r9 &: P_1 & \to & \ P_0, & \qquad r10 &: T_1 & \to & \ T_0, \\
r11 &: P_0 & \to & \ \lambda, & \qquad r12 &: T_0 & \to & \ \lambda, \\
r13 &: P_1 & \to & \ \lambda, & \qquad r14 &: T_1 & \to & \ \lambda, \\
r15 &: P_1 & \to & \ P_2, & \qquad r16 &: T_1 & \to & \ T_2, \\
r17 &: P_2 & \to & \ P_1, & \qquad r18 &: T_2 & \to & \ T_1, \\
r19 &: P_2 & \to & \ \lambda, & \qquad r20 &: T_2 & \to & \ \lambda, \\
r21 &: P_2 T_2 & \to & \ C, & \qquad r22 &: C & \to & \ P_2 T_2, \\
r23 &: C & \to & \ C_N, & \qquad r24 &: C_N & \to & \ C, \\
r25 &: C & \to & \ \lambda, & \qquad r26 &: C_N & \to & \ \lambda.
\end{aligned}
\tag{5}
$$

In these rules the symbol λ as usual represents the null string. In this way rules in the form $\lambda \to X$ are production rules, and rules in the form $X \to \lambda$ are degradation rules.

Furthermore, for each element X that is present in the system we introduce a *transparent rule* in the form $X \to X$. These rules do not cause any change in the system. Rather, they are needed to model elements that do not take part in a reaction (for example, reactants that are spatially far from each other) [2].

Note that, besides the radical differences existing between the differential and the rewriting system, our model differs from the continuous one especially in what concerns the formation of the PER-TIM complex—expressed in our system by rule $r21$. This rule is, in fact, cooperative and in this case we use the *limiter* Λ_{r21}, discussed in Section 2, in order to calculate the variation of P_2, T_2, and C.

As we have previously seen, each rule is coupled with a reaction map. According to the formulas proposed in the original model, we have come up with the following maps:

$$F_{r1} = v_{sP} \frac{K_{IP}^n}{K_{1P}^n + C_N^n},$$

$$F_{r2} = v_{sT} \frac{K_{IT}^n}{K_{1T}^n + C_N^n},$$

$$F_{r3} = \frac{v_{mP}}{K_{mP} + M_P} + K_d,$$

$$F_{r4} = \frac{v_{mT}}{K_{mT} + M_T} + K_d,$$

$$F_{r5} = K_{sP},$$

$$F_{r6} = K_{sT},$$

$$F_{r7} = \frac{v_{1P}}{K_{1P} + P_0},$$

$$F_{r8} = \frac{v_{1T}}{K_{1T} + T_0},$$

$$F_{r9} = \frac{v_{2P}}{K_{2P} + P_1},$$

$$F_{r10} = \frac{v_{2T}}{K_{2T} + T_1},$$

$$F_{r11} = K_d,$$

$$F_{r12} = K_d,$$

$$F_{r13} = K_d,$$

$$F_{r14} = K_d,$$

$$F_{r15} = \frac{v_{3P}}{K_{3P} + P_1},$$

$$F_{r16} = \frac{v_{3T}}{K_{3T} + T_1},$$

$$F_{r17} = \frac{v_{4P}}{K_{4P} + P_2},$$

$$F_{r18} = \frac{v_{4T}}{K_{4T} + T_2},$$

$$F_{r19} = K_d + \frac{v_{dT}}{K_{dT} + T_2},$$

$$F_{r20} = K_d + \frac{v_{dP}}{K_{dP} + P_2},$$

$$F_{r21} = K_3,$$

$$F_{r22} = K_4,$$

$$F_{r23} = K_1,$$

$$F_{r24} = K_2,$$

$$F_{r25} = K_{dC},$$

$$F_{r26} = K_{dN}.$$

(6)

Moreover, in agreement with [12], we choose the following set of parameters (reported here dimensionless): $v_{sP} = v_{sT} = 1$, $v_{mP} = v_{mT} = 0.7$, $K_{mP} =$

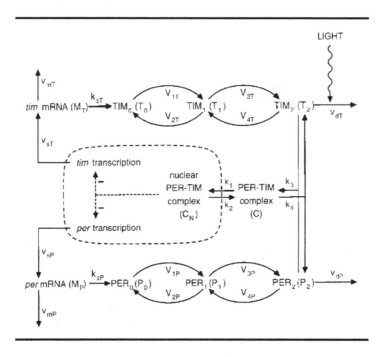

Fig. 1. Model for circadian rhythms in *Drosophila* (from Leloup and Goldbeter [12])

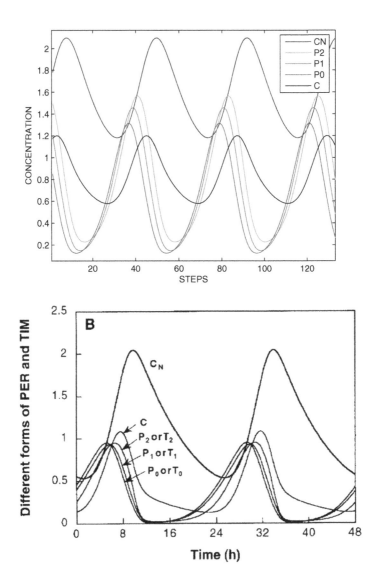

Fig. 2. Above: plots for C_N, P_2, P_1, P_0, and C obtained using the metabolic algorithm (elements ordered starting from the highest to the lowest maximum peak value, as in the legend at the top-right corner). Below: plots for C_N, P_2, P_1, P_0, and C (from Leloup and Goldbeter [12]).

$K_{mT} = 0.2$, $K_{sP} = K_{sT} = 0.9$, $v_{dP} = v_{dT} = 2$, $K_1 = 0.6$, $K_2 = 0.2$, $K_3 = 0.5$, $K_4 = 0.2$, $K_{IP} = K_{IT} = 1$, $K_{dP} = K_{dT} = 0.2$, $n = 4$ $K_{1P} = K_{1T} = K_{2P} = K_{2T} = K_{3P} = K_{3T} = K_{4P} = K_{4T} = 2$, $K_d = K_{dC} = K_{dN} = 0.01$, $v_{1P} = v_{1T} = v_{1P} = v_{1T} = 8$, $v_{2P} = v_{2T} = v_{4P} = v_{4T} = 1$. Note that the different interpretation given by $r21$ to the formation of the PER-TIM compound, compared to that formalized by a numerical equation (typically as the product of two reactants weighted by a proper kinetic constant rate), suggested to employ different values for the variables K_3 and K_4 as opposite to the values chosen in the continuous model, respectively set to 1.2 and 0.6. In addition to that we have coupled a constant reaction map $F_r = 1$ to every transparent rule r.

Figure 2 (above) shows the salient result we have obtained by simulating circadian rhythms using the membrane model. In this simulation, changes of variable have been applied to all concentrations in order to magnify the dynamics of our system by a scale factor 10^4. The resulting, magnified concentrations have been finally scaled back by the same factor to display amounts of substance that could be directly compared to those found in [12]. Otherwise, the effects of rounding arising in our simulation would have overwhelmed the natural characteristics of the cyrcadian dynamics.

Plots figure out the state along 130 transitions of the system, i.e., every plot describes the evolution along discrete time of the corresponding element in the k-tuple forming the state. It can be seen that a stable oscillatory dynamics is achieved using the symbolic approach.

Such plots are compared to the numerical solution of the corresponding differential equation model, reported in Figure 2 (below). It can be noted that the relative temporal shifts between concentration peaks are preserved by our simulation. This means that comparable dynamic behaviors exist for the two models. In particular, the membrane system correctly models the sequence of concentration peaks of the phosphorilating PER protein (P_0, P_1, and P_2), followed by the peak in the concentration of the cytosolic PER-TIM complex C and, finally, by its nuclear counterpart C_N. This dynamic behavior corresponds to results obtained by Leloup and Goldbeter, which, in their turn, match with experimental observations [26].

4   Toward a Characterization of Oscillations

For what we have seen in the previous example, oscillation is perhaps the most important emergent property featured by a biochemical system. Investigating its onsets, temporal extension, robustness against parameter changes, characteristic evolution along time, deviation from an ideal periodic track, is crucial for extracting many properties inherently present in the system structure. These properties range from the topology of the signal transduction network underlying the communication flows that are active in the system, to its distinctive parameters which determine the modalities by which this evolution develops along time.

Curiously, oscillation is not yet well defined. On one hand, this depends on the generality of the phenomenon. Oscillation in fact includes concepts such as quasi-periodicity, recurrence, periodic chaotic attraction [8]. On the other hand, it is precisely that generality that most biochemical systems exhibit: in some sense, oscillation is a weak but, at the same time, one of the strongest and most distinctive properties shown by nonlinear systems. It is with these questions in mind that we try to formalize oscillation.

Let us consider a state transition dynamics $\mathcal{S} = (S, q)$, in which q maps states into sets of states: $q : S \longrightarrow \mathcal{P}(S)$ [14, 15]. In $\mathcal{S}$, let us consider a *local* trajectory T made of states $X_0, X_1, \ldots, X_n$ such that X_i is obtained by repeatedly applying m_i times the transition function to X_{i-1} for each $i = 1, \ldots, m$ (note that we conveniently extend q to work over sets, i.e., $q(X) = \bigcup_{s \in X} q(s)$):

$$T : \quad X_0 \xrightarrow{q^{(m_1)}} X_1 \xrightarrow{q^{(m_2)}} \cdots \xrightarrow{q^{(m_i)}} X_i \xrightarrow{q^{(m_{i+1})}} \cdots \xrightarrow{q^{(m_n-1)}} X_{n-1} \xrightarrow{q^{(m_n)}} X_n, \quad (7)$$

with

$$X_i \subseteq q^{(m_i)}(X_{i-1}) = \underbrace{(q \circ q \circ \cdots \circ q)}_{m_i \text{ times}}(X_{i-1}), \quad i = 1, 2, \ldots \quad (8)$$

Definition 1. *A local trajectory T in $\mathcal{S}$ oscillates around x_0 with respect to a (state observation) function $\mu : S \longrightarrow \mathbb{R}$ if T exists such that*

- $\mu(X_i) \geq x_0$ *for i even (odd),*
- $\mu(X_i) < x_0$ *for i odd (even).*

Clearly, this definition does not prevent that several oscillations exist in one single sequence. In particular, it does not exclude that inner oscillations are present in between adjacent states in T. For instance, it may be likely that T oscillates also around x_1, and that this oscillation appears within states traced by the local trajectory between X_k and X_{k-1}. And so on.

Whether this definition can form an initial basis to a future theoretical development, enriching the wide amount of literature already existing on Fourier and, more general, spectral analysis, will be a matter of forthcoming research. We are now working on this definition in an attempt to find a more insightful interpretation of the oscillation *per se*.

5   Concluding Remarks

Our experience with the representation of several biochemical phenomena, including the circadian model we have presented here, suggests that membrane systems are promising candidates for providing accurate models of such phenomena provided their versatility in dealing with discrete (that is, symbolic) representations of the information and its transmission along peculiar communication channels such as cell ports and signal transduction networks.

This first attempt of symbolic modeling of the circadian cycle in *Drosophila* yet has not considered the effect of light on the degradation of the phosphorilated TIM. We want to include this effect in a forthcoming session of further tests of our algorithm, still relying on the well-documented figures proposed in [12]. Even more interesting will be comparing our symbolic algorithm to some well-known stochastic simulation methods that are used when the molecules involved in a biochemical process are few, in a way that the deterministic approach turns out to be no longer suitable. Surprising analogies exist in fact between the symbolic and the stochastic approach to the simulation of circadian rhythms when our algorithm is set to work over populations rather than concentrations, i.e., over discrete rather than continuous domains [7, 4].

In parallel, an analysis focusing on the ultimate meaning of the behaviors we observe in a dynamical system is needed, since, if successful, this analysis will become a useful way to extract important structural information from a system, even independently of its physical (*viz.* biological for us) nature: such kind of analyses have already provided powerful conceptual frameworks based on control theory [24] that have found fertile applications, for instance, in the identification of "black-box" systems—as biological systems still are, at least to some extent [11].

A possible roadmap to follow along this research perhaps starts from properly defining basic dynamic concepts, oscillation *in primis* for its major importance in any dynamic phenomenon. We will try to move along this roadmap in the next few months.

References

1. L. Bianco, F. Fontana, G. Franco, V. Manca: P systems for biological dynamics. In *Applications of Membrane Computing* (G. Ciobanu, Gh. Păun, M.J. Pérez-Jiménez, eds.), Springer, Berlin, 2006, 81–126.
2. L. Bianco, F. Fontana, V. Manca: Metabolic algorithm with time-varying reaction maps. In *Proc. of the Third Brainstorming Week on Membrane Computing*, Sevilla, Spain, 2005, 43–62.
3. L. Bianco, F. Fontana, V. Manca: Reaction-driven membrane systems. In *Proc. Advances in Natural Computation, First International Conference*, ICNC 2005, Changsha, China, August 27-29, 2005, Part II (L. Wang, K. Chen, Y.S. Ong, eds.), LNCS 3611, Springer, Berlin, 2005, 1155–1158.
4. D.T. Gillespie: Exact stochastic simulation of coupled chemical reactions. *J. of Phys. Chem.*, 81 (1977), 2340–2361.
5. A. Goldbeter: Computational approaches to cellular rhythms. *Nature*, 420 (2002), 238–244.
6. A. Goldbeter: *Biochemical Oscillations and Cellular Rhythms. The Molecular Bases of Periodic and Chaotic Behaviour.* Cambridge University Press, New York, 2004.
7. D. Gonze, J. Halloy, A. Goldbeter: Stochastic model for circadian oscillations: Emergence of a biological rhythm. *Int. J. of Quantum Chemistry*, 98 (2004), 228–238.
8. R.C. Hilborn: *Chaos and Nonlinear Dynamics.* Oxford University Press, Oxford, UK, 2000.
9. D.S. Jones, B.D. Sleeman: *Differential Equations and Mathematical Biology.* Chapman & Hall/CRC, London, UK, 2003.
10. T. Kailath: *Linear Systems.* Prentice-Hall, Englewood Cliffs, 1980.
11. H. Kitano: Computational systems biology. *Nature*, 420 (2002), 206–210.
12. J.C. Leloup, A. Goldbeter: A model for circadian rhythms in *Drosophila* incorporating the formation of a complex between the PER and TIM proteins. *J. of Biological Rhythms*, 13 (1998), 70–87.
13. A. Lindenmayer: Mathematical models for cellular interaction in development. *J. of Theoretical Biology*, 18 (1968), 280–315, Part I and II.

14. V. Manca, L. Bianco, F. Fontana: Evolutions and oscillations of P systems: Applications to biological phenomena. In [16], 63–84.

15. V. Manca, G. Franco, G. Scollo: State transition dynamics: Basic concepts and molecular computing perspectives. In *Molecular Computational Models - Unconventional Approaches* (M. Gheorghe, ed.), Idea Group, 2004.

16. G. Mauri, Gh. Păun, M.J. Pérez-Jiménez, G. Rozenberg, A. Salomaa, eds.: *Membrane Computing, 5th International Workshop, WMC 2004, Milan, Italy, June 14-16, 2004, Revised Selected and Invited Papers*. LNCS 3365, Springer, Berlin, 2005.

17. Gh. Păun: Computing with membranes. *J. Comput. System Sci.*, 61 (2000), 108–143

18. Gh. Păun: *Membrane Computing. An Introduction*. Springer, Berlin, 2002.

19. M.J. Pérez-Jiménez, F.J. Romero-Campero: Modelling EGFR signalling network using continuous membrane systems. In *Proceedings of the Third International Workshop on Computational Methods in Systems Biology 2005* (CMSB 2005) (G. Plotkin, ed.), University of Edinburgh, UK, 2005.

20. P. Prusinkiewicz, M. Hammel, J. Hanan, R. Mech: Visual models of plant development. In [21], Volume III: *Beyond Words*, 535–597.

21. G. Rozenberg, A. Salomaa, eds.: *Handbook of Formal Languages*. Springer, Berlin, 1997.

22. I. Stamatopoulou, M. Gheorghe, P. Kefalas: Modelling dynamic organization of biology-inspired multi-agent systems with communicating X-machines and population P systems. In [16], 389–403.

23. Y. Suzuki, H. Tanaka: Chemical oscillation in symbolic chemical systems and its behavioral pattern. In *Proc. International Conference on Complex Systems* (Y. Bar-Yam, ed.), Nashua, NH, 1997.

24. T.L. Vincent, W.J. Grantham: *Nonlinear and Optimal Control Systems*. Wiley, New York, 1997.

25. V. Volterra: Fluctuations in the abundance of a species considered mathematically. *Nature*, 118 (1926), 558–560.

26. H. Zeng: Constitutive overexpression of the drosophila period protein inhibits period mRNA cycling. *The EMBO Journal*, 13 (1994), 3590–3598.

P Systems, Petri Nets, and Program Machines

Pierluigi Frisco

Department of Computer Science,
School of Engineering, Computer Science and Mathematics,
University of Exeter, Harrison Building, North Park Road,
Exeter, EX4 4QF, U.K
P.Frisco@exeter.ac.uk

Abstract. Some features capturing the computational completeness of
P systems with maximal parallelism, priorities or zero-test using symbol
objects are studied through Petri nets.

The obtained results are not limited to P systems.

1   Introduction

Membrane systems (also called *P systems*) are a new class of distributed and parallel theoretical computing devices introduced in [19]. In the seminal paper the
author considers systems based on a hierarchically arranged, finite *cell-structure*
consisting of several cell-membranes embedded in a main membrane called the
skin. The membranes delimit *regions* where *objects*, elements of a finite set, and
evolution rules can be placed.

In [19] the author examines three ways to view P systems: transition, rewriting and splicing P systems. Starting from these, several variants were considered
[26, 20]. These variants can be divided in two main categories: P systems using
symbol objects and P systems using string objects. Several proofs of computational universality of P systems using symbol objects are based on a simulation
of program machines.

In this research we try to discover and study the principles underlying the
P systems using symbol objects that happen to be computationally complete.
A similar study but limited to specific variants of (tissue) P systems has been
reported in [4]. We focused our attention on the processes carried out by these
systems and we used Petri nets as a tool for our research. Links between P
systems and Petri nets have been already investigated [27, 22, 11, 12].

The obtained results are not limited to P systems.

2   Basic Definitions

We assume the reader to have familiarity with basic concepts of formal language
theory [10], in particular with the topic of P systems [20], Petri nets [23] and
program machines [16]. In the following subsections we recall particular aspects
relevant to our presentation.

R. Freund et al. (Eds.): WMC 2005, LNCS 3850, pp. 209–223, 2006.

2.1   General

We indicate with $\mathbb{N}$ the set of natural numbers while $\mathbb{N}_0 = \{0\} \cup \mathbb{N}$. We use $\mathbb{N}_0 \mathsf{RE}$ to denote the family of recursively enumerable sets of natural numbers. For $k \in \mathbb{N}_0$, $\mathbb{N}_k \cdot \mathsf{RE}$ equals the family of recursively enumerable sets with elements greater than or equal to k.

Let V be a finite set of objects. With V^* we indicate the free monoid generated by V with the operation of concatenation; λ indicates the empty word. A *multiset* (over V) is a function $M : V \to \mathbb{N}_0 \cup \{+\infty\}$; for $a \in V$, $M(a)$ defines the *multiplicity* of a in the multiset M. We will say that an element a of a multiset M has *infinite multiplicity* if $M(a) = +\infty$. In case the multiplicity of an element of a multiset is 1 we will indicate just the element, otherwise $(a, M(a))$ or $a^{M(a)}$ (that is, the symbol a repeated $M(a)$ times) is indicated. The *support* of a multiset M is the set $supp(M) = \{a \in V \mid M(a) > 0\}$. The *size* of a multiset is defined by the function $|\cdot| : (V \to \mathbb{N}_0 \cup \{+\infty\}) \to \mathbb{N}_0 \cup \{+\infty\}$, where for a multiset M over V, $|M| = \sum_{a \in supp(M)} M(a)$. The symbol ϕ indicates the *empty multiset*, that is, the multiset whose support is the empty set $\emptyset$.

Let $M_1, M_2 : V \to \mathbb{N}_0 \cup \{+\infty\}$ be two multisets. The *union* of M_1 and M_2 is the multiset $M_1 \cup M_2 : V \to \mathbb{N}_0 \cup \{+\infty\}$ defined by $(M_1 \cup M_2)(a) = M_1(a) + M_2(a)$, for all $a \in V$. The *difference* $M_1 \backslash M_2$ is here defined only when M_2 is *included* in M_1 (which means that $M_1(a) \geq M_2(a)$ for all $a \in V$) and it is the multiset $M_1 \backslash M_2 : V \to \mathbb{N}_0 \cup \{+\infty\}$ given by $(M_1 \backslash M_2)(a) = M_1(a) - M_2(a)$ for all $a \in V$. Of course, if $M_1(a) = +\infty$ and $M_2(a)$ is finite, then $M_1(a) \backslash M_2(a) = +\infty$. If $M_2(a) = +\infty$, then by convention, $M_1(a) \backslash M_2(a) = 0$.

2.2   P Systems

In this subsection we do not give the definition of a specific P system, rather we give a general definition for P systems whose content of the membrane compartments are multisets of objects.

Let us consider the construct $\Pi = (V, \mu, L_1, \ldots, L_m, R, fin)$, where:

V is a set of objects;

$\mu = (N, E)$ is a *directed graph* underlying Π. The set $N \subset \mathbb{N}$ contains *vertices*; for simplicity we define $N = \{1, \ldots, m\}$. Each vertex in N defines a *membrane* of Π. The set $E \subseteq N \times N$ defines directed *edges* between vertices indicated by (i, j).

L_i over $V \to \mathbb{N}_0 \cup \{+\infty\}$ are the multisets associated with membranes $i \in N$. They define the input of the system. If an object belongs to the support of a multiset associated with a membrane, then we will say that the object is present into the membrane.

R is a finite set of *rules* describing operations on one or two multisets of objects. As we are not considering a specific P system we do not give a definition of the rules.

$fin \in N$ defines the *final membrane* indicating the multiset output of the system when a certain condition is met. This condition can be, for instance, the impossibility to apply any rule (as in P systems with symport/antiport [18, 13, 8, 2, 25]) or the presence of an object in a specific membrane (as in conformon-P systems [6]).

A *configuration* of Π is an m-tuple $(M_1, \ldots, M_m)$ of multisets over $V \times \mathbb{N}_0 \cup \{+\infty\}$. From two configurations $(M_1, \ldots, M_m), (M'_1, \ldots, M'_m)$ of Π we write $(M_1, \ldots, M_m) \Rightarrow (M'_1, \ldots, M'_m)$ indicating a *transition* from $(M_1, \ldots, M_m)$ to $(M'_1, \ldots, M'_m)$ obtained by means of the parallel application of a multiset of rules. In a transition $M_j \neq M'_j$ for at least a $1 \leq j \leq m$. If no rule is applied to a multiset M_i, then $M_i = M'_i$. Notice that transitions could be applied under the requirement of *maximal parallelism* that is, a multiset of rules cannot be applied if there is a strictly larger multiset of rules that could be applied.

A *computation* is a finite sequence of transitions between configurations of a system Π starting from $(L_1, \ldots, L_m)$ and ending with a configuration that meets certain conditions. The result of a computation is given by the multiset of objects present in membrane fin in the final configuration. The set of all such multisets is indicated by $L(\Pi)$.

2.3 Petri Nets

Definition 1. *A Petri net is a quadruple $M = (P, T, F, C_{in})$, where:*

i) (P, T, F) is a net, that is:
    1. P and T are sets with $P \cap T = \emptyset$;
    2. $F \subseteq (P \times T) \cup (T \times P)$;
    3. for every $t \in T$ there exist $p, q \in P$ such that $(p, t), (t, q) \in F$;
    4. for every $t \in T$ and $p, q, \in P$, if $(p, t), (t, q) \in F$, then $p \neq q$.
ii) $C_{in} \subseteq P$ is the initial configuration.

Elements of P are called *places* (graphically represented with circles), elements of T are called *transitions* (graphically represented with rectangles), elements of $X = P \cup T$ are called *elements (of M)*, F is called the *flow relation* and, in general, a $C \subseteq P$ is a *configuration*. Graphically, a configuration is represented by placing a 'token' (i.e., a dot) in every circle corresponding to a place in C.

Given a Petri net $M = (P, T, F, C_{in})$, (P, T, F) is the *underlying net* of M.

A *directed edge-labelled tree* is a tree provided with a labelling function for its edges. Given a Petri net $M = (P, T, F, C_{in})$ we define the *sequential configuration graph of M*, denoted by $SCG(M)$, as a directed edge-labelled tree having elements in $\mathbb{C}_M$ (the set of all *reachable configurations*) as vertices, C_{in} as root, $E = \{(C, D) \mid C, D \in \mathbb{C}_M, t \in T, C[t\rangle D\}$ as set of directed edges and $label : E \to T$ as labelling function. If $e = (C, D) \in E$, then $label(e) = t$ if $C[t\rangle D$ (that is, if $t \in T$ fires from C to D).

Moreover, $U_{C,D} = \{U_i \subseteq T \mid U_i \text{ is a concurrent step from } C \text{ to } D\}$ is the *set of concurrent steps from C to D* and $U_{C,D}^{max} = \{U \mid |U| \geq |V| \ \forall U, V \in U_{C,D}\}$ is the *maximal set of concurrent steps from C to D*.

The *configuration graph of M*, denoted by $CG(M)$, is similar to the $SCG(M)$ but it has $E = \{(C, D) \mid C, D \in \mathbb{C}_M, U \subseteq T, C[U\rangle D\}$ and $label : E \to \mathcal{P}(T)$

(where, given a set A, $\mathcal{P}(A)$ indicates its *power set*, the set of all subsets of A). If $e = (C, D) \in E$, then $label(e) = U$ if $C[U\rangle D$ (that is, $U \subseteq T$ is a *concurrent step* from C to D).

The *configuration graph with maximal concurrency* of M, denoted by $CGMC(M)$, is similar to the $CG(M)$ but it has $E = \{(C, D) \mid C, D \in \mathbb{C}_M, U \in U_{C,D}^{max}\}$ and $label : E \to \mathcal{P}(T)$ is such that if $e = (C, D) \in E$, then $label(e) = U \in U_{C,D}^{max}$.

The definition of Petri nets can be extended to the one of *place/transition systems*, *P/T systems* for short, allowing a place to contain more than one token and more than one token to be removed/added from/to places as a consequence of a firing.

Definition 2. *A P/T system is a tuple $M = (P, T, F, W, K, C_{in})$, where:*

  i) *(P, T, F) is a net (see Definition 1);*
  ii) *$W : F \to \mathbb{N}$ is a weight function;*
  iii) *$K : P \to \mathbb{N} \cup \{+\infty\}$ is a capacity function;*
  iv) *$C_{in} : P \to \mathbb{N}_0$ is the initial configuration.*

A *configuration* of a P/T system is a multiset over P; if we consider a linear order on the elements of P, then a configuration can be regarded as a vector (this fact will be used in Definition 3). The dynamic behaviour of a P/T system is analogous to the one of a Petri net, but considering the weight and capacity functions.

A P/T system M with *maximal concurrency* is such that for each $C, D \in \mathbb{C}_M$ if there is a $U \subseteq T$ such that $C[U\rangle D$, then $U \in U_{C,D}^{max}$.

Petri nets can be regarded as a specific kind of a P/T systems having $W : F \to \{1\}$ and $K : P \to \{1\}$ as weight and capacity functions, respectively. Moreover, a P/T system can be regarded as a 'compressed' Petri net; given a P/T system it is always possible to create a Petri net modelling the same process of the P/T system.

Definition 3. *Given a P/T system $M = (P, T, F, W, K, C_{in})$ a vector $i : P \to \mathbb{Z}$ is a p-invariant of M if for all configurations C, D of M and all $t \in T$, if $C[t\rangle D$, then $C \cdot i = D \cdot i$ (in this case a configuration is regarded as a vector).*

2.4   Program Machines

Non-rewriting Turing machines were introduced by M. L. Minsky in [15] and then reconsidered in [16] under the name of *program machines*.

Formally a *program machine* with n counters ($n \in \mathbb{N}$), each counter able to store any element in $\mathbb{N}_0$, is defined as $M = (S, R, s_0, f)$, where S is a finite set of *states*, $s_0, f \in S$ are respectively called the *initial* and *final* states, R is the finite set of *instructions* of the form $(s, op(l), v, w)$, with $s, v, w \in S$, $s \neq f$, $op(l) \in \{l_+, l_-\}$, $1 \leq l \leq n$.

A *configuration* of a program machine M with n counters is given by an element in the $n + 1$-tuples $S \times \mathbb{N}_0^n$. Given two configurations $(s, val(l_1), \ldots, val(l_n)), (s', val(l_1'), \ldots, val(l_n'))$ (where $val : \mathbb{N} \to \mathbb{N}_0$ is the function returning the content of a counter) we define a *computational step* as $(s, \quad val(l_1), \quad \ldots, \quad val(l_n)) \vdash (s', val(l_1'), \ldots, val(l_n'))$ if $(s, op(l), v, w) \in R$ and:

- if $op(l) = l_-$, $l = l_i$ and $val(l_i) \neq 0$, then $s' = v$, $val(l_i') = val(l_i) - 1$, $val(l_j') = val(l_j)$, $j \neq i$, $1 \leq j \leq n$;
  if $op(l) = l_-$, $l = l_i$ and $val(l_i) = 0$, then $s' = w$, $val(l_j') = val(l_j)$, $1 \leq j \leq n$;
  (informally: in state s if the content of counter l is greater than 0, then subtract 1 from that counter and change state into v, otherwise change state into w)
- if $op(l) = l_+$, $l = l_i$, then $s' = v, val(l_i') = val(l_i) + 1$, $val(l_j') = val(l_j)$, $j \neq i$, $1 \leq j \leq n$;
  (informally: in state s add 1 to counter l and change state into v).

The reflexive and transitive closure of $\vdash$ is indicated by $\vdash^*$.

A *computation* is a finite sequence of transitions between configurations of a program machine M starting from the initial configuration $(s_0, l_1, \ldots, l_n)$ with $val(l_1) \neq 0$, $val(l_j) = 0$, $2 \leq j \leq n$ and ending with a configuration from which no computational step is possible. If the last of such configurations has f as state, then we say that M *accepts* $val(l_1)$. The set of numbers accepted by M is defined as $L(M) = \{val(l_1) \mid (s_0, val(l_1), \ldots, val(l_n)) \vdash^* (f, val(l_1''), \ldots, val(l_n''))\}$.

2.5 From P to P

Throughout this paper we only consider systems, of the kind introduced in the previous section, whose set of configurations contains some elements which are *final*, i.e., there is no transition from a final configuration to any other configuration.

The results present in Section 5 are related to the simulation of one system performed by another one. A simulation is a relation from the set of subsets of the configurations of a system, the *simulating* one, to the set of configurations of another (different) system, the *simulated* one.

This relation (mapping) induces a partition in the set of configurations of the simulating system and associates the final configurations of this system with the final configurations of the simulated one.

Now we formally define a *simulation* between two systems.

Given a set A we define with $Sub(A) = \{A_1, \ldots, A_t\}, A_i \subseteq A, 1 \leq i \leq t$, a *subdivision* of A into subsets. If $Sub(A)$ is such that $\bigcup_{i=1}^{t} A_i = A$ and $A_p \cap A_q = \emptyset, p \neq q, 1 \leq p, q \leq t$, then $Sub(A)$ is a *partition* of A indicated with $Part(A)$.

Let S, S' be two different systems with $\mathbb{C} = \{c_1, c_2, \ldots, c_v\}$ and $\mathbb{C}' = \{c_1', c_2', \ldots, c_{v'}'\}$ their respective sets of configurations.

A computation of a system S is a finite sequence of configurations (in which it can be that not all configurations of the system are present).

Given the set of configurations $\mathbb{C}$ of a system S it is possible to distinguish one subset $F_\mathbb{C}$ in it: the set of *final* configurations (all sharing certain termination criteria). The last configuration in all computations of S is an element of $F_\mathbb{C}$.

Let us denote with $\Rightarrow$ ($\Rightarrow'$) the transition from one configuration to another in a computation of S (S'). Moreover, let $\Rightarrow^*$ ($\Rightarrow'^*$) be the reflexive and transitive closure of $\Rightarrow$ ($\Rightarrow'$).

We will say that S can simulate S' if there is a relation $Sim \subseteq Sub(\mathbb{C}) \times \mathbb{C}'$ such that:

1. for each $c'_{g'}, c'_{h'} \in \mathbb{C}', g' \neq h'$, such that $c'_{g'} \Rightarrow' c'_{h'}$ there are $G, H \in Sub(\mathbb{C})$ such that $Sim(G) = c'_{g'}$ and $Sim(H) = c'_{h'}$ and $c_g \Rightarrow c_h$ for each $c_g \in G$ and $c_h \in H$;
2. for each $c'_{f'} \in F_{\mathbb{C}'}$ there is $F \in Sub(\mathbb{C}), F = F_\mathbb{C}$, such that $Sim(F) = c'_{f'}$.

So, if $b' \Rightarrow'^* e', e' \in F_{\mathbb{C}'}$, then there are $B, E \in Sub(\mathbb{C}), E = F_\mathbb{C}$, such that $Sim(B) = b', Sim(E) = e'$, and $b \Rightarrow^* e$ for each $b \in B$ and $e \in F_\mathbb{C}$. In this case we can also write $B \Rightarrow^* E$.

S is called the *simulating* system and S' the *simulated* system.

Notice that neither all elements in $Sub(\mathbb{C})$ are in relation with an element $l' \in \mathbb{C}'$, nor for each element in $\mathbb{C}'$ there is $L \in Sub(\mathbb{C})$ such that $Sim(L) = l'$.

Lemma 1. *Given two systems S and S' the simulation relation $Sim \subseteq Sub(\mathbb{C}) \times \mathbb{C}'$ induces a partition in $\mathbb{C}$.*

So we can say that if S can simulate S', then there is a relation $Sim \subseteq Part(\mathbb{C}) \times \mathbb{C}'$.

Given two systems it is possible to have several relations defining different simulations.

3   Maximal Parallelism, Priorities and Indication of Emptiness

Several proofs of the computational completeness of (tissue) P systems using symbol objects are based on the simulation of program machines and use either maximal parallelism [18], or priorities [24], or indication of emptiness of the counters (of the simulated program machine) [6]. With *indication of emptiness* we mean that in the P system there is a configuration associated with the one(s) of the program machine in which one of the counters is zero (i.e., is empty). For some of these variants (for instance, [7, 6]) it is proved that when these elements are missing, then the computational power is reduced to the one of partially blind program machines (see also [4]).

These facts suggest that maximal parallelism, priorities and indication of emptiness are different aspects of the same feature, that is, that they are equivalent. To our knowledge there is no direct proof of this (an indirect proof would be to consider one computational device and show that with either maximal parallelism, priorities or indication of emptiness it is computationally complete).

In this section we prove that, for P/T systems maximal concurrency, priorities and indication of emptiness are equivalent.

In [3] it is indicated that P/T systems with maximal concurrency (there called *maximum strategy*) can perform the test for zero (addressed by us as the *0-test*) simulating rule (s, l_-, v, w) (addressed by us as *0-rule*) of a program machine. This simulation is performed by the net underlying the P/T system with maximal concurrency depicted in Figure 1. The same P/T system simulates the 0-rule if the firing of transition t_2 has priority on the firing of transition t_5 (and maximal concurrency is not present). In this P/T system the number of tokens that can be present in p_c is unbounded. It is important for us to notice that in the P/T system simulating the program machine there are as many such P/T systems performing the 0-test as many 0-rules present in the simulated program machine. Moreover, as the program machine can be in only one state per time, then at most one place p_s in a P/T system performing a 0-test can have a token.

If we transform the net underlying the P/T system present in Figure 1 into a Petri net, then we obtain the net depicted in Figure 2 (without considering the dashed place and edge) where, if we consider the presence of priorities (and the absence of maximal parallelism), all the $t_2^i, i \in \mathbb{N}$, have priority on t_5. In Figure 2, if the counter c of the simulated program machine has value $i, i \in \mathbb{N}$, then a place $p_{c=i}$ has a token (we will discuss the case $i = 0$ in a while).

It should be clear that neither the just mentioned P/T system, nor the Petri net perform the 0-test if maximal parallelism and priorities are not considered. In the net underlying the P/T system in Figure 1 it can be, for instance, that if at least one token is present in p_c and one token is present in p_s, then the system can fire t_1, t_3 and t_5 in sequence reaching a configuration having one token in p_w.

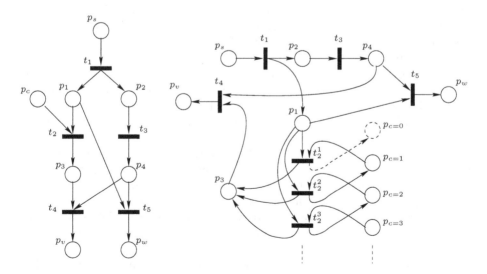

Fig. 1. Net underlying the P/T system for the 0-test

Fig. 2. Net underlying the Petri net for the 0-test

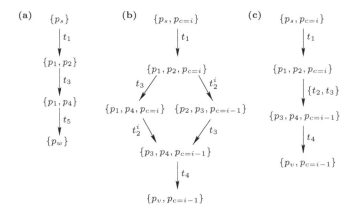

Fig. 3. (a), (b) SCG for the 0-test with priorities, **(a), (b)** CG for the 0-test with maximal parallelism, $i \in \mathbb{N}$

Fig. 4. 'Reduced' (S)CGs, $i \in \mathbb{N}$

As in the net underlying the P/T system in Figure 1 the place p_c can contain arbitrarily many tokens, then in the net underlying the Petri net in Figure 2 the number of transitions t_2^i and of places $p_{c=i}, i \in \mathbb{N}$, is infinite.

The CGMC and the SCG (in case of priorities) for all the permitted initial configurations of the net underlying the Petri net depicted in Figure 2 are represented in Figure 3.

The graphs depicted in Figure 3 are such that, once in the root, the system can only evolve toward the configuration at the bottom. So we can write a 'reduced' graph. This is done in Figure 4.a and Figure 4.c.

As in each configuration of a program machine a counter can have only one value, a Petri net simulating it would have $\sum_{i=1}^{\infty} p_{c=i} = 1$ as p-invariant (where $p_{c=i}$ are the places in the net depicted in Figure 2). If in the same net we consider the dashed place $p_{c=0}$ and the dashed edge incoming this place, then its 'behaviour' is not changed, but it is actually enlarged to model a program machine also when a counter c is empty. The configuration graphs are changed adding the place $p_{c=0}$ to every configuration in Figure 3.a. This means that its 'reduced' configuration graph changes into the one depicted in Figure 4.b.

If we now consider the 'reduced' configuration graphs depicted in Figure 4.b and Figure 4.c, then we can create another net underlying a Petri net implementing the 0-test. This is depicted in Figure 5. Because of the edges from $p'_{c=0}$ to $t_2'^0$ and vice versa, what is depicted in Figure 5 is not a net underlying a

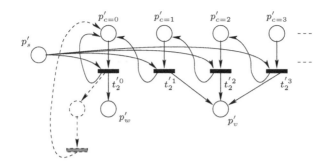

Fig. 5. Net underlying the 'reduced' Petri net for the 0-test

Petri net as defined in Definition 1 (as point 4 is not satisfied). We can overcome this by simply removing the edge from $t_2'^0$ to $p_{c=0}'$ and adding the dashed place, transition and edges.

The net underlying the Petri net depicted in Figure 5 can be regarded as a rewriting of the one depicted in Figure 2. Such a rewriting implements the 0-test without maximal concurrency and priorities but with an infinity of places and transitions.

Recalling (from Section 2.3) that a Petri net can be regarded as a specific kind of a P/T system we can say that:

Theorem 1. *For a P/T system,*

1. *finite number of places + unbounded number of tokens in a place + maximal concurrency,*
2. *finite number of places + unbounded number of tokens in a place + priorities,*
3. *infinite number of places and transitions (that is, indication of emptiness)*

are similar ways to perform the 0-test.

It is important to notice that the net underlying the Petri net depicted in Figure 5 performs more than just the 0-test, it performs the i-test for $i \in \mathbb{N}_0$.

4   0-Test and 0-Gamble

In this section we will show that two ways to simulate the 0-rule are equivalent. The proof uses nets and building blocks.

The 0-test can be performed by nets different from the one depicted in Figure 1. Several papers on variants of P systems using symbol objects use another mapping (from P systems to program machines) to simulate the 0-rule (s, l_-, v, w).

This procedure, addressed by us as the *0-gamble*, can be represented by the net underlying the P/T system depicted in Figure 6 where maximal concurrency or priorities (transition t_4 has priority on transition t_6) are present.

Let us say that once in state p_s the system 'gambles' one of two cases: either the counter is empty or it is not. If the gamble is correct, then the system will

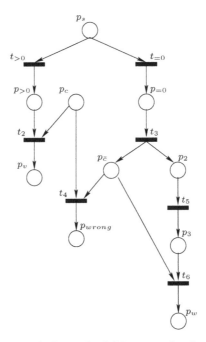

Fig. 6. Net underlying the P/T system for the 0-gamble

evolve in state p_w or p_v respectively, in case of wrong gamble it will go into the state p_{wrong} or it will block, respectively.

It is interesting to notice what happens when the system gambles that the counter in not empty. In this case the places $p_{\bar{c}}$ and p_2 get a token and then either p_{wrong} or p_{s_0} will get a token.

The presence of the place $p_{\bar{c}}$ is of interest for our discussion. Following what indicated in [8] we can name this place 'conflicting counter'. A similar concept has been used also in [5]. Even if explicitly defined in the just mentioned papers, the concept of 'conflicting counter' was already implicitly present in all the proofs of P systems using symbol objects generating $\mathbb{N} \cdot \mathbf{RE}$ and using the 0-gamble ([18], for instance).

Some of these proofs were so made that once in p_w the computation could still enter the p_{wrong} place (for instance, Theorem 1 in [7]).

At this point we can wonder on the relation between the 0-test (Figure 1) and the 0-gamble (Figure 6).

Before studying this further, let us introduce the nets depicted in Figure 7. We call these nets *building blocks*.

Both the 0-test and the 0-gamble are implemented by a combination of the building blocks. In the net underlying the P/T system for the 0-test (Figure 1) $\{p_c, p_1, p_3\}$, $\{p_3, p_4, p_v\}$ and $\{p_1, p_4, p_v\}$ are building blocks of type **b**; $\{p_s, p_1, p_2\}$ is a building block of type **c** and $\{p_2, p_4\}$ is a building block of type **d**. In the net underlying the P/T system for the 0-gamble (Figure 6) $\{p_s, p_{>0}, p_{=0}\}$ is a building block of type **a**; $\{p_{>0}, p_c, p_v\}$, $\{p_c, p_{\bar{c}}, p_{wrong}\}$ and $\{p_{\bar{c}}, p_3, p_w\}$ are

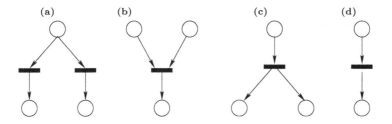

Fig. 7. Building blocks: **(a)** nondeterminism, **(b)** join, **(c)** fork, **(d)** determinism

building blocks of type **b**; $\{p_{=0}, p_{\bar{c}}, p_2\}$ is a building block of type **c** and $\{p_2, p_3\}$ is a building block of type **d**. In this figure we also see that the relative arrangement of pairs of building blocks is the one indicated in Table 1.

At this point we can say that:

Theorem 2. *A necessary condition such that a system S with maximal parallelism or priorities using symbol objects can implement the 0-test (or the 0-gamble) is that there is a mapping from S to a net underlying a P/T system such that it is possible to have a sequence of sets of configurations in S associated with the subsequent firing of transitions present in the pairs of building blocks listed above.*

The previous theorem does not give a sufficient condition as the system could have features (limits in the number of tokens present in a place, limits on the firing of transitions, etc.) not allowing it to perform the 0-test even if its process can be described by the building blocks and that pairs of building blocks can be combined in the ways listed in Table 1.

As the relative arrangements of the pairs of building blocks present in the 0-test are part of the relative arrangements of building blocks present in the 0-gamble, then we can say that:

Corollary 1. *If a system with maximal parallelism or priorities using symbol objects can implement the 0-gamble, then it can implement the 0-test.*

Table 1. Pairs of building blocks for the 0-test and the 0-gamble (with **d**)

0-test	**c-b, c-d, b-b, d-b**
0-gamble	**a-b, a-c, b-b, c-b, c-d, d-b**

Table 2. Pairs of building blocks for the 0-test and the 0-gamble (without **d**)

0-test	**c-b, b-b**
0-gamble	**a-b, a-c, b-b, c-b**

Both in the 0-test (Figure 1) and the 0-gamble (Figure 6) the building block d can be substituted by the building block **c** followed by the building block **b** without affecting the behaviour of the P/T system. If we consider this, the relative arrangements of pairs of building blocks indicated in Table 1 changes into the one indicated in Table 2.

5   Unifying Results

In this section we generalise the result obtained in Section 3 showing that maximal parallelism, priorities and indication of emptiness are equivalent concepts for systems using symbol objects. To do so we use the same technique used in Section 4.

The capability to simulate the 0-rule is only one of the operations needed for a system using symbol objects to simulate a program machine. The system has also to simulate the rule (s, l_+, v, w) (adding 1 to a counter) and to simulate nondeterminism (see Section 2.4). These two operations can be simulated by the building blocks **c** and **a** respectively. The operations of simulating a 0-rule, addition of 1 and simulating nondeterminism, can be performed by the system in any order. If we consider that the simulation of the 0-test can be followed by the simulation of nondeterminism, then it has to be possible that the building block **b** (as in Figure 1 both p_v and p_w are in such building block) is followed by the building block **a**. Reasoning in a similar way we obtain the pairs of building blocks listed in Table 3.

Table 3.   Pairs of building blocks for 0-test (0-gamble), fork and nondeterminism

0-test, non det.	**b-a**	0-gamble, non det.	**b-a**
non det., 0-test	**a-c**	non det., 0-gamble	**a-c**
fork, 0-test	**c-b, c-c**	fork, 0-gamble	**c-b, c-a**
0-test, fork	**b-c**	0-gamble, fork	**b-c**
fork, non det.	**c-a**	fork, non det.	**c-a**
non det., fork	**a-c**	non det., fork	**a-c**

This implies that:

Corollary 2. *A necessary condition such that a system S with maximal parallelism or priorities using symbol objects can simulate a program machine is that there is a mapping from S to a net underlying a P/T system such that it is possible to have a sequence of sets of configurations in S associated with any subsequent firing of transitions present in the pairs of building blocks listed in Table 1 and Table 3.*

Reasoning in a similar way we can say that

Corollary 3. *A necessary condition such that a system S using symbol objects can simulate a P/T system with indication of emptiness is that there is a mapping*

Table 4. Pairs of building blocks for indication of emptiness, fork and nondeterminism

inside ind. empty	**b-c**
ind. empty., non det.	**c-a**
non det., ind. empty.	**a-b**
fork, ind. empty.	**c-b**
ind. empty, fork	**c-c**
fork, non det.	**c-a**
non det., fork	**a-c**

from S to a net underlying a P/T system such that it is possible to have a sequence of sets of configurations in S associated with any subsequent firing of transitions present in the pairs of building blocks listed in Table 4.

Now we are ready to state the main result of this paper.

Theorem 3. *Let $X = \{maximal\ parallelism,\ indication\ of\ emptiness,\ priorities\}$ and let D provided with $x \in X$ be a device using symbol objects which is computationally complete. Let D' be similar to D but with $x' \in X, x' \neq x$.*

1. *If $x =$ 'maximal parallelism' and $x' =$ 'priorities', then D' with x' is also computationally complete (similarly if $x =$ 'priorities' and $x' =$ 'maximal parallelism');*
2. *If $x =$ 'maximal parallelism' and $x' =$ 'indication of emptiness', then a necessary condition for D' with x' to be computationally complete is the presence of a mapping from D' to the net underlying a P/T system such that it is possible to have a sequence of sets of configurations in D' associated with the subsequent firing of the transitions present in the pair of building blocks **c-c** (similarly if $x =$ 'priorities');*
3. *If $x =$ 'indication of emptiness' and $x' =$ 'maximal parallelism', then a necessary condition for D' with x' to be computationally complete is the presence of a mapping from D' to the net underlying a P/T system such that it is possible to have a sequence of sets of configurations in D' associated with the subsequent firing of the transitions present in the pairs of building blocks **b-b** and **b-a** (similarly if $x' =$ 'priorities').*

In the previous theorem, if $x' =$ 'indication of emptiness' then, more than being able to arrange the building blocks as indicated, D' needs a finite way to address the infinite number of places that are created.

6   Final Remarks

How can the results obtained in the previous sections be of any use in the study of the computational power of a system using symbol objects?

Given a computability system S using symbol objects one can prove that it is computationally complete using Theorem 3, and not trying the simulation of a computationally complete device. As Theorem 3 states only a necessary condition it has also to be proved that there are no limitations affecting the work of S.

More relevant consequences are present in case a system S using symbol objects cannot fulfil what stated in Theorem 3. Not verifying the necessary condition present in that theorem S cannot be computationally complete.

At the present time we do not know if the building blocks **a**, **b** and **c** represent a base for nets underlying a P/T systems generating $\mathbb{N} \cdot \mathrm{RE}$. For sure they do not represent a base for a general net.

Our intention is to go further on the line of this research trying to give an answer to the following questions:

How computationally powerful is a P/T system having an underlying net composed by proper subsets of the building blocks depicted in Figure 7? (in this respect the computational differences between program machine and partially blind program machine [9] and the infinite hierarchy described in [17] are going to be of help)

How the computational power is affected if we limit the kind of relative arrangements of pairs of building blocks?

What happens if we allow the P/T system having as underlying net the one depicted in Figure 2 to have as p-invariant $\sum_{i=1}^{\infty} p_{c=i} = n, n \in \mathbb{N}_0$? (this means that more than one place of the kind $p_{c=i}$ can have a token or that some of them have more than one token).

Is it possible to extend these results to systems not using symbol objects?

Our ultimate question on this subject is: is it possible to create an hierarchy of computational power based on building blocks, their combinations and the functions W and K (see Definition 2)?

Acknowledgements

This work has been supported by the research grant NAL/01143/G of The Nuffield Foundation.

References

1. A. Alhazov, C. Martín-Vide, Gh. Păun, eds.: *Preproceedings of the Workshop on Membrane Computing, WMC-2003*. Rovira i Virgili University, Tarragona, 2003.
2. F. Bernardini, M. Gheorghe: On the power of minimal symport/antiport. In [1], 72–83.
3. H.-D. Burkhard: Ordered firing in Petri nets. *Journal of Information Processing and Cybernetics*, 17, 2–3 (1981), 71–86.
4. R. Freund: Asynchronous P systems and P systems working in the sequential mode. In [14], 12–28.
5. R. Freund, M. Oswald: P systems with activated/prohibited membrane channels. In [21], 261–269.

6. P. Frisco: The conformon-P system: A molecular and cell biology-inspired computability model. *Theoretical Computer Science*, 312, 2-3 (2004), 295–319.
7. P. Frisco: About P systems with symport/antiport. *Soft Computing*, 9, 9 (2005), 664–672.
8. P. Frisco, H.J. Hoogeboom: Simulating counter automata by P systems with symport/antiport. In [21], 288–301.
9. S.A. Greibach: Remarks on blind and partially blind one-way multicounter machines. *Theoretical Computer Science*, 7 (1978), 311–324.
10. J.E. Hopcroft, D.Ullman: *Introduction to Automata Theory, Languages, and Computation*. Addison-Wesley, 1979.
11. O.H. Ibarra, Z. Dang, O. Egecioglu: Catalytic P systems, semilinear sets, and vector addition systems. *Theoretical Computer Science*, 312, 1-2 (2004), 379–399.
12. J. Kleijn, M. Koutny, G. Rozenberg: Towards a Petri net semantics for membrane systems. In this volume.
13. C. Martín-Vide, A. Păun, G. Păun: On the power of P systems with symport rules. *The Journal of Universal Computer Science*, 8 (2002), 317–331.
14. G. Mauri, G. Păun, C. Zandron, eds.: *Preproceedings of the Fifth Workshop on Membrane Computing, WMC-2004*. Universitá degli studi di Milano Bicocca, 2004.
15. M.L. Minsky: Recursive unsolvability of Post's problem of "tag" and other topics in theory of Turing machines. *Annals of Mathematics*, 74, 3 (1961), 437–455.
16. M.L. Minsky: *Computation: Finite and Infinite Machines*. Automatic computation. Prentice-Hall, 1967.
17. B. Monien: Two-way multihead automata over a one-letter alphabet. *Informatique Thèorique et Applications*, 14, 1 (1980), 67–82.
18. A. Păun, Gh. Păun: The power of communication: P systems with symport/antiport. *New Generation Computing*, 20, 3 (2002), 295–306.
19. Gh. Păun: Computing with membranes. *Journal of Computer and System Sciences*, 61 (2000), 108–143.
20. Gh. Păun: *Membrane Computing. An Introduction*. Springer, Berlin, 2002.
21. Gh. Păun, G. Rozenberg, A. Salomaa, C. Zandron, eds.: *Membrane Computing: International Workshop, WMC-CdeA 2002, Curtea de Arges, Romania, August 19-23, 2002. Revised Papers*. LNCS 2597, Springer, Berlin, 2002.
22. Z. Qi, J. You: P systems and Petri nets. In [1], 387–403.
23. W. Reisig, G. Rozenberg, eds.: *Lectures on Petri Nets I: Basic Models*. LNCS 1491, Springer, Berlin, 1998.
24. P. Sosík: The power of catalysts and priorities in membrane systems. *Grammars*, 6, 1 (2003), 13–24.
25. G. Vaszil: On the size of P systems with minimal symport/antiport. In [14], 422–431.
26. C. Zandron: P-systems web page: `http://psystems.disco.unimib.it`.
27. S. Dal Zilio, E. Formenti: On the dynamics of PB systems. In [1], 197–208.

On the Power of Dissolution in
P Systems with Active Membranes

Miguel A. Gutiérrez–Naranjo, Mario J. Pérez–Jiménez, Agustín Riscos–Núñez,
and Francisco J. Romero–Campero

Research Group on Natural Computing,
Department of Computer Science and Artificial Intelligence,
University of Sevilla, Avda. Reina Mercedes s/n, 41012 Sevilla, Spain
{magutier, marper, ariscosn, fran}@us.es

Abstract. In this paper we study membrane dissolution rules in the
framework of P systems with active membranes but without using electrical charges. More precisely, we prove that the polynomial computational complexity class associated with the class of recognizer P systems
with active membranes, without polarizations and without dissolution
coincides with the standard complexity class **P**. Furthermore, we demonstrate that if we consider dissolution rules, then the resulting complexity
class contains the class **NP**.

1 Introduction

Membrane Computing is inspired by the structure and functioning of living cells,
and it provides a new non–deterministic model of computation which starts from
the assumption that the processes taking place in the compartmental structure
of a living cell can be interpreted as computations. The devices of this model
are called *P systems*.

Roughly speaking, a P system consists of a cell-like membrane structure, in the
compartments of which one places multisets of objects which evolve according
to given rules in a synchronous non–deterministic maximally parallel manner.

In this paper we work with P systems with active membranes. This model was
introduced in [7], abstracting the way of obtaining new membranes through the
process of *mitosis* (membrane division) and providing a tool able to construct an
exponential workspace in linear time. In these devices membranes are considered
to have polarizations, one of the "electrical charges" $0, -, +$, and several times
the problem was formulated whether or not these polarizations are necessary in
order to obtain polynomial time solutions to **NP**–complete problems. The last
result is that from [1], where it is proved that two polarizations suffice.

In the literature, P systems with active membranes have been successfully
used to design (uniform) solutions to well-known **NP**–complete problems, such
as SAT [12], *Subset Sum* [9], *Knapsack* [10], *Bin Packing* [11], *Partition* [3], and
the *Common Algorithmic Problem* [13].

The present paper can be considered as a contribution to the interesting
problem of characterizing the tractability in terms of descriptional resources
required in membrane systems.

R. Freund et al. (Eds.): WMC 2005, LNCS 3850, pp. 224–240, 2006.
© Springer-Verlag Berlin Heidelberg 2006

Specifically, in the framework of recognizer P systems with membrane division but not using polarizations, we prove the following: (a) the class of problems which can be solved in a polynomial time by a family of such P systems *without dissolution* is equal to class **P**, and (b) the class of problems which can be solved in a polynomial time by a family of such P systems *with dissolution* contains the class **NP**. Hence, we show a surprising role of the –apparently "innocent"– operation of membrane dissolution, as it makes the difference between efficiency and non–efficiency for polarizationless P systems with membrane division.

The paper is organized as follows. In the next section some preliminary ideas about recognizer membrane systems and polynomial complexity classes are introduced. In Section 3 we present a characterization of the class **P** through the polynomial complexity class associated with recognizer P systems with active membranes, without polarization and without dissolution. In Section 4 we show that every **NP**–complete problem can be solved in a semi–uniform way by families of recognizer P systems using membrane dissolution rules and division for elementary and non–elementary membranes. Conclusions and some final remarks are given in Section 5.

2 Preliminaries

2.1 Recognizer P Systems

In the structure and functioning of a cell, biological *membranes* play an essential role. The cell is separated from its environment by means of a *skin membrane*, and it is internally compartmentalized by means of *internal membranes*.

The main *syntactic* ingredients of a cell–like membrane system (P system) are the *membrane structure*, the *multisets*, and the *evolution rules*.

– A *membrane structure* consists of several membranes arranged hierarchically inside a main membrane (the *skin*), and delimiting *regions* (the space in–between a membrane and the immediately inner membranes, if any). When a membrane has no membrane inside, it is called *elementary*. A membrane structure can be considered as a rooted tree, where the nodes are called *membranes*, the root is called *skin*, and the leaves are called *elementary membranes*.
– Regions defined by a membrane structure can contain objects, corresponding to chemical substances present in the compartments of a cell. These objects can be described by symbols or by strings of symbols, in such a way that *multisets of objects* are placed in the regions of the membrane structure.
– The objects can evolve according to given *evolution rules*, associated with the regions (hence, with the membranes).

The *semantics* of the cell–like membrane systems is defined through a non–deterministic and synchronous model (a global clock is assumed) as follows:

– A *configuration* of a cell–like membrane system consists of a membrane structure and a family of multisets of objects associated with each region of the structure. At the beginning, there is a configuration called the *initial config-uration* of the system.

- In each time unit a given configuration is transformed in another configura-tion by applying the evolution rules to the objects placed inside the regions of the configurations, in a non–deterministic, maximally parallel manner (the rules are chosen in a non–deterministic way, and in each region all objects that can evolve must do it). In this way, we get *transitions* from one config-uration of the system to the next one.
- A *computation* of the system is a (finite or infinite) sequence of configurations such that each configuration –except the initial one– is obtained from the previous one by a transition.
- A computation which reaches a configuration where no more rules can be ap-plied to the existing objects and membranes, is called a *halting computation*.
- The result of a halting computation is usually defined through the multiset associated with a specific output membrane (or the environment) in the final configuration.

In this paper we use membrane computing as a framework to address the reso-lution of decision problems. In order to solve this kind of problems and having in mind that solving them is equivalent to recognizing the language associated with them, we consider P systems as *language recognizer* devices.

Definition 1. *A P system with input is a tuple (Π, Σ, i_Π), where: (a) Π is a P system with working alphabet Γ, with p membranes labelled with $1, \ldots, p$, and initial multisets $\mathcal{M}_1, \ldots, \mathcal{M}_p$ associated with them; (b) Σ is an (input) alphabet strictly contained in Γ and the initial multisets are over $\Gamma - \Sigma$; (c) i_Π is the label of a distinguished (input) membrane.*

The computations of a P system with input in the form of a multiset over Σ are defined in a natural way, but the initial configuration of (Π, Σ, i_Π) must be the initial configuration of the system Π to which we add the input multiset. More formally,

Definition 2. *Let (Π, Σ, i_Π) be a P system with input. Let Γ be the working alphabet of Π, μ the membrane structure, and $\mathcal{M}_1, \ldots, \mathcal{M}_p$ the initial multisets of Π. Let m be a multiset over Σ. The initial configuration of (Π, Σ, i_Π) with input m is $(\mu, \mathcal{M}_1, \ldots, \mathcal{M}_{i_\Pi} \cup m, \ldots, \mathcal{M}_p)$.*

Let (Π, Σ, i_Π) be a P system with input. Let Γ be the working alphabet of Π, μ the membrane structure, and $\mathcal{M}_1, \ldots, \mathcal{M}_p$ the initial multisets of Π. Let m be a multiset over Σ. Then we denote $\mathcal{M}_j^* = \{(a, j) : a \in \mathcal{M}_j\}$, for $1 \leq j \leq p$, and $m^* = \{(a, i_\Pi) : a \in m\}$.

Let us recall that a decision problem X is a pair (I_X, θ_X) where I_X is a language over a finite alphabet (its elements are called *instances*) and θ_X is a predicate (a total boolean function) over I_X.

Definition 3. *Let $X = (I_X, \theta_X)$ be a decision problem. Let $\mathbf{\Pi} = (\Pi(n))_{n \in \mathbf{N}}$ be a family of P systems with input. A polynomial encoding from X to $\mathbf{\Pi}$ is a pair (cod, s) of polynomial time computable functions over I_X such that for each*

instance $w \in I_X$, $s(w)$ *is a natural number and* $cod(w)$ *is an input multiset for the system* $\Pi(s(w))$.

Polynomial encodings are stable under polynomial time reductions [12]. More precisely, the following proposition holds.

Proposition 1. *Let* X_1, X_2 *be decision problems. Let* r *be a polynomial time reduction from* X_1 *to* X_2. *Let* (cod, s) *be a polynomial encoding from* X_2 *to* Π. *Then* $(cod \circ r, s \circ r)$ *is a polynomial encoding from* X_1 *to* Π.

Definition 4. *A* recognizer P system *is a P system with input and external output such that:*

1. *The working alphabet contains two distinguished elements* **yes** *and* **no**.
2. *All computations halt.*
3. *If* $\mathcal{C}$ *is a computation of the system, then either the object* **yes** *or the object* **no** *(but not both) must have been released into the environment, and only in the last step of the computation.*

In recognizer P systems, we say that a computation is an *accepting computation* (respectively, *rejecting computation*) if the object **yes** (respectively, **no**) appears in the environment associated with the corresponding halting configuration.

2.2 Recognizer P Systems with Active Membranes and Without Polarizations

A particularly interesting class of membrane systems are the systems with active membranes, where the membrane division can be used in order to solve computationally hard problems in polynomial or even linear time, by a space–time trade-off.

In this paper we work with a variant of P systems with active membranes that does not use polarizations.

Definition 5. *A P system with active membranes and without polarizations is a P system with* Γ *as working alphabet, with* H *as the finite set of labels for membranes, and where the rules are of the following forms:*

(a) $[a \rightarrow u]_h$ *for* $h \in H$, $a \in \Gamma$, $u \in \Gamma^*$. *This is an object evolution rule, associated with a membrane labelled with* h: *an object* $a \in \Gamma$ *belonging to that membrane evolves to a string* $u \in \Gamma^*$.

(b) $a[\ ]_h \rightarrow [b]_h$ *for* $h \in H$, $a, b \in \Gamma$. *An object from the region immediately outside a membrane labelled with* h *is introduced in this membrane, possibly transformed into another object.*

(c) $[a]_h \rightarrow b[\ ]_h$ *for* $h \in H$, $a, b \in \Gamma$. *An object is sent out from membrane labelled with* h *to the region immediately outside, possibly transformed into another object.*

(d) $[a]_h \rightarrow b$ *for* $h \in H$, $a, b \in \Gamma$: *A membrane labelled with* h *is dissolved in reaction with an object. The skin is never dissolved.*

(e) $[a]_h \rightarrow [b]_h [c]_h$ for $h \in H$, $a, b, c \in \Gamma$. An elementary membrane can be divided into two membranes with the same label, possibly transforming some objects.

These rules are applied according to the following principles:

- All the rules are applied in parallel and in a maximal manner. In one step, one object of a membrane can be used by only one rule (chosen in a non–deterministic way), but any object which can evolve by one rule of any form, must evolve.
- If at the same time a membrane labelled with h is divided by a rule of type (e) and there are objects in this membrane which evolve by means of rules of type (a), then we suppose that first the evolution rules of type (a) are used, and then the division is produced. Of course, this process takes only one step.
- The rules associated with membranes labelled with h are used for all copies of this membrane. At one step, a membrane can be the subject of *only one* rule of types (b)-(e).

Let us note that in this framework we shall work without cooperation, without priorities, with cell division rules for elementary membranes, and without changing the labels of membranes. But we shall explicitly mention in each case whether we use dissolution or not.

We denote by $\mathcal{AM}^0_{-d}$ (respectively, $\mathcal{AM}^0_{+d}$) the class of all recognizer P systems with active membranes without polarizations and without using dissolution (respectively, using dissolution).

2.3 Polynomial Complexity Classes in Recognizer P Systems

Definition 6. *Let $X = (I_X, \theta_X)$ be a decision problem. Let $\mathbf{\Pi} = (\Pi(w))_{w \in I_X}$ be a family of recognizer membrane systems without input.*

- **$\mathbf{\Pi}$ is sound** *with regard to X if for each instance of the problem $w \in I_X$, if there exists an accepting computation of $\Pi(w)$, then $\theta_X(w) = 1$.*
- **$\mathbf{\Pi}$ is complete** *with regard to X if for each instance of the problem $w \in I_X$, if $\theta_X(w) = 1$, then every computation of $\Pi(w)$ is an accepting computation.*

These concepts can be extended to families of recognizer P systems with input membrane.

Definition 7. *Let $X = (I_X, \theta_X)$ be a decision problem. Let $\mathbf{\Pi} = (\Pi(n))_{n \in \mathbf{N}}$ be a family of recognizer P systems with input. Let (cod, s) be a polynomial encoding from X to $\mathbf{\Pi}$.*

- *We say that the family $\mathbf{\Pi}$ is sound with regard to (X, cod, s) if the following holds: for each instance of the problem $w \in I_X$, if there exists an accepting computation of $\Pi(s(w))$ with input $cod(w)$, then $\theta_X(w) = 1$.*

- *We say that the family Π is complete with regard to (X, cod, s) if the following holds: for each instance of the problem $w \in I_X$, if $\theta_X(w) = 1$, then every computation of $\Pi(s(w))$ with input $cod(w)$ is an accepting computation.*

The first results about *solvability* of **NP**–complete problems in polynomial time (even linear) by membrane systems were given by Gh. Păun [6], C. Zandron, C. Ferretti and G. Mauri [14], S.N. Krishna and R. Rama [4], and A. Obtulowicz [5] in the framework of P systems that lack an input membrane. Thus, the constructive proofs of such results need to design *one* system for *each* instance of the problem.

This method for solving problems provides a *specific purpose* algorithmic solution in the following sense: if we wanted to follow this approach for solving some decision problem in a laboratory, then the system constructed to solve a concrete instance would be useless when trying to solve another instance.

Now, we formalize these ideas in the following definition.

Definition 8. *Let $\mathcal{R}$ be a class of recognizer P systems without input membrane. A decision problem $X = (I_X, \theta_X)$ is solvable in polynomial time by a family, $\Pi = (\Pi(w))_{w \in I_X}$, of P systems from $\mathcal{R}$, and we denote this by $X \in \mathbf{PMC}_{\mathcal{R}}^*$, if:*

- *Π is polynomially uniform by Turing machines, that is, there exists a deterministic Turing machine working in polynomial time which constructs the system $\Pi(w)$ from the instance $w \in I_X$.*
- *Π is polynomially bounded, that is, there exists a polynomial function $p(n)$ such that for each $w \in I_X$, all computations of $\Pi(w)$ halt in at most $p(|w|)$ steps.*
- *Π is sound and complete with regard to X.*

Next, we propose to solve a decision problem through a family of P systems constructed in polynomial time by a Turing machine, and verifying that each element of the family processes, in a specified sense, all the instances of *equivalent* size. We say that these solutions are *uniform solutions*.

Definition 9. *Let $\mathcal{R}$ be a class of recognizer P systems with input membrane. A decision problem $X = (I_X, \theta_X)$ is solvable in polynomial time by a family $\Pi = (\Pi(n))_{n \in \mathbf{N}}$, of P systems from $\mathcal{R}$, and we denote this by $X \in \mathbf{PMC}_{\mathcal{R}}$, if the following holds:*

- *The family Π is polynomially uniform by Turing machines.*
- *There exists a polynomial encoding (cod, s) from I_X to Π such that*
  - *The family Π is polynomially bounded with regard to (X, cod, s); that is, there exists a polynomial function p, such that for each $u \in I_X$ every computation of $\Pi(s(u))$ with input $cod(u)$ is halting and, moreover, it performs at most $p(|u|)$ steps.*
  - *The family Π is sound and complete with regard to (X, cod, s).*

It is easy to see that the classes $\mathbf{PMC}_{\mathcal{R}}^*$ and $\mathbf{PMC}_{\mathcal{R}}$ are closed under polynomial–time reduction and complement (see [8] for details).

3 Characterizing the Tractability by Recognizer P Systems with Active Membranes

Let Π be a recognizer P system with active membranes without polarizations and <u>without dissolution</u>. Let R be the set of rules associated with Π.

Each rule can be considered, in a certain sense, as a *dependency* between the object triggering the rule and the object or objects produced by its application.

We can consider a general pattern $(a, h) \rightarrow (a_1, h')(a_2, h') \dots (a_s, h')$, for rules of types $(a), (b), (c), (e)$, where:

- The rules of type (a) correspond to the case $h = h'$ and $s \geq 1$.
- The rules of type (b) correspond to the case $h = f(h')$ and $s = 1$.
- The rules of type (c) correspond to the case $h' = f(h)$ and $s = 1$.
- The rules of type (e) correspond to the case $h = h'$ and $s = 2$.

If h is the label of a membrane, then $f(h)$ denotes the label of the father of the membrane labelled with h. We adopt the convention that the father of the skin membrane is the environment (and we denote by *environment* the label associated with the environment of the system).

For example, let us consider a general rule $(a, h) \rightarrow (a_1, h') \dots (a_s, h')$. Then we can interpret that from the object a in membrane labelled with h we can *reach* the objects $a_1, \dots, a_s$ in membrane labelled with h'.

Next, we formalize these ideas in the following definition.

Definition 10. *Let Π be a recognizer P system with active membranes without polarizations and without dissolution. Let R be the set of rules associated with Π. The dependency graph associated with Π is the directed graph $G_\Pi = (V_\Pi, E_\Pi)$ defined as follows:*

$$V_\Pi = VL_\Pi \cup VR_\Pi,$$

$$VL_\Pi = \{(a, h) \in \Gamma \times H : \ \exists u \in \Gamma^* \ ([a \rightarrow u]_h \in R) \ \vee$$

$$\exists b \in \Gamma \ ([a]_h \rightarrow [\ ]_h b \in R) \ \vee$$

$$\exists b \in \Gamma \ \exists h' \in H \ (h = f(h') \wedge a[\ ]_{h'} \rightarrow [b]_{h'} \in R) \ \vee$$

$$\exists b, c \in \Gamma \ ([a]_h \rightarrow [b]_h[c]_h \in R)\},$$

$$VR_\Pi = \{(b, h) \in \Gamma \times H : \ \exists a \in \Gamma \ \exists u \in \Gamma^* \ ([a \rightarrow u]_h \in R \wedge b \in alph(u)) \ \vee$$

$$\exists a \in \Gamma \ \exists h' \in H \ (h = f(h') \wedge [a]_{h'} \rightarrow [\ ]_{h'} b \in R) \ \vee$$

$$\exists a \in \Gamma \ (a[\ ]_h \rightarrow [b]_h \in R) \ \vee$$

$$\exists a, c \in \Gamma \ ([a]_h \rightarrow [b]_h[c]_h \in R)\},$$

$$E_\Pi = \{((a,h),(b,h')) : \exists u \in \Gamma^* \ ([a \to u]_h \in R \wedge b \in alph(u) \wedge h = h') \vee$$

$$([a]_h \to [\ ]_h b \in R \ \wedge \ h' = f(h)) \vee$$

$$(a[\ ]_{h'} \to [b]_{h'} \in R \ \wedge h \ = f(h')) \vee$$

$$\exists c \in \Gamma \ ([a]_h \to [b]_h[c]_h \in R \wedge h = h')\}.$$

Proposition 2. *Let Π be a recognizer P system with active membranes without polarizations and without dissolution. Let R be the set of rules associated with Π. There exists a Turing machine that constructs the dependency graph associated with Π, G_Π, in polynomial time (that is, in a time bounded by a polynomial function depending on the total number of rules and the maximum length of the rules).*

Proof. A deterministic algorithm that, given a P system Π with the set R of rules, constructs the corresponding dependency graph, is the following:

```
Input: Π (with R as its set of rules)
```
$V_\Pi \leftarrow \emptyset; \ E_\Pi \leftarrow \emptyset$
```
for each rule r ∈ R of Π do
```
$\quad$ `if` $r = [a \to u]_h \wedge$ `alph`$(u) = \{a_1, \ldots, a_s\}$ `then`

$$V_\Pi \leftarrow V_\Pi \cup \bigcup_{j=1}^{s}\{(a,h),(a_j,h)\}; \ \ E_\Pi \leftarrow E_\Pi \cup \bigcup_{j=1}^{s}\{((a,h),(a_j,h))\}$$

$\quad$ `if` $r = [a]_h \to [\ ]_h b$ `then`

$\qquad V_\Pi \leftarrow V_\Pi \cup \{(a,h),(b,f(h))\};$
$\qquad E_\Pi \leftarrow E_\Pi \cup \{((a,h),(b,f(h)))\}$

$\quad$ `if` $r = a[\ ]_h \to [b]_h$ `then`

$\qquad V_\Pi \leftarrow V_\Pi \cup \{(a,f(h)),(b,h)\};$
$\qquad E_\Pi \leftarrow E_\Pi \cup \{((a,f(h)),(b,h))\}$

$\quad$ `if` $r = [a]_h \to [b]_h[c]_h$ `then`

$\qquad V_\Pi \leftarrow V_\Pi \cup \{(a,h),(b,h),(c,h)\};$
$\qquad E_\Pi \leftarrow E_\Pi \cup \{((a,h),(b,h)),((a,h),(c,h))\}$

The running time of this algorithm is bounded by $O(|R| \cdot q)$, where q is the value $\max\{length(r) : \ r \in R\}$.

Proposition 3. *Let $\Pi = (\Gamma, \Sigma, H, \mathcal{M}_1, \ldots, \mathcal{M}_p, R_1, \ldots, R_p, i_\Pi)$ be a recognizer P system with active membranes without polarizations and without dissolution. Let Δ_Π be defined as follows:*

$$\Delta_\Pi = \{(a,h) \in \Gamma \times H : \text{there exists a path (within the dependency graph)}$$
$$\text{from } (a,h) \text{ to } (\textbf{yes}, environment)\}.$$

Then, there exists a Turing machine that constructs the set Δ_Π in polynomial time (that is, in a time bounded by a polynomial function depending on the total number of rules and the maximum length of the rules).

Proof. We can construct the set Δ_Π from Π as follows:

- We construct the dependency graph G_Π associated with Π.
- Then we consider the following algorithm:

> **Input:** $G_\Pi = (V_\Pi, E_\Pi)$
> $\Delta_\Pi \leftarrow \emptyset$
>   **for each** $(a, h) \in V_\Pi$ **do**
>   **if reachability** $(G_\Pi, (a, h), (\text{yes}, environment)) = \text{yes}$ **then**
> $\Delta_\Pi \leftarrow \Delta_\Pi \cup \{(a, h)\}$

The running time of this algorithm is of the order $O(|V_\Pi| \cdot |V_\Pi|^2)$, hence[1] it is of the order $O(|\Gamma|^3 \cdot |H|^3)$.

Next, given a family of recognizer P systems solving a decision problem, we will characterize the acceptance of an instance of the problem, w, using the set $\Delta_{\Pi(s(w))}$ associated with the system $\Pi(s(w))$, that processes the given instance w. More precisely, the instance is accepted by the system if and only if there is an object in the initial configuration of the system $\Pi(s(w))$ with input $cod(w)$ such that there exists a path in the associated dependency graph starting from that object and reaching the object **yes** in the environment.

Proposition 4. *Let $X = (I_X, \theta_X)$ be a decision problem. Let $\mathbf{\Pi} = (\Pi(n))_{n \in \mathbf{N}}$ be a family of recognizer P systems with input membrane solving X, according to Definition 9. Let (cod, s) be the polynomial encoding associated with that solution. Then, for each instance w of the problem X the following assertions are equivalent:*

*(a) $\theta_X(w) = 1$ (that is, the answer to the problem is **yes** for w).*

(b) $\Delta_{\Pi(s(w))} \cap ((cod(w))^* \cup \bigcup\limits_{j=1}^{p} \mathcal{M}_j^*) \neq \emptyset$, where $\mathcal{M}_1, \ldots, \mathcal{M}_p$ are the initial multisets of the system $\Pi(s(w))$.

---

[1] The Reachability Problem is the following: *given a (directed or undirected) graph, G, and two nodes a, b, determine whether or not the node b is reachable from a, that is, whether or not there exists a path in the graph from a to b.* It is easy to design an algorithm running in polynomial time solving this problem. For example, given a (directed or undirected) graph, G, and two nodes a, b, we consider a depth–first–search with source a, and we check if b is in the tree of the computation forest whose root is a. The total running time of this algorithm is $O(|V| + |E|)$, that is, in the worst case is quadratic in the number of nodes. Morover, this algorithm needs to store a linear number of items (it can be proved that there exists another polynomial time algorithm which uses $O(\log^2(|V|))$ space).

Proof. Let $w \in I_X$. Then $\theta_X(w) = 1$ if and only if there exists an accepting computation of the system $\Pi(s(w))$ with input multiset $cod(w)$. But this condition is equivalent to the following: in the initial configuration of $\Pi(s(w))$ with input multiset $cod(w)$ there exists at least one object $a \in \Gamma$ in a membrane labelled with h such that in the dependency graph the node (**yes**, *environment*) is reachable from (a, h).

Hence, $\theta_X(w) = 1$ if and only if $\Delta_{\Pi(s(w))} \cap \mathcal{M}_j^* \neq \emptyset$ for some $j \in \{1, \ldots, p\}$, or $\Delta_{\Pi(s(w))} \cap (cod(w))^* \neq \emptyset$.

Theorem 1. $\mathbf{P} = \mathbf{PMC}_{\mathcal{AM}_{-d}^0}$.

Proof. We have $\mathbf{P} \subseteq \mathbf{PMC}_{\mathcal{AM}_{-d}^0}$ because the class $\mathbf{PMC}_{\mathcal{AM}_{-d}^0}$ is closed under polynomial time reduction. Next, we show that $\mathbf{PMC}_{\mathcal{AM}_{-d}^0} \subseteq \mathbf{P}$. Let $X \in \mathbf{PMC}_{\mathcal{AM}_{-d}^0}$ and let $\mathbf{\Pi} = (\Pi(n))_{n \in \mathbf{N}}$ be a family of recognizer P systems with input membrane solving X, according to Definition 9. Let (cod, s) be the polynomial encoding associated with that solution.

We consider the following deterministic algorithm:

```
Input: An instance w of X
    - Construct the system Π(s(w)) with input multiset cod(w).
    - Construct the dependency graph G_{Π(s(w))} associated with Π(s(w)).
    - Construct the set Δ_{Π(s(w))} as indicated in Proposition 3
```
$\quad answer \leftarrow \mathbf{no}; \ j \leftarrow 1$

$\quad \mathbf{while} \ j \leq p \ \wedge \ answer = \mathbf{no} \ \mathbf{do}$

$\quad\quad \mathbf{if} \ \Delta_{\Pi(s(w))} \cap \mathcal{M}_j^* \neq \emptyset \ \mathbf{then}$

$\quad\quad\quad answer \leftarrow \mathbf{yes}$

$\quad\quad j \leftarrow j + 1$

$\quad \mathbf{endwhile}$

$\quad \mathbf{if} \ \Delta_{\Pi(s(w))} \cap (cod(w))^* \neq \emptyset \ \mathbf{then}$

$\quad\quad answer \leftarrow \mathbf{yes}$

On one hand, the answer of this algorithm is **yes** if and only if there exists a pair (a, h) belonging to $\Delta_{\Pi(s(w))}$ such that the symbol a appears in the membrane labelled with h in the initial configuration (with input the multiset $cod(w)$).

On the other hand, a pair (a, h) belongs to $\Delta_{\Pi(s(w))}$ if and only if there exists a path from (a, h) to (**yes**, *environment*), that is, if and only if we can obtain an accepting computation of $\Pi(s(w))$ with input $cod(w)$. Hence, the algorithm above described solves the problem X.

The cost to determine whether or not $\Delta_{\Pi(s(w))} \cap \mathcal{M}_j^* \neq \emptyset$ (or $\Delta_{\Pi(s(w))} \cap (cod(w))^* \neq \emptyset$) is of the order $O(|\Gamma|^2 \cdot |H|^2)$.

Hence, the running time of this algorithm can be bounded by $f(|w|) + O(|R| \cdot q) + O(p \cdot |\Gamma|^2 \cdot |H|^2)$, where f is the (total) cost of a polynomial encoding from X to $\mathbf{\Pi}$, R is the set of rules of $\Pi(s(w))$, H is the set of labels for membranes of $\Pi(s(w))$, p is the number of (initial) membranes of $\Pi(s(w))$, and $q = \max$ $\{length(r): r \in R\}$. But from Definition 9 we have that all involved parameters are polynomials in $|w|$. That is, the algorithm is polynomial in the size $|w|$ of the input.

Now, we consider *division rules for non–elementary membranes*, that is, rules of the following form $[\, [\ ]_{h_1} [\ ]_{h_2}\,]_{h_0} \rightarrow [\, [\ ]_{h_1}\,]_{h_0} [\, [\ ]_{h_2}\,]_{h_0}$, where h_0, h_1, h_2 are labels: if the membrane with label h_0 contains other membranes than those with labels h_1, h_2, then such membranes and their contents are duplicated and placed in both new copies of the membrane h_0; all membranes and objects placed inside membranes h_1, h_2, as well as the objects from membrane h_0 placed outside membranes h_1 and h_2, are reproduced in the new copies of membrane h_0. We denote by $\mathcal{AM}^0_{-d,+ne}$ the class of all recognizer P systems with active membranes without polarization, without membrane dissolution rules, and using division rules for elementary and non–elementary membranes.

If $\Pi \in \mathcal{AM}^0_{-d,+ne}$, then we define the dependency graph associated with Π as the directed graph G_Π from Definition 10, that is, the division rules for non–elementary membranes do not add any node or edge to the dependency graph.

Then, the proof of Theorem 1 provides the following result:

Theorem 2. $\mathbf{P} = \mathbf{PMC}_{\mathcal{AM}^0_{-d,+ne}}$.

Now, we study similar characterizations of $\mathbf{P}$ dealing with semi–uniform solutions in the framework of recognizer P systems with active membranes without polarizations and without dissolution.

Proposition 5. *Let $X = (I_X, \theta_X)$ be a decision problem. Let $\mathbf{\Pi} = (\Pi(w))_{w \in I_X}$ be a family of recognizer P systems without input membrane solving X, according to Definition 8. Then, for each instance w of the problem X the following assertions are equivalent:*

(a) $\theta_X(w) = 1$ *(that is, the answer to the problem is* **yes** *for w).*

(b) $\Delta_{\Pi(w)} \cap (\bigcup_{j=1}^{p} \mathcal{M}_j^*) \neq \emptyset$, *where $\mathcal{M}_1, \ldots, \mathcal{M}_p$ are the initial multisets of the system $\Pi(w)$.*

Proof. Let $w \in I_X$. Then $\theta_X(w) = 1$ if and only if there exists an accepting computation of the system $\Pi(w)$. But this condition is equivalent to the following: in the initial configuration of $\Pi(w)$ there exists an object $a \in \Gamma$ in a membrane labelled with h such that in the dependency graph the node $(\mathbf{yes}, environment)$ is reachable from (a, h).

Hence, $\theta_X(w) = 1$ if and only if $\Delta_{\Pi(w)} \cap \mathcal{M}_j^* \neq \emptyset$ for some $j \in \{1, \ldots, p\}$.

Theorem 3. $\mathbf{P} = \mathbf{PMC}^*_{\mathcal{AM}^0_{-d}}$.

Proof. The proof of this result is analogous to the proof of Theorem 1, taking into account that in this case we are dealing with a semi-uniform solution. That is, in the previous theorem an instance $w \in I_X$ was processed by the P system $\Pi(s(w))$ with input $cod(w)$, and now such instance is processed by $\Pi(w)$.

Bearing in mind that division rules for non–elementary membranes do not influence the construction of the dependency graph, we have:

Theorem 4. $\mathbf{P} = \mathbf{PMC}^*_{\mathcal{AM}^0_{-d,+ne}}$.

We can consider a three dimensional representation of the above theorems, where $+u$ (respectively, $-u$) stands for uniform (respectively, semi–uniform) solutions.

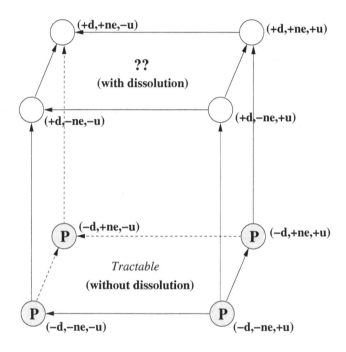

Fig. 1. Characterizations of **P** by P systems

What happens if we consider dissolution rules in the framework of recognizer P systems with active membranes and without polarizations? Will it be possible to solve **NP**–complete problems in that framework? In the next section we will affirmatively answer to this question.

4   Computational Efficiency Using Dissolution Rules

In this section we show that the class of decision problems solvable in polynomial time in a semi–uniform way by families of recognizer P systems with active membranes, without polarization, and using membrane dissolution rules and division rules for elementary and non–elementary membranes, contains the standard complexity class **NP**.

For that, we describe a family of such recognizer membrane systems which solves the Subset Sum problem in linear time and in a semi–uniform way.

The Subset Sum problem is the following one: *Given a finite set A, a weight function, $w : A \rightarrow \mathbf{N}$, and a constant $k \in \mathbf{N}$, determine whether or not there exists a subset $B \subseteq A$ such that $w(B) = k$.*

Proposition 6. *The Subset Sum problem belongs to the class* $\mathbf{PMC}^*_{\mathcal{AM}^0_{+d,+ne}}$.

Sketch of the Proof. We will use a tuple $u = (n, (w_1, \ldots, w_n), k)$ to represent an instance of the problem, where n stands for the size of $A = \{a_1, \ldots, a_n\}$, $w_i = w(a_i)$, and k is the constant given as input for the problem.

We propose here a solution to this problem based on a brute force algorithm implemented in the framework of P systems with active membranes, without polarizations, with dissolution, and using division for elementary and non–elementary membranes.

The idea of the design is better understood if we divide the solution to the problem into several stages:

- *Generation stage*: for every subset of A, a membrane is generated via membrane division.
- *Weight calculation stage*: in each membrane the weight of the associated subset is calculated. This stage will take place in parallel with the previous one.
- *Checking stage*: for each membrane it is checked whether or not the weight of its associated subset is exactly k. This stage cannot start before the previous ones are over.
- *Output stage*: when the previous stage has been completed in all membranes, the system sends out the answer to the environment.

For each instance $u = (n, (w_1, \ldots, w_n), k)$ of the Subset Sum problem we consider the P system with active membranes, without polarization, without input membrane

$$\Pi(u) = (\Gamma(u), H(u), \mu, \mathcal{M}_0, \mathcal{M}_1, \ldots, \mathcal{M}_{k+3}, R(u))$$

defined as follows:
- Working alphabet:

$$\Gamma(u) = \{d_0, \ldots, d_{2n+1}, a_1, \ldots, a_n, e_1, \ldots, e_n\} \cup \{b, s, c, \underline{c}, z_0, \ldots, z_{2n+k+5}, \text{yes}, \text{no}\}.$$

- $H(u) = \{0, 1, 2, 3, \ldots, k + 3\}$.
- Initial membrane structure: $\mu = [\,[\,[\,[\cdots[\,[\,]_0\,]_1 \cdots]_k\,]_{k+1}\,]_{k+2}\,]_{k+3}$.
- Initial multisets:
  $\mathcal{M}_0 = d_0$, $\mathcal{M}_{k+2} = z_0$ and $\mathcal{M}_i = \emptyset$, for every $i \in \{1, \ldots, k, k+1, k+3\}$.
- The set of evolution rules, $R(u)$, consists of the following rules:

(a) $[d_{2i} \rightarrow a_{i+1}d_{2i+1}]_0$ for $i \in \{0, \ldots, n\}$,
       $[d_{2i+1} \rightarrow d_{2i+2}]_0$ for $i \in \{0, \ldots, n-1\}$.

The goal of the counter d_i is to control the apparition of an object a_j only in the odd steps. The importance of these objects will be explained in the next set of rules.

(b) $\begin{rcases} [a_i]_0 \rightarrow [e_i]_0\,[b]_0 \\ [e_i \rightarrow s^{w_i}]_0 \end{rcases}$ for $i \in \{1, \ldots, n\}$.

The object a_i triggers the rule for division of elementary membranes. After the division, in one membrane is placed an object e_i and in the other one an object b. The object b remains inactive whereas the object e_i evolves in the next step to as many copies of object s as the weight w_i.

(c) $[\,[\,]_i\,[\,]_i\,]_{i+1} \rightarrow [\,[\,]_i\,]_{i+1}\,[\,[\,]_i\,]_{i+1}$ for $i \in \{1, \ldots, k\}$.

This is the set of rules for the division of non-elementary membranes. These three first set of rules produce a membrane structure with 2^n branches. On each of the leaves of the tree we have a membrane with as many objects s as the weight of a possible subset, S, of A.

(d) $[d_{2n+1}]_0 \rightarrow b$,
       $[s]_i \rightarrow c$ for $i \in \{1, \ldots, k+1\}$.

When the generation stage has finished, the object d_{2n+1} dissolves the membrane with label 0. At this point, the elements s start to dissolve membranes. If there are enough objects s, all the membranes of the branch with labels $1, \ldots, k+1$ are dissolved. Otherwise, the branch remains inactive.

(e) $[c \rightarrow \underline{c}]_{k+1}$.

This is a waiting step and the key of the computation. If in a branch the encoded weight of the subset, w_S, is less than k, the branch becomes inactive. Otherwise all the membranes of the branch are dissolved until reaching the membrane with label $k + 1$. If $w_S = k$ then in this membrane there are no objects s that dissolve it and the object $\underline{c}$ remains in the membrane. On the contrary, if $w_S > k$, then the membrane is dissolved in the same step in which $\underline{c}$ is produced and $\underline{c}$ goes to the membrane with label $k + 2$.

(f) $[z_i \rightarrow z_{i+1}]_{k+2}$ for $i \in \{0, \ldots, 2n+k+4\}$,
       $[\underline{c}]_{k+1} \rightarrow$ yes,
       $[yes]_{k+2} \rightarrow$ yes,
       $[z_{2n+k+5}]_{k+2} \rightarrow$ no.

If one of the subsets of A has weight k, then an object $\underline{c}$ appears in a membrane with label $k+1$. This object dissolves the membrane and sends an object yes to the membrane with label $k + 2$. In this membrane we keep a counter z_i along the computation. If at some step an object $\underline{c}$ has sent an object yes to this membrane, this object will dissolve the membrane in the next step preventing that the object z_{2n+k+5} appears in the membrane. Otherwise, if the object $\underline{c}$ is never produced, then we eventually get an object z_{2n+k+5} in the membrane with label $k + 2$. In the following step this membrane is dissolved and an element no is sent to the membrane with label $k + 3$.

(g) $[no]_{k+3} \rightarrow$ no $[\,]_{k+3}$,
       $[yes]_{k+3} \rightarrow$ yes $[\,]_{k+3}$.

From above, we know that the membrane with label $k+3$ (recall that this is the skin membrane) is reached by one and only one of the objects yes or no. The rules in group (g) send that object to the environment in the last step of the computation. □

Theorem 5. $\mathbf{NP} \cup \mathbf{co\text{-}NP} \subseteq \mathbf{PMC}^*_{\mathcal{AM}^0_{+d,+ne}}$.

Proof. It suffices to remark that the Subset Sum problem is $\mathbf{NP}$–complete, belonging to the class $\mathbf{PMC}^*_{\mathcal{AM}^0_{+d,+ne}}$, and this class is stable under polynomial-time reduction and closed under complement.

Remark 1. A. Alhazov et al. in [2] showed that $\mathbf{SAT} \in \mathbf{PMC}^*_{\mathcal{AM}^0_{+d,+ne}}$. Hence the result in Theorem 5 can also be deduced from this remark.

The following picture illustrates the results obtained in this paper.

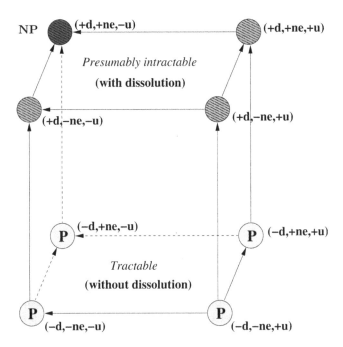

Fig. 2. A borderline between the tractability and the (presumable) intractability

5   Conclusions

A conjecture known in the membrane computing area under the name of the P–conjecture asserts that the polynomial–time solvability by deterministic Turing machines is equivalent to the polynomial–time solvability by recognizer P systems with active membranes and without polarizations, that is, that conjecture can be expressed by the equality $\mathbf{P} = \mathbf{PMC}_{\mathcal{AM}^0}$, where $\mathcal{AM}^0$ is the class of all recognizer P systems with active membranes and without polarization.

In this paper we provide a *partial affirmative* answer to the P–conjecture in the case that the P systems from $\mathcal{AM}^0$ do not use dissolution rules. Besides, a *partial negative* answer to the P–conjecture is given when we use semi–uniform solutions and membrane division rules for elementary and non–elementary membranes (and supposing that $\mathbf{P} \neq \mathbf{NP}$).

We have used the concept of *dependency graph* that initially was defined to help to design strategies that allow to choose short computations of recognizer membrane systems. In this paper we work with dependency graphs associated with a variant of recognizer P systems with active membranes. In this way we are able to characterize accepting computations of these systems through the reachability of a distinguished node of the graph from other nodes associated with the initial configuration.

We have shown that it is possible to solve in polynomial time and in a uniform way through recognizer P systems with active membranes without polarizations and without dissolution *only* problems which are tractable in the standard sense. Morover, if in this framework we consider membrane dissolution rules, then we can solve $\mathbf{NP}$–complete problems in polynomial time, in a semi–uniform way and using division for elementary and non–elementary membranes.

Acknowledgement

The authors wish to acknowledge the support of the project TIC2002-04220-C03-01 of the Ministerio de Ciencia y Tecnología of Spain, cofinanced by FEDER funds.

References

1. A. Alhazov, R. Freund, Gh. Păun: P systems with active membranes and two polarizations. *Proceedings of the Second Brainstorming Week on Membrane Computing* (Gh. Păun, A. Riscos-Núñez, A. Romero-Jiménez, F. Sancho-Caparrini, eds.), Report RGNC 01/04, 2004, 20–35.
2. A. Alhazov, L. Pan, Gh. Păun: Trading polarizations for labels in P systems with active membranes. *Acta Informaticae*, 41, 2-3 (2004), 111-144.
3. M.A. Gutiérrez-Naranjo, M.J. Pérez-Jiménez, A. Riscos-Núñez: A fast P system for finding a balanced 2-partition. *Soft Computing*, 9, 9(2005), 673–678.
4. S.N. Krishna, R. Rama: A variant of P systems with active membranes: Solving NP–complete problems. *Romanian Journal of Information Science and Technology*, 2, 4 (1999), 357–367.
5. A. Obtulowicz: Deterministic P systems for solving SAT problem. *Romanian Journal of Information Science and Technology*, 4, 1–2 (2001), 551–558.
6. Gh. Păun: P systems with active membranes: Attacking NP–complete problems. *Journal of Automata, Languages and Combinatorics*, 6, 1 (2001), 75–90.

7. Gh. Păun: Computing with membranes: Attacking **NP**–complete problems. In *Unconventional Models of Computation, UMC'2K* (I. Antoniou, C. Calude, M.J. Dinneen, eds.), Springer–Verlag, 2000, 94–115.

8. M.J. Pérez–Jiménez: An approach to computational complexity in Membrane Computing. In *Membrane Computing, 5th International Workshop, WMC5, Revised Selected and Invited Papers* (G. Mauri, Gh. Păun, M. J. Pérez-Jiménez, Gr. Rozenberg, A. Salomaa, eds.), LNCS 3365 (2005), 85-109.

9. M.J. Pérez-Jiménez, A. Riscos-Núñez: Solving the Subset-Sum problem by active membranes. *New Generation Computing*, 23, 4(2005), 367–384.

10. M.J. Pérez-Jiménez, A. Riscos-Núñez: A linear–time solution to the Knapsack problem using P systems with active membranes. In *Membrane Computing* (C. Martín-Vide, Gh. Păun, G. Rozenberg, A. Salomaa, eds.), LNCS 2933 (2004), 250–268.

11. M.J. Pérez-Jiménez, F.J. Romero-Campero: Solving the Bin Packing problem by recognizer P systems with active membranes. *Proceedings of the Second Brainstorming Week on Membrane Computing* (Gh. Păun, A. Riscos-Núñez, A. Romero-Jiménez, F. Sancho-Caparrini, eds.), Report RGNC 01/04, University of Seville, 2004, 414–430.

12. M.J. Pérez-Jiménez, A. Romero-Jiménez, F. Sancho-Caparrini: A polynomial complexity class in P systems using membrane division. *Proceedings of the 5th Workshop on Descriptional Complexity of Formal Systems, DCFS 2003* (E. Csuhaj-Varjú, C. Kintala, D. Wotschke, G. Vaszil, eds.), 2003, 284-294.

13. M.J. Pérez-Jiménez, F.J. Romero–Campero: Attacking the Common Algorithmic Problem by recognizer P systems. In *Machines, Computations and Universality, MCU'2004, Saint Petesburg, Russia, September 2004, Revised Selected Papers* (M. Margenstern, ed.), LNCS 3354 (2005), 304-315.

14. C. Zandron, C. Ferreti, G. Mauri: Solving NP-complete problems using P systems with active membranes. In *Unconventional Models of Computation, UMC'2K* (I. Antoniou, C. Calude, M.J. Dinneen, eds.), Springer–Verlag, 2000, 289–301.

A Linear Solution for QSAT with Membrane Creation

Miguel A. Gutiérrez-Naranjo, Mario J. Pérez-Jiménez,
and Francisco J. Romero-Campero

Research Group on Natural Computing,
Department of Computer Science and Artificial Intelligence,
University of Sevilla, Avda. Reina Mercedes s/n 41012, Sevilla, Spain
{magutier, marper, fran}@us.es

Abstract. The usefulness of P systems with membrane creation for solving **NP** problems has been previously proved (see [2,3]), but, up to now, it was an open problem whether such P systems were able to solve **PSPACE**-complete problems in polynomial time. In this paper we give an answer to this question by presenting a uniform family of P system with membrane creation which solves the QSAT-problem in linear time.

1 Introduction

The power of P systems as a tool for efficiently solving **NP** problems has been widely proved. Many examples have been proposed in the framework of P systems with active membranes (with polarizations) and in the framework of P systems with membrane creation.

The complexity class of **NP** problems deals with the *time* needed to solve a problem, i.e., **NP** is the class of problems which can be *solved* by a non-deterministic one-tape Turing machine program where the number of steps is polynomially bounded (see [1]). The key of solving such problems in polynomial time by means of P systems is the creation of an exponential amount of workspace (membranes) in polynomial time.

When we consider the resources needed in a computation, we obviously have to consider the *time*, i.e., the number of steps of our device, but in practice, we also need to consider the amount of memory or storage required by the computation. If we consider a Turing machine computation, the *space* is the number of distinct tape squares visited by the write-read head of the machine. Since the number of visited squares cannot be greater than the number of steps in the computation, we have that, if the number of steps is polynomially bounded, then the number of visited squares is also polynomially bounded. Therefore, any problem solvable in polynomial time is also solvable in polynomial space.

PSPACE (respectively, **NPSPACE**) is the class of decision problems that are solvable by a deterministic (respectively, non–deterministic) Turing machine using a polynomial amount of space. These complexity classes are closed under

R. Freund et al. (Eds.): WMC 2005, LNCS 3850, pp. 241–252, 2006.
© Springer-Verlag Berlin Heidelberg 2006

polynomial time reduction. Savitch's theorem says that each non–deterministic Turing machine using $f(n)$ space can be simulated by a deterministic Turing machine using only $f(n)^2$ space (for time complexity, such a simulation seems to require an exponential increase in time). Bearing in mind that a Turing machine running in $f(n) \geq n$ time can use at most $f(n)$ space we have $\mathbf{P} \subseteq \mathbf{PSPACE}$ and $\mathbf{NP} \subseteq \mathbf{NPSPACE}$. So, $\mathbf{P} \subseteq \mathbf{NP} \subseteq \mathbf{NPSPACE} = \mathbf{PSPACE}$. It is unknown whether any of these containments are strict.

A decision problem in $\mathbf{PSPACE}$ such that every problem in $\mathbf{PSPACE}$ is polynomial time reducible to it, is called $\mathbf{PSPACE}$–complete. If a $\mathbf{PSPACE}$–complete problem belongs to $\mathbf{P}$ (respectively, $\mathbf{NP}$), then $\mathbf{P} = \mathbf{PSPACE}$ (respectively, $\mathbf{NP} = \mathbf{PSPACE}$).

In this paper, we present the first polynomial time solution to the QSAT problem, a well known $\mathbf{PSPACE}$-complete problem (see L.J. Stockmeyer and A.R. Meyer in [14]) using a family of recognizer P systems with membrane creation. Taking into account that the class of all decision problems solvable in polynomial time by a family of such P systems is closed under polynomial–time reduction, this result shows that all $\mathbf{PSPACE}$ problems can be solved in polynomial time by P systems with membrane creation.

The paper is organized as follows. In the next section, recognizer P systems are briefly described. In Section 3 the variant of P systems with membrane creation are recalled with a short discussion about their semantics. A linear–time solution to the QSAT problem is presented in the following section, with a short overview of the computation. Finally, some conclusions are given in the last section.

2   Recognizer P Systems

Recognizer P systems were introduced in [13] and are the natural framework to study and solve decision problems, since deciding whether an instance of a problem has an affirmative or negative answer is equivalent to deciding if a string belongs or not to the language associated with the problem.

In the literature, recognizer P systems are associated with P systems with *input* in a natural way. The data related to an instance of the decision problem has to be provided to the P system in order to compute the appropriate answer. This is done by codifying each instance as a multiset placed in an *input membrane*. The output of the computation (**yes** or **no**) is sent to the environment. In this way, P systems with input and external output are devices which can be seen as black boxes, in which the user provides the data before the computation starts and the P system sends to the environment the output in the last step of the computation. Another important feature of P systems is the non-determinism. The design of a family of recognizer P system has to consider it, because all possibilities in the non-deterministic computations must produce the same answer. This can be summarized in the following definitions.

Definition 1. *A P system with input is a tuple (Π, Σ, i_Π), where: (a) Π is a P system, with working alphabet Γ, with p membranes labelled by $1, \ldots, p$, and initial multisets $w_1, \ldots, w_p$ associated with them; (b) Σ is an (input) alphabet strictly contained in Γ; the initial multisets are over $\Gamma - \Sigma$; and (c) i_Π is the label of a distinguished (input) membrane.*

Let m be a multiset over Σ. The *initial configuration of* (Π, Σ, i_Π) *with input* m is $(\mu, w_1, \ldots, w_{i_\Pi} \cup m, \ldots, w_p)$.

Definition 2. *A* recognizer P system *is a P system with input, (Π, Σ, i_Π), and with external output such that:*

1. *The working alphabet contains two distinguished elements* yes, no.
2. *All computations halt.*
3. *If $\mathcal{C}$ is a computation of Π, then either the object* yes *or the object* no *(but not both) must have been released into the environment, and only in the last step of the computation.*

We say that $\mathcal{C}$ is an accepting computation (respectively, rejecting computation) if the object yes (respectively, no) appears in the environment associated with the corresponding halting configuration of $\mathcal{C}$.

Definition 3. *Let $\mathcal{F}$ be a class of recognizer P systems. We say that a decision problem $X = (I_X, \theta_X)$ is solvable in polynomial time by a family $\mathbf{\Pi} = (\Pi(n))_{n \in \mathbb{N}}$, of $\mathcal{F}$, and we denote this by $X \in \mathbf{PMC}_\mathcal{F}$, if the following holds:*

- *The family $\mathbf{\Pi}$ is* polynomially uniform by Turing machines, *that is, there exists a deterministic Turing machine constructing $\Pi(n)$ from $n \in \mathbb{N}$ in polynomial time.*
- *There exists a pair (cod, s) of polynomial-time computable functions over I_X such that:*
  - *for each instance $u \in I_X$, $s(u)$ is a natural number and $cod(u)$ is an input multiset of the system $\Pi(s(u))$;*
  - *the family $\mathbf{\Pi}$ is polynomially bounded with regard to (X, cod, s), that is, there exists a polynomial function p, such that for each $u \in I_X$ every computation of $\Pi(s(u))$ with input $cod(u)$ is halting and, moreover, it performs at most $p(|u|)$ steps;*
  - *the family $\mathbf{\Pi}$ is sound with regard to (X, cod, s), that is, for each $u \in I_X$, if there exists an accepting computation of $\Pi(s(u))$ with input $cod(u)$, then $\theta_X(u) = 1$;*
  - *the family $\mathbf{\Pi}$ is complete with regard to (X, cod, s), that is, for each $u \in I_X$, if $\theta_X(u) = 1$, then every computation of $\Pi(s(u))$ with input $cod(u)$ is an accepting one.*

In the above definition we have imposed to every P system $\Pi(n)$ to be *confluent*, in the following sense: every computation of a system with the *same* input must always give the *same* answer.

It can be proved that $\mathbf{PMC}_\mathcal{F}$ is closed under polynomial–time reduction and complement (see [13]). In this paper we will deal with the class $\mathcal{MC}$ of recognizer P systems with membrane creation.

3   P Systems with Membrane Creation

In this section we recall the description of cellular devices (P systems) with membrane creation.

Basically, a P system[1] consists of a hierarchical membrane structure where each membrane has associated a multiset of objects and a set of rules expressing how these objects can evolve. The *membrane structure* of a P system is a hierarchical arrangement of membranes embedded in a *skin* membrane, which separates the system from its *environment*. A membrane without any membrane inside is called *elementary*. Each membrane determines a *region* (the space enclosed between the membrane and the membranes immediately inside it), which can contain a multiset of *objects*. Associated with the regions there are *rules* that can transform and move those objects.

There are two ways of producing new membranes in living cells: *mitosis* (membrane division) and *autopoiesis* (membrane creation, see [5]). Both ways of generating new membranes have given rise to different variants of P systems: *P systems with active membranes*, where the new workspace is generated by membrane division, and *P systems with membrane creation*, where the new membranes are created from objects. Both models have been proved to be universal, but up to now there is no theoretical result proving that these models simulate each other in polynomial time. P systems with active membranes have been successfully used to design solutions to **NP**-complete problems, as SAT [13], Subset Sum [10], Knapsack [11], Bin Packing [12], and Partition [4], but as Gh. Păun pointed out in [9] *"membrane division was much more carefully investigated than membrane creation as a way to obtain tractable solutions to hard problems"*. The first results in this way have recently appeared, showing that **NP** problems can also be solved in this framework (see [2, 3]).

Recall that a *P system with membrane creation* is a construct of the form $\Pi = (O, H, \mu, w_1, \ldots, w_m, R)$, where:

1. $m \geq 1$ is the initial degree of the system; O is the alphabet of *objects* and H is a finite set of *labels* for membranes;
2. μ is a *membrane structure* consisting of m membranes labelled (not necessarily in a one-to-one manner) with elements of H and $w_1, \ldots, w_m$ are strings over O, describing the *multisets of objects* placed in the m regions of μ;
3. R is a finite set of *rules*, of the following forms:
   (a) $[a \rightarrow v]_h$ where $h \in H$, $a \in O$, and v is a string over O describing a multiset of objects. These are *object evolution rules* associated with membranes and depending only on the label of the membrane.
   (b) $a[\ ]_h \rightarrow [b]_h$ where $h \in H$, $a, b \in O$. These are *send-in communication rules*. An object is introduced in the membrane, possibly modified.
   (c) $[a]_h \rightarrow [\ ]_h b$ where $h \in H$, $a, b \in O$. These are *send-out communication rules*. An object is sent out of the membrane, possibly modified.

---

[1] A layman-oriented introduction can be found in [8], a comprehensive monograph in [7], and the latest information about P systems is available at [15].

(d) $[a]_h \rightarrow b$ where $h \in H$, $a, b \in O$. These are *dissolution rules*. In reaction with an object, a membrane is dissolved, while the object specified in the rule can be modified.

(e) $[a \rightarrow [v]_{h_2}]_{h_1}$ where $h_1, h_2 \in H$, $a \in O$, and v is a string over O describing a multiset of objects. These are *creation rules*. In reaction with an object, a new membrane is created. This new membrane is placed inside of the membrane of the object which triggers the rule and has associated an initial multiset and a label.

Rules are applied according to the following principles:

– Rules from (a) to (d) are used as usual in the framework of membrane computing, that is, in a maximally parallel way. In one step, each object in a membrane can only be used for one rule (non-deterministically chosen when there are several possibilities), but any object which can evolve by a rule of any form must do it (with the restrictions indicated below).

– Rules of type (e) are used also in a maximally parallel way. Each object a in a membrane labelled with h_1 produces a new membrane with label h_2 placing in it the multiset of objects described by the string v.

– If a membrane is dissolved, its content (multiset and interior membranes) becomes part of the immediately external one. The skin membrane is never dissolved.

– All the elements which are not involved in any of the operations to be applied remain unchanged.

– The rules associated with the label h are used for all membranes with this label, irrespective of whether or not the membrane is an initial one or it was obtained by creation.

– Several rules can be applied to different objects in the same membrane simultaneously. The exception are the rules of type (d) since a membrane can be dissolved only once.

We denote by $\mathcal{MC}$ the class of recognizer P systems with membrane creation.

4   Solving QSAT in Linear Time

In this section we design a family of recognizer P systems with membrane creation (and using dissolution rules) which solves the QSAT problem (the quantified satisfiability problem).

Given a Boolean formula $\varphi(x_1, \ldots, x_n)$ in conjunctive normal form, with Boolean variables $x_1, \ldots, x_n$, the sentence $\varphi^* = \exists x_1 \forall x_2 \ldots Q_n x_n \varphi(x_1, \ldots, x_n)$ (where Q_n is $\exists$ if n is odd, and Q_n is $\forall$, otherwise) is said to be the (existential) *fully quantified* formula associated with $\varphi(x_1, \ldots, x_n)$.

We say that φ^* is satisfiable if there exists a truth assignment, σ, over $\{i \mid 1 \leq i \leq n \land i \text{ odd}\}$ such that each extension, σ^*, of σ over $\{1, \ldots, n\}$ verify $\sigma^*(\varphi(x_1, \ldots, x_n)) = 1$.

The QSAT problem is the following one: *Given a Boolean formula* $\varphi(x_1, \ldots, x_n)$ *in conjunctive normal form, determine whether or not the (existential) fully quantified formula* $\varphi^* = \exists x_1 \forall x_2 \ldots Q_n x_n \varphi(x_1, \ldots, x_n)$ *is satisfiable.*

It is well known that QSAT is a **PSPACE**–complete problem [6].

Next, we provide a polynomial time solution of QSAT by a family of recognizer P systems with membrane creation and *using dissolution rules*, according to Definition 3. We will address the resolution via a brute force algorithm, in the framework of recognizer P systems with membrane creation, which consists in the following phases:

- Generation and Evaluation Stage: Using membrane creation we will generate all possible truth assignments associated with the formula and evaluate it on each one. Specifically, we construct a binary complete tree where the leaves encode all possible truth assignment associated with the formula, and the nodes whose level is even (respectively, odd) are codified by an OR gate (respectively, AND gate). In this stage, the values of the formula corresponding to each truth assignment is obtained in the leaves.
- Checking Stage: In each membrane we check whether or not the formula evaluates true on the truth assignment associated with it. Specifically, we proceed to compute the output of that Boolean circuit (that only have gates AND, OR) from the inputs obtained in the leaves by propagating values along the wires and computing the respective gates until the output gate (the root of the tree) has assigned a value.
- Output Stage: The system sends out to the environment the right answer according to the result of the previous stage.

Let us consider the pair function $\langle \, , \, \rangle$ defined by $\langle n, m \rangle = ((n + m)(n + m + 1)/2) + n$. This function is polynomial-time computable (it is primitive recursive and bijective from $\mathbb{N}^2$ onto $\mathbb{N}$). For any given Boolean formula, $\varphi(x_1, \ldots, x_n) = C_1 \wedge \cdots \wedge C_m$, in conjunctive normal form, with n variables and m clauses, we construct a P system $\Pi(\langle n, m \rangle)$ processing the (existential) fully quantified formula φ^* associated with φ (when an appropriate input is supplied). The family presented here is:

$$\mathbf{\Pi} = \{(\Pi(\langle n, m \rangle), \Sigma(\langle n, m \rangle), i(\langle n, m \rangle)) \mid (n, m) \in \mathbb{N}^2\}.$$

For each element of the family, the input alphabet is

$$\Sigma(\langle n, m \rangle) = \{x_{i,j}, \overline{x}_{i,j} \mid 1 \leq i \leq m, 1 \leq j \leq n\}$$

the input membrane is $i(\langle n, m \rangle) = t$, and the P system

$$\Pi(\langle n, m \rangle) = (\Gamma(\langle n, m \rangle), H(\langle n, m \rangle), \mu, w_s, w_{<t, \vee>}, R(\langle n, m \rangle))$$

is defined as follows:

- Working alphabet:

$$\Gamma(\langle n, m\rangle) = \Sigma(\langle n, m\rangle)$$
$$\cup\ \{z_{j,c} \mid j \in \{0, \ldots n\},\ c \in \{\wedge, \vee\}\}$$
$$\cup\ \{z_{j,c,l} \mid j \in \{0, \ldots, n-1\},\ c \in \{\wedge, \vee\}\, l \in \{t, f\}\}$$
$$\cup\ \{x_{i,j,l}, \overline{x}_{i,j,l} \mid j \in \{1, \ldots, n\},\ i \in \{1, \ldots, m\},\ l \in \{t, f\}\}$$
$$\cup\ \{x_{i,j} \mid j \in \{1, \ldots, n\},\ i \in \{1, \ldots, m\}\}$$
$$\cup\ \{r_i, r_{i,t}, r_{i,f} \mid i \in \{1, \ldots, m\}\}$$
$$\cup\ \{d_1, \ldots, d_m, q, t_0, \ldots, t_4, ans_0, \ldots, ans_5, \mathsf{yes}, \mathsf{no}\}$$
$$\cup\ \{yes_\vee, yes^*, no_\vee, \underline{no}_\vee, yes_\wedge, no_\wedge, no^*, yes_\wedge, \underline{yes}_\wedge, no_\vee, \underline{no}_\wedge\}$$
$$\cup\ \{YES, NO\}.$$

- The set of labels, $H(\langle n, m\rangle)$, is

$$\{< l, c > \mid l \in \{t, f\}, c \in \{\wedge, \vee\}\} \cup \{a, s, 1, \ldots, m\}.$$

- Initial membrane structure: $\mu = [\ [\ ]_{<t,\vee>}]_s$.
- Initial multiset: $w_s = \emptyset$, $w_{<t,\vee>} = \{z_{0,\wedge,t}\ z_{0,\wedge,f}\}$.
- Input membrane: $i(\langle n, m\rangle =< t, \vee >$.
- The set of evolution rules, $R(\langle n, m\rangle)$, consists of the following rules (recall that λ denotes the empty string and if c is $\wedge$ then $\overline{c}$ is $\vee$ and if c is $\vee$ then $\overline{c}$ is $\wedge$):

1. $\left.\begin{array}{l} [z_{j,c} \to z_{j,c,t}, z_{j,c,f}]_{<l,\overline{c}>} \\ [z_{j,c,l} \to [z_{j+1,\overline{c}}]_{<l,c>}]_{<l',\overline{c}>} \end{array}\right\}$ for $\begin{array}{l} l, l' \in \{t, f\}, \quad c \in \{\vee, \wedge\}, \\ j \in \{0, \ldots, n-1\}. \end{array}$

The goal of these rules is to create one membrane for each truth assignment to the variables of the formula. Firstly, the object $z_{j,c}$ evolves to two objects, one for the assignment *true* (the object $z_{j,c,t}$), and a second one for the assignment *false* (the object $z_{j,c,f}$). In a second step these objects will create two membranes. The new membrane with t in its label represents the assignment $x_{j+1} = true$; on the other hand, the new membrane with f in its label represents the assignment $x_{j+1} = false$.

2. $\left.\begin{array}{l} [x_{i,j} \to x_{i,j,t} x_{i,j,f}]_{<l,c>} \\ [\overline{x}_{i,j} \to \overline{x}_{i,j,t} \overline{x}_{i,j,f}]_{<l,c>} \\ [r_i \to r_{i,t} r_{i,f}]_{<l,c>} \end{array}\right\}$ for $\begin{array}{l} l \in \{t, f\} \quad i \in \{1, \ldots, m\}, \\ c \in \{\vee, \wedge\} \quad j \in \{1, \ldots, n\}. \end{array}$

These rules duplicate the objects representing the formula so it can be evaluated on the two possible assignments, $x_j = true$ ($x_{i,j,t}, \overline{x}_{i,j,t}$) and $x_j = false$ ($x_{i,j,f}, \overline{x}_{i,j,f}$). The objects r_i are also duplicated ($r_{i,t}, r_{i,f}$) in order to keep track of the clauses that evaluate true on the previous assignments to the variables.

3. $\left.\begin{array}{l} x_{i,1,t}[\ ]_{<t,c>} \to [r_i]_{<t,c>} \\ \overline{x}_{i,1,t}[\ ]_{<t,c>} \to [\lambda]_{<t,c>} \\ x_{i,1,f}[\ ]_{<f,c>} \to [\lambda]_{<f,c>} \\ \overline{x}_{i,1,f}[\ ]_{<f,c>} \to [r_i]_{<f,c>} \end{array}\right\}$ for $\begin{array}{l} i \in \{1, \ldots, m\}, \\ c \in \{\vee, \wedge\}. \end{array}$

According to these rules the formula is evaluated in the two possible truth assignments for the variable that is being analyzed. The objects $x_{i,1,t}$ (resp. $\overline{x}_{i,1,f}$) get into the membrane with t in its label (resp. f) being transformed into the objects r_i representing that the clause number i evaluates true on the assignment $x_{j+1} = true$ (resp. $x_{j+1} = false$). On the other hand, the objects $\overline{x}_{i,1,t}$ (resp. $x_{i,1,t}$) get into the membrane with f in its label (resp. t) producing no objects. This represents that these objects do not make the clause true in the assignment $x_{j+1} = true$ (resp. $x_{j+1} = false$).

4.
$$
\left.
\begin{array}{l}
x_{i,j,l}[\,]_{<l,c>} \rightarrow [x_{i,j-1}]_{<l,c>} \\
\overline{x}_{i,j,t}[\,]_{<l,c>} \rightarrow [\overline{x}_{i,j-1}]_{<l,c>} \\
r_{i,t}[\,]_{<l,c>} \rightarrow [r_i]_{<l,c>}
\end{array}
\right\}
\text{ for }
\begin{array}{l}
l \in \{t,f\}, \quad i \in \{1,\ldots,m\}, \\
c \in \{\vee,\wedge\}, \quad j \in \{2,\ldots,n\}.
\end{array}
$$

In order to analyze the next variable the second subscript of the objects $x_{i,j,l}$ and $\overline{x}_{i,j,l}$ are decreased when they are sent into the corresponding membrane labelled with l. Moreover, following the last rule, the objects $r_{i,l}$ get into the new membranes to keep track of the clauses that evaluate true on the previous truth assignments.

5. $[z_{n,c} \rightarrow d_1 \ldots d_m q]_{<l,\overline{c}>}$ } for $l \in \{t,f\}$ and $c \in \{\vee,\wedge\}$.

At the end of the generation stage the object z_n will produce the objects $d_1,\ldots,d_m$ and yes_0, which will take part in the checking stage.

6.
$$
\left.
\begin{array}{ll}
[d_i \rightarrow [t_0]_i]_{<l,c>} & \\
r_{i,t}[\,]_i \rightarrow [r_i]_i & [r_i]_i \rightarrow \lambda \\
[t_s \rightarrow t_{s+1}]_i & [t_2]_i \rightarrow t_3
\end{array}
\right\}
\text{ for }
\begin{array}{l}
i \in \{1,\ldots,m\}, \\
s \in \{0,1\}, \quad c \in \{\vee,\wedge\}.
\end{array}
$$

Following these rules each object d_i creates a new membrane with label i where the object t_0 is placed; this object will act as a counter. The object r_i gets into the membrane labelled with i and dissolves it preventing the counter, t_i, from reaching the object t_2. The fact that the object t_2 appears in a membrane with label i means that there is no object r_i, that is, the clause number i does not evaluate true on the truth assignment associated with the membrane; therefore neither does the formula evaluate true on the associated truth assignment.

7.
$$
\left.
\begin{array}{ll}
[q \rightarrow [ans_0]_a]_{<l,c>} & \\
t_3[\,]_a \rightarrow [t_4]_a & [t_4]_a \rightarrow \lambda \\
[ans_h \rightarrow ans_{h+1}]_a, & [ans_5]_a \rightarrow \textbf{yes} \\
[ans_5 \rightarrow \textbf{no}]_{<l,c>} &
\end{array}
\right\}
\text{ for }
\begin{array}{l}
l \in \{t,f\} \quad c \in \{\vee,\wedge\}, \\
h = 0,\ldots,4.
\end{array}
$$

The object q creates a membrane with label a where the object ans_0 is placed. The object ans_h evolves to the object ans_{h+1}; at the same time the objects t_3 can get into the membrane labelled with a and dissolve it preventing the object **yes** from being sent out from this membrane.

8.
$$
\left.
\begin{array}{ll}
[yes]_{<l,c>} \rightarrow yes_{\bar{c}} & [no]_{<l,c>} \rightarrow no_{\bar{c}} \\
[yes_\vee]_{<l,\vee>} \rightarrow yes^* & [no_\vee \rightarrow \underline{no}_\vee]_{<l,\vee>} \\
[yes^* \rightarrow yes_\wedge]_{<l,\wedge>} & [\underline{no}_\vee]_{<l,\vee>} \rightarrow no_\wedge \\
[\underline{no}_\vee \rightarrow \lambda]_{<l,\wedge>} & [yes_\vee \rightarrow \lambda]_{<l,\wedge>} \\
[no_\wedge]_{<l,\wedge>} \rightarrow no^* & [yes_\wedge \rightarrow \underline{yes}_\wedge]_{<l,\wedge>} \\
[no^* \rightarrow no_\vee]_{<l,\vee>} & [\underline{yes}_\wedge]_{<l,\wedge>} \rightarrow yes_\vee \\
[\underline{no}_\wedge \rightarrow \lambda]_{<l,\vee>} & [\underline{yes}_\wedge \rightarrow \lambda]_{<l,\vee>} \\
[yes^*]_s \rightarrow yes\,[\,]_s & [no_\wedge]_s \rightarrow no\,[\,]_s
\end{array}
\right\}
\text{ for } l \in \{t, f\}.
$$

This set of rules controls the output stage. After the evaluation stage, from each working membrane we obtain an object *yes* or *no* depending on whether the truth assignment associated with this membrane satisfies or not the formula. On the contrary to the SAT problem, in QSAT it is not enough that one truth assignment satisfies the formula, but the final answer is YES if an appropriate combination of truth assignments according to the quantifiers $\exists$ and $\forall$ are founded.

4.1 An Overview of the Computation

First of all we define a polynomial encoding of the QSAT problem in the family $\mathbf{\Pi}$ constructed in the previous section. Given a Boolean formula in conjunctive normal form, $\varphi = C_1 \wedge \cdots \wedge C_m$ such that $Var(\varphi) = \{x_1, \ldots, x_n\}$, and being φ^* the (existential) fully quantified formula associated with it, we define $s(\varphi^*) = \langle n, m \rangle$ (recall the bijection mentioned in the previous section) and $cod(\varphi^*) = \{x_{i,j} \mid x_j \in C_i\} \cup \{\overline{x}_{i,j} \mid \neg x_{i,j} \in C_i\}$.

Next we describe informally how the recognizer P system with membrane creation $\Pi(s(\varphi^*))$ with input $cod(\varphi^*)$ works.

In the initial configuration we have the input multiset $cod(\varphi)$ and the objects $z_{0,\wedge,t}$ and $z_{0,\wedge,f}$ placed in the input membrane (membrane labelled with $< t, \vee >$). In the first step of the computation the object $z_{0,\wedge,t}$ creates a new membrane with label $< t, \vee >$ which represents the assignment $x_1 = true$ and the object $z_{0,\wedge,f}$ creates a new membrane with label $< f, \vee >$ which represents the assignment $x_1 = false$. The second component of the labels, i.e., $\wedge$ and $\vee$ will be used in the output stage.

In these two new membranes the object $z_{1,\vee}$ is placed. At the same time the input multiset representing the formula φ is duplicated following the two first rules in group 2. In the next step, according to the rules in group 3, the formula is evaluated on the two possible truth assignments for x_1. In the same step the rules in group 4 decrease the second subscript of the objects representing the formula ($x_{i,j,l}, \overline{x}_{i,j,l}$ with $j \geq 2$) in order to analyze the next variable. Moreover, at the same time, the object $z_{1,c}$ produces the object $z_{1,c,t}$ and $z_{1,c,f}$ ($c \in \{\wedge, \vee\}$) and the system is ready to analyze the next variable. In this way, the generation and evaluation stages go until all the possible assignments to the variables are generated and the formula is evaluated on each one of them. Observe that it takes two steps to generate the possible assignments for a variable and to evaluate the formula on them; therefore the generation and evaluation stages take $2n$ steps.

The checking stage starts when the object $z_{n,c}$ produces the objects $d_1, \ldots, d_m$ and the object q. In the first step of the checking stage each object d_i, for $i = 1, \ldots, m$, creates a new membrane labelled with i where the object t_0 is placed, and the object q creates a new membrane with label a placing the object yes_0 in it.

The objects $r_{i,t}$, which indicate that the clause number i evaluates true on the truth assignment associated with the membrane, are sent into the membranes by the last rule in group 4 so the system keeps track of the clauses that are true. The objects $r_{i,t}$ get into the membrane with label i and dissolves it in the following two steps preventing the counter t_2 from dissolving the membrane and producing the object t_3 according to the last rule in group 6. If for some i there is no object r_i (this means that the clause i does not evaluate true on the associated assignment) the object t_2 will dissolve the membrane labelled with i producing the object t_3 that will get into the membrane with label a where the object ans_h evolves following the rules in 7. The object t_4 dissolves the membrane with label a preventing the production of the object ans_5. Therefore the checking stage takes 6 steps.

Finally the output stage takes place according to the rules in group 8. If some object ans_5 is present in any membrane with label $< l, c >, (l \in \{t, f\}, c \in \{\wedge, \vee\})$, this means that there exists at least one clauses not satisfied by the truth assignment associated with the membrane, and by the last rule in group 7, we obtain no in this membrane. Otherwise, the object ans_5 will be inside the membrane with label a, it will dissolve the membrane, and send yes to the working membrane.

At this point, in each of the 2^n working membranes we have an object yes or no depending on if the associated truth assignment satisfies or not the formula φ. In the last steps we control the flow of the objects yes and no from the working membranes to the environment. Basically, the process is the following. If there are one object yes inside a membrane with $\vee$ in its label, this object dissolves the membrane and sends out another yes. If this does not happen, i.e., if two objects no are inside a membrane with label $\vee$, the membrane is dissolved and no is sent out. Analogously, if there are one object no inside a membrane with $\wedge$ in its label, this object dissolves the membrane and sends out another no. Otherwise, if two objects yes are inside a membrane with label $\vee$, the membrane is dissolved and yes is sent out.

Consequently, the family Π of recognizer P systems with membrane creation using dissolution rules solves in polynomial time QSAT according to Definition 3. Hence, we have:

Theorem 1. QSAT $\in$ **PMC**$_{\mathcal{MC}}$

From this theorem we deduce the following result:

Corollary 1. PSPACE $\subseteq$ **PMC**$_{\mathcal{MC}}$

Proof. It suffices to make the following remarks: the QSAT problem is **PSPACE**–complete, QSAT $\in$ **PMC**$_{\mathcal{MC}}$, and the complexity class **PMC**$_{\mathcal{MC}}$ is closed under polynomial time reduction. $\qquad\square$

5   Conclusions and Future Work

P systems are computational devices whose power has to be studied in a deeper extent. In the last time, several paper have explored this power, both in the framework of P systems with active membranes and P systems with membrane creation. These papers have shown that **NP**-complete problems are solvable (in polynomial time) by families of recognizer of P systems of these types, according to Definition 3. In this paper we have shown that **PSPACE**–complete problems can also be solved (in polynomial time) by families of recognizer P systems with membrane creation, in a uniform way.

Both models (active membranes and membrane creation) have been proved to be universal, but up to now there is no theoretical result proving that these models simulate each other in polynomial time. The specific techniques for designing solutions to concrete problems (generation, evaluation, checking, and output stages) are quite different, so the simulation of one model in the other one is not a trivial question. This seems an interesting open problem to be considered in the future.

Acknowledgement

This work is supported by Ministerio de Ciencia y Tecnología of Spain, by *Plan Nacional de I+D+I (2000–2003)* (TIC2002-04220-C03-01), cofinanced by FEDER funds. F.J. Romero-Campero also acknowledges a FPU fellowship from the same Ministerio.

References

1. M.R. Garey, D.S. Johnson: *Computers and Intractability A Guide to the theory of NP-Completeness.* W.H. Freeman and Company, 1979.
2. M.A. Gutiérrez-Naranjo, M.J. Pérez-Jiménez, F.J. Romero-Campero: A linear solution of Subset Sum Problem by using Mmmbrane creation. In *Mechanisms, Symbols and Models Underlying Using Cognition, First International Work-Conference on the Interplay Between Natural and Artificial Computation, IWINAC 2005* (J. Mira, J.R. Alvarez, eds.). LNCS 3561, Springer, Berlin, 2005, 258–267.
3. M.A. Gutiérrez-Naranjo, M.J. Pérez-Jiménez, F.J. Romero-Campero: Solving SAT with Membrane Creation. In *Computability in Europe 2005, CiE 2005: New Computational Paradigms* (S. Barry Cooper, B. Lowe, L. Torenvliet, eds.), Report ILLC X-2005-01, University of Amsterdam, 82–91.
4. M.A. Gutiérrez-Naranjo, M.J. Pérez-Jiménez, A. Riscos-Núñez: A fast P system for finding a balanced 2-partition. *Soft Computing*, 9, 9 (2005), 673–678.
5. P.L. Luisi: The chemical implementation of autopoiesis,   *Self-Production of Supramolecular Structures* (G.R. Fleishaker et al., eds.), Kluwer, Dordrecht, 1994.
6. C.H. Papadimitriou: *Computational Complexity.* Addison-Wesley, Reading, Mass., 1994.
7. Gh. Păun: *Membrane Computing. An Introduction*, Springer, Berlin, 2002.
8. Gh. Păun, M.J. Pérez-Jiménez: Recent computing models inspired from biology: DNA and membrane computing, *Theoria*, 18, 46 (2003), 72–84.

9. Gh. Păun: Further open problems in membrane computing. *Proceedings of the Second Brainstorming Week on Membrane Computing* (Gh. Păun, A. Riscos-núñez, A. Romero-Jiménez, F. Sancho-Caparrini, eds.), Report RGNC 01/04, University of Seville, 2004, 354–365.

10. M.J. Pérez-Jiménez, A. Riscos-Núñez: Solving the Subset-Sum problem by active membranes. *New Generation Computing*, 23, 4 (2005), 367–384.

11. M.J. Pérez-Jiménez, A. Riscos-Núñez: A linear solution for the Knapsack problem using active membranes. *Membrane Computing. International Workshop, WMC2003, Tarragona, Spain, July 2003, Revised Papers* (C. Martín-Vide, G. Mauri, Gh. Păun, G. Rozenberg, A. Salomaa, eds.), LNCS 2933, Springer, Berlin, 2004, 250–268.

12. M.J. Pérez-Jiménez, F.J. Romero-Campero: Solving the BIN PACKING problem by recognizer P systems with active membranes. In *Proceedings of the Second Brainstorming Week on Membrane Computing* (Gh. Păun, A. Riscos-Núñez, A. Romero-Jiménez, F. Sancho-Caparrini, eds.), Report RGNC 01/04, University of Seville, 2004, 414–430.

13. M.J. Pérez-Jiménez, A. Romero-Jiménez, F. Sancho-Caparrini: A polynomial complexity class in P systems using membrane division. In *Proceedings of the 5th Workshop on Descriptional Complexity of Formal Systems, DCFS 2003* (E. Csuhaj-Varjú, C. Kintala, D. Wotschke, Gy. Vaszyl, eds.), 2003, 284–294.

14. L.J. Stockmeyer, A.R. Meyer: Word problems requiring exponential time. *Proc. 5th ACM Symp. on the Theory of Computing*, 1973, 1–9.

15. P systems web page `http://psystems.disco.unimib.it/`

On Symport/Antiport P Systems
and Semilinear Sets

Oscar H. Ibarra[1], Sara Woodworth[1], Hsu-Chun Yen[2], and Zhe Dang[3]

[1] Department of Computer Science,
University of California, Santa Barbara, CA 93106, USA
ibarra@cs.ucsb.edu
[2] Department of Electrical Engineering,
National Taiwan University, Taipei, Taiwan 106, R.O.C
[3] School of Electrical Engineering and Computer Science,
Washington State University, Pullman, WA 99164, USA

Abstract. We introduce some restricted models of symport/antiport P systems that are used as acceptors (respectively, generators) of sets of tuples of non-negative integers and show that they characterize precisely the semilinear sets. Specifically, we prove that a set $R \subseteq \mathbf{N}^k$ is accepted (respectively, generated) by a restricted system if and only if R is a semilinear set. We also show that "slight" extensions of the models will allow them to accept (respectively, generate) non-semilinear sets. In fact, for these extensions, the emptiness problem is undecidable.

1 Introduction

A general problem of clear interest in the area of membrane computing or P systems is to find classes of non-universal P systems that correspond to (i.e., characterize) known families of languages or subsets of $\mathbf{N}^k$ (where $\mathbf{N}$ is the set of non-negative integers, and k is a positive integer), and to investigate their closure and decidability properties. For example, P system characterizations of Parikh images or of length sets of ET0L languages, bounded languages accepted by multihead finite automata, and context-sensitive languages are known (see, e.g., [6, 8, 5, 1]). Here, we give characterizations of semilinear sets in terms of restricted models of symport/antiport systems.

A popular model in membrane computing is the symport/antiport P system first introduced in [9]. It is a system whose rules closely resemble the way membranes transport objects between themselves in a purely communicating manner. Symport/antiport systems (SA systems) have rules of the form (u, out), (v, in), and $(u, out; v, in)$ where u, v are multisets that are represented as strings (the order in which the symbols are written is not important, since we are only interested in the multiplicities of each symbol). A rule of the form (u, out) in membrane i sends the elements of u from membrane i out to the membrane (directly) containing i. A rule of the form (v, in) in membrane i transports the elements of v into membrane i from the membrane enclosing i. Hence this rule can only be used when the elements of v exist in the outer membrane. A rule

R. Freund et al. (Eds.): WMC 2005, LNCS 3850, pp. 253–271, 2006.
© Springer-Verlag Berlin Heidelberg 2006

of the form $(u, out; v, in)$ simultaneously sends u out of the membrane i while transporting v into membrane i. Hence this rule cannot be applied unless membrane i contains the elements in u and the membrane surrounding i contains the elements in v. The rules are applied in a non-deterministic maximally parallel manner. In general, the number of times a particular rule is applied at anyone step can be unbounded. We require that the application of the rules is maximal: all objects, from all membranes, which *can be* the subject of local evolution rules *have to* evolve simultaneously. Note that there may be several maximal multisets of rules applicable in a step, but we non-deterministically select only one such multiset to apply.

Formally, an SA system is defined as

$$\Pi = (V, H, \mu, w_1, \ldots, w_{|H|}, E, R_1, \ldots, R_{|H|}, i_o),$$

where V is the set of objects (symbols) the system uses. H is the set of membrane labels. The membrane structure of the system is defined in μ. The initial multiset of objects within membrane i is represented by w_i, and the rules are given in the set R_i. E is the set of objects which can be found within the environment, and i_o is the designated output membrane. (When the system is used as a recognizer or acceptor, there is no need to specify i_o.) A large number of papers have been written concerning symport/antiport systems. For example, it has been shown that "minimal" such systems (with respect to the number of membranes, the number of objects, the maximum "size" of the rules) are universal in the sense that they can simulate the computation of Turing machines or, equivalently, counter machines. See the P system website at `http://psystems.disco.unimib.it` for papers about symport/antiport systems and in the general area of membrane computing, and in particular the monograph [10]. In this paper, we introduce restricted models of symport/antiport systems that are used as acceptors or generators of sets of tuples of non-negative integers and show that they characterize exactly the semilinear sets.

First, we look at systems that are acceptors. One model is called *simple SA*. The system consists of $k + 1$ membranes, arranged in a 2-level structure: membranes $m_1, m_2, \ldots, m_k$ (the *input membranes*) are at the same level and enclosed in membrane m_{k+1} (the *skin membrane*). The set of objects is $V = F \cup \{o\}$, where F is a *finite* set of objects not containing the distinguished symbol o. The restriction is that in the rules of the forms (v, in) and $(u, out; v, in)$, v does not contain o's. Thus, the number of o's in each membrane can only be decreased. The environment initially contains a fixed (finite) multiset over F. The system accepts a k-tuple $(n_1, \ldots, n_k)$ of non-negative integers if, when the k input membranes are given $o^{n_1}, \ldots, o^{n_k}$ and no o's in membrane m_{k+1} (with some fixed strings $w_1, \ldots, w_{k+1} \in F^*$ in membranes $m_1, \ldots, m_{k+1}$, respectively), the system halts (i.e., no rule in any of the membranes is applicable). We show that a set $R \subseteq \mathbf{N}^k$ is accepted by a simple SA if and only if it is a semilinear set. (This result generalizes to the case when there is an infinite supply of o's in the environment, and the v's can contain o's in the rules in the skin membrane m_{k+1}.) As a consequence, the class of sets of tuples accepted by these SAs are closed under union, intersection, and complementation. Moreover, the emptiness, disjointness, containment, and equivalence problems for simple SAs are decidable. When the model is generalized to a multi-level structure, the set of tuples accepted need no longer be semilinear. In particular, suppose we have a k-membrane SA, where membrane m_i is enclosed in membrane m_{i+1} for $1 \leq i \leq k-1$. Membrane m_1 is the only input membrane and membrane m_k is the skin membrane. Again, in the rules (v, in) and $(u, out; v, in)$, v does not contain o's. We call this model a k-*membrane cascade SA*. Note that the system accepts a subset of $\mathbf{N}$. We show that 3-membrane cascade SAs can accept non-semilinear subsets of $\mathbf{N}$. We also prove that their emptiness problem is undecidable by showing that they can simulate the computations of two-counter machines.

The k-membrane cascade SA's can be generalized. A k-*membrane extended cascade SA* has a set of objects $V = F \cup \Sigma_r$, where now the input alphabet is $\Sigma_r = \{a_1, \ldots, a_r\}$ ($r \geq 1$). Again the rules are restricted in that in the rules of the forms (v, in) and $(u, out; v, in)$, v does not contain any symbol in Σ_r. The environment initially contains only a fixed multiset over F. Also, there are fixed strings $w_1, \ldots, w_k \in F^*$ such that the system starts with $w_1 a_1^{n_1} \ldots a_r^{n_r}$ in membrane m_1 (the input membrane) and w_i in membrane m_i for $2 \leq i \leq k$. If the system halts, then we say that the r-tuple $(n_1, \ldots, n_r)$ is accepted. We show that a set $R \subseteq \mathbf{N}^r$ is accepted by a 1-membrane extended cascade SA if and only if it is semilinear. However, 2-membrane extended cascade SAs can accept non-semilinear sets, and their emptiness problem is undecidable, even for $r = 2$ (i.e., there are two symbols in the input alphabet). Note that for the case $r = 1$ (i.e., Σ contains only a single symbol), the set of unary numbers is semilinear (since this is a special case of the result above for 2-level simple SA).

We then consider symport/antiport models that are used as generators. One such model is a 2-level symport/antiport system with membranes $m_1, \ldots, m_k$, m_{k+1}, where membranes $m_1, \ldots, m_k$ are at the same level, and they are enclosed in the skin membrane m_{k+1}. There is an infinite supply of o's in the environment (but the initial multiplicities of symbols in F in the environment are fixed). We require that for membranes $m_1, \ldots, m_k$, in the rules of the forms (u, out) and (u, out, v, in), u does not contain o's. Note that there is no restriction on the rules in the skin membrane. We say that $(n_1, \ldots, n_k)$ is generated if, when started with no o's in the system and fixed $w_i \in F^*$ in membrane m_i ($1 \leq i \leq k+1$), the system halts with $o^{n_1}, \ldots, o^{n_k}$ in membranes $m_1, \ldots, m_k$. We call this system a *simple SA generator*. We show that a set $R \subseteq \mathbf{N}^k$ is generated by a simple SA generator if and only if R is a semilinear set. Again, generalizing the model to have at least 3 levels would allow it to generate a non-semilinear set. In fact, for any recursively enumerable (RE) set R, the set $\{2^n \mid n \in R\}$ can be accepted by a 3-level system, while R can be accepted by a 4-level system.

We also look at a 1-membrane symport/antiport system with a set of objects $V = F \cup \Sigma_r$, where $\Sigma_r = \{a_1, \ldots, a_r\}$, and whose rules are restricted so that in the rules of the forms (u, out) and $(u, out; v, in)$, u does not contain any symbol in Σ_r. Thus symbols in Σ_r can only be transported from the environment into the membrane (note that, by the restriction, once these symbols enter the membrane, they remain in the membrane). The system starts with a fixed string $w \in F^*$. The environment initially contains a fixed multiset over F and an infinite supply of each a_i $(1 \le i \le r)$. We show that the sets of r-tuples generated by these systems are exactly the semilinear sets over $\mathbf{N}^r$. However, when there are 2 membranes, where again, the second (i.e., innermost) membrane cannot transport symbols in Σ_r into the first (skin) membrane, the set of tuples generated by such a system need not be semilinear. In fact, for any RE set R, the set $\{(2^n, 0) \mid n \in R\}$ can be generated by a 2-membrane system with input alphabet Σ_2, while the set $\{(n, 0, 0) \mid n \in R\}$ can be generated by a 2-membrane system with input alphabet Σ_3.

2   Restricted SA Acceptors and Semilinear Sets

We first introduce a restricted model of a symport/antiport system [9] which is used as an acceptor of tuples of non-negative integers. A *simple SA Π* is defined as follows:

1. The alphabet of objects is $V = F \cup \{o\}$, where F is a finite set and o is a distinguished object.
2. There are $k + 1$ membranes $(k \ge 1)$ arranged in a 2-level structure: membranes $m_1, m_2, \ldots, m_k$ (the *input membranes*) are at the same level and enclosed in membrane m_{k+1} (the *skin membrane*).
3. At the start of the computation the k input membranes are given $o^{n_1}, \ldots, o^{n_k}$, respectively, for some non-negative integers $n_1, \ldots, n_k$ (the skin membrane initially does not contain any o).
4. Also, at the start of the computation, there are fixed strings, i.e., multisets $w_1, \ldots, w_{k+1} \in F^*$, in membranes $m_1, \ldots, m_{k+1}$, respectively. Thus, the w_i's do not contain any o.
5. The environment initially only contains a fixed (finite) multiset over F. Of course, symbols that are exported to the environment from the skin membrane during the computation can be retrieved from the environment.
6. Each membrane has a set R_i of rules (some may be empty) The rules are of the forms:
   (a) (u, out),
   (b) (v, in),
   (c) $(u, out; v, in)$,

   where $u, v \in V^+$. A rule of type (a) transports multiset u from the membrane containing the rule into the surrounding membrane (if the membrane contains u). A rule of type (b) imports multiset v from the surrounding membrane into the membrane containing the rule (if the surrounding membrane contains v). A rule of type (c) simultaneously transports u to the surrounding membrane and imports v from the surrounding membrane (if the membrane contains u and the surrounding membrane contains v).

The restriction is:

In the rules of types (b) and (c), v **does not** contain o's. This just means that the number of o's in any membrane can only be decreased and cannot be increased.

7. As usual in a P system, the rules are applied in a non-deterministic maximally parallel manner.

Notice that the fixed multisets over F given initially in the membranes as well as in the environment are part of the specification of the simple SA Π (which we do not always explicitly state). We say that a tuple $(n_1, \ldots, n_k)$ is accepted by Π if, when the k input membranes are given $o^{n_1}, \ldots, o^{n_k}$ respectively, the system halts (i.e., none of the rules is applicable). The set of all such tuples is denoted by $R(\Pi)$.

Simple SAs are intimately related to counter machines. Let M be a nondeterministic multicounter machine all of whose counters are reversal-bounded. A counter is reversal-bounded if the number of alternations between non-decreasing mode and non-increasing mode during any computation is at most a fixed number. The first k counters are input counters. We say that M accepts $(n_1, \ldots, n_k)$ if, when started in its start state with counter i set to n_i $(1 \leq i \leq k)$ and the other counters to zero, M halts in an accepting state with all counters zero. The set of all such tuples accepted by M is denoted by $R(M)$. We call M a *reversal-bounded (multi) counter machine*.

A special case is a counter machine with only k counters (the input counters) each of whose counters can only be decremented. Moreover, at every step, the machine decrements exactly one counter. We call this machine a *decreasing counter machine*.

We can augment a reversal-bounded multicounter machine with an unrestricted counter, i.e., a free counter. This counter can make an unbounded number of reversals. We call such a machine *reversal-bounded counter machine with a free-counter*.

Convention: In our definition of counter machines above, acceptance is by "accepting state". Clearly, given a counter machine M, we can easily construct an equivalent machine M' which accepts if and only if it eventually halts in some state (accepting or not). M' simulates M faithfully. If M enters an accepting state, then M' halts. If M halts in a rejecting state, say s, then M' goes into an infinite loop by executing the following (where c is some counter of the machine):

s : If counter c is non-zero, then decrement c and go to state s, else go to state s

The reason we need the second mode of acceptance is that in our constructions characterizing the different SA systems by counter machines, the equivalences are of the form: The SA halts (i.e., accepts) if and only if the machine halts. All the machines discussed in the paper can easily be converted to ones whose mode of acceptance is by halting.

Next we recall the definition of a semilinear set [3]. Let $\mathbf{N}$ be the set of non-negative integers and k be a positive integer. A subset R of $\mathbf{N}^k$ is a *linear set* if there exist vectors $v_0, v_1, \ldots, v_t$ in $\mathbf{N}^k$ such that

$$R = \{v \mid v = v_0 + m_1 v_1 + \ldots + m_t v_t, \ m_i \in \mathbf{N}\}.$$

The vectors v_0 (referred to as the *constant vector*) and $v_1, v_2, \ldots, v_t$ (referred to as the *periods*) are called the *generators* of the linear set R. The set $R \subseteq \mathbf{N}^k$ is *semilinear* if it is a finite union of linear sets. The empty set is a trivial (semi)linear set, where the set of generators is empty. Every finite subset of $\mathbf{N}^k$ is semilinear – it is a finite union of linear sets whose generators are constant vectors. It is also clear that the semilinear sets are closed under (finite) union. It is also known that they are closed under complementation and intersection.

Theorem 1. *Let $R \subseteq \mathbf{N}^k$. Then the following statements are equivalent:*

1. *R is a semilinear set.*
2. *R is accepted by a reversal-bounded counter machine with a free counter.*
3. *R is accepted by a reversal-bounded counter machine.*
4. *R is accepted by a decreasing counter machine.*

Proof. It is obvious that (4) implies (3) and (3) implies (2). From the definition of a semilinear set, it is easy to construct, given a semilinear set R, a decreasing counter machine M accepting R. Since M is non-deterministic, it is sufficient to describe the construction of M when R is a linear set. So suppose, $R = \{v \mid v = v_0 + m_1 v_1 + \ldots + m_t v_t, \ m_i \in \mathbf{N}\} \subseteq \mathbf{N}^k$, with $v_i = (v_{i1}, \ldots, v_{ik})$ for $0 \leq i \leq t$. M, when given $(n_1, \ldots, n_k)$ in its counters, applies the constant vector v_0 to decrement the counters simultaneously by $v_{01}, \ldots, v_{0k}$, respectively. Then M non-deterministically guesses the number of times m_i to apply v_i to the counters (again, decreasing the counters simultaneously by the amounts $m_i v_{i1}, \ldots, m_i v_{ik}$, respectively for $1 \leq i \leq t$. If all the counters become zero at the same time, M accepts. Thus, (1) implies (4). That (2) implies (1) is a trivial consequence of a result in [4], which showed that if a bounded language $L \subseteq a_1^* \ldots a_k^*$ (where $a_1, \ldots, a_k$ are distinct symbols and $n_1, \ldots, n_k$ are non-negative integers) is accepted by a non-deterministic finite automaton augmented with reversal-bounded counters and one unrestricted counter, then the set $\{(n_1, \ldots, n_k) \mid a_1^{n_1} \ldots a_k^{n_k} \in L\}$ is semilinear.

Lemma 1. *Let Π be a simple SA. Then $R(\Pi)$ can be accepted by a reversal-bounded counter machine with a free counter M.*

Proof. We construct a counter machine M with $k + 1$ counters to simulate Π. The intuitive idea behind the simulation is the following. The first k counters are reversal-bounded (the input counters) and the last is the free counter. Initially, the input counters are set to $n_1, \ldots, n_k$, respectively. The free counter will keep track of the current number of o's in the skin membrane (at the start, there is none). The initial configuration $(w_1, \ldots, w_k, w_{k+1})$ and the rules $(R_1, \ldots, R_{k+1})$ are stored in the finite-state control of M. The finite-state control keeps track of the numbers of non-o symbols and their distributions within the membranes and the environment (this can be done since their total multiplicities remain the same (as ones initially given as fixed constants in the definition of Π) at any time, independent of the n_i's). M simulates each non-deterministic maximally parallel step of Π by several moves. Clearly, because of the restrictions on the rules, the counters keeping track of the multiplicities of o's in the input membranes are only decremented. Special care has to be taken when simulating a rule of type either (u, out) or $(u, out; v, in)$ when u contains multiple copies of o's. In order to tell whether such a rule is applicable or not, for each membrane we associate a finite buffer of size d (where d is the maximum number of o's that can be thrown out by a single rule in the membrane) to the finite control of M to keep track of the first d o's in the membrane while using the counter of M associated with the membrane to hold the number of the remaining o's. By doing so, checking whether the above rule is applicable can be done by examining the contents of the finite buffer associated with the membrane in which the rule resides.

Now in a maximally parallel step, some (possibly all) of the input membranes can transport o's to the skin membrane and the skin membrane itself can also transport some o's to the environment. However, the total number of o's transferred from the input membranes to the skin membrane and the total number of o's transferred from the skin membrane to the environment may have no relationship, so the free counter may be decremented and incremented an unbounded number of times during the computation. This is the reason why we need a free counter. It follows from the description that M can simulate the computation of Π.

We now prove the converse of Lemma 1.

Lemma 2. *Let M be a reversal-bounded counter machine with a free counter. Then $R(M)$ can be accepted by a simple SA Π.*

Proof. By the proof of Theorem 1, we may assume that M is a decreasing counter machine with k counters accepting $R(M) \subseteq \mathbf{N}^k$. Thus M, when started in its initial state with $n_1, \ldots, n_k$ in the counters halts in an accepting state if $(n_1, \ldots, n_k)$ is in $R(M)$. Moreover, at each step of the computation, before it halts, M decrements exactly one counter (there are no increments).

We will construct a simple SA Π simulating M. As defined, Π will have a 2-level structure with k input membranes $m_1, \ldots, m_k$ (at the same level) enclosed by the skin membrane m_{k+1}. The k input membranes will keep track of the values of the counters. The construction of Π follows the construction in [11] where a two-level SA system is shown to simulate a multicounter machine. In the construction, each of the inner membranes represents a counter and the multiplicity of the distinguished symbol o within each membrane represents the value of that counter. The rules associated with each subtract instruction in the construction adhere to the restrictions required by a simple SA system. Since M has no increment instructions, the associated Π, by the construction in [11], is a simple SA. We omit the details.

From Theorem 1 and Lemmas 1 and 2, we have:

Theorem 2. *Let $R \subseteq \mathbf{N}^k$. Then the following statements are equivalent:*

1. *R is a semilinear set.*
2. *R is accepted by a reversal-bounded counter machine with a free counter.*
3. *R is accepted by a reversal-bounded counter machine.*
4. *R is accepted by a decreasing counter machine.*
5. *R is accepted by a simple SA.*

Note that in a simple SA, the number of o's in the membranes cannot be increased, since in the rules of the form (v, in) and $(u, out; v, in)$ we do not allow v to contain o's. We can generalize the model. The environment can have an infinite supply of o's, and in the rules of the forms (v, in) and $(u, out; v, in)$ in the skin membrane, v is in F^+o^*. Thus v can contain o's but must contain at least one symbol in F. (We do not allow v to only contain o's since, otherwise, the system will not halt because there is an infinite supply of o's in the environment.) Thus the number of o's in the skin membrane can increase during the computation by importing o's from the environment. Call this model *simple SA*$^+$. Clearly the construction in Lemma 1 still works when Π is a simple SA$^+$. The only modification is that in the simulation of a maximally parallel step of Π by M, we also need to consider the o's that may be brought into the skin membrane from the environment by the (v, in) and $(u, out; v, in)$ rules. Thus, we have:

Corollary 1. *Let $R \subseteq \mathbf{N}^k$. Then the following statements are equivalent: items (1), (2), (3), (4), (5) of Theorem 2, and (6): R is accepted by a simple SA$^+$.*

The following corollary follows from known results concerning semilinear sets.

Corollary 2. *Let k be any positive integer. Then:*

1. *The class of subsets of $\mathbf{N}^k$ accepted by simple SAs is closed under union, intersection, and complementation.*
2. *The membership, disjointness, containment, and equivalence problems for simple SAs accepting subsets of $\mathbf{N}^k$ are decidable.*

3   Cascade Counter Machines and Cascade SAs

In this section, we will show that Theorem 2 does not generalize to the case when the simple SA has a 3-level structure. In particular, consider a simple SA with only three membranes m_1, m_2, m_3, where membrane m_1 is enclosed in m_2, and m_2 is enclosed in m_3 (the skin membrane). Initially, membrane m_1 contains the input o^n. The same restriction (i.e., in the rules of the forms (v, in) and $(u, out; v, in)$, v does contain o's) applies. We will show that such a system can accept a non-semilinear set. In fact, the emptiness problem for such systems is undecidable. To facilitate the proofs, we first introduce the notion of cascade counter machines.

3.1   Cascade Counter Machines

A k-counter cascade machine M is a finite-state machine with k counters, c_1, ..., c_k. The instructions of M are of the following forms:

$$s \to (s', c_i := c_i - 1; c_{i+1} := c_{i+1} + 1) \text{ (decrement } c_i \text{ then increment } c_{i+1})$$
$$s \to (s' \text{ if } c_i \text{ is zero else } s'') \text{ (test if } c_i = 0)$$
$$s \to (s', c_k := c_k - 1) \text{ (counter } c_k \text{ can be independently decremented)}$$

Notice that in the above, it is implicit that M cannot increment c_1 (there is no such instruction). We say that a non-negative integer n is accepted if M, when started in its initial state with counter values $(n, 0, \ldots, 0)$ eventually enters an accepting state.

We first show that the emptiness problem for deterministic 3-counter cascade machines is undecidable by showing how a 3-counter cascade machine with initial counter values $(n, 0, 0)$ can simulate the computation of a deterministic (unrestricted) 2-counter machine with initial counter values $(0, 0)$. The former accepts some n if and only if the latter halts. The result then follows from the undecidability of the halting problem for 2-counter machines [7].

So suppose that M is a deterministic (unrestricted) 2-counter machine. We show that M can be simulated by a deterministic 3-counter cascade machine M' with counters c_1, c_2, c_3. The two counters x_1 and x_2 of M are simulated by c_2 and c_3 of M', respectively. Clearly, testing if counter x_i is zero for $i = 1, 2$ can be directly simulated in M'. Incrementing/decrementing counters x_1 and x_2 of M can also be simulated in M':

1. When M increments x_1, M' performs the following: Decrement c_1, increment c_2.
2. When M increments x_2, M' performs the following: Decrement c_1, increment c_2, decrement c_2, increment c_3.
3. When M decrements x_1, M' performs the following: Decrement c_2, increment c_3, decrement c_3.
4. When M decrements x_2, M' also decrements c_3.

During the simulation, if c_1 is zero when an instruction being simulated calls for decrementing c_1, M' rejects. Note that all state transitions in M are simulated faithfully by M'. It follows that we can construct M' so that it accepts the input n (initially given in c_1) if and only if n is "big" enough to allow the simulation of M to completion. If M does not halt or n is not big enough to carry out the simulation (at some point), M' goes into an infinite loop or rejects. It follows that the emptiness problem for deterministic 3-counter cascade machines is undecidable.

Example. We now give an example of a deterministic 3-counter cascade machine M accepting a non-semilinear set. Starting with $c_1 = n, c_2 = 0, c_3 = 0$,

1. If c_1 is zero, M rejects.
2. M configures the counters to contain: $c_1 = n - 1, c_2 = 0, c_3 = 1$.
3. If c_1 is zero, M accepts.

4. Set $k = 1$.
5. Starting with values: $c_1 = n - (1 + 3 + \ldots + (2k - 1)), c_2 = 0, c_3 = (2k - 1)$,

   (*) M iteratively decrements c_3 by 1 while decrementing c_1 by 1 and incrementing c_2 by 1 until $c_3 = 0$. Then M decrements c_1 by 2 and increments c_2 by 2 (this is done in two steps). After that, M iteratively decrements c_2 by 1 while incrementing c_3 by 1 until $c_2 = 0$.
   – If c_1 becomes zero before the completion of (*), M rejects.
   – If $c_1 = 0$ after the completion of (*), M accepts, else M sets $k := k + 1$ and goes back to (*).

Clearly, the values of the counters when k becomes $k + 1$ are: $c_1 = n - (1 + 3 + \ldots + (2k - 1) + (2k + 1)) = n - (k + 1)^2, c_2 = 0, c_3 = (2k + 1)$. It follows that M can be constructed to accept the set $\{n^2 \mid n \geq 1\}$, which is not semilinear.

From the above discussion and example, we have:

Theorem 3. *Deterministic 3-counter cascade machines can accept non-semilinear sets. Moreover, their emptiness problem is undecidable.*

Remark 1. The construction of the deterministic 3-counter cascade machine in the example above can be modified to accept the set $R_1 = \{2n^2 \mid n \geq 1\}$. Now define for each $k \geq 1$, the set $R_k = \{2n^{2^k} \mid n \geq 1\}$. One can show by essentially iterating the construction in the example that R_k can be accepted by a deterministic $(2 + k)$-counter cascade machine. We believe (but have no proof at this time), that the R_k's form an infinite hierarchy: R_{k+1} can be accepted by a deterministic $(2 + k)$-counter cascade machine but cannot be accepted by any deterministic or non-deterministic $(2 + (k - 1))$-counter cascade machine. Note that 1- and 2- counter cascade machines are equivalent — both accept exactly the semilinear sets.

It is interesting to observe that for a k-counter cascade machine M, if counter c_1 cannot be tested for zero, then either $R(M) = \emptyset$ (if M never enters an accepting state regardless of the input initially given in c_1) or there exists an $m \in \mathbf{N}$ such that $R(M) = \{n \mid n \geq m, n \in \mathbf{N}\}$ (m is the smallest input for which M accepts). Hence, for cascade counter machines lacking the capability of testing counter c_1 for zero, they accept only semilinear sets. The emptiness problem, nevertheless, remains undecidable for such a restricted class of cascade counter machines, implying that the semilinear sets associated with such machines are not effective.

We conclude this section by noting that Theorem 3 is not true for (deterministic or non-deterministic) 2-counter cascade machines. In fact, consider a non-deterministic machine M which has $k + 1$ counters, where the first k counters are initially set to input values $n_1, \ldots, n_k$, respectively, and the last counter set to zero. The computation is restricted in that the first k counters can only be decremented, but the last counter can be decremented/incremented independently. It follows from Theorem 1 that these machines accept exactly the semiliner sets.

3.2 Cascade SAs

A cascade SA has k membranes $m_1, \ldots, m_k$ (for some k) that are nested: For $1 \leq i \leq k-1$, membrane m_i is enclosed in membrane m_{i+1}. The input membrane, m_1, initially contains o^n for some n. Again, in the rules of the forms (v, in) and $(u, out; v, in)$, v does not contain o's. There are fixed multisets $w_1, \ldots, w_k$ not containing o's in membranes $m_1, \ldots, m_k$ initially. The environment initially contains a fixed multiset of symbols.

The connection between cascade counter machines and cascade SAs is given by the following theorem.

Theorem 4. *Let $k \geq 1$ be a positive integer. A set $Q \subseteq \mathbf{N}$ is accepted by a k-membrane cascade SA if and only if it can be accepted by a k-counter cascade machine.*

Proof. Let Π be a k-membrane cascade SA. We construct an equivalent k-counter cascade machine M. We associate a counter c_i for every membrane m_i to keep track of the number of o's in membrane m_i during the computation. The construction of M simulating Π is straightforward, following the strategy in the proof of Lemma 1.

We now prove the converse. Let M be a k-counter cascade machine. For notational convenience we will assume the program instructions for M are labelled $l_0, l_1, \ldots, l_n$ and begin with instruction l_0. We also assume they are written in the form l_i: $(SUB(r), l_s, l_t)$ meaning that when instruction l_i is executed, counter r is decremented. If counter r was initially positive (meaning it was able to be decremented), the machine will next execute the instruction l_s, otherwise it will execute the instruction l_t. Also, since M is a cascade counter machine, each decrement from counter r where $r < k$ must be followed by an instruction which increments the counter $r + 1$. Hence, we can incorporate each increment instruction into its preceding decrement instruction. (In the case where we decrement counter r and $r = k$, no increment instruction follows since the decremented value is thrown out of the system.) In this way we can consider the program for M to consist entirely of decrement instructions. We now construct an equivalent k-membrane cascade SA Π which simulates each decrement instruction of M. The membrane structure of Π is a set of nested membranes which each corresponds to a counter in M. The skin membrane also acts as program control membrane. Formally, the simulation occurs by creating the following cascade SA membrane system from a given cascade counter machine:

$$\Pi = (V, H, \mu, w_{m_1}, \ldots, w_{m_k}, E, R_{m_1}, \ldots, R_{m_k})$$

where
$V = \{l_{i1}, l_{i2}, l_{i3}, l_{i4}, d_{ij} \mid l_i \text{ is an instruction label of the form } l_i:$
        $(SUB(r), l_s, l_t) \text{ where } r \neq k \text{ and } 0 \leq j \leq 2(k-r)+1\} \cup$
        $\{l_{i1}, l_{i2}, l_{i3} \mid l_i \text{ is an instruction label of the form } l_i : (SUB(r), l_j, l_s)$
        $\text{where } r = k\} \cup \{d_0, d_1\} \cup \{c, c', c_1, \ldots, c_m\} \cup \{o\},$
$H = \{m_1, m_2, \ldots, m_k\},$

$$\mu = [_{m_k}[_{m_{k-1}} \cdots [_{m_1}\ ]_{m_1} \cdots]_{m_{k-1}}]_{m_k},$$
$$w_{m_1} = c_1 o^n,$$
$$w_{m_i} = c_i \text{ for all } 1 < i < k,$$
$$w_{m_k} = l_{01}c_k \text{ (since } l_0 \text{ is the first instruction to execute),}$$
$$E = \text{one copy of each element in } V \text{ except } o \text{ and } l_{01}.$$

The rule sets $(R_{m_1}, \ldots, R_{m_k})$ are created based on the cascade machine's program. Initially we create the rule $(d_0, out; d_1, in)$ within R_{m_k}. For each rule of the form $l_i : (SUB(r), l_s, l_t)$ where $r \neq k$ we add the following rules:

1. R_{m_k} contains:
   (a) $(l_{i1}, out; l_{i2}cd_0d_{i0}, in)$,
   (b) $(d_{ij}, out; d_{i(j+1)}, in)$ where $0 \leq j \leq 2(k - r)$,
   (c) $(d_1d_{i[2(k-r)+1]}, out; l_{i4}c', in)$,
   (d) $(l_{i2}d_1, out; l_{i3}, in)$,
   (e) $(l_{i3}cd_{i[2(k-r)+1]}, out; l_{s1}, in)$,
   (f) $(l_{i2}l_{i4}, out; l_{t1}, in)$,
   (g) (cc', out);
2. R_{m_n} where $k \geq n > r$ contains:
   (a) $(l_{i2}c, in)$,
   (b) $(l_{i2}c_r, out)$,
   (c) $(l_{i3}c_r, in)$,
   (d) $(l_{i3}c, out)$,
   (e) $(l_{i4}c', in)$,
   (f) $(l_{i2}l_{i4}, out)$,
   (g) (cc', out);
3. R_{m_r} contains:
   (a) $(c_r, out; l_{i2}c, in)$,
   (b) $(l_{i2}o, out)$,
   (c) $(l_{i3}c_r, in)$,
   (d) $(l_{i3}c, out)$,
   (e) $(l_{i2}, out; c_rc', in)$,
   (f) (cc', out).

For a rule of the form $l_i : (SUB(r), l_s, l_t)$ where $r = k$ we create the following rules:

4. $R_{m_r} = R_{m_k}$ contains:
   (a) $(l_{i1}, out; l_{i2}d_0, in)$,
   (b) $(l_{i2}o, out; l_{i3}, in)$,
   (c) $(l_{i3}d_1, out; l_{s1}, in)$,
   (d) $(l_{i2}d_1, out; l_{t1}, in)$.

Informally, the above simulation operates as follows. The process of simulating a single subtract instruction $l_i : (SUB(r), l_s, l_t)$ if $r \neq k$ begins by the presence of the object l_{i1} within the outermost membrane (m_k). This object is used to bring in the necessary execution objects l_{i2}, c, d_0, and d_{i0} using rule 1a. The objects l_{i2} and c are used cooperatively and are drawn deeper through the membrane hierarchy until they have reached the membrane m_{r+1}. Here they are drawn into membrane m_r while the object c_r is thrown out.

If membrane m_r contains an o object (meaning counter r is not empty) the objects l_{i2} and o are thrown out into membrane m_{r+1}. This simulates both the current subtract instruction along with the add instruction we know must follow. Now, the objects l_{i2} and c_r are used cooperatively and are thrown out of each membrane until they located in the skin membrane.

While this has been occurring, the delay objects in the skin membrane have been being incremented. The d objects are delay objects and are used to delay certain execution steps. During each step of computation, their subscripts are incremented by one. The object d_0 only changes to d_1 to delay an action for a single step while the object d_{i0} increments to $d_{i[2(k-r)+1]}$. This number $(2(k-r)+1)$ corresponds to the number of steps plus one that l_{i2} will take to travel to membrane r and back if membrane r contains a o. This allows us to determine whether the object l_{i2} is stuck in membrane r.

If the membrane m_r contains an o (meaning counter r is not zero), objects l_{i2} and c_r will return to the skin membrane in $2(k-r)$ steps and rule 1d is applicable before $d_{i[2(k-r)+1]}$ has been brought into the membrane. So, l_{i2} and d_2 are thrown out into the environment and object l_{i3} is brought into the system. Now the objects c and c_r must be swapped to their original positions. This occurs by having objects l_{i3} and c_r work cooperatively to move deeper through the membranes to membrane r and then objects l_{i3} and c work cooperatively to be thrown out of each membrane until they return to the skin membrane. At this point, everything is completed and all objects are in the correct location. So objects l_{i3}, c, and $d_{i[2(k-r)+1]}$ are thrown out into the environment while object l_{s1} is brought in. At this point, instruction l_i is complete and instruction l_s will execute next.

If the objects l_{i2} and c_r have not returned to the skin membrane after $2(k-r)+1$ steps, then the membrane r must not have contained an o. At this point, the objects d_1 and $d_{i[2(k-r)+1]}$ are thrown out of the skin membrane and objects l_{i4} and c' are brought in. Now, objects l_{i4} and c' work cooperatively to move deeper through the membranes to membrane m_{r+1}. Object c' is drawn into membrane m_r while object l_{i2} is thrown out. At this point, membrane m_r contains the objects c and c' while membrane m_{r+1} contains the objects l_{i2} and l_{i4}. These pairs of objects work cooperatively to be thrown out of each membrane. The pair $l_{i2}l_{i4}$ will get to the skin membrane a step ahead of the pair cc'. The objects l_{i2} and l_{i4} are thrown out into the environment while bringing in the object l_{t1}. During the next step the pair cc' will be thrown out into the environment. At this point, instruction l_i is complete and instruction l_t will execute next.

If the instruction to be simulated is of the form $l_i : (SUB(r), l_s, l_t)$ where $r = k$, the simulation is much simpler. In this case, since the instruction is immediately placed within the counter membrane, only a single delay object is needed along with the instruction object l_{i2}. If membrane k contains an o, it is thrown out during the next step along with the object l_{i2} and the object l_{i3} is brought in allowing the final step to clean up and bring in the instruction object l_{s1}. If l_{i2} is still in membrane m after one step, the delay object can cooperate with object l_{i2} to bring in the next instruction object l_{t1}.

Consequently, these cascade SA rules simulate the operation of M.

From Theorems 3 and 4, we have,

Corollary 3. *3-membrane cascade SAs can accept non-semilinear sets. Moreover, their emptiness problem is undecidable.*

A careful examination of the proof of Theorem 4 reveals that the degree of maximal parallelism for the constructed SA is finite (i.e., at every step of the computation, the size of the multiset of applicable rules is bounded by some fixed integer). Hence, Corollary 3 holds even if the 3-membrane cascade SAs have a bounded degree of maximal parallelism.

4   Another SA Acceptor Characterizing the Semilinear Sets

The k-membrane cascade SA of the previous section can be generalized. A k-*membrane extended cascade SA* has a set of objects $V = F \cup \Sigma_r$, where now the input alphabet is $\Sigma_r = \{a_1, \ldots, a_r\}$ $(r \geq 1)$. Again the rules are restricted in that in the rules of the forms (v, in) and $(u, out; v, in)$, v does not contain any symbol in Σ_r. The environment initially contains only F. There are fixed strings $w_i \in F^*$ such that the system starts with $w_1 a_1^{n_1} \ldots a_r^{n_r}$ in membrane m_1 (the input membrane) and w_i in membrane m_i for $2 \leq i \leq k$. If the system halts, then we say that the r-tuple $(n_1, \ldots, n_r)$ is accepted.

Next consider a finite-state device M with a finite-state control and a "bag" that can hold a multiset of symbols. M starts in its initial state with the bag containing a multiset $a_1^{n_1} \ldots a_r^{n_r}$. The instructions of M are of the following form:

$$q \rightarrow (q' \text{ delete } a_i \text{ from the bag if it is in the bag else } q'')$$

Thus, from state q, M removes a_i from the bag if it is in the bag and goes to state q'; otherwise, M goes to state q''. The initial multiset in the bag is accepted if M enters an accepting state. We call this device a *1-bag automaton*. A 1-bag automaton is like a multiset automaton studied in [2]. Although the notion is not the same, the idea is quite similar.

We can generalize the 1-bag automaton to a *k-bag automaton*, where now, a symbol is deleted from bag i if and only if it is exported into bag $i + 1$. A symbol can be deleted from the k-th bag independently.

Lemma 3. *A set $R \subseteq \mathbf{N}^r$ is accepted by a 1-bag automaton if and only if it is accepted by a decreasing r-counter machine.*

Proof. Clearly, deleting a_i from the bag corresponds to decrementing counter i $(1 \leq i \leq r)$.

Theorem 5. *Let $k \geq 1$. A set of tuples R is accepted by a k-membrane extended cascade SA if and only if R is accepted by a k-bag automaton.*

Proof. The proof for the "only if" part is a straightforward generalization of the proof of the first part of Theorem 1 (which was for $k + 1$). For the second part, let M be a k-bag automaton. We construct a k-membrane extended cascade SA Π equivalent to M, in the same manner as the construction of Theorem 4 where each membrane corresponds to a bag. The rules can be created by mapping each subtraction rule of the form $l_i : (SUB(r), l_s, l_t)$ to the bag rule of the form $q \to (q'$ delete a_i from the bag if it is in the bag else $q'')$ as follows. The instruction labels of a counter machine can also be viewed as states so we can say l_i corresponds to q, l_s corresponds to q', and l_t corresponds to q''. The bag associated with q corresponds to the counter r. The additional difference is that the bag also specifies the object (a_i) in Σ which should be thrown out of the bag. Hence, we can create Π to simulate M using the techniques in Theorem 4 and the above mapping along with the following changes. The set V will now additionally contain the set of objects $\{a_1, \ldots, a_r\}$ rather than the single object $\{o\}$. Then the multiset $w_{m_1} = c_1 a_1^{n_1} \ldots a_r^{n_r}$ replaces the multiset $c_1 o^n$. Also, the rules 3b: $(l_{i2}o, out)$ and 4b: $(l_{i2}o, out; l_{i3}, in)$ will be changed to $(q_2 a_i, out)$ and $(q_2 a_i, out; s_3, in)$, respectively. Clearly, this k-membrane extended cascade SA now simulates a k-bag automaton.

Theorem 6. *A set $R \subseteq \mathbf{N}^r$ is accepted by a 1-membrane extended cascade SA if and only if it is a semilinear set.*

Proof. Let Π be a 1-membrane extended cascade SA with input alphabet Σ_r. We can easily construct a decreasing r-counter machine M which, when the counters are initially given $n_1, \ldots, n_r$, simulates the computation of Π on $wa_1^{n_1} \ldots a_r^{n_r}$. The simulation is straightforward, as in Lemma 1. It follows from Theorem 1 that $R(\Pi)$ is a semilinear set.

For the converse, by Lemma 3 we need only show that a 1-bag automaton can be simulated by a 1-membrane extended cascade SA. This follows from Theorem 5.

Let $\Sigma_2 = \{a_1, a_2\}$. Using the ideas in the example of the previous section, we can easily construct a 2-bag automaton accepting the non-semilinear set $\{(n_1, n_2) \mid n_1, n_2 \geq 0, n_1 + n_2 = m^2 \text{ for some } m \geq 1\}$. It is also easy to construct a 2-bag automaton with input alphabet Σ_2 that simulates the computations of a 2-counter automaton. The values of the counters are represented in the second bag. The number of a_1's (resp., a_2's) in that bag denotes the value of the first (resp., second) counter. The a_1's and the a_2's in the first bag are the suppliers (sources) of the "increments" for the two counters in the second bag.

From the above discussion and Theorem 5, we have,

Theorem 7. *2-bag automata (and, hence, 2-membrane extended cascade SAs) can accept non-semilinear sets. Moreover, their emptiness problem is undecidable.*

5   Restricted Symport/Antiport Systems as Generators

In this section, we look at symport/antiport systems used as generators of tuples. We only state the results; the proofs will be given in the full paper.

In the definition of a k-membrane cascade SA, the input o^n is initially given in m_1 (the innermost membrane) with no o's in the other membranes. The computation is such that the o's can only be exported from membrane m_i to membrane m_{i+1} (or to the environment in the case of m_k).

Now consider a system Π which is a generator of tuples and the cascading (flow of o's) is from the environment to the innermost membrane. More precisely, let $m_1, \ldots, m_k$ be the membranes of Π, where m_i is enclosed in m_{i+1} for $1 \leq i \leq k - 1$ (m_1 is the innermost membrane and m_k is the skin membrane). Initially, there are no o's in the membranes, but there is an infinite supply of o's in the environment. There may also be a finite supply of other symbols in the environment initially. The rules of the forms (u, out) and $(u, out; v, in)$ are restricted in that u cannot contain o's. Thus the o's can only be moved from the environment to membrane m_k and from m_{i+1} to m_i for $1 \leq i \leq k-1$. (Note that once o's reach membrane m_1, they remain there.) The set of numbers generated by Π is $G(\Pi) = \{n \mid \Pi$ halts with o^n in the skin membrane $m_k\}$. It is important to point out that the skin membrane is the output membrane. We call this new model a k-membrane reverse-cascade SA.

Theorem 8.   1. 1-membrane and 2-membrane reverse-cascade SAs are equivalent, and they generate exactly the semilinear sets over $\mathbf{N}$.

 2. 3-membrane reverse-cascade SAs can generate non-semilinear sets. In fact, for any recursively enumerable (RE) set $R \subseteq \mathbf{N}$, the set $\{2^n \mid n \in R\}$ can be generated by a 3-membrane reverse-cascade SA. (Hence, their emptiness problem is undecidable.)

 3. Any RE set R can be generated by a 4-membrane reverse-cascade SA.

The proof of Theorem 8 involves the use of a counter machine similar to the k-counter cascade machine in Section 3. Define a k-counter reverse-cascade machine M as a non-deterministic machine with k counters $c_1, \ldots, c_k$. M starts in its initial state with all counters zero. As usual, the counters can be incremented/decremented and tested for zero but with the following restrictions:

1. If counter c_{i+1} is decremented, it must be followed by an increment of counter c_i for $1 \leq i \leq k - 1$, and this is the only way counter c_i can be incremented.
2. Counter c_k can be incremented independently.
3. Counter c_1 cannot be decremented. (Thus, c_1 is non-decreasing, hence, essentially useless. The reason is that once it becomes positive, it will remain positive, and can no longer affect the computation. We include this counter for convenience.)

We say that M generates a non-negative integer n if it halts with value n in counter c_k, and the set of all such numbers generated is the set generated by M.

It can be shown that for any $k \geq 1$, a set $R \subseteq \mathbf{N}$ is generated by a k-membrane reverse-cascade SA if and only if it can be generated by a k-counter reverse-cascade machine. Then to prove items (1), (2), and (3) of Theorem 8, we need only show that they hold for 1-counter/2-counter, 3-counter, and 4-counter reverse-cascade machines, respectively.

Remark 2. We believe that the 4 membranes in Theorem 8, item (3) is best possible. We think that there are RE sets (even recursive sets) that cannot be generated by 3-counter reverse-cascade machines based on the following discussion.

By definition, in a 3-counter reverse-cascade machine M, with three counters, c_1, c_2, c_3, counter c_1 cannot be decremented. So, in fact, the computation of M can be simulated by a machine M' with only two counters, d_1, d_2. Again, the only restriction is that if d_2 is decremented, it must be followed by an increment of d_1, and this is the only way d_1 can be incremented. But now, we allow d_1 to be decremented independently and, as before, d_2 can be incremented independently.

We conjecture that there is an RE set (even a recursive set) that cannot be generated by a 2-counter machine M' as defined above. (Note that by definition, the generated number is in counter d_2 when the machine halts.) However, we have no formal proof at this time.

We can generalize the reverse-cascade SA by using, instead of only one input symbol o, a set of symbols $\Sigma_r = \{a_1, \ldots, a_r\}$ as input symbols, again with the restriction that these symbols can only be moved from the environment to membrane m_k and from m_{i+1} to m_i for $1 \leq i \leq k-1$. Now the system generates a set of r-tuples of non-negative integers in the skin membrane when it halts. We can prove:

Theorem 9.   *1. 1-membrane reverse-cascade SAs with input alphabet $\Sigma_r = \{a_1, \ldots, a_r\}$ generate exactly the semilinear sets over $\mathbf{N}^r$.*

   2. 2-membrane reverse-cascade SAs with input alphabet $\Sigma_2 = \{a_1, a_2\}$ can generate non-semilinear sets over $\mathbf{N}^2$. In fact, for any RE set R, the set $\{(2^n, 0) \mid n \in R\}$ can be generated by a 2-membrane reverse-cascade SA with input alphabet Σ_2.

   3. For any RE set R, the set $\{(n, 0) \mid n \in R\}$ can be generated by a 3-membrane reverse-cascade SA with input alphabet Σ_2.

   4. For any RE set R, the set $\{(n, 0, 0) \mid n \in R\}$ can be generated by a 2-membrane reverse-cascade SA with input alphabet Σ_3.

Remark 3. Again, as in Remark 2, we believe that Theorem 9, item (3), does not hold for 2-membrane reverse-cascade SAs with input alphabet Σ_2.

In the definition of a reverse-cascade SA, the skin membrane is the output membrane. We now consider the model where the output membrane is the innermost membrane m_1 (and not the skin membrane). Similar to Theorem 8, we can prove the following (but item (3) is weaker):

Theorem 10. *Under the assumption that the output membrane is the innermost membrane m_1 (and not the skin membrane), we have:*

1. *1-membrane and 2-membrane reverse-cascade SAs are equivalent, and they generate exactly the semilinear sets over* $\mathbf{N}$.
2. *3-membrane reverse-cascade SAs can generate non-semilinear sets (e.g., the set $\{n^2 \mid n \geq 1\}$). Moreover, their emptiness problem is undecidable.*
3. *Any RE set R can be generated by a 5-membrane reverse-cascade SA.*

Remark 4. It does not seem that item (3) of the above theorem holds for a 4-membrane reverse-cascade SA, but we have no proof at this time.

Finally, consider a 2-level symport/antiport system Π has membranes $m_1, m_1, \ldots, m_{k+1}$, where $m_1, \ldots, m_k$ are at the same level, and they are enclosed in the skin membrane m_{k+1}. The environment contains F initially and an infinite supply of o's. We require that for membranes $m_1, \ldots, m_k$, in the rules of the forms (u, out) and (u, out, v, in), u does not contain o's. Note that there is no restriction on the rules in the skin membrane. For this system, we say that $(n_1, \ldots, n_k)$ is generated if, when Π is started with no o's in the system and fixed $w_i \in F^*$ in m_i ($1 \leq i \leq k+1$), Π halts with $o^{n_1}, \ldots, o^{n_k}$ in membranes $m_1, \ldots, m_k$. Call the system just described a *simple SA generator*. We can show the following:

Theorem 11. *A set $R \subseteq \mathbf{N}^k$ is generated by a simple SA generator if and only if R is a semilinear set.*

The theorem above no longer holds when the simple SA generator is extended to a 3-level structure, as Theorem 10, item (2) shows.

6 Conclusion

In this paper, we introduced restricted models of symport/antiport P systems and proved that they characterize precisely the semilinear sets. We also showed that "slight" generalizations of the models allowed them to accept non-semilinear sets, and made their emptiness problem undecidable. We also looked at related models that are used as generators of sets of tuples. Some models generate exactly the semilinear sets; others generate the recursively enumerable sets. We mentioned some interesting open questions in Remarks 1–4.

Acknowledgements

The work of Oscar H. Ibarra and Sara Woodworth was supported in part by NSF Grants CCR-0208595 and CCF-0430945. The work of Hsu-Chun Yen was supported in part by NSC Grant 93-2213-E-002-003, Taiwan. The work of Zhe Dang was supported in part by NSF Grant CCF-0430531.

References

1. E. Csuhaj-Varjú, O.H. Ibarra, G. Vaszil: On the computational complexity of P automata. *Proc DNA10*, Milano, 2004 (C. Ferretti, G. Mauri, C. Zandron, eds.), LNCS 3384, Springer, Berlin, 2005, 76–89.
2. E. Csuhaj-Varjú, C. Martín-Vide, V. Mitrana: Multiset automata. In *Multiset Processing. Mathematical, Computer Science, Molecular Computing Points of View* (C.S. Calude, Gh. Păun, G. Rozenberg, A. Salomaa, eds.), LNCS 2235, Springer, Berlin, 2001 69–84.
3. S. Ginsburg: *The Mathematical Theory of Context-Free Languages.* McGraw-Hill, New York, 1966.
4. O.H. Ibarra: Reversal-bounded multicounter machines and their decision problems. *Journal of the ACM*, 25 (1978), 116–133.
5. O.H. Ibarra: On membrane hierarchy in P systems. *Theoretical Computer Science*, 334 (2005), 115–129.
6. M. Ito, C. Martín-Vide, Gh. Păun: A characterization of Parikh sets of ETOL languages in terms of P systems. In *Words, Semigroups, and Transductions* (M. Ito, Gh. Păun, and S. Yu, eds.), World Scientific, Singapore, 2001, 239–253.
7. M. Minsky: Recursive unsolvability of Post's problem of Tag and other topics in the theory of Turing machines. *Ann. of Math.*, 74 (1961), 437–455.
8. C. Martín-Vide, Gh. Păun, J. Pazos, A. Rodríguez-Patón: Tissue P systems. *Theoretical Computer Science*, 296 (2003), 295–326.
9. A. Păun, Gh. Păun: The power of communication: P systems with symport/antiport. *New Generation Computing*, 20, 3 (2002), 295–306.
10. Gh. Păun: *Membrane Computing. An Introduction.* Springer, Berlin, 2002.
11. Gh. Păun, J. Pazos, M. Pérez-Jiménez, A. Rodríguez-Patón: Symport/antiport P systems with three objects are universal. *Fundamenta Informaticae*, 64, 1-4 (2005), 353–367.

Boolean Circuits and a DNA Algorithm in Membrane Computing

Mihai Ionescu and Tseren-Onolt Ishdorj

Research Group on Mathematical Linguistics,
Pl. Imperial Tàrraco 1, 43005 Tarragona, Spain
armandmihai.ionescu@urv.net, itsot@yahoo.com

Abstract. In the present paper we propose a way to simulate Boolean gates and circuits in the framework of P systems with active membranes using inhibiting/de-inhibiting rules. This new approach on the simulation of Boolean gates has the advantage of a self-embedded synchronization, an extra system to solve this problem not being needed. Moreover, the number of membranes and objects we use for the simulation of Boolean gates is only two. **NP**-complete problems, particularly `CIRCUIT-SAT`, are also considered here. In addition, we simulate a 'DNA-like' way of (experimentally) solving `SAT` problem using the tools given by polarization, merging, and separation in P systems.

1 Introduction

P systems are a class of distributed parallel computing devices of a biochemical type, which can be seen as a general computing architecture where various types of objects can be processed by various operations.

In membrane computing, P systems with active membranes have a special place, because they provide biologically inspired tools to solve computationally hard problems. In [6] the computational power of a class of P systems using catalytic and non-cooperative inhibiting/de-inhibiting rules was explored, and in [7] such a controlling mechanism was investigated in the framework of P systems with active membranes.

Boolean circuits are well-known classical computing devices, which incorporate features of parallelism. Various possibilities to simulate Boolean circuits by P systems with promoters/inhibitors, mobile catalysts, and weak priorities for rules were considered in [8].

In this paper, we propose a model to simulate Boolean circuits by inhibiting/de-inhibiting P systems with active membranes (AID P Systems). The idea behind the simulation of such a circuit is to construct a global AID P system for the whole circuit having distributed sub-AID P systems for each gate. The sub-AID P systems work in a parallel manner producing a unique output as the result of the computation of the whole system. One can see a correspondence between the concept of *inhibition* (which means *blocking* the execution of a rule in a membrane) and the term *switch-off* frequently used in the theory of circuits, and conversely, between *de-inhibition* and *switching on* some parts of the circuits.

R. Freund et al. (Eds.): WMC 2005, LNCS 3850, pp. 272–291, 2006.

Using this model to simulate Boolean circuits, we do not need an extra system to coordinate the entrance of the two inputs in an AND or an OR gate as presented in [8]. Here, the inputs wait for each other and produce the right result when the circuit is simulated. We say that the system has a self-embedded synchronization. As a consequence of the ability of AID P systems to simulate specific Boolean circuits, we also consider the Boolean CIRCUIT-SAT problem (which is **NP**-complete).

The second proposal of this paper is the construction of a 'DNA-like' system for solving SAT problem, following the original idea of Lipton presented in [13], this time, using the properties of merging and separation operations from membrane computing. The motivation behind this proposal is to create a model as close as possible to the experimental results on solving the problem mentioned above by using DNA strands (see [4], [24]). We only say here that the main idea in such a simulation is to consider the test tubes used in the experiments as being membranes, and, of course, the DNA-strands contained in such a test tube as being the objects inside membranes. For a detailed presentation of this concept we refer the reader to Section 6.

In the following section we will recall some of the notions regarding P systems with active membranes, Boolean gates, circuits, and the DNA way of solving SAT we will use in the next sections.

2   Preliminaries

We assume the reader to be familiar with the fundamentals of formal language theory and complexity theory (e.g., from [17, 25, 23]), as well as with the basics of membrane computing (e.g., from [20]).

2.1   P Systems with Active Membranes

Informally speaking, in P systems with polarizations and active membranes the following types of rules are used:

(a) multiset rewriting rules,
(b) rules for introducing objects into membranes,
(c) rules for sending objects out of membranes,
(d) rules for dissolving membranes,
(e) rules for dividing elementary membranes, and
(h) rules for separating membranes, see [2, 19, 22, 15, 16].

The rules of type (a) are applied in a parallel way (all objects which can evolve by such rules have to evolve), while the rules of types (b), (c), (d), (e), (g), (h) are used sequentially, in the sense that one membrane can be used by at most one rule of these types at a time. In total, the rules are used in the non-deterministic maximally parallel manner: all objects and all membranes which can evolve, should evolve. Only halting computations give a result, in the form of the number (or the vector) of objects expelled into the environment during the computation.

In this paper we will make use only of some of the mentioned active membranes rules, so we define P systems with active membranes using only such rules.

A P system *with active membranes* (and electrical charges) is a construct

$$\Pi = (O, H, \mu, w_1, \ldots, w_m, R) \tag{1}$$

where:

- $m \geq 1$ (the initial degree of the system);
- O is the alphabet of *objects*;
- H is a finite set of *labels* for membranes;
- μ is a *membrane structure*, consisting of m membranes, labeled (not necessarily in a one-to-one manner) with elements of H;
- $w_1, \ldots, w_m$ are strings over O, describing the *multisets of objects* placed in the m regions of μ;
- R is a finite set of *developmental rules*, of the following forms:
  - (a) $[\, a \to v \,]_h^e$,
    for $h \in H, e \in \{+, -, 0\}, a \in O, v \in O^*$
    (object evolution rules, associated with membranes and depending on the label and the charge of the membranes, but not directly involving the membranes, in the sense that the membranes are neither taking part in the application of these rules nor are they modified by them);

  - (c) $[\, a \,]_h^{e_1} \to [\ ]_h^{e_2} b$,
    for $h \in H, e_1, e_2 \in \{+, -, 0\}, a, b \in O$
    (communication rules; an object is sent out of the membrane, possibly modified during this process; also the polarization of the membrane can be modified, but not its label);

  - (g) $[\ ]_h^{e_1} [\ ]_h^{e_2} \to [\ ]_h^{e_3}$,
    for $h \in H, e_1, e_2, e_3 \in \{+, -, 0\}$
    (merging rules for elementary membranes; in reaction of two membranes, they are merged into a single membrane; the objects of the former membranes are put together in the new membrane);

  - (h) $[\ ]_h^{e_1} \to [\, K \,]_h^{e_2} [\, \neg K \,]_h^{e_3}$,
    for $h \in H, e_1, e_2, e_3 \in \{+, -, 0\}, K \subseteq O$
    (separation rules for elementary membranes; the contents of membrane h is split into two membranes, the first one containing all objects from K and the second one containing all objects which are not in K).

The set H of labels has been specified because it is also possible to allow the change of membrane labels. For instance, a separation rule can be of the more general form

(h') $[\ ]_{h_1}^{e_1} \to [\, K \,]_{h_2}^{e_2} [\, \neg K \,]_{h_3}^{e_3}$,
   for $h_1, h_2, h_3 \in H, e_1, e_2, e_3 \in \{+, -, 0\}$.

The change of labels can also be considered for other types of rules.

P systems with active membranes without electrical charges were also considered and investigated (see [2, 3, 1, 12]). Let us consider now some rules of types without polarizations. They are of the following forms ("no electrical charges" means "neutral polarization"; as above, O is the alphabet of objects and H is the set of labels of membranes):

(a_0) $[\ a \rightarrow v\ ]_h$, where $a \in O, v \in O^*$, and $h \in H$,
(b_0) $a[\ ]_h \rightarrow [\ b\ ]_h$, where $a, b \in O$ and $h \in H$,
(c_0) $[\ a\ ]_h \rightarrow [\ ]_h b$, where $a, b \in O$ and $h \in H$,
(g_0) $[\ ]_h[\ ]_h \rightarrow [\ ]_h$, where $h \in H$,
(h_0) $[\ ]_h \rightarrow [\ K\ ]_h[\ \neg K\ ]_h$, where $K \subseteq O$ and $h \in H$,
(i_0) $[\ [\ O\ ]_h\ ]_h \rightarrow [\ ]_h O$, where $h \in H$.

We recommend the reader unfamiliar with these rules to consult the references mentioned above for a better understanding of their functionality.

The subscript 0 indicates the fact that we do not use polarization for membranes. When the rules of a given type (α_0) are able to change the label(s) of the involved membranes, we denote that type of rules by (α_0'). For example, the primed versions of merging and separation rules are of the following forms:

(g_0') $[\ ]_{h_1}[\ ]_{h_2} \rightarrow [\ ]_{h_3}$, for $h_1, h_2, h_3 \in H$.
(h_0') $[\ ]_{h_1} \rightarrow [\ K\ ]_{h_2}[\ \neg K\ ]_{h_3}$, for $h_1, h_2, h_3 \in H$.

To understand the difference of uniform construction and semi-uniform construction of P systems, we recall some notions about solving decidability problems in the membrane computing framework.

Given a decision question X, we say that it can be solved in polynomial (linear) time by recognizing P systems in a uniform way, if, informally speaking, we can construct in polynomial time a family of recognizing P systems $\Pi_n, n \in \mathbb{N}$, associated with the sizes n of instances $X(n)$ of the problem, such that the system Π_n, starting from the code of some Π_n, will always stop in a polynomial (linear, respectively) number of steps, sending out the object **yes** if the instance $X(n)$ has a positive answer and the object **no** if the instance $X(n)$ has a negative answer.

In [19], the complexity classes related to P systems are defined in the semi-uniform way: P systems are constructed – in polynomial time – starting not from the size n, but from an instance $X(n)$. For a clearer description of the difference between uniform and semi-uniform constructions, the reader is referred to [22].

2.2 Inhibiting/De-inhibiting (AID) P Systems with Active Membranes

The basic idea of the AID P systems is that, when a rule (acting on the membranes or on the objects) is inhibited, then it cannot be applied until another rule de-inhibits it. The application of a rule can inhibit other rules (and in particular may inhibit itself).

A P system *with active membranes and inhibiting/de-inhibiting mechanism*, in short, an AID P system, without electrical charges and without using catalysts, is a construct

$$\Pi = (O, H, I, \mu, w_1, \ldots, w_m, R), \tag{2}$$

where:

- $m \geq 1$ is the initial degree of the system;
- O is the alphabet of *objects*;
- H is a finite set of *labels* for membranes;
- I is a finite set of *labels* for rules;
- μ is a *membrane structure*, consisting of m membranes, labeled with elements of H;
- $w_1, \ldots, w_m$ are strings over O, describing the *multisets of objects* placed in the m regions of μ;
- R is a finite set of *developmental rules*. Here are some examples:
  - (b_0) $r : a[\ ]_h \to [\ b]_h \langle S \rangle$, for $r \in I, h \in H, a, b \in O, S \subseteq I$(communication rules; an object is introduced in the membrane during this process);
  - (c_0) $r : [\ a\ ]_h \to [\ ]_h b \langle S \rangle$, for $r \in I, h \in H, a, b \in O, S \subseteq I$(communication rules; an object is sent out of the membrane during this process).

The rules in R are written as $r_j : \neg r \langle S \rangle$ or as $r_j : r \langle S \rangle$, where $r_j \in I$ and r is a rule of types $(a_0) - (l_0)$ $((k_0)$ indicates replicative-distribution rules, of the form $r : a[\ ]_{h_1}[\ ]_{h_2} \to [\ u]_{h_1}[\ v]_{h_2}$, for $h_1, h_2 \in H, a \in O, u, v \in O^*$, with h_1, h_2 sibling membranes and (l_0) indicates rules $r : [\ a[\ ]_{h_1}]_{h_2} \to [\ [\ u]_{h_1}]_{h_2} v$, for $h_1, h_2 \in H, a \in O, u, v \in O^*$ – for nested membranes) from $[1, 2, 6]$; S is a string that represents a subset of I.

The AID P systems work like general P systems with active membranes. The only difference consists in the fact that, in each step, only the non-inhibited rules can be used. When a rule $r_j : r \langle S \rangle$ is applied, the rules whose labels are specified in S are inhibited (if they were de-inhibited) or de-inhibited (if they were inhibited). Now, starting from an initial configuration, the system evolves according to the rules and objects present in the membranes, in a non-deterministic maximally parallel manner, and according to a universal clock. The system will make a successful computation if and only if it halts, meaning there is no applicable rule to the objects present in the halting configuration.

The result of a successful computation is the number of objects present in the output membrane (or in the environment) in a halting configuration of Π. If the computation never halts, then we will have no output.

2.3   Boolean Functions and Circuits

An n-ary *Boolean function* is a function

$$f : \{true, false\}^n \mapsto \{true, false\}; \tag{3}$$

$\neg$ (negation) is a unary Boolean function (the other unary functions are the constant functions and the identity function). We say that the Boolean expression

φ with variables $x_1, \ldots, x_n$ *expresses* the n-ary Boolean function f if, for any n-tuple of truth values $t = (t_1, \ldots, t_n)$, $f(t)$ is *true* if $T \vDash \varphi$, and $f(t)$ is false if $T \nvDash \varphi$, where $T(x) = t_i$ for $i = 1, \ldots, n$.

There are three primary Boolean functions that are widely used:

(1) the NOT function, which takes only one input, and the output is true when the input is false, and vice-versa.

(2) the AND function – the output of an AND function is true only if all its inputs are true.

(3) the OR function – the output of an OR function is true if at least one of its inputs is true.

Both AND and OR can have any number of inputs, with a minimum of two.

Any n-ary Boolean function f can be expressed as a Boolean expression φ_f involving variables $x_1, \ldots, x_n$.

There is a potentially more economical way than these expressions for representing Boolean functions, namely *Boolean circuits*. A Boolean circuit is a graph $C = (V, E)$, where the nodes in $V = \{1, \ldots, n\}$ are called the *gates* of C. The graph C has a rather special structure. First, there are no cycles in the graph, so we can assume that all edges are of the form (i, j), where $i < j$. All nodes in the graph have in-degree (number of incoming edges) equal to 0, 1, or 2. Moreover, each gate $i \in V$ has a *sort* $s(i)$ associated with it, where

$$s(i) \in \{true, false, \vee, \wedge, \neg\} \cup \{x_1, x_2, \ldots\}.$$

If $s(i) \in \{true, false\} \cup \{x_1, x_2, \ldots\}$, then the in-degree of i is 0, that is, i must not have any incoming edges. Gates with no incoming edges are called the *inputs* of C. If $s(i) = \neg$, then i has in-degree one. If $s(i) \in \{\vee, \wedge\}$, then the in-degree of i must be two. Finally, node n (the largest numbered gate in the circuit, which necessarily has no outgoing edges) is called the *output gate* of the circuit.

This concludes our definition of the *syntax* of circuits. The *semantics* of circuits specifies a truth value for each appropriate truth assignment. We let $X(C)$ be the set of all Boolean variables that appear in the circuit C (that is, $X(C) = \{x \in X \mid s(i) = x \text{ for some gate } i \text{ of } C\}$). We say that a truth assignment T is appropriate for C if it is defined for all variables in $X(C)$. Given such a T, *the truth value of gate $i \in V$, $T(i)$*, is defined, by induction on i, as follows:

If $s(i) = true$, then $T(i) = true$, and similarly if $s(i) = false$. If $s(i) \in X$, then $T(i) = T(s(i))$. If now $s(i) = \neg$, there is a unique gate $j < i$ such that $(j, i) \in E$. By induction, we know $T(j)$, and then $T(i)$ is *true* if $T(j) = false$, and vice-versa.

If $s(i) = \vee$, then there are two edges (j, i) and (j', i) entering i. $T(i)$ is then *true* if only if at least one of $T(j)$, $T(j')$ is *true*. If $s(i) = \wedge$, then $T(i)$ is *true* if only if both $T(j)$ and $T(j')$ are *true*, where (j, i) and (j', i) are the incoming edges. Finally, *the value of the circuit, $T(C)$*, is $T(n)$, where n is the output gate.

2.4   Brief Description of Solving SAT in DNA Computing

Lipton's DNA-based solution of the satisfiability problem [13] uses some of the basic operations in DNA Computing:

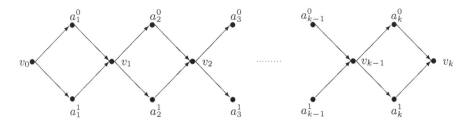

Fig. 1. A graph associated with a truth assignment

    – *merge* (given test tubes N_1 and N_2, we consider their union, understood as a multiset),

    – *separate* (given a test tube N and a word w over the alphabet A, C, T, G, produce two test tubes $+(N, w)$ and $-(N, w)$, where $+(N, w)$ consists of all strands in N which contain w as a (consecutive substring), while $-(N, w)$ is its negation), and

    – *detect* (given a tube N, return *true* if N contains at least one DNA strand, otherwise return *false*).

We begin with a graphical description of truth assignments. Assume that we are dealing with a propositional formula containing k variables. Consider the directed graph depicted in Fig. 1:

There are 2^k paths from v_0 to v_k, none of the paths being Hamiltonian. One can observe that in each of the v_i nodes $(i \neq k)$ there are two independent choices (0 or 1). The construction of the graph prevents the (unwanted) possibility of choosing for the same variable both 0 and 1 values. Moreover, the paths and the truth assignments for the variables $x_1, x_2, \ldots, x_k$ have a natural one-to-one correspondence.

Each vertex of the graph is encoded by a random oligonucleotide of length 20 and an arc between two vertices will be the Watson-Crick complementation of the last half and the first half of the start and end nodes, respectively. More precisely, consider the encodings s_i and s_j of two vertices such that there is an edge $e_{i,j}$ from the former to the latter. If $s_i = s'_i s''_i$, where s'_i and s''_i have equal length, and similarly, $s_j = s'_j s''_j$, then the edge $e_{i,j}$ is encoded by the Watson-Crick complement of $s''_i s'_j$.

Now, having encoded all the possible truth assignments with the help of the operations mentioned above and strictly depending on the clauses given in the SAT problem, an algorithm (based on separation, merging, and, only in the end, detection) will select the right solution(s) of the given problem. An example is presented in Section 6 where we compare the two (DNA and P-based) ways of solving a particular, simple SAT problem.

3   Simulating Logical Gates

In this section we present AID P systems which simulate logical gates. We will consider that the input for a gate is given in the inner membrane, while the output will be computed and sent out to the outer region.

3.1   Simulation of AND Gate

Lemma 1. *Boolean AND gate can be simulated by AID P systems with rules of types (b'_0) and (c'_0), using two membranes and two objects (only the input), in at most four steps.*

Proof. We construct the AID P system

$$\Pi_{AND} = (\{0,1\}, \{0,1,s\}, \{r_i \mid 0 \le i \le 9\}, [\ [\ ]_0]_s, \lambda, \lambda, R),$$

with the set R consisting of the following rules:

$$r_1 : [\ 0]_0 \to [\ ]_1 0,$$
$$r_2 : [\ 0]_1 \to [\ ]_0 \lambda \langle r_2 r_8 \rangle,$$
$$r_3 : [\ 1]_0 \to [\ ]_1 1 \langle r_2 r_4 r_5 r_6 \rangle,$$
$$r_4 : [\ 1]_1 \to [\ ]_0 \lambda \langle r_2 r_8 \rangle,$$
$$r_5 : \neg[\ 0]_1 \to [\ ]_1 0 \langle r_5 r_7 \rangle,$$
$$r_6 : \neg[\ 1]_1 \to [\ ]_1 \lambda \langle r_4 r_6 r_9 \rangle,$$
$$r_7 : \neg 1[\ ]_1 \to [\ \lambda]_0 \langle r_4 r_6 r_7 r_8 \rangle,$$
$$r_8 : \neg[\ 0]_s \to [\ ]_s 0 \langle r_2 r_8 \rangle,$$
$$r_9 : \neg[\ 1]_s \to [\ ]_s 1 \langle r_2 r_5 r_9 \rangle.$$

Initially, we place the input values x_1 and x_2 in the membrane with label 0 from the membrane structure. Depending on the value of the initial variables x_1 and x_2, the rules we apply for each of the four cases are: r_1, r_2, r_8 for 00, r_1, r_4, r_8 for 01, r_3, r_5, r_7, r_8 for 10, and r_3, r_6, r_9 for 11.

More precisely, if two symbols 1 are in membrane 0, in the first step, rule r_3 is applied, a symbol 1 is expelled and the membrane label is changed to 1. At the same time, according to the inhibition/de-inhibition concept, rules r_2 and r_4 are inhibited, while rules r_5 and r_6 are de-inhibited and ready to be used. In the second step we notice that only rule r_6 can be applied, thus, object 1, placed inside membrane labeled 1 is transformed, on its way out, into λ. One may notice that rule r_6, after having been applied, restores the original status of rules r_4 and itself, and also de-inhibits rule r_9. In the third step, rule r_9 performs and the right answer 1 is sent out the skin membrane, while rules $r_2, r_5,$ and r_9 come back to their original status.

In other words, after these three steps, our system has sent out of the skin membrane the right answer (given the input 11) and comes back to its initial configuration, thus being ready for a new input.

In the case when the input is 01 or 10, we can start by using r_1 or r_3. Let us examine the second case. Rule r_3 sends 1 out of membrane 0 and changes its label to 1. At the same time, rules r_2 and r_4 are inhibited, while rules r_5 and r_6 are de-inhibited. The only rule we can use in the second step is r_5 which expels 0 out of membrane 1, inhibits itself and de-inhibits rule r_7. In this moment we have the following configuration of our system: $[\,[\ ]_1 01\,]_s$. We now apply rule r_7 which transforms object 1 to λ on its way in the inner membrane and changes its label from 1 to 0. Rule r_7 de-inhibits the inhibited rule r_4, inhibits r_6 and itself, and de-inhibits rule r_8. The fourth step is the one in which the right answer 0 is sent out of the skin membrane, while the system gets back to its initial configuration.

Thus, our system gives the right answer, in four steps, when we have input 01. In the other two cases (when we have the input 01 and start by using first the rule r_1, or the input is 00) our system performs the rules mentioned above; the details being left to the reader.   □

3.2   Simulation of OR Gate

Lemma 2. *A Boolean OR gate with fan-in at most 2 can be simulated by AID P systems with rules of types (b'_0) and (c'_0), using two membranes and two objects (only the input), at most four steps.*

Proof. We construct the AID P system

$$\Pi_{OR} = (\{0,1\}, \{o,1,s\}, \{r_i \mid 0 \le i \le 9\}, [\,[\ ]_0\,]_s, \lambda, \lambda, R),$$

with the following set of R of rules:

$$r_1 : [\,1\,]_0 \rightarrow [\ ]_1 1,$$
$$r_2 : [\,1\,]_1 \rightarrow [\ ]_0 \lambda \langle r_2 r_8 \rangle,$$
$$r_3 : [\,0\,]_0 \rightarrow [\ ]_1 0 \langle r_2 r_4 r_5 r_6 \rangle,$$
$$r_4 : [\,0\,]_1 \rightarrow [\ ]_0 \lambda \langle r_2 r_8 \rangle,$$
$$r_5 : \neg[\,1\,]_1 \rightarrow [\ ]_1 1 \langle r_5 r_7 \rangle,$$
$$r_6 : \neg[\,0\,]_1 \rightarrow [\ ]_1 \lambda \langle r_4 r_6 r_9 \rangle,$$
$$r_7 : \neg 0[\ ]_1 \rightarrow [\ \lambda]_0 \langle r_4 r_6 r_7 r_8 \rangle,$$
$$r_8 : \neg[\,1\,]_s \rightarrow [\ ]_s 1 \langle r_2 r_8 \rangle,$$
$$r_9 : \neg[\,0\,]_s \rightarrow [\ ]_s 0 \langle r_2 r_5 r_9 \rangle.$$

As in the case of the AND gate, we place initial values x_1 and x_2 in the membrane labeled 0 from the membrane structure. The succession of rules we apply for each case is (as expected due to the duality of the system) the following: r_3, r_6, r_9 for 00, r_3, r_5, r_7, r_8 for 01, r_1, r_4, r_8 for 10, and r_1, r_2, r_8 for 11.

We only give here the details of the case when x_1 and x_2 are both 1. Our system has the following initial configuration: $[\,[\,11\,]_0\,]_s$. As mentioned above, the only rule we can apply is r_1, and our system evolves to the following configuration: $[\,[\,1\,]_1 1\,]_s$. The next rule we can apply is r_2 through which the object in membrane 1 is transformed into λ and the membrane label changes to 0, the system evolving to $[\,[\ ]_0 1\,]_s$. After having applied rule r_2, rule r_8 is de-inhibited while rule r_2 is inhibited. We now can apply r_8, which sends out of the skin membrane the answer 1 and restores the initial configuration of the system inhibiting rule r_8 and de-inhibiting rule r_2.

We have shown how our systems expels, in three steps, the right answer, given the input 11.

The details of the behavior of the system in the other three cases are left to the reader. □

3.3 Simulation of NOT Gate

Lemma 3. *A Boolean (unary) NOT gate can be simulated by AID P systems with rules of type (b_0) in one step.*

Proof. We construct the AID P system

$$\Pi_{NOT} = (\{0,1\}, \{s\}, \{r_0, r_1\}, [\ ]_s, \lambda, \{r_0 : [\ 0]_s \to [\ ]_s 1, r_1 : [\ 1]_s \to [\ ]_s 0\}).$$

The correct simulation of the NOT gate is obvious. □

4 Simulating Circuits

We give now an example of how to construct a global AID P system which simulates a Boolean circuit, designed for evaluating a Boolean function, using the distributed sub-AID P systems in it, namely including Π_{AND}, Π_{OR}, and Π_{NOT} constructed in the previous section.

4.1 An Example

We take into consideration the same example used in [8], namely we consider the function $f : \{0,1\}^4 \to \{0,1\}$ given by the formula

$$f(x_1, x_2, x_3, x_4) = (x_1 \wedge x_2) \vee \neg(x_3 \wedge x_4).$$

The corresponding circuit is depicted in Fig. 2 and its assigned membrane structure in Fig 3; one can see that the circuit has a tree as its underlying graph, with the leaves as input gates and the root as output gate.

We simulate this circuit with the P system

$$\Pi_C = (\Pi_{AND}^{(1)}, \Pi_{AND}^{(2)}, \Pi_{NOT}^{(3)}, \Pi_{OR}^{(4)})$$

constructed from the distributed sub-AID P systems which work in parallel in the global P system, and we obtain a unique result in the following way:

1. for every gate of the circuit with inputs from input gates, we have an appropriate P system simulating it, with the innermost membrane containing the input values;
2. for every gate which has at least one input coming as an output of a previous gate, we construct an appropriate P system to simulate it by embedding in a membrane the "environments" of the P systems which compute the gates at the previous level.

For the particular formula

$$(x_1 \wedge x_2) \vee \neg(x_3 \wedge x_4)$$

and the circuit depicted in Figure 2 we will have:

- $\Pi_{AND}^{(1)}$ computes the first AND$_1$ gate $(x_1 \wedge x_2)$ with inputs x_1 and x_2.
- $\Pi_{AND}^{(2)}$ computes the second AND$_2$ gate $(x_3 \wedge x_4)$ with inputs x_3 and x_4; these two P systems, $\Pi_{AND}^{(1)}$ and $\Pi_{AND}^{(2)}$, act in parallel.
- $\Pi_{NOT}^{(3)}$ computes the NOT gate $\neg(x_3 \wedge x_4)$ with input $(x_3 \wedge x_4)$; while $\Pi_{NOT}^{(3)}$ is working, the output value of the first AND$_1$ gate performs the rules that can be applied (in $\Pi_{OR}^{(4)}$) and at a point waits for the second input (namely, the output of $\Pi_{NOT}^{(3)}$) to come.
- after the second input has entered the inner membrane of the OR gate, the P system $\Pi_{OR}^{(4)}$ will be able to complete its task; the result of the computation for the OR gate (which is the result of the global P system), is sent into the environment of the whole system.

The idea we want to stress here is that, as noticed from the explanations given above, our system has a self-embedded synchronization. By this we mean that if either of the gates AND or OR receives only one (part of the) input from an upper level of the tree, the gate will wait for the other part of the input to come in order to expel the output. In that way, an extra synchronization system, as considered in [8], is not needed in AID P Systems.

Based on the previous explanations the following result holds:

Theorem 1. *Every Boolean circuit α whose underlying graph structure is a rooted tree, can be simulated by a P system, Π_α, in linear time. Π_α is constructed from AID P systems of type Π_{AND}, Π_{OR} and Π_{NOT}, by reproducing the structure of the tree associated to the circuit in the architecture of the membrane structure.*

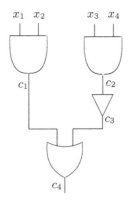

Fig. 2. Boolean Circuit

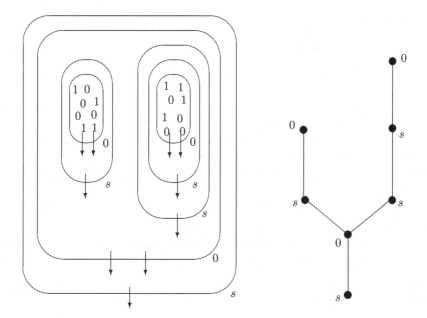

Fig. 3. Membrane structure associated with circuit from Fig. 2

Property 1. Any Boolean circuit α, with n gates, can be simulated using at most $2n$ membranes.

Proof. Let us consider the worst case in which our circuit contains only OR and AND gates. Then it is obvious that for the individual simulation of these gates we use $2n$ membranes (every gate is simulated by using two membranes). In fact, this coincides exactly with the upper bound stated in the property due to the embedded synchronization and the fact we do not need additional membranes in order to simulate it.   □

5   CIRCUIT-SAT Efficiency

There is an interesting computational problem related to circuits, CIRCUIT-SAT. Given a circuit C, is there a truth assignment T appropriate to C such that $T(C) = true$? It is easy to show that CIRCUIT-SAT is computationally equivalent to SAT, and thus presumably very hard.

We can now appeal to a well-known construction to reduce a CIRCUIT-SAT instance to a CNF formula. Given a circuit C, we will construct a CNF formula φ_C such that there is an assignment to the inputs of C producing an output 1 if and only if the formula φ_C is satisfiable. The formula φ_C will have $n + |C|$ variables, where $|C|$ denotes the number of gates in C; if C acts on inputs $x_1, \ldots, x_n$ and contains gates $g_1, \ldots, g_{|C|}$, then φ_C will have variable set $\{x_1, \ldots, x_n, g_1, \ldots, g_{|C|}\}$. For each gate $g \in C$, we define a set of clauses as follows:

1. if $c = AND(a, b)$, then add $(\neg c \vee a), (\neg c \vee b), (c \vee \neg a \vee \neg b)$;
2. if $c = OR(a, b)$, then add $(c \vee \neg a), (c \vee \neg b), (\neg c \vee a \vee b)$;
3. if $c = NOT(a)$, then add $(c \vee a), (\neg c \vee \neg a)$.

The formula φ_C is simply the conjunction of all the clauses over all the gates of C.

We assume below that C consists of gates from a standard complete basis such as AND, OR, NOT and that each gate has fan-in at most 2. Our results can easily be generalized to allow other gates (e.g., with a larger fan-in); the final bounds are interesting as long as the number of clauses per gate and the maximum fan-in in the circuit have constant upper bounds. Recall that a circuit C is a directed acyclic graph (DAG).

We define the underlying undirected graph as G_C:

Definition 1. *Given a circuit C with inputs $X = \{x_1, \ldots, x_n\}$ and gates $S = \{g_1, \ldots, g_s\}$, let $G_C = (V, E)$ be the undirected and unweighted graph with $V = X \cup S$ and $E = \{\{x, y\} \mid x$ is an input to gate y or vice versa$\}$.*

Theorem 2. *For a circuit C containing gates from $\{AND, OR, NOT\}$, the CIRCUIT-SAT instance for C can be solved by an AID P system.*

Proof. We only give a sketch of the proof.

We know that a propositional formula φ_C in CNF is simply the conjunction of all the clauses over all the gates of C. In our previous example, for the Boolean circuit considered in Section 4, φ_C is:

$$\begin{aligned}
\varphi_C = &(\neg c_1 \vee x_1) \wedge (\neg c_1 \vee x_2) \wedge (c_1 \vee \neg x_1 \vee \neg x_2) \wedge \\
&(\neg c_2 \vee x_3) \wedge (\neg c_2 \vee x_4) \wedge (c_2 \vee \neg x_3 \vee \neg x_4) \wedge \\
&(c_2 \vee c_3) \wedge (\neg c_2 \vee \neg c_3) \wedge \\
&(\neg c_1 \vee c_4) \wedge (\neg c_3 \vee c_4) \wedge (\neg c_4 \vee c_1 \vee c_3).
\end{aligned}$$

There are already known algorithms which solve SAT (written as Boolean propositional formula in CNF) with P systems with active membranes (see [1, 2, 7, 14, 15, 19]). Then our φ_C can be solved easily following the proof ideas from these papers.

We have left the technical details of the proof to the reader.   □

6   A DNA-Like Proposal to Solve SAT

For a better understanding of the proposed system we start with an example and then we give the general details.

Let us begin with the example promised in Subsection 2.4, which was first considered in [13] and later mentioned in [21]. Starting from this example we will make a connection between the classical DNA way of solving satisfiability and the 'DNA-like' way of solving it with P systems using the tools of merging and separation of the membranes, and polarizations.

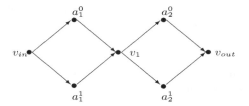

Fig. 4. The graph associated with formula α

Consider the propositional formula
$$\alpha = (x_1 \vee x_2) \wedge (\neg x_1 \vee \neg x_2).$$
Thus, we have two variables with the corresponding graph as depicted in Fig. 4.

As mentioned in Section 2.4, each of the four paths through this graph corresponds to one of the four truth assignments for the variables x_1 and x_2. The core of the procedure of solving SAT with DNA strands is the operation of *separation*. Let us denote by N_0 the initial test tube which contains all four paths (strands) from the initial to the final vertex of the graph. If we apply the operation separate, forming the test tube $+(N_0, a_1^1)$, we get those truth assignments where x_1 assumes the value 1 (true).

A truth assignment is denoted by a two-bit sequence in the natural way. Thus, 01 stands for the assignment $x_1 = 0$, $x_2 = 1$. A similar notation is also used if there are more than two variables. This simple notation of bit sequences is extended to the DNA strands resulting from our basic graphs. Thus, the strand $v_{in} a_1^0 v_1 a_2^1 v_{out}$ is simply denoted by 01.

Following the idea in [21], by $S(N, i, j)$ we denote the test tube of such strands in N where the i-th bit equals j, $j = 0, 1$. Thus, as we observed above, $S(N, i, j)$ results from N by the operation *separate*:
$$S(N, i, j) = +(N, a_i^j).$$

The tube of such strands in N, where the i-th bit equals the complement of j is also considered:
$$S^-(N, i, j) = -(N, a_i^j).$$

Here is the algorithm of solving SAT for the propositional formula α:

    (1) $input(N_0)$,

    (2) $N_1 = S(N_0, 1, 1)$,

    (3) $N_1' = S^-(N_0, 1, 1)$,

    (4) $N_2 = S(N_1', 2, 1)$,

    (5) $merge(N_1, N_2) = N_3$,

    (6) $N_4 = S(N_3, 1, 0)$,

    (7) $N_4' = S^-(N_3, 1, 0)$,

    (8) $N_5 = S(N_4', 2, 0)$,

    (9) $merge(N_4, N_5) = N_6$,

    (10) $detect(N_6)$.

The program is based on exhaustive search. The initial tube at step (1) contains all possible truth-assignments. The test tube at step (5) contains the assignments satisfying the *first clause* of the propositional formula α. (Either x_1 or x_2 must assume the value 1. At step (2) we have those assignments for which x_1 is 1. Of the remaining ones we still take, at step (4), those for which x_2 is 1.) The assignments in this tube, N_3, are filtered further to yield at step (9) those assignments that also satisfy the second clause of the propositional formula α.

Let us now consider the same propositional formula α and solve it using the new technique we propose here, namely P systems, using polarizations and separation/merging rules following closely the principle of separation/merging as above.

We start our computation having in one membrane, labeled $(1,1)$, all truth assignments plus the instances of the given problem (α) encoded as follows:

- truth assignments
  $$00 - a_{1,1}^0, a_{1,2}^0, \quad 01 - a_{2,1}^0, a_{2,2}^1$$
  $$10 - a_{3,1}^1, a_{3,2}^0, \quad 11 - a_{4,1}^1, a_{4,2}^1$$
  More precisely, $a_{1,2}^0$ says that first position – (1) in the subscript indicates the truth-assignment, the second position – (2) indicates the place in the assignment of the value indicated by the superscript - (0).

- clauses
  - $(x_1 \vee x_2) - x_{1,1}^1, x_{1,2}^1,$
  - $(\neg x_1 \vee \neg x_2) - x_{2,1}^0, x_{2,2}^0.$

  Here, by $x_{1,2}^1$ we understand that in the first instance of the formula – (1), variable x_2 (2) is not negated (1).

In the given example, one can imagine 12 objects (given by the sum of the 4 truth assignments (8 objects) and 4 variables of the propositional formula) of two types, a and x, floating in the membrane labeled $(1,1)$, but, at any time, picking any of these objects we can precisely state which is its value and position/value in the set of string of truth assignments/clauses. In other words, a more clear image is that of some "strings" of two types floating inside that cell (membrane), an image very close to the one of the initial test tube N_0 having all truth assignments encoded as we previously saw.

This last image is also very close to the biological image of DNA in an eukaryotic cell enclosed in the *nuclear envelope* through *inner nuclear membrane* and *outer nuclear membrane*.

Coming back to our example, we now want to separate the membrane labeled $(1,1)$ having the polarization 1 into two membranes – one containing the truth assignments which have 1 on the first position (10 and 11, encoded as $a_{3,1}^1, a_{3,2}^0$, and $a_{4,1}^1, a_{4,2}^1$, respectively), the variable which is on the first position on the first clause (namely $x_{1,1}^1$) and the variables from the other clause ($x_{2,1}^0$, and $x_{2,2}^0$), while the second contains the rest of the truth assignments (00 and 01) plus the second variable of the first clause ($x_{1,2}^1$). This step simulates the steps (2) and (3) from the DNA variant of the example. (Fig. 5 shows how the example is processed by the two techniques in parallel.)

(1) $input(N_0)$

    (1_P) input membrane labeled $1, 1$

(2) $N_1 = S(N_0, 1, 1)$

(3) $N_1' = S^-(N_0, 1, 1)$

    (2_P) separation of membrane labeled $1, 1$

(4) $N_2 = S(N_1', 2, 1)$

    (3_P) separation of membrane labeled $1, 2$

(5) $merge(N_1, N_2) = N_3$

    (4_P) merge between membranes $1, 1$ and $1, 2$ to membrane $2, 1$

(6) $N_4 = S(N_3, 1, 0)$

(7) $N_4' = S^-(N_3, 1, 0)$

    (5_P) separation of membrane $2, 1$

(8) $N_5 = S(N_4', 2, 0)$

    (6_P) separation of membrane $2, 2$

(9) $merge(N_4, N_5) = N_6$

    (7_P) merge between membranes $2, 1$ and $2, 2$ to membrane $3, 1$

(10) $detect(N_6)$

    (8_P) detect if there is at least one solution

Fig. 5. Simulation of DNA (rules (1)-(10)) and DNA-like (rules (1_P)-(8_P)) models in parallel

This is done by applying rule r_1:

$r_1 : [\ ]_{1,1}^1 \rightarrow [\ X_{1,1}]_{1,1}^0 [\ X_{1,2}]_{1,2}^1$, where
    $X_{1,1} = \{11, 10, \neg x_1, \neg x_2, x_1\}$,
    $X_{1,2} = \neg X_{1,1} = \{x_2\}$.

(We remind the reader that in showing our procedure we start from an example and only after it we define the general framework).

We continue the computation by separating the membrane labeled $(1, 2)$ with polarization 1 into two membranes labeled $(1, 2)$ and $(1, 3)$ with polarizations 0 and 1, respectively. The first membrane will contain the truth assignments that have 0 on the first position and 1 on the second position (so, only 01) plus the variable x_2 from the first clause. The second membrane is the negation of the above one, thus containing only the truth assignment 00.

A schematic way of solving the problem (by r_1 we mean the application of the general rule r_1, etc.) is depicted in Fig. 6.

In the next step, membranes labeled $(1, 1)$ and $(1, 2)$ will merge and form membrane $(2, 1)$. The rule of merging is given below:

$$[\ ]_{1,1}^0 [\ ]_{1,2}^0 \rightarrow [\ ]_{2,1}^1.$$

The membrane labeled $(2, 1)$ contains strings 10, 11, 01 plus variables x_1, x_2, $\neg x_1$, and $\neg x_2$.

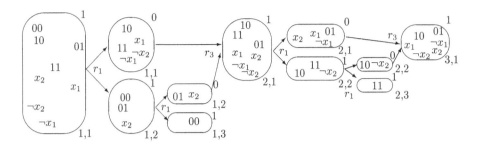

Fig. 6. Schematic representation of solving α

In this phase of the computation, our procedure has computed the *first clause* of the formula and continues with the second one.

From the membrane labeled $(2, 1)$ we separate, using the rule r_1 (applicable to membrane $(2, 1)$), those truth assignments which begin with 0 from those that do not begin with 0. Thus, the membrane labeled $2, 1$ (with polarization 0) will contain the truth assignment 01 and the variables x_1, x_2, and $\neg x_1$, while membrane labeled $(2, 2)$ will contain the rest of the objects (namely, the truth assignments 10 and 11 plus the variable $\neg x_2$).

In this step we separate the second membrane produced in the previous step into two membranes, one (with polarization 0) containing the truth assignments that have 0 on the second position (so only 10) and variable $\neg x_2$, and the other one containing only the string 11. We now merge the two last membranes having polarization 0 ($(2, 1)$, and $(2, 2)$), thus completing the seventh step of the computation.

One can notice that the answer to our particular problem floats into the membrane labeled $(3, 1)$ (produced by the union of membranes labeled $(2, 1)$ and $(2, 2)$). So, now, we are in the stage of *detecting* the result of our problem.

For detection, we will use the following rules:

$r_4 : [\, a_{i,j}^k \,]_{3,1}^1 \to [\ ]_{3,1}^1 1$
    (where $a_{i,j}^k \in \{a_{2,1}^0, a_{2,2}^1, a_{3,1}^1, a_{3,2}^0\}$ is non-deterministically chosen),

$r_5 : [\ ]_{1,4}^1 [\ ]_{2,4}^1 \to [\ ]_{2,4}^1$,

$r_6 : [\, 1 \,]_{0,0}^0 \to [\ ]_{0,0}^1 yes$.

In the last step of the computation, which is done through rule r_6, the correct answer *yes* is sent to the environment, meaning that our problem has at least one solution.

The example we considered here has, as we have seen, at least one solution to the given problem. In the general case, if there is no solution to the given problem, the system will expel to the environment the answer **no**.

The problem with this solution is that we first have to produce 2^n truth assignments for variables. In membrane computing, this can be done in various ways – see, e.g., [16], [1], [15] – by using membrane division, separation, etc.

However, the respective truth assignments are obtained in 2^n separate membranes. By merging operations, we could put together these truth assignments in a single membrane, but, in order not to "mix" them, we have to encode them separately. This, however, assumes using an exponential number of objects, and thus the system itself has exponential size. For the moment, we do not know how to overcome this difficulty.

7   Final Remarks

In this paper we have introduced a new way of simulating Boolean gates and circuits, as an answer to a question formulated in [6]: simulate Boolean circuits with P systems using the inhibiting/de-inhibiting controlling mechanism of computation, as introduced and investigated in [6, 7]. This idea is very attractive because apart from using less biological resources (only two objects and two types of rules for the simulation of Boolean gates) than the previous simulations, we also proposed a system which has a self-embedded synchronization of the objects in the circuit without having to coordinate the computation like in other systems.

We have also proposed an approach to solving the SAT problem simulating, in P systems with active membranes, the way this problem is effectively solved in laboratories using DNA strands. Technical details of this proposal still remain to be fixed, but we hope that this is a step ahead in our way to the laboratory. In addressing the problem mentioned above we have used polarized/non-polarized P systems, while membranes are capable of merge/separate, changing or not-changing their labels. We found very natural to compare (and study the computational bridge between the) two notions from Natural Computing both having the tools of merging/separation already defined. Actually, such an attempt was already done in [11], but using different protocols of DNA computing and different operations with membranes in P systems.

In the end we invite the reader to investigate, using the new tools (uniformly way of solving SAT, but following Lipton's algorithm) presented above, other NP-hard problems, or to try to solve the proposed problem using P systems with different features.

Acknowledgments. The work of first author was supported by the fellowship "Formación de Profesorado Universitario" from the Spanish Ministry of Education, Culture and Sport. The work of the second author was supported by the grant 2002CAJAL-BURV4 from Rovira i Virgili University, Spain.

References

1. A. Alhazov, T.-O. Ishdorj: Membrane operations in P systems with active membranes. In *Second Brainstorming Week on Membrane Computing* (Gh. Păun, A. Riscos-Núñez, A. Romero-Jiménez, F. Sancho-Caparrini, eds.), Technical report of Research Group on Natural Computing, University of Seville, TR 01/2004, 37–44.
2. A. Alhazov, L. Pan, Gh. Păun: Trading polarizations for labels in P systems with active membranes. *Acta Informatica*, 41, 2-3 (2004), 111–144.

3. A. Alhazov, L. Pan: Polarizationless P systems with active membranes. *Grammars*, 7 (2004), 141–159.

4. R.S. Braich, N. Chelyapov, C. Johnson, R.W.K. Rothemund, L. Adleman: Solution to a 20-variable 3-SAT problem on a DNA computer. *Science*, 296, 5567 (2002), 499–502

5. C. Calude, Gh. Păun, G. Rozenberg, A. Salomaa, eds.: *Multiset Processing. Mathematical, Computer Science, Molecular Computing Points of View*. LNCS 2235, Springer, Berlin, 2001.

6. M. Cavaliere, M. Ionescu, T.-O. Ishdorj: Inhibiting/de-inhibiting rules in P systems. In *Membrane Computing, International Workshop, WMC5, Milano, Italy, 2004, Selected Papers* (G. Mauri, Gh. Păun, M.J. Pérez-Jiménez, G. Rozenberg, A. Salomaa, eds.), LNCS 3365, Springer, Berlin, 2005 224–238

7. M. Cavaliere, M. Ionescu, T.-O. Ishdorj: Inhibiting/de-inhibiting P systems with active membranes. In *Cellular Computing (Complexity Aspects), ESP PESC Exploratory Workshop*, Sevilla, 2005, 117–130

8. R. Ceterchi, D. Sburlan: Simulating Boolean circuits with P systems. *Membrane Computing, International Workshop, WMC 2003, Tarragona, July 2003, Selected Papers* (C. Martin-Vide, G. Mauri, Gh. Păun, G. Rozenberg, A. Salomaa, eds.), LNCS 2933, Springer, Berlin, 2004 104–122

9. J. Dassow, Gh. Păun: *Regulated Rewriting in Formal Language Theory*. Springer, Berlin, 1989.

10. M.R. Garey, D.J. Johnson: *Computers and Intractability. A Guide to the Theory of NP-Completeness*. Freeman WH, San Francisco, 1979.

11. T. Head: Aqueous simulations of membrane computations. *Romanian Journal of Information Science and Technology*, 5 (2002).

12. M. Ionescu, T.-O. Ishdorj: Replicative–distributed rules in P systems with active membranes. *Proceedings of First International Colloquium on Theoretical Aspects of Computing*, Guiyang, China, September 20-24, 2004 UNU/IIST Report No. 310, 263–278, and LNCS 4705, Springer, Berlin, 2005, 69–84.

13. R.J. Lipton: Using DNA to solve NP-complete problems.*Science*, 268 (1995), 542–545.

14. L. Pan, A. Alhazov, T.-O. Ishdorj: Further remarks on P systems with active membranes, separation, merging and release rules. *Soft Computing*, 9, 9 (2005), 686–690.

15. L. Pan, T.-O. Ishdorj: P systems with active membranes and separation rules. *Journal of Universal Computer Science*, 10, 5 (2004), 630–649.

16. L. Pan, A. Alhazov: Solving HPP and SAT by P systems with active membranes and separation rules. Submitted, 2005.

17. C.P. Papadimitriou: *Computational Complexity*. Addison-Wesley, Reading, MA, 1994.

18. Gh. Păun: Computing with membranes. *Journal of Computer and System Sciences*, 61,1 (2000), 108–143, and TUCS Research Report 208, 1998.

19. Gh. Păun: P systems with active membranes: Attacking NP-complete problems. *Journal of Automata, Languages and Combinatorics*, 6, 1 (2001), 75–90.

20. Gh. Păun: *Membrane Computing: An Introduction*. Springer, Berlin, 2002.

21. Gh. Păun, G. Rozenberg, A. Salomaa: *DNA Computing. New Computing Paradigms*. Springer-Verlag, Berlin, 1998.

22. M.J. Pérez-Jiménez, A. Romero-Jiménez, F. Sancho-Caparrini: Complexity classes in models of cellular computation with membranes. *Natural Computing*, 2, 3 (2003), 265–285.

23. G. Rozenberg, A. Salomaa, eds.: *Handbook of Formal Languages*. Springer-Verlag, Berlin, 1997.

24. K. Sakamoto, H. Gounzu, K. Komiya, D. Kiga, S. Yokoyama, T. Yokomori, M. Hagiya: Molecular computation by DNA hairpin formation. *Science*, 288 (2000), 1223–1226.

25. A. Salomaa: *Formal Languages*. Academic Press, New York, 1973.

Towards a Petri Net Semantics for Membrane Systems

Jetty H.C.M. Kleijn[1], Maciej Koutny[2], and Grzegorz Rozenberg[1,3]

[1] LIACS, Leiden University,
P.O. Box 9512, NL-2300 RA Leiden, The Netherlands
{kleijn, rozenber}@liacs.nl
[2] School of Computing Science, University of Newcastle,
Newcastle upon Tyne, NE1 7RU, United Kingdom
Maciej.Koutny@ncl.ac.uk
[3] Department of Computer Science,
University of Colorado at Boulder, Boulder, CO 80309-0347, USA

Abstract. We consider the modelling of the behaviour of membrane systems using Petri nets. First, a systematic, structural link is established between a basic class of membrane systems and Petri nets. To capture the compartmentisation of membrane systems, localities are proposed as an extension of Petri nets. This leads to a locally maximal concurrency semantics for Petri nets. We indicate how processes for these nets could be defined which should be of use in order to describe what is actually going on during a computation of a membrane system.

1 Introduction

In the past 7 years *membrane systems*, also known as *P systems*, have received a lot of attention and in the process became a prominent new computational model [18, 17, 19, 1]. They are inspired by the compartmentisation of living cells and its effect on their functioning. A key structural notion is that of a *membrane* by which a system is divided into compartments where chemical reactions can take place. These reactions transform multisets of objects present in the compartments into new objects, possibly transferring objects to neighbouring compartments, including the environment. Consequently, the behavioural aspects of membrane systems are based on sets of *reaction rules* defined for each compartment. A distinguishing feature of membrane systems is that the system is assumed to evolve in a synchronous fashion, meaning that there is a global clock common for all the compartments. Within each time unit, the system is transformed by the rules which are applied in a maximally concurrent fashion (this means that no further rules in any compartment could have been applied in the same time unit). These transformations are applied starting from an initial distribution of objects. Depending on the exact formalisation of the model, the notion of a successful (or halting) computation is defined together with its output, e.g., the number of objects sent to the environment.

R. Freund et al. (Eds.): WMC 2005, LNCS 3850, pp. 292–309, 2006.
© Springer-Verlag Berlin Heidelberg 2006

The above describes the functionality of the basic membrane system model, according to [18, 19]. In addition, many different extensions and modifications of that basic model have been proposed and studied, such as priorities and catalysts. Moreover, those studies have been mostly focussed on the computational power of the models considered, including various aspects of complexity.

Given the existing body of results on the possible outcomes of computations of membrane systems, we feel that we are now in a position to also investigate and describe what is actually going on during a computation. The situation may be compared to that in the field of the semantics of programming languages based on input-output relations where the operational semantics was added to deal with the correctness of potentially non-terminating and concurrent programs. In this paper we propose to undertake this endeavour using the Petri net model (see, e.g., [21]). The reason is that they have local transformation rules and support the modelling of causality and concurrency in a direct and explicit way. In a nutshell, a Petri net is a bipartite directed graph consisting of two kinds of nodes, called *places* and *transitions*. Places together with their markings indicate the local availability of resources and thus can be used to represent objects in specific compartments, whereas transitions are actions which can occur depending on local conditions related to the availability of resources and thus can be used to represent reaction rules associated with specific compartments. When a transition occurs it consumes resources from its input places and produces items in its output places thus mimicking the effect of a reaction rule.

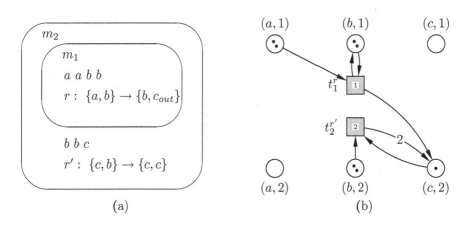

Fig. 1. A membrane system (a), and the corresponding Petri net (b)

The basic idea of modelling a membrane system using a Petri net can be explained through an example shown in Figure 1(a). The system depicted there consists of two nested membranes (the inner membrane m_1 and the outer membrane m_2), two rules (rule r associated with the compartment c_1 inside the inner membrane, and rule r' associated with the compartment c_2 surrounded by m_2, i.e., in-between the two membranes), and three symbols denoting molecules (a, b, and c). Initially, the compartment c_1 contains two copies of both a and b, and c_2 contains two copies of b and a single copy of c. To model this membrane system using a Petri net, we introduce a separate place (x, j) for each kind of molecule x and compartment c_j. As usual, places are drawn as circles with the number of the currently associated resources represented as tokens (small black dots). For each rule r associated with a compartment c_i we introduce a separate transition t_i^r, drawn as a rectangle. Transitions are connected to places by weighted directed arcs, and if no weight is shown it is by default equal to 1. If the transformation described by a rule r of compartment c_i consumes k copies of molecule x from compartment c_j, then we introduce a k weighted arc from place (x, j) to transition t_i^r, and similarly for molecules produced by transformations. Finally, assuming that initially compartment c_j contained n copies of molecule x, we introduce n tokens into place (x, j). The resulting Petri net is depicted in Figure 1(b). As argued later on, Petri nets derived in this way can be used to describe issues related to concurrency in the behaviour of the original membrane systems.

Applying Petri nets to model membrane systems is by no means an original idea. Since multiset calculus is basic for membrane systems and also for computing the token distribution in Petri nets [3], some connections have already been established. Some authors have in fact already proposed to interpret reaction rules of membrane systems using Petri net transitions, e.g., [5, 20]. Our aim is to demonstrate that a relationship between Petri nets and membrane systems can be established at the system level. We achieve this by defining a class of Petri nets suitable for the study of behavioural aspects of membrane systems and other systems exhibiting a mix of synchronous and asynchronous execution rules. This latter feature is motivated by the observation that the assumed strict global synchronicity of the membrane systems is not always reasonable from the biological point of view as already observed in [18]. In fact, [8] proposes to drop this assumption completely and considers fully asynchronous and sequential membrane systems; also the membrane systems of [5] are sequential, whereas [4] advocates that reactions are assigned their own execution times and uses a form of local synchronicity.

We intend to demonstrate that Petri nets obtained from membrane systems in the way described above provide a suitable model to capture and investigate the behavioural properties of membrane systems. In this sense the paper is more directed towards the computations taking place in membrane systems. After recalling the definition of membrane systems, we introduce a general class of Petri nets which can be used to define their formal concurrency semantics. This concurrency semantics will be built upon a well established technique of *unfolding* Petri nets, leading to *processes* which formalise concurrent execution histories. The paper deliberately avoids going into full technical details of the formal presentation, aiming instead at conveying the basic ideas of our proposal. Most of the formalities and proofs are delegated to the companion paper [14].

In this paper, a multiset (over a set X) is a function $m : X \to \mathbb{N}$. By $\mathbb{N}^X$ we denote the set of multisets over X. For two multisets m and m' over X, we denote $m \leq m'$ if $m(x) \leq m'(x)$ for all $x \in X$. Moreover, a subset of X may be viewed through its characteristic function as a multiset over X, and for a multiset m we denote $x \in m$ if $m(x) \geq 1$. The sum of two multisets m and m' over X is given by $(m + m')(x) \stackrel{\text{df}}{=} m(x) + m'(x)$, the difference by $(m - m')(x) \stackrel{\text{df}}{=} \max\{0, m(x) - m'(x)\}$, as a total function extending set difference. The multiplication of m by a natural number n is given by $(n \cdot m)(x) \stackrel{\text{df}}{=} n \cdot m(x)$. Moreover, any finite sum $m_1 + \cdots + m_k$ will also be denoted as $\sum_{i \in \{1,\ldots,k\}} m_i$.

2 Basic Membrane Systems

For the purposes of this paper, it suffices to consider the most basic definition of membrane systems [17, 19]. Throughout the paper a *membrane system* (of degree $m \geq 1$) is a construct

$$\Pi \stackrel{\text{df}}{=} (V, \mu, w_1^0, \ldots, w_m^0, R_1, \ldots, R_m),$$

where:

- V is a finite *alphabet* consisting of (names of) objects;
- μ is a *membrane structure* given by a rooted tree with m nodes, representing the membranes, as illustrated in Figure 2 – without loss of generality, we assume that the nodes are given as the integers $1, \ldots, m$, and $(i, j) \in \mu$ will mean that there is an edge from i (parent) to j (child) in the tree of μ;
- each w_i^0 is a multiset of objects initially associated with membrane i;
- each R_i is a finite set of *evolution rules* r associated with membrane i, of the form

$$lhs^r \to rhs^r,$$

where lhs^r — the left hand side of r – is a non-empty multiset over V, and rhs^r — the right hand side of r – is a non-empty multiset over

$$V \cup \{a_{out} \mid a \in V\} \cup \{a_{in_j} \mid a \in V \text{ and } (i,j) \in \mu\}.$$

Symbols a_{in_j} represent objects a that will be sent to a child node j and a_{out} stands for an a that will be sent out to the parent node. Without loss of generality,[1] we additionally assume that no evolution rule r associated with the root of the membrane structure uses any a_{out} in rhs^r.

A membrane system Π as above evolves from configuration to configuration as a consequence of the application of (multisets of) evolution rules in each membrane. Formally, a *configuration* is a tuple $C \stackrel{\text{df}}{=} (w_1, \ldots, w_m)$ where each w_i is a multiset of object names; we define a *vector multi-rule* $\boldsymbol{R}$ as an element of $\mathbb{N}^{R_1} \times \cdots \times \mathbb{N}^{R_m}$. Given a vector multi-rule $\boldsymbol{R} = (\widehat{R}_1, \ldots, \widehat{R}_m)$, we use as

---

[1] Since the environment can always be modelled by adding a new root to the membrane structure.

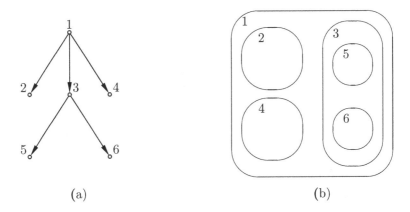

Fig. 2. A membrane structure (a); and the corresponding compartments (b)

additional notation $lhs_i = \sum_{r \in R_i} \widehat{R}_i(r) \cdot lhs^r$ for the multiset of all objects in the left hand sides of the rules in $\widehat{R}_i$ and, similarly, $rhs_i = \sum_{r \in R_i} \widehat{R}_i(r) \cdot rhs^r$ is the multiset of all — possibly indexed — objects in the right hand sides.

Given two configurations, $C = (w_1, \ldots, w_m)$ and $C' = (w'_1, \ldots, w'_m)$, C can *evolve* into C' if there exists a vector multi-rule $\boldsymbol{R} = (\widehat{R}_1, \ldots, \widehat{R}_m)$ such that for every $1 \le i \le m$, the following hold

(i) $lhs_i \le w_i$;
(ii) there is no rule r in R_i such that $lhs^r + lhs_i \le w_i$; and
(iii) for each object $a \in V$,

$$w'_i(a) = w_i(a) - lhs_i(a) + rhs_i(a) + rhs_{parent(i)}(a_{in_i}) + \sum_{(i,j) \in \mu} rhs_j(a_{out}),$$

where $parent(i)$ is the father membrane of i unless i is the root in which case $parent(i)$ is undefined and $rhs_{parent(i)}(a_{in_i})$ is omitted. Note that any j in the last term must be a child membrane of i.

By (i), the configuration C has in each membrane i enough occurrences of objects for the application of the multiset of evolution rules $\widehat{R}_i$. Maximal concurrency is captured by (ii) according to which in none of the membranes an additional evolution rule can be applied. Observe that some of the $\widehat{R}_i$'s in $\boldsymbol{R}$ may be empty i.e., no evolution rules associated with the corresponding membranes i can be used. Finally, (iii) describes the effect of the application of the rules in $\boldsymbol{R}$.

By $C \xRightarrow{\boldsymbol{R}} C'$ we denote that C evolves into C' due to the application of $\boldsymbol{R}$. Note that the evolution of C is non-deterministic in the sense that there may be different vector multi-rules applicable to C as described above. A (finite) *computation* of Π is now a (finite) sequence of evolutions starting from the initial configuration $C_0 \overset{\text{df}}{=} (w^0_1, \ldots, w^0_m)$.

3   Petri Nets

We first recall the key notions of the standard Petri net model. A *PT-net* is a tuple $N \overset{\text{df}}{=} (P, T, W, M_0)$ such that P and T are finite disjoint sets; $W : (T \times P) \cup (P \times T) \to \mathbb{N}$ is a multiset; and M_0 is a multiset of places. The elements of P and T are respectively the *places* and *transitions*, W is the *weight function* of N, and M_0 is the *initial* marking. In diagrams, places are drawn as circles, and transitions as rectangles. If $W(x, y) \geq 1$ for some $(x, y) \in (T \times P) \cup (P \times T)$, then (x, y) is an *arc* leading from x to y. As usual, arcs are annotated with their weight if this is 2 or more. We assume that, for every $t \in T$, there are places p and q such that $W(p, t) \geq 1$ and $W(t, q) \geq 1$.

Places represent local states, while markings are global states of systems represented by PT-nets. Transitions represent actions which may occur at a given marking and then lead to a new marking (the weight function specifies what resources are consumed and produced during the execution of such actions).

Figure 3 shows a PT-net model of a simple one-producer / two-consumers concurrent system, where the producer is represented by the initial token in place p and the consumers by the two tokens in place r. Using transition a, the producer repeatedly produces new items (tokens) and *adds* them to place q (intuitively, a buffer between the producer and the two consumers) from where they can be *taken* by one of the two consumers, and then *used* by executing transition u. Rather than producing a new item, the producer may at any time *cancel* the production cycle by executing transition c.

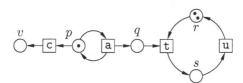

Fig. 3. PT-net of the one-producer / two-consumers system

The *pre-* and *post-multiset* of a transition $t \in T$ are multisets of places given, for all $p \in P$, by:

$$\text{PRE}_N(t)(p) \overset{\text{df}}{=} W(p, t) \quad \text{and} \quad \text{POST}_N(t)(p) \overset{\text{df}}{=} W(t, p).$$

Both notations extend to multisets of transitions U:

$$\text{PRE}_N(U) \overset{\text{df}}{=} \sum_{t \in U} U(t) \cdot \text{PRE}_N(t) \quad \text{and} \quad \text{POST}_N(U) \overset{\text{df}}{=} \sum_{t \in U} U(t) \cdot \text{POST}_N(t).$$

A *step* is a multiset of transitions, $U : T \to \mathbb{N}$. It is *enabled* at a marking M if $M \geq \text{PRE}_N(U)$. We denote this by $M[U\rangle$. Thus, in order for U to be enabled at M, for each place p, the number of tokens in p under M should at least be equal to the total number of tokens that are needed as an input to U, respecting the weights of the input arcs. Moreover, U is a *maximal step* at M if $M[U\rangle$ and there is no transition t such that $M[U + \{t\}\rangle$.

If U is enabled at M, then it can be *executed* leading to the marking $M' \stackrel{\mathrm{df}}{=} M - \mathrm{PRE}_N(U) + \mathrm{POST}_N(U)$. This means that the execution of U 'consumes' from each place p exactly $W(p, t)$ tokens for each occurrence of a transition $t \in U$ that has p as an input place, and 'produces' in each place p exactly $W(t, p)$ tokens for each occurrence of a transition $t \in U$ with p as an output place. If the execution of U leads from M to M' we write $M[U\rangle M'$. Whenever U is a maximal step at M, we will also write $M[U\rangle_{max} M'$.

A finite sequence $\sigma = U_1 \ldots U_n$ of non-empty steps is a *step sequence* from the initial marking M_0 if there are markings $M_1 \ldots M_n$ of N satisfying $M_{i-1}[U_i\rangle M_i$ for every $i \leq n$. Such a σ is also called a step sequence from M_0 to M_n, and M_n itself is called a *reachable* marking.

In the same way, we can define step sequences consisting of maximal steps, and markings reachable through such step sequences. Together, they define the *maximal concurrency semantics* of the PT-net N as considered, for instance, in [11].

The example PT-net in Figure 3 admits an infinite number of step sequences. For example, $\sigma = \{a\}\{t, a\}\{u, t\}$ models the following scenario: (i) the producer produces an item which is then deposited into the buffer; (ii) the producer produces another item and, at the same time, one of the consumers takes the previously produced item from the buffer; and (iii) the consumer who retrieved the first item produced uses it and, at the same time, the second consumer removes the second item produced from the buffer. In Figure 4 we show how this scenario changes the current marking (global state) of the PT-net. As far as the maximal concurrency semantics is concerned, $\sigma = \{a\}\{t, a\}\{u, t\}$ is not allowed: though the first two steps executed are maximal, $\{u, t\}$ is not since, for instance, the step $\{a, u, t\}$ is enabled after the execution of $\{a\}\{t, a\}$, and $\sigma' = \{a\}\{t, a\}\{a, u, t\}$ rather than σ is part of the maximal concurrency semantics of the PT-net in Figure 3.

3.1   Petri Nets with Localities

In order to represent the compartmentisation of membrane systems we now introduce a novel extension of the basic net model of PT-nets, by adding the notion of located transitions and locally maximally concurrent executions of co-located transitions. In the proposed way of specifying locality for the transitions in a PT-net, each transition belongs to a fixed unique locality. The exact mechanism for achieving this is to introduce a partition of the set of all transitions, using a locality mapping $\mathfrak{L}$. Intuitively, two transitions for which $\mathfrak{L}$ returns the same value will be co-located.

A *PT-net with localities* (or PTL-net) is a tuple $NL \stackrel{\mathrm{df}}{=} (P, T, W, M_0, \mathfrak{L})$, where $\mathrm{UND}(NL) \stackrel{\mathrm{df}}{=} (P, T, W, M_0)$ is the *underlying* PT-net and $\mathfrak{L} : T \to \mathbb{N}$ is a *location mapping* for the transition set T. In the diagrams of PTL-nets, transitions are

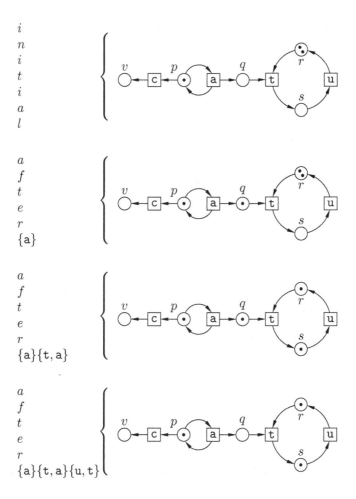

Fig. 4. Executing the PT-net according to $\{a\}\{t, a\}\{u, t\}$

shaded rectangles with the locality being shown in the middle. Note that $\mathcal{L}$ is merely a labelling of transitions, it is not meant as a renaming (as used later for occurrence nets).

The two execution semantics already defined for PT-nets carry over to PTL-nets, after assuming that all the notations concerning the places and transitions of a PTL-net are as in the underlying PT-net, together with the notions of marking, (maximal) step and the result of executing a step.

3.2   Membrane Systems as Petri Nets

In this section, we make our proposal on how membrane systems can be interpreted by Petri nets more precise. Given the definitions of membrane systems and Petri nets with localities, the construction sketched in the introduction can be implemented as follows.

Let $\Pi = (V, \mu, w_1^0, \ldots, w_m^0, R_1, \ldots, R_m)$ be a membrane system of degree m. Then the corresponding PTL-net is $NL_\Pi \stackrel{\text{df}}{=} (P, T, W, M_0, \mathfrak{L})$ where the various components are defined thus:

- $P \stackrel{\text{df}}{=} V \times \{1, \ldots, m\}$;
- $T \stackrel{\text{df}}{=} T_1 \cup \ldots \cup T_m$ where each T_i contains a distinct transition t_i^r for every evolution rule $r \in R_i$;
- for every place $p = (a, j) \in P$ and every transition $t = t_i^r \in T$,

$$W(p, t) \stackrel{\text{df}}{=} \begin{cases} lhs^r(a) & \text{if } i = j, \\ 0 & \text{otherwise,} \end{cases}$$

$$W(t, p) \stackrel{\text{df}}{=} \begin{cases} rhs^r(a) & \text{if } i = j, \\ rhs^r(a_{out}) & \text{if } (j, i) \in \mu, \\ rhs^r(a_{in_j}) & \text{if } (i, j) \in \mu, \\ 0 & \text{otherwise;} \end{cases}$$

- for every place $p = (a, j) \in P$, its initial marking is $M_0(p) \stackrel{\text{df}}{=} w_j(a)$;.
- for every transition $t = t_i^r \in T$, its locality is $\mathfrak{L}(t) \stackrel{\text{df}}{=} i$.

To capture the very tight correspondence between the membrane system Π and the PTL-net NL_Π, we introduce a straightforward bijection between configurations of Π and markings of NL_Π, based on the correspondence of object locations and places.

Let $C = (w_1, \ldots, w_m)$ be a configuration of Π. Then the corresponding marking $\phi(C)$ of NL_Π is given by $\phi(C)(a, i) \stackrel{\text{df}}{=} w_i(a)$, for every place (a, i) of NL_Π. Similarly, for any vector multi-rule $\boldsymbol{R} = (\widehat{R}_1, \ldots, \widehat{R}_m)$ of Π, we define a multiset $\psi(\boldsymbol{R})$ of transitions of NL_Π such that $\psi(\boldsymbol{R})(t_i^r) \stackrel{\text{df}}{=} \widehat{R}_i(r)$ for every $t_i^r \in T$. It is clear that ϕ is a bijection from the configurations of Π to the markings of NL_Π, and that ψ is a bijection from vector multi-rules of Π to steps of NL_Π.

It should be clear that not every PTL-net can be obtained from a membrane system using the transformation described above. For example, in any net NL_Π, two transitions sharing an input place will always have the same locality assigned by $\mathfrak{L}$.

We now can formulate a fundamental property concerning the relationship between the dynamics of the membrane system Π and that of the corresponding PTL-net:

$$C \stackrel{\boldsymbol{R}}{\Longrightarrow} C' \quad \text{if and only if} \quad \phi(C) \, [\psi(\boldsymbol{R})\rangle_{max} \, \phi(C').$$

Since the initial configuration of Π corresponds through ϕ to the initial marking of NL_Π, the above immediately implies that the computations of Π coincide with the maximal concurrency semantics of the PTL net NL_Π.

The reader might by now have observed that the membrane structure of Π is used in the definitions of the static structure of the PTL-net NL_Π (i.e., in the definitions of places, transitions and the weight function), but as far as maximal concurrency semantics is concerned, the locality information for transitions in the form of the mapping $\mathfrak{L}$ of NL_Π is not relevant (the structure of Petri nets explicitly supports the locality aspects of the resources consumed and produced by transitions). However, it allows us to define local synchronicity presented next.

3.3   Locally Maximal Concurrency Semantics of PTL-Nets

Consider the PTL-model of the producer/consumer example as depicted in Figure 5. It conveys, in particular, the information that transitions a and c are assigned one locality, whereas transitions t and u are assigned another locality. This reflects the view that the producer operates away from the two consumers.

To define a right semantical model reflecting this distribution of computing agents, we need to change the enabling condition for steps. Now, intuitively, only those steps are allowed to occur which are maximally concurrent within the localities given by $\mathfrak{L}$.

In a PTL-net $NL = (P, T, W, M_0, \mathfrak{L})$, a step $U : T \rightarrow \mathbb{N}$ is *locally max-enabled* at a marking M if it is enabled at M in $\text{UND}(NL)$ and, in addition, there is no transition t such that $\mathfrak{L}(t) \in \mathfrak{L}(U)$ and $U+\{t\}$ is still enabled at M in $\text{UND}(NL)$. Thus a step which is locally max-enabled at a marking is not necessarily a maximal step at that marking. The induced notions of a locally maximal step sequence and marking reachability are then defined as usual using the just defined notion of enabledness.

We now can look at the impact the various definitions of enabledness have on the set of legal behaviours of a Petri net. Looking at the PT-net N in Figure 3 and PTL-net NL in Figure 5, we can observe the following. First of all, the step sequence $\{a\}\{t, a\}\{u, t\}$, which was possible for N, is a legal behaviour of NL under the locally maximal concurrency semantics as are many others, like $\{a\}\{a\}\{a\}$ and $\{a\}\{a\}\{t, t\}$. (Recall here that $\{a\}\{t, a\}\{u, t\}$ was disallowed by the maximal concurrency semantics.) However, there are also step sequences of N which are not part of the locally maximal concurrency semantics of NL; e.g., $\sigma = \{a\}\{t, a\}\{t\}$ since after executing $\{a\}\{t, a\}$ it is possible to execute step $\{u, t\}$ which is strictly greater than $\{t\}$ and transitions t and u are co-located.

Coming back to the example shown in Figure 1(b), we have the following step sequences in the maximal concurrency semantics: the empty sequence,

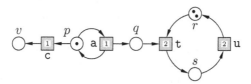

Fig. 5. PTL-net of the one-producer / two-consumers system

$\{t_1^r, t_1^r, t_2^{r'}\}$ and $\{t_1^r, t_1^r, t_2^{r'}\}\{t_2^{r'}\}$. The locally maximal concurrency semantics, on the other hand, yields several additional step sequences, like $\{t_1^r, t_1^r\}\{t_2^{r'}, t_2^{r'}\}$ and $\{t_2^{r'}\}\{t_1^r, t_1^r\}\{t_2^{r'}\}$. Note further that it does not allow $\{t_1^r, t_1^r\}\{t_2^{r'}\}$ which, in turn, is allowed by the standard step sequence semantics.

To summarise, PT-nets admit both standard and maximal concurrency semantics, while for PTL-nets we have in addition locally maximal concurrency semantics. In particular, this means that we cannot identify the exact semantical model just by looking at a net's structure; we always need to specify which execution semantics is being used.

4   Causality and Concurrency

All three variants of step sequence semantics of a Petri net considered in this paper provide important insights into the concurrency aspects of the underlying systems. They are, however, still sequential in nature in the sense that steps occur ordered thus obscuring the true causal relationships between the occurrences of transitions. On the other hand, information on causal relationship is often of high importance for system analysis and/or design. Petri nets can easily support a formal approach where this information is readily available as was recognised a long time ago, see [16] where it was proposed to unfold behaviours into structures allowing an explicit representation of causality, conflict and concurrency. A well-established way of developing such a semantics for the standard PT-nets is based on a class of acyclic Petri nets, called *occurrence nets* [22]. What one essentially tries to achieve is to trace the changes of markings due to transitions being executed along some legal behaviour of the original PT-net, and in doing so record which resources were consumed and produced.

In this section, we first explain the main ideas behind the causality semantics based on standard step sequences of PT-nets. After that, we show how this approach could be adapted to work for the locally maximal concurrency semantics of PTL-nets. Note that the maximal concurrency semantics of a PT-net coincides with the locally maximal concurrency semantics of this PT-net after extending it to a PTL-net with all transitions mapped to the same locality; hence we will only consider explicitly the locally maximal concurrency semantics.

4.1   Causal Behaviours of PT-Nets

Looking at the sequence $\sigma = \{a\}\{t, a\}\{u, t\}$ of executions in Figure 4, it is not immediate that transition u could have occurred before the second occurrence of transition a or, in other words, that the former is not causally dependent on the latter.

Figure 6 illustrates the idea in which we *unfold* the scenario represented by σ. The initial stage shows just the initial marking which includes two separate (labelled) *conditions* (this is how places are called in occurrence nets) to represent the two initial tokens in place r. Executing step $\{a\}$ consumes the p-condition, creates an a-event (this is how transitions are called in occurrence

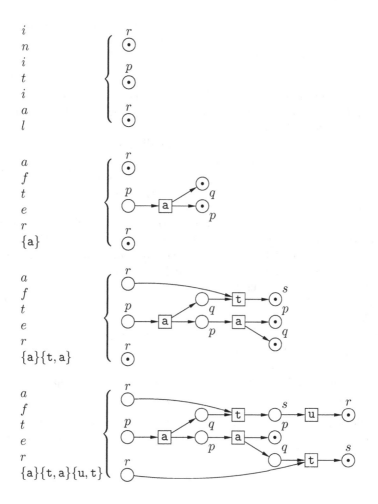

Fig. 6. Constructing an occurrence net corresponding to $\{a\}\{t, a\}\{u, t\}$

nets), as well as two new conditions: a p-condition and a q-condition. An important point is to notice that we create a fresh p-condition rather than a loop back to the initial one since we want to distinguish between different occurrences of the same token; as a result the occurrence net being constructed will be an acyclic graph. Another important point is that the environment of the generated a-event corresponds exactly to the environment of transition a; namely, it consumes a p-token and creates a p-token and a q-token. After that, executing step $\{t, a\}$ consists in consuming three conditions and creating two events and three fresh conditions, and similarly for the last step $\{u, t\}$. And, as a final result, we obtain an acyclic net labelled with places and transitions of the original PT-net; it is called a *process* of the original PT-net. The process net has a default initial marking consisting of a token in each of the conditions without an incoming arc.

It is now possible to look both at the structure of the process net and the executions which are possible from its default initial marking, making some important observations relating to:

- *Causality.* The causality relationships among the executed transitions can be read-off by following directed paths between the events; for example in Figure 6, the lower t-event is caused by both a-events, while the upper one is caused only by the leftmost a-event.
- *Concurrency.* Events for which there is no directed path from one to another can be thought of as concurrent.
- *Reachability.* Any maximal set of conditions for which there is no directed path from one condition to another corresponds to a reachable marking of the original PT-net.
- *Representation.* The step sequence on the basis of which the process was created can be executed from the initial default marking in the occurrence net. So the original behaviour has been retained. In Figure 6, there are 13 different step sequences generated by the process net defined by $\sigma = \{a\}\{t, a\}\{u, t\}$, including σ itself.
- *Soundness.* Any step sequence which can be executed from the default initial marking to the default final marking (consisting of tokens placed in each of the conditions without an outgoing arc) of the process net is also a legal step sequence of the original PT-net. Processes provide a highly compressed representation of step sequence behaviours of the original PT-net (this feature has been exploited to a significant degree in the development of efficient model checking algorithms for PT-nets).

The above observations on the process nets of the standard PT-nets lead us to consider a similar treatment for the PTL-net model and their locally maximal concurrency semantics.

4.2   Causal Behaviours of PTL-Nets

As a first attempt, we simply adopt the unfolding strategy as in the PT-net case. We only ensure that the step sequence consists of (locally) maximal steps. Moreover, we preserve the localities of the transitions in the events created while constructing the occurrence net. Figure 7 shows the result for the PTL-net of Figure 5 and the step sequence $\{a\}\{t, a\}$ which is allowed in the maximal and thus also in the locally maximal concurrency semantics (both the occurrence net and its default initial marking are depicted). Although this is straightforward, we still need an argument that the resulting process is what one would want to take for further analyses. In particular, one would want to retain the soundness of the previous construction. In the case of our example, we can execute the occurrence net and conclude that under the maximal rule it admits the original sequence, whereas under the locally maximal rule it admits two more step sequences, $\{a\}\{t\}\{a\}$ and $\{a\}\{a\}\{t\}$. Clearly $\{a\}\{t\}\{a\}$ is a legal step sequence of the original PTL-net in the locally maximal concurrency semantics. However $\{a\}\{a\}\{t\}$ is not, since after $\{a\}\{a\}$, two occurrences of t are enabled (due to

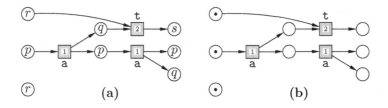

Fig. 7. Process net corresponding to the step sequence $\{a\}\{t, a\}$ **(a)**; and its default initial marking **(b)**

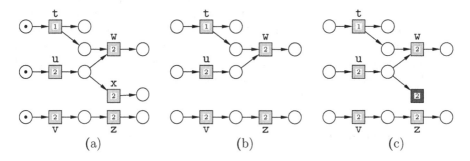

Fig. 8. PTL-net **(a)**; an occurrence net constructed from step sequence $\{t, u, v\}\{w, z\}$ **(b)**; and a barbed process **(c)**

auto-concurrency). Thus, in general it would be too hasty to accept the standard unfolding routine as satisfactory since information on (additional) enabledness may be lost.

Consider, for example, the PTL-net in Figure 8(a) and its step sequence $\{t, u, v\}\{w, z\}$ consisting of locally maximal steps. Proceeding as in the previous case, we obtain an occurrence net shown in Figure 8(b). Now the problem is that it has an execution from the default initial marking (using only locally maximal steps) which corresponds to $\{u, v\}\{t, z\}\{w\}$. This step sequence, however, is not a locally maximal step sequence of the original PTL-net as in the second step it is possible to add transition x which is co-located with transition z.

An intuitive reason why the standard construction fails to work for the PTL-net in Figure 8(a) is that such an unfolding 'forgets' that transition x was enabled at a stage where transition w was selected. Then, delaying the execution of the w-event, creates a situation where the executed step (though locally maximal within the occurrence net since the knowledge of the enabledness of x is lost) does not correspond to a locally maximal step within the PTL-net.

Our approach to cope with these problems in [14] is to equip occurrence nets generated by PTL-nets with additional *barb-events*, represented by darkly shaded rectangles. Barb-events are not labelled with transition names and are not meant to be executed; rather, they are used in the calculation of the enabled sets of events. Such occurrence nets are called *barbed* processes. Rather than providing a full formal definition of how barb-events are added during the un-folding procedure, which we give in the companion paper [14], we only mention here that it is based on checking for the existence of locally newly enabled transitions not (yet) included in the executed scenario, e.g., since another co-located transition was selected. Figure 8(c) illustrates the modified construction for the net in Figure 8(a,b).

After executing $\{u, v\}$, it is now impossible to select $\{t, z\}$ since there is a record in the form of the barb-event that such a step would not be maximal in the locality to which transition $\{z\}$ belongs. The only way of continuing is to execute $\{t\}$ and after that $\{z, w\}$, generating a legal step sequence $\{u, v\}\{t\}\{z, w\}$.

Finally, we return to the example shown in figure 7. Recall that for this occurrence net we can execute under the maximal rule $\{a\}\{a\}\{t\}$, which is not a legal step sequence of the original PTL-net in the locally maximal concurrency semantics. Using barb-events this is no longer the case as the barbed process will contain a barb-event with locality 2 and two inputs: the bottom r-condition and the bottom q-condition. As a result, one cannot execute a single t after $\{a\}\{a\}$ under the locally maximal rule.

5   Summary and Conclusions

In this paper we have proposed an approach to the modelling of the behaviour of membrane systems through a class of Petri nets with localities (PTL-nets).

We gave first a formal translation for a basic class of membrane systems, and argued that the structure of the (maximally concurrent) computations of such membrane systems is faithfully reflected by the maximal concurrency semantics of the corresponding PTL-nets. This corresponds to the situation whereby all the rules are governed by a single global clock which corresponds to the case of maximally concurrent executions, as investigated in [11]. Hence the results on the reachability of certain markings (or, equivalently, configurations in membrane systems) developed there could form the basis of an investigation, e.g., whether a particular combination of molecules in certain compartments can happen in the legal evolutions of a membrane system.

After that we moved to a less centralised view of concurrent executions, as already advocated e.g., in [8], and defined a locally maximal concurrency semantics for PTL-nets. However, in case of individual localities for all transitions, we are not exactly dealing with the asynchronous or sequential systems, proposed by [8]. Since we maintain the requirement of locally maximal concurrency executions, the resulting systems exhibit maximal *autoconcurrency*.

In the model of PTL-nets there are no additional requirements on the relationship between transitions and their localities; in particular, as already mentioned, transitions with shared input places do not have to be co-located. Moreover, the flow of resources among the localities does not necessarily follow a tree-like structure. In fact, PTL-nets with their locally maximal concurrency semantics constitute a very general framework in which membrane systems and even con-glomerates of membrane systems (organisms) can be expressed and studied.

An important feature characterising the proposed basic PTL-net model is its robustness, in the sense of being easily extendable to handle salient features of more sophisticated membrane systems. Examples of such features are: (i) priorities among rules which can be dealt with using Petri nets with priorities, e.g., as in [2]; (ii) catalysts governing the enabling of the reaction rules purely by their presence which can be dealt with using Petri nets with read arcs, e.g., as in [24]; (iii) substances forbidding certain reactions which can be dealt with using Petri nets with inhibitor arcs, e.g., as in [13]; and (iv) dissolution of membranes which can be dealt with using Petri nets with transfer arcs; e.g., as in [23, 6]. We could also consider membrane systems with rules having variable discrete durations, by suitably exploiting the locally maximal concurrency semantics of PTL-nets. Further investigation is also needed into the relationship between various P systems and a wide variety of restricted/extended Petri nets, such as [9, 10].

We finally outlined how a causality based semantics of PTL-nets could be defined and used to analyse the intricate details of concurrent computations of membrane systems. The proposed semantics is based on the unfolding of PTL-nets with the novel feature of *barb-events* needed to reflect choices in the locally maximal executions. Among the potential benefits of the proposed unfolding-based semantics is the efficient model checking approach to the verification of properties of concurrent systems modelled as Petri nets [7, 15, 12].

Summarising, we have developed a new systematic link between Petri nets and membrane systems which (hopefully) is useful for both areas. We see this formalisation only as a beginning of the research into the representation of the behaviour of membrane systems through concurrent processes.

Clearly, one could simply use the basic model of PT-nets and simulate by 'brute force' the behaviour of membrane systems. In general, however, a biologist's interest will be in how a system functions and not just in what is delivered at the end. From the modelling point of view it is therefore more convenient to include localities as a direct interpretation of 'where is what'. This also provides the possibility to introduce a notion of local synchronicity as opposed to a global clock governing the evolution of a system. The process semantics of PT-nets provides an additional formal tool to study how a system functions rather than what it computes. Whereas step sequences can be viewed as ordered by a clock, processes can be used to represent causalities. Moreover using (infinite) processes, also ongoing (potentially infinite) system behaviour can be investigated, which is also interesting from a biological point of view.

For PT-nets the notion of locality inspired by membrane systems is a new interesting feature. The process semantics for PTL-nets working under the (locally) maximal concurrency semantics still has to be developed. In this paper we have briefly indicated how the technical problems could be solved. In addition, a proper notion of causality (order relation) based on processes (see the semantical scheme of [13]) and relevant for the biologically motivated membrane systems has to be identified as well.

Acknowledgments. The authors are grateful to Hendrik Jan Hoogeboom for his comments on an earlier version of this paper. We would also like to thank the anonymous referees for their constructive comments. This research was supported by the EPSRC project CASINO.

References

1. Membrane systems web page: http://psystems.disco.unimib.it/
2. E. Best, M. Koutny: Petri net semantics of priority systems. *Theoretical Computer Science*, 96 (1992), 175–215.
3. C.S. Calude, Gh. Păun, G. Rozenberg, A. Salomaa, eds.: *Multiset Processing. Mathematical, Computer Science, and Molecular Computing Points of View.* LNCS 2235, Springer, Berlin, 2001.
4. M. Cavaliere, D. Sburlan: Time-independent P systems. In *Membrane Computing, International Workshop, WMC5, Milano, Italy, 2004, Selected Papers* (G. Mauri et al., eds.), LNCS 3365, Springer, Berlin, 2005, 239–258.
5. DS. al Zilio, E. Formenti: On the dynamics of PB systems: a Petri net view. In *Membrane Computing, International Workshop, WMC 2003, Tarragona, July 2003, Selected Papers* (C. Martin-Vide et al., eds.) , LNCS 2933, Springer-Verlag, Berlin, 2004, 153–167.
6. C. Dufourd: *Réseaux de Petri avec Reset/Transfert: Décidabilité et Indécidabilité.* PhD Thesis, ENS Cachan, 1998.
7. J. Esparza, S. Römer, W. Vogler: An improvement of McMillan's unfolding algorithm. *Formal Methods in System Design*, 20 (2002), 285–310.
8. R. Freund: Asynchronous P systems and P systems working in the sequential mode. In *Membrane Computing, International Workshop, WMC5, Milano, Italy, 2004, Selected Papers* (G. Mauri et al., eds.), LNCS 3365, Springer, Berlin, 2005, 36–62.
9. O.H. Ibarra, Z. Dang, O. Egecioglu: Catalytic P systems, semilinear sets, and vector addition systems. *Theoretical Computer Science*, 312 (2004), 379–399.
10. O.H. Ibarra, H.C. Yen, Z. Dang: The power of maximal parallelism in P systems. *Proceedings of DLT 2004, Auckland* (C.S. Calude, E. Calude, M.J. Dinneed, eds.), LNCS 3340, Springer, Berlin, 2004, 212–224.
11. R. Janicki, P.E. Lauer, M. Koutny, R. Devillers: Concurrent and maximally concurrent evolution of nonsequential systems. *Theoretical Computer Science*, 43 (1986), 213–238.
12. V. Khomenko, M. Koutny, W. Vogler: Canonical prefixes of Petri net unfoldings. *Acta Informatica*, 40 (2003), 95–118.
13. H.C.M. Kleijn, M. Koutny: Process semantics of general inhibitor nets. *Information and Computation*, 190 (2004), 18–69.
14. H.C.M. Kleijn, M. Koutny, G. Rozenberg: Processes of Petri nets with localities. Manuscript, 2005.
15. K.L. McMillan: Using unfoldings to avoid state explosion problem in the Verification of Asynchronous Circuits. In *Proceedings CAV 1992* (G. von Bochmann, D.K. Probst, eds.), LNCS 663, Springer, Berlin, 1992.
16. M. Nielsen, G. Plotkin, G. Winskel: Petri nets, event structures and domains, Part I. *Theoretical Computer Science*, 13 (1980), 85–108.
17. Gh. Păun: Computing with membranes. An introduction. *Bulletin of the EATCS*, 67 (1999), 139–152.
18. Gh. Păun: *Membrane Computing, An Introduction.* Springer, Berlin, 2002.

19. Gh. Păun, G. Rozenberg: A guide to membrane computing. *Theoretical Computer Science*, 287 (2002), 73–100.

20. Z. Qi, J. You, H. Mao: P systems and Petri nets. In *Membrane Computing, International Workshop, WMC 2003, Tarragona, July 2003, Selected Papers* (C. Martin-Vide et al., eds.), LNCS 2933, Springer, Berlin, 2004, 286–303.

21. W. Reisig, G. Rozenberg, eds.: *Lectures on Petri Nets*. LNCS 1491 and 1492, Springer, Berlin, 1998.

22. G. Rozenberg, J. Engelfriet: Elementary net systems. In [21]

23. R. Valk: Self-modifying nets, a natural extension of Petri nets. In *Proceedings of ICALP 1978* (G. Ausiello, C. Böhm, eds.) LNCS 62, Springer, Berlin, 1978.

24. W. Vogler: Partial order semantics and read arcs. *Theoretical Computer Science*, 286 (2002), 33–63.

Quantum Sequential P Systems with Unit Rules and Energy Assigned to Membranes

Alberto Leporati, Giancarlo Mauri, and Claudio Zandron

Dipartimento di Informatica, Sistemistica e Comunicazione,
Università degli Studi di Milano – Bicocca,
Via Bicocca degli Arcimboldi 8, 20126 Milano, Italy
{leporati, mauri, zandron}@disco.unimib.it

Abstract. We propose a quantum version of P systems with unit rules and energy assigned to membranes. Differently from the classical version, the new quantum P systems do not need to use priorities over rules to be computationally complete. We also propose a quantum version of register machines as a tool to study the computational power of quantum models of computation.

1 Introduction

P systems (also called *membrane systems*) have been introduced in [21] as a new class of distributed and parallel computing devices, inspired by the structure and functioning of living cells. The basic model consists of a hierarchical structure composed by several membranes, embedded into a main membrane called the *skin*. Membranes divide the Euclidean space into *regions*, that contain some *objects* (represented by symbols of an alphabet) and *evolution rules*. Using these rules, the objects may evolve and/or move from a region to a neighboring one. A *computation* starts from an initial configuration of the system and terminates when no evolution rule can be applied. Usually, the result of a computation is the multiset of objects contained in an *output membrane* or emitted from the skin of the system.

In this paper, starting from the ideas exposed in [17], we propose a *quantum* version of P systems with unit rules and energy assigned to membranes, which have recently appeared in [10]. The proposed quantum P systems are sequential; moreover, at every computation step only one rule can be applied, and hence they are in some sense deterministic. Differently from the classical version, the amount of energy assigned to a membrane is not a property of the membrane itself, but is instead represented by the energy level of a quantum harmonic oscillator which is contained in the region enclosed by the membrane. Another notable difference between the classical and the quantum version of our P systems is that in the quantum version only one rule is assigned to each membrane. As a consequence, we obtain computational completeness without the need to assign priorities to rules, as it is done in the classical case.

R. Freund et al. (Eds.): WMC 2005, LNCS 3850, pp. 310–325, 2006.

In what follows we assume the reader is already familiar with the basic notions and the terminology underlying P systems. For a systematic introduction, we refer the reader to [22]. The latest information about P systems can be found in [25].

This is by no means the first time that energy is considered in P systems. We recall in particular [1, 9, 24, 14, 18, 19, 17].

The paper is organized as follows. In section 2 some preliminaries are given: in particular, we recall register machines (section 2.1), classical P systems with unit rules and energy assigned to membranes [10], together with their computational capabilities (section 2.2), and some notions of quantum computing (section 2.3). In section 3 we define the quantum version of such P systems, and in section 4 we establish their computational completeness. In section 5 we introduce a quantum version of register machines, as a tool to study present and future quantum computational models. Conclusions are given in section 6.

2 Preliminaries

2.1 Register Machines

A *deterministic n–register machine* is a construct $M = (n, P, l_0, l_h)$, where n is the number of registers, P is a finite set of instructions injectively labelled with a given set $lab(M)$, l_0 is the label of the first instruction to be executed, and l_h is the label of the last instruction of P. Registers contain non-negative integer values. Without loss of generality, we can assume $lab(M) = \{1, 2, \ldots, m\}$, $l_0 = 1$ and $l_h = m$. The instructions of P have the following forms:

- $j : (INC(r), k)$, with $j, k \in lab(M)$.
  This instruction increments the value contained in register r, and then jumps to instruction k.
- $j : (DEC(r), k, l)$, with $j, k, l \in lab(M)$.
  If the value contained in register r is positive then decrement it and jump to instruction k. If the value of r is zero then jump to instruction l (without altering the contents of the register).
- $m : Halt$.
  Stop the machine. Note that this instruction can only be assigned to the final label m.

Register machines provide a simple universal computational model. Indeed, the results proved in [11] (based on the results established in [20]) as well as in [12] and [13] immediately lead to the following proposition.

Proposition 1. *For any partial recursive function $f : \mathbf{N}^\alpha \to \mathbf{N}^\beta$ there exists a deterministic $(\max\{\alpha, \beta\} + 2)$–register machine M computing f in such a way that, when starting with $(n_1, \ldots, n_\alpha) \in \mathbf{N}^\alpha$ in registers 1 to α, M has computed $f(n_1, \ldots, n_\alpha) = (r_1, \ldots, r_\beta)$ if it halts in the final label l_h with registers 1 to β containing r_1 to r_β, and all other registers being empty; if the final label cannot be reached, then $f(n_1, \ldots, n_\alpha)$ remains undefined.*

2.2   P Systems with Unit Rules and Energy Assigned to Membranes

A P system with unit rules and energy assigned to membranes [10] of degree $d + 1$ is a construct Π of the form

$$\Pi = (A, \mu, e_0, \ldots, e_d, w_0, \ldots, w_d, R_0, \ldots, R_d),$$

where:

- A is an alphabet of *objects*;
- μ is a *membrane structure*, with the membranes labelled by numbers $0, \ldots, d$ in a one-to-one manner;
- $e_0, \ldots, e_d$ are the initial energy values assigned to the membranes $0, \ldots, d$. In what follows we assume that $e_0, \ldots, e_d$ are non-negative integers;
- $w_0, \ldots, w_d$ are multisets over A associated with the regions $0, \ldots, d$ of μ;
- $R_0, \ldots, R_d$ are finite sets of *unit rules* associated with the membranes $0, \ldots, d$. Each rule has the form $(\alpha : a, \Delta e, b)$, where $\alpha \in \{in, out\}$, $a, b \in A$, and $|\Delta e|$ is the amount of energy that — for $\Delta e \geq 0$ — is added to or — for $\Delta e < 0$ — is subtracted from e_i (the energy assigned to membrane i) by the application of the rule.

By writing $(\alpha_i : a, \Delta e, b)$ instead of $(\alpha : a, \Delta e, b) \in R_i$, we can specify only one set of rules R with

$$R = \{(\alpha_i : a, \Delta e, b) \mid (\alpha : a, \Delta e, b) \in R_i, 0 \leq i \leq d\}.$$

The *initial configuration* of Π consists of $e_0, \ldots, e_d$ and $w_0, \ldots, w_d$. The transition from a configuration to another one is performed by non-deterministically choosing one rule from some R_i and applying it (observe that here we consider a sequential model of applying the rules instead of choosing rules in a maximally parallel way, as it is often required in P systems). Applying $(in_i : a, \Delta e, b)$ means that an object a (being in the membrane immediately outside of i) is changed into b while entering membrane i, thereby changing the energy value e_i of membrane i by Δe. On the other hand, the application of a rule $(out_i : a, \Delta e, b)$ changes object a into b while leaving membrane i, and changes the energy value e_i by Δe. The rules can be applied only if the amount e_i of energy assigned to membrane i fulfills the requirement $e_i + \Delta e \geq 0$. Moreover, we use some sort of local priorities: if there are two or more applicable rules in membrane i, then one of the rules with $\max |\Delta e|$ has to be used.

A sequence of transitions is called a *computation*; it is *successful* if and only if it halts. The *result* of a successful computation is considered to be the distribution of energies among the membranes (a non-halting computation does not produce a result). If we consider the energy distribution of the membrane structure as the input to be analysed, we obtain a model for accepting sets of (vectors of) non-negative integers.

The following result, proved in [10], establishes computational completeness for this model of P systems.

Proposition 2. *Every partial recursive function* $f : \mathbf{N}^\alpha \to \mathbf{N}^\beta$ *can be computed by a P system with unit rules and energy assigned to membranes with (at most)* $\max\{\alpha, \beta\} + 3$ *membranes.*

It is interesting to note that the proof of this proposition is obtained by simulating register machines. In the simulation, a P system is defined which contains one subsystem for each register of the simulated machine. The contents of the register is expressed as the energy value e_i assigned to the i-th subsystem. A single object is present in the system at every computation step, which stores the label of the instruction of P currently simulated. Increment instructions are simulated in two steps by using the rules $(in_i : p_j, 1, \widetilde{p}_j)$ and $(out_i : \widetilde{p}_j, 0, p_k)$. Decrement instructions are also simulated in two steps, by using the rules $(in_i : p_j, 0, \widetilde{p}_j)$ and $(out_i : \widetilde{p}_j, -1, p_k)$ or $(out_i : \widetilde{p}_j, 0, p_l)$. The use of priorities associated to these last rules is crucial to correctly simulate a decrement instruction. For the details of the proof we refer the reader to [10].

On the other hand, by omitting the priority feature we do not get systems with universal computational power. Precisely, in [10] it is proved that P systems with unit rules and energy assigned to membranes without priorities and with an arbitrary number of membranes characterize the family $PsMAT^\lambda$ of Parikh sets generated by context–free matrix grammars (with λ-rules).

2.3   Quantum Computers

From an abstract point of view, a quantum computer can be considered as made up of interacting parts. The elementary units (memory cells) that compose these parts are two–levels quantum systems called *qubits*. A qubit is typically implemented using the energy levels of a two–levels atom, or the two spin states of a spin–$\frac{1}{2}$ atomic nucleus, or a polarization photon. The mathematical description — independent of the practical realization — of a single qubit is based on the two–dimensional complex Hilbert space $\mathbb{C}^2$. The boolean truth values 0 and 1 are represented in this framework by the unit vectors of the canonical orthonormal basis, called the *computational basis* of $\mathbb{C}^2$:

$$|0\rangle = \begin{bmatrix} 1 \\ 0 \end{bmatrix}, \qquad |1\rangle = \begin{bmatrix} 0 \\ 1 \end{bmatrix}.$$

Qubits are thus the quantum extension of the classical notion of bit, but whereas bits can only take two different values, 0 and 1, qubits are not confined to their two basis (also *pure*) states, $|0\rangle$ and $|1\rangle$, but can also exist in states which are coherent superpositions such as $\psi = c_0 |0\rangle + c_1 |1\rangle$, where c_0 and c_1 are complex numbers satisfying the condition $|c_0|^2 + |c_1|^2 = 1$. Performing a measurement of the state alters it. Indeed, performing a measurement on a qubit in the above superposition will return 0 with probability $|c_0|^2$ and 1 with probability $|c_1|^2$; the state of the qubit after the measurement (*post–measurement state*) will be $|0\rangle$ or $|1\rangle$, depending on the outcome.

A *quantum register* of size n (also called an n–*register*) is mathematically described by the Hilbert space $\otimes^n \mathbb{C}^2 = \underbrace{\mathbb{C}^2 \otimes \ldots \otimes \mathbb{C}^2}_{n \text{ times}}$, representing a set of n

qubits labelled by the index $i \in \{1, \ldots, n\}$. An n–*configuration* (also *pattern*) is a vector $|x_1\rangle \otimes \ldots \otimes |x_n\rangle \in \otimes^n \mathbb{C}^2$, usually written as $|x_1, \ldots, x_n\rangle$, considered as a quantum realization of the boolean tuple $(x_1, \ldots, x_n)$. Let us recall that the dimension of $\otimes^n \mathbb{C}^2$ is 2^n and that $\{|x_1, \ldots, x_n\rangle \mid x_i \in \{0, 1\}\}$ is an orthonormal basis of this space, called the n–register *computational basis*.

Computations are performed as follows. Each qubit of a given n–register is prepared in some particular pure state ($|0\rangle$ or $|1\rangle$) in order to realize the required n–configuration $|x_1, \ldots, x_n\rangle$, quantum realization of an input boolean tuple of length n. Then, a linear operator $G : \otimes^n \mathbb{C}^2 \to \otimes^n \mathbb{C}^2$ is applied to the n–register. The application of G has the effect of transforming the n–configuration $|x_1, \ldots, x_n\rangle$ into a new n–configuration $G(|x_1, \ldots, x_n\rangle) = |y_1, \ldots, y_n\rangle$, which is the quantum realization of the output tuple of the computer. We interpret such modification as a computation step performed by the quantum computer. The action of the operator G on a superposition $\Phi = \sum c^{i_1 \cdots i_n} |x_{i_1}, \ldots, x_{i_n}\rangle$, expressed as a linear combination of the elements of the n–register basis, is obtained by linearity: $G(\Phi) = \sum c^{i_1 \cdots i_n} G(|x_{i_1}, \ldots, x_{i_n}\rangle)$. We recall that linear operators which act on n–registers can be represented as order 2^n square matrices of complex entries. Usually (but not in this paper) such operators, as well as the corresponding matrices, are required to be unitary. In particular, this implies that the implemented operations are logically reversible (an operation is *logically reversible* if its inputs can always be deduced from its outputs).

All these notions can be easily extended to quantum systems which have $d > 2$ pure states. In this setting, the d–valued versions of qubits are usually called *qudits* [15]. As it happens with qubits, a qudit is typically implemented using the energy levels of an atom or a nuclear spin. The mathematical description — independent of the practical realization — of a single qudit is based on the d–dimensional complex Hilbert space $\mathbb{C}^d$. In particular, the pure states $|0\rangle, \left|\frac{1}{d-1}\right\rangle, \left|\frac{2}{d-1}\right\rangle, \ldots, \left|\frac{d-2}{d-1}\right\rangle, |1\rangle$ are represented by the unit vectors of the canonical orthonormal basis, called the *computational basis* of $\mathbb{C}^d$:

$$|0\rangle = \begin{bmatrix} 1 \\ 0 \\ \vdots \\ 0 \\ 0 \end{bmatrix}, \quad \left|\frac{1}{d-1}\right\rangle = \begin{bmatrix} 0 \\ 1 \\ \vdots \\ 0 \\ 0 \end{bmatrix}, \quad \cdots, \quad \left|\frac{d-2}{d-1}\right\rangle = \begin{bmatrix} 0 \\ 0 \\ \vdots \\ 1 \\ 0 \end{bmatrix}, \quad |1\rangle = \begin{bmatrix} 0 \\ 0 \\ \vdots \\ 0 \\ 1 \end{bmatrix}.$$

As before, a *quantum register* of size n can be defined as a collection of n qudits. It is mathematically described by the Hilbert space $\otimes^n \mathbb{C}^d$. An n–*configuration* is now a vector $|x_1\rangle \otimes \ldots \otimes |x_n\rangle \in \otimes^n \mathbb{C}^d$, simply written as $|x_1, \ldots, x_n\rangle$, for x_i running on $L_d = \left\{0, \frac{1}{d-1}, \frac{2}{d-1}, \ldots, \frac{d-2}{d-1}, 1\right\}$. An n–configuration can be viewed as the quantum realization of the "classical" tuple $(x_1, \ldots, x_n) \in L_d^n$. The dimension of $\otimes^n \mathbb{C}^d$ is d^n and the set $\{|x_1, \ldots, x_n\rangle \mid x_i \in L_d\}$ of all n–configurations is an orthonormal basis of this space, called the n–register *com-*

putational basis. Notice that the set L_d can also be interpreted as a set of truth values, where 0 denotes falsity, 1 denotes truth and the other elements indicate different degrees of indefiniteness.

Let us now consider the set $\mathcal{E}_d = \left\{ \varepsilon_0, \varepsilon_{\frac{1}{d-1}}, \varepsilon_{\frac{2}{d-1}}, \ldots, \varepsilon_{\frac{d-2}{d-1}}, \varepsilon_1 \right\} \subseteq \mathbb{R}$ of real values; we can think to such quantities as energy values. To each element $v \in L_d$ (and hence to each object $|v\rangle \in A$) we associate the energy level ε_v; moreover, let us assume that the values of $\mathcal{E}_d$ are all positive, equispaced, and ordered according to the corresponding objects: $0 < \varepsilon_0 < \varepsilon_{\frac{1}{d-1}} < \cdots < \varepsilon_{\frac{d-2}{d-1}} < \varepsilon_1$. If we denote by $\Delta\varepsilon$ the gap between two adjacent energy levels then the following linear relation holds:

$$\varepsilon_k = \varepsilon_0 + \Delta\varepsilon \, (d-1) \, k \qquad\qquad \forall \, k \in L_d. \qquad (1)$$

Notice that it is not required that $\varepsilon_0 = \Delta\varepsilon$. As explained in [17], the values ε_k can be thought of as the energy eigenvalues of the infinite dimensional quantum harmonic oscillator truncated at the $(d-1)$-th excited level (see Fig. 1), whose

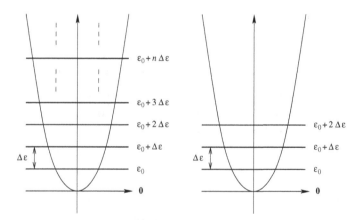

Fig. 1. Energy levels of the infinite dimensional (on the left) and of the truncated (on the right) quantum harmonic oscillator

Hamiltonian on $\mathbb{C}^d$ is

$$H = \begin{bmatrix} \varepsilon_0 & 0 & \cdots & & 0 \\ 0 & \varepsilon_0 + \Delta\varepsilon & \cdots & & 0 \\ \vdots & \vdots & \ddots & & \vdots \\ 0 & 0 & \cdots & \varepsilon_0 + (d-1)\Delta\varepsilon \end{bmatrix}. \qquad (2)$$

The unit vector $|H = \varepsilon_k\rangle = \left| \frac{k}{d-1} \right\rangle$, for $k \in \{0, 1, \ldots, d-1\}$, is the eigenvector of the state of energy $\varepsilon_0 + k\Delta\varepsilon$. To modify the state of a qudit we can use the creation and annihilation operators on the Hilbert space $\mathbb{C}^d$, which are defined respectively as

$$a^\dagger = \begin{bmatrix} 0 & 0 & \cdots & 0 & 0 \\ 1 & 0 & \cdots & 0 & 0 \\ 0 & \sqrt{2} & \cdots & 0 & 0 \\ \vdots & \vdots & \ddots & \vdots & \vdots \\ 0 & 0 & \cdots & \sqrt{d-1} & 0 \end{bmatrix}, \qquad a = \begin{bmatrix} 0 & 1 & 0 & \cdots & 0 \\ 0 & 0 & \sqrt{2} & \cdots & 0 \\ \vdots & \vdots & \vdots & \ddots & \vdots \\ 0 & 0 & 0 & \cdots & \sqrt{d-1} \\ 0 & 0 & 0 & \cdots & 0 \end{bmatrix}.$$

It is easily verified that the action of $a^\dagger$ on the vectors of the canonical orthonormal basis of $\mathbb{C}^d$ is

$$a^\dagger \left| \frac{k}{d-1} \right\rangle = \sqrt{k+1} \left| \frac{k+1}{d-1} \right\rangle \qquad \text{for } k \in \{0, 1, \ldots, d-2\},$$

$$a^\dagger \left| 1 \right\rangle = \mathbf{0},$$

whereas the action of a is

$$a \left| \frac{k}{d-1} \right\rangle = \sqrt{k} \left| \frac{k-1}{d-1} \right\rangle \qquad \text{for } k \in \{1, 2, \ldots, d-1\},$$

$$a \left| 0 \right\rangle = \mathbf{0}.$$

Using $a^\dagger$ and a we can also introduce the following operators:

$$N = a^\dagger a = \begin{bmatrix} 0 & 0 & 0 & \cdots & 0 \\ 0 & 1 & 0 & \cdots & 0 \\ 0 & 0 & 2 & \cdots & 0 \\ \vdots & \vdots & \vdots & \ddots & \vdots \\ 0 & 0 & 0 & \cdots & d-1 \end{bmatrix}, \qquad aa^\dagger = \begin{bmatrix} 1 & 0 & \cdots & 0 & 0 \\ 0 & 2 & \cdots & 0 & 0 \\ \vdots & \vdots & \ddots & \vdots & \vdots \\ 0 & 0 & \cdots & d-1 & 0 \\ 0 & 0 & \cdots & 0 & 0 \end{bmatrix}.$$

The eigenvalues of the self–adjoint operator N are $0, 1, 2, \ldots, d-1$, and the eigenvector corresponding to the generic eigenvalue k is $|N = k\rangle = \left| \frac{k}{d-1} \right\rangle$. This corresponds to the notation adopted in [15], where the qudit base states are denoted by $|0\rangle, |1\rangle, \ldots, |d-1\rangle$, and it is assumed that a qudit can exist in a superposition

$$c_0 |0\rangle + c_1 |1\rangle + \ldots + c_{d-1} |d-1\rangle$$

of the d base states, with $c_i \in \mathbb{C}$ for $i \in \{0, 1, \ldots, d-1\}$ and $|c_0|^2 + |c_1|^2 + \ldots + |c_{d-1}|^2 = 1$.

One possible physical interpretation of N is that it describes the *number of particles* of physical systems consisting of a maximum number of $d-1$ particles. In order to add a particle to the k particles state $|N = k\rangle$ (thus making it switch to the "next" state $|N = k+1\rangle$) we apply the creation operator $a^\dagger$, while to remove a particle from this system (thus making it switch to the "previous" state $|N = k-1\rangle$) we apply the annihilation operator a. Since the maximum number of particles that can be simultaneously in the system is $d-1$, the application of the creation operator to a full $d-1$ particles system does not have any effect on the system, and returns as a result the null vector. Analogously, the application of the annihilation operator to an empty particle system does not affect the system and returns the null vector as a result.

Another physical interpretation of operators $a^\dagger$ and a, by operator N, follows from the possibility of expressing the Hamiltonian (2) as

$$H = \varepsilon_0 \operatorname{Id} + \Delta\varepsilon \operatorname{N} = \varepsilon_0 \operatorname{Id} + \Delta\varepsilon \, a^\dagger a.$$

In this case $a^\dagger$ (resp., a) realizes the transition from the eigenstate of energy $\varepsilon_k = \varepsilon_0 + k \, \Delta\varepsilon$ to the "next" (resp., "previous") eigenstate of energy $\varepsilon_{k+1} = \varepsilon_0 + (k+1) \, \Delta\varepsilon$ (resp., $\varepsilon_{k-1} = \varepsilon_0 + (k-1) \, \Delta\varepsilon$) for any $0 \le k < d-1$ (resp., $0 < k \le d-1$), while it collapses the last excited (resp., ground) state of energy $\varepsilon_0 + (d-1) \, \Delta\varepsilon$ (resp., ε_0) to the null vector.

The collection of all linear operators on $\mathbb{C}^d$ is a d^2-dimensional linear space whose canonical basis is

$$\{E_{x,y} = |y\rangle \langle x| \mid x, y \in L_d\}.$$

Since $E_{x,y} |x\rangle = |y\rangle$ and $E_{x,y} |z\rangle = \mathbf{0}$ for every $z \in L_d$ such that $z \ne x$, this operator transforms the unit vector $|x\rangle$ into the unit vector $|y\rangle$, collapsing all the other vectors of the canonical orthonormal basis of $\mathbb{C}^d$ to the null vector. Each of the operators $E_{x,y}$ can be expressed, using the whole algebraic structure of the associative algebra of operators, as a suitable composition of creation and annihilation operators, as explained in [17].

3   Quantum P Systems with Unit Rules and Energy Assigned to Membranes

Let us now define a quantum version of P systems with unit rules and energy assigned to membranes. All the elements of the model (multisets, the membrane hierarchy, configurations, and computations) are defined just like the corresponding elements of the classical P systems, but for objects and rules.

The objects of A are represented as pure states of a quantum system. If the alphabet contains $d \ge 2$ elements, then without loss of generality we can put $A = \left\{ |0\rangle, \left|\frac{1}{d-1}\right\rangle, \left|\frac{2}{d-1}\right\rangle, \ldots, \left|\frac{d-2}{d-1}\right\rangle, |1\rangle \right\}$, that is, $A = \{|a\rangle \mid a \in L_d\}$. As stated above, the quantum system will also be able to assume as a state any superposition of the kind

$$c_0 |0\rangle + c_{\frac{1}{d-1}} \left|\frac{1}{d-1}\right\rangle + \ldots + c_{\frac{d-2}{d-1}} \left|\frac{d-2}{d-1}\right\rangle + c_1 |1\rangle,$$

with $c_0, c_{\frac{1}{d-1}}, \ldots, c_{\frac{d-2}{d-1}}, c_1 \in \mathbb{C}$ such that $\sum_{i=0}^{d-1} \left|c_{\frac{i}{d-1}}\right|^2 = 1$. A multiset is simply a collection of quantum systems, each in its own state.

The membrane structure is defined just like in the classical case. In order to represent the energy values assigned to membranes we must use quantum systems which can exist in an infinite (countable) number of states. Hence we assume that every membrane of the quantum P system has an associated infinite dimensional quantum harmonic oscillator whose state represents the energy value assigned to the membrane. To modify the state of such harmonic oscillator we can use the infinite dimensional version of the creation ($a^\dagger$) and annihilation (a) operators described above, which are commonly used in quantum mechanics. The actions of $a^\dagger$ and a on the state of an infinite dimensional harmonic oscillator are analogous to the actions on the states of truncated harmonic oscillators; the only difference is that in the former case there is no state with maximum energy, and hence the creation operator never produces the null vector. Also in this case it is possible to express operators $E_{x,y} = |y\rangle\langle x|$ as appropriate compositions of $a^\dagger$ and a.

The initial configuration of a quantum P system with unit rules and energy assigned to membranes of degree $d+1$ consists of $e_0, \ldots, e_d$, the initial energy values assigned to the membranes, and $w_0, \ldots, w_d$, the multisets of objects initially present in the regions $0, \ldots, d$ determined by the membrane structure.

Rules are defined as (n, d)–functions, that is, functions of the kind $f : A^n \to A^n$. Such functions are not necessarily bijections on A^n: they can be arbitrary mappings. This means that the linear operators which realize such functions are not necessarily unitary. To write these linear operators we use an extension of the *Conditional Quantum Control* technique introduced in [2]. Such operators are sums of "local" operators, each being a tensor product of suitable compositions of the operators $a^\dagger$ and a. An equivalent formulation is possible, using spin–rising (J_+) and spin–lowering (J_-) operators, following the lines illustrated in [17].

The quantum realization of a "controlled behavior" can be obtained by making use of the operators $E_{X,X} = |X\rangle\langle X|$, for $X \in L_d$. For simplicity, let us first consider the case of a $(2, 2)$–function, that is, a two–input/two–output boolean function. For a reason that will be clear in a moment, we call *control qubit* and *target qubit* the first and the second input, respectively. If we want to realize a linear operator performing the condition: "if the control qubit is $|1\rangle$ then the operator O_1 is applied to the target qubit (and the control qubit is left unchanged)", then we can build the operator $E_{1,1} \otimes O_1$, where $E_{1,1} = |1\rangle\langle 1|$ checks for the condition "the control qubit is $|1\rangle$" and O_1 is the operator which acts on the target qubit $|x_2\rangle$. Note that if the control qubit is $|0\rangle$ then the operator $E_{1,1} \otimes O_1$ produces the null vector of $\mathbb{C}^2 \otimes \mathbb{C}^2$. Similarly, $E_{0,0} \otimes O_0$, with $E_{0,0} = |0\rangle\langle 0|$, realizes the condition "if the control qubit is $|0\rangle$ then the operator O_0 is applied to the target qubit $|x_2\rangle$ (and the control qubit is left unchanged)".

The same applies to (n, d)–functions, where the first k qudits are used as *control qudits* and the remaining $n - k$ are used as *target qudits*. We can thus realize any controlled behavior of the kind: "if the control qudits are in the (basis) states $X = |x_1, x_2, \ldots, x_k\rangle$, then apply the operator O_X to target qudits" (and leave the control qudits unaltered). The global operator that describes the behavior of the (n, d)–function has thus the form

$$|0\rangle\langle 0| \otimes O_0 + |1\rangle\langle 1| \otimes O_1 + \ldots + |d^k - 1\rangle\langle d^k - 1| \otimes O_{d^k-1} = \sum_{X=0}^{d^k-1} |X\rangle\langle X| \otimes O_X,$$

where $E_{X,X} = |X\rangle \langle X|$ is the orthogonal projection of the Hilbert space $\otimes^k \mathbb{C}^d$ which selects the X-th control configuration, and collapses to the null vector all the other configurations.

We can now precisely describe how rules are defined in our model of quantum P systems. As in the classical case, rules are associated to membranes rather than to the regions enclosed by them. Each rule of R_i is an operator of the form

$$|y\rangle \langle x| \otimes O, \qquad \text{with } x, y \in L_d, \tag{3}$$

where O is a linear operator which can be expressed by an appropriate composition of operators $a^\dagger$ and a. The part $|y\rangle \langle x|$ is the *guard* of the rule: it makes the rule "active" (that is, the rule produces an effect) if and only if a quantum system in the basis state $|x\rangle$ is present. The semantics of rule (3) is the following: If an object in state $|x\rangle$ is present in the region immediately outside membrane i, then the state of the object is changed to $|y\rangle$ and the operator O is applied to the state of the infinite dimensional harmonic oscillator associated with the membrane. Notice that the application of O can result in the null vector, so that the rule has no effect even if its guard is satisfied; this fact is equivalent to the condition $e_i + \Delta e \geq 0$ on the energy of membrane i required in the classical case. Differently from the classical case, no local priorities are assigned to the rules. If two or more rules are associated to membrane i, then they are summed. This means that, indeed, we can think to each membrane as having only one rule with many guards. When an object is present, the inactive parts of the rule (those for which the guard is not satisfied) produce the null operator as a result. If the region in which the object occurs contains two or more membranes, then all their rules are applied to the object. Observe that the object which activates the rules never crosses the membranes. This means that the objects specified in the initial configuration can change their state but never move to a different region. Notwithstanding, transmission of information between different membranes is possible, since different objects may modify in different ways the energy state of the harmonic oscillators associated with the membranes.

The application of one or more rules determines a *transition* between two configurations. A *halting configuration* is a configuration in which no rule can be applied. A sequence of transitions is a *computation*. A computation is *successful* if and only if it *halts*, that is, reaches a halting configuration. The *result* of a successful computation is considered to be the distribution of energies among the membranes in the halting configuration. A non-halting computation does not produce a result. Just like in the classical case, if we consider the energy distribution of the membrane structure as the input to be analyzed, we obtain a model for accepting sets of (vectors of) non-negative integers.

4   Computational Completeness

In this section we prove that quantum P systems with unit rules and energy assigned to membranes are computationally complete, that is, they are able to compute any partial recursive function $f : \mathbf{N}^\alpha \rightarrow \mathbf{N}^\beta$. As in the classical case, the proof is obtained by simulating register machines.

Theorem 1. *Every partial recursive function $f : \mathbf{N}^\alpha \to \mathbf{N}^\beta$ can be computed by a quantum P system with unit rules and energy assigned to membranes with (at most) $\max\{\alpha, \beta\} + 3$ membranes.*

Proof. Let $M = (n, P, 1, m)$ be a deterministic n–register machine that computes f. Let m be the number of instructions of P. The initial instruction of P has the label 1, and the halting instruction has the label m. Observe that, according to Proposition 1, $n = \max\{\alpha, \beta\} + 2$ is enough.

The input values $x_1, \ldots, x_\alpha$ are expected to be in the first α registers, and the output values are expected to be in registers 1 to β at the end of a successful computation. Moreover, without loss of generality, we may assume that at the beginning of a computation all the registers except (eventually) the registers 1 to α contain zero.

We construct the quantum P system

$$\Pi = (A, \mu, e_0, \ldots, e_n, w_0, \ldots, w_n, R_0, \ldots, R_n),$$

where:

- $A = \{|j\rangle \mid j \in L_m\}$,
- $\mu = [_0[_1\ ]_1 \cdots [_\alpha\ ]_\alpha \cdots [_n\ ]_n]_0$,
- $e_i = \begin{cases} |\varepsilon_{x_i}\rangle & \text{for } 1 \leq i \leq \alpha, \\ |\varepsilon_0\rangle & \text{for } \alpha + 1 \leq i \leq n, \\ 0 & \text{(the null vector) for } i = 0, \end{cases}$
- $w_0 = |0\rangle$,
- $w_i = \emptyset \qquad \text{for } 1 \leq i \leq n$,
- $R_0 = \emptyset$,
- $R_i = \sum_{j=1}^{m} O_{i_j} \qquad \text{for } 1 \leq i \leq n$,

   where the O_{i_j}'s are local operators which simulate instructions of the kind $j : (INC(i), k)$ and $j : (DEC(i), k, l)$ (one local operator for each increment or decrement operation which affects register i). The details on how the O_{i_j}'s are defined are given below.

The value contained in register i, $1 \leq i \leq n$, is represented by the energy value $e_i = |\varepsilon_{x_i}\rangle$ of the infinite dimensional quantum harmonic oscillator associated with membrane i. Figure 2 depicts a typical configuration of Π. The skin contains one object of the kind $|j\rangle$, $j \in L_m$, which mimics the program counter of machine M. Precisely, if the program counter of M has the value $k \in \{1, 2, \ldots, m\}$ then the object present in region 0 is $\left|\frac{k-1}{m-1}\right\rangle$. In order to avoid cumbersome notation, in what follows we denote by $|p_k\rangle$ the state $\left|\frac{k-1}{m-1}\right\rangle$ of the quantum system which mimics the program counter.

The sets of rules R_i depend upon the instructions of P. Precisely, the simulation works as follows.

1. Increment instructions $j : (INC(i), k)$ are simulated by a guarded rule of the kind $|p_k\rangle \langle p_j| \otimes a^\dagger \in R_i$.

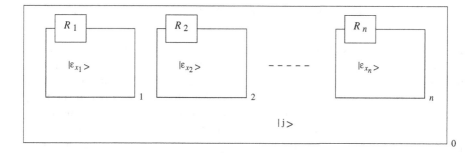

Fig. 2. A configuration of the simulating P system

If the object $|p_j\rangle$ is present in region 0, then the rule transforms it into object $|p_k\rangle$ and increments the energy level of the harmonic oscillator contained in membrane i.

2. Decrement instructions $j : (DEC(i), k, l)$ are simulated by a guarded rule of the kind

$$|p_l\rangle \langle p_j| \otimes |\varepsilon_0\rangle \langle \varepsilon_0| + |p_k\rangle \langle p_j| \otimes a \in R_i.$$

In fact, let us assume that the object $|p_j\rangle$ is present in region 0 (if $|p_j\rangle$ is not present then the above rule produces the null operator), and let us denote by O the above rule. The harmonic oscillator may be in the base state $|\varepsilon_0\rangle$ or in a base state $|\varepsilon_x\rangle$ with x a positive integer.
If the state of the harmonic oscillator is $|\varepsilon_0\rangle$, then the rule produces

$$O(|p_j\rangle \otimes |\varepsilon_0\rangle) =$$
$$= (|p_l\rangle \langle p_j| \otimes |\varepsilon_0\rangle \langle \varepsilon_0|)(|p_j\rangle \otimes |\varepsilon_0\rangle) + (|p_k\rangle \langle p_j| \otimes a)(|p_j\rangle \otimes |\varepsilon_0\rangle) =$$
$$= |p_l\rangle \otimes |\varepsilon_0\rangle + |p_k\rangle \otimes \mathbf{0} = |p_l\rangle \otimes |\varepsilon_0\rangle ,$$

that is, the state of the oscillator is unaltered and the program counter is set to $|p_l\rangle$.
If the state of the harmonic oscillator is $|\varepsilon_x\rangle$, for a positive integer x, then the rule produces

$$O(|p_j\rangle \otimes |\varepsilon_x\rangle) =$$
$$= (|p_l\rangle \langle p_j| \otimes |\varepsilon_0\rangle \langle \varepsilon_0|)(|p_j\rangle \otimes |\varepsilon_x\rangle) + (|p_k\rangle \langle p_j| \otimes a)(|p_j\rangle \otimes |\varepsilon_x\rangle) =$$
$$= |p_l\rangle \otimes \mathbf{0} + |p_k\rangle \otimes a |\varepsilon_x\rangle = |p_k\rangle \otimes |\varepsilon_{x-1}\rangle ,$$

that is, the energy level of the harmonic oscillator is decremented and the program counter is set to $|p_k\rangle$.

The set R_i of rules is obtained by summing all the operators which affect (increment or decrement) register i. The Halt instruction is simply simulated by doing nothing with the object $|p_m\rangle$ when it appears in region 0.

It is apparent from the description given above that after the simulation of each instruction every energy value e_i equals the value contained in register i, with $1 \leq i \leq m$. Hence, when the halting symbol $|p_m\rangle$ appears in region 0, the energy values $e_1, \ldots, e_\beta$ equal the output of the program P. $\square$

Let us conclude this section by observing that, in order to obtain computational completeness, it is not necessary that the objects cross the membranes. This fact avoids one of the problems raised in [17]: the existence of a "magic" quantum transportation mechanism which is able to move objects according to the target contained in the rule (and working against the so called "tunnel effect"). In quantum P systems with unit rules and energy assigned to membranes, the only problem is to keep the object $|p_j\rangle$ localised in region 0, so that it never enters into the other regions. In other words, the major problem of this kind of quantum P systems is to oppose the tunnel effect.

5   Quantum Register Machines

The P system illustrated in Fig. 2, which has been used to prove Theorem 1, suggests to define also a quantum version of register machines.

A *quantum n–register machine* is defined exactly as in the classical case, as a four–tuple $M = (n, P, l_0, l_h)$. For simplicity, also the instructions of P are denoted in the usual way:

$$j : (INC(i), k) \qquad \text{and} \qquad j : (DEC(i), k, l).$$

This time, however, these instructions are appropriate linear operators acting on the Hilbert space whose vectors describe the (global) state of M.

The structure of the machine resembles the P system which has been used to prove Theorem 1. Each register of the machine is an infinite dimensional quantum harmonic oscillator, capable to assume the base states $|\varepsilon_0\rangle, |\varepsilon_1\rangle, |\varepsilon_2\rangle, \ldots$, corresponding to its energy levels. The program counter of the machine is instead realized through a quantum system capable to assume m different base states, from the set $\{|x\rangle \mid x \in L_m\}$.

A *configuration* of M is given by the value of the program counter and the values contained in the registers. From a mathematical point of view, a configuration of M is a (base) vector of the Hilbert space $\mathbb{C}^m \otimes (\otimes^n \mathcal{H})$, where $\mathcal{H}$ is the Hilbert space associated with every quantum harmonic oscillator. Notice that here we are just interested in simulating a classical machine behavior, and hence we do not care about superpositions of states. A transition between two configurations is obtained by executing one instruction of P (the one pointed at by the program counter).

The instruction $j : (INC(r), k)$ is defined as the operator

$$O_{j,r,k}^{INC} = |p_k\rangle \langle p_j| \otimes \left(\otimes^{r-1}\mathbb{I}\right) \otimes a^\dagger \otimes \left(\otimes^{n-r}\mathbb{I}\right),$$

with $\mathbb{I}$ the identity operator on $\mathcal{H}$, whereas the instruction $j : (DEC(r), k, l)$ is defined as the operator

$$O_{j,r,k,l}^{DEC} = |p_l\rangle \langle p_j| \otimes \left(\otimes^{r-1}\mathbb{I}\right) \otimes |\varepsilon_0\rangle \langle \varepsilon_0| \otimes \left(\otimes^{n-r}\mathbb{I}\right) + $$
$$|p_k\rangle \langle p_j| \otimes \left(\otimes^{r-1}\mathbb{I}\right) \otimes a \otimes \left(\otimes^{n-r}\mathbb{I}\right).$$

Hence the program P can be formally defined as the sum O_P of all these operators:

$$O_P = \sum_{j,r,k} O_{j,r,k}^{INC} + \sum_{j,r,k,l} O_{j,r,k,l}^{DEC}.$$

Thus O_P is the global operator which describes a computation step of M. The Halt instruction is simply executed by doing nothing when the program counter assumes the value $|p_m\rangle$. For such value, the application of O_P results in the null operator.

From the definition of the system, it is apparent that any classical deterministic n–register machine can be simulated by a corresponding quantum n–register machine: the simulation proceeds exactly as described in the proof of Theorem 1. As a consequence, also quantum n–register machines are computationally complete.

It should also be evident that the proof of Theorem 1 can be modified to show that quantum P systems are able to simulate quantum register machines. Indeed, the notable difference between the quantum P systems described above and quantum register machines is that in the latter model we modify the values contained in registers using *global* operators (if a given register need not be modified then the identity operator is applied to its state) whereas in the former model we operate locally, on a smaller Hilbert space. Hence, as it happens in classical P systems, membranes are used to divide the site where the computation occurs into independent local areas. The effect of each rule is local, in the sense that the rule affects only the state of one subsystem. Due to the simulations mentioned above, we can order these computational models with respect to their computational power, as follows:

deterministic register machines		quantum register machines		quantum P systems with unit rules and energy assigned to membranes
	$\leq$		$\leq$	

Quantum register machines can thus be used as a tool to study the computational power of other quantum models of computation, just like it happens in the classical case.

6   Conclusions and Directions for Future Research

In this paper we have introduced a quantum version of P systems with unit rules and energy assigned to membranes. Objects are represented as pure states in a finite Hilbert space, whereas rules are defined as generic functions which map the alphabet into itself. Such functions are implemented using a generalization of the Conditional Quantum Control technique, and may yield non-unitary operators. Energy values are associated to membranes by incorporating an infinite dimensional quantum harmonic oscillator in every membrane. For the application of rules leading from one configuration of the system to the next configuration we consider a sequential model, instead of the usual model of maximal parallelism.

The input of a computation is given by the distribution of energy values carried by the membranes. Analogously, the result of a successful computation is the distribution of energy values at the end of the computation.

In this paper we have proved that such quantum model of computation is computationally complete, that is, it is able to compute any partial recursive function $f : \mathbf{N}^\alpha \to \mathbf{N}^\beta$. This result has been obtained by simulating classical deterministic register machines. We have also proposed quantum register machines as a tool to study the computational power of present and future quantum computational models.

It is currently an open problem, as well as an interesting direction for future research, to precisely assess the computational power of quantum P systems and quantum register machines. Concerning the power of quantum P systems we note that, in analogy with other models of quantum computers, there is the possibility to initialize the system with a multiset of objects whose state is a superposition of classical (pure) states. As a result, the computation will transform such input multiset to an output multiset which is obtained by linearity as a superposition of the results of the computation on every single classical state. As usual, when we measure the state of the systems which occur into the output multiset we will obtain a pure state as a result, according to the probability distribution which is induced by the coefficients of the superposition. An interesting question, not afforded in this paper, is whether the measurement of the state of an object into a region should have only *local* effects, or instead make the global configuration of the P system collapse to a classical state. Another interesting aspect of quantum P systems to be investigated is their behavior when some quantum systems in the initial configuration are in an entangled state.

References

1. G. Alford: Membrane systems with heat control. In *Pre-Proceedings of Workshop on Membrane Computing, WMC-CdeA2002, Curtea de Argeş, Romania* (Gh. Păun, C. Zandron, eds.), 2002. Electronic version available in [25].
2. A. Barenco, D. Deutsch, A. Ekert, R. Jozsa: Conditional quantum control and logic gates. *Physical Review Letters*, 74 (1995), 4083–4086.
3. P. Benioff: Quantum mechanical hamiltonian models of discrete processes. *Journal of Mathematical Physics*, 22 (1981), 495–507.
4. P. Benioff: Quantum mechanical hamiltonian models of computers. *Annals of the New York Academy of Science*, 480 (1986), 475–486.
5. D. Deutsch: Quantum theory, the Church–Turing principle, and the universal quantum computer. *Proceedings of the Royal Society of London*, A 400 (1985), 97–117.
6. R.P. Feynman R P: Simulating physics with computers. *International Journal of Theoretical Physics*, 21, 6–7 (1982), 467–488.
7. R.P. Feynman: Quantum mechanical computers. *Optics News*, 11 (1985), 11–20.
8. R. Freund: Sequential P-systems. *Romanian Journal of Information Science and Technology*, 4, 1–2 (2001), 77–88.
9. R. Freund: Energy-controlled P systems. In *Membrane Computing. International Workshop, WMC 2002, Curtea de Argeş, Romania, August 2002. Revised Papers* (Gh. Păun, G. Rozenberg, A. Salomaa, C. Zandron, eds.), LNCS 2597, Springer, Berlin, 2003, 247–260.

10. R. Freund, A. Leporati, M. Oswald, C. Zandron: Sequential P systems with unit rules and energy assigned to membranes. In *Machines, Computations and Universality, MCU 2004* (M. Margenstern, ed.), LNCS 3354, Springer, Berlin, 2005, 200–210.

11. R. Freund, M. Oswald: GP systems with forbidding context. *Fundamenta Informaticae*, 49, 1–3 (2002), 81–102.

12. R. Freund, Gh. Păun: On the number of non-terminals in graph-controlled, programmed, and matrix grammars. In *Machines, Computations and Universality, MCU 2001* (M. Margenstern, Y. Rogozhin, eds.), LNCS 2055, Springer, Berlin, 2001, 82–101.

13. R. Freund, Gh. Păun: From regulated rewriting to computing with membranes: collapsing hierarchies. *Theoretical Computer Science*, 312 (2004), 143–188.

14. P. Frisco: The conformon–P system: a molecular and cell biology–inspired computability model. *Theoretical Computer Science*, 312 (2004), 295–319.

15. D. Gottesman: Fault-tolerant quantum computation with higher-dimensional systems. *Chaos, Solitons, and Fractals*, 10 (1999), 1749–1758.

16. J. Gruska: *Quantum computing*. McGraw–Hill, New York, 1999.

17. A. Leporati, D. Pescini, C. Zandron: Quantum energy–based P systems. In *Proceedings of the First Brainstorming Workshop on Uncertainty in Membrane Computing*, Palma de Mallorca, Spain, 2004, 145–168.

18. A. Leporati, C. Zandron, G. Mauri: Simulating the Fredkin gate with energy–based P systems. *Journal of Universal Computer Science*, 10, 5 (2004), 600–619.

19. A. Leporati, C. Zandron, G. Mauri: Universal families of reversible P systems. In *Machines, Computations and Universality, MCU 2004* (M. Margenstern, ed.), LNCS 3354, Springer, Berlin, 2005, 257–268.

20. M.L. Minsky: *Finite and Infinite Machines*. Prentice Hall, Englewood Cliffs, New Jersey, 1967.

21. Gh. Păun: Computing with Membranes. *Journal of Computer and System Sciences*, 1, 61 (2000), 108–143. See also Turku Centre for Computer Science – TUCS Report No. 208, 1998.

22. Gh. Păun: *Membrane Computing – An Introduction*. Springer, Berlin, 2002.

23. Gh. Păun, A. Riscos-Nuñez, A. Romero-Jiménez, F. Sancho Caparrini, eds.: *Proc. Second Brainstorming Week on Membrane Computing*, Seville, Spain. Department of Computer Sciences and Artificial Intelligence, University of Seville TR 01/2004.

24. Gh. Păun, Y. Suzuki, H. Tanaka: P systems with energy accounting. *International Journal Computer Math.*, 78, 3 (2001), 343–364.

25. The P systems Web page: http://psystems.disco.unimib.it/

Editing Distances Between Membrane Structures

Damián López and José M. Sempere

Departamento de Sistemas Informáticos y Computación,
Universidad Politécnica de Valencia, 46071 Valencia, Spain
{dlopez, jsempere}@dsic.upv.es

Abstract. In this work we propose an efficient solution to calculate the minimum editing distance between membrane structures of arbitrary P systems. We use a new model of tree automata based on multisets of states and symbols linked to the finite control. This new model accepts a set of trees with symmetries between their internal nodes (*mirrored trees*). Once we have calculated the editing distance between an arbitrary tree and an arbitrary multiset tree automaton, we can translate the classical operations of insertion, deletion and substitution into rule applications of membrane dissolving and membrane creation.

1 Introduction

One of the main components of P systems is the membrane structure. This structure evolves during the computation time due to the application of rules associated to the membranes. The membrane structure can be represented by a tree in which the internal nodes denote regions which have inner regions inside. The root of the tree is always associated to the skin membrane of the P system.

The relation between regions and trees has been recently strengthened by Freund *et al.* [7]. These authors have established that any recursively enumerable set of trees can be generated by a P system with active membranes and string objects. So, P systems can be viewed as tree generators.

In this work we use multiset tree automata to accept and handle the tree structures defined by P systems [16]. This model is an extension of classical tree automata [8] in which the states and symbols of the finite control form *multisets*. Multiset theory has been linked to parallel processing as showed in [2].

The main aspect we will solve in this work is the one related to *editing structural configurations* of P systems. Recently, Csuhaj-Varjú *et al.* [4] have proposed editing distances between configurations of P systems. Here, we restrict our solution only to the structural configuration of P systems, that is, the membrane structure underlying any P system configuration. The multiset tree automata model that we propose in this work will be useful to calculate the trees associated with membrane structures. Here we can take advantage of a previous work on editing distances between trees and tree automata [10].

The structure of this work is as follows. First we introduce basic definitions and notation about multisets, tree languages and automata and P systems. In section

R. Freund et al. (Eds.): WMC 2005, LNCS 3850, pp. 326–341, 2006.

3, we introduce the model of multiset tree automata, we define the relation of *mirroring* between trees and we establish some results between tree automata, multiset tree automata, and mirroring trees. In section 4, we use previous results about editing distances between trees and tree automata in order to solve the minimum editing distance between membrane structures. Finally, we state some conclusions and give some guidelines for future works.

2   Notation and Definitions

In the sequel we will provide some concepts from formal language theory, membrane computing, and multiset processing. Further details can be found in the books [15], [12], and [2].

Multisets

First, we will provide some definitions from multiset theory as exposed in [17].

Definition 1. *Let D be a set. A multiset over D is a pair $\langle D, f \rangle$ where $f : D \longrightarrow \mathbb{N}$ is a function.*

Definition 2. *Suppose that $A = \langle D, f \rangle$ and $B = \langle D, g \rangle$ are two multisets. The removal of multiset B from A, denoted by $A \ominus B$, is the multiset $C = \langle D, h \rangle$ where for all $a \in D$ $h(a) = max(f(a) - g(a), 0)$.*

Definition 3. *Let $A = \langle D, f \rangle$ be a multiset; we will say that A is empty if for all $a \in D$, $f(a) = 0$.*

Definition 4. *Let $A = \langle D, f \rangle$ and $B = \langle D, g \rangle$ be two multisets. Their sum, denoted by $A \oplus B$, is the multiset $C = \langle D, h \rangle$, where for all $a \in D$ $h(a) = f(a) + g(a)$.*

Definition 5. *Let $A = \langle D, f \rangle$ and $B = \langle D, g \rangle$ be two multisets. We will say that $A = B$ if for all $a \in D$ $f(a) = g(a)$.*

The number of elements that a multiset contains can be finite. In such case, the multiset will be finite too. The size of any multiset M, denoted by $|M|$ will be the number of elements that it contains. We are specially interested in the class of multisets that we call *bounded multisets*. They are multisets that hold the property that the sum of all the elements is bounded by a constant n. Formally, we will denote by $\mathcal{M}_n(D)$ the set of all multisets $\langle D, f \rangle$ such that $\sum_{a \in D} f(a) = n$.

A concept that is quite useful to work with sets and multisets is the *Parikh mapping*. Formally, a Parikh mapping can be viewed as the application $\Psi : D^* \to \mathbb{N}^n$ where $D = \{d_1, d_2, \ldots, d_n\}$ and D^* is the set of strings defined by D. Given an element $x \in D^*$ we define $\Psi(x) = (\#_{d_1}(x), \ldots, \#_{d_n}(x))$ where $\#_{d_j}(x)$ denotes the number of occurrences of d_j in x.

Later, we will use tuples of symbols and states as strings and we will apply the Parikh mapping as defined above.

Tree Automata and Tree Languages

Now, we will introduce some concepts from tree languages and automata as exposed in [3, 8]. First, a *ranked alphabet* is the pair (V, r) where V is an alphabet and r is a finite relation in $V \times \mathbb{N}$. We denote by V_n the subset $\{\sigma \in V \mid (\sigma, n) \in r\}$. Given (V, r) we define $maxarity(V)$ as the maximum integer n such that $(\sigma, n) \in r$.

For every ranked alphabet (V, r), the set of trees over V, is denoted by V^T and defined inductively as follows:

$a \in V^T$ for every $a \in V_0$,

$\sigma(t_1, \ldots, t_n) \in V^T$ whenever $\sigma \in V_n$ and $t_1, \ldots, t_n \in V^T$, $n > 0$,

and let a *tree language* over V be defined as a subset of V^T.

Given the tuple $l = \langle 1, 2, \ldots, k \rangle$ we will denote the set of permutations of l by $perm(l)$. Let $t = \sigma(t_1, \ldots, t_n)$ be a tree over V^T, we will denote the set of permutations of t at first level by $perm_1(t)$. Formally, $perm_1(t) = \{\sigma(t_{i_1}, \ldots, t_{i_n}) \mid \langle i_1, i_2, \ldots, i_n \rangle \in perm(\langle 1, 2, \ldots, n \rangle)\}$.

Let $\mathbb{N}^*$ be the set of finite strings of natural numbers, separated by dots, formed using the product as the composition rule and the empty word λ as the identity. Let the prefix relation $\leq$ in $\mathbb{N}^*$ be defined by the condition that $u \leq v$ if and only if $u \cdot w = v$ for some $w \in \mathbb{N}^*$ $(u, v \in \mathbb{N}^*)$. A finite subset D of $\mathbb{N}^*$ is called a *tree domain* if:

$$u \leq v, \text{ where } v \in D \text{ implies } u \in D, \text{ and}$$
$$u \cdot i \in D \text{ whenever } u \cdot j \in D \ (1 \leq i \leq j).$$

Each tree domain D could be seen as an unlabelled tree whose nodes correspond to the elements of D where the hierarchy relation is the prefix order. Thus, each tree t over V can be seen as an application $t : D \rightarrow V$. The set D is called the *domain of the tree* t, and denoted by $dom(t)$. The elements of the tree domain $dom(t)$ are called *positions* or *nodes* of the tree t. We denote by $t(x)$ the label of a given node x in $dom(t)$.

Let the level of $x \in dom(t)$ be denoted by $level(x)$. Intuitively, the level of a node measures its distance from the root of the tree. Then, we can define the depth of a tree t as $depth(t) = max\{level(x) \mid x \in dom(t)\}$. In the same way, for any tree t, we denote the size of the tree by $|t|$ and the set of subtrees of t (denoted with $Sub(t)$) as follows:

$$Sub(a) = \{a\} \text{ for all } a \in V_0,$$
$$Sub(t) = \{t\} \cup \bigcup_{i=1,\ldots,n} Sub(t_i) \text{ for } t = \sigma(t_1, \ldots, t_n) \ (n > 0).$$

For any set of trees T, $Sub(T) = \bigcup_{t \in T} Sub(t)$. Given a tree $t = \sigma(t_1, \ldots, t_n)$, the root of t will be denoted as $root(t)$ and defined as $root(t) = \sigma$. If $t = a$, then $root(t) = a$. The successors of a tree $t = \sigma(t_1, \ldots, t_n)$ will be defined as $H^t = \langle root(t_1), \ldots, root(t_n) \rangle$.

Definition 6. *A finite deterministic tree automaton is defined by the tuple* $A = (Q, V, \delta, F)$, *where Q is a finite set of states, V is a ranked alphabet, $Q \cap V = \emptyset$, $F \subseteq Q$ is a set of final states, and $\delta = \bigcup_{i:V_i \neq \emptyset} \delta_i$ is a set of transition functions defined as follows:*

$$\delta_n : (V_n \times (Q \cup V_0)^n) \to Q \qquad n > 0,$$
$$\delta_0(a) = a \qquad \forall a \in V_0.$$

Given the state $q \in Q$, we define the *ancestors* of the state q, denoted by $Anc(q)$, as the set of strings

$$Anc(q) = \{p_1 \ldots p_n \mid p_i \in Q \cup V_0 \wedge \delta_n(\sigma, p_1, \ldots, p_n) = q \in \delta\}.$$

From now on, we will refer to finite deterministic tree automata simply as *tree automata*. We suggest [3, 8] for other definitions on tree automata.

The transition function δ is extended to a function $\delta : V^T \to Q \cup V_0$ on trees as follows:

$$\delta(a) = a \text{ for any } a \in V_0,$$
$$\delta(t) = \delta_n(\sigma, \delta(t_1), \ldots, \delta(t_n)) \text{ for } t = \sigma(t_1, \ldots, t_n) \ (n > 0).$$

Note that the symbol δ denotes both the set of transition functions of the automaton and the extension of these functions to operate on trees. In addition, one can observe that the tree automaton A cannot accept any tree of depth zero.

Given a finite set of trees T, let the *subtree automaton* for T be defined as $AB_T = (Q, V, \delta, F)$, where:

$$Q = Sub(T),$$
$$F = T,$$
$$\delta_n(\sigma, u_1, \ldots, u_n) = \sigma(u_1, \ldots, u_n) \qquad \sigma(u_1, \ldots, u_n) \in Q,$$
$$\delta_0(a) = a \qquad a \in V_0.$$

P Systems

Finally, we will introduce some basic concepts from the theory of membrane systems taken from [12]. A general P system of degree m is a construct

$$\Pi = (V, T, C, \mu, w_1, \ldots, w_m, (R_1, \rho_1), \ldots, (R_m, \rho_m), i_0),$$

where:

- V is an alphabet (the *objects*),
- $T \subseteq V$ (the *output alphabet*),
- $C \subseteq V, C \cap T = \emptyset$ (the *catalysts*),
- μ is a membrane structure consisting of m membranes,
- $w_i, 1 \leq i \leq m$ is a string representing a multiset over V associated with the region i,

- R_i, $1 \leq i \leq m$ is a finite set of *evolution rules* over V associated with the ith region and ρ_i is a partial order relation over R_i specifying a *priority*. An evolution rule is a pair (u, v) (or $u \to v$), where u is a string over V and $v = v'$ or $v = v'\delta$, where v' is a string over

$$\{a_{here}, a_{out}, a_{in_j} \mid a \in V, 1 \leq j \leq m\},$$

and δ is an special symbol not in V (it defines the *membrane dissolving action*),

- i_0 is a number between 1 and m and it specifies the *output* membrane of Π, or $i_0 = \infty$ and in this case the output is read outside the system).

The language generated by Π in external mode ($i_0 = \infty$) is denoted by $L(\Pi)$ and it is defined as the set of strings that can be defined by collecting the objects that leave the system by arranging them in the leaving order (if several objects leave the system at the same time, then all permutations are allowed). The set of numbers that represent the objects in the output membrane i_0 will be denote by $N(\Pi)$. Obviously, both sets $L(\Pi)$ and $N(\Pi)$ are defined only for *halting computations*.

Some kinds of P systems which have been proposed focus on the creation, division, and modification of membrane structures. There have been several works in which these operations have been proposed (see, for example, [1, 11, 12, 13]).

In the following, we enumerate some kinds of rules which are able to modify the membrane structure:

1. 2-division: $[_h a]_h \to [_{h'} b]_{h'} [_{h''} c]_{h''}$,
2. Creation: $a \to [_h b]_h$,
3. Dissolving: $[_h a]_h \to b$.

The power of P systems with the previous operations and other ones (e.g., *exocytosis, endocytosis*, etc.) has been widely studied in the literature.

3   Multiset Tree Automata and Mirrored Trees

We will extend some definitions of tree automata and tree languages over multisets. We will introduce the concept of multiset tree automata and then we will characterize the set of trees that they accept, as exposed in [16]. Observe that our approach is different from Csuhaj-Varjú *et al.* [5] and from Kudlek *et al.* [9] where the authors consider the case that *bags of objects* are analyzed by an abstract machine. Here, we do not consider *bags of (sub)trees* but we introduce bags of states and symbols in the finite control of the automata.

Given any tree automaton $A = (Q, V, \delta, F)$ and $\delta_n(\sigma, p_1, p_2, \ldots, p_n) \in \delta$, we can associate to δ_n the multiset $\langle Q \cup V_0, f \rangle \in \mathcal{M}_n(Q \cup V_0)$ where f is defined by $\Psi(p_1 p_2 \ldots p_n)$. The multiset defined in such way will be denoted by $M_\Psi(\delta_n)$. Alternatively, we can define $M_\Psi(\delta_n)$ as $M_\Psi(p_1) \oplus M_\Psi(p_2) \oplus \cdots \oplus M_\Psi(p_n)$ where $M_\Psi(p_i) \in \mathcal{M}_1(Q \cup V_0)$ for all $1 \leq i \leq n$. Observe that if $\delta_n(\sigma, p_1, p_2, \ldots, p_n) \in \delta$, $\delta_n'(\sigma, p_1', p_2', \ldots, p_n') \in \delta$, and $M_\Psi(\delta_n) = M_\Psi(\delta_n')$ then δ_n and δ_n' are defined over the same set of states and symbols but in different order (that is, the multiset induced by $\langle p_1 p_2 \ldots p_n \rangle$ equals the one induced by $\langle p'_1 p'_2 \ldots p'_n \rangle$).

Now, we can define a *multiset tree automaton* that performs a bottom-up parsing as in the tree automaton case.

Definition 7. *A multiset tree automaton is defined by the tuple* $MA = (Q, V, \delta, F)$, *where Q is a finite set of states, V is a ranked alphabet with* $maxarity(V) = n$, $Q \cap V = \emptyset$, $F \subseteq Q$ *is a set of final states, and δ is a set of transition functions defined as follows:*

$$\delta = \bigcup_{\substack{1 \leq i \leq n \\ V_i \neq \emptyset}} \delta_i,$$

$$\delta_i : (V_i \times \mathcal{M}_i(Q \cup V_0)) \rightarrow \mathcal{P}(\mathcal{M}_1(Q)) \qquad i = 1, \ldots, n,$$
$$\delta_0(a) = M_\Psi(a) \in \mathcal{M}_1(Q \cup V_0) \qquad \forall a \in V_0.$$

We can take notice that every tree automaton A defines a multiset tree automaton MA as follows

Definition 8. *Let $A = (Q, V, \delta, F)$ be a tree automaton. The multiset tree automaton induced by A is defined by the tuple* $MA = (Q, V, \delta', F)$ *where each δ' is defined as follows:* $M_\Psi(r) \in \delta'_n(\sigma, M)$ *if* $\delta_n(\sigma, p_1, p_2, \ldots, p_n) = r$ *and* $M_\Psi(\delta_n) = M$.

Observe that, in the general case, the multiset tree automaton induced by A is non-deterministic.

As in the case of tree automata, δ' could also be extended to operate on trees. Here, the automaton carries out a bottom-up parsing where the tuples of states and/or symbols are transformed by using the Parikh mapping Ψ to obtain the multisets in $\mathcal{M}_n(Q \cup V_0)$. If the analysis is completed and δ' returns a multiset with at least one final state, then the input tree is accepted. So, δ' can be extended as follows:

$\delta'(a) = M_\Psi(a)$ for any $a \in V_0$,
$\delta'(t) = \{M \in \delta'_n(\sigma, M_1 \oplus \cdots \oplus M_n) \mid M_i \in \delta'(t_i)\ 1 \leq i \leq n\}$,
   for $t = \sigma(t_1, \ldots, t_n)$ $(n > 0)$.

Formally, every multiset tree automaton MA accepts the following language

$$L(MA) = \{t \in V^T \mid M_\Psi(q) \in \delta'(t), q \in F\}.$$

Another extension which will be useful is the one related to the ancestors of every state. So, we define $Anc_\Psi(q) = \{M \mid M_\Psi(q) \in \delta_n(\sigma, M)\}$. The following two results characterize the relation between the languages accepted by tree automata and the multiset tree automata induced by them.

Theorem 1. *(Sempere and López, [16]) Let* $A = (Q, V, \delta, F)$ *be a tree automaton,* $MA = (Q, V, \delta', F)$ *be the multiset tree automaton induced by A and* $t = \sigma(t_1, \ldots, t_n) \in V^T$. *If* $\delta(t) = q$, *then* $M_\Psi(q) \in \delta'(t)$.

Corollary 1. *(Sempere and López, [16]) Let $A = (Q, V, \delta, F)$ be a tree automaton and $MA = (Q, V, \delta', F)$ be the multiset tree automaton induced by A. If $t \in L(A)$, then $t \in L(MA)$.*

Mirrored Equivalent Trees

We will introduce the concept of *mirroring* in tree structures as it was exposed in [16]. Informally speaking, two trees will be related by mirroring if some permutations at the structural level make the difference among them. For example, the trees of Figure 1 have identical subtrees except that some internal nodes have changed their order.

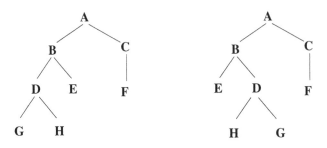

Fig. 1. Two mirrored trees

We propose a definition that relates all the trees with this mirroring property. For any other concepts used in this section, we refer to the previous section 2 on tree automata.

Definition 9. *Let (V, r) be a ranked alphabet and t and s be two trees from V^T. We say that t and s are mirror equivalent, denoted by $t \bowtie s$, if one of the following conditions holds:*

1. $t = s = a \in V_0$,
2. $t \in perm_1(s)$,
3. $t = \sigma(t_1, \ldots, t_n)$, $s = \sigma(s_1, \ldots, s_n)$ *and there exists* $\langle s^1, s^2, \ldots, s^k \rangle \in perm(\langle s_1, s_2, \ldots, s_n \rangle)$ *such that* $t_i \bowtie s^i$ *for all* $1 \leq i \leq n$.

The following results characterize the set of trees accepted by a multiset tree automaton induced by a tree automaton.

Theorem 2. *(Sempere and López, [16]) Let $A = (Q, V, \delta, F)$ be a tree automaton, $t = \sigma(t_1, \ldots, t_n) \in V^T$, and $s = \sigma(s_1, \ldots, s_n) \in V^T$. Let $MA = (Q, V, \delta', F)$ be the multiset tree automaton induced by A. If $t \bowtie s$, then $\delta'(t) = \delta'(s)$.*

Note that the converse result of this theorem is not generally true. For instance, consider the trees $t = \sigma(a)$ and $s = \sigma(a, \sigma(a))$ and the tree automaton with the following transition function:

$$\delta_1(\sigma, a) = q_1 \in F, \qquad \delta_2(\sigma, a, q_1) = q_1 \in F.$$

It is easy to see that $\delta'(t) = \delta'(s)$ but t is not mirror equivalent to s.

Corollary 2. *(Sempere and López, [16]) Let $A = (Q, V, \delta, F)$ be a tree automaton, $MA = (Q, V, \delta', F)$ the multiset tree automaton induced by A and $t \in V^T$. If $t \in L(MA)$, then $s \in L(MA)$ for any $s \in V^T$ such that $t \bowtie s$.*

The last results were useful to propose an algorithm to determine whether two trees are mirror equivalent or not [16]: given two trees s and t, we can establish in time $\mathcal{O}((min\{|t|, |s|\})^2)$ if $t \bowtie s$.

4   Solving the Membrane Structure Recognition Problem

Recently, in [7], a way to generate trees by membrane systems has been proposed. Initially, any membrane structure can be represented by a tree taking the membrane structure as a hierarchical order between regions. Freund *et al.* [7] have taken advantage of a variant of P systems with active membranes and string objects. Active membranes have an electrical charge (*polarization*) together with a set of rules that allow the membrane to change polarizations, move objects (strings), dissolving the membrane, 2-dividing the membrane, etc. They have proved that any recursively enumerable tree language can be generated by a P system.

A way to recognize two identical membrane structures by taking advantage of tree representations was proposed in [16]. For example, let us see Figure 2, in which we represent a membrane structure with different trees.

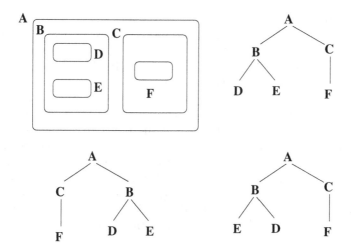

Fig. 2. A membrane structure together with different representations by trees

Obviously, the initial order of a membrane structure can be fixed. Anyway, whenever the system evolves (by membrane dissolving, division, creation, etc.) this order can be somehow ambiguous. Furthermore, the initial order of a P system is only a naming convention given that the membrane structure of any

P system can be renamed without changing its behavior due to the parallelism (observe that if this mechanism were sequential, then the ordering could be important for the final output).

The representation by trees could be essential for the analysis of the dynamic behavior of P systems. Whenever we work with trees to represent the membrane structure of a given P system, we can find a *mirroring effect*. Again, look at Figure 2: the three different trees proposed for the membrane structure have a mirroring property, that is, some subtrees at a given level of the tree have been permuted.

The method that we propose to establish if two membrane structures μ and $\mu\prime$ are identical is based on the algorithm proposed in [16]. First, we represent μ and $\mu\prime$ by t and s respectively. Then, we apply the proposed algorithm and, if $t \bowtie s$ we can affirm that μ and $\mu\prime$ are identical.

5   Editing Distances Between Membrane Structures

The study of relations between membrane structures is proposed in the sequel. The main problem we address is the following:

Let μ and $\mu\prime$ be two membrane structures corresponding to arbitrary P systems. What is the minimum set of membrane rule applications needed to transform one into the other?

The solution to the last problem can be approached by using multiset tree automata and editing distances between trees and tree automata. A previous work [10], considered the case of tree automata. Here, we will extend the previous results to multiset tree automata as described in previous sections.

First, we will describe the method employed in [10], in order to give the main components of the editing distance calculation.

Given a tree automaton $A = (Q, V, \delta, F)$ and a tree t, the distance between t and A can be established as the minimum in the set $\{D(t, q) \mid q \in F\}$, where $D(t, q)$ is the minimum distance of the tree t to the state q. The distance $D(t, q)$ evaluates the number of operations needed to reduce the tree t to the state q according to the function δ in automata A. Some operations involved in the distance refer to operations for trees as *Insertion, Deletion* and *Substitution*. We consider the costs for these operations as exposed in [10]. Observe that these costs are usually defined by taking into account the sizes of the trees. So, the bigger tree involved in the operation, the bigger cost to handle it:

- Insertion
  $\forall a \in V \ I(a) = 1$
  $I(\sigma(t_1, t_2, \ldots, t_k)) = 1 + \sum_{\forall j} I(t_j),$
- Deletion
  $\forall a \in V \ B(a) = 1$
  $B(\sigma(t_1, t_2, \ldots, t_k)) = 1 + \sum_{\forall j} B(t_j),$

− Substitution

$$\forall a \in V \ S(a, a) = 0$$
$$\forall a, b \in V \ S(a, b) = 1$$
$$S(\sigma(t_1, t_2, \ldots, t_k), a) = B(\sigma(t_1, t_2, \ldots, t_k)) + I(a)$$
$$S(a, \sigma(t_1, t_2, \ldots, t_k)) = B(a) + I(\sigma(t_1, t_2, \ldots, t_k)).$$

So, the distance of every (sub)tree to a tree automaton will involve every ancestor of each state of the automata together with the substructures of the tree. If we have to reduce the structure $\sigma(s_1, s_2, \ldots, s_n)$ to the state q such that $Anc(q)$ contains $\langle p_1, \ldots, p_m \rangle$, we will have to modify substructures s_i or we will have to insert states p_j at the minimum cost.

The edition cost of every tree to every state of the automaton can be calculated by considering the set of ancestors of the state and the set of successors of the tree. Then we can apply a dynamic programming scheme that takes into account previous calculations which can be stored in a distance matrix. For additional details of this method we refer the reader to [10].

The main components used to calculate the distance of a tree t to a multiset tree automaton MA are the same as in the tree automata case with the following remarks:

1. The successors of any node in the tree are considered as a multiset instead of a sequence.
2. The ancestors of every state in the automaton form a multiset.
3. The editing costs for trees and states are the same as in the tree automata.
4. The calculation of the edit distance is performed by using a edition matrix which can be obtained by using a dynamic programming strategy with some differences which will be explained later.

We propose **Algorithm 1** which obtains the distance from a tree t to a multiset tree automaton MA. Note that the target of the algorithm is to force the automaton to accept the tree. Therefore the set of edit operations is not fully needed. The algorithm use edit operations for substitution (reduction) of a tree to a state of the automaton, deletion of a (sub)tree and insertion of a state. Intuitively, the substitution of a tree by a state of the automaton could be seen as the substitution of the tree by the nearest tree that could be reduced to the state.

The error-correcting analysis method is shown in **Algorithm 1**. First the cost of the basic operations are obtained (i.e., insertion cost of a state and deletion of a subtree). Each of the calculations carried out are stored in a distance matrix indexed by the set of subtrees and the set of states of the automaton. This matrix is first initialized and the basic distances are stored. Distances between symbols in V_0 and between any symbol and any state of the automaton are also considered.

Note that the key problem of the algorithm is to find, for any subtree $t' = \sigma(t_1, \ldots, t_n)$ of t and any transition $\delta(\sigma, M) = M_\Psi(p)$, with $M \in Anc_\Psi(p)$, the matching of minimum cost between each t_i and the states and symbols in M. This problem can be reduced to the *minimum cost maximum matching* or

---

Algorithm 1. Algorithm to obtain the minimum distance from a tree t to the nearest tree in $L(MA)$.

Input:

    A multiset tree automaton $A = (Q, V, \delta, F)$.

    A tree t.

Output:

    Edit distance from t to the automaton A.

Method:

    /* initialization */

    $\forall t' \in Sub(t)$ $B[t'] = |t'|$ $end\forall$

    $\forall a \in V_0$ $I[a] = 1$ $end\forall$

    $\forall q \in Q$

        $I[q] = min\{|t'| \; : \; \delta(t') = q\}$

        $\forall t' \in Sub(t)$

            $D[t', q] = \infty$

        $end\forall$

    $end\forall$

    $\forall a, b \in V_0$

$$D[a, b] = \begin{cases} 1 & \text{if } a \neq b \\ 0 & \text{otherwise} \end{cases}$$

        $D[a, q] = 1 + I[q] \; : \; q \in Q$

    $end\forall$

    /* iteration */

    $\forall t' = \sigma(t'_1, \ldots, t'_n) \in Sub(t)$ /* postorder traverse */

        $\forall \delta(\sigma, M) = M_\Psi(p)$

            $D[t', p] = min(D[t', p], MMC(t', \delta(\sigma, M)))$

        $end\forall$

    $end\forall$

    $Return(min\{D[t', q] \; : \; q \in F\})$

  EndMethod:

---

maximum bipartite matching problem [14]. It is known that this problem can be solved in polinomial time by reducing it to the *minimum cost maximum flow* (MCMF) problem (see also [14]). This scheme is similar to the one proposed in [18] where the author considers distances between unordered trees.

Briefly, MCMF looks for obtaining, for a given graph $G = (V, E)$ in which functions *capacity* and *cost* are defined among the edges, the best way (with lower cost) to send the maximum flow between two nodes of the graph. The flow has to take into account the capacity constraint. The cost function measures the penalization of each unit of flow. Several solutions have been implemented to solve this problem and their complexities depend on the number of nodes n and the number of edges of the graph m. A proper algorithm for our purposes could be the one by Edmons and Karp [6] because its complexity depends only on the number of nodes of the graph ($\mathcal{O}(n^3)$).

Given a tree $t = \sigma(t_1, \ldots, t_n)$ and a transition $M_\Psi(p) \in \delta(\sigma, M)$, the minimum cost matching between t_i and the states in M can be obtained by the subroutine

MMC. First, this subroutine builds the directed graph from the parameters and set the proper capacities and costs functions among the edges. Then, a general solution could be run in order to solve the matching. The subroutine is shown in **Algorithm 2**.

Intuitively, each successor tree and each state (namely nodes t_i and q_j respectively) have their own nodes in the graph. Each node in one set is connected with all the nodes in the other. These connections model the reduction (substitution) of each tree to each state. Therefore, the capacity of these edges is set to 1 (these edges can be used only once) and the cost is set to the distance between each tree and each state. Note that this distance is always available due to the postorder traverse of the tree.

Algorithm 2. MMC Subroutine to obtain the Maximum Matching of Minimum Cost.

Input:
    A multiset tree automaton transition $\delta(\sigma, M) = M_\Psi(p)$.
    A tree $t = \sigma(t_1, \ldots, t_n)$.

Output:
    Minimum cost of the maximum match between $\{t_1, \ldots, t_n\}$
    and M.

Method:
    /* construction of the graph */
    Let $G = (V, E)$ where:
        $V = \{t_1, \ldots, t_n\} \cup M \cup \{s, ss, iq, dt\}$
        $(t_i, q_j) \in E, \ \forall q_j \in M; \ i : 1..n$
        $(t_i, dt) \in E, \ i : 1..n$
        $(iq, q_j) \in E, \ \forall q_j \in M$
        $(s, t_i) \in E, \ i : 1..n$
        $(q_j, ss) \in E, \ \forall q_j \in M$
        $(s, iq), (dt, ss) \in E$
    /* set capacities of each edge */
        $c(t_i, q_j) = 1, \ \forall q_j \in M; \ i : 1..n$
        $c(t_i, dt) = 1, \ i : 1..n$
        $c(iq, q_j) = \#_{q_j}(M), \ i : 1..n$
        $c(s, t_i) = 1, \ i : 1..n$
        $c(q_j, ss) = \#_{q_j}(M), \ \forall q_j \in M$
        $c(s, iq) = |M|, \ c(dt, ss) = n$
    /* set cost of each edge */
        $d(t_i, q_j) = D[t_i, q_j], \ \forall q_j \in M; \ i : 1..n$
        $d(t_i, dt) = B[t_i], \ i : 1..n$
        $d(iq, q_j) = I[q_j], \ \forall q_j \in M$
        $d(s, t_i) = 0, \ i : 1..n$
        $d(q_j, ss) = 0, \ \forall q_j \in M$
        $d(s, iq) = 0$
        $d(dt, ss) = 0$
    Return($MinCostMaxFlow(G)$)
  EndMethod:

The set of edit operations we consider also takes into account the insertion of a state. The node iq and the connections between this node and the nodes q_j model the insertion operation. Thus, the cost of these edges is set to the insertion cost of the state. Note that the number of insertions of each state is bounded by the number of occurrences of the state in M, therefore, the capacities of these edges is set to this value.

In the same way, in order to model the deletion of trees, the node dt and the connections with the successor trees are considered in the graph. Each tree can be deleted only once, therefore the capacity of these edges is set to 1. Obviously, the cost of these edges is set to the cost of deleting the corresponding tree.

The construction of the graph also considers a source node s. This node is connected to the tree nodes, with connectivity 1 and cost 0 (these edges must be selected without cost). The node s is also connected to the node iq and the cost of this edge is set to 0. Note that the number of state insertions is bounded by the number of states, therefore, the capacity of this edge is set to $|M|$. The cost of this connection is set to 0.

Finally, the graph construction considers a sink node ss. This node is connected with the state nodes q_j with cost 0. Note that the edition process aims to fit the set of successors with the multiset of ancestors, thus, the capacity of the edges must be set to the number of occurrences of each state. The node dt is also connected with the node ss with cost 0. This edge models the tree deletions, therefore, the capacity of the connection must be set to the number of trees that can be deleted.

Example 1. Let us consider the tree $t = \sigma(\sigma(b, \sigma(a, \sigma(a, b), a)), \sigma(a, \sigma(a, a)))$ and the automaton defined by the following transition functions with $q_3 \in F$:

$$\delta(\sigma, aq_1 a) = q_1, \quad \delta(\sigma, bq_2) = q_2, \quad \delta(\sigma, aa) = q_1,$$
$$\delta(\sigma, b) = q_2, \qquad \delta(\sigma, q_1 q_2) = q_3.$$

First, the insertion and deletion costs are obtained. They are shown in the following tables

t_1	t_2	t_3	t_4	t_5	t_6
3	6	8	3	5	14

Deletion costs

q_1	q_2	q_3
3	2	6

Insertion costs

Then, the editing process considers the first postorder subtree $\sigma(a, b)$ and the first transition $\delta(\sigma, aq_1 a) = q_1$. The process starts with the construction of the graph shown in Figure 3.

Solid lines in Figure 3 show the minimum cost matching. The distance is stored in the matrix of distances. Note that this cost is improved when the transition $\delta(\sigma, aa) = q_1$ is considered. The following table shows an intermediate state of the matrix.

D_A	t_1	t_2	t_3	t_4	t_5	t_6
q_1	1	1				
q_2	1	3				
q_3	7					

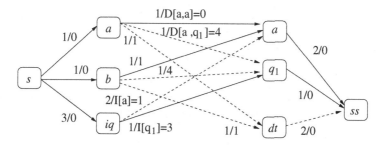

Fig. 3. Underlying graph to obtain the distance of the first postorder subtree to the first transition of the automaton. Edge labels show the capacity/cost. Solid lines show the best matching.

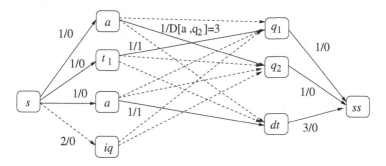

Fig. 4. Underlying graph to obtain the distance of the second postorder subtree to the transition of the automaton $\delta(\sigma, q_1 q_2) = q_3$. Solid lines show the best matching.

We now compute the distance of the second postorder subtree, $\sigma(a, \sigma(a, b), a)$, to the state q_3. The underlying graph is shown in Figure 4. The best matching is indicated in solid lines.

Observe that the minimum editing distance that we have calculated can be established in terms of operations which have a translation into membrane rules. Let us consider that μ is the membrane structure which is accepted by the multiset tree automaton MA and μ' is represented by a tree t. We have the following correspondences between edition operations and membrane rules:

1. Insertion of state q

   Let us suppose that the insertion is produced to match the ancestors of a state p. The minimum tree that can be reduced to q is t_j. The operations needed to achieve this goal in the membrane structure are membrane creation at region p in order to obtain membrane structure t_j.

2. Reduction of tree t_i to state q

   Let us suppose that the tree which can be reduced to q with a minimal cost is t_j, according with the δ function of the automaton. The operations needed to make this reduction are the ones involved to transform t_i to t_j at a region k. These operations consider again membrane creation and dissolving depending on the operations involved in the minimum distance from t_i to t_j.

3. Substitution of a by b
   The region a is dissolved and created with a new label.
4. Deletion of tree t_i
   Let us suppose that t_i is a membrane structure at region k. The deletion consists of several membrane dissolving of structure t_i.

6   Conclusions and Future Work

We have proposed a method to calculate the minimum number of membrane rules needed to transform a membrane structure into a different one. The number of rules needed, if so, establishes an editing distance between P systems by taking into account only membrane modifications. This measure can provide new definitions about *structural confluence* in P systems, that is, structural agreement during evolution.

Observe that we have worked with a simplified version of P systems. That is, the objects inside any region do not influence the editing distance. A future research will consider how the objects can be taken into account to calculate the editing distance.

Acknowledgements

Work supported by the Spanish CICYT under contract TIC2003-09319-C03-02. The authors are grateful to the anonymous referees which have made several sharp remarks on the first version of this work. Special thanks are given to Mario Pérez-Jiménez for useful discussions during the *3rd Brainstorming Week on Membrane Computing* which was held in Sevilla from 31st January to 4th February 2005.

References

1. A. Alhazov, T.O. Ishdorj: Membrane operations in P systems with active membranes. In *Proceedings of the Second Brainstorming Week on Membrane Computing* (Gh. Păun, A. Riscos-Núñez, A. Romero-Jiménez, F. Sancho Caparrini, eds.). TR 01/04 of RGNC. Sevilla University, 2004, 37–844.
2. C. Calude, Gh. Păun, G. Rozenberg, A. Salomaa: *Multiset Processing. Mathematical, Computer Science, Molecular Computing Points of View.* LNCS 2235, Springer, Berlin, 2001.
3. H. Comon, M. Dauchet, R. Gilleron, F. Jacquemard, D. Lugiez, S. Tison, M. Tommasi: Tree automata techniques and applications. Available on: `http://www.grappa.univ-lille3.fr/tata` (1997).
4. E. Csuhaj-Varjú, A. Di Nola, Gh. Păun, M. Pérez-Jiménez, G. Vaszil: Editing configurations of P systems. *Proc. Third Brainstorming Week on Membrane Computing*, Sevilla, 2005, RGNC Report 01/2005, 131–155.

5. E. Csuhaj-Varjú, C. Martín-Vide, V. Mitrana: Multiset automata. In [2], 69–83.
6. J. Edmonds, R.M. Karp: Theoretical improvements in algorithmic efficiency for network flow problems. *Journal of the ACM*, 19, 2 (1972), 248–264.
7. R. Freund, M. Oswald, A. Păun: P systems generating trees. In *Pre-proceedings of Fifth Workshop on Membrane Computing, WMC5, Milano, June 2004* (G. Mauri, Gh. Păun, C. Zandron, eds.), MolCoNet project IST-2001-32008, 2004, 221–232.
8. F. Gécseg, M. Steinby: Tree languages. In vol. 3 of [15], 1–69.
9. M. Kudlek, C. Martín-Vide, Gh. Păun: Towards a formal macroset theory. In [2], 123–133.
10. D. López, J.M. Sempere, P. García: Error correcting analysis for tree languages. *International Journal of Pattern Recognition and Artificial Intelligence*, 14, 3 (2000), 357–368.
11. A. Păun: On P systems with active membranes. In: *Proceedings of Conference on Unconventionals Models of Computation*, Brussels, 2000, 187-201.
12. Gh. Păun: *Membrane Computing. An Introduction.* Springer, Berlin, 2002.
13. Gh. Păun, Y. Suzuki, H. Tanaka, T. Yokomori: On the power of membrane division in P systems. *Theoretical Computer Sci.*, 324, 1 (2004), 61–85.
14. R.L. Rivest T.H. Cormen, C.E. Leiserson, C. Stein: *Introduction to Algorithms.* MIT Press and McGraw-Hill, second edition, 2001.
15. G. Rozenberg, A. Salomaa, eds.: *Handbook of Formal Languages.* Springer, Berlin, 1997.
16. J.M. Sempere, D. López: Recognizing membrane structures with tree automata. In *Proceedings of the 3rd Brainstorming Week on Membrane Computing 2005* (M.A. Gutirrez Naranjo, A. Riscos-Núñez, F.J. Romero-Campero, D. Sburlan, eds.), RGNC Report 01/2005 Research Group on Natural Computing, Sevilla University, Fénix Editora, 2005, 305–316.
17. A. Syropoulos: Mathematics of multisets. In [2], 347–358.
18. K. Zhang: A constrained edit distance between unordered labelled trees. *Algorithmica*, 15 (1996), 205–222.

Relational Membrane Systems

Adam Obtułowicz

Institute of Mathematics,
Polish Academy of Sciences,
Śniadeckich 8, P.O. Box 21 00-956 Warsaw, Poland
adamo@impan.gov.pl

Abstract. The notion of a relational membrane system is introduced as a generalization of the notion of a membrane system defined in [8]. A representation of certain relational membrane systems by some hereditary finite sets is given. Evolutive transformations of relational membrane systems with mobile membranes according to simultaneous application of some evolution rules are described by using the representation.

1 Introduction

We continue the discussion initiated in [7], concerning the interconnections between membrane computing, cf. [8], and Gandy's mechanisms, cf. [5].

We propose in the paper an approach to evolution processes of membrane systems with active membranes, where membrane systems are represented by certain hereditary finite sets in a way different from the representations of membrane systems given in [7].

The approach is restricted to some narrow class of evolution rules related to some development evolution rules discussed in [6] and to process the capabilities "can enter in an ambient", "can exit out of an ambient", "can open an ambient", introduced in [3]. We focus more on membrane mobility than on transformations of membrane contents with respect to the objects contained in the regions of membranes during an evolution process.

We expect that the methods contained in this approach can be extended and modified to introduce mathematical models (by means of denotational semantics) of formal systems like Ambient Calculus [3] and Brane Calculi [1], [4], where these models, based on hereditary finite sets, may have also an immediate physical or biochemical interpretation.

We introduce in Section 2 a notion of a relational membrane system which comprises a wide class of membrane systems, including fuzzy membrane systems, and other structures related to membrane systems. The relational membrane systems belonging to a certain class have a simple representation by some hereditary finite sets which we use in Section 3 to discuss in detail the possible transformations of membrane systems according to simultaneous applications of evolution rules as mentioned above. The transformations are described simply in terms of union, intersection, difference of sets, and an operation assigning to a set x

R. Freund et al. (Eds.): WMC 2005, LNCS 3850, pp. 342–355, 2006.
© Springer-Verlag Berlin Heidelberg 2006

the one element set $\{x\}$. The description is possible due to the representation of relational membrane systems by hereditary finite sets given in Section 2.

2   Relational Membrane Systems and Their Representation by Hereditary Finite Sets

Both membrane computing approach and Gandy's mechanism approach to computing devices concern hierarchically organized systems, where the hierarchical organization of a given system is determined by the nesting relation of the less complex parts of the system in the more complex parts of the system.

In membrane computing approach the nesting relation which determines the hierarchical organization of a given membrane system is modelled by the tree whose nodes are membranes of the system, where membranes correspond to the parts of the system and for all two different membranes of the system there is no common membrane which is nested immediately in both of them.

In Gandy's mechanism approach the nesting relation which determines the hierarchical organization of a given system is modelled by the restriction of the membership relation $\in$ to the union $\mathrm{WTC}(x) \cup L$ for that hereditary finite set x which is a model of the whole system, where $\mathrm{WTC}(x)$ is the weak transitive closure of x and L is a set of urelements (see the Appendix). In this case urelements are elementary (indecomposable) parts and the elements of $\mathrm{WTC}(x)$ are composite parts, where for two different composite parts there may exist a common composite part which is nested in both of them.

Thus the considered approaches are different because of the shape of models used in them.

We introduce and discuss a notion of a relational membrane system which is a generalization of models used in these approaches and which includes the case of a fuzzy nesting relation appearing in practice.

Let $\mathcal{D} = \{N, [0, 1]\}$, where N is the set of natural numbers with 0 and $[0, 1]$ is the closed unit interval.

For a set $D \in \mathcal{D}$ we define a [finite] D-relational membrane system S to be given by a function $\mathcal{E}_S : \mathbb{U}_S \times \mathbb{U}_S \to D$, a distinguished proper subset $\mathbb{O}_S$ of [a finite] $\mathbb{U}_S$, and a distinguished element $r_S \in \mathbb{U}_S - \mathbb{O}_S$ such that the following conditions hold:

i) $\mathcal{E}_S(m, a) = 0$ for all $m \in \mathbb{U}_S$ and $a \in \mathbb{O}_S$,
ii) the *underlying graph* G_S of S with the set V_S of vertices given by

$$V_S = \mathbb{U}_S - \mathbb{O}_S,$$

and the set E_S of edges given by

$$E_S = \{(m, m') \in V_S \times V_S \mid \mathcal{E}_S(m', m) > 0\}$$

is a *rooted graph with the root* r_S, i.e., G_S is an acyclic graph and for every $m \in V_S$ there exists a natural number $n > 0$ and a route $m_1 \ldots m_n$ in G_S whose first element m_1 is r_S and the last element m_n is m (a *route* in a directed graph G is meant to be a finite string $v_1 \ldots v_n$ with $n > 0$ of vertices of G such that, if $n > 1$, then (v_i, v_{i+1}) is an edge of G for all i with $1 \le i < n$).

The sets $\mathbb{U}_S, \mathbb{O}_S, \mathbb{U}_S - \mathbb{O}_S$ are called the *universe* of S, the *set of objects* of S, the *set of membranes* of S, respectively, the function $\mathcal{E}_S$ is called the *immediate nesting relation* of S, and r_S is called the *root* or the *skin* of S.

The immediate nesting relation $\mathcal{E}_S$ of a D-relational membrane system S is interpreted in the following way:

— for $D = N$ the value $\mathcal{E}_S(x, y)$ means that exactly $\mathcal{E}_S(x, y)$ copies of part x are immediately nested in part y,
— for $D = [0, 1]$ the value $\mathcal{E}_S(x, y)$ means that with the certainty degree $\mathcal{E}_S(x, y)$ part x is immediately nested in part y.

Thus $[0, 1]$-relational membrane systems are fuzzy relational membrane systems.

If S is a finite N-relational membrane system whose underlying graph G_S is a tree, i.e., for every $m \in V_S$ there exist a unique route in G_S whose first element is r_S and the last element is m, and the following condition holds:

iii) $\mathcal{E}_S(m, m') \leq 1$ for all $m, m' \in \mathbb{U}_S - \mathbb{O}_S,$

then S is a usual membrane system whose set of membranes is $\mathbb{U}_S - \mathbb{O}_S$, the set of objects is $\mathbb{O}_S$, G_S is the membrane structure of S in Păun's sense, and for all $m \in \mathbb{U}_S - \mathbb{O}_S$ and $a \in \mathbb{O}_S$ the value $\mathcal{E}_S(a, m)$ means that exactly $\mathcal{E}_S(a, m)$ copies of a are contained in the region of m.

For every hereditary finite set x with urelements in L the characteristic function of the restriction of the membership relation $\in$ to the set $\mathrm{WTC}(x) \cup L$ is the immediate nesting relation of that N-relational membrane system whose universe is $\mathrm{WTC}(x) \cup L$ and the set of objects is L.

We introduce a notion of homomorphism of relational membrane systems to describe certain relationships between relational membrane systems in mathematical way.

For $D \in \mathcal{D}$ and two D-relational membrane systems with $\mathbb{O}_S = \mathbb{O}_{S'}$ we define a *homomorphism of S into S'* to be a mapping $h : \mathbb{U}_S \to \mathbb{U}_{S'}$, written $h : S \to S'$, such that the following two conditions hold:

H_1) $h(a) = a$ for every $a \in \mathbb{O}_S$,
H_2) $\mathcal{E}_S(x_1, x_2) \leq \mathcal{E}_{S'}\big(h(x_1), h(x_2)\big)$ for all $x_1, x_2 \in \mathbb{U}_S$.

A homomorphism h of a relational membrane system S into a relational membrane system S' is called an *isomorphism* of S into S' if there exists a homomorphism $h^- : S' \to S$, called the *inverse of h*, such that

$$h^-(h(x)) = x \text{ for all } x \in \mathbb{U}_S \quad \text{and} \quad h(h^-(x')) = x' \text{ for all } x' \in \mathbb{U}_{S'}.$$

We say that two D-relational membrane systems S and S' with $\mathbb{O}_S = \mathbb{O}_{S'}$ are *isomorphic* or that S *is isomorphic to* S' if there exists an isomorphism of S into S'.

The relationship of two relational membrane systems such that they are isomorphic is a kind of structural equivalence of these systems in the sense that they differ only in the mathematical presentation or physical interpretation of membranes themselves.

We give below a useful representation of certain N-relational membrane systems by hereditary finite sets.

We say that an N-relational membrane system S is a *Boolean relational membrane system* if S satisfies the condition

iv) $$\mathcal{E}_S(x,y) \leq 1 \quad \text{for all } x, y \in \mathbb{U}_S.$$

For a finite Boolean relational membrane system S one constructs a hereditary finite set $\mathrm{hf}(S)$ over $\mathbb{U}_S$ which is defined inductively by

$$\mathrm{hf}(S) = \{a \in \mathbb{O}_S \,|\, \mathcal{E}_S(a, r_S) > 0\} \cup \{r_S\}$$
$$\cup \{\mathrm{hf}(S(m)) \,|\, \mathcal{E}_S(m, r_S) > 0 \text{ and } m \in \mathbb{U}_S - \mathbb{O}_S\},$$

where $S(m)$ is that subsystem of S whose immediate nesting relation $\mathcal{E}_{S(m)}$ is the restriction of $\mathcal{E}_S$ to the set

$$\mathbb{U}_{S(m)} = \{m' \in \mathbb{U}_S - \mathbb{O}_S \,|\, \text{there exists a route in } G_S$$
$$\text{with the first element } m \text{ and the last element } m'\} \cup \mathbb{O}_S$$

and m is the root of $S(m)$.

Theorem 1. *Let S be a finite Boolean relational membrane system. Then S is isomorphic to that N-relational membrane system S' whose universe is $\mathrm{WTC}(\mathrm{hf}(S)) \cup \mathbb{O}_S$ and the immediate nesting relation $\mathcal{E}_{S'}$ of S' is the characteristic function of the restriction of the membership relation $\in$ to $\mathrm{WTC}(\mathrm{hf}(S)) \cup \mathbb{O}_S$.*

Proof. A mapping $h : \mathbb{U}_S \to \mathrm{WTC}(\mathrm{hf}(S)) \cup \mathbb{O}_S$ given by $h(a) = a$ for every $a \in \mathbb{O}_S$ and $h(m) = \mathrm{hf}(S(m))$ for every $m \in \mathbb{U}_S - \mathbb{O}_S$ is an isomorphism of S into S', where for the inverse h^- of h the value $h^-(y)$ is that unique $m \in \mathbb{U}_S - \mathbb{O}_S$ which belongs to y for every $y \in \mathrm{WTC}(\mathrm{hf}(S))$. $\qquad\square$

We shall use the following notions in Section 3.

Let $\mathfrak{M}$ be a family of pairwise disjoint non-empty sets of urelements in L and let x be a hereditary finite set over L. We say that x is *determined by* $\mathfrak{M}$ if the following conditions hold:

M_1) $\{y \cap \bigcup \mathfrak{M} \,|\, y \in \mathrm{WTC}(x)\} = \mathfrak{M}$,
M_2) $y \cap \bigcup \mathfrak{M} = y' \cap \bigcup \mathfrak{M}$ implies $y = y'$ for all y, y' in $\mathrm{WTC}(x)$.

Corollary 1. *Let S be an N-relational membrane system which is Boolean. Then $\mathrm{hf}(S)$ is a hereditary finite set determined by $\mathfrak{M} = \{\{m\} \,|\, m \in \mathbb{U}_S - \mathbb{O}_S\}$.*

Proof. It is a consequence of Theorem 1. $\qquad\square$

We say that a hereditary finite set x is a *tree-like hereditary finite set* if the graph $G_x = (V_x, E_x)$ with the set $V_x = \mathrm{WTC}(x)$ of vertices and the set $E_x = \{(y, z) \,|\, z \in y \text{ and } \{y, z\} \subseteq \mathrm{WTC}(x)\}$ of edges is a tree with the root x.

Corollary 2. *If the underlying graph G_S of a Boolean N-relational membrane system is a tree, then* $\mathrm{hf}(S)$ *is a tree-like hereditary finite set.*

Proof. It is a consequence of Theorem 1.   □

The representation of S by $\mathrm{hf}(S)$ appears useful for a discussion of certain evolutive transformations of N-relational membrane systems which are determined by simultaneous applications of different evolution rules. Namely, these evolutive transformations can be described in terms of hereditary finite sets $\mathrm{hf}(S)$ by using set theoretical operations of union, intersection, difference of sets, and that unary operation $\{?\}$ whose value is $\{x\}$ for a hereditary finite set x. We present a description of evolutive transformations of hereditary finite sets in Section 3.

3   Evolutive Transformations of Hereditary Finite Sets

We consider those evolutive transformations of hereditary finite set into hereditary finite sets which are determined by evolution rules written in Păun's manner as the parentheses expressions:

$R_1)$ $[a] \to b$ (*dissolution rule*),
$R_2)$ $[a][b] \to [c[d]]$ (*in-rule*),
$R_3)$ $[[a]b] \to [c][d]$ (*out-rule*),

where a, b, c, d are urelements, but their occurrence in the above expressions is not obligatory.

We adopt the following notation for evolution rules. For a rule R of the form given in $R_1)$

$$\mathrm{left}(R) = \{a\} \quad \text{and} \quad \mathrm{right}(R) = \{b\},$$

eventually $\mathrm{right}(R) = \varnothing$ for R of the form $[a] \to \,.$

For a rule R of the form given in $R_2)$ or $R_3)$

$$\mathrm{left}_1(R) = \{a\}, \quad \mathrm{left}_2(R) = \{b\}, \quad \mathrm{right}_1(R) = \{c\}, \quad \text{and} \quad \mathrm{right}_2(R) = \{d\},$$

if a, b, c, d occur in the rules, otherwise $\mathrm{left}_i(R)$ and $\mathrm{right}_i(R)$ are empty for $i \in \{1, 2\}$.

The single applications from the top of the above rules to hereditary finite sets are described in the following way:

— if $a \in y \in x \in \mathrm{HF}$, then the dissolution rule $[a] \to b$ *can be applied to* x *and the result of its application is a new hereditary finite set of the form*

$$(x - \{y\}) \cup (y - \{a\}) \cup \{b\},$$

— if $a \in y \in x \in \mathrm{HF}$, $b \in z \in x$, and $z \neq y$, then the in-rule $[a][b] \to [b[a]]$ *can be applied to* x *and the result of its application is a new hereditary finite set of the form*

$$(x - \{y, z\}) \cup \{z \cup \{y\}\},$$

— if $a \in z \in y \in x \in$ HF and $y - \{z\} \neq \varnothing$, then the out-rule $[[a]] \rightarrow [a][\ ]$ *can be applied to* x and the result of its application is a new hereditary finite set of the form

$$(x - \{y\}) \cup \{y - \{z\}, z\}.$$

The results of application are similar for arbitrary objects occurring in the rules.

The above described single applications of evolution rules R_1), R_2), R_3) from the top determine evolutive transformations of hereditary finite sets into the new hereditary finite sets from the top. One sees that these rules are related to some development evolution rules discussed in [6] and to process capabilities "can enter in an ambient", "can exit out of an ambient", "can open an ambient", introduced in [3]. We describe by using $\cup$, $-$, and $\{?\}$ a more complicated case of evolutive transformations of hereditary finite sets, where these transformations are determined by simultaneous applications of many different rules to many different elements of WTC(x) for a hereditary finite set x to be transformed.

The evolutive transformations of hereditary finite sets considered above can be "transferred" to N-relational membrane systems by using the construction of hf(S) (see Theorem 1 and Corollary 1) to define evolutive transformations of N-relational membrane systems themselves.

We restrict our considerations to tree-like hereditary finite sets which are closely related to the usual membrane systems of [8] (see Corollary 2 in this paper).

Let x be a tree-like hereditary finite set determined by a family $\mathfrak{M}$ of pairwise disjoint non-empty sets and let x belong to the set HF of hereditary finite sets over the set $L = \mathbb{O} \cup \bigcup \mathfrak{M}$ of urelements with $\mathbb{O} \cap \bigcup \mathfrak{M} \neq \varnothing$ for $\mathbb{O}$ meant as a set of objects. By a *local action over* x we mean an ordered pair $\mathfrak{a} = (P^{\mathfrak{a}}, R^{\mathfrak{a}})$, where $P^{\mathfrak{a}}$ is a bijection from dom$(\mathfrak{a})$ into scope$(\mathfrak{a})$ with scope$(\mathfrak{a}) \subset$ WTC(x) and $R^{\mathfrak{a}}$ is an evolution rule such that

a_1) if $R^{\mathfrak{a}}$ is a dissolution rule of the form $[a] \rightarrow b$, then dom$(\mathfrak{a}) = \{0, 1\}$, $P^{\mathfrak{a}}(1) \in P^{\mathfrak{a}}(0)$, and $a \in P^{\mathfrak{a}}(1)$,

a_2) if $R^{\mathfrak{a}}$ is an in-rule $[a][b] \rightarrow [c[d]]$, then dom$(\mathfrak{a}) = \{0, 1, 2\}$, $\{P^{\mathfrak{a}}(1), P^{\mathfrak{a}}(2)\} \subset P^{\mathfrak{a}}(0)$, $a \in P^{\mathfrak{a}}(1)$, and $b \in P^{\mathfrak{a}}(2)$,

a_3) if $R^{\mathfrak{a}}$ is an out-rule $[a[b]] \rightarrow [c][d]$, then dom$(\mathfrak{a}) = \{0, 1, 2\}$, $b \in P^{\mathfrak{a}}(2) \in P^{\mathfrak{a}}(1) \in P^{\mathfrak{a}}(0)$, and $a \in P^{\mathfrak{a}}(1)$.

For a local action $\mathfrak{a}$ over x the bijection $P^{\mathfrak{a}}$ is meant as a *place of application* of the rule $R^{\mathfrak{a}}$, where it will be seen later than one can interpret scope$(\mathfrak{a})$ as the scope of the local transformation of x according to the rule $R^{\mathfrak{a}}$.

Let $\mathcal{A}$ be a set of local actions over x. For a set $y \in$ WTC(x) and a set $z \subseteq y$ we write $\mathcal{A} \upharpoonright (y - z)$ to denote the set of local actions $\mathfrak{a}$ over $y - z$ such that $\mathfrak{a} \in \mathcal{A}$ or $P^{\mathfrak{a}}(0) = y - z$ with $\mathfrak{a}^* = (P^{\mathfrak{a}^*}, R^{\mathfrak{a}}) \in \mathcal{A}$ for $P^{\mathfrak{a}^*} : $ dom$(\mathfrak{a}) \rightarrow$ (scope$(\mathfrak{a}) - \{y - z\}) \cup \{y\}$ with $P^{\mathfrak{a}^*}(i) = P^{\mathfrak{a}}(i)$ for all $i \in$ dom$(\mathfrak{a}) - \{0\}$. If $z = \varnothing$, then $\mathcal{A} \upharpoonright (y - z) = \mathcal{A} \upharpoonright y$ is simply the set of those local actions over y which belong to $\mathcal{A}$. If $z = y$, then $\mathcal{A} \upharpoonright (y - z) = \mathcal{A} \upharpoonright \varnothing = \varnothing$.

For a set $\mathcal{A}$ of local actions over x we adopt the following notation

$$\mathcal{A}_\alpha = \{\mathfrak{a} \in \mathcal{A} \mid R^{\mathfrak{a}} \text{ is an } \alpha\text{-rule}\} \quad \text{for} \quad \alpha \in \{\text{in}, \text{out}\},$$
$$\mathcal{A}_{\text{diss}} = \{\mathfrak{a} \in \mathcal{A} \mid R^{\mathfrak{a}} \text{ is a dissolution rule}\}.$$

We define now a property of sets $\mathcal{A}$ of local actions over tree-like hereditary finite sets x such that if $\mathcal{A}$ has this property, then one can construct the result of transformation of x with respect to $\mathcal{A}$ in a consistent (unambigous) way, where x is transformed according to simultaneous application of the rules R^a in places P^a, respectively for all $a \in \mathcal{A}$.

A set $\mathcal{A}$ of local actions over x is called a *proper set of local actions over x* if the following conditions hold:

(C_0) for all local actions a, a' in $\mathcal{A}$ if $P^a = P^{a'}$, then $R^a = R^{a'}$,

(C_1) for all local actions a, a' in $\mathcal{A}$ if $a \neq a'$, then $\mathrm{scope}(a) \cap \mathrm{scope}(a') = \varnothing$ or the disjunction of the following conditions holds:

$(C_{1,1})$ $P^a(0) = P^{a'}(0)$ and $(\mathrm{scope}(a) - \{P^a(0)\}) \cap (\mathrm{scope}(a') - \{P^{a'}(0)\}) = \varnothing$,

$(C_{1,2})$ if $\{a, a'\} \subseteq \mathcal{A}_{\mathrm{diss}}$, then $P^a(0) = P^{a'}(1)$,

$(C_{1,3})$ if $\{a, a'\} \subseteq \mathcal{A}_{\mathrm{in}}$, then $P^a(1) = P^{a'}(1)$ or $P^{a'}(0) \in \{P^a(1), P^a(2)\}$,

$(C_{1,4})$ if $\{a, a'\} \subseteq \mathcal{A}_{\mathrm{out}}$, then $P^a(0) = P^{a'}(2)$
or $\{P^a(1), P^a(2)\} \cap \{P^{a'}(0), P^{a'}(1)\} = \{P^a(1)\}$,

$(C_{1,5})$ if $a \in \mathcal{A}_{\mathrm{diss}}$ and $a' \in \mathcal{A}_{\mathrm{in}}$, then $P^a(1) = P^{a'}(0)$
or $P^a(0) \in \{P^{a'}(1), P^{a'}(2)\}$,

$(C_{1,6})$ if $a \in \mathcal{A}_{\mathrm{diss}}$ and $a' \in \mathcal{A}_{\mathrm{out}}$, then $P^a(1) = P^{a'}(0)$ or $\{P^a(0), P^a(1)\} \cap \{P^{a'}(1), P^{a'}(2)\} = \{P^a(0)\}$,

$(C_{1,7})$ if $a \in \mathcal{A}_{\mathrm{in}}$ and $a' \in \mathcal{A}_{\mathrm{out}}$, then $P^a(1) = P^{a'}(1)$ or $P^{a'}(0) \in \{P^a(1), P^a(2)\}$
or $\mathrm{scope}(a) \cap \{P^{a'}(1), P^{a'}(2)\} = \{P^a(0)\}$.

We adopt the following conventions to explain and illustrate the notion of a proper set of local actions.

For a tree-like non-empty hereditary finite set x whose content is not specified (or is not important for considerations) we illustrate x by a drawing given by the triangle below whose bottom vertex is labelled by x.

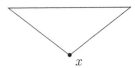

For a tree-like non-empty hereditary finite set x whose content is not specified we illustrate one-element set $\{x\}$ by a drawing given by a triangle with an arrow glued to the bottom vertex of the triangle as below

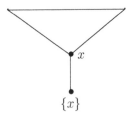

where the bottom vertex of the drawing is that vertex which is labelled by $\{x\}$.

If a tree-like hereditary finite set x is such that $x = u \cup w$ for hereditary finite sets u, w with $(\mathrm{HF} \cap u) \cap (\mathrm{HF} \cap w) = \varnothing$ such that there are given the drawings used for illustrations of u and w, respectively, then we illustrate x by the drawing below

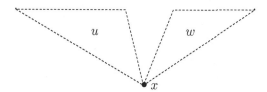

where the meta-triangles labelled by u and w contain the drawing used to illustrate u and the drawing used to illustrate w, respectively. In the above drawing which illustrates $x = u \cup w$ the bottom vertex labelled by x is the result of gluing of the bottom vertex of the drawing used to illustrate u and the bottom vertex of the drawing used to illustrate w. Here the intersection of the set of vertices of the drawing for u and the set of vertices of the drawing for w is the one-element set containing the result of gluing described above, which is the vertex labelled by x.

Thus for tree-like hereditary finite sets x, y, z such that $z \in y \in x$ one can illustrate x by the drawing

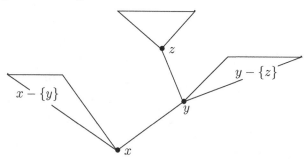

where the contents of $x - \{y\}$, $y - \{z\}$, and z are not specified.

We explain and illustrate the conditions $(C_{1,1})$–$(C_{1,7})$, where, to simplify the considerations, we assume that the objects do not occur in the evolution rules.

Ad $(C_{1,1})$. For two different local actions $\mathfrak{a} \in \mathcal{A}_{\mathrm{diss}}$ and $\mathfrak{a}' \in \mathcal{A}_{\mathrm{out}}$ satisfying $(C_{1,1})$ the places $P^{\mathfrak{a}}$ and $P^{\mathfrak{a}'}$ are illustrated in Fig. 1(a). The result of simultaneous application of the rules $R^{\mathfrak{a}}$ and $R^{\mathfrak{a}'}$ in places $P^{\mathfrak{a}}$ and $P^{\mathfrak{a}'}$, respectively, is illustrated in Fig. 1(b), where $P^{\mathfrak{a}}(1)$ is "dissolved" in $P^{\mathfrak{a}}(0)$ and $P^{\mathfrak{a}'}(2)$ is "sent out" of $P^{\mathfrak{a}'}(1)$ into $P^{\mathfrak{a}}(0) = P^{\mathfrak{a}'}(0)$. The remaining cases of $\mathfrak{a}$ and $\mathfrak{a}'$ satisfying $(C_{1,1})$ are explained and illustrated in a similar way.

Ad $(C_{1,2})$. For two different local actions $\mathfrak{a}, \mathfrak{a}'$ belonging to $\mathcal{A}_{\mathrm{diss}}$ with $P^{\mathfrak{a}}(0) = P^{\mathfrak{a}'}(1)$ the places $P^{\mathfrak{a}}$ and $P^{\mathfrak{a}'}$ are illustrated in Fig. 2(a). The result of simultaneous application of the rules $R^{\mathfrak{a}}$ and $R^{\mathfrak{a}'}$ in places $P^{\mathfrak{a}}$ and $P^{\mathfrak{a}'}$, respectively, is illustrated in Fig. 2(b), where both $P^{\mathfrak{a}}(1)$ and $P^{\mathfrak{a}'}(1) - \{P^{\mathfrak{a}}(1)\}$ are "dissolved" simultaneously in $P^{\mathfrak{a}'}(0)$.

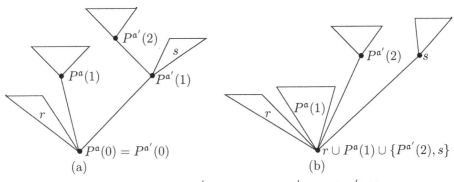

(a)

(b)

where $r = P^{\mathfrak{a}}(0) - \{P^{\mathfrak{a}}(1), P^{\mathfrak{a}'}(1)\}$ and $s = P^{\mathfrak{a}'}(1) - \{P^{\mathfrak{a}'}(2)\}$

Fig. 1

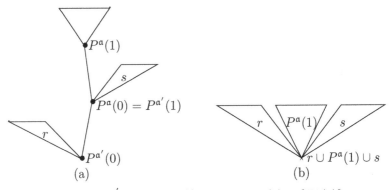

(a)

(b)

where $r = P^{\mathfrak{a}'}(0) - \{P^{\mathfrak{a}}(0)\}$ and $s = P^{\mathfrak{a}}(0) - \{P^{\mathfrak{a}}(1)\}$

Fig. 2

Ad $(C_{1,3})$. For two different local actions $\mathfrak{a}, \mathfrak{a}'$ belonging to $\mathcal{A}_{\text{in}}$ with $P^{\mathfrak{a}}(1) = P^{\mathfrak{a}'}(1)$ the places $P^{\mathfrak{a}}$ and $P^{\mathfrak{a}'}$ are illustrated in Fig. 3(a). The result of simultaneous application of the rules $R^{\mathfrak{a}}$ and $R^{\mathfrak{a}'}$ in these places $P^{\mathfrak{a}}$ and $P^{\mathfrak{a}'}$, respectively, is illustrated in Fig. 3(b), where both $P^{\mathfrak{a}}(2)$ and $P^{\mathfrak{a}'}(2)$ are "sent into" $P^{\mathfrak{a}}(1) = P^{\mathfrak{a}'}(1)$ simultaneously. We point out that for all two different local actions $\mathfrak{a}$ and $\mathfrak{a}'$ with $\text{scope}(\mathfrak{a}) \cap \text{scope}(\mathfrak{a}') \neq \varnothing$ the condition $(C_{1,3})$ implies $P^{\mathfrak{a}}(1) \neq P^{\mathfrak{a}'}(2)$, which excludes the case where simultaneous application of $R^{\mathfrak{a}}$ and $R^{\mathfrak{a}'}$ in places $P^{\mathfrak{a}}$ and $P^{\mathfrak{a}'}$ is ambiguous. The remaining cases of $\mathfrak{a}$ and $\mathfrak{a}'$ satisfying $(C_{1,3})$ are explained and illustrated in a similar way.

Ad $(C_{1,4})$. For two different local actions $\mathfrak{a}, \mathfrak{a}'$ belonging to $\mathcal{A}_{\text{out}}$ we explain the case of $\{P^{\mathfrak{a}}(1), P^{\mathfrak{a}}(2)\} \cap \{P^{\mathfrak{a}'}(0), P^{\mathfrak{a}'}(1)\} = \{P^{\mathfrak{a}}(1)\}$ which is equivalent to the disjunction of the following two conditions:

i) $P^{\mathfrak{a}'}(0) = P^{\mathfrak{a}}(1)$ and $P^{\mathfrak{a}'}(1) \neq P^{\mathfrak{a}}(2)$,
ii) $P^{\mathfrak{a}}(1) = P^{\mathfrak{a}'}(1)$.

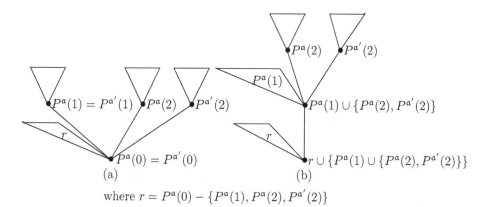

where $r = P^a(0) - \{P^a(1), P^a(2), P^{a'}(2)\}$

Fig. 3

The places P^a and $P^{a'}$ for the case i) are illustrated in Fig. 4(a). The result of simultaneous application of R^a and $R^{a'}$ in these places P^a and $P^{a'}$, respectively, is illustrated in Fig. 4(b), where $P^a(2)$ and $P^{a'}(2)$ are simultaneously "sent out" of $P^a(1)$ into $P^a(0)$ and of $P^{a'}(2)$ into $P^{a'}(0) = P^a(1)$, respectively. The condition $P^{a'}(1) \neq P^a(2)$ in i) excludes the case where simultaneous application of R^a and $R^{a'}$ in places P^a and $P^{a'}$ is ambiguous. The case ii) and the remaining cases in $(C_{1,4})$ are explained and illustrated in a similar way.

Ad $(C_{1,5})$. One explains and illustrates this condition in a way similar to $(C_{1,1})$ and $(C_{1,3})$.

Ad $(C_{1,6})$. One explains and illustrates this condition in a way similar to $(C_{1,4})$. We point out here that for two different local actions $a \in \mathcal{A}_{\text{diss}}$ and $a' \in \mathcal{A}_{\text{out}}$ with scope$(a) \cap$ scope$(a') \neq \varnothing$ the condition

$$\{P^a(0), P^a(1)\} \cap \{P^{a'}(1), P^{a'}(2\} = \{P^a(0)\}$$

is equivalent to the disjunction of the following two conditions:

iii) $P^a(0) = P^{a'}(1)$ and $P^a(1) \neq P^{a'}(2)$,
iv) $P^a(0) = P^{a'}(2)$.

The condition $P^a(1) \neq P^{a'}(2)$ in iii) excludes the case where simultaneous application of R^a and $R^{a'}$ in the places P^a and $P^{a'}$ is ambiguous.

Ad $(C_{1,7})$. For two different local actions $a \in \mathcal{A}_{\text{in}}$ and $a' \in \mathcal{A}_{\text{out}}$ we explain the case of scope$(a) \cap \{P^{a'}(1), P^{a'}(2)\} = \{P^a(0)\}$ which is equivalent to the disjunction of the following two conditions:

v) $P^a(0) = P^{a'}(1)$ and $P^{a'}(2) \notin \{P^a(1), P^a(2)\}$,
vi) $P^a(0) = P^{a'}(2)$.

The places P^a and $P^{a'}$ in the case v) are illustrated in Fig. 5(a). The result of simultaneous application of R^a and $R^{a'}$ in these places P^a and $P^{a'}$, respectively, is illustrated in Fig. 5(b), where $P^a(2)$ is "sent into" $P^a(1)$ and $P^{a'}(2)$ is "sent

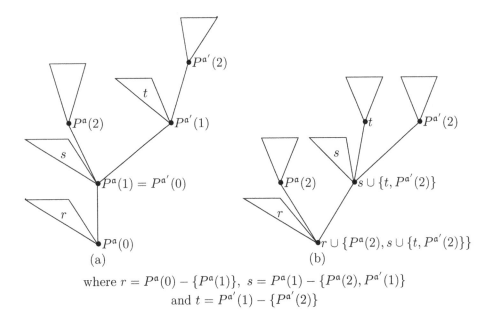

where $r = P^{\mathfrak{a}}(0) - \{P^{\mathfrak{a}}(1)\}$, $s = P^{\mathfrak{a}}(1) - \{P^{\mathfrak{a}}(2), P^{\mathfrak{a}'}(1)\}$
and $t = P^{\mathfrak{a}'}(1) - \{P^{\mathfrak{a}'}(2)\}$

Fig. 4

out" of $P^{\mathfrak{a}'}(1) = P^{\mathfrak{a}}(0)$ into $P^{\mathfrak{a}'}(0)$ simultaneously. The condition $P^{\mathfrak{a}'}(2) \notin \{P^{\mathfrak{a}}(1), P^{\mathfrak{a}}(2)\}$ in v) excludes the case where simultaneous application of $R^{\mathfrak{a}}$ and $R^{\mathfrak{a}'}$ in the places $P^{\mathfrak{a}}$ and $P^{\mathfrak{a}'}$ is ambiguous. The case vi) and the remaining cases in $(C_{1,7})$ are explained and illustrated in a similar way.

Let $\mathcal{A}$ be a proper set of local actions over a tree-like hereditary finite set x determined by a family $\mathfrak{M}$ for x belonging to the set HF of hereditary finite sets over the set $L = \mathbb{O} \cup \bigcup \mathfrak{M}$ of urelements with $\mathbb{O} \cap \bigcup \mathfrak{M} = \varnothing$ for $\mathbb{O}$ meant as a set of objects. By the *result of evolutive transformation of x with respect to $\mathcal{A}$* we mean a set, denoted by $\mathrm{Ap}(\mathcal{A}, x)$, which is defined inductively (with respect to the number of elements of $\mathcal{A}$ and the depth of x) by the following equations:

1) $\mathrm{Ap}(\varnothing, x) = x$ and $\mathrm{Ap}(\varnothing, \varnothing) = \varnothing$,
2) if $\mathcal{A} \neq \varnothing$, then $\mathrm{Ap}(\mathcal{A}, x) = (L \cap x) \cup \mathrm{Ap}^{\bullet}(\mathcal{A}, x)$ for

$$\mathrm{Ap}^{\bullet}(\mathcal{A}, x) = \bigcup_{1 \leq i \leq 4} \mathrm{Ap}_i(\mathcal{A}, x),$$

where
- $\mathrm{Ap}_1(\mathcal{A}, x) = \{\mathrm{Ap}(\mathcal{A} \upharpoonright y, y) \mid y \in x \cap \mathrm{HF}$ and $y \notin \bigcup\{\mathrm{scope}(\mathfrak{a}) \mid \mathfrak{a} \in \mathcal{A}\}$,
- $\mathrm{Ap}_2(\mathcal{A}, x) = \bigcup\{\mathrm{Ap}^{\bullet}(\mathcal{A} \upharpoonright P^{\mathfrak{a}}(1), P^{\mathfrak{a}}(1)) \cup Z^{\mathfrak{a}}_{\mathrm{diss}} \mid P^{\mathfrak{a}}(0) = x$ and $\mathfrak{a} \in \mathcal{A}_{\mathrm{diss}}\}$
  for
  $$Z^{\mathfrak{a}}_{\mathrm{diss}} = ((P^{\mathfrak{a}}(1) \cap \mathbb{O}) - \mathrm{left}(R^{\mathfrak{a}})) \cup \mathrm{right}(R^{\mathfrak{a}}),$$

- $\mathrm{Ap}_3(\mathcal{A}, x) = \{\mathrm{Ap}^{\bullet}(\mathcal{A} \upharpoonright P^{\mathfrak{a}}(2), P^{\mathfrak{a}}(2)) \cup Z^{\mathfrak{a},2}_{\mathrm{out}} \mid P^{\mathfrak{a}}(0) = x$ and $\mathfrak{a} \in \mathcal{A}_{\mathrm{out}}\}$
  for
  $$Z^{\mathfrak{a},2}_{\mathrm{out}} = ((P^{\mathfrak{a}}(2) \cap L) - \mathrm{left}_2(R^{\mathfrak{a}})) \cup \mathrm{right}_2(R^{\mathfrak{a}}),$$

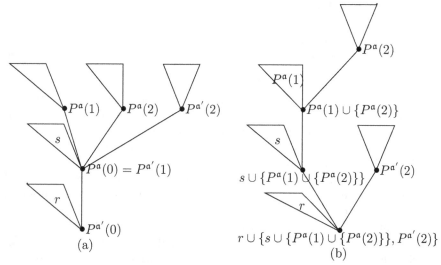

where $r = P^{a'}(0) - \{P^{a'}(1)\}$ and $s = P^a(0) - \{P^a(1), P^a(2), P^{a'}(2)\}$

Fig. 5

- $\mathrm{Ap}_4(\mathcal{A}, x) = \{\mathrm{Ap}^\bullet(\mathcal{A} \restriction (y - P^y), y - P^y) \cup Q^y \cup Z^y \mid y \in \mathrm{INOUT}_{\mathcal{A}}^x\}$ for

$$\mathrm{INOUT}_{\mathcal{A}}^x = \{P^a(1) \mid P^a(0) = x \text{ and } a \in \mathcal{A}_{\mathrm{in}} \cup \mathcal{A}_{\mathrm{out}}\},$$
$$P^y = \{P^a(2) \mid P^a(1) = y \text{ and } \mathcal{A} \in \mathcal{A}_{\mathrm{out}}\},$$
$$Q^y = \{\mathrm{Ap}^\bullet(\mathcal{A} \restriction P^a(2), P^a(2)) \cup Z_{\mathrm{in}}^{a,2} \mid P^a(1) = y \text{ and } a \in \mathcal{A}_{\mathrm{in}}\}$$

with

$$Z_{\mathrm{in}}^{a,2} = \big((P^a(2) \cap L) - \mathrm{left}_2(R^a)\big) \cup \mathrm{right}_2(R^a),$$
$$Z^y = \big((y \cap L) - \bigcup\{\mathrm{left}_1(R^a) \mid y = P^a(1) \text{ and } a \in \mathcal{A}_{\mathrm{in}} \cup \mathcal{A}_{\mathrm{out}}\}\big)$$
$$\cup \bigcup\{\mathrm{right}_1(R^a) \mid y = P^a(1) \text{ and } a \in \mathcal{A}_{\mathrm{in}} \cup \mathcal{A}_{\mathrm{out}}\}.$$

The result $\mathrm{Ap}(\mathcal{A}, x)$ of evolutive transformation of x with respect to $\mathcal{A}$ is the result of simultaneous application of the rules R^a in places P^a, respectively for $a \in \mathcal{A}$, such that $\mathrm{Ap}(\mathcal{A}, x)$ inherits some basic properties of x which are described in the following theorem.

Theorem 2. *Let x be a tree-like hereditary finite set determined by a family $\mathfrak{M}$ of pairwise disjoint non-empty sets and let $\mathcal{A}$ be a proper set of local action over x. Then $\mathrm{Ap}(\mathcal{A}, x)$ is a tree-like hereditary finite set determined by $\mathfrak{M}' = \mathfrak{M} - \{P^a(1) \cap \bigcup \mathfrak{M} \mid a \in \mathcal{A}_{\mathrm{diss}}\}$.*

Proof. One proves the theorem by induction on the number of elements of $\mathcal{A}$ and the depth of x. □

4   Concluding Remarks

We point out here those aspects and features of methods introduced in the paper which may determine some future investigations in the area of membrane computing.

- One can see that the class of proper sets $\mathcal{A}$ of local actions over tree-like hereditary finite sets x is maximal with respect to the definition of $\mathrm{Ap}(\mathcal{A}, x)$, in the sense that for any class of sets $\mathcal{A}$ of local actions properly containing the class of proper sets of local actions the definition of $\mathrm{Ap}(\mathcal{A}, x)$ is not correct and may require some modifications. The investigations of those classes of sets of local actions which properly contain the class of proper sets of local actions may shed more light on massively parallel processes of evolution of membrane systems with mobile membranes.
- If we define a *P system* to be an ordered pair $\Pi = (x_0, \mathbb{R})$ with x_0 being a tree-like hereditary finite set determined by some family of sets and $\mathbb{R}$ being a set of evolution rules of the form R_1)–R_3), then the definition of a proper set of local actions and the definition of $\mathrm{Ap}(\mathcal{A}, x)$ provide a simple uniform treatment of processes generated by Π. Namely, the processes *generated by Π* can be defined simply in a uniform way as sequences $x_0, \ldots, x_n, \ldots$, maybe infinite, of tree-like hereditary finite sets such that $x_{n+1} = \mathrm{Ap}(\mathcal{A}_n, x_n)$ (see Theorem 2), where $\mathcal{A}_n$ is a maximal proper set of local actions over x_n with $\{R^{\mathfrak{a}} \,|\, \mathfrak{a} \in \mathcal{A}_n\} \subseteq \mathbb{R}$. A uniform treatment means, among others, that the "next state" relation is given simply by the equation $\mathrm{Ap}(\mathcal{A}, x) = y$, where a treatment of x and y up to some structural equivalence (isomorphism) of membrane systems is not required. The treatment "up to structural equivalence" is required for some other presentations of membrane systems, different from that by hereditary finite sets; for instance, a syntactical presentation of membrane systems by expressions requires the treatment "up to structural equivalence".
- The notion of a hereditary finite set, the concept of a proper set of local actions defined for wider classes of evolution rules than those of the forms R_1)–R_3), and appropriate modifications of the definition of $\mathrm{Ap}(\mathcal{A}, x)$ may give rise to mathematical models (by means of denotational semantics) of formal systems like Ambient Calculus [3], [2] and Brane Calculi [1], [4], where the models may have some immediate physical or biochemical interpretation. We have already some partial results in this respect.

References

1. L. Cardelli: Brane calculi. Interactions of biological membranes. In *Proc. Computational Methods in System Biology* (CMSB 2004), Paris, France, May 2004. LNCS 3082, Springer, Berlin, 2004, 257–280.
2. L. Cardelli, A.D. Gordon: Mobile ambients. In *Foundations of Software Science and Computation Structures*, LNCS 1378, Springer, Berlin, 1998, 140–155.
3. L. Cardelli, A.D. Gordon: Mobile ambients. Coordination. *Theoret. Comput. Sci.*, 240 (2000), 177–213.

4. L. Cardelli, Gh. Păun: An universality result for (mem)brane calculus based on mate/drip operations. In *Proc. Cellular Computing (Complexity Aspects)* (M.A. Gutiérrez-Naranjo et al., eds.), ESF PESC Exploratory Workshop, January 31–February 2, 2005, Fenix Editora, Sevilla, 2005, 75–94.
5. R. Gandy: Church's thesis and principles for mechanisms. In *The Kleene Symposium* (J. Barwise et al., eds.), North-Holland, Amsterdam, 1980, 123–148.
6. S.N. Krishna: On the efficiency of a variant of P systems with mobile membranes. In *Proc. Cellular Computing (Complexity Aspects)* (M.A. Gutiérrez-Naranjo et al., eds.), ESF PESC Exploratory Workshop, January 31–February 2, 2005, Fenix Editora, Sevilla, 2005, 237–245.
7. A. Obtułowicz: Gandy's principles for mechanisms and membrane computing. In *Proc. Cellular Computing (Complexity Aspects)* (M.A. Gutiérrez-Naranjo et al., eds.), ESF PESC Exploratory Workshop, January 31–February 2, 2005, Fenix Editora, Sevilla, 2005, 267–276.
8. Gh. Păun: *Membrane Computing. An Introduction.* Springer, Berlin, 2002.

Appendix

For a potentially infinite set L of labels or names which are *urelements*, i.e., they are not (treated as) sets themselves, we define inductively a family of sets HF_i for natural numbers $i \geq 0$ such that

$$\mathrm{HF}_0 = \varnothing,$$
$$\mathrm{HF}_{i+1} = \text{the set of nonempty finite subsets of } L \cup \mathrm{HF}_i.$$

The elements of the union $\mathrm{HF} = \bigcup\{\mathrm{HF}_i \mid i \geq 0\} \cup \{\varnothing\}$ are called *hereditary finite sets over* L or *hereditary finite sets with urelements* in L, or simply *hereditary finite sets* if there is no risk of confusion.

For $x \in \mathrm{HF}$ we define its weak transitive closure $\mathrm{WTC}(x)$ by

$$\mathrm{WTC}(x) = \bigcup\{\mathrm{WTC}(y) \mid y \in x \text{ and } y \in \mathrm{HF}\} \cup \{x\}$$

and the *depth of* x to be the smallest natural number i for which $x \in \mathrm{HF}_i$.

On the Rule Complexity
of Universal Tissue P Systems

Yurii Rogozhin[1] and Sergey Verlan[2]

[1] Institute of Mathematics and Computer Science,
Academy of Sciences of Moldova,
Str. Academiei 5, Chişinău, Moldova
`rogozhin@math.md`
[2] LACL, Université Paris XII, France
`verlan@univ-paris12.fr`

Abstract. In the last time several attempts to decrease different complexity parameters (number of membranes, size of rules, number of objects etc.) of universal P systems were done. In this article we consider another parameter which was not investigated yet: the number of rules. We show that 8 rules suffice to recognise any recursively enumerable language if splicing tissue P systems are considered.

1 Introduction

P systems were introduced by Gh. Păun in [5] as distributed parallel computing devices of biochemical inspiration, specifically, starting from the structure and the functioning of a living cell. The cell is considered as a set of compartments (membranes) nested one in another and which contain objects and evolution rules. The basic model does not specify neither the nature of these objects, nor the nature of rules. Numerous variants specify these two parameters by obtaining a lot of different models of computing (see [11] for a comprehensive bibliography).

The inspiration for *tissue P systems* comes from two sides. On one hand, P systems previously introduced may be viewed as transformations of labels associated to nodes of a tree. Therefore, it is natural to consider same transformations on a graph. On the other hand, they may be obtained by following the same reflections as for P systems, but starting from a tissue of cells and not from a single cell.

Tissue P systems were first considered by Gh. Păun and T. Yokomori in [8] and [9]. They have richer possibilities and the advantages of new topology have to be investigated.

There are many results dealing with the descriptional complexity of (tissue) P systems. In most of the cases, the main complexity parameter of such systems – the number of membranes/cells is investigated. Recently, other parameters such as the size of rules or the number of objects started to be investigated. For example, in [6, 1] systems having a minimal number of objects are investigated.

R. Freund et al. (Eds.): WMC 2005, LNCS 3850, pp. 356–362, 2006.
© Springer-Verlag Berlin Heidelberg 2006

In this article we consider another complexity parameter, *the number of rules*, which has not been investigated yet. We take a particular class of tissue P systems, *splicing tissue P systems*, which is a mixture of tissue P systems and splicing Head systems and which were introduced by Gh. Păun in [5]. In this case, we show that systems having 8 rules are universal and that they can recognise any recursively enumerable language modulo a suitable codification.

2 Definitions

We do not present here definitions concerning concepts of the theory of formal languages. We refer to [3] and [10] for more details. We only remark that we denote the empty word by ε.

A *tag system* of degree $m > 0$, see [2] and [4], is a triplet $T = (m, V, P)$, where $V = \{a_1, \ldots, a_{n+1}\}$ is an alphabet and P is a set of productions of form $a_i \to P_i, 1 \leq i \leq n, P_i \in V^*$. The symbol a_{n+1} is called the halting symbol. A configuration of the system T is a word w. We pass from the configuration $w = a_{i_1} \ldots a_{i_m} w'$ to the next configuration z by erasing the first m symbols of w and by adding P_{i_1} to the end of the word: $w \Rightarrow z$, if $z = w' P_{i_1}$.

The computation of T over the word $x \in V^*$ is a sequence of configurations $x \Rightarrow \ldots \Rightarrow y$, where either $y = a_{n+1} a_{i_1} \ldots a_{i_{m-1}} y'$, or $y' = y$ and $|y'| < m$, where $|w|$ is the length of word w. In this case we say that T halts on x and that y' is the result of the computation of T over x. We say that T recognises the language L if for all $x \in L$, T halts on x, and T halts only on words from L.

We note that tag systems of degree 2 are able to recognise the family of recursively enumerable languages, see [2] and [4]. Moreover, systems constructed in [2] have non-empty productions and halt only by reaching the symbol a_{n+1} in first position.

2.1 Splicing Operation

By an (abstract) *molecule* we understand a word over an alphabet.

A *splicing rule* (over an alphabet V) is a 4-tuple (u_1, u_2, u_3, u_4) where $u_1, u_2, u_3, u_4 \in V^*$. It is frequently written as $u_1 \# u_2 \$ u_3 \# u_4$, $\{\$, \#\} \notin V$, or in two dimensions as $\dfrac{u_1 | u_2}{u_3 | u_4}$. Strings $u_1 u_2$ and $u_3 u_4$ are called splicing *sites*. The *diameter* of splicing rule $u_1 \# u_2 \$ u_3 \# u_4$ is the vector $(|w_1|, |w_2|, |w_3|, |w_4|)$.

We say that a word x *matches* rule r if x contains an occurrence of one of the two sites of r. We also say that x and y are *complementary* with respect to a rule r if x contains one site of r and y contains the other one. In this case we also say that x or y may *enter* rule r. When x and y can enter a rule $r = u_1 \# u_2 \$ u_3 \# u_4$, i.e., we have $x = x_1 u_1 u_2 x_2$ and $y = y_1 u_3 u_4 y_2$, it is possible to define the application of r to couple x, y. The result of this application is w and z where $w = x_1 u_1 u_4 y_2$ and $z = y_1 u_3 u_2 x_2$. We also say that x and y are spliced and w and z are the result of this splicing. We write this as follows: $(x, y) \vdash_r (w, z)$ or

$$\frac{x_1 u_1 | u_2 x_2}{y_1 u_3 | u_4 y_2} \quad \vdash_r \quad \frac{x_1 u_1 u_4 y_2}{y_1 u_3 u_2 x_2} .$$

The pair $\sigma = (V, R)$ where V is an alphabet and R is a set of splicing rules is called a *splicing scheme* or an H-scheme.

For a splicing scheme $\sigma = (V, R)$ and for a language $L \subseteq V^*$ we define:

$$\sigma(L) \overset{\text{def}}{=} \{w, z \in V^* \mid \exists x, y \in L, \exists r \in R : (x, y) \vdash_r (w, z)\}.$$

Now we can introduce the iteration of the splicing operation.

$$\sigma^0(L) = L,$$
$$\sigma^{i+1}(L) = \sigma^i(L) \cup \sigma(\sigma^i(L)), \ i \geq 0,$$
$$\sigma^*(L) = \cup_{i \geq 0} \sigma^i(L).$$

The iterated splicing preserves the regularity of a language:

Theorem 1. *[7] Let $L \subseteq T^*$ be a regular language and let $\sigma = (T, R)$ be a splicing scheme. Then language $\sigma^*(L)$ is regular.*

2.2 Splicing Tissue P Systems

A *splicing tissue P system* of degree $m \geq 1$ is a construct

$$\Pi = (V, T, G, A_1, \ldots, A_m, R_1, \ldots, R_m),$$

where V is a finite alphabet, $T \subseteq V$ is the terminal alphabet, and G is the underlying directed labeled graph of the system. The graph G has m nodes (cells) numbered from 1 to m. Each node has a label that contains a set of strings (a language) over V. The symbols $A_1, \ldots, A_m$ are finite sets of strings over V that give initial labels of nodes of G. Symbols R_i, $1 \leq i \leq m$, are finite sets of rules (associated to regions) of the form $(r; tar_1, tar_2)$, where r is a splicing rule: $r = u_1 \# u_2 \$ u_3 \# u_4$ and $tar_1, tar_2 \in \{here, go_j, out\}$, $1 \leq j \leq m$, are target indicators.

A *configuration* of Π is an m-tuple $(N_1, \ldots, N_m)$, where $N_i \subseteq V^*$. A *transition* between two configurations $(N_1, \ldots, N_m) \Rightarrow (N_1', \ldots, N_m')$ is defined as follows. In order to pass from one configuration to another, splicing rules of each node are applied in parallel to all possible words that belong to the label of that node. After that, the result of each splicing is distributed according to target indicators. More exactly, if there are x, y in N_i and $r = (u_1 \# u_2 \$ u_3 \# u_4; tar_1; tar_2)$ in R_i, such that $(x, y) \vdash_r (w, z)$, then words w and z are sent to nodes indicated by tar_1, respectively tar_2. We write this as follows $(x, y) \vdash_r (w, z)(tar_1, tar_2)$. If $tar_k = here$, $k = 1, 2$, then the word remains in node i; if $tar_k = go_j$, then the word is sent to node j (it is clear that there must be an edge (i, j) in G); if $tar_k = out$, the word is sent outside of the system.

Since the words are present in an arbitrary number of copies, after the application of rule r in node i, words x and y are still present in the same node.

A *computation* in a splicing tissue P system Π is a sequence of transitions between configurations of Π which starts from the initial configuration $(A_1, \ldots, A_m)$. The result of the computation consists of all words over terminal alphabet T which are sent outside the system at some moment of the computation. We denote by $L(\Pi)$ the language generated by system Π.

We also define the notion of an *input* for the system above. An input word for a system Π is simply a word w over the non-terminal alphabet of Π. The computation of Π on input w is obtained by adding w to the axioms of A_1 and after that by evolving Π as usual.

We denote by $ELStP_m(spl, go)$ the family of languages generated by tissue splicing P systems having a degree at most m.

We shall consider a restriction of splicing tissue P systems. A *restricted splicing tissue P system* is a splicing tissue P systems which has the property that for any rule $(r; tar_1, tar_2)$ either $tar_1 = tar_2 = go_j$, or $tar_1 = tar_2 = out$. This means that both resulting strings are moved over the same connection. In this case, we may associate splicing rules to corresponding edges. If both targets are out, then we associate the splicing rule with an edge going to a special node called out. A restricted splicing tissue P system will be denoted as $(V, T, G, A_1, \ldots, A_m, R)$, where V, T, G, and A_i, $1 \le i \le m$, have the same meaning as before and R is a set of splicing rules associated to edges.

3 Main Results

Let $V = \{a_1, \ldots, a_n\}$ be an alphabet. Consider coding functions c and $\bar{c}$ defined as follows: $c(a_i) = \alpha^i \beta$ and $\bar{c}(a_i) = \beta \alpha^i$. We extend these functions to words and put $c(w) = c(b_1) \ldots c(b_m)$ if $w = b_1 \ldots b_m$.

Theorem 2. *Let $TS = (2, V, P)$ be a tag system and $w \in V^*$. Then, there is a restricted splicing tissue P system $\Pi = (V', T, G, A_1, \ldots, A_m, R)$, having 8 rules, which given the word $Xc(w)Y$ as input simulates TS on input w, i.e. such that:*

1. *for any word w on which TS halts producing the result w', the system Π produce an unique result $Xc(w')Y$.*
2. *for any word w on which TS does not halt, the system Π computes infinitely without producing a result.*

Proof. Firstly we give the definition of Π and after that we show that Π correctly simulates TS.

We construct the system Π as follows.

Let $|V| = n$. Then we consider

$$V' = \{\alpha, \beta, X, Y, Z\}, \; T = \{X, Y, \alpha, \beta\}.$$

The graph G and rules from R are given in Figure 1.
The initial languages A_j are given as follows.

$$A_1 = \{Zc(P_i)\bar{c}(a_i)Y \mid a_i \to P_i \in P\} \cup \{XZ\},$$
$$A_2 = \{ZY\},$$
$$A_3 = A_4 = A_5 = \{XZ\}.$$

The main idea of the construction is the following. The word $X\alpha^j \beta c(bw)Y$ in node 1 encodes the current configuration of TS. Using rule 1 one attaches

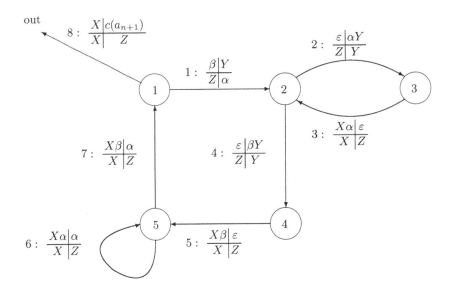

Fig. 1. The graph and the rules of out system

a production P_i and a symbol a_i, $1 \le i \le n$, at the end of the word (in this way a guess is made about the first symbol of the word). As a result, the words $X\alpha^j\beta c(bwP_i)\beta\alpha^i Y$ are generated. After that, the indices of the first and the last symbol are decreased simultaneously by taking off one α (since all symbols are coded in the unary alphabet, this decreases the index of the symbol). This work is done by rules 2 and 3. When the same number of α is present at both ends of a string, *i.e.*, both indices coincide, the system removes one more symbol and the string returns to node 1 where it may be processed again. The check for equality is made by rules 4 and 5. Since rule 4 (resp. 5) checks presence of β at the end (resp. beginning) of the string, the test is successful if and only if both ends of the string contain β ($X\beta c(bwP_j)\beta Y$). Now the second symbol (b) is eliminated by rules 6 and 7. Rule 6 eliminates α's from $c(b)$ and when β is reached, *i.e.*, b is erased, the resulting string $Xc(wP_j)Y$ is passed to node 1. It is quite obvious that the system simulates in this way the productions of the tag system.

When a symbol a_{n+1} begins the string, rule 8 is used and the resulting string is sent outside of the system. Hence, Π simulates TS.

Conversely, it is clear that a successful computation in TS may be reconstructed from a successful computation in Π. For this it is enough to look at strings of the form $Xc(w)Y$ in node 1. □

Remark 1. It is clear that the alphabet V' may be reduced to two elements by reencoding letters X, Y, Z, α, β in the binary alphabet.

Therefore the system constructed above needs 8 rules, 2 symbols, and $n + 5$ initial axioms. The diameter is given in the following table:

Rule(s)	Diameter
1	$(1,1,1,1)$
2, 4	$(0,2,1,1)$
3, 5	$(2,0,1,1)$
6, 7	$(2,1,1,1)$
8	$(1, n+2, 1, 1)$

It is easy to observe that if we put $c(a_{n+1}) = \beta\beta$, then the last diameter becomes $(1, 2, 1, 1)$, hence the diameter of the whole system is $(2, 2, 1, 1)$.

4 Conclusions

In this work we investigated a new complexity parameter for (tissue) P systems – the number of rules – which was not investigated before. We showed that it is possible to construct a universal system having only 8 rules. In order to achieve this, we used a particular class of splicing tissue P systems. An open problem raised by this result is if the above number is minimal. Other open problems concern the minimal number of rules in the case of ordinary P systems or P systems with symbol-objects.

Acknowledgements

The first author acknowledge the U.S. Civilian Research and Development Foundation (CRDF) and the Moldovan Research and Development Association (MRDA), Award No. MM2-3034 for providing a challenging and fruitful framework for cooperation.

References

1. A. Alhazov, R. Freund, M. Oswald: Tissue P systems with antiport rules and small numbers of symbols and cells. In *Proceedings of the ESF Exploratory Workshop on Cellular Computing (Complexity Aspects)*, Sevilla (Spain), January 31st - February 2nd, 2005, 7–22.
2. J. Cocke, M. Minsky: Universality of tag systems with p=2. *Journal of the ACM*, 11 (1964), 15–20.
3. J. Hopcroft, R. Motwani, J. Ullman: *Introduction to Automata Theory, Languages, and Computation*. Addison-Wesley, Reading, Mass., 2nd edition, 2001.
4. M. Minsky: *Computations: Finite and Infinite Machines*. Prentice Hall, Englewood Cliffts, NJ, 1967.
5. G. Păun: Computing with membranes. *Journal of Computer and System Sciences*, 1 (2000), 108–143. Also TUCS Report No. 208, 1998.
6. G. Păun, J. Pazos, M. J. Pérez-Jiménez, A. Rodriguez-Patón: Symport/antiport P Systems with three objects are universal. *Fundamenta Informaticae*, 64 (2005), 345–358.
7. G. Păun, G. Rozenberg, A. Salomaa: *DNA Computing: New Computing Paradigms*. Springer-Verlag, Berlin, 1998.

8. G. Păun, Y. Sakakibara, T. Yokomori: P systems on graphs of restricted forms. *Publicationes Mathematicae Debrecen*, 60 (2002), 635–660.

9. G. Păun, T. Yokomori: Membrane computing based on splicing. In *DNA Based Computers V* (E. Winfree, D.K. Gifford, eds.), volume 54 of *DIMACS Series in Discrete Mathematics and Theoretical Computer Science*, American Mathematical Society, 1999, 217–232.

10. G. Rozenberg, A. Salomaa, eds.: *Handbook of Formal Languages, 3 volumes*. Springer Verlag, Berlin, 1997.

11. The P systems web page: `http://psystems.disco.unimib.it/`.

Non-cooperative P Systems with Priorities Characterize PsET0L

Dragoş Sburlan[1,2]

[1] Department of Computer Science and Artificial Intelligence,
University of Sevilla,
Avda Reina Mercedes s/n 41012, Sevilla, Spain
[2] Department of Informatics and Numerical Methods,
Ovidius University of Constantza,
124 Mamaia Bd., Constantza, Romania
dsburlan@univ-ovidius.ro

Abstract. The paper answers an open problem from [4], proving that transition P systems with non-cooperative rules using priorities generate exactly the Parikh images of ET0L languages.

1 Introduction

The classical model of P systems with priorities has been introduced in [3] and since then the field of membrane computing has grown considerably, nowadays becoming more and more a framework for modeling various phenomena occurring in cells.

The model of P systems with priorities was initially used to describe the biochemical reactions occurring in the cell. There, priority relations (in the form of a partial order relation) among the rules from each region expressed the following phenomenon: if a biochemical reaction r_1 is more active than a reaction r_2 and it consumes a given resource (energy, for example) from the region, then the reaction r_2 cannot take place despite the availability of all necessary input objects.

In the attempt to make use of these features to design new bio-inspired computational devices, the current trend was to decrease as much as possible the level of cooperation between the objects participating into the rules while maintaining the currently obtained results. The mathematical interest was also the opposite problem, namely to see which is the upper bound of cooperation such that the systems are not anymore universal, knowing that almost for all variants of P systems universality results were obtained.

This bring us to the topic of the paper – it determines the computational power of the classical P system model with strong priorities when only non-cooperative rules are used: such systems generate exactly the Parikh images of ET0L languages.

We assume the reader familiar with basic notions of P systems with priorities among rules and P systems with promoters/inhibitors at the level of rules. For

R. Freund et al. (Eds.): WMC 2005, LNCS 3850, pp. 363–370, 2006.

more details regarding these topics we refer to [1], [2] and [7]. In addition, we assume known the basic notions and results about Lindenmayer systems (see [5] and [6] for details).

We denote by $PsP_m(ncoo, \alpha)$, $\alpha \in \{pri, inh\}$, the family of sets of vectors of numbers, computed by P systems of degree at most m, $m \geq 1$, using non-cooperative rules ($ncoo$) and priorities among rules ($\alpha = pri$) or inhibitors at the level of rules ($\alpha = inh$).

2   Some Known Results

In [7] it was proved that P systems with non-cooperative rules and inhibitors at the level of rules generates exactly the $PsET0L$, the family of Parikh images of ET0L languages. For the sake of clarity, we sketch the proof of the inclusion $PsET0L \supseteq PsP(ncoo, inh)$, pointing out some relevant details for the present work.

Here are the outlines of the proof:

- First we have shown the equivalence between P systems with non-cooperative inhibited rules using m membranes, and P systems with non-cooperative inhibited rules and only one membrane with a similar construction as it will be presented in the proof of Lemma 1.
- We have shown that any P system with non-cooperative inhibited rules is equivalent with a P system with non-cooperative inhibited rules, one region, and having the alphabet made out of two disjoint sets, the set of terminals and of non-terminals; in addition, all the rules have a non-terminal on their left-hand side; moreover, the set is complete, i.e., for each symbol in the nonterminal alphabet there exists at least one rule having it on the left-hand side.
- For a given set of inhibited rules, we have defined *saturated* classes of rules, i.e., we have found the sets containing rules that does not mutually forbids each other.
  Let V be an alphabet and $R = \{r_1, r_2, \ldots, r_k\}$ be a set of rules over V, of the form $r_i : (A_i \rightarrow \alpha_i|_{\neg B_i})$, $A_i, B_i \in V$, $A_i \neq B_i$, $\alpha_i \in V^*$, $1 \leq i \leq k$. For a rule $r : (A \rightarrow \alpha|_{\neg B}) \in R$ let us denote $left(r) = A$ and $inh(r) = B$.
  Two rules $r_i, r_j \in R$ are said to be in the *non-excluding inhibiting relation*, and we denote this by $r_i \equiv_{nei} r_j$, iff $left(r_i) \neq inh(r_j)$ and $left(r_j) \neq inh(r_i)$.
  A subset $W \subseteq R$ is said to be *saturated* (or *complete*) with respect to non-excluding inhibiting relation $\equiv_{nei}$ iff $(\forall)\ r_i, r_j \in W$, $r_i \equiv_{nei} r_j$, and $(\forall)\ r_i \in R \setminus W$, $(\exists)\ r_j \in W$ such that $r_i \not\equiv_{nei} r_j$.
- We have constructed an ET0L system $H = (V, T, \omega, \Delta)$, with the set $T = \{T_1, T_2, \ldots, T_k\}$, having as tables all the saturated sets $\{\overline{T_1}, \overline{T_1}, \ldots, \overline{T_k}\}$ (but with rules without inhibiting conditions and, in addition, with some other rules as will be explained later). Remark that from the way we have defined the saturated subsets, the conditions on the rules can be omitted (observe that two rules $r_1 : (a_1 \rightarrow \alpha_1|_{\neg b_1}$ and $r_2 : (a_2 \rightarrow \alpha_2|_{\neg b_2})$ can simultaneously

rewrite symbols a_1 and a_2 iff $b_1 \neq a_2$ and $a_1 \neq b_2$) in case we divide them in different tables. In addition, we have added to each table all context-free rules of the P system that does not violate the saturation relation considered for the table. We also have added rules of the type $b \to \#$ if rules $\{a \to \alpha \mid a \to \alpha|_{\neg b} \in \overline{T_i}\} \in T_i$ and $\# \to \#$; in this way we have assured that if we have chosen the "wrong" table, the computation will never stop since the $\#$ is produced (and therefore $\# \to \#$ will always be executed no matter which table is chosen).

In [4] it was shown in a straightforward manner that $PsP_1(ncoo, pri) \supseteq PsET0L$ by simulating the computation of an arbitrary two table ET0L system H with a P system with non-cooperative rules and priorities. In addition, catalytic P systems with priorities proved to be universal when only one catalyst is used. The remaining open problem ($Q2$ in [4]) was whether or not non-cooperative systems with priorities are universal. Here we deal with this problem.

3   P Systems with Priorities – New Results

P systems with priorities characterize $PsET0L$, the family of Parikh images of ET0L languages. In the proof of this result we will need the notions of P systems with inhibitors (see [1] for the introductory paper on this topic).

The following lemma shows that P systems with non-cooperative rules and priorities, having only one membrane, equal in computational power the ones having the same features, but with $m > 1$ membranes.

Lemma 1. $PsP_m(ncoo, pri) = PsP_1(ncoo, pri), m \geq 1$.

Proof. The inclusion $PsP_m(ncoo, pri) \supseteq PsP_1(ncoo, pri)$ is trivial. For the proof of the inclusion $PsP_m(ncoo, pri) \subseteq PsP_1(ncoo, pri)$, we construct a P system $\Pi_1 = (V, C, \mu, w, R, \vartheta)$ that simulates the computation of P system $\overline{\Pi_m} = (\overline{V}, \overline{C}, \overline{\mu}, \overline{w_1}, \ldots, \overline{w_m}, \overline{R_1}, \ldots, \overline{R_m}, \overline{\vartheta})$ in the following way.

First, denote by $\mathcal{L} = \{1, 2, \ldots, m\}$ the set of labels of the regions in $\overline{\Pi_m}$. Then, we define:

- $V = \{a_i \mid a \in \overline{V}, i \in \mathcal{L}\}$,
- $C = \overline{C} = \emptyset$.

Let $h : \overline{V}^* \times \mathcal{L} \to V^*$ be a mapping such that

1) $h(a, i) = a_i, a \in \overline{V}, i \in \mathcal{L}$,
2) $h(\lambda, j) = \lambda, j \in \mathcal{L}$,
3) $h(x_1 x_2, j) = h(x_1, j)h(x_2, j), x_1, x_2 \in \overline{V}^*, j \in \mathcal{L}$.

- Denote $w = h(\overline{w_1})h(\overline{w_2}) \ldots h(\overline{w_m})$, where $\overline{w_i}$ is the multiset present in region $i \in \mathcal{L}$ of $\overline{\Pi_m}$ at the beginning of the computation.
- R is defined as follows. For each rule $a \to \alpha \in \overline{R_i}$, $a \in \overline{V}$, $\alpha \in \{c, c_{out}, c_{in} \mid c \in \overline{V}\}^*$, $i \in \mathcal{L}$, we add to R the rule $h(a, i) \to \alpha'$ where α' is the corresponding string over $\{h(c, i), h(c, j), h(c, k) \mid c \in \overline{V}, i, j, k \in \mathcal{L}\}$, j being the label of the

outer region of i, and k being the label of an inner region of i. In addition, we inherit the existing priority relations among the rules.

- $\vartheta = 1$.

In other words, for the P system with a single region that simulates a P system with m regions, we have encoded the regions labels into objects (the subscript associated to an object indicates the region where the corresponding object belongs) and we have expressed the rules of regions by the corresponding encoded objects. In this way we ensured that, when simulating $\overline{\Pi_m}$ with Π_1, both the parallelism at the level of regions and at the level of whole system $\overline{\Pi_m}$ is respected. In addition, one can remark that whenever $\overline{\Pi_m}$ halts, Π_1 halts as well. Moreover, when Π_1 halts, we will have in the output region of Π_1 all the objects corresponding to the multisets present in all regions of $\overline{\Pi_m}$.

However, in the output multiset w_{Π_1} of Π_1 we can distinguish the output multiset $w_{\overline{\Pi_m}}$ of $\overline{\Pi_m}$ because we know which are the objects corresponding to the output region of $\overline{\Pi_m}$ (they are the objects that have as index $\overline{\vartheta}$). Therefore, we have to delete the unnecessary objects that remain in the output region of Π_1 in a halting configuration since we want to show that Π_1 and $\overline{\Pi_m}$ generate exactly the same set of vectors of numbers. We will modify the rules presented above in the following manner.

We add to the vocabulary V a new symbol D (the object D stands for the "deletion command") and we replace each rule $a_i \rightarrow \alpha' \in R$ by

$$a_i \rightarrow \alpha' D \in R,$$

of course, maintaining the priority relations among the rules. In addition, we add the following rules (with the corresponding priority relation)

$$\boxed{D \rightarrow \lambda} > \boxed{a_i \rightarrow \lambda}, \text{ for all } a_i \in V, \, i \neq \overline{\vartheta}.$$

One can remark that in this way we produce at each computational step at least one object D and also, in the same time, we delete the already existing object(s) D. If there exist rules that can be executed (i.e., there will be objects D) rules of type $a_i \rightarrow \lambda$ cannot be applied because they are locked according to the priority relations. When the computation halts, objects D are not produced anymore, and so, the deletion rules can start and erase the remaining unnecessary objects. Consequently, we have shown that both systems generate the same family of vectors of natural numbers, hence we have $PsP_m(ncoo, pri) \subseteq PsP_1(ncoo, pri)$.

Consequently, we have that $PsP_m(ncoo, pri) = PsP_1(ncoo, pri)$.   □

Now, we can prove the following result that shows the equality between the class of sets of vectors generated by P systems with non-cooperative rules and priorities, and the class of Parikh images of languages generated by ET0L systems.

Theorem 1. $PsP_m(ncoo, pri) = PsP_m(ncoo, inh) = PsET0L$.

Proof. In [4] it was shown that $PsP(ncoo, pri) \supseteq PsET0L$. In [7] was shown that $PsP(ncoo, inh) = PsET0L$ following a procedure as the one roughly described in Section 1. Here we will show that $PsP(ncoo, inh) \supseteq PsP(ncoo, pri)$ and hence, $PsP(ncoo, pri) = PsET0L$. Here is how we proceed.

Let us consider an arbitrary P system $\widetilde{\Pi}$ with m membranes, non-cooperative rules, and with a priority relations among rules. According to Lemma 1 we know that we can construct an equivalent P system $\overline{\Pi} = (\overline{V}, \overline{C}, \overline{\mu}, \overline{w}, \overline{R}, \overline{\vartheta})$ where:

- $\overline{V} = \{X_1, X_2, \ldots, X_r\}$,
- $\overline{C} = \emptyset$,
- $\overline{\mu} = [\,]_1$,
- $\overline{w} \in \overline{V}^*$.
- The set $\overline{R}$ is defined by the sequences of rules:

$$\boxed{X_{(1,1)} \to \alpha_{(1,1)}} > \boxed{X_{(1,2)} \to \alpha_{(1,2)}} > \cdots > \boxed{X_{(1,k_1)} \to \alpha_{(1,k_1)}}$$

$$\ldots$$

$$\boxed{X_{(p,1)} \to \alpha_{(p,1)}} > \boxed{X_{(p,2)} \to \alpha_{(p,2)}} > \cdots > \boxed{X_{(p,k_p)} \to \alpha_{(p,k_p)}}$$

with $X_{(i,j)} \in \overline{V}$, such that $X_{(i,j_1)} \neq X_{(i,j_2)}$, for all $j_1 \neq j_2$, $1 \leq i \leq p$, and $\alpha_{i,j} \in \overline{V}^*$, $1 \leq i \leq p$, $1 \leq j \leq k_i$. In addition, without loosing the generality, we will assume that $k_1 \geq k_2 \geq \ldots \geq k_p$.

Recall that we assumed that $X_{(i,j_1)} \neq X_{(i,j_2)}$, for all $j_1 \neq j_2$, $1 \leq i \leq p$, because in case $X_{(i,j_1)} = X_{(i,j_2)}$, the rule $X_{(i,j_2)} \to \alpha_{(i,j_2)}$ will never be applied since the rule $X_{(i,j_1)} \to \alpha_{(i,j_1)}$, having a grater priority, is applied first (of course, if it fulfills all required conditions).

We construct a P system $\Pi = (V, C, \mu, w, R, \vartheta)$ with non-cooperative inhibited rules that simulates the moves of $\overline{\Pi}$ and which is defined as follows.

- $V = \overline{V} \cup \{\overline{X} \mid X \in \overline{V}\} \cup \{A_{(i,j)}, U_{(i,j)} \mid 1 \leq i \leq p, 1 \leq j \leq k_i\}$
  $\cup \{S, T, H, \#\} \cup \{W_i \mid 1 \leq i \leq k_1 + 1\}$,
- $C = \emptyset$,
- $\mu = [\,]_1$,
- $w = STH\overline{w}$.

- The set of rules R is defined as follows.
  ⋄ We add to R the rules:

$$X_i \to \overline{X_i}TA_{(1,1)}A_{(1,2)} \cdots A_{(1,k_1)} \cdots \cdots A_{(p,1)} \cdots A_{(p,k_p)}, \ 1 \leq i \leq k,$$

$$S \to U_{(1,0)}U_{(2,0)} \cdots U_{(p,0)}WTHA_{(1,1)}A_{(1,2)} \cdots A_{(1,k_1)} \cdots \cdots A_{(p,1)} \cdots A_{(p,k_p)},$$

$$W \to W_1THA_{(1,1)}A_{(1,2)} \cdots A_{(1,k_1)} \cdots \cdots A_{(p,1)} \cdots A_{(p,k_p)},$$

$$W_1 \to W_2THA_{(1,1)}A_{(1,2)} \cdots A_{(1,k_1)} \cdots \cdots A_{(p,1)} \cdots A_{(p,k_p)},$$

$$\ldots$$

$$W_{k_1} \to W_{k_1+1}THA_{(1,1)}A_{(1,2)} \cdots A_{(1,k_1)} \cdots \cdots A_{(p,1)} \cdots A_{(p,k_p)},$$

$$W_{k_1+1} \to SH,$$

$$T \to \lambda,$$

$$A_{(i,j)} \to \lambda, \ 1 \leq i \leq p, 1 \leq j \leq k_i.$$

⋄ For each sequence of rules belonging to $\overline{R}$:

$$\boxed{X_{(i,1)} \to \alpha_{(i,1)}} > \boxed{X_{(i,2)} \to \alpha_{(i,2)}} > \cdots > \boxed{X_{(i,k_i)} \to \alpha_{(i,k_i)}}$$

we add to R the rules:

$$U_{(i,0)} \to U_{(i,1)}|_{\neg \overline{X_{(1,1)}}},$$
$$U_{(i,1)} \to U_{(i,2)}|_{\neg \overline{X_{(1,2)}}},$$
$$\ldots$$
$$U_{(i,k_i)} \to U_{(i,k_i+1)}|_{\neg \overline{X_{(1,k_1)}}},$$

$$U_{(i,0)} \to A_{(i,2)} A_{(i,3)} \cdots A_{(i,r)}|_{\neg T},$$
$$U_{(i,1)} \to A_{(i,1)} A_{(i,3)} A_{(i,4)} \cdots A_{(i,r)}|_{\neg T},$$
$$\ldots$$
$$U_{(i,k_i)} \to A_{(i,1)} \cdots A_{(i,k_1)} A_{(i,k_1+2)} \cdots A_{(i,r)}|_{\neg T},$$
$$U_{(i,k_i+1)} \to A_{(i,1)} \cdots A_{(i,r)}|_{\neg T},$$

$$\overline{X_{(i,j)}} \to \alpha_{(i,j)}|_{\neg A_{(i,j)}}, \quad 1 \le j \le k_i.$$

⋄ Also, we add the rules:

$$S \to \lambda,$$
$$X_i \to \#|_{\neg H} \text{ iff there exits a rule } X_i \to \alpha_i \in R,$$
$$\# \to \#,$$
$$H \to \lambda,$$
$$\overline{X_{(i,j)}} \to X_{(i,j)}|_{\neg H}.$$

Let us see how the simulation works. First, observe that (as a general technique) when we want to execute a certain non-cooperative rule r at a certain moment during the computation, then we might activate it using an inhibitor; however, this means that all the time during the computation we have to generate the symbol representing the inhibitor, to delete at each step all previously created inhibitors, and only when we actually want to execute r we omit its generation.

We start the computation by executing the rule

$$X_i \to \overline{X_i} T A_{(1,1)} A_{(1,2)} \cdots A_{(1,k_1)} \cdots \cdots A_{(p,1)} \cdots A_{(p,k_p)}, \quad 1 \le i \le k.$$

This rule is responsible for "painting" all objects X_i that correspond to objects in $\overline{V}$. In the same time we create the objects:

$$A_{(1,1)}, A_{(1,2)}, \ldots, A_{(1,k_1)}, \ldots \ldots, A_{(p,1)}, \ldots, A_{(p,k_p)},$$

$1 \le i \le k$, that will be used as "flags", indicating which rules cannot be applied (here the simulation of any rule from $\overline{\Pi}$ is forbidden – all objects are present). In addition, we create the object T that represents as well a flag, its role being to indicate when the selected rules will be effectively applied.

In the same time, the rule

$$S \to U_{(1,0)} U_{(2,0)} \cdots U_{(k,0)} W T H A_{(1,1)} A_{(1,2)} \cdots A_{(1,k_1)} \cdots \cdots A_{(p,1)} \cdots A_{(p,k_p)}$$

is executed. All objects $U_{(i,0)}$, $1 \leq i \leq p$, represent the starting points for the sequences of rules of type:

$$U_{(i,0)} \rightarrow U_{(i,1)}|_{\neg \overline{X_{(1,1)}}},$$
$$U_{(i,1)} \rightarrow U_{(i,2)}|_{\neg \overline{X_{(1,2)}}},$$
$$\cdots$$
$$U_{(i,k_i)} \rightarrow U_{(i,k_i+1)}|_{\neg \overline{X_{(1,k_1)}}}.$$

Such a sequence (that corresponds to $X_{(i,1)} \rightarrow \alpha_{(i,1)} > \cdots > X_{(i,k_i)} \rightarrow \alpha_{(i,k_i)} \in \overline{R}$ is used to check which rules from $\overline{R}$ can be applied. Depending where this sequence stops we will know what rules we have to apply. This information will be stored in the objects $U_{(i,j)}$.

Remark that along with objects $U_{(i,0)}$, $1 \leq i \leq p$, the object W is produced. This object will be used by the cycle (let us call it the "waiting" cycle):

$$W \rightarrow W_1 THA_{(1,1)}A_{(1,2)} \cdots A_{(1,k_1)} \cdots \cdots A_{(p,1)} \cdots A_{(p,k_p)},$$
$$W_1 \rightarrow W_2 THA_{(1,1)}A_{(1,2)} \cdots A_{(1,k_1)} \cdots \cdots A_{(p,1)} \cdots A_{(p,k_p)},$$
$$\cdots$$
$$W_{k_1} \rightarrow W_{k_1+1}THA_{(1,1)}A_{(1,2)} \cdots A_{(1,k_1)} \cdots \cdots A_{(p,1)} \cdots A_{(p,k_p)},$$
$$W_{k_1+1} \rightarrow SH,$$

which produces "enough" time (more than the maximum length of the sequences of rules in $\overline{R}$) objects $A_{(1,1)}A_{(1,2)} \cdots A_{(1,k_1)} \cdots \cdots A_{(p,1)} \cdots A_{(p,k_p)}$ which forbids the application of any rule that corresponds to a rule in $\overline{R}$. In the last step of the cycle we omit the creation of object T. The absence of object T means that we can apply one of the rules:

$$U_{(i,0)} \rightarrow A_{(i,2)}A_{(i,3)} \cdots A_{(i,r)}|_{\neg T},$$
$$U_{(i,1)} \rightarrow A_{(i,1)} A_{(i,3)}A_{(i,4)} \cdots A_{(i,r)}|_{\neg T},$$
$$\cdots$$
$$U_{(i,k_i)} \rightarrow A_{(i,1)} \cdots A_{(i,k_1)} A_{(i,k_1+2)} \cdots A_{(i,r)}|_{\neg T},$$
$$U_{(i,k_i+1)} \rightarrow A_{(i,1)} \cdots A_{(i,r)}|_{\neg T}.$$

In this way we are able to select which are the rules (that corresponds to rules in $\overline{R}$) that can be applied, namely:

$$\overline{X_{(i,j)}} \rightarrow \alpha_{(i,j)}|_{\neg A_{(i,j)}}, \ 1 \leq j \leq k_i.$$

Now, observe that all the time the "waiting" cycle is active (that is, we intend to make a simulation of a step in $\overline{\Pi}$) the object H is created. Also, the already existing objects H are deleted by the rule $H \rightarrow \lambda$. This object will help us to finish the simulation. Here are the details.

Non-deterministically, object S might also be deleted by the rule $S \rightarrow \lambda$. If this happen, then the object H is not produced anymore and so, the rules $\overline{X_{(i,j)}} \rightarrow X_{(i,j)}|_{\neg H}$ and $X_{(i,j)} \rightarrow \#|_{\neg H}$ are executed. So, basically, if symbol $\#$ appears, then the computation will not stop because the rule $\# \rightarrow \#$ will be always executed.

In case the symbol $\#$ is not produced then the computation eventually stops if the computation of $\overline{\Pi}$ stops. This is due to the fact that the cycle involving object S might be always executed. However, the system Π will generate in a non-deterministic manner (if object S is deleted and there is no symbol $\#$) the same set of vectors as $\overline{\Pi}$.

Therefore, we have that $PsP_m(ncoo, pri) = PsP_m(ncoo, inh) = PsET0L.$ $\square$

4   Concluding Remarks

Here we have proved that P systems with strong priorities characterize $PsET0L$, the Parikh images of ET0L languages. Recall now that in the sequential case, forbidden random context grammars equals in computational power ordered grammars. From this perspective, the result $PsP(ncoo, pri) = PsP(ncoo, inh) = PsET0L$ surprises also because here the maximal parallelism proved not to influence the equality between the classes of sets of vectors generated by P systems with priorities and with inhibitors.

In addition, the equality with the class of Parikh images of ET0L languages gives us "for free" all decidability results known for the family of ET0L languages. For example, it is of a mathematical interest (but not only) to mention that reachability and membership problems for ET0L systems are decidable.

Acknowledgements. I would like to thank to all members of the Research Group on Natural Computing from University of Seville, for the friendly and stimulating scientific environment provided.

References

1. P. Bottoni, C. Martín-Vide, Gh. Păun, G. Rozenberg: Membrane systems with promoters/inhibitors. *Acta Informatica*, 38 (2002), 695–720.
2. M. Ionescu, D. Sburlan: On P systems with promoters/inhibitors. *Journal of Universal Computer Science*, 10 (2004), 581–599.
3. Gh. Păun: Computing with membranes. *Journal of Computer and System Sciences*, 61, (2000), 108–143.
4. Gh. Păun: *Membrane Computing. An Introduction.* Springer, Berlin, 2002.
5. G. Rozenberg, A. Salomaa: *The Mathematical Theory of L Systems.* Academic Press, New York, 1980.
6. G. Rozenberg, A. Salomaa, eds.: *Handbook of Formal Languages.* Springer, Berlin, 1997.
7. D. Sburlan: Further results on P systems with promoters/inhibitors. *Intern. J. Found. Computer Sci.*, to appear.

Author Index

Lecture Notes in Computer Science

For information about Vols. 1–3742

please contact your bookseller or Springer

Vol. 3791: A. Adi, S. Stoutenburg, S. Tabet (Eds.), Rules and Rule Markup Languages for the Semantic Web. X, 225 pages. 2005.

Vol. 3790: G. Alonso (Ed.), Middleware 2005. XIII, 443 pages. 2005.

Vol. 3789: A. Gelbukh, Á. de Albornoz, H. Terashima-Marín (Eds.), MICAI 2005: Advances in Artificial Intelligence. XXVI, 1198 pages. 2005. (Sublibrary LNAI).

Vol. 3788: B. Roy (Ed.), Advances in Cryptology - ASI-ACRYPT 2005. XIV, 703 pages. 2005.

Vol. 3785: K.-K. Lau, R. Banach (Eds.), Formal Methods and Software Engineering. XIV, 496 pages. 2005.

Vol. 3784: J. Tao, T. Tan, R.W. Picard (Eds.), Affective Computing and Intelligent Interaction. XIX, 1008 pages. 2005.

Vol. 3783: S. Qing, W. Mao, J. Lopez, G. Wang (Eds.), Information and Communications Security. XIV, 492 pages. 2005.

Vol. 3781: S.Z. Li, Z. Sun, T. Tan, S. Pankanti, G. Chollet, D. Zhang (Eds.), Advances in Biometric Person Authentication. XI, 250 pages. 2005.

Vol. 3780: K. Yi (Ed.), Programming Languages and Systems. XI, 435 pages. 2005.

Vol. 3779: H. Jin, D. Reed, W. Jiang (Eds.), Network and Parallel Computing. XV, 513 pages. 2005.

Vol. 3778: C. Atkinson, C. Bunse, H.-G. Gross, C. Peper (Eds.), Component-Based Software Development for Embedded Systems. VIII, 345 pages. 2005.

Vol. 3777: O.B. Lupanov, O.M. Kasim-Zade, A.V. Chaskin, K. Steinhöfel (Eds.), Stochastic Algorithms: Foundations and Applications. VIII, 239 pages. 2005.

Vol. 3776: S.K. Pal, S. Bandyopadhyay, S. Biswas (Eds.), Pattern Recognition and Machine Intelligence. XXIV, 808 pages. 2005.

Vol. 3775: J. Schönwälder, J. Serrat (Eds.), Ambient Networks. XIII, 281 pages. 2005.

Vol. 3774: G. Bierman, C. Koch (Eds.), Database Programming Languages. X, 295 pages. 2005.

Vol. 3773: A. Sanfeliu, M.L. Cortés (Eds.), Progress in Pattern Recognition, Image Analysis and Applications. XX, 1094 pages. 2005.

Vol. 3772: M. Consens, G. Navarro (Eds.), String Processing and Information Retrieval. XIV, 406 pages. 2005.

Vol. 3771: J.M.T. Romijn, G.P. Smith, J. van de Pol (Eds.), Integrated Formal Methods. XI, 407 pages. 2005.

Vol. 3770: J. Akoka, S.W. Liddle, I.-Y. Song, M. Bertolotto, I. Comyn-Wattiau, W.-J. van den Heuvel, M. Kolp, J. Trujillo, C. Kop, H.C. Mayr (Eds.), Perspectives in Conceptual Modeling. XXII, 476 pages. 2005.

Vol. 3769: D.A. Bader, M. Parashar, V. Sridhar, V.K. Prasanna (Eds.), High Performance Computing – HiPC 2005. XXVIII, 550 pages. 2005.

Vol. 3768: Y.-S. Ho, H.J. Kim (Eds.), Advances in Multimedia Information Processing - PCM 2005, Part II. XXVIII, 1088 pages. 2005.

Vol. 3767: Y.-S. Ho, H.J. Kim (Eds.), Advances in Multimedia Information Processing - PCM 2005, Part I. XXVIII, 1022 pages. 2005.

Vol. 3766: N. Sebe, M.S. Lew, T.S. Huang (Eds.), Computer Vision in Human-Computer Interaction. X, 231 pages. 2005.

Vol. 3765: Y. Liu, T. Jiang, C. Zhang (Eds.), Computer Vision for Biomedical Image Applications. X, 563 pages. 2005.

Vol. 3764: S. Tixeuil, T. Herman (Eds.), Self-Stabilizing Systems. VIII, 229 pages. 2005.

Vol. 3762: R. Meersman, Z. Tari, P. Herrero (Eds.), On the Move to Meaningful Internet Systems 2005: OTM 2005 Workshops. XXXI, 1228 pages. 2005.

Vol. 3761: R. Meersman, Z. Tari (Eds.), On the Move to Meaningful Internet Systems 2005: CoopIS, DOA, and ODBASE, Part II. XXVII, 653 pages. 2005.

Vol. 3760: R. Meersman, Z. Tari (Eds.), On the Move to Meaningful Internet Systems 2005: CoopIS, DOA, and ODBASE, Part I. XXVII, 921 pages. 2005.

Vol. 3759: G. Chen, Y. Pan, M. Guo, J. Lu (Eds.), Parallel and Distributed Processing and Applications - ISPA 2005 Workshops. XIII, 669 pages. 2005.

Vol. 3758: Y. Pan, D.-x. Chen, M. Guo, J. Cao, J.J. Dongarra (Eds.), Parallel and Distributed Processing and Applications. XXIII, 1162 pages. 2005.

Vol. 3757: A. Rangarajan, B. Vemuri, A.L. Yuille (Eds.), Energy Minimization Methods in Computer Vision and Pattern Recognition. XII, 666 pages. 2005.

Vol. 3756: J. Cao, W. Nejdl, M. Xu (Eds.), Advanced Parallel Processing Technologies. XIV, 526 pages. 2005.

Vol. 3754: J. Dalmau Royo, G. Hasegawa (Eds.), Management of Multimedia Networks and Services. XII, 384 pages. 2005.

Vol. 3753: O.F. Olsen, L.M.J. Florack, A. Kuijper (Eds.), Deep Structure, Singularities, and Computer Vision. X, 259 pages. 2005.

Vol. 3752: N. Paragios, O. Faugeras, T. Chan, C. Schnörr (Eds.), Variational, Geometric, and Level Set Methods in Computer Vision. XI, 369 pages. 2005.

Vol. 3751: T. Magedanz, E.R.M. Madeira, P. Dini (Eds.), Operations and Management in IP-Based Networks. X, 213 pages. 2005.

Vol. 3750: J.S. Duncan, G. Gerig (Eds.), Medical Image Computing and Computer-Assisted Intervention – MICCAI 2005, Part II. XL, 1018 pages. 2005.

Vol. 3749: J.S. Duncan, G. Gerig (Eds.), Medical Image Computing and Computer-Assisted Intervention – MICCAI 2005, Part I. XXXIX, 942 pages. 2005.

Vol. 3748: A. Hartman, D. Kreische (Eds.), Model Driven Architecture – Foundations and Applications. IX, 349 pages. 2005.

Vol. 3747: C.A. Maziero, J.G. Silva, A.M.S. Andrade, F.M.d. Assis Silva (Eds.), Dependable Computing. XV, 267 pages. 2005.

Vol. 3746: P. Bozanis, E.N. Houstis (Eds.), Advances in Informatics. XIX, 879 pages. 2005.

Vol. 3745: J.L. Oliveira, V. Maojo, F. Martín-Sánchez, A.S. Pereira (Eds.), Biological and Medical Data Analysis. XII, 422 pages. 2005. (Sublibrary LNBI).

Vol. 3744: T. Magedanz, A. Karmouch, S. Pierre, I.S. Venieris (Eds.), Mobility Aware Technologies and Applications. XIV, 418 pages. 2005.